World in Transition

Members of the German Advisory Council on Global Change (WBGU)

(as of 31 October 2004)

Professor Dr Hartmut Graßl, chair
Director of the Max Planck Institute for Meteorology, Hamburg

Professor Dr Renate Schubert, vice chair
Professor for Economics at the Swiss Federal Institute for Technology and Head of the Center for Economic Research at the ETH Zurich, Switzerland

Professor Dr Astrid Epiney
Professor for International Law, European Law and Swiss Public Law and Director at the Institute for European Law, Université de Fribourg, Switzerland

Professor Dr Margareta E. Kulessa
Professor of Economics and European Economic Politics at the Mainz Unversity of Applied Sciences

Professor Dr Joachim Luther
Director of the Fraunhofer Institute for Solar Energy Systems, Freiburg/Breisgau

Professor Dr Franz Nuscheler
Director of the Institute for Development and Peace, Duisburg

Professor Dr Dr Rainer Sauerborn
Medical Director of the Department of Tropical Hygiene and Public Health at the University of Heidelberg

Professor Dr Hans-Joachim Schellnhuber, C. B. E.
Director of the Potsdam Institute for Climate Impact Research (PIK) and Research Director of the Tyndall Centre for Climate Change Research in Norwich, United Kingdom

Professor Dr Ernst-Detlef Schulze
Director at the Max Planck Institute of Biogeochemistry in Jena

German Advisory Council on Global Change

World in Transition:

Fighting Poverty through Environmental Policy

Earthscan

London and Sterling, VA

German Advisory Council on Global Change (WBGU)
Secretariat
Reichpietschufer 60-62, 8th Floor
D-10785 Berlin, Germany

http://www.wbgu.de

German edition published in 2004, entitled
Welt im Wandel: Armutsbekämpfung durch Umweltpolitik.
Springer-Verlag Berlin, Heidelberg, New York, 2004
ISBN 3-540-24987-7

First published by Earthscan in the UK and USA in 2005

ISBN-13   978-1-85383-883-5
ISBN-10   1-85383-883-7

Printed and bound in the UK by Cromwell Press Ltd
Translation by Christopher Hay, Darmstadt
Cover design by Meinhard Schulz-Baldes using the following illustrations:
Coffee picker in India (Margot Weiß), road construction in Guatemala (Nina Michaelis), cattle in Burkina Faso, children in Burkina
Faso, PATECORE-Project Burkina Faso, antenatal class in Nouna, World Summit on Sustainable Development in Johannesburg (all
Meinhard Schulz-Baldes)

For a full list of publications please contact:
Earthscan
8-12 Camden High Street
London, NW1 0JH, UK
Ph: +44 (0)20 7387 8558
Fax: +44 (0)20 7387 8998
Email: earthinfo@earthscan.co.uk
Web: www.earthscan.co.uk

22883 Quicksilver Drive, Sterling, VA 20166-2012, USA

Earthscan publishes in association with WWF-UK and the International Institute for Environment and Development

A catalogue record for this book is available from the British Library

Library of Congress Cataloging-in-Publication Data
    Wissenschaftlicher Beirat der Bundesregierung Globale Umweltveränderungen (Germany)
    World in transition : Fighting Poverty through Environmental Policy / German Advisory Council on Global Change.
    p. cm.
    Includes bibliographical references (p.).
    ISBN-13   978-1-85383-883-5
    ISBN-10   1-85383-883-7
    1. Poverty--Environmental policy--Germany. 2. Millennium Development Goals--Global change--International institutions.
    3. Sustainable development--Development policy--Governance. I. Title

    QH77.G3 W57 2001
    333.95'16'0943--dc21
                                                                                    2001023313

    This book is printed on elemental chlorine-free paper

Council Staff and Acknowledgments

Secretariat

Scientific Staff

Prof Dr Meinhard Schulz-Baldes
(Secretary-General)

Dr Carsten Loose
(Deputy Secretary-General)

Dr Ursula Fuentes Hutfilter (until 26.10.2003)

Dipl Umweltwiss Tim Hasler

Dipl Pol Lena Kempmann

Dr Nina V Michaelis

Dr Benno Pilardeaux
(Media and Public Relations)

Dr Astrid Schulz (from 01.02.2004)

Administration, Editorial work and Secretariat

Vesna Karic-Fazlic (Accountant)

Martina Schneider-Kremer, MA (Editorial work)

Margot Weiß (Secretariat)

Scientific Staff to the Council Members

Dr Carsten Agert (Fraunhofer Institute for Solar Energy Systems, Freiburg)

Anayo Fidelis Akunne, BA MPH (Department of Tropical Hygiene, University Heidelberg)

Lic Oec HSG Carolin Feindor (ETH Zurich, Switzerland, from 01.08.2004 until 31.10.2004)

Dr Thomas Fues (Institute for Development and Peace, Duisburg, until 01.07.2004)

Dr Jacques Léonardi (Max Planck Institute for Meteorology, Hamburg)

Dr Franziska Matthies (Tyndall Centre for Climate Change Research, Norwich, UK)

Dipl Volksw Kristina Nienhaus (Akademie für Technikfolgenabschätzung in Baden-Württemberg, Stuttgart, until 31.07.2004)

Dipl Volksw Matthias Oschinski (University Mainz, from 01.03.2004)

Dipl Volksw Marc Ringel (University Mainz, until 01.03.2004)

Dr Martin Scheyli (University Fribourg, Switzerland, from 01.09.2004)

Dr Angelika Thuille (Max Planck Institute for Biogeochemistry, Jena)

WBGU owes a debt of gratitude to the important contributions and support provided by other members of the research community. This report builds on the following expert studies:

- Prof Dr Friedrich O. Beese (Institut für Bodenkunde und Walderernährung, Göttingen University): Ernährungssicherung als Produktions- bzw. Verteilungsproblem.
- Prof Dr Frank Biermann (Amsterdam Free University) and Steffen Bauer, MA (Berlin University): United Nations Development Programme (UNDP) and United Nations Environment Programme (UNEP).
- Junior Professor Dr Tanja Brühl (Institut für Vergleichende Politikwissenschaft und Internationale Beziehungen, University of Frankfurt am Main): Funktionsweise und Effektivität der GEF.
- Dr Walter Eberlei (Institut für Politikwissenschaft am Institut für Entwicklung und Frieden, INEF, Duisburg) in cooperation with Arne Wunder (Bielefeld): Umweltrelevante Aspekte in Poverty Reduction Strategies.
- Dr Gerhard Petschel-Held, Dipl Geoökol Diana Sietz, Dipl Phys Oliver Walkenhorst and Carsten Walter (Potsdam Institute for Climate Impact Research PIK) in cooperation with Nick Brooks and Franziska Matthies (Tyndall Centre, Norwich, UK): Armut und Umwelt in Burkina Faso: Entwicklung und Anwendung eines Matrixkonzeptes zur Beschreibung differenzierter Anfälligkeiten gegenüber dem globalen Wandel.
- Prof Dr Peter Proksch (Institut für Pharmazeutische Biologie, Düsseldorf University): Bedeutung von Naturstoffen für die Pharmazie.
- Prof Dr Peter-Tobias Stoll (Institut für Völkerrecht, Göttingen University) in cooperation with Dipl Ing agr Stephanie Franck, Susanne Reyes-Knoche, Dipl Jur Focke Höhne: Armutsbekämpfung und Zugang zu genetischen Ressourcen.

WBGU also wishes to thank all those who, in numerous instances, promoted the progress of this report through their comments and advice:

Melchior Landolt (GTZ Burkina Faso) and Dr Hannelore Kußerow (Department of Geosciences, Berlin Free University) for their review of the vulnerability study ('Armut und Umwelt in Burkina Faso') and Bettina Führmann (Institute for Development and Peace, Duisburg) for input on the theme of European development policy.

WBGU is much indebted to the persons who received the WBGU delegation visiting Burkina Faso from 9 to 19 February 2004, and to the organizers of the visit. Many experts from politics, administration and science offered guided tours, prepared presentations and were available for in-depth discussions and conversations.

In particular, WBGU wishes to thank the Burkinabè team of organizers: Dr Bocar Koujaté (Nouna Health Research Centre), Kimsé Ouédraogo (Environment Ministry, Ouagadougou) and Yazoumé Yé (Heidelberg University).

Warmest thanks also go to Ambassador Marc-Ulrich von Schweinitz, to Milan Simandl, permanent representative of the German Embassy in Burkina Faso, to Environment Minister Dr Laurent Sédéogo (Environment Ministry, Ouagadougou) and to the representatives of various departments of the Environment Ministry of Burkina Faso.

WBGU thanks Christopher Hay (Übersetzungsbüro für Umweltwissenschaften, Seeheim-Jugenheim, Germany) for his expert translation of this report into English from the German original.

Contents

Boxes

Tables

Figures

Acronyms and Abbreviations

ABS	Access to Genetic Resources and Benefit-Sharing
ACC	Administrative Committee on Coordination (UN)
ADB	Asian Development Bank
AfDB	African Development Bank
AIDS	Acquired Immune Deficiency Syndrome
ASEAN	Association of South-East Asian Nations
BDI	Bundesverband der Deutschen Industrie [Federation of German Industries]
BMI	Body Mass Index
BMVEL	Bundesministerium für Verbraucherschutz, Ernährung und Landwirtschaft [Federal Ministry of Consumer Protection, Food and Agriculture (Germany)]
BMU	Bundesministerium für Umwelt, Naturschutz und Reaktorsicherheit [Federal Ministry for Environment, Nature Conservation and Reactor Safety (Germany)]
BMZ	Bundesministerium für wirtschaftliche Zusammenarbeit und Entwicklung [Federal Ministry for Economic Cooperation and Development (Germany)]
BUND	Bund für Umwelt und Naturschutz Deutschland [Friends of the Earth Germany]
CAS	Country Assistance Strategy (World Bank)
CBD	Convention on Biological Diversity
CDCF	Community Development Carbon Fund (World Bank)
CDF	Comprehensive Development Framework (World Bank)
CDM	Clean Development Mechanism (Kyoto Protocol)
CEB	United Nations System Chief Executive Board for Coordination
CESCR	International Covenant on Economic, Social and Cultural Rights (UN)
CGIAR	Consultative Group on International Agricultural Research
CIMMYT	Centro Internacional de Maiz y Trigo (Mexico)
CIS	Commonwealth of Independent States
CITES	Convention on International Trade in Endangered Species of Wild Fauna and Flora (UN)
CFC	Chlorofluorocarbon
COP	Conference of the Parties
CSD	Commission on Sustainable Development (UN)
CSP	Country Strategy Papers
CSR	Corporate Social Responsibility
DAC	Development Assistance Committee (OECD)
DALYs	Disability Adjusted Life Years
DED	Deutscher Entwicklungsdienst [German Development Service]
DFID	Department for International Development (UK)
DIVERSITAS	International Programme of Biodiversity Sience
EADI	European Association of Development Research and Training Institutes
EBRD	European Bank for Reconstruction and Development
ECHO	Humanitarian Aid Office of the European Commission (EU)

EC	European Community
ECOSOC	United Nations Economic and Social Council
EDF	European Development Fund
EEAC	European Environment and Sustainable Development Advisory Councils
EEC	European Economic Community
EIB	European Investment Bank
EU	European Union
FAO	Food and Agriculture Organization of the United Nations
FC	Financial Cooperation
FDI	Foreign Direct Investment
GATS	General Agreement on Trade in Services
GATT	General Agreement on Tariffs and Trade
GDP	Gross Domestic Product
GEF	Global Environment Facility (UNDP, UNEP, World Bank)
GEM	Gender Empowerment Measure (UNDP)
GEO	Global Environmental Organization (recommended)
GFATM	Global Fund to Fight AIDS, Tuberculosis and Malaria (UN)
GNI	Gross National Income
GTZ	Gesellschaft für Technische Zusammenarbeit [German Society on Development Cooperation]
HDI	Human Development Index
HFC	Hydrofluorocarbons
HIPC-Initiative	Heavily Indebted Poor Countries Initiative
HIV	Human Immunodeficiency Virus
HPI	Human Poverty Index
IAEA	International Atomic Energy Agency
IBD	Islamic Development Bank
IBRD	International Bank for Reconstruction and Development (World Bank)
ICARDA	International Center for Agricultural Research in the Dry Areas, Syrien
ICSU	International Council for Science
ICT	Information and Communication Technologies
IDA	International Development Agency (World Bank)
IFAD	International Fund for Agricultural Development (FAO)
IFC	International Finance Corporation (World Bank Group)
IFF	International Finance Facility (recommended)
IFF	Intergovernmental Forum on Forests (UN)
IFPRI	International Food Policy Research Institute (FAO)
IGEC	Intergovernmental Panel on Global Environmental Change (recommended)
IHDP	International Human Dimensions Programme on Global Environmental Change (ISSC, ICSU)
IIASA	International Institute for Applied Systems Analysis (Laxenburg, Austria)
ILO	International Labour Organization (UN)
IMF	International Monetary Fund
IMO	International Maritime Organization (UN)
IMWR	Integrated Water Resources Management
IOM	International Organization for Migration
IPCC	Intergovernmental Panel on Climate Change (WMO, UNEP)
IPBD	Intergovernmental Panel on Biological Diversity (recommended)
IPEA	Instituto de Pesquisa Econômica Aplicada (Brazil)
IPF	Intergovernmental Panel on Forests (UN)
IPLS	Intergovernmental Panel on Land and Soils (recommended)
IPPC	International Plant Protection Convention (FAO)
IPSE	Intergovernmental Panel on Sustainable Energy (recommended)
IRRI	International Rice Research Institute, Philippines
ISDR	International Strategy for Disaster Reduction (UN)
IUCN	The World Conservation Union

JI	Joint Implementation (Kyoto Protocol)
JPoI	Johannesburg Plan of Implementation (WSSD)
KfW	German Development Bank
LDCs	Least Developed Countries
LDCF	Least Developed Countries Fund (UNFCCC)
LICs	Low Income Countries
LISHD	Letter of Intent for Sustainable Human Development (PRSP)
MA	Millennium Ecosystem Assessment (UN)
MAI	Multilateral Agreement on Investment (WTO)
MDGs	Millennium Development Goals (UN)
MEA	Multilateral Environmental Agreements
MIGA	Multilateral Investment Guarantee Agency (World Bank Group)
NAP	National Action Programme
NAPAs	National Adaptation Programmes of Action (UNFCCC)
NEPAD	New Partnership for Africa's Development
NGO	Non-governmental Organization
NICs	Newly Industrializing Countries
NIEs	Newly Industrializing Economies
NIS	Newly Independent States (= former CIS and Baltic States)
NSSD	National Strategies for Sustainable Development
ODA	Official Development Assistance
OECD	Organisation for Economic Co-operation and Development
OPEC	Organization of Petroleum Exporting Countries
OSPAR	Convention for the Protection of the Marine Environment of the North-East Atlantic 'Oslo Paris Convention'
PATECORE	Projet d'aménagement des terroirs et conservation des ressources dans le plateau central, Burkina Faso
PCBs	Polychlorinated Biphenyls
PHARE	European Union Initiative Providing Grant Finance to Support its Partner Countries in Central and Eastern Europe
PIC	Prior Informed Consent
PIC Convention	Convention on the Prior Informed Consent Procedure for Certain Hazardous Chemicals and Pesticides in International Trade
POP	Persistent Organic Pollutant
PPA	Participatory Poverty Assessments (World Bank)
PPP	Purchasing Power Parity
PRGF	Poverty Reduction and Growth Facility (IMF)
PRSP	Poverty Reduction Strategy Paper (Governments, IMF, World Bank)
RNE	Rat für Nachhaltige Entwicklung [German Council for Sustainable Development]
SAPARD	Special Accession Programme for Agricultural and Rural Development (EU)
SCCF	Special Climate Change Fund (UNFCCC)
SGP	Small Grant Programme (GEF)
SIA	Sustainable Impact Assessment (EU)
SPS	Sanitary and Phytosanitary Agreement (WTO)
SRES	Special Report on Emission Scenarios (IPCC)
SRU	Rat von Sachverständigen für Umweltfragen [Council of Environmental Experts (Germany)]
STABEX	System for the Stabilization of Export Earnings (EU)
TACIS	Technical Assistance to the Commonwealth of Independent States (EU)
TBT	Agreement on Technical Barriers to Trade (WTO)
TC	Technical Cooperation
TNC	Transnational Corporation
TRIPS	Trade-Related Aspects of Intellectual Property Rights (WTO)
TTB	Technical Barriers to Trade (WTO)
UN	United Nations

UNCCD	United Nations Convention to Combat Desertification in Countries Experiencing Serious Drought and/or Desertification, Particularly in Africa
UNCDF	United Nations Capital Development Fund
UNCED	United Nations Conference on Environment and Development
UNCHE	United Nations Conference on the Human Environment
UNCHS	United Nations Centre for Human Settlements (now UN HABITAT)
UNDESA	UN Department of Economic and Social Affairs
UNDP	United Nations Development Programme
UNEO	United Nations Environment Organization (recommended)
UNEP	United Nations Environment Programme
UNEP TIE	UNEP Division of Technology, Industry and Economics
UNESCO	United Nations Educational, Scientific and Cultural Organization
UNFCCC	United Nations Framework Convention on Climate Change
UNFF	United Nations Forum on Forests
UNFfD	UN Conference on Financing for Development
UNFPA	United Nations Fund for Population Activities
UNGA	United Nations General Assembly
UN HABITAT	United Nations Human Settlements Programme (former UNCHS)
UNHCR	United Nations High Commissioner on Refugees
UNIDO	United Nations Industrial Development Organisation
UNIFEM	United Nations Development Fund for Women
UNU	United Nations University
UNV	United Nations Volunteers Programme
WBGU	Wissenschaftlicher Beirat der Bundesregierung Globale Umweltveränderungen [German Advisory Council on Global Change]
WCD	World Commission on Dams
WCED	World Commission on Environment and Development
WERCP	World Energy Research Coordination Programme (recommended)
WEHAB	Water, Energy, Health, Agriculture and Biodiversity Initiative (WSSD)
WFP	World Food Programme (UN, FAO)
WHO	World Health Organization (UN)
WIPO	World Intellectual Property Organization
WMO	World Meteorological Organization (UN)
WSSD	World Summit on Sustainable Development
WTO	World Trade Organization
WWF	World Wide Fund for Nature
YLLs	Years of Life Lost

Summary for Policy-makers

1
The challenges of poverty reduction and environmental policy

1.1
The vision of the Rio Earth Summit

At the start of the 21st century, fighting poverty and protecting the environment are two of the most urgent challenges facing the international community. Narrowing the massive disparities in the satisfaction of basic needs and distribution of prosperity must be a primary objective. Extreme poverty, such as that prevailing above all in sub-Saharan Africa and South Asia, is the most obvious manifestation of the untenable imbalance in the world's social system.

Human intervention in the natural environment is already jeopardizing natural life-support systems, especially those utilized by the poor, in many regions of the world. Unless countermeasures are adopted, environmental changes will have an even more life-threatening impact in future. While those who are responsible for global and transboundary environmental problems, such as climate change, are predominantly based in the industrialized countries, the vast majority of those affected live in the developing world. Poor groups are especially vulnerable to environmental changes as these people are more exposed to risks which threaten their survival (disease, hunger, harvest losses, etc.) and have very few coping and adaptive capacities.

So it is important to remind ourselves of the conclusion drawn at the Earth Summit in Rio de Janeiro (United Nations Conference on Environment and Development – UNCED, 1992): environmental and development policies are inextricably linked – and this must apply to any promising long-term strategy aimed at reducing poverty worldwide and narrowing the potentially explosive North-South divide. To this end, poverty reduction and environmental protection must be forged into a coherent policy from the local to the global level. Only an integrated approach which involves civil-society actors can fulfil the guid-ing vision of sustainable development. In the spirit of Rio, the German Advisory Council on Global Change (WBGU) presents the following hypothesis: *Global environmental policies are prerequisite to global poverty reduction.*

1.2
An integrated analysis of poverty, environmental change and relevant political processes

The recommendations for action set out in this report are based on an analysis of the systemic links between poverty (income poverty, diseases, malnutrition, and lack of education, social stability and social capital) and environmental changes (climate change, water pollution and lack of water resources, soil degradation, loss of biological diversity and resources, and air pollution). The manifestations of and interactions between poverty and environmental problems are investigated in their various forms. This type of integrated analysis is nothing new; what is new, however, is the consistent linking of a holistic approach with the following key questions: which institutional arrangements offer ways of coping with these problems, and where must gaps be closed? To this end, WBGU has evaluated major international political processes and developed recommendations on policy coherence. It also presents various recommendations on further research to identify the strategic gaps in theoretical and practical knowledge.

1.3
Deficits in global poverty reduction and environmental policies

WBGU's analysis reveals that the existing institutional architecture is too weak to solve poverty and environmental problems any time soon. It also shows that although most of the political processes studied perform key functions in terms of identifying themes, raising awareness and establishing a conceptual framework for individual policy areas, the lack of coordination between poverty reduction and environmental policy is still a major shortcoming. The weakness of the United Nations is an ubiquitous and recurrent problem. Moreover, international trade and economic policy is not adequately geared towards the goals of poverty reduction and environmental protection. Poor policy implementation and inadequate funding are other major flaws.

Above all, there is too little recognition of the need for a new development paradigm. In particular, the principle that economic growth must be decoupled from resource consumption as far as possible is not adequately embedded in all policy areas. Moreover, the strategic option of leapfrogging stages of technological development is given too little consideration by international environment and development policy actors, even though there are successful examples of this approach.

2
Recommendations on policy coherence

2.1
Drawing on synergies generated by coupling poverty reduction with environmental policy

WBGU's analysis and assessment of political processes has revealed that the impact of poverty reduction and environmental policy can be greatly enhanced by dovetailing the two realms. The targeted coupling of these two policy areas can help resolve goal conflicts and ensure that financial resources are deployed more effectively. These are not the only two policy areas in need of dovetailing. Trade and economic policy, for example, must also not conflict with internationally agreed environmental and poverty reduction targets. Although this position is generally endorsed by the international community, there is still a major gap between the pledges made and their actual implementation.

Compensation for the negative impacts of environmental changes and the assumption of liability

BEARING THE COSTS OF ENVIRONMENTAL DAMAGE IN LINE WITH THE 'POLLUTER PAYS' PRINCIPLE
Industrialized countries are responsible for a substantial proportion of the emissions of persistent trace gases and modifications to natural biogeochemical cycles which trigger global environmental changes such as climate change. Very often, it is the developing countries which are most severely affected by

the negative impacts. The payment of compensation for the ongoing environmental damage caused since the problem was identified would take account of the industrialized countries' responsibility and could help reduce the vulnerability of poor people in developing countries, e.g. to climate change, and thus fight poverty. On the issue of climate change in particular, WBGU recommends that states be obliged to pay appropriate compensation for climate damage in line with their contribution to global warming, taking 1990 as a baseline year for the calculation of their emissions.

MAKING PRIVATE ENTERPRISES LIABLE FOR ENVIRONMENTAL DAMAGE
Enterprises which cause environmental damage through their use of natural resources or their environmentally harmful activities should – in line with the 'polluter pays' principle – face liability under civil law. Appropriate regulations should be established in both national and international law. The – inadequate – sectoral environmental liability regimes which exist at international level (e.g. in the law of the sea or in relation to transboundary movements of hazardous wastes) should be reinforced and extended to other environmental media (e.g. freshwater regimes). The focus should be on strict (absolute) liability. Here, the object of protection should be the environment *per se*, irrespective of property status and economic value. Ongoing efforts to conclude cross-sectoral international agreements on environmental liability in civil law should also continue.

Making the global economy more socially and environmentally responsible

USING INTERNATIONAL TRADE AS A LEVER
Germany should intensify its efforts within the EU and multilateral organizations such as the World Trade Organization (WTO) to ensure that the developing countries' products are granted free access to the industrialized countries' markets. Industrialized and newly industrializing countries should open up their markets to products from developing countries to the maximum extent and abolish agricultural subsidies which distort competition. The only trade policy concessions which should be demanded from the developing countries are those which have a direct and beneficial impact on poverty reduction and global environmental protection, e.g. easier market access for goods required by the poor, or zero tariffs on goods whose use eases environmental stress (such as renewables technology). The negotiations in the Doha Round, resumed in 2004, offer a useful oppor-

tunity to use trade as a 'lever' for the benefit of the developing countries.

HARMONIZING THE WTO RULES WITH
ENVIRONMENTAL PROTECTION
Within the WTO, the precautionary principle should be given far greater priority, and multilateral environmental agreements should take precedence over WTO agreements. An appropriate addition to the exemptions contained in the GATT/WTO treaty could ensure, for example, that programmes and standards adopted under international environmental conventions are not challenged by any decision taken within the WTO's dispute settlement mechanism. Cooperation between the WTO and UNEP should be intensified. The German Federal Government should continue to lobby pro-actively for these objectives at the WTO negotiations.

INSTITUTIONALIZING ENVIRONMENTAL AND SOCIAL
STANDARDS
It is becoming increasingly important to establish more binding environmental and social codes of conduct at institutional level for multinational corporations, state export guarantee schemes and the private banking sector. WBGU recommends that the Federal Government continue to work actively for the implementation of the OECD Guidelines for Multinational Enterprises. A system to monitor compliance with codes of conduct should be established at EU level. These voluntary commitments should be incorporated progressively into binding international law. Environmental standards should also be introduced for exports of used industrial goods. The granting of export credit guarantees by Euler Hermes Kreditversicherungs-AG should be brought into line with existing OECD standards at last.

Expanding environmental policies as a prerequisite for poverty reduction

Preserving the integrity of the local environment, protecting and managing resources in line with sustainability criteria, and preventing hazardous environmental changes are key prerequisites for poverty reduction. Poor people suffer most acutely from local environmental problems such as water pollution or soil degradation which put their health and life-support systems at risk. Environmental protection therefore directly contributes to poverty reduction, and maintaining the natural environment can help reduce vulnerability at the same time.

As examples, various recommendations on ways of integrating poverty reduction into environmental schemes are as follows: As part of climate protection,

WBGU recommends that the Federal Government work actively for an international commitment on the preservation of carbon stocks in terrestrial ecosystems (e.g. primary forests, wetlands, grasslands), perhaps in the form of a protocol to the United Nations Framework Convention on Climate Change. To encourage the integrated management of water resources, international funding should be pooled and deployed, as a priority, in the most water-poor regions where there is a high level of water-borne diseases. Access to clean drinking water should be recognized as a fundamental right under binding international law. In soil protection, salinization is a serious problem, so a global monitoring system for the early detection of salinization should be established. To reduce indoor air pollution, WBGU has proposed the replacement of traditional biomass with modern fuels. To this end, funding should be provided for pilot projects which aim to establish a distributed energy supply, e.g. using biogenic liquefied natural gas.

Reducing vulnerability through adaptation

People with adequate entitlements, such as access to education and healthcare, are better able to cope with environmentally related pressures. This aspect of poverty reduction is becoming more important in light of the predictions being made in environmental research, for even if preventive policies are implemented rigorously, many environmental changes can no longer be prevented. German development cooperation should therefore develop a strategic framework aimed at reducing vulnerability to both gradual and abrupt environmental changes.

SAFEGUARDING THE CAPACITY FOR POLITICAL
ACTION
WBGU recommends that a new field of action be established in development cooperation, i.e. 'adaptation to expected global environmental changes'. In particular, the German poverty reduction strategy currently being pursued must be adapted in anticipation of the likely regional impacts of global environmental changes.

REDUCING RISKS AND VULNERABILITY THROUGH
DEVELOPMENT COOPERATION
WBGU recommends the inclusion of disaster risk management in the Poverty Reduction Strategy Papers (PRSPs) and the integration of disaster mitigation into the implementation of the UN Millennium Development Goals (MDGs). Disaster prevention should also become a new sectoral priority in development cooperation.

ADOPTING A LONG-TERM PERSPECTIVE IN
NATIONAL ENVIRONMENTAL PLANNING IN THE
DEVELOPING COUNTRIES

Promoting environmentally relevant spatial planning as part of development cooperation is strategically important, especially in terms of boosting coping capacities. Among other things, the development and enforcement of effective environmental laws, the production of national environmental statistics, and policy coherence play a key role in this context. WBGU recommends that national environmental planning in the developing countries focus to a greater extent on these long-term impacts.

ESTABLISHING RISK PREVENTION INSTITUTIONS

Risk and vulnerability assessments provide information which is urgently needed in the planning of risk prevention schemes. An international risk and vulnerability assessment programme should therefore be established, whose task would be to develop 'Disaster Risk Indices' to identify priorities for resource use based on cost-benefit analysis.

Protecting the environment through poverty reduction

The significance of poverty's negative impacts on the natural environment is often overestimated – prosperity and industrialization play a far greater role in causing environmental change. Nonetheless, the poor are often forced to over-exploit the natural resources which generally form the basis of their livelihoods. Combating poverty through better provision of basic services, enhanced rights of participation and entitlements along with better income-generation opportunities can reduce the pressure on local ecosystems.

COUPLING POVERTY REDUCTION STRATEGY PAPERS
WITH ENVIRONMENTAL STRATEGIES

Since 1999, the submission of a PRSP has been a prerequisite for debt relief and concessionary loans from the World Bank, the IMF and G7. WBGU welcomes this linkage in principle. However, too little priority has been given to environmental aspects so far. As environmental policy is prerequisite for poverty reduction, the PRSPs should include consistent environmental strategies from the outset. They should also address any potential conflicts between the objectives of economic development, poverty reduction and environmental policy.

BOOSTING LOCAL COMMUNITIES' ENTITLEMENTS
AND PROPERTY RIGHTS

Better participation by local and indigenous communities in decisions on biological resources and conservation areas, as well as improved entitlements to ecosystem services, can help lessen the negative incentives which encourage over-exploitation of sensitive ecosystems at local level. Appropriate framework conditions (e.g. good governance, secure entitlements) are a key prerequisite here. WBGU recommends that the developing countries be given targeted support to develop these framework conditions in order to open up long-term prospects for the use of ecosystem services.

IMPROVING CONDITIONS IN URBAN SLUMS AND
OVERCOMING ENERGY POVERTY

A water and sanitation infrastructure, waste disposal services, modern energy supply and transportation systems are vital to combat urban poverty. They also help to protect the local environment and reduce the pressure on adjacent ecosystems. Integrated development plans for urban slums are therefore essential, not only to combat poverty but also to prevent further environmental damage. WBGU therefore recommends that the German Programme of Action 2015 focus especially on water and energy issues.

2.2
Reforming the UN and enhancing environmental protection in the international system

WBGU considers that the major challenges of environmental protection and poverty reduction can only be mastered with the assistance of global rules and effective international organizations, i.e. global governance. This means reinforcing international law and intensifying multilateral cooperation. To this end, a major reform of the international institutional system is essential. The UN is a cumbersome organization which must improve its capacity to steer policy and become the institutional backbone of a global environmental and development partnership. This does not mean weakening the international financial institutions and the World Trade Organization, but integrating them more fully into a coherent global governance architecture under the UN's political leadership. Environment and development issues are key to the future of humankind. They should therefore be given the same high priority as security issues in the UN's institutional system.

The vision: Subsuming ECOSOC into a Council on Global Development and Environment

Establishing a new lead agency in the UN system is the most promising way to overcome the much-lamented lack of coherence in the international institutional system and improve the enforceability of sustainability goals. As a long-term vision, WBGU therefore recommends that a Council on Global Development and Environment be established to replace the Economic and Social Committee (ECOSOC). This new Council would provide the strategic and policy framework, coordinate the activities of the multilateral organizations working on development and environment – including the International Monetary Fund and the World Bank – and focus their activities towards the guiding vision of sustainable development. This would not only ensure that the problems of environment and poverty are given adequate priority within the UN system; it would also overcome the international financial institutions' *de facto* externalization out of the UN system. However, this will only be successful if the new Council's decisions have more binding force than ECOSOC decisions in providing policy direction. The new body should be composed of around a dozen permanent members from the key industrialized and developing countries and the same number of other representatives of the world's regions, elected on a rotating basis. The permanent members should not have a veto, and decisions would require not only an overall majority but also separate majorities among the industrialized and the developing countries respectively (North-South parity).

Since an amendment to the UN Charter would be necessary to establish the new Council, this reform project can only be achieved over the long term. In the meantime, the Chief Executives Board for Coordination should be utilized to better effect in coordinating the UN institutions. The Board is a forum which brings together the executive heads of the UN programmes, specialized agencies and funds, as well as the WTO, the World Bank and the IMF.

Enhancing the status of environmental policy in the UN system

WBGU reiterates its recommendation, which has now been taken up by the German Federal Government, for UNEP to be converted into a UN specialized agency. This would enhance the importance attached to environmental issues within the UN system and improve coordination on environmental work. The new agency would also ensure that poverty reduction and economic development in the poor countries are integrated into global environmental policy and a fair division of burdens is established at global level. In parallel, the Global Ministerial Environment Forum should play a greater role in promoting international cooperation on environmental issues, and should also have the capacity to make recommendations to other UN organizations involved in environmental activities.

The UN Commission on Sustainable Development

Due to its institutional weakness, the UN Commission on Sustainable Development (CSD) has been unable to fulfil its mandate satisfactorily until now. WBGU considers that the CSD's status should be enhanced through the appointment of a high-ranking figure – akin to the UN High Commissioner for Human Rights – as its permanent chair. Above all, the CSD chair could mediate, should conflicts arise, between the agencies working on sustainable development.

Improving participation in the international institutions

The UN system's guiding role in future policy development and the greater focus on environmental and development issues will also depend on enhanced participation. This means, firstly, that civil-society actors (enterprises, interest groups and non-governmental organizations) must be involved in consultation mechanisms and dialogue processes. Secondly, it means that the developing countries must play a greater role in multilateral decision-making bodies. This applies especially to the financial institutions (IMF, World Bank) and the regional development banks, which are currently dominated by the OECD countries. This power imbalance impedes the development of a global environmental and development partnership which is key to solving the problems of the environment and poverty. WBGU therefore welcomes the German Federal Government's initiative which aims to modify the voting arithmetic in the decision-making bodies of the Bretton Woods Institutions.

Strengthening the environmental component of the Millennium Development Goals

The MDGs are milestones on the path towards global poverty reduction. Through their adoption, the international community has committed itself, for the first time, to quantifiable goals and a fixed timetable. However, the strong focus on social policy deficits implies that poverty reduction can be viewed separately from the condition of the world's natural life-support systems. WBGU therefore recommends that the environmental policy objectives set forth in the MDGs be reinforced and that meaningful indicators be agreed in this area. The UN Conference to review the progress made in the achievement of the MDGs (the 'Millennium Summit 2000+5') in September 2005 offers a good political opportunity to take these steps.

Enhancing cooperation between the Rio Conventions

Cooperation between the UN Framework Convention on Climate Change, the Convention on Biological Diversity and the UN Convention to Combat Desertification, as well as in the thematic fields covered by these Conventions, is extremely unsatisfactory. This is particularly true when conflicting objectives arise. The Joint Liaison Group – a forum comprising representatives of the secretariats of the three Rio Conventions – offers an opportunity to address these problems and identify not only win-win situations but also conflicting objectives. Furthermore, thematic working groups consisting of an equal number of representatives from each Convention secretariat could offer an additional opportunity to exchange views on mutual interests and propose possible solutions to the relevant Conferences of the Parties. In many cases, joint development of strategies within the framework of the Conventions may be a positive way forward. The integration of the Rio Conventions into development cooperation, as proposed by the OECD, would ensure policy coherence among the donor countries.

Improving policy advice

Knowledge and evaluation are key to the development of viable policies for the future. In order to predict and identify global environmental and development problems and map out options for action, the role of scientific policy advice should be enhanced. WBGU recommends that the knowledge base available to policymakers be improved through the production of regular assessment reports. To this end, panels – akin to the IPCC – should be established to deal with the issues of land, soils and biodiversity. The option of establishing an Intergovernmental Panel on Poverty and Vulnerability should also be explored.

2.3
Driving forward local implementation

Since the adoption of Agenda 21 in 1992 and the breakthrough of the concept of sustainable development, a heightened awareness of the link between environment and development has emerged. The international community has agreed on a shared guiding vision of the overall direction and goals of global development. Yet in practice, economic development or power politics often still take precedence over sustainability. The guiding vision can only be implemented successfully if national and local actors are recognized as the driving forces behind this process. The transition from the development and adoption of global action plans to their practical implementation by local and national actors is mostly unsatisfactory. In view of the increasing number of international conventions, the international community must turn its attention to the widening gap between pledges and practice as a matter of urgency.

AGREEING QUANTITATIVE TARGETS AND DEVELOPING INDICATOR SYSTEMS
Quantitative and time-bound targets should not only be set at an overarching level, as in the MDGs; they are required in each separate field of action in global environmental and development policy. This approach is already being adopted in the Convention on Biological Diversity and the Kyoto Protocol, for example. But time-bound quantitative targets have not yet been established for other political processes, such as the Convention to Combat Desertification. The setting of targets makes it easier to assess political processes and their impacts at a later stage and should therefore be introduced in all areas of environment and development policy. Furthermore, ongoing monitoring of the impacts of measures through the use of appropriate indicator systems is an essential prerequisite which, although often called for, is still not fully implemented in practice.

COORDINATE THE SEPARATE IMPLEMENTATION PATHWAYS OF ENVIRONMENTAL CONVENTIONS
The implementation pathways of the environmental conventions, the National Strategies for Sustainable Development, and the National Action Plans to combat poverty generally run concurrently in many countries and are poorly coordinated. Implementation should therefore be streamlined in a consistent and coherent way at national and local level in order to improve the effectiveness and impact of the resources deployed. Integrated measures at local level could form practical fields of action.

IMPROVING DONOR COORDINATION
The greater part of official development assistance (ODA) is granted through bilateral approval procedures. Efforts are under way to improve the coordination of the development funding provided by donor countries, but are hindered by national interests:

- The OECD's Development Assistance Committee (DAC) is seeking to ensure that the international commitments undertaken at Monterrey 2002 are honoured, that development cooperation becomes more effective, and that it is targeted more specifically towards poverty reduction. The German Action Plan on Harmonization of Donor Practices points in the right direction. The German Federal Government should also work for better donor coordination in international forums, such as the DAC's High-Level Forum on Harmonization and Aid Effectiveness and the forthcoming UN Conference to review the progress made in the achievement of the MDGs in September 2005.
- The Treaty on European Union merely assigns a 'supplementary' role to the European Commission in European development policy, making it more difficult to achieve effective coordination and coherence within the EU. WBGU recommends greater communitization of development policy and its integration into the Common Foreign and Security Policy. This is especially important for the priority region of sub-Saharan Africa, where more intensive development policies at Community level could achieve substantially more than the bilateral efforts of the EU Member States, now numbering 25 in all.

MAINSTREAMING OF OBJECTIVES
The Federal Government should ensure that trade, economic, security and foreign policies do not conflict with development and environmental policy objectives. This means in Germany, for example, involving all the relevant ministries in decisions to grant Hermes credit guarantees and enhancing the role of the Interministerial Committee. Furthermore, the public profile of the Committee of State Secretaries for Sustainable Development ('Green Cabinet') should be enhanced in order to reinforce its key role in agenda-setting. In industrialized and developing countries alike, environmental policy should be taken seriously both as an independent policy field in its own right and as a cross-cutting task.

2.4
Promoting good governance

Global governance not only requires effective multilateral institutions and the rigorous implementation of international agreements at regional and national level. It also requires good governance in the partner countries – i.e. the rule of law, legal certainty for citizens and enterprises, respect for basic human rights, government accountability, and anti-corruption measures.

In WBGU's view, it is sensible to link development cooperation to good governance criteria (conditionality). Within the development cooperation framework, more assistance should be granted to recipient states which are willing to reform and are taking positive action. To this end, non-purpose-specific funding (budget aid) should be provided as well – albeit subject to regular reviews.

Fragile states with a weak political infrastructure need help to develop well-functioning administrative and legal structures and effective environmental management systems. For security and humanitarian reasons too, the international community cannot afford to write off failing or collapsed states as hopeless cases. It must find ways of maintaining or restoring these states' monopoly of power as a prerequisite for peace, stability, development and environmental protection. Failing states should therefore still receive humanitarian aid and assistance with institution-building. The anti-corruption campaigns being spearheaded by international NGOs and national actors should also be supported. Germany should ratify the UN Convention Against Corruption at the earliest opportunity.

2.5
Securing the funding

WBGU estimates the additional resources (international transfer from industrialized to developing countries) needed to implement internationally agreed poverty and environmental targets to run in the low hundreds of thousand millions of US dollars per year. Biodiversity conservation and compliance with the 'global warming guard rail' established by WBGU, i.e. a maximum tolerable temperature increase, are also likely to be achievable with global financial resources less than US\$400,000 million, on average, annually. A prerequisite, however, is that all measures are embedded in a coherent sustainable development strategy. In the climate policy field, adaptation and compensation funds must also be adequately funded. For the purposes of comparison, the OECD countries' annual spending on agricultural subsidies total around US\$350,000 million, while annual global military expenditure amounts to almost US\$1,000,0000 million. Global GDP stood at around US\$36,000,000 million in 2003. In WBGU's view, the internationally agreed targets on poverty and environment are affordable.

POVERTY REDUCTION AND ENVIRONMENTAL
PROTECTION ARE WORTHWHILE FOR THE
INDUSTRIALIZED COUNTRIES TOO

Besides their ethical responsibility, poverty reduction and environmental protection accord with the
industrialized countries' pragmatic interests as well.
At least four positive dividends can be anticipated
for industrialized countries:

- *Environmental dividend:* By protecting global
  public goods, environmental damage is reduced in
  the industrialized countries too.
- *Development dividend:* Reducing poverty and
  environmental damage worldwide creates markets for export products and investors from industrialized countries.
- *Trade dividend:* The abolition of subsidies in the
  industrialized countries will boost world trade.
  The industrialized countries will also benefit, e.g.
  because they will be able to import products more
  cheaply. Production efficiency will also increase
  over the medium to long term.
- *Security dividend:* By maintaining natural life-support systems and successfully reducing poverty, the
  numbers of refugees fleeing from environmental
  damage and poverty will decrease. Furthermore,
  improved living conditions, better entitlements
  and more participation rights will reduce an enabling environment for terrorism.

DISMANTLING ENVIRONMENTALLY HARMFUL
SUBSIDIES AND TRADE BARRIERS

Every year, environmentally harmful subsidies
amounting to around US$850,000 million worldwide
are paid to agriculture, the fossil fuel and nuclear
energy sectors, transport, the water industry, fisheries and forestry. Significant funding could be released
by slashing these subsidies and allocating a proportion of the resources to development and environmental policy. If the OECD countries abolished all
their trade barriers for agricultural goods and other
products from developing countries, the developing
countries could increase their revenue by at least
US$40,000 million per year.

FURTHER DEVELOPMENT OF THE CLEAN
DEVELOPMENT MECHANISM AND EMISSIONS
TRADING

WBGU recommends that a positive decision be
adopted as soon as possible on the eligibility of CDM
emissions reductions in future Kyoto commitment
periods. This would give investors planning security and thus ensure that investment flows are not
jeopardized in the current commitment period. In a
future expansion of emissions trading to include all
newly industrializing and developing countries, emissions trading would replace the CDM and could thus

lead to a substantial transfer of financial resources
to poorer countries. WBGU recommends that at the
forthcoming negotiations, the German Federal Government press for the rapid integration of all states
into a contraction and convergence regime.

ESTABLISHING A COMPENSATION FUND FOR
CLIMATE DAMAGE

In addition to the provision of regular and more generous financial resources for the existing adaptation
funds, WBGU recommends that polluters be required
to make further payments into an international fund
as compensation for the damage sustained by developing countries as a result of climate change. In principle, all countries should undertake payment commitments, which should be commensurate not only with
their current emissions but also with their cumulative
greenhouse gas emissions since the baseline year of
1990. Because it is impossible to predict future damage and its distribution with certainty, some measure
of flexibility is required as regards the total resources
available to the fund and the payments per tonne of
CO_2 equivalent. Transparent rules should therefore
be agreed so that the payment commitments can be
adapted not only to the damage caused over time, but
also to the countries' economic performance.

CREATING INSURANCE MARKETS AND EXPANDING
MICROFINANCING

In order to reduce the vulnerability of the poor,
WBGU recommends that development cooperation
further increase its support for micro-credit schemes
in developing countries. The launch of micro insurance schemes for the purpose of risk spreading in the
event of individual hardship (e.g. illness) should also
be considered as an element of risk management.
Measures to develop and expand an international
insurance fund to guard against damage caused by
natural disasters, e.g. harvest losses, flooding or pests,
should also be driven forward. WBGU also recommends exploring the extent to which weather derivatives, disaster loans and similar capital market products can be deployed and developed further in order
to generate funding for this type of insurance scheme.
At the G8 Summit in 2003, it was agreed that the
introduction of insurance against hunger would be
explored as an option. At the forthcoming G8 Summit, the German Federal Government should lobby
for the continuation and expansion of this initiative.

BOOSTING OFFICIAL DEVELOPMENT ASSISTANCE

Official development assistance (ODA) is very
important, particularly for the least developed countries. In WBGU's view, it is necessary to establish
a binding timetable to achieve, at the least, the target of spending 0.7 per cent of gross national income

on ODA. Germany's announcement that it plans to allocate 0.33 per cent of gross national income to ODA in 2006, thus increasing its ODA to more than €7,000 million annually, is a first step. As the next step, WBGU recommends an increase to 0.5 per cent by 2010.

WIDENING DEBT RELIEF

Further debt relief is essential to promote economic development in developing countries. WBGU endorses in principle an expansion of the HIPC Initiative to include heavily indebted middle-income countries. This would allow these countries to benefit from being released from a proportion, e.g. 10–20 per cent, of their debt. However, the expansion of debt relief cannot take place at the expense of other development financing: debt relief should not be factored into ODA, which is what often happens at present.

The G8 Summit in July 2005 will focus on, among other things, poverty reduction and climate protection. In this context, WBGU welcomes the British Government's announcement to cancel more of the poorest developing countries' debts. The German Federal Government should follow suit.

LEVYING USER CHARGES AND INTRODUCING NON-UTILIZATION OBLIGATION PAYMENTS

As recommended in earlier reports, user charges should be levied on aviation and the use of the seas. In addition, in order to protect environmental resources whose preservation is a common concern and responsibility of all humankind, but which cannot be defined as global public goods in the strict sense, a system of non-utilization obligation payments should be introduced.

3
Breathing life into the Global Partnership for Environment and Development

The international community will only master the major challenges of environmental protection and poverty reduction if the industrialized and the developing countries embark on a new type of cooperation. A 'global partnership' was agreed at the Earth Summit in Rio de Janeiro in 1992 and, in the 2000 Millennium Declaration, was described by all the heads of state and government as one of the most important goals of international politics – although the environmental dimension was neglected in this context. To date, the partnership forged between the industrialized and developing countries has failed to develop the momentum necessary to resolve the key problems of poverty and environmental degrada-

tion. With increasing resource consumption, worsening environmental damage and rising population figures, the scope for action is narrowing. WBGU therefore recommends that declarations of intent be followed by swift action and that the global partnership be taken seriously.

The governments of the developing countries have a responsibility to improve the performance, transparency and management of their public sectors, legal certainty for their citizens, and decision-makers' accountability. They should also boost poor people's entitlements and rights of participation and take seriously the environmental dimension of sustainability. Without fundamental economic, social and political reforms and a change of behaviour on the part of their elites in particular, the developing countries' efforts to free themselves from the all-pervasive problems of poverty, environmental degradation and violence are bound to fail.

For their part, the industrialized countries must change their consumption and production patterns at home while supporting viable modernization processes in developing countries. The present gap between the wealthy countries' rhetoric and their actual policies is undermining the developing countries' trust and confidence and impeding joint progress. The industrialized countries should honour the pledges that they have made: to open up their markets to products from the developing countries, to cancel the poorest countries' debt, and to provide more generous development assistance. At the very least, they should fulfil the voluntary commitments undertaken at the International Conference on Financing for Development in Monterrey.

Over the long term, an integrated approach which links poverty reduction and environmental policy affords major opportunities to the developing and industrialized countries alike.

Introduction

At the dawn of the 21st century, poverty reduction and environmental protection count among the greatest challenges facing the global community.

Human intervention in the natural environment is already endangering livelihoods across large parts of the world. Without concerted action, the impacts of such interventions will jeopardize people's survival to an even greater extent in the future. Pressure on the environment can only be expected to escalate, above all because of climate change which is increasingly in evidence. Similar trends in other environmental dimensions – such as water scarcity and pollution, soil degradation and biodiversity loss – are neither slowing nor showing any signs of reversing.

Extreme poverty, which is most prevalent in sub-Saharan Africa and South Asia, is the clearest expression of an untenable social imbalance in the world. Policies aiming to reduce poverty must address concrete and pressing concerns – not least the huge disparities in the satisfaction of basic needs and distribution of wealth. The people living in absolute poverty in developing countries will be the people affected most severely by anticipated environmental changes. This further intensifies the pressure to act. The poor suffer from lack of entitlements and property rights, social participation and access to resources. This is expressed not only in income poverty, but also in undernourishment, disease, inadequate education and a lack of social capital and societal stability.

In September 2000, 191 nations meeting in New York stated in the final declaration of the Millennium Summit their resolve to act against war and poverty more vigorously, to protect the environment more effectively and to strengthen the United Nations. The Millennium Development Goals adopted at that summit are milestones on the path towards eliminating poverty worldwide. However, their strong focus on social policy deficits suggests that poverty reduction can be achieved without engaging with the condition of the natural resources which sustain all life. In fact, integrating environment and development interests and giving greater consideration to both is the only way to meet basic needs, improve living standards for all, conserve and make sustainable use of ecosystems, and safeguard peace and security.

The international community needs to recall the consensus that emerged from the Rio de Janeiro Earth Summit in 1992 that environmental protection and poverty reduction are inseparable. This demands coherent policy design by government and civil society actors, from local to global level. Three questions guide the German Advisory Council on Global Change (WBGU) in its present report:

- What have been the responses of the international community to global environmental problems and poverty, and what progress has been made?
- Have suitable instruments, institutions and measures been developed to meet the challenges?
- To what extent have environment and development issues been integrated within coherent policies?

The recommendations for action presented in this report flow from an analysis of the systemic linkages between dimensions of poverty (income poverty, disease, undernourishment, lack of education, lack of social capital and societal stability) and environmental changes (climate change, water scarcity and pollution, soil degradation, loss of biological diversity and resources, air pollution). Such integrated analyses are not new. What is new is the rigorous linking of this synoptic assessment with the question of which institutional arrangements can tackle the problems most effectively, and where gaps remain to be closed. With this aim, WBGU has assessed key international policy processes and has developed recommendations for policy coherence. The result is a new framework for policy-makers.

Integrative environment and development policy – The Rio vision

Human beings are at the centre of concerns for sustainable development. They are entitled to a healthy and productive life in harmony with nature.
PRINCIPLE I OF THE RIO DECLARATION

2.1
The Rio process

2.1.1
The Earth Summit in Rio de Janeiro

'Rio' stands for a vision. In 1992, more than 100 heads of state and government committed to the guiding vision of sustainable development at the United Nations Conference on Environment and Development (UNCED) held in Rio de Janeiro. Although this guiding vision continues to lack conceptual clarity in various respects, the Rio process has contributed decisively to formulating the relevant challenges for environmental protection and social and economic development. It has established the long-term sustainability of natural life-support systems as an indispensable component of development that meets the needs of both present and future generations. The Earth Summit invoked the vision of a global partnership, not only between environment and development, but also between North and South. Rio de Janeiro thus became the starting point for a new quality of cooperation in global environment and development policy.

In the years before, an internationally coordinated environmental policy had gradually become a recognized need. As early as 1972, the United Nations convened a World Conference on the Human Environment in Stockholm. Despite a series of treaties, conventions and protocols concerned with environmental protection, the 1980s were widely considered a 'lost decade' – due to the cold war and the arms race, the mounting debt crisis of developing countries and their sceptical attitude to environmental concerns. Then, the World Commission on Environ-

ment and Development, commissioned by the UN to identify new ways to harmonize environmental and development goals, gained great importance. In 1987 the Commission published its report under the title Our Common Future, which became known as the 'Brundlandt Report'. This had a seminal impact on the international debate on environment and development policy, and was instrumental in initiating the Rio de Janeiro Earth Summit in 1992. The Commission developed in its report for the first time the guiding vision of sustainable development 'that meets the needs of the present without compromising the ability of future generations to meet their own needs and choose their lifestyle' (WCED, 1987).

In the following years, industrialized countries began to realize that the global environmental crisis is rooted in the conception of welfare that they are pursuing. The developing countries, for their part, gradually realized that environmentally sustainable development is in their very own best interest. The Earth Summit furthermore coincided with the end of the East-West conflict, in a period of great hope that there might be a peace dividend for development policy. The new global political situation presented the prospect of the United Nations exerting greater influence upon global environment and development policy.

The Earth Summit gave key impulses to environment and development policy that continue to resonate today (SEF, 1993; Eisermann, 2003):

- The final Rio Declaration on Environment and Development formulated fundamental rights and responsibilities of states vis-à-vis the environment.
- The 27 principles proclaimed in the declaration include the sovereign right of states to exploit their own resources, and the responsibility to ensure that such activities do not cause damage to the environment or other states (Principle 2).
- For the first time, the industrialized countries acknowledged officially that they bear the principal responsibility for the environmental crisis and thus also for turning development paths around. The principle of 'common but differentiated

responsibilities' holds key importance for North-South relations (Principle 7).

- The declaration also recognized the precautionary principle (Principle 15), the polluter pays principle and a commitment to establish liability and compensation (Principle 13), the internalization of environmental costs (Principle 16) and the rights of local communities and indigenous peoples.
- Overall, international awareness of the extent of environmental degradation and poverty and of the linkages among environmental concerns, social equity and economic development was heightened.
- With Agenda 21, a comprehensive and detailed programme of action for sustainable development was adopted; this is not, however, binding upon governments.
- In the meantime, many governments have elaborated national strategies for sustainable development.
- In cities and municipalities, the vision of Rio de Janeiro has launched numerous Local Agenda 21 initiatives.
- The Earth Summit was a breakthrough for extended participation opportunities for non-governmental organizations (NGOs) and other sectors of society such as indigenous peoples, youth, women, representations of local authorities, labour unions and the private sector.
- The social and environmental responsibility of the private sector was made an issue. Companies joined forces in organizations such as the World Business Council for Sustainable Development.

Furthermore, the Commission on Sustainable Development (CSD) was created, establishing a permanent forum within the UN system to support governments in implementing Agenda 21.

The Earth Summit also generated crucial momentum for the further development of international environmental law. Three new conventions have emerged: the Climate Change Convention with its Kyoto Protocol, the Biodiversity Convention with its Cartagena Protocol on Biosafety and the Desertification Convention. An attempt to initiate an intergovernmental convention on forests failed in Rio de Janeiro, but a Statement of Forest Principles was adopted, providing a starting point for debate on how to elaborate effective forest conservation approaches. To implement the statement, the CSD set up the Intergovernmental Panel on Forests in 1995, from which emerged the Intergovernmental Forum on Forests in 1997 and finally the United Nations Forum on Forests (UNFF) with universal membership in 2000.

The Global Environment Facility (GEF) was presented at the summit as a new financing instrument. Following a German-French initiative, GEF was established by the United Nations development and environment programmes (UNDP and UNEP) and the World Bank in 1991. Today it serves as the financing mechanism for the Rio conventions.

2.1.2
World Conferences in the 1990s

The Rio de Janeiro Earth Summit became a reference point for a series of major world conferences held in the 1990s which put key aspects of sustainable development on the agenda (Box 2.1-1). Following the model developed in Rio de Janeiro, governmental negotiations became increasingly open to the participation of non-state actors such as NGOs, labour unions and the private sector. In some instances, the outcomes of these conferences had a major impact upon the direction and design of global policy processes and institutions (Fues and Hamm, 2001). In 1995, for instance, the Copenhagen Summit engendered an enhanced status of social policy goals within development cooperation activities.

2.1.3
Millennium Declaration

The world conferences culminated in September 2000 in the Millennium Summit in New York. In the final declaration 191 nations declared their resolve, in the

---

Box 2.1-1

UN world conferences since Rio de Janeiro

1993	Second World Conference on Human Rights in Vienna
1994	Third International Conference on Population and Development in Cairo
1995	World Summit for Social Development in Copenhagen
1995	Fourth World Conference on Women in Beijing
1996	World Food Summit in Rome
1997	Second United Nations Conference on Human Settlements (Habitat II) in Istanbul
1997	Rio+5 in New York
2000	Social Summit+5 in Geneva
2001	Third United Nations Conference on the Least Developed Countries in Brussels
2002	International Conference on Financing for Development in Monterrey
2002	World Food Summit+5 in Rome
2002	World Summit on Sustainable Development in Johannesburg
2003	World Summit on the Information Society in Geneva

presence of 147 heads of state and government, to act against poverty and war more vigorously, protect the environment more effectively and strengthen the United Nations (UN, 2000). The report of the UN Secretary-General drew together the development goals contained in the Millennium Declaration in the form of a road map and assigned indicators to them (Millennium Development Goals – MDGs; UN, 2001c). The OECD countries had already agreed on most of these goals four years previously, terming them International Development Goals. They encapsulate the main outcomes of the world conferences held in the previous decade (OECD, 1996). The United Nations Millennium Declaration bestowed global recognition and validity upon these goals.

The MDGs are made up of eight goals which are detailed, operationalized and made suitable for monitoring by a set of 18 targets and 48 indicators (Table 2.1-1). Most goals and targets are quantified and have a time horizon, generally the year 2015 (from a 1990 baseline). The MDGs aim to halve by that year the proportion of people living in extreme income poverty, to reduce infant, child and maternal mortality, to achieve universal primary education and to ensure universal access to reproductive health services (such as access to contraceptives, prenatal care and the attendance of births by skilled health personnel). Furthermore, by the year 2005 boys and girls are to have equal access to primary schooling as a step towards ensuring gender equality and enabling women to determine their own lives. The goal of environmental sustainability (MDG 7) is far less differentiated. Under that goal, strategies for sustainable development are to be implemented, the loss of environmental resources reversed, the proportion of people without access to safe drinking water halved and the lives of slum dwellers improved. The eighth goal – 'Develop a global partnership for development' – relates to the strategies by which the mutually reinforcing goals of sustainable development are to be attained.

2.1.4
World Summit on Sustainable Development

In 2002, one decade after the highly promising launch of the Rio process, the World Summit on Sustainable Development (WSSD) was held in Johannesburg to review progress, address new global challenges and advance the implementation of Agenda 21. The resulting Johannesburg Plan of Implementation formulates a number of key additions to the Millennium Declaration that have immediate relevance to the living conditions of the poor.

In the water sector, the Millennium Goals were limited to the supply of drinking water. Johannesburg has now set timebound targets for improved access to sanitation (Table 2.1-2). The call to develop integrated water resources management and water efficiency plans is important with regard to drinking water supply for the poor. A further key extension of the MDGs is the goal of achieving sustainable energy supply for all. However, governments were unable to agree quantitative targets for the expansion of renewable energy sources and energy efficiency standards.

The Plan of Implementation further calls for application by 2010 of the ecosystem approach to promote sustainable use of the oceans, and for restoration by 2015 of a natural balance for all fish stocks. It further sets the goal of achieving by 2010 a significant reduction in the current rate of loss of biological diversity. Governments also agreed to negotiate within the context of the Convention on Biological Diversity an international regime on access to genetic resources and benefit-sharing (Section 3.2.3). The call to accelerate implementation of international proposals for forest conservation is also poverty-relevant.

The Plan of Implementation further urges the elaboration of national strategies for sustainable development and the beginning of their implementation by 2005. Other important points contained in the WSSD Plan of Implementation are its recognition of corporate social and environmental responsibility, and its highlighting of the International Labour Organization's core labour standards as a basis for promoting welfare worldwide.

The summit made no significant new contributions on the linkages between sustainable development, globalization and world trade. Nor could the international community muster sufficient political will to upgrade the competencies or resources of multilateral institutions in the environment and development realm, such as UNEP, UNDP or CSD. The German proposal, supported by the EU, to set up a United Nations World Commission on Sustainability and Globalization as post-Johannesburg agenda was not followed. The CSD was affirmed as the central body for sustainable development within the UN system, charged with monitoring, reviewing and coordinating Agenda 21, the programme of further implementation of Agenda 21, and the Johannesburg Plan of Implementation. The partnership initiatives launched in Johannesburg are important innovations. They forge new alliances for sustainable development among governments, companies and civil society actors.

WSSD took place in a sobering atmosphere within a changed global policy setting. The years since the Rio de Janeiro Earth Summit have been marked by turbulence in the global economy, the international

Table 2.1-1
The development goals set out in the United Nations Millennium Declaration.
Source: after UN, 2004b

GOAL 1	ERADICATE EXTREME POVERTY AND HUNGER	INDICATORS
Target 1	Halve, between 1990 and 2015, the proportion of people whose income is less than US$1 per day.	1. Proportion of population below US$1 per day 2. Poverty gap ratio (incidence and depth of poverty) 3. Share of poorest quintile in national consumption
Target 2	Halve, between 1990 and 2015, the proportion of people who suffer from hunger.	4. Prevalence of underweight children (under five years of age) 5. Proportion of population below minimum level of dietary energy consumption
GOAL 2	ACHIEVE UNIVERSAL PRIMARY EDUCATION	INDICATORS
Target 3	Ensure that, by 2015, children everywhere – boys and girls alike – will be able to complete a full course of primary schooling.	6. Net enrolment ratio in primary education 7. Proportion of pupils starting grade 1 who reach grade 5 8. Literacy rate of 15–24 year olds
GOAL 3	PROMOTE GENDER EQUALITY AND EMPOWER WOMEN	INDICATORS
Target 4	Eliminate gender disparity in primary and secondary education, preferably by 2005, and in all levels of education no later than 2015.	9. Ratio of girls to boys in primary, secondary and tertiary education 10. Ratio of literate women to men, 15–24 years old 11. Share of women in wage employment in the non-agricultural sector 12. Proportion of seats held by women in national parliament
GOAL 4	REDUCE CHILD MORTALITY	INDICATORS
Target 5	Reduce by two-thirds, between 1990 and 2015, the under-five mortality rate.	13. Under-five mortality rate 14. Infant mortality rate 15. Proportion of 1 year-old children immunized against measles
GOAL 5	IMPROVE MATERNAL HEALTH	INDICATORS
Target 6	Reduce by three-quarters, between 1990 and 2015, the maternal mortality ratio.	16. Maternal mortality ratio 17. Proportion of births attended by skilled health personnel
GOAL 6	COMBAT HIV/AIDS, MALARIA AND OTHER DISEASES	INDICATORS
Target 7	Have halted by 2015 and begun to reverse the spread of HIV/AIDS.	18. HIV/AIDS prevalence 19. Condom use rate of the contraceptive prevalence rate 20. Ratio of school attendance of orphans to school attendance of non-orphans aged 10–14 years
Target 8	Have halted by 2015 and begun to reverse the incidence of malaria and other major diseases.	21. Prevalence and death rates associated with malaria 22. Proportion of population in malaria-risk areas using effective malaria prevention and treatment measures 23. Prevalence and death rates associated with tuberculosis 24. Proportion of TB cases detected and cured under DOTS (*Directly Observed Treatment Short Course* – internationally recommended TB control strategy)
GOAL 7	ENSURE ENVIRONMENTAL SUSTAINABILITY	INDICATORS
Target 9	Integrate the principles of sustainable development into country policies and programmes, and reverse the loss of environmental resources.	25. Proportion of land area covered by forest 26. Ratio of area protected to maintain biological diversity to surface area 27. Energy use per US$ GDP (purchasing power parity) 28. CO_2 emissions and consumption of ozone-depleting CFCs 29. Proportion of population using solid fuels

▶

GOAL 7	ENSURE ENVIRONMENTAL SUSTAINABILITY	INDICATORS
Target 10	Halve by 2015 the proportion of people without sustainable access to safe drinking water and sanitation.	30. Proportion of population with sustainable access to an improved water source 31. Proportion of people with access to improved sanitation
Target 11	To have achieved by 2020 a significant improvement in the lives of at least 100 million slum dwellers.	32. Proportion of households with access to secure tenure

GOAL 8	DEVELOP A GLOBAL PARTNERSHIP FOR DEVELOPMENT	INDICATORS
Target 12	Develop further an open, rule-based, predictable, non-discriminatory trading and financial system. Includes a commitment to good governance, development and poverty reduction – both nationally and internationally.	*Official development assistance (ODA)* 33. Net ODA, total and to least developed countries (LDCs) 34. Proportion of ODA to basic social services (basic education, primary health care, nutrition, drinking water supply, sanitation and waste management) 35. Proportion of ODA that is untied
Target 13	Address the special needs of the least developed countries (LDCs). Includes: tariff and quota-free access for LDC exports; intensified programme of debt relief within the context of the enhanced HIPC Initiative and cancellation of official bilateral debt; and more generous ODA for countries committed to poverty reduction.	36. ODA received in landlocked developing countries as proportion of their GNIs 37. ODA received in small island developing states as proportion of their GNIs *Market access* 38. Proportion of total developed country imports (by value and excluding arms) from developing countries and from LDCs, admitted free of duties and quotas 39. Average tariffs and quotas imposed by developed countries on agricultural products and textiles and clothing from developing countries
Target 14	Address the special needs of landlocked and small island developing states (through the Barbados Programme and the outcome of the 22nd special session of the General Assembly).	40. Domestic and export agricultural subsidies in OECD countries as percentage of their GNI 41. Proportion of ODA provided to help build trade capacity
Target 15	Deal comprehensively with the debt problems of developing countries through national and international measures in order to make debt sustainable in the long term.	42. Number of countries reaching HIPC Initiative decision and completion points 43. Debt relief committed under HIPC Initiative 44. Debt service as percentage of exports of goods and services
Target 16	In cooperation with developing countries, develop and implement strategies for decent and productive work for youth.	45. Unemployment rate of young people aged 15–24 years
Target 17	In cooperation with pharmaceutical companies, provide access to affordable essential drugs in developing countries.	46. Proportion of population with access to affordable essential drugs on a sustainable basis
Target 18	In cooperation with the private sector, make available the benefits of new technologies, especially information and communications.	47. Number of telephone lines and cellular subscribers 48. Number of PC and Internet users

struggle against terrorism, wars, and great reticence on the part of superpower USA with regard to multilateral commitments. Against this backdrop, it is a positive achievement that Johannesburg succeeded in keeping global sustainability policy on course. What is more, the summit not only defended and affirmed the value of multilateral agreements, but also forged a new kind of multilateralism. This is exemplified in the field of energy policy, where new forms of organization have emerged in the form of networks among states willing to move the agenda forward – a 'multi-speed multilateralism' is appearing (Hauff, 2002). Results to date are thus ambivalent. Only specific implementation in the various policy fields will allow a final judgement on Johannesburg.

Table 2.1-2
Goals contained in the WSSD Plan of Implementation (Johannesburg goals).
Source: UN, 2002a

Theme	Goal	Time	Reference paragraph
Education	Recommend to the United Nations General Assembly that it consider adopting a decade of education for sustainable development, starting in 2005.	2005	124d
Education, health	Improve health literacy on a global basis.	2010	54e
Health	Reduce HIV prevalence among young men and women aged 15–24 by 25% in the most affected countries by 2005 and globally by 2010. Combat malaria, tuberculosis and other diseases.	2005/ 2010	55
Health, water	Halve the proportion of people who have no access to sanitation.	2015	8, 25
Water	Develop integrated water resources management and water efficiency plans by 2005, with support to developing countries.	2005	26
Oceans	Establish a regular process under the United Nations for global assessment of the state of the marine environment.	2004	36b
Oceans	Apply the ecosystem approach for a sustainable development of oceans by 2010.	2010	30d
Oceans, fisheries	Put into effect the international plans of action of the United Nations Food and Agriculture Organization (FAO): The international plan of action to prevent, deter and eliminate illegal, unreported and unregulated fishing by 2004; and the international plan of action for the management of fishing capacity by 2005.	2004/2005	31d
Oceans, fisheries	Develop and facilitate the use of diverse approaches and tools, including the ecosystem approach, the elimination of destructive fishing practices, the establishment of marine protected areas, including representative networks by 2012 and time/area closures for the protection of nursery grounds and periods, proper coastal land use and watershed planning and the integration of marine and coastal areas management into key sectors.	2012	32c
Oceans, fisheries	Maintain or restore stocks to levels that can produce the maximum sustainable yield with the aim of achieving these goals for depleted stocks on an urgent basis and where possible not later than 2015.	2015	31a
Forests	Accelerate implementation of the Intergovernmental Panel on Forests (IPF)/ Intergovernmental Forum on Forests (IFF) proposals for action by countries and by the Collaborative Partnership on Forests, and intensify efforts on reporting to the United Nations Forum on Forests to contribute to an assessment of progress in 2005.	2005	45g
Biological diversity	Reduce significantly the current rate of loss of biological diversity.	2010	44
Chemicals	Further develop a strategic approach to international chemicals management based on the Bahia Declaration and Priorities for Action of the Intergovernmental Forum on Chemical Safety (IFCS).	2005	23b
Chemicals	Encourage countries to implement the new globally harmonized system for the classification and labelling of chemicals as soon as possible with a view to having the system fully operational by 2008.	2008	23c
Chemicals	Achieve that chemicals are used and produced in ways that lead to the minimization of significant adverse effects on human health and the environment.	2020	23c
Atmosphere	Facilitate implementation of the Montreal Protocol on Substances that Deplete the Ozone Layer by ensuring adequate replenishment of its fund by 2003/2005.	2003/2005	39b
Atmosphere	Ensure access by developing countries to affordable, accessible, cost-effective, safe and environmentally sound alternatives to ozone-depleting substances, and assist them in complying with the phase-out schedule for these substances under the Montreal Protocol.	2010	39d
National sustainability strategies	Take immediate steps to make progress in the formulation and elaboration of national strategies for sustainable development and begin their implementation by 2005.	2005	162b
Sustainable production & consumption	Encourage and promote the development of a 10-year framework of programmes in support of regional and national initiatives to accelerate the shift towards sustainable patterns of consumption and production.	2012	15

2.1.5
Assessing the Rio process

The hopes placed on a new 'Earth politics', on a new 'development paradigm' and on the dawn of an 'environment century' have faded. Since the mid-1990s at the latest, it has become clear that Agenda 21 and the new conventions lack the strength to transform the Rio de Janeiro decisions into practical politics. Environmental policy concerns appear to be losing support, in contrast to international poverty reduction. Nonetheless, despite intensified poverty reduction efforts, for many countries attainment of the Millennium Development Goals remains a remote prospect (Section 3.6). The challenges of sustainable development will not be met by conventional development approaches alone, such as economic growth, technological progress and financial transfers. These need to be joined by a new quality of North-South cooperation, the first outlines of which are only just emerging.

Institutional fragmentation at international level, combined with inadequate financial resources, is preventing the implementation of effective strategies. Sustainability policy within the UN context is hampered by the circumstance that key decisions are taken in other international organizations. A realignment of the World Bank and the International Monetary Fund, for instance, with the objectives of sustainable development has been insufficient until now at the operative level. There is an urgent need for improved, more integrative mainstreaming of sustainability policy within the international institutional architecture and national governments alike. The strong movement of globalization critics reveals the widespread unease with economic globalization and its consequences. The calls for equity, equality, democracy and freedom are vociferous (Brand and Görg, 2002). The guiding vision of sustainable development has indeed experienced a quite unexpected breadth of dissemination and transferral to the most varied policy areas since 1992. But as yet the vision has neither been made comprehensible and practical for a broader public, nor have efforts succeeded to align national and international policies with it.

The overall assessment is thus: The desired dovetailing of environment and development policy has remained inadequate until now. The world is at a strategic juncture. If development trajectories are not put on a sustainable path soon, the opportunities to resolve global environment and development problems will be missed.

2.2
Concerted environment and development policy at a global scale

2.2.1
Rio vision: A rediscovery within the context of poverty reduction

Beyond all lofty avowals, sustainability policy must address concrete and pressing concerns – not least the huge disparities in the satisfaction of basic needs and distribution of wealth across our planet. Extreme poverty such as prevails above all in sub-Saharan Africa and South Asia is the clearest expression of an untenable social imbalance in the world.

Of late, there has been an outpouring of academic analyses and policy initiatives to solve these problems within a global welfare policy approach (Sachs, 2004). Unfortunately most of these revert to the mindset of the 1960s and 1970s – as if the ecological life-support systems on which humanity depends were a handout made by nature to a civilization committed to permanent economic growth. It is therefore high time to recall the consensus established by the Rio de Janeiro Earth Summit: Environment and development policy are inseparable – especially within the context of any strategy that is to combat worldwide poverty over the long term and reduce the dangerous volatility of the North-South gradient.

The German Advisory Council on Global Change (WBGU) formulates the key hypothesis of this report in the spirit of the Rio de Janeiro Earth Summit: Global environmental policy are prerequisite to poverty reduction. Indeed, if aligned carefully, these basic elements of a global sustainability strategy can even amplify and drive each other.

This hypothesis is supported by the realization that poverty and the associated socio-economic disparities cannot be overcome permanently through reactive transfers and repairs, but only through proactive investments to enhance the structural preconditions for people to develop their own, competitive outputs. Safeguarding sustainable environmental conditions in the relevant regions of the world is thus an essential structural policy measure.

The nexus of environment and development is characterized specifically by the following aspects:
- Global environmental policy, pursued through, for instance, the targeted prevention of dangerous climatic changes (WBGU, 2003), is indispensable in order to prevent a massive deterioration of the living and production conditions in most developing countries (and numerous industrialized countries). Empirical findings and theoretical consider-

ations show that such a deterioration would exacerbate socio-economic inequalities.

- Environmental policy instruments and mechanisms can generate significant welfare effects – intended or as side-effects. For example, the worldwide transformation of energy systems needed for reasons for climate protection requires a huge transfer of capital from the present industrialized countries to the present developing countries (WBGU, 2004), which can be utilized for the sustainable industrialization of the latter. Many equatorial states could become exporters of solar electricity in this way and thus free themselves from the cash crop trap on world markets.

- In concert with direct development policy activities, the above positive welfare effects of environmental policy could bring about a substantial reduction of poverty and inequality in many countries. Conversely, if steered carefully, this process can be expected to trigger a series of effects that reduce environmental pressures, for instance reduced utilization pressure upon fragile natural resources such as tropical forests or steppes.

- Welfare-driven environmental protection effects in developing countries could in turn amplify the effects of direct global environmental policy, for instance by freeing resources for sustainable investment in industrialized countries. The environmental changes already unavoidable today will impose major adaptation costs upon the industrialized states, which will certainly heat up the debate on the purpose of development cooperation.

- Finally, the sustainability of our present model of civilization will depend upon whether the global polarity between rich and poor countries can be reduced. Developing countries now not only have the power to impose political blockades (based not least upon ethical reasons), but also occupy a key position in terms of the preservation or destruction of the global environment. It is not acceptable that the present industrialized countries use the ecosphere to generate their welfare and at the same time refuse responsibility for maintaining this ecosphere. Taking on this responsibility means according developing countries more political clout. This is an essential precondition for a global partnership for sustainability, without which the Earth System will shift beyond control.

2.2.2
Rio transmission: Applying a systems metaphor

WBGU's core message formulated in the previous section can be illustrated using a simple image. At first, global environmental policy and global devel-

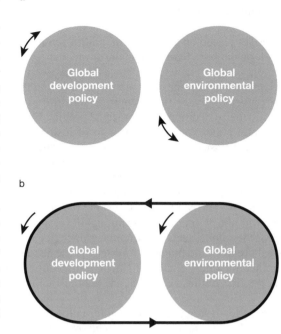

Figure 2.2-1a, b
Illustration of the two principal realms of global sustainability policy (a) and of a coupling of environment and development policy within a simple mechanical model (b).
Source: WBGU

opment policy are represented by two large flywheels which initially move unsynchronized and independently in the 'Rio space' (Fig. 2.2.1a).

In this model, coherence means coupling the flywheels to achieve a certain type of dynamics. As a metaphor of this coupling, we may imagine a transmission belt that establishes a concerted movement of the gear pair (Fig. 2.2.1b). The two policy wheels rotate in the same direction, thus moving both policy realms forward at the same time. We assume, however, that the environmental policy flywheel is the primary driving force transmitting its momentum to the development policy wheel.

Naturally this image is too coarse to be of direct use for the concrete improvement of policy coherence. We must therefore characterize the structures in greater detail and identify the specific activity areas of global sustainability policy in a further step. These are the principal elements of environment and development policy, such as the package of measures taken by industrialized countries to combat absolute poverty worldwide, or the system of environmental agreements adopted under the United Nations umbrella (Fig. 2.2-2, Table 2.2-1). This presentation makes no claim to be exhaustive, nor to separate neatly the principal policy areas. Its purpose is merely

Table 2.2-1
Policy elements: Options for global sustainability policy.
Source: WBGU

Policy areas	Characterization
Promotion of sustainable economic growth	Economic growth that is environmentally sustainable and contributes to combating poverty and reducing major disparities.
Reduction of major disparities	Mitigation of extreme socio-economic inequality, both domestic and global.
Poverty reduction	Poverty encompasses lack of income, health, food, education and social capital.
Good governance	Safeguarding an independent judiciary, efficient public administration, governmental accountability and legal stability.
Development cooperation	A generic term covering all inputs under technical, financial and human resources cooperation. It is performed by private and public bodies in both industrialized and developing countries. Development cooperation inputs can be provided either in material (e.g. loans or subsidies) or non-material form (e.g. provision of technical expertise, training).
Enhancing the operability of markets	Measures to improve market mechanisms, especially in order to raise macro-economic efficiency and stimulate innovation (e.g. removal of environmentally harmful subsidies, reduction of protectionism, internalization of external costs and benefits, competition policy).
Debt relief	Remission (in part or in full) of the debt owed to foreign creditors by heavily indebted developing countries, in order to free resources for environmental protection and poverty reduction and permit sustainable economic development.
Sustainable investment	Investment that contributes directly to sustainable development (e.g. environmental protection, basic social services) as well as measures to safeguard or help ensure that private-sector investment meets macro-economic, social and environmental standards.
Vulnerability reduction	The key concern is the vulnerability of the poor to environmental changes. This can be reduced through adaptation to or prevention of environment-related pressures.
Sustainable consumption and production patterns	Change in lifestyles and patterns of production in the direction of forms of natural resource use that have less impact or are more efficient, with the goal of preventing their scarcity as far as possible and reducing environmental impacts.
Technology transfer	Transfer of environmentally sound technologies, e.g. for energy production, transportation systems or waste management.
Resource conservation and management	Sustainable use of natural resources such as forests or fish stocks, but also of non-renewable resources such as soils, water (e.g. fossil aquifers), mineral oil, coal, mineral ores, etc.
Prevention of dangerous environmental changes	Prevention of dangerous climate change (compliance with WBGU climate guard rail) and other global environmental changes entailing potentially intolerable consequences.
Crisis and conflict prevention	Strengthening the capacity of societies to handle their conflicts in a constructive and peaceful manner, taking a preventive approach to tackle causes at root.
Maintenance of ecological integrity and diversity	Preservation of ecosystem services (flood protection, CO_2 storage, etc.) and biological diversity (ecosystem protection, species conservation, prevention of genetic impoverishment).
Financing and governance instruments	Instruments that generate financial resources for global environmental policy and poverty reduction on the one hand, and steer the behaviour of actors towards more sustainable paths on the other.
Compensation payments	International payments by states that have generated transboundary environmental impacts to the states damaged thereby.

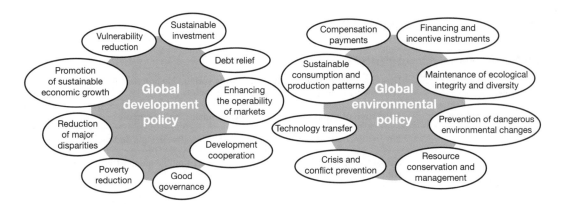

Figure 2.2-2
The elements of the Rio transmission system. The ellipses in the diagram symbolize the policy areas which can be assumed to play a key role in the concertation of global environment and development strategies.
Source: WBGU

to provide an impression of the tools and instruments that are in principle available to implement a coherent, programmatic approach.

The policy elements presented here have developed largely in isolation from each other. They need concertation within the Rio transmission to improve their effectiveness.

2.2.3
Rio strategies: Making the coherence principle operable

The idea of coupling global environment and development policy in such a way that they run in the same direction, as indicated in Figure 2.2-1b, needs to be transferred to the level of policy elements as shown schematically in Figure 2.2-2. To that end, more complex transmission belts need to be identified that attach directly to the policy elements and couple these for optimal synergy. WBGU introduces the concept of 'Rio strategies' for such types of coupling. Here the basic concept is merely illustrated (Fig. 2.2-3). Section 5.2 of the present report elaborates and details two specific examples of such strategies for concerted sustainability policy.

The strategy outlined in Figure 2.2-3 aims specifically to cope with the climate change problem (building upon the notes made in Section 2.2.1). Taking the prevention of dangerous environmental changes as starting point, financing instruments applied within the climate regime could generate a cascade of welfare effects via intensified sustainable investment in energy supply and key infrastructure, including stronger economic growth in the developing countries. This could lead on to mitigation effects with regard to land-use-related greenhouse gas emis-

sions. Debt relief motivated by this climate protection strategy could deliver a great reduction in pressure on environmental resources (here: greenhouse gas sources and sinks). Section 5.2 takes up this strategy, illustrating its concrete implementation in the form of a package of policy measures, and analysing in detail the actors involved in the Rio transmission system.

The poor integration of measures within the Rio space is doubtlessly due in part to the lack of coordination among principal actors (such as the World Bank, UNEP or FAO), as the analysis in Chapter 4 shows. None of these global players has sufficient range on its own to realize a closed strategic loop between the two great poles – the prevention of dangerous environmental changes and the elimination of absolute poverty. However, most of these actors do carry so much clout that if they are not integrated sufficiently it becomes impossible to realize a coherent Rio strategy. Fig. 2.2-4 illustrates this situation. Clearly such a constellation hampers optimal linkage of environment and development policy, or even makes it impossible. WBGU holds the view that overarching orchestration will be indispensable, (re)assigning competencies unequivocally. Restructuring the institutional architecture, such as WBGU has already outlined for the environmental realm in its 2000 report, would be a key precondition.

2.3
Principles of sustainable development in international law and ways to render them operable

The concept of sustainable development is not clearly defined. Notably, it is unclear what the relationship is

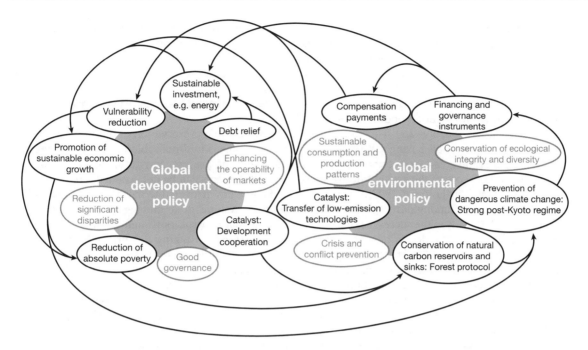

Figure 2.2-3
A possible Rio strategy for climate protection, symbolized by the coupling (arrows) of suitable policy elements. Note that multi-branched transmission mechanisms can be utilized, policy impacts can be concentrated greatly (e.g. sustainable investment) and where transmission loops are closed the strategy is self-reinforcing.
Source: WBGU

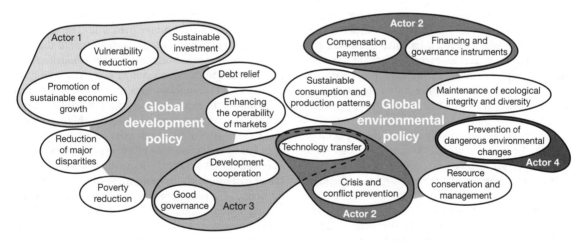

Figure 2.2-4
Schematic of the possible positions of principal actors. The policy landscape is fragmented among different realms of influence (indicated by different shading). Some of these are separate, while some overlap, which tends to create competition. The purpose of this Figure is merely to visualize the principle – the actors do not necessarily represent any specific institutions.
Source: WBGU

between environmental, developmental and socio-political objectives, whether the independence of each individual objective is retained and what the legal nature of the concept is or should be (Epiney and Scheyli, 1998). This debate shall not be taken up here, especially considering its limited productivity.

Rather, the following reflections proceed from two insights which are essentially undisputed and have gained prominence through the discourse on the concept of sustainable development and the stress on its role as a leading principle of international politics:

- In addition to its intragenerational perspective the concept of sustainable development embraces the perspective of future generations (intergenerational perspective). This entails developing human behaviour and politics in such a way that the needs of the present generation are met without endangering the essential conditions for life of future generations (Section 2.1). Thus the notion of the present generation having a responsibility for future generations is of key importance. This can be termed the core of the concept of sustainable development (Bartholomäi, 1997).
- The diverse linkages among different global policies (Section 2.2) leads to the success of one policy depending closely on the design of other policies and vice versa. In terms of the theme of the present report, for instance, advancing environmental degradation precludes sustained elimination of poverty. Similarly, poverty has a negative impact on the state of the environment. Thus, effective and sustainable policy-making always demands taking comprehensive account of the effects of other policies.

Both these categories of insights or concerns are scarcely operable as such. Proceeding from this understanding, the international community has developed a set of principles that establish necessary preconditions for the protection of present and future generations and/or for taking into account the linkages among different policies – the focus being placed here on environmental policy on the one hand and poverty-reduction or development policies on the other. These principles of sustainable development are generally and politically recognized; their legal nature – that is whether and to what extent these principles can give rise to binding legal obligations, in particular for states – is in part subject to differing opinion. They can be grouped around four major axes, each of which expresses its own perspective on the preconditions for realizing the above two insights and encompasses a range of subaspects. These four axes or lines of orientation are: The protection of natural life-support systems as an overarching objective (Section 2.3.1), taking into account the interplay between different policy areas (principle of integration, Section 2.3.2), the principle of the commensurability of measures taken to implement concrete policy goals (Section 2.3.3) and the question of minimum standards for the institutional architecture needed to implement sustainable development (Section 2.3.4).

Concerning the relationship between these different principles, it must be noted that they each represent fundamentally independent principles – although clearly some aspects, such as the balancing of different interests or concerns, can play a role in the context of several principles, whereby such aspects may pull in different directions.

2.3.1
Protecting natural life-support systems

The sustainable preservation of our natural life-support systems is indispensable if we are to safeguard the rights of present and future generations. Two basic statements can be deduced from this.

Firstly, any irreversible harm to our natural life-support systems that endangers supraregional or even global control loops and equilibrium must be avoided. Only by taking this principle into account will it be possible to ensure that natural life-support systems are left intact and are adequate for present and future generations. This can be translated into action in some areas using 'ecological guard rails' (Section 3.6). This principle is widely recognized as such; however, its normative density and precision are not sufficient to derive legally relevant strictures. At most, as the concept of sustainable development is a principle in international law, and as the principle of protecting natural life-support systems flows from that concept, the latter could be accorded the status of a guiding principle (Epiney and Scheyli, 1998).

Secondly, the idea of sustainable protection of our natural life-support systems highlights the significance of the precautionary principle. The basic idea behind this principle is that, in cases where there is a lack of full scientific certainty or knowledge, it justifies action and can even oblige countries to act in a certain way. The weight which the precautionary principle brings to bear in international environmental law can be summarized as follows: where countries must make decisions about courses of action which could have a detrimental effect on the environment, they should take a future-focussed approach. Action taken early should stop potential pollution from even occurring. Furthermore, the precautionary principle in international law places countries under an obligation to regulate or even ban outright those activities or substances that could cause serious environmental degradation – especially where risks to the environment are high due to long-term or irreversible damage – even if no clear scientific proof of the potential damage has been obtained. The precautionary principle has been enshrined in many international treaties. See for example Article 3(3) of the Framework Convention on Climate Change, Article 2(1) of the Alpine Convention, Article 4(3)(f) of the Bamako Convention and Article 2(2)(a) of the OSPAR Convention. The principle has also been acknowledged in other important documents, for example, it constitutes Principle 15 of the Rio Declaration.

The case law of the international courts now also contains references to the principle; in the literature on international law the precautionary principle is increasingly being considered to be part of international custom (Sands, 2003). However, the principle does not contain any precise models for how to proceed during its application, as it is only a basic guideline for choosing a course of action. Nevertheless, a relatively firm set of instructions for action can be derived from the principle in individual cases. Take for example the 1999 Decision of the International Tribunal for the Law of the Sea in the Southern Bluefin Tuna case. Despite scientific uncertainty about the stock levels necessary to ensure the survival of the species, the Court decided to order a precautionary measure within the meaning of Article 290(5) of the Convention on the Law of the Sea: experimental fishing of the relevant species was to cease immediately (Marr, 2000).

The precautionary principle is closely linked to a series of other principles, which could be described as principles for the implementation or practical application of the precautionary principle:

- The *principle of using the best available technology and the best environmental practice* is aimed at ensuring that, even where there is a lack of certainty about the environmental damage that will arise from a particular course of action, the latest techniques not entailing excessive cost will be applied.
- The *principle that environmental damage should be rectified at source* dictates that pollution must be tackled as soon as possible after it has occurred and as close as possible to its source. Like the precautionary principle, the principle of rectification at source aims to ensure that pollution is tackled as early as possible.
- The *polluter pays principle* should be viewed as an allocation of responsibility for reducing or preventing pollution and/or for bearing the cost of a particular measure. Given that the polluter is obliged to bear the cost, the principle is aimed at reducing or preventing pollution; thus it also promotes the precautionary principle.

These principles have also been adopted in many international law documents (Epiney and Scheyli, 1998). However, apart from the principle of using the best available technology and the best environmental practice, there has not yet been sufficient continuity of acknowledgement in international jurisprudence that these principles are international custom. This does not alter the fact that these principles are important for the legal and political aspects of environmental policy making, especially as they can and should form a starting point and act as a guide for international legal and national policy.

2.3.2
The principle of integration, with particular consideration of equity

Discussion of the concept of sustainable development has raised awareness of the significant linkages between measures in different policy areas. If such recognition were translated into a principle to be considered in policy making, it would be called the principle of integration. The thrust of this principle can be summarized as follows: that implications for other policies should always be considered during policy making and, conversely, that achievement against objectives in one policy area is always conditional on measures taken in other policy areas. Generally speaking, it is a question of observing and considering the varied and highly complex interactions between different policies and measures in different areas. As this principle – which we will call the principle of integration – is of a general nature, the scope for operationalizing it is limited. It can, however, provide the backdrop for a series of additional principles, which are important for the interplay between environmental policy and poverty. These include the following:

- The fundamental requirement is to take equity into account. Some equity principles have emerged in international case law in relation to specific areas or specific questions. Hence the aim to uphold both inter- and intra-generational equity, equality of opportunity between men and women and solidarity between and within countries (equitable burden sharing).
- The principle of common, but differentiated responsibilities has also been enshrined in various international treaties (e.g. Art. 3(1) of the Convention on Climate Change) and documents (such as Principle 7 of the Rio Declaration). This states that all countries bear a common responsibility for protecting the natural environment, but that burdens should be shared according to the pressure each country has put on the global environment and according to each country's financial and technological resources.

A clear connection emerges here with rule-of-law requirements and especially with bans on discrimination. As regards discrimination, recent consideration of gender mainstreaming has highlighted the need for all policies to address gender issues.

For the most part, the principles described here are general postulates of equity. As such, the scope for operationalizing them is very limited; they first need to be translated into concrete terms in the various areas. These principles therefore have no claim to be legally binding, but should be considered as policy making guidelines, which form the basis for further obligations on countries.

2.3.3
The proportionality principle

Closely allied to the principle of integration is the proportionality principle. The general thrust of this is that measures taken must be designed to achieve their intended objective and other interests must not be disadvantaged more than absolutely necessary in order to reach that objective (necessity). When assessing the benefit of a measure, it is necessary to ensure that other targets of protection are not put at an excessive disadvantage. Thus every (environmental) policy initiative must be examined to check that it does not have a disproportionate effect on economic and social policy objectives. The converse also applies, i.e. economic and social policy measures must be drawn up in such a way that they do not imply a disproportionate impact upon the realization of environmental policy objectives.

2.3.4
The institutional framework

Sustainable development can only become a reality if a certain minimum standard is upheld for constitutional (rule of law) and institutional principles and frameworks and if suitable institutions exist to put the principles into practice. The following rights and principles are particularly important in this context:
- *Human rights* are defined in many international treaties and are for the most part considered to form part of international custom. These rights guarantee the citizen fundamental, individual, legally enforceable rights in relation to 'their' own country. In addition to the traditional protective rights (such as the right to life and the right to freedom from harm), bans on discrimination (especially on the basis of sex or race) and rights of entitlement also come into play. In this report, entitlements are of particular importance. International decisions, especially those made by the Committee on Economic, Social and Cultural Rights indicate that entitlements can to some extent become a reality and can thus place the State under justiciable obligations. For example, the concept of a *minimum core content* assumes that a certain minimum content can be defined for most entitlements and that in cases of non-fulfilment the corresponding obligation has therefore been infringed. This can be illustrated with reference to the right to food: nutritional requirements for human beings

can be determined both quantitatively and qualitatively, also implying a right to clean drinking water. Where the limits are not respected, the country concerned is said to have infringed this right, unless it can justify its position, especially on the grounds of force *majeure* or the impossibility of performance. Furthermore, the core content of such entitlements can in the long term only be guaranteed on condition that resources are managed sustainably. This can be illustrated using the example of water: if water resources are not managed sustainably, there is a danger that, in many regions and within the foreseeable future, clean drinking water will cease to be available (Epiney, 2003).
- The principle of *participation* is also important: policies can only succeed in the long term if sufficient, effective involvement of the public in general and affected persons in particular in the implementation of environmental and development policy is given. However, it is not possible, given the current state of development, to formulate general, universally acknowledged principles beyond the general rule that public participation is necessary. Instead, rights to and responsibilities for participation arise within individual policies. One example of this is environmental impact assessment (EIA) law; another, in the European context, would be the Aarhus Convention on Access to Information, Public Participation in Decision-making and Access to Justice in Environmental Matters.
- In addition to this, the general requirement to consider minimum constitutional standards and principles of *good governance* should be noted. This relates to minimum requirements for the manner in which a state or a government is run, which are highly significant for the effective implementation of policy objectives. It should be noted that this type of principle does not normally become legally binding.
- Finally, suitable *institutional arrangements* need to be set up at both national and international levels to ensure policy is made in a way that safeguards sustainability. Particular attention should be paid in this context to the interface between environmental and development policy.

2.3.5
Rendering the principles operable

WGBU has developed the idea of guard rails to operationalize the concept of sustainable development (WBGU, 1997, 2003b). Guard rails are limits on damage and can be defined quantitatively; a breach of these limits would give rise either immediately or in future to intolerable consequences so significant that even major utility gains could not compensate for the damage (WBGU, 2001a). Thus guard rails form a type of barrier, separating sustainable from unsustainable system states.

For global climate change, the global aggregated danger threshold (or guard rail) is estimated to be a rise in the global average temperature of over 2°C above pre-industrial levels. The overall long-term rate of warming should not exceed 0.2°C per decade (WBGU, 1995, 2003a). The Earth System is currently in the sustainable area as regards climate change, but is on a high-speed collision course with the guard rail (Section 3.3.1).

If a system is in the non-sustainable area, it must be steered by appropriate measures in such a way that it moves through the guard rail into the sustainable area. If a system is in the sustainable area, there are no further requirements upon it at first. The system can develop in the free interplay of forces. Only if the system, moving within the sustainable area, is on course for collision with a guard rail, must measures be taken to prevent it crossing the rail. If systems do not breach the guard rail, this does not mean that all socioeconomic abuse or ecological damage will be avoided in all regions, as global guard rails do not take into account the fact that the effects of global change can vary significantly from region to region and sector to sector.

As guard rails can shift due to future advances in knowledge, compliance with present guard rails is only a necessary criterion of sustainability, but it is not sufficient. In any case, the guard rails defined by WGBU can only be seen as suggestions. The task of setting the level above which degradation cannot be tolerated must not be left to science alone. Instead, it should be performed – with the support of scientists – as part of a world-wide, democratic decision making process (WBGU, 2003).

Guard rails are not objectives. They are not desirable values or states, but minimum requirements that need to be obeyed if sustainability is to be achieved. However, where guard rail limits are breached or where it appears that this is imminent, quantitative and time-bound goals may be derived from the relevant guard rails. Goals are political declarations of intent. Thus the Millennium Development Goals should be interpreted as interim targets, which should allow for as rapid a transition as possible between the current situation and the sustainable area, given what is achievable from a political and societal point of view (Section 2.1.3). A failure to achieve the MDGs is undesirable from a political and ethical perspective, but it does not follow that the realization of sustainable development will be fundamentally impossible as a result.

The present report begins by defining only the ecological guard rails and working with 'goals' in the social realm. The first reason for this is that, if the ecological guard rail limits are breached, irreversible loss of our natural life-support systems occurs, whereas if societal guard rail limits are breached, this is negative in both the short and long term, but not fundamentally irreversible. The second reason is that an international catalogue of social goals already exists in the shape of the MDGs; this is not perfect (Section 3.6), but it is sufficient to set the initial direction.

Poverty, vulnerability and environmental change – The setting and trends **3**

This chapter explores the systemic linkages between poverty and environmental factors. First of all, Section 3.1.1 outlines various concepts of poverty. Section 3.1.2 goes on to present the main strands of vulnerability research, a branch of science concerned with the vulnerability of societies to crisis such as disaster and conflict, and to environmental change. Building upon that analytical foundation, Section 3.2 presents the dimensions of poverty examined by the present report: income and asset poverty, disease, undernourishment, lack of education, lack of social capital and societal stability. Section 3.3 then sets out the main global environmental changes, concentrating particularly upon their interactions with the dimensions of poverty. The presentations of the dimensions of poverty and environmental changes all conclude with a discussion of the prospects for attaining relevant international goals.

The vulnerability of poor groups is determined not only by environmental changes, but also, to a great degree, by the global setting. Key factors are demographic development, the future development of the global economy and technological development. Section 3.4 provides an analysis of the potential trajectories of these contextual factors, their linkages with vulnerability, and possible points of leverage for policy action.

The knowledge currently available precludes any global, quantitative analysis of vulnerability; the issues are too complex and data availability too poor. Moreover, such an analysis would operate at a level of aggregation that might make any concrete recommendations for action thus obtained appear dubious. At the regional or local level, however, if appropriate data are available, a cogent analysis of vulnerability is indeed possible. WBGU performs such an analysis in Section 3.5 with two case studies on Burkina Faso and northeast Brazil. These case studies are concerned less with delivering precise policy recommendations than with illustrating the basic approach of this new methodology.

Section 3.6 makes the link to the policy level. The synoptic analysis of international goals and their financeability provided in that section sets the scene for the analysis of relevant policy processes performed in Chapter 4.

3.1
Conceptual fundamentals

3.1.1
Poverty as a multidimensional concept

People who live in extreme poverty are directly dependent on natural resources and functioning ecosystems in their daily struggle for survival. They are the ones who are especially affected by changes in the natural environment, a phenomenon which will gain in significance over the coming decades (Watts and Bohle, 1993). In order to analyse the relationship between poverty and the environment in more detail, the following section introduces first the concept of poverty used by WBGU. The focus in this report is on poverty in developing and newly industrializing countries (Box 3.1-1). This type of poverty is different from that found in industrialized countries. For although 130 million people in industrialized countries live on less than 50 per cent of the average income and are designated as poor (UNDP, 2001a), this relative poverty is manifested less in an experience of need that threatens people's survival than in a low standard of living and a lack of opportunities for participation in civil society.

Income indicators are widely used nowadays as a means of measuring the poverty experienced by countries and by people; on the data available international comparisons are relatively easy on this basis. However, they have been criticized as being inadequate, particularly in the context of development policy (Reddy and Pogge, 2002; UNDP, 2003c; Section 3.2.1). The reason for this, in addition to certain methodological and conceptual difficulties, is that they fail to reflect the fact that poverty means more than simply having insufficient income.

WBGU has taken a broad concept of poverty as a basis for this report, regarding poverty as a lack of access and entitlements in the broadest sense. The work of Amartya Sen, who devised the concept of capabilities in the 1970s and 1980s, should be mentioned here in particular (Sen, 1981; Drèze and Sen, 1989). Starting out from the notion of entitlements, he developed a definition of poverty that not only addresses the issue of material well-being but also that of opportunities: these arise out of what poor people are able or unable to do (capabilities), and from what they do or do not do (functions) (Sen, 1999). The understanding of poverty is thus broadened since it includes as an indicator a person's capacity to reach certain goals. Poverty then encompasses inadequate nutrition, poor health and health care provision, inadequate education and a lack of social networks and participatory opportunities, in addition to a low per capita income and unequal income distribution (Section 3.2). Usually it is particular sections of the population, such as children, older people, women, the rural population, indigenous communities, etc., who are affected to a greater than proportional extent by poverty (Box 3.1-2).

The Human Development Index (HDI) and the Human Poverty Index (HPI) of the United Nations Development Programme are indicators that take into account other dimensions besides income (Box 3.1-3).

Human development, according to Sen, is aimed at removing the sources of unfreedom and the barriers that limit an individual's capacity to make choices and to act. Linked implicitly to this is the demand for civil and political rights and for participation in decisions at different levels of society (Box 3.1-4).

Poor people themselves frequently give expression to a broad understanding of poverty that goes beyond income poverty (Robb, 1999; Chambers, 1995; Jodha, 1991). For some years now the World Bank and other organizations have been conducting Participatory Poverty Assessments, especially in connection with participatory processes undertaken in the course of devising Poverty Reduction Strategy Papers (Section 4.2.10). Participatory approaches to poverty require the direct involvement of poor people in defining and measuring poverty.

WBGU thus conceives of poverty as a multidimensional, dynamic, gender- and location-specific phenomenon. In WBGU's view, the aim of poverty reduction policy should be to improve the range of opportunities available to poor people and groups in developing countries. In order to achieve this, it is necessary to look in particular at the interactions between poverty and changes in the natural environment.

3.1.2
The vulnerability of the poor to environmental change

Poor people in developing countries are especially affected by environmental change because they are much more exposed to existential risks, such as disease, hunger, loss of income and so on, and therefore have only limited coping and adaptive capacities. In order to reduce poor people's vulnerability to environmental change, it is necessary first to understand the factors and structures that generate and perpetuate vulnerability and thereby obstruct the quest for human security. Both internal factors (e.g. social structure, land use) and external factors (e.g. integra-

Box 3.1-2

Examples of particularly vulnerable groups

Children, elderly people, women, rural populations, indigenous communities, and so forth, often possess a lesser degree of political and civil rights as well as access to income, health care, nutrition, or education than other social groups and thus are more directly affected by environmental crises.

DISADVANTAGING OF WOMEN
Women and girls are particularly exposed to physical and psychological violence, have lower literacy and school enrolment rates, and are mostly underrepresented in political decision-making bodies. As a result, they have little influence on the shaping of societal change. The prevailing inheritance, family and land laws often prevent economic autonomy and accumulation of capital in the hands of women. As a consequence, very many women lead economically insecure lives. Approximately 70 per cent of the people living in poverty are women. To support the family, women depend mostly upon natural resources such as water or firewood, whose mounting shortage necessitates increased time and effort. Therefore, women are especially affected by environmental changes. Amartya Sen has highlighted the need to strengthen the role of women through education, creation of income opportunities, and the guarantee of property rights. Through this empowerment of women, their capabilities are to be strengthened and the key roles taken into account that they play when coping with pivotal development problems such as child mortality or population growth.

DISADVANTAGING OF INDIGENOUS COMMUNITIES
According to United Nations estimates, there are roughly 350 million indigenous people worldwide, 70 per cent of which live in Asia. Some 70 countries harbour indigenous people. However, the identification and definition of indigenous people is controversial. Even today, numerous governments do not recognize the designation indigenous people because it implies a right to self-determination. Therefore, the United Nations Working Group uses the designation 'indigenous community'. In all societies, indigenous people have been marginalized and excluded for centuries. Therefore, today they belong almost without exception to the most disadvantaged and vulnerable groups. Per capita income is considerably lower than that of non-indigenous groups, illiteracy rates are several times higher, health care is worse, unemployment is higher. If one asks the indigenous people themselves, poverty is a consequence of disregard of their rights and identities as autonomous peoples. Today, large portions of indigenous population groups no longer live in traditional structures, but as peasants or day labourers on the outskirts of cities. The remaining indigenous people who live traditionally often tie their cultures closely with the natural environment. Usually, there is a pronounced responsibility to preserve ancestral land for use by subsequent generations. The physical and cultural survival of these indigenous peoples who live traditionally is dependent upon the protection of their land and their natural resources. Therefore, one of the main demands of indigenous interest groups is access to land and natural resources.

DISADVANTAGING OF PEOPLE IN RURAL AREAS
On average, rural people have lower income, poorer educational and health status, as well as inferior access to drinking water and sanitary facilities than do people in cities. Poverty in the city is commonly characterized by unemployment, employment in the informal sector, life in slums, high population density, health problems caused by air pollution, contaminated water, toxic waste, as well as loss of social networks. In contrast, rural poverty is characterized mostly by lack of tenure, semi-feudal conditions, dominance of the agricultural sector, a subsistence economy, and lack of access to social services. Many landless people are forced to secure a livelihood for themselves on marginal land. In rural regions, peasants, landless people, indigenous people, refugees, women, and nomads are under the greatest threat. In most developing countries, there is an urban bias that has been scarcely taken into sufficient consideration within the context of lending policies of the International Monetary Fund and World Bank during past decades and even today. For example, only very few resources flow into the strengthening of the rural financial infrastructure. Lack of microcredit opportunities diminishes the prospects of rural populations to escape poverty (Section 5.6). These causes drove the pronounced migration to the cities during the 20th century. This urbanization trend will continue in forthcoming decades: The World Bank predicts that 4,000 million of the 7,000 million people in developing and transition countries will be living in urban areas in the year 2030 and 5,000–6,000 million of 8,000 million people in 2050.

Sources: Engelhard and Otto, 2001; OECD, 2002b; Sen, 1981, 1999; UN, 2001a; Psacharopoulos and Patrinos, 1994; Feiring, 2003; IFAD, 2001; Ekbom and Bojö, 1999; World Bank, 2003d

tion of a country into the global economy, impact of global climate change) need to be taken into account. The guiding question is: What makes an individual or a social group especially vulnerable?

While conventional concepts of poverty emphasize levels of income and consumption and expanded concepts of poverty focus on people's capabilities and opportunities (Drèze and Sen, 1989), concepts of vulnerability concentrate on the loss of factors such as income or entitlements, through which people's very existence is put at risk. Such concepts of vulnerability unpick the notion of poverty and look at it from the point of view of the processes, mechanisms and changing range of options that pose a threat to people's capacity to secure their survival in a sustainable way, both now and in the future. Thus, they are particularly well suited to examining the impact of current and predicted environmental change on the situation of the poor.

Vulnerability research developed from the late 1980s onwards out of disaster research and research on food security, and has also been gaining currency since the end of the 1990s in studies on global change. In addition to research networks such as the International Human Dimensions Programme on Global Environmental Change (IHDP), the concept has taken hold in policy think-tanks such as the IPCC and has also been taken up by the United Nations

Box 3.1-3

Measuring the multiple dimensions of poverty – the Human Development and Human Poverty Index

The United Nations Development Programme (UNDP) has taken on board Sen's expanded notion of poverty: 'Poverty means being deprived of the most important basic necessities. These include a long and healthy life, an appropriate material provision and participation in the life of the society'. Since single indicators fail to do justice to this approach, the programme introduced an aggregated indicator in 1990 – the Human Development Index (HDI). In this index, the three dimensions of health, education and standard of living are rendered operational through life expectancy at birth, the literacy and school enrolment rate, and a weighted per capita income.

Whereas the HDI is intended to measure the overall progress in a country's human development, the Human Poverty Index (HPI) introduced in 1997 reflects the way in which this progress is distributed, and measures the proportion of people who have no share in development. The HPI is similar in its construction to the HDI (Table 3.1-1).

The advantage of the HDI and HPI is that they are able to depict deficiencies and progress that cannot be captured in monetary terms. However, criticism can be directed at the high level of aggregation of the indicators as well as the problem that weaknesses in one dimension may be compensated for by strengths in another. Currently no conceptual basis exists for such a differentiation. Finally, certain important dimensions, such as political freedom, insecurity and social exclusion, are not taken into consideration. .

Sources: UNDP, 1997; Kanbur, 2002; Ravaillon, 2003

Index	Life span	Knowledge	Standard of living
HDI	Life expectancy at birth	Adult literacy and school enrolment rates	Per capita gross domestic product (purchasing power in US$)
HPI	Probability at birth of not reaching the age of 40	Adult literacy rate	Inadequate provision, measured by the proportion of a population without access to clean water and by the proportion of underweight children less than 5 years old

Table 3.1-1
Composition of HDI and HPI.
Source: UNDP, 2003c

Box 3.1-4

Poverty and human rights

Human poverty and deprivation are a manifestation of serious human rights abuses. International law protects the economic, social and cultural rights of the individual that became legally binding in the Universal Declaration of Human Rights of 1948. Known as ESC rights, they were fleshed out in the International Covenant on Social, Economic and Cultural Rights (Social Covenant) which was adopted by the UN General Assembly in 1966 and which entered into force in 1976. By June 2004, 149 States had ratified the Social Covenant. Directly relevant to poverty are for example the rights to social security (Art. 9), food (Art. 11), health (Art. 12), education (Art. 13) and participation in cultural life (Art. 15). A special UN committee (Committee on Economic, Social and Cultural Rights) which began its work in 1987 carries responsibility for monitoring the observance of the Social Covenant. In addition to dealing with country reports by governments and NGOs, the com-

mittee contributes towards the conceptual development of SEC rights through its so-called general commentaries, for example relating to the rights of the handicapped (1994) and the right to water (2002). In contrast to the Civil Covenant, no individual complaints procedure has been established to-date. And yet since 1996 the Contracting States have had access to the UN Human Rights Commission's draft of such an Optional Protocol. Countless States have reservations about it as they reject raising the value of ESC rights to a position of equality with political rights and civil liberties. The Social Covenant also has international legal relevance for development cooperation as Article 2 embodies the reciprocal obligation of the Contracting States to fulfil the ESC standards. Thus international assistance programmes' focus on poverty is no longer at the discretion of the donor countries but rather a consequence of international legal obligations. The reference to human rights norms leads to a shift of perspective in development policies. The starting point of a rights-based North-South cooperation process is the universally recognized Conventions, not the interests or one-sided intentions of the donor or receiving party.

(Bohle, 2001; IPCC, 2001b; Kasperson and Kasperson, 2001b). UNEP, FAO, the International Decade for Natural Disaster Reduction (IDNDR, now ISDR) as well as the current report to the UN General Assembly 'World Social Situation 2003' all address various aspects of vulnerability research or even place them at the centre of their considerations (UNGA, 2003). The World Bank has also been working with this concept more recently. The concept of vulnerability is increasingly being taken note of by the implementing organizations because it offers a framework for developing policy options. The following sections present the most important strands in vulnerability research, upon which basis the integrative analytical concept for vulnerability assessment developed by WBGU is introduced. Finally, this analytical concept will be applied in Section 3.5.

3.1.2.1
Approaches in vulnerability research

Conceptual notions of vulnerability are many and varied in this still young field of research that encompasses so many different disciplines (Sections 3.1.2.2, 3.1.3.3). Developing a common language that can straddle these different disciplines represents a considerable challenge. The WBGU vulnerability analysis presented in this report (Section 3.5) is therefore only one of many possible methodologies for approaching the study of the poverty-environment nexus. This is illustrated in the following overview of the most important research approaches, which indicates that vulnerability research is characterized, to a greater extent than in other fields, by quite heterogeneous approaches, data problems and inadequacies of methods and models (Corell et al., 2001). Up until now, efforts to bring together within an integrative concept the factors that play a role in vulnerability on the different spatial scales (locally, regionally, globally) with their systemic impacts (such as ecosystem degradation, harm to economic and social systems) and their impacts on specific social groups (such as limitations of scope for action, impoverishment, existential crisis, death) have been only of limited success. WBGU addresses these two aspects of impact in Sections 3.2 (dimensions of poverty) and 3.3 (environmental change).

At a workshop organized by the Stockholm Environment Institute in 2001 an attempt was made to outline an integrative concept for analysing vulnerability (Kasperson and Kasperson, 2001a). This involved extending the focus of research from concentration on a single stress event to analysing a whole package of negative impacts and stress factors. Environmental and societal factors both play a role in this. The human/environment system is being regarded as a whole that includes different systemic levels and actor groups. Fig. 3.1-1 shows the main elements of this approach to integrated vulnerability research (Kasperson and Kasperson, 2001b).

As far as the aims of the present report are concerned, it makes sense to draw a distinction between social and biophysical vulnerability (Brooks and Adger, 2003). Whereas the biophysical vulnerability approach essentially accords with the view of natural disaster research and deals with systemic vulnerabilities and risks in particular – such as potential eco-

system degradation and damage to the economy – the field of social vulnerability deals with the susceptibility of humans and of the conditions necessary for their survival within a social system.

3.1.2.2
Biophysical vulnerability

Biophysical vulnerability (Brooks and Adger, 2003) is predominantly about the vulnerability of systems, although some studies of this kind also identify crisis-prone regions and locations (Kasperson et al., 1995). The focus of interest here is the exposure of a system or a region and its potential sensitivity to, e.g., environmental crises. The probability of such events occurring and the extent of the damage caused also play an important role in the analysis. Biophysical vulnerability and (environmental) risk are broadly equivalent (Brooks and Adger, 2003).

The IPCC has proposed a widely used definition of vulnerability for this field of research. It is described as the extent to which a system is vulnerable to the adverse effects of climate change (including climate variability and extreme events) and to what extent it is unable to adapt to such impacts. Vulnerability is a function of the type, extent and speed of climatic fluctuations to which a system is exposed, as well as its sensitivity and adaptive capacity. The impact may be either direct (such as a change in agricultural yield as a response to a change in average temperatures or temperature variability) or indirect (such as damage caused by recurrent coastal flooding, itself a result of rising sea levels).

Analyses of biophysical vulnerability can produce vulnerability maps, which depict the probabilities of certain disasters occurring (earthquakes, droughts, heavy rainfall, storms, technological accidents, and epidemics; Hewitt, 1997) or the number of people at risk. These vulnerability maps provide a basis for planning crisis prevention measures. The first global vulnerability analysis looked at the consequences of a potential rise in sea levels (Nicholls and Hoozemans, 2000).

The aspect of environmental change that has been studied most comprehensively in relation to biophysical vulnerability is global climate change (Hoozemans et al., 1993; Parry and Livermore, 1999) and its indirect consequences, such as an increase in weather extremes or changes in the water cycle and sea levels (Nicholls et al., 1995; Nicholls and Hoozemans, 2000). Brooks and Adger (2003) have undertaken a retrospective analysis of the vulnerability of specific countries to climate change over a period going back three decades (up to 2000). Their analysis was based on country-related data about deaths from

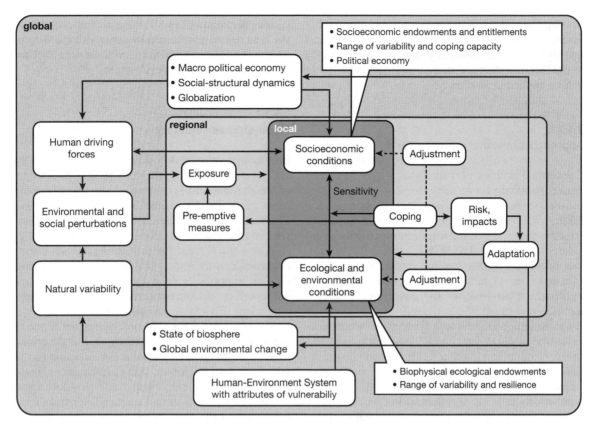

Figure 3.1-1
Elements of an integrated vulnerability analysis. Starting from the observation that the causes of vulnerability differ according to their spatial dimension and their scope of impact, the analysis differentiates between local, regional and global factors. Factors with the widest scope of impact include global environmental change (Section 3.3) and the global economic system (Section 3.4). In the regional/local context vulnerability is determined chiefly by the exposure of a system or a social group to stress as well as the existing capacity to deal with or adapt to adversities (Section 3.2). Irrespective of analytical level, both environmental and social systems and the social groups affected are included in the overall assessment of vulnerability. Source: Kasperson and Kasperson, 2001b

natural disasters and about people severely affected by weather-related natural disasters. This study, like many others on the same subject, shows that developing countries are the ones most under threat from climate change.

Prompted by the International Decade for Natural Disaster Reduction (IDNDR, now ISDR) declared by the United Nations, various studies emerged during the 1990s on natural disasters, and in particular on how to prevent them and how to cope with them (e.g. Feldbrügge and von Braun, 2002; DFG, 1993). The increasing significance of risks from nature is also reflected in the growing number of regular reports on the issue. The International Red Cross publishes an annual world disaster report, which addresses the consequences of natural disasters in particular, along with issues of prediction and coping strategies (IFRC, 2002). The reinsurance Munich Re publishes regular statistics about the costs of natural disasters around the world along with world maps of natural risks (Münchner Rück, 2002a–c, 2003). In addition,

UNDP published a Disaster Profile for the Least Developed Countries in 2001 and the 'Disaster Risk' vulnerability report in 2004.

Vulnerability analyses also deal with the development of other kinds of environmental change, usually related to specific regions (e.g. loss of biological diversity, soil degradation, water scarcity). For example, WBGU has developed a criticality index for regional vulnerability to freshwater crises and has produced a global overview on this basis (WBGU, 1998a). In all areas of environmental change, the interaction between specific factors – such as cumulation, overlaps and positive feedback loops between, say, climate change, soil degradation and freshwater scarcity – is becoming increasingly significant. Attempts are currently being made to produce an overall view, and to this end the IHDP core project Global Environmental Change and Human Security is engaged in developing an Index of Human Insecurity (Lonergan et al., 2000; Box 3.1-5). In addition, a framework concept for quantitative assessment of vulner-

Box 3.1-5

Approaches to operationalization: Vulnerability indices

INITIAL SUGGESTIONS FROM UNEP REGARDING A
VULNERABILITY INDEX FOR CLIMATE CHANGE
The UN Environment Programme has begun to develop
some ideas for a vulnerability index using climate change
as an example. According to UNEP such an index can be
formulated as a function of vulnerability, criticality, adaptive capacity and disaster event. Due to a lack of data and
models, however, it is not possible currently to produce
a robust global analysis of these interconnected factors.
An initial approach, so UNEP believes, would be to link
sectoral vulnerability (in agriculture, say) to climatic risks.
One example of such a domain of vulnerability is subsistence agriculture in semi-arid regions.

A second approach, according to UNEP, would be to
start with measurements that have already been used, such
as the Human Development Index (HDI) and its relationship to vulnerability in specific sectors. In view of evident
deficiencies in securing elementary assets in sub-Saharan
Africa, for example, it is obvious that the consequences of
climate change may pose a particularly serious threat here.
The vulnerability of specific social groups, however, cannot
be adequately portrayed using these sorts of aggregated
data. Further social scientific research would be required
for this.

VULNERABILITY-RESILIENCE INDICATOR
The Pacific Northwest National Laboratory has been commissioned by the US Department of Energy to develop a
quantitative method for measuring vulnerability to climate
change. A total of 17 indicators were set up in five sensitivity sectors (food security, settlements and infrastructure,
health, ecosystems and availability of fresh water) and three
coping capacity sectors (human capital, economic efficiency
and adaptive capacity of the environment). The difference
between aggregated sensitivity (negative value) and coping
capacity (positive value) produces a vulnerability resilience
indicator. This was calculated for the present and future
conditions of 38 countries. Of these, Canada proves to be
the least vulnerable and Yemen the most vulnerable to climate change. Additionally, three different scenarios were
calculated up to the year 2095.

INDEX OF HUMAN INSECURITY
The Index of Human Insecurity was developed for the Global Environmental Change and Human Security Project of

the IHDP. It identifies vulnerable or insecure regions, both
currently and in the future, with the aim of supporting decision makers in the field of development cooperation. The
index comprises a total of 16 indicators taken from the different spheres of the environment, the economy, society and
institutions.

GLOBAL RISK VULNERABILITY INDEX
In 2004 UNDP published a report entitled Reducing Disaster Risk, which contained the first ever Global Risk Vulnerability Index (GRVI). This index serves to identify the
essential factors for determining the risk configuration
of a country. Now that nationally differentiated GRVIs
have been developed, it is possible to make a comparison
between countries and to capture changes in vulnerability.
The Center for Natural Risks and Development at the University of Bonn (ZENEB) is coordinating Germany's contribution.

ENVIRONMENTAL VULNERABILITY INDEX
The South Pacific Applied Geoscience Commission
(SOPAC) is working on an *environmental vulnerability
index*. The aim is to develop an indicator that is capable
of distinguishing between natural and human-influenced
events in depictions of the state of the environment. The
objective is to produce a list of states placed in the order of
their vulnerability to environmental change. Three aspects
of vulnerability have been identified in order to do this:
Risks to the environment (natural and anthropogenic), the
capacity of the environment to cope with risks (resilience
of the ecological system) and the integrity of the ecosystem (the state of the environment on the basis of past influences). 57 environmental indicators were identified and
grouped in three sub-indices. A first version of this index
was produced for Australia, Fiji and Tuvalu.

FOOD INSECURITY AND VULNERABILITY INFORMATION
AND MAPPING SYSTEM
FAO has been using the Food Insecurity and Vulnerability Information and Mapping System (FIVIMS) for some
years now to provide vulnerability analyses for localizing regions that are potentially vulnerable to food crises.
FIVIMS supports the integration of national reporting systems into the international information network. At country level, FIVIMS works together with a range of information systems that collate regionally and nationally relevant
information about food insecurity and vulnerability to food
crises.

Sources: UNEP, 2001; Brenkert et al., 2001; Lonergan et al.,
2000; UNDP, 2004a

ability to environmental stress has been developed
using security diagrams.

The influence of climate change on agriculture
worldwide has been relatively comprehensively
studied, regional conditions and adaptive capacity
representing the crucial determinants (IPCC, 2001b;
Fischer et al., 2002; Fig. 3.1-2). Great uncertainty still
exists about the impacts of climate change on yields in
agriculture and predictive uncertainty varies greatly
from region to region. The central issue here is the
link between freshwater scarcity and agricultural
production. The International Food Policy Research

Institute has published a study on this issue (IFPRI,
2003). Following on from this, Downing (2002) produced a systematic overview of potentially worrying
developments in food security by way of response to
the IPCC's Third Assessment Report and thus presented a first systematic assessment of the impacts of
climate change on food security.

A future-oriented policy of poverty reduction
must make use of such studies to understand the
links between poverty and the environment at the
stage of strategy development and, given that one is
operating in conditions of uncertainty, must compare

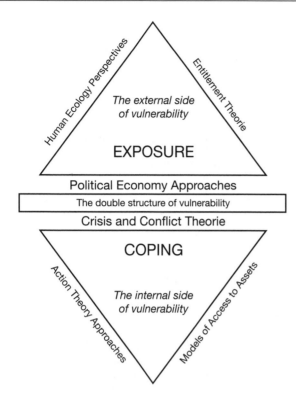

Figure 3.1-2
Analytical framework for social vulnerability. Two sides
are identified. The exposure of a society is established by
studying the 'external' side. This includes taking into account
environmental change, changing entitlements and the political
economy of the relevant social environment. Study of the
'internal' side of vulnerability involves drawing on theories
of conflict and action as well as models depicting access
to resources, in order to explain how risks and stresses are
actually coped with by those affected.
Source: Bohle, 2001

them regularly and repeatedly with the latest scientific prognoses.

3.1.2.3
Social vulnerability

In their description of the Guatemala earthquake of
1976 as a 'classquake', Blaikie et al. (1994) indicated
the extent to which social status plays a role in people's vulnerability to harm from environmental crises. This type of approach is typical of the research
strand that can be summarized under the rubric of
social vulnerability (Brooks and Adger, 2003). Chambers (1989) defines (social) vulnerability as 'the risk
of being exposed to a situation of stress and to the
difficulties of coping with it. Vulnerability has two
sides: an external side of the shocks, stress and risks
to which a household is exposed; and an internal side
of defencelessness and a lack of coping capacity'. This
is a reference to the risk faced by a household (or a

social group) of getting into a situation where it is
no longer able to maintain its already marginal livelihood and enters into a state of existential crisis (hunger, family breakdown, impoverishment or death;
Hulme and Shepherd, 2003).

Bohle et al. (1993) have developed an analytical
framework for vulnerability and have likewise identified two sides (Fig. 3.1-2). The exposure of a society is established by looking at the 'external' side of
vulnerability. This includes looking at environmental change, changing entitlements and the political
economy of the relevant livelihood system. Study of
the 'internal' aspect of vulnerability seeks to show
how risks and stress are actually coped with by those
affected. This involves using theories of conflict and
theories of action as well as models of access to
resources.

The research strand that deals with social vulnerability concentrates on the ways social stability may be compromised (Section 3.2) and on strategies for securing livelihoods. Social vulnerability is
determined, among other things, by factors such as
income and income distribution, social status, availability of and access to food and health care provision, the housing situation and the functioning of
social networks and ethnic affiliations. Formal institutions, such as the state, and informal institutions,
such as networks, play an important role in the allocation and distribution of access rights and entitlements in a society (Chambers, 1989; Pryer, 1990; Winchester, 1992; Bohle et al., 1993; DFG, 1993; Downing,
1993; Blaikie et al., 1994; Feldbrügge and von Braun,
2002). Indicators for social vulnerability are found
in the resources available to households, their socio-
economic setting and their dependency on the state
of the environment. Any study of adaptive and coping capacities must also consider the obstacles to the
development of such capacities.

The environmental dimension of vulnerability is
linked by Watts and Bohle (1993) to Sen's entitlements approach (Section 3.1.1). They inquire as to
how changes in relationships of exchange and environmental change prevent people from, say, being
able to purchase or produce food. One core term in
this analytical concept is marginality (Weber, 2002):
Individuals or social groups are vulnerable because
they have only a limited share – or none at all – in the
resources, achievements, services and opportunities
offered by society. Thus, vulnerability is also a result
of social power relations at local, national and global level. This basic structural vulnerability becomes
transformed into a crisis when certain critical events
occur. These may be droughts, earthquakes, storms
or floods. The people affected are no longer able to
respond adequately to the crisis, and help from the
outside is either inadequate or non-existent, leading

eventually to a complete breakdown in people's livelihood system and to a dependence on external aid. Policies aimed at preventing poverty among specific target groups must therefore take into account the living conditions of different social groups. The processes that increase or reduce social vulnerability to environmental change need to be identified.

Social vulnerability and the dimensions of poverty looked at in Section 3.1.1 are of crucial importance in discussions about sustainable livelihoods: 'A livelihood comprises the capabilities, assets and activities required for a means of living. A livelihood is sustainable when it can cope with and recover from stresses and shocks and maintain or enhance its assets and endowments both now and in the future, while not undermining the natural resource base' (Chambers and Conway, 1992). This concept, which refers to poor people's circumstances in the context of their vulnerability to crises and shocks, has been the subject of intense debate since the mid-1990s, especially in the English-speaking world. Ever since the World Summit for Social Development in Copenhagen in 1995, the normative principles of the sustainable livelihood concept have gradually been finding their way into development policy and practice.

If a policy of poverty reduction in the context of impending regional and global environmental change is to be a success, it is necessary first to uncover the factors that determine vulnerability and to establish their structural causes. The study of social vulnerability should therefore include an investigation into individuals' entitlements to resources and basic needs and the distribution of these entitlements within a society (or social group). This requires applying qualitative research methods to

- the institutional context from which these entitlements result and are distributed among social groups (Adger and Kelly, 1999);
- the role of formal mechanisms of risk distribution, such as health and pension insurance for sustainable livelihoods.

3.1.2.4
Requirements for integrated vulnerability analyses

The above presentation of the two main strands of vulnerability research (social and biophysical vulnerability) shows that a comprehensive understanding of the problems that arise for poor people as a result of environmental change can only be acquired by taking account of both research approaches. Integrated vulnerability analyses at the human/environment interface are needed in order to comprehend the new problems for poverty reduction that

are becoming apparent at the start of the twenty-first century. It is only by identifying current and future regional hotspots and especially vulnerable groups that suitable instruments for preventing and coping with crises can begin to be developed.

One way of integrating social and biophysical vulnerabilities is suggested by the concept of 'differentiated vulnerability' (Corell et al., 2001; Petschel-Held et al., 2004; Section 3.5). The emphasis here is on the fact that harmful impacts are unequally distributed in social, spatial and temporal terms, and that the extent of the harm caused depends on the various cultural and socio-economic conditions that exist in a society. The key question is: 'Which parts of the system are vulnerable to which perturbations?' In WBGU's view this kind of multidimensional vulnerability assessment needs to contain the following elements (Section 6.2.1):

- Scenarios of significant development trends that influence the sensitivity of social systems and their coping capacity. A differentiation should be made in particular between dimensions of poverty (Section 3.2), social groups and different scales.
- Scenarios that address the impacts of global environmental change upon the livelihood conditions of poor people (exposure). A differentiation should be made here between gradual impacts and abrupt impacts.
- Analyses of the sensitivity of social and natural systems to an exposure, and of the significance of multiple perturbations and their temporal dynamic.
- Analyses of the responses displayed by societies and the natural environment, especially the capacity of the coupled system to cope with perturbations or to learn from them (adaptation). Consideration should be given especially to critical thresholds and positive feedback loops.
- Analyses of the coping capacities of social systems and livelihood systems.

To give an example of how the concept can be rendered operational, Section 3.5 presents these elements in an integrated analysis of regional vulnerability using two case studies.

3.2
Dimensions of poverty

3.2.1
Income and asset poverty

As has been shown in Section 3.1.1, poverty is often equated with income poverty alone, and thus reduced to a single dimension. In the opinion of WBGU, this view is unduly narrow. Nevertheless, income and asset poverty and the absence of material security are core elements of poverty. They are determined by the scale of the other dimensions of poverty, and intensify them considerably in response. Acute income poverty and asset poverty compel the poor to adopt short-term strategies and prevent them from investing sufficiently in their own health, in education, or in political participation. Even the natural resources their lives depend upon are often jeopardized.

3.2.1.1
Income and asset poverty affect all other dimensions

Material security may be derived from regular income, from the commitment of production factors such as labour, land, physical capital and human capital, or from existing assets. Effective mutual organizations or systems of social security represent another potential source. Without work or decent pay, without adequate access to land, capital, education and information, and cut off from functioning commodity and factor markets, the incomes of the poor fluctuate heavily and are often barely enough to meet basic needs. Poor people are rarely in a position to put any money aside. Moreover, many developing countries have no formal systems of social security which could effectively cushion the poor in the event of emer-

gencies such as incapacity to work. In old age, most poor people are dependent upon their families, the social group or the village community. In the course of industrialization and urbanization, and the associated individualization of society, these informal systems of social security are increasingly disintegrating (Section 3.2.5).

There are strong interactions between the absence of material security and the other dimensions of poverty (Section 3.2.2–3.2.5). The income and asset poor are generally at higher risk of disease because they are unable to afford basics like clean drinking water. With limited or no access to a modern energy supply, they often have no choice but to cook and heat with fuels which are harmful to their health (Box 3.2-1). Likewise, it is virtually impossible to ensure an adequate diet without income or assets, e.g. the necessary land for subsistence farming. Last but not least, there is a relationship between a lack of material security and a lack of education. This is due firstly to the direct costs of education (e.g. school fees, clothing and transport) and secondly to the fact that adults and often also children have to work all day to scrape together sufficient income to live on. This in turn conspires to restrict their opportunities for exerting political influence, and hence their power to change the underlying conditions in their own favour.

Box 3.2-1

Energy poverty

Energy, in the form of light, heat, mechanical power or electricity, is essential in every society. Access to a modern energy supply is an important prerequisite for the achievement of the Millennium Development Goals. Energy underpins incomes, education, social participation and health. It frees women, in particular, from such time-consuming and laborious work as gathering firewood or fetching water. In the year 2000, 1,600 million people or 27 per cent of the world population were without access to electricity. Of these people, 99 per cent live in developing countries, and 80 per cent of those in rural areas. This energy poverty correlates with a low human development index. Moreover, the use of wood and manure for cooking and heating causes major health problems, affecting women and young children most of all. In the year 2000, WHO attributed 1.6 million deaths to the risk factor of indoor air pollution. According to estimates from the International Energy Agency, without targeted measures the number of people cooking and heating with traditional biomass is likely to rise from its current 2,400 million to 2,600 million people by the year 2030.

The energy sector, particularly in developing countries, suffers from inefficiency and mismanagement. In the year 1992, state energy subsidies in developing countries

amounted to US$50,000 million in total. In many cases, the needy target groups are not the ones to benefit from these subsidies, which also impede the development of sustainable technologies. To develop their energy supply, developing countries therefore need human resources and financial and technical support at all levels. One possible way forward could be strategic energy partnerships between industrialized and developing countries, as announced at the World Summit on Sustainable Development (WSSD) in 2002. Without enabling framework conditions at national and international level and without coherent sector policies, however, these initiatives and projects have little prospect of success. Thus the aim must be long-term structural reform of international policy processes, so that they support global sustainable development.

WBGU has called upon the international community to work towards a target of providing all people with access to a modern energy supply by 2020. Contributory elements of this policy would include putting the new World Bank policy into practice, integrating the issue of sustainable energy supply into the Poverty Reduction Strategy Papers (PRSPs), strengthening the role of regional development banks, making use of innovative financing instruments, and enabling developing countries to act more effectively by strengthening capacity.

Sources: IEA, 2002; WBGU, 2004

Box 3.2-2

Measuring income poverty: Methodological and conceptual difficulties

On account of the shortage of data, in conjunction with conceptual problems, it is extremely difficult to measure poverty in its multidimensional complexity. Absolute income poverty is a key indicator which gives a useful measure of progress for the evaluation of poverty reduction. The statistic calculated is the number of people or the proportion of the population living on less than a certain income per day. This predetermined amount is known as the poverty line. Because the concepts and criteria underlying the definition of the income-based poverty line are different in each country, the national poverty line will vary from one country to another. In order to achieve international comparability, the World Bank draws the line for extreme poverty at US$1 per person per day (measured in terms of US$ purchasing power parity). In recent years, a parallel poverty line of US$2 per day has been applied to medium-income countries.

With the poverty line as the basis, reference can be made to other indicators of extreme poverty. These are the poverty gap (average difference between the income of the poor and the poverty line) and the *headcount index* (percentage of the population living below the poverty line in terms of per capita consumption). While the UNDP emphasises the necessity of an international poverty line, it also acknowledges: 'Because of enormous methodological and conceptual inconsistencies, poverty data calculated using international poverty lines are extremely problematic and can lead to misleading poverty rates.'

For methodological reasons, incomes are seldom recorded directly, but determined indirectly from household expenditure on specific groups of products (the shopping basket method). Poverty lines, however, are often based on the prices of goods which the poor do not even consume. Neither is any allowance made for differences between the shopping baskets or purchasing power of people in urban and rural areas. Given this disagreement over how poverty should be measured, it is by no means easy to monitor the implementation of the Millennium Development Goal of halving poverty (MDG 1; Section 2.1). Nevertheless, the data situation has become more comprehensive and reliable since the international community reached agreement on the MDGs.

Sources: Brachinger and Schubert, 2003; UNDP, 2003c; Reddy and Pogge, 2002; Glewwe and van der Gaag, 1988

3.2.1.2
Situation and trends

In the year 2000 some 1,100 million people had to survive on less than US$1 per day, and 2,700 million on less than US$2 a day (World Bank, 2003e). In certain countries, the majority of people are poor by this definition. In Zambia and Nigeria for instance, it would apply to between 70 per cent (US$1) and 90 per cent (US$2) of the population (World Bank, 2003d). Similarly, a substantial part of the population lives below these poverty lines in other countries in sub-Saharan Africa, South and South-East Asia and Latin America. Moreover, there are numerous developing countries for which figures cannot even be quoted because of a lack of data. Even where poverty figures are available, they are often based on specific national poverty lines so that data from different countries are not comparable (Box 3.2-2).

In the 1990s, the proportion of the world population living in extreme income poverty (<US$1 per day) fell from 28.3 per cent (1990) to 21.6 per cent (2000) (World Bank, 2003e). This is attributable in large part to the achievements of China. Due to population growth, however, the absolute number of poor people worldwide has only fallen modestly from 1,200 million (1990) to 1,100 million (2000). The trend varies greatly in the different regions of the world: whereas absolute income poverty has fallen significantly in East and South Asia, for example, both as a percentage and in absolute terms, it has risen slightly in Latin America and increased substantially in Europe, Central Asia and sub-Saharan Africa (Fig. 3.2-1). About half of all people in sub-Saharan Africa still live on less than US$1 per day. In 2000, 82 million more of its inhabitants were living in extreme poverty than in 1990.

The World Bank predicts that whilst the proportion of people living in poverty will indeed be halved from its year 2000 level by 2015, not all regions will benefit equally. In sub-Saharan Africa, the number

Table 3.2-1

Number of people living in poverty on less than US$1 per day (forecast for 2015).
Source: World Bank, 2003e

	Number [millions of people]			Proportion of population [%]		
	1990	2000	2015	1990	2000	2015
East Asia and Pacific	470	261	44	29.4	14.5	2.3
(excl. China)	110	57	3	24.1	10.6	0.5
Europe and Central Asia	6	20	6	1.4	4.2	1.3
Latin America and Caribbean	48	56	46	11.0	10.8	7.6
Middle East and North Africa	5	8	4	2.1	2.8	1.2
South Asia	466	432	268	41.5	31.9	16.4
Sub-Saharan Africa	241	323	366	47.4	49.0	42.3
Total	*1,237*	*1,100*	*734*	*28.3*	*21.6*	*12.5*
(excl. China)	877	896	692	27.2	23.3	15.4

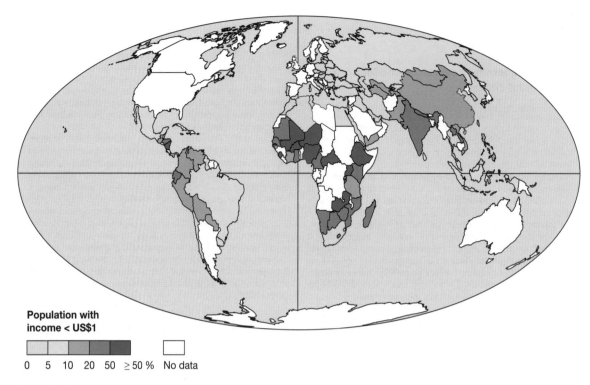

Population with income < US$1

0   5   10   20   50   ≥ 50 %   No data

Figure 3.2-1
Proportion of population with income below US$1 per person per day.
Source: World Bank, 2004e

of people living in poverty will rise and is likely to constitute more than 42 per cent of the total population. In contrast, Asia will continue to be the driver of poverty reduction (Table 3.2-1). The World Bank prognosis must be interpreted with caution, however, because it is based on an exceedingly optimistic scenario of future economic development (World Bank, 2003e; Nuscheler, 2004).

3.2.1.3
Disparities

In many countries, both absolute poverty and vast disparities in income occur at the same time. This inequality in distribution is most pronounced in many South American and African countries (Table 3.2-3; Box 3.2-3). Within individual countries, further disparities exist between urban and rural populations. Worldwide, 75 per cent of those living in extreme poverty (some 900 million people with an income of less than US$1 per day) belong to rural populations. In 1998, the number of rural poor in Burkino Faso was around 3.2 times the number of urban poor. Brazil had 3.1 times as many rural poor as urban poor in 1995. Disparities in the incomes of the rural population result primarily from the distribution of land ownership (Table 3.2-2). Poor people often have too

little land, if any at all, to support a decent livelihood, and their soils tend to be degraded and of poor quality. Shortages of water for irrigation are not unusual. According to a study by Nelson et al. (1997) this situation applies to 634 million poor people, of whom 375 million live in Asia (IFAD, 2001).

Frequently there are also major differences in the economic status of women and men. The UNDP estimates that in many countries, women's income is less than 40 per cent of men's. It amounts to as little as 27 per cent in Peru and 30 per cent in Yemen. Compared with countries like Germany (52 per cent), the USA (62 per cent) and especially the Scandinavian countries (around 75 per cent), these figures are very low (UNDP, 2004b). In part, this is certainly due to the educational disadvantages faced by girls and women, and to discrimination against them in law. However, another important factor is the entirely inadequate recording of statistical data on the value created in the household and in subsistence farming.

3.2.1.4
Income and asset poverty and the environment

Income and asset poverty lead to economic emergencies in which the poor, for lack of other alternatives, are forced to resort to short-term survival strat-

Box 3.2-3

The Gini coefficient and the Gini index

The Gini coefficient is the most commonly used measure of personal income and land distribution within a country or a region. The Gini coefficient of income distribution, for example, is determined from a graph on which the cumulative percentage of national income is plotted on the y-axis

Figure 3.2-2
Example of a Lorenz curve and the Gini coefficient.
Source: WBGU after Dichtl and Issing, 1994

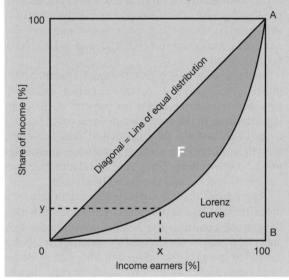

while the percentage of income earners is plotted on the x-axis. The diagonal on this graph (0A) represents absolute equality of distribution within a country (Fig. 3.2-2). The curve (known as the Lorenz curve) reflects the actual distribution, i.e. what percentage of the population receives what percentage of income. The more rounded this curve is, the greater the inequality of distribution in the country. The Gini coefficient is the ratio of the area between the Lorenz curve and the diagonal (F) and the area below the diagonal (0AB). Consequently its value will be 1 in the case of extreme inequality of distribution, and 0 if distribution is perfectly equal. The weakness of the Gini coefficient is that two areas of equal size, and hence two Gini coefficients with identical numerical values do not necessarily reflect the same profile of distribution, i.e. they can be arrived at by way of different Lorenz curves. Although two curves may produce the same area, inequality may be skewed towards the lower incomes in one case and the higher incomes in the other. Internationally, the indicator used is the Gini index (Gini coefficient x 100).

In South American and African countries, inequality is particularly pronounced. Brazil and Nicaragua, for example, have a Gini index of approx. 55, while that of Honduras and Guatemala is approx. 48. The Gini index is 62.9 for Sierra Leone, 61.3 for the Central African Republic, and 59.3 for South Africa. In Burkina Faso the Gini index is around 48.2. In Asia the concentration is somewhat less striking. Indonesia for instance has a Gini index of 34.3; in Bangladesh it is 31.8, in Sri Lanka 34.4, in China 44.7, and in India 32.5. In many industrialized countries, the index is around 35. It is particularly low in Japan and Sweden (25). Germany has a Gini index of 28.3, in contrast to 40.8 in the USA where distribution is relatively unequal.

Sources: Dichtl and Issing, 1994; Hemmer, 2002; UNDP, 2004b

egies. Then natural resources are overexploited and the 'freely' accessible environment, often the sole remaining capital asset and consumable resource, is overused. People end up overfarming or overgrazing land, clearing forests, leaving 'scorched earth', and poaching protected wild animals (Section 3.3). However, this in no way implies that wealth and material security would generate comparatively fewer environmental impacts. As incomes rise and consumer behaviour becomes routine, the higher level of consumption often intensifies other strains on the environment. These may include rising CO_2 emissions, for instance, as a consequence of the growth of motorized transport (Section 3.3.1). Furthermore, higher incomes also alter methods of production. Agricultural practices can then be detrimental to the environment; for example, the harmful effects of heavy machinery and pesticide use on soil structure and soil organisms.

3.2.1.5
International goals on income and asset security

The Millennium Development Goal of halving the proportion of people with per capita income of less than US$1 per day between 1990 and 2015 (MDG 1) seems most likely to be achieved if measured as a global average. From a regional perspective, significant progress in South-East Asia and elsewhere contrasts with deterioration or stagnation in West Asia and sub-Saharan Africa (Fig. 3.2-3).

3.2.2
Disease

3.2.2.1
Disease as a dimension of poverty

Both mortality patterns and disease profiles in developing countries exhibit typical differences from those in industrialized countries: high infant, child and maternal mortality rates are characteristic of the

Table 3.2-2
Distribution of land ownership (on the Gini coefficient, see Box 3.2-3).
Source: Griffin et al., 2002 (in IFAD, 2001)

	Time frame	Gini coefficient
SUB-SAHARAN AFRICA		
Kenya	1981–1990	0.77
Nigeria	1973	0.37
Botswana	1991–2000	0.49
LATIN AMERICA		
Colombia	1981–1990	0.77
Brazil	1971–1980	0.85
Mexico	1961–1970	0.75
SOUTH ASIA		
Bangladesh	1995	0.65
India	1981–1990	0.59
Pakistan	1981–1990	0.58
SOUTH-EAST ASIA		
Indonesia	1971–1980	0.56
Malaysia	1971–1980	0.58
Philippines	1980	0.61
NEAR EAST AND NORTH AFRICA		
Morocco	1981	0.47
Syria	1979	0.59
Tunisia	1980	0.58
EAST ASIA		
China	1995	0.43
South Korea	1971–1980	0.30
Taiwan	1961–1970	0.47

less constant, especially for maternal mortality (UN, 2004b).

Disease is a fundamental attribute of poverty and reinforces it. The importance of health promotion measures as part of poverty reduction strategies is largely undisputed by development economists (World Bank, 1993; WHO, 2001; Sachs and Malaney, 2002; OECD and WHO, 2003). Good health enables higher labour productivity, and thus higher individual and macro-economic income. Healthy, well-nourished children attain better results at school. Finally, it has been demonstrated that if children have a higher probability of survival there is a reduction in the fertility rate, which has positive implications for the material situation of poor households and for environmental resources (OECD and WHO, 2003; Section 3.5.1).

Sachs and Malaney (2002) found evidence that malaria, for example, is an important contributory and reinforcing factor for poverty in developing countries. In the event that malaria could be controlled successfully, they calculated that economic growth would rise by a whole percentage point. Figure 3.2-4 shows the geographical correlation between per capita income and the extent of malaria.

Apart from the discrepancies in health between industrialized and developing countries, even within developing countries the health indicators for rich and poor people (as defined by income) are poles apart. For instance, the infant mortality rate in Brazil is six times higher in the lowest income class than in the highest (Menezes et al., 1996).

As can be seen from the comparison of a district in Burkina Faso with the figures for sub-Saharan Africa, with the exception of malaria the most common diseases of the poor are not tropical diseases but infectious diseases such as respiratory infections, diarrhoea and measles, along with undernourishment and complications at birth (Table 3.2-3). Statis-

vulnerable groups in society. Infant mortality rates are 17 times higher than in industrialized countries, and maternal mortality is 100 times higher (Garenne et al., 1997; World Bank, 2004c). Although mortality rates in developing countries have fallen in recent decades, the relative disparity has remained more or decades, the relative disparity has remained more or

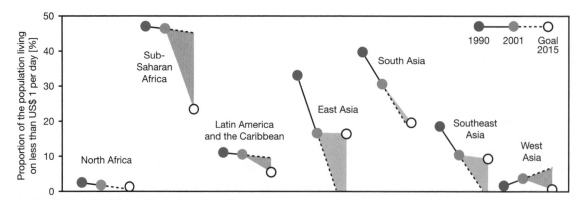

Figure 3.2-3
Situation and trends for the Millennium Development Goal of halving absolute income poverty (MDG 1).
Source: UN, 2004b

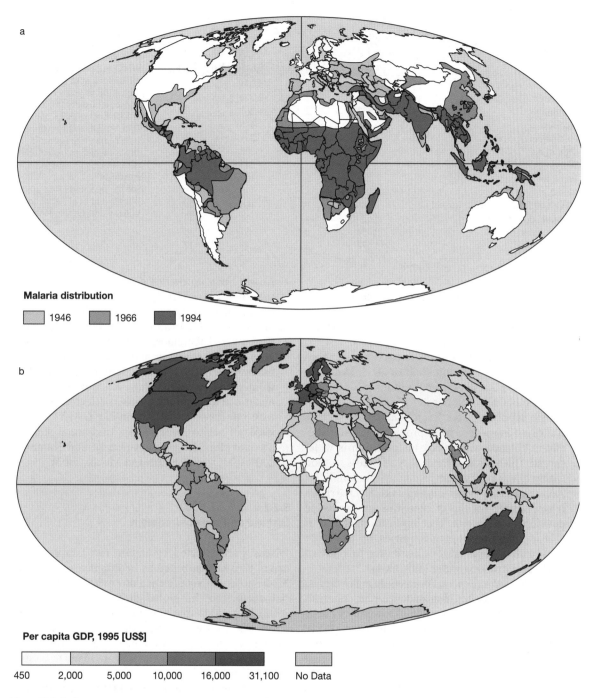

Figure 3.2-4a, b
World maps showing the distribution of malaria (a) and per capita income (b).
Source: Sachs and Malaney, 2002

tics on the causes of disease and death in developing countries are based on estimates because of the poor availability of data. The table shows that survey data from research projects can reveal a substantially different ranking of health problems from that yielded by means of estimates, which are necessarily based on highly aggregated and incomplete health report-

ing data. For example, according to WHO estimates of causes of mortality in sub-Saharan Africa, under-nourishment is ranked in fifteenth place, whereas a study from Burkina Faso places it fifth.

Disease	Sub-Saharan Africa (WHO estimate)			Nouna (survey data)	
	DALYs [rank]	YLLs [thousands]	[rank]	YLLs [thousands]	[rank]
Malaria	4	24,385	3	3,034	1
Diarrhoea	1	31,393	1	2,244	2
Pneumonia	2	29,533	2	1,281	3
Accidents	3	16,459	6	448	4
Undernourishment	17	3,285	15	281	5
Meningitis	30	756	28	266	6
Worm infections	34	58	38	243	7
Perinatal diseases	6	1,750	5	199	8
Measles	5	19,923	4	176	9
HIV/AIDS	11	7,020	9	168	10
Complications at birth	10	5,530	11	65	13
Tuberculosis	9	9,434	8	57	15
Injuries	7	14,572	7	49	17

Table 3.2-3
Ranking of diseases in Nouna in rural Burkina Faso, compared with WHO estimated rankings for sub-Saharan Africa. Measured in years lost due to premature death (Years of Life Lost – YLLs) or in DALYs (Disability Adjusted Life Years), a measure of disease which takes account of morbidity as well as mortality.
Source: adapted after Würthwein et al., 2001 and Murray and Lopez, 1996

3.2.2.2
Poverty amplifies susceptibility to disease

Poverty breeds disease. The causes are many and varied:

- *Access to food:* Undernourishment is a major contributory factor in around half of all child deaths. As Section 3.2.3 shows, recurrent infections are as much to blame for undernourishment as an inadequate supply of food. Even in countries such as Burkina Faso where food production is statistically in balance with needs, malnutrition is widespread. This indicates inequality of access to food within developing countries, and within families.

- *Access to clean water and sanitation:* Diarrhoea is responsible for the greatest disease burden in developing countries. The implication of this is that in many developing countries, up to 80 per cent of all diseases must be attributed to a lack of clean, safe drinking water (WI, 2004).

- *Access to health services:* Poor people make far less use of health services. In most developing countries the demand for health services is lower by a factor of 30 than in OECD countries (0.3 as opposed to 10 visits to the doctor per person per year; Sauerborn et al., 1994); this despite the substantially higher incidence of disease. In Burkina Faso, for example, more than three-quarters of children with malaria are not presented for health service treatment, nor do they receive effective medication (Krause and Sauerborn, 2000). Women and children from rural areas and poor households have the least access to health services. The price elasticity of demand for outpatient care for children in Burkina Faso is more than four times the average elasticity (Sauerborn et al., 1994), which means that any rise in the price of health services leads to a disproportionate fall in demand from these vulnerable population groups.

- *Living environment and access to a modern energy supply:* Cramped living conditions encourage the spread of respiratory infections, which rank second in the table of diseases in developing countries, and of tuberculosis and meningitis (Hodgson et al., 2001). Cooking and heating indoors with biomass fuel or coal is detrimental to the health of women and babies, causing even more illness than malaria in terms of the numbers affected. Respiratory infections cause 98 million DALYs worldwide, of which cooking on traditional hearths accounts for 35.7 per cent (Ezzati and Kammen, 2001; WHO, 2002; Smith and Mehta, 2003).

3.2.2.3
Disease and the environment

Diseases are affected by certain risk factors, which can in turn be controlled by health measures. Figure 3.2-5 shows the significance of environment-related risk factors to the global disease burden (WHO, 2002). In its 2002 annual report, the WHO attributes around 28 per cent of the global disease burden to these risk factors. In developing countries, the health impacts of environmental factors are likely to be substantially greater.

Firstly, figure 3.2-5 lists risk factors with an obvious link to the environment, such as inadequate water supply and sanitation, which causes infections such as diarrhoea. What is less well known is that smoke inside dwellings – most often from cooking and heating with wood and coal – is a far more serious risk factor than air pollution in cities.

Secondly, the figure shows the significance of undernourishment as a risk factor. Global environmental change threatens to worsen the food supply situation in developing countries, through shortage of fresh water, land degradation and particularly

Figure 3.2-5
Disease burden caused
by risk factors sensitive to
environmental change.
Source: WHO, 2002;
Ezzati et al., 2003

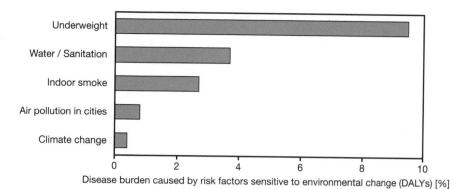

soil salinization, and in sub-Saharan Africa above all, through climate change. The relationship between food production and nutritional status is complex (Section 3.2.3). Nevertheless, a decline in production would in all probability lead to a substantial increase in undernourishment in developing countries, especially among children. This effect is intensified by the interaction between infectious diseases, diarrhoea and undernourishment, described in Section 3.2.3.

Global environmental change thus threatens to amplify especially the diseases of poverty: infectious diseases, undernourishment and lung complaints caused by toxic smoke in living quarters (Sauerborn et al., 2004).

3.2.2.4
International goals on health

Health is an integral component of development. This insight has been articulated in the Millennium Development Goals. The following are the goals which refer to health (Table 2.1-1):
* *MDG 1:* To halve hunger and material poverty by the year 2015 (Section 3.2.3).
* *MDG 4:* To reduce under-five child mortality by two-thirds of its current rate between 1990 and 2015.
* *MDG 5:* To reduce maternal mortality by three-quarters between 1990 and 2015.
* *MDG 6:* To halt, and begin to reverse, the spread of HIV/AIDS and other major diseases by 2015.
* *MDG 7:* By the same date, to halve the proportion of people without sustainable and affordable access to safe drinking water.
* *MDG 8:* To ensure access to essential drugs in cooperation with the pharmaceutical industry.
Additional key targets on health were formulated at the World Summit for Sustainable Development in Johannesburg in the year 2002 (Section 2.1.4.):
* The proportion of people without basic sanitation is to be halved by the year 2015. This is a decisive improvement upon MDG 7.

* Cases of HIV infection in young men and women aged between fifteen and twenty-four are to be reduced by 25 per cent by the year 2005 in the worst affected countries in Africa, and worldwide by 2010. This is a very ambitious target which goes far beyond MDG 6, although it departs from the time frame and target group specified in this Millennium Goal.
* Chemical substances which are harmful to human health and to the environment are no longer to be produced nor used by the year 2020. This Johannesburg target is ambitious and its implementation is difficult to verify in the absence of indicators.
As regards the evaluation of progress in developing countries, it must first be noted that the statistical data available on mortality is extraordinarily patchy and unreliable. In developing countries there are barely functioning systems for reporting deaths, particularly of children. Health indicators (MDG 4 and 5) are therefore based, of necessity, on rudimentary estimates. Another reason for caution when interpreting data on implementation of the MDGs is the reference year. All the MDG indicators take figures from the year 1990 as their reference point. Thus the first decade of the comparison time frame predates the agreement of any MDGs, and long precedes any of the measures taken to implement them. The Secretary-General of the UN, Kofi Annan himself rightly points out that it is not valid simply to project a comparison between 1990–2002, which in fact is more of a base-line for the present trend (UN, 2004b). In spite of all these caveats, a few key trends can be identified nevertheless:
* *MDG 4:* Between 1990 and 2002, developing countries recorded a drop in infant mortality from 92 to 71 deaths per 1000 births. It will only be possible to achieve a two-thirds reduction by the year 2015 by taking additional drastic steps. Furthermore some groups of developing countries are closer than others to meeting the target (Fig. 3.2-6). The largest gap between the goal and the present reality is

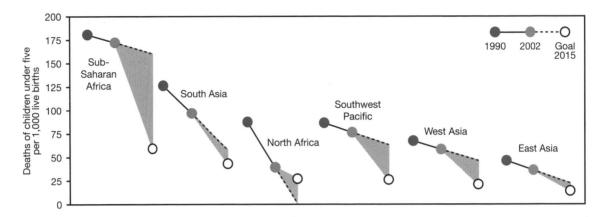

Figure 3.2-6
Situation and trends for the Millennium Development Goal of reducing infant mortality by two-thirds (MDG 4).
Source: UN, 2004b

in sub-Saharan Africa. There the fall in infant mortality between 1990 and 2002 was only 6 per cent.

- *MDG 5:* For assessment of the reduction in maternal mortality, no figures from later than the year 2000 are available (UN, 2004b).
- *MDG 6:* There was no decrease in the proportion of people infected with HIV between 2001 and 2003. The prevalence of HIV actually rose in East and South Asia (UN, 2004b). There is no data from more recently than the year 2000 on the number of malaria deaths per 100,000 children under five (UN, 2004b). Regarding the incidence of tuberculosis and the number of resulting deaths, there was no significant change between the years 2000 and 2002 (UN, 2004b).
- *MDG 7:* Access to clean drinking water has improved slightly worldwide (Section 3.3.2).

The availability of data for health indicators is in urgent need of improvement, particularly in relation to infant and maternal mortality. It is nevertheless foreseeable that if current trends in the health sector continue, the MDGs will not be met in most regions, a prospect most clearly indicated in sub-Saharan Africa.

3.2.3
Undernourishment

3.2.3.1
Situation and Trends

According to the FAO definition (2001b), food security is a situation in which the people concerned have access to enough nutritionally adequate and safe food for their physiological needs and dietary habits and preferences and to guarantee an active and healthy life. So undernourishment should not simply be equated with a lack of food (Box 3.2-4). An equally important cause may be acute and recurrent or chronic (infectious) diseases. In simplified terms, undernourishment can be explained as an energy input-output deficit, where the requirement for energy and essential nutrients exceeds the intake of food. The three aspects which dictate requirements for energy and essential nutrients are maintaining body temperature and basic metabolic processes, physical exertion (e.g. agricultural labour), and infectious diseases.

A deficit in the intake of essential nutrients and energy can occur if insufficient quantities of food are eaten, or if inadequate levels of nutrients are absorbed in the intestine, because of diarrhoea for instance. Both causes of undernourishment occur in combination with various other factors in the three

Box 3.2-4

Measuring nutritional status

A population's nutritional status is generally surveyed using simple anthropometric measures. It is important to distinguish between acute (wasting) and chronic malnutrition (stunting). Wasting can set in quite rapidly, e.g. in the event of an infectious disease or an acute food shortage, and can subside equally rapidly. The main indicator used is the quotient of height to weight. Stunting, in contrast, is the consequence of a long-term or recurrent shortfall of food. It is usually measured by the quotient of height to age. Stunting is used beyond the health sector as an indicator of social deprivation. The same is true of birth weight, which is a measure of chronic prenatal malnutrition. The standard Body Mass Index (weight/height^2) used in industrialized countries is primarily intended for measuring obesity in adults, and is inappropriate for diagnosing malnutrition in children.

population groups which are most susceptible to undernourishment:

- *Unborn children:* Heavy agricultural labour, maternal malaria and anaemia are the most important causes of intra-uterine growth retardation. This has far-reaching consequences, since children do not make up the missed growth, show greater susceptibility to infections, and exhibit cognitive deficits which can impair their later learning success. Maternal deprivation of food, on the other hand, only affects the foetus's weight gain in periods of extreme hunger.
- *Infants (6-24 months):* The key causes are infectious diseases, e.g. recurrent diarrhoea, and insufficient quantity and quality of food at the time of weaning from mother's milk onto solids.
- *Women of reproductive age:* Besides frequent pregnancies, insufficient food intake and frequent infectious diseases are the principal causes of undernourishment. Women who have pregnancies in close succession are the worst affected.

A series of feedback loops can reinforce undernourishment and stunt development (Fig. 3.2-7).

Today around 840 million people worldwide are undernourished (Fig. 3.2-8; FAO 2003b). Children in particular are affected: around 30 per cent of all five-year-olds suffer from undernourishment (UNICEF, 2000). The vast majority of undernourished people live in India, sub-Saharan Africa, other parts of Asia and the Southwest Pacific, and in China (Fig. 3.2-9). In the year 2000, undernourishment claimed 3.7 million lives, 1.8 million of them in Africa. There undernourishment is the cause of around 50 per cent of all deaths of children aged under five (Pelletier et al., 1995; UN SCN, 2004).

Admittedly, in the past 20 years the number of people who are undernourished has fallen worldwide. However, this is solely attributable to the major reduction achieved in East and South-East Asia. In sub-Saharan Africa, in the Near East, in Latin America and in South Asia the situation remains as bad as ever. In mid-2003, 36 countries had been affected by food emergencies for at least two years and were dependent on international food aid. Many of them have been in this position for ten years or more (Fig. 3.2-10).

3.2.3.2
Undernourishment as a dimension of poverty

Undernourishment is a key attribute of poverty and reinforces it. Undernourishment in developing countries is also a barrier to economic growth. Better nutrition and lower risk of disease were the basis for the development of the modern industrialized states (Fogel, 1990; McKeown, 1989). Arcand (2001) estimates that per capita GDP in sub-Saharan Africa would be around double its current value, had it been possible to overcome hunger in the 1960s. This involves not only increasing the supply of food, but also making improvements in the health and education sectors.

According to FAO (2003a), although the world population has doubled in the last 40 years, food production per head of the population has grown by more than one-quarter and at approx. 2,800kcal exceeds the average energy requirement of 2,000–2,600kcal. During the same period, the proportion of the world population living on less than 2,200kcal per head per day has fallen from 57 per cent to 10 per

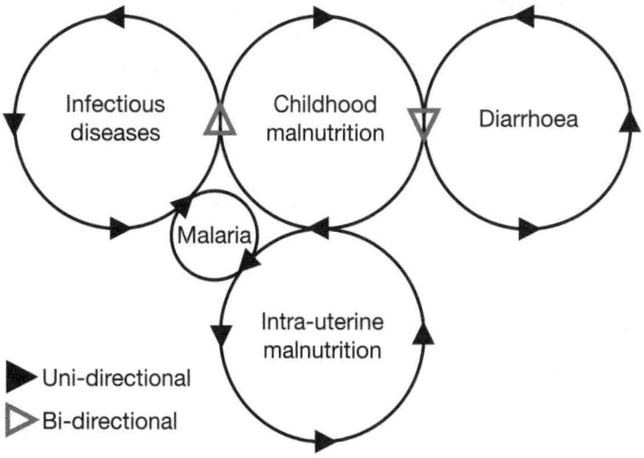

Figure 3.2-7
Positive feedback loops between infectious diseases, malnutrition (pre-natal and childhood) and diarrhoea.
Source: WBGU

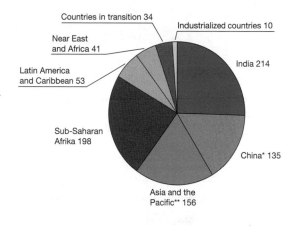

Figure 3.2-8
Numbers of people undernourished (in millions) by world region (1999–2001). * including Taiwan, ** excluding China and India.
Source: FAO, 2003b

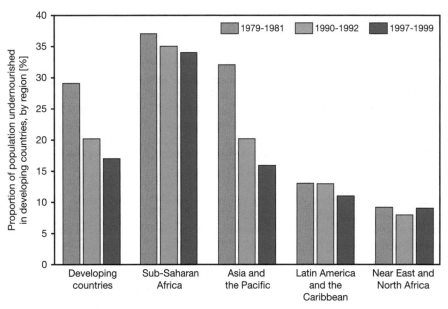

Figure 3.2-9
Percentage of population undernourished in developing countries and regional breakdown, for the years 1979–81, 1990–92 and 1997–99 (estimates).
Source: FAO, 2003b

cent; that is, from 1,890 to 570 million people. However, calorie intake is not the sole criterion for adequate nutrition. Even in poor countries there is often sufficient food on average, despite sometimes severe famines. For example, Burkina Faso has been producing enough food to meet its own national per capita requirements for the last ten years. Nonetheless, the proportion of undernourished children is not falling.

Frequent causes of food emergencies in countries with an adequate food supply are the hoarding of food surpluses for speculative purposes, an inadequate transport infrastructure, high transport costs and organizational shortcomings. Areas suffering shortages can therefore be impossible to reach. Another level on which there is unequal distribution of food is the household. As with the provision of health services, it is women, children and the eld-

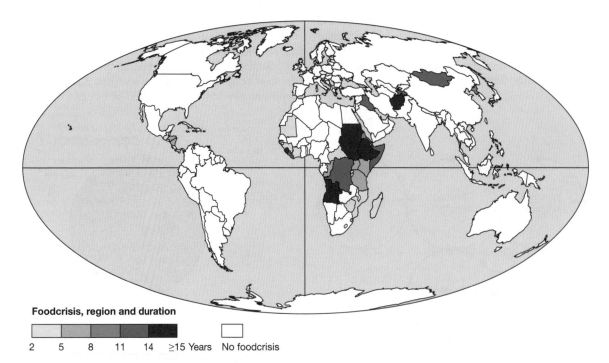

Figure 3.2-10
Countries affected by food emergencies in 2003, and duration of emergency.
Source: FAO, 2003b

erly who lose out (Haddad et al., 1996). Girls in particular receive a comparatively small share of food in many households (Dasgupta, 1987). Food insecurity is currently a distribution problem and not a production problem.

3.2.3.3
Food security and the environment

Undernourishment and famines can also be the result of lost harvests or crop failures caused by environmental changes. According to forecasts by the IPCC (2001c), agriculture in developing countries will suffer the worst negative impacts of climate change. Risk factors include the predicted increase in natural disasters and unfavourable shifts in regional precipitation regimes (rainstorms, droughts). Added to these, the effects of environmental degradation are insidious and can be cumulative. For instance, in places which are already susceptible to food shortages and fresh water crises, the combined effects of regional rises in temperature (heat stress), fresh water shortages (drought stress) and salinization can be expected to result in lost harvests (WBGU, 2003).

Thus far, agricultural production has been able to satisfy the increasing needs of a growing world population and, indeed, even significantly improve the level of supply. The study 'World Agriculture: Towards 2015/30' paints the following picture of the future: an annual 1.4 per cent rise in cereal production is needed up until 2015. From then until 2030 it will have to increase by 1.2 per cent per year (FAO, 2003a). In 2030 some 2,800 million tonnes of cereal will be required worldwide, which is double the 1980 level. This is based on population figures of 7,200 million for the year 2015 and 8,300 million for the year 2030. Although the growth rates for agricultural production in developing countries are higher than those in industrialized and transition countries, their cereal deficit will rise to 265 million tonnes in the year 2030, which corresponds to around 14 per cent of their total requirements. FAO believes that worldwide there is still sufficient unutilized potential, in terms of land, water and yield improvements, to meet the growing need.

DEMAND FOR LAND AND SOIL DEGRADATION
Since the rural poor in developing countries usually only have poor soils at their disposal (Section 3.3.3), there is a close link between poverty and soil degradation. Subsistence farmers and their families have to abandon this low-yielding land as progressive soil degradation reduces its productivity below the minimum needed to support themselves. Then they have

no choice but to take new land, e.g. by forest clearance (Barbier, 1997), or else migrate to the cities.

In order to meet the growing need for food, agricultural production worldwide must be increased. The greater part of these production increases will be achieved by means of an ongoing expansion of the land area used for agriculture. In addition, according to FAO forecasts, growing demand will be met by productivity increases and more intensive production (FAO, 2002). By 2030, it is estimated that in developing countries around 20 per cent of the rise in production will come from the expansion of land area, 70 per cent from increases in yield and 10 per cent from shorter fallow periods and multiple cropping. The area of arable land in developing countries will rise, according to FAO (2002), from 885 million ha in the year 1998 to 1,063 million ha in 2030, more than 80 per cent of which will be in Africa and South America. This will largely be created at the expense of forest – 12 per cent of the 1,400 million ha of fully stocked forests in industrialized countries, and 30 per cent of a similar forest area in developing countries, would be suitable or very suitable for agricultural use.

The land already in use is at risk of soil degradation in many cases (WBGU, 1994; Section 3.3). It is estimated that 1,900 million ha were degraded by human activity between 1940 and 1990 (Oldeman et al., 1991). This equates to 15 per cent of the total area. 65 per cent of agriculturally used land exhibits symptoms of degradation, according to these estimates, 25 per cent of which is moderate and 40 per cent severe or very severe. Hotspots for soil degradation are South and South-East Asia.

There are ways of reducing soil degradation, e.g. by increasing the proportion of rain-fed farming on land on gradients of less than 5 per cent at low risk of erosion, concentrating animal husbandry so as to relieve marginal land, using minimal soil tillage, higher crop densities with fertilizer use and irrigation, nitrogen-fixing crops, agroforestry and mixed cropping. In future, irrigation will play an even more important role in feeding the human race, particularly in developing countries. Steps must be taken to prevent soil salinization and increase the efficiency of water use. This objective is subject to constraints depending on the soil type and the availability of water, however.

3.2.3.4
The role of transgenic crops

On the question of how far transgenic crops can contribute to improving food security, there are widely divergent opinions. While proponents of modern biotechnology see it as a means of ensuring sufficient food production even in times of population growth, opponents emphasise the risks and problems associated with this technology (Masood, 2003).

The UN Millennium Project Hunger Task Force found the principal reasons for the decline in agricultural production in Africa between 1980 and 1995 to be low soil fertility, inappropriate irrigation, inflated fertilizer prices, poor transport routes and insufficient access to loans (UN Millennium Project, 2004d). If these obstacles are not overcome, transgenic crops will not solve the problem of hunger (Masood, 2003) because, for physical and physiological reasons, it is impossible to increase drought- and salt-resistance substantially. Non-governmental organizations like ActionAid point out that only one per cent of research into transgenic crops takes the needs of small-scale farmers into consideration. The overwhelming majority of research funding is committed to the development of technologies for large-scale farmers and multinational corporations, whereas hardly any work is taking place on modifying crop plants for marginal sites, which include millet, manioc and beans (Huang et al., 2002).

The development of transgenic crops has so far been focused on a narrow range of applications, most prominently crops with herbicide resistance or the ability to produce substances derived from the bacteria *Bacillus thuringensis* (Bt toxins) which are toxic to certain groups of insects. In a few cases, however, the transgenic crop research taking place also addresses the needs of developing countries. For example, research is being conducted in China on rice, potatoes and peanuts, crops which have been neglected by research in industrialized countries. In other developing countries, research is in progress on sugar cane, papaya and other tropical crops. Here, more than in the industrialized countries, questions of biological safety are a central concern. Fewer than one per cent of experiments with genetically modified crops in developing countries were conducted with the objective of increasing yield (Huang et al., 2002).

Risks
- Many long-term environmental effects have not been sufficiently studied. These include the impacts of genetically modified organisms upon the biodiversity of wild and cultivated plant and animal species, the effects of Bt toxin over several trophic levels and its accumulation in the soil, the effects of any outcrossing of transgenic traits into wild populations, and the development of multiple resistances.
- There is insufficient knowledge about the potential of transgenic foods to trigger allergies.

- When the same corporation is the supplier of transgenic herbicide-resistant crops and corresponding plant protection products, replacing traditional crop varieties, small farmers are driven into dependency. Just six European and North American companies control 98 per cent of the market for genetically modified crops and 70 per cent of global pesticide use. Some 91 per cent of transgenic crops cultivated worldwide originate from one firm's seed (Monsanto).
- For subsistence farmers in developing countries, it is extremely important to have unhindered access to plant genetic material for seed multiplication in preparation for breeding work, and for exchange within farming communities. When genetically modified crops are used, this access is barred by variety protection or even patent law, whereby licensing costs are entailed. Agrarian communities living and working within traditional structures often lack the financial means to meet such costs (Stoll, 2004).

Benefits and opportunities
- The use of Bt cotton results in time savings, lower labour costs, higher yields and a reduction in pesticide use, which lowers the health risk to small farmers.
- In future, transgenic crops which are currently at the research stage may represent opportunities for developing countries. For example they may prove to have higher nutritional value and yields, greater tolerance of abiotic stress (drought, flooding, salt, aluminium) or resistance to nematodes, bacteria, fungi or viruses.
- Dietary Vitamin A deficiency can be remedied by implanting specialized genes in rice (golden rice). However, critical investigation of vitamin content, bioavailability and stability remains to be carried out. It is also worth weighing up whether there are not simpler and better alternatives (e.g. adding vitamins to staple foods, vegetable-growing campaigns, etc.).

Conclusions
The Nuffield Council on Bioethics (2003) comes to the conclusion that the possible costs, benefits and risks associated with the use of certain transgenic crops can only be evaluated on a case-by-case basis. Any recommendation to use or avoid a transgenic plant must therefore take account of the specific situation of the prospective country of use and its farmers. The critical question is what impact the production of the genetically modified crop will have in comparison with the alternatives. All possible courses of action must be compared with regard to their effect on human health, nutrition, the environment, and

the associated costs. Since transgenic crops can clearly contribute to progress in agriculture in certain cases, the Nuffield Council recommends responsible research into their potential benefits as a means of contributing to poverty reduction and improvement of the nutritional situation in developing countries (Nuffield Council on Bioethics, 2003). In many cases, however, the same ends could be achieved using conventional methods.

3.2.3.5
International goals on undernourishment

In its most recent prognosis on the future development of global agriculture, FAO takes the view that the supply of food for the world population will be better in 2015 than it is today (FAO, 2003a). It does not expect the Millennium Development Goal of halving hunger by 2015 to be achieved, however (Fig. 3.2-11). Once again, certain groups of countries, particularly in sub-Saharan Africa, West Asia and the Southwest Pacific, may well fall significantly short of meeting this target.

FAO forecasts that the number of undernourished people will fall from its current level of 840 million to 440 million by the year 2015, but only if the full spectrum of causes of undernourishment have been overcome successfully by that time, particularly in Africa and South Asia (Section 3.2.3.1).

3.2.4
Lack of education

3.2.4.1
Lack of education amplifies poverty

A lack of education cements and accentuates other dimensions of poverty. At the same time, educational opportunities are reduced by material insecurity, disease and undernourishment (UNESCO, 2003b; Bruns et al., 2003). Basic education is particularly important. It increases opportunities for market participation, facilitates the adoption of new technologies, increases organizational ability, including within the informal sector, and can thus contribute both to the socio-economic advancement of individual households and to wider economic development. For example, World Bank studies show that where four years of schooling are completed, the productivity of small agricultural businesses will rise across the board (BMZ, 1999a). Adequate basic education also contributes to improvements in public health (Section 3.2.3), e.g. in disease prevention or family planning. Basic education is also a prerequisite for participation in society and democratic checks and balances. For the individual, education is a critical step towards self-realization and personal development.

Over and above basic education, secondary and vocational education also make valuable contributions to promoting social and economic development, and thus support the fight against poverty, at least indirectly. This is true of both formal and informal education. In particular, the opportunity for permanent initial and continuing education and training (lifelong learning) increases people's adaptability to socio-economic and technological change, ena-

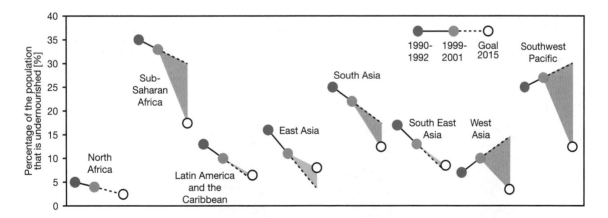

Figure 3.2-11
Situation and trends for the Millennium Development Goal of halving the number of undernourished people (MDG 1).
Source: UN, 2004b

bling them to exert more influence over it at the same time (World Bank, 2003a).

Higher education performs important functions for the education system as a whole, e.g. through teacher training. University graduates play a part in solving many development-related challenges in business, government and society. Since the non-university research sector in developing countries often has a relatively weak institutional infrastructure, universities have a leading role to play in research and scientific advisory work. Despite the fact that well-educated academics are frequently recruited to work in industrialized countries, they will often contribute to development in their home countries by way of resource and knowledge transfer (Lowell and Findley, 2001). Alongside the conventional education sector, access to information and communications technologies can also contribute to poverty reduction if the information concerned meets the country's needs (Section 3.4.3).

Although higher as well as informal education are of the utmost importance for a country's development, particularly in that they give previously disadvantaged groups fairer access to professional opportunities and life chances, the following section will deal mainly with basic education because of its tremendous potential to overcome poverty. But basic education alone does not alleviate hunger or create wealth. How far basic education can develop its potential to reduce individual poverty and bring about sustainable development depends crucially on the social, political, legal, micro-economic and macro-economic framework conditions.

3.2.4.2
Situation and trends

In developing countries today, 84 per cent of all children of compulsory school age are enrolled in school (UNESCO, 2003b). Many countries in East Asia, the Southwest Pacific, Latin America and the Caribbean achieve almost universal primary education. China and India have made considerable strides in this area. Even today, though, there are still over 100 million children worldwide who are not given the opportunity to attend primary school (UNESCO, 2003b). In sub-Saharan Africa, over 40 per cent of children do not go to school. While this is a smaller proportion than in 1990, in terms of raw numbers the statistic has risen due to population growth. According to estimates from UNESCO, if the current trend continues, in another decade there will still be 76 million children without access to basic education (Fig. 3.2-12).

Moreover, many children do not complete primary school. In numerous countries in Africa, over half of children enrolled in school end their education prematurely, and in almost all countries, it is girls more often than boys who drop out. Over half of developing countries look unlikely to succeed in guaranteeing that all children receive a full primary education by the year 2015 (Bruns et al., 2003).

The proportion of adults who can read and write rose between 1970 and 2000 from 46 per cent to almost 80 per cent worldwide (85 per cent of all men and 74 per cent of all women). Nevertheless, there are still 862 million adults and young people over the age of 15 who cannot read and write (UNESCO, 2003b). In the least developed countries, one person in two is illiterate. Projections for the year 2015 indicate that while the number of illiterates will decrease overall

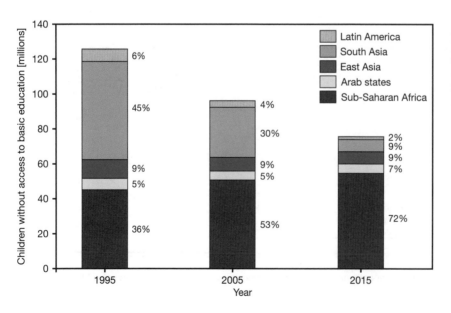

Figure 3.2-12
Number and regional distribution of children without access to basic education. 1995 and forecast for 2005 and 2015.
Source: Watkins, 2000 after UNESCO, 1997

Table 3.2-4
Literacy rate and number of illiterates in the population over the age of 15. Estimates for 1990 and 2000, projection for 2015.
Source: UNESCO, 2003b

	Literacy rate [%]			Number of illiterates [millions of people]			Change the number of illiterates [%]	
	1990	2000	2015	1990	2000	2015	1990–2000	2000–2015
World	75	80	85	879	862	799	-2	-7
Developed and transition countries	98	99	99	22	15	8	-32	-50
Developing countries	67	74	81	857	847	792	-1	-7
Sub-Saharan Africa	49	60	74	131	136	133	4	-2
Arab states	50	60	72	62	68	71	8	5
East Asia and Pacific	80	87	93	233	186	114	-20	-39
South and West Asia	48	55	66	382	412	437	8	6
Latin America and Caribbean	85	89	93	42	39	33	-6	-16

by about 7 per cent worldwide, it will continue to rise in South and West Asia and in the Arab states (Table 3.2-4). Unless additional efforts are made, there will still be some 800 million illiterate people worldwide in 2015.

It is generally acknowledged that the quality of schooling has not kept pace with its quantitative expansion. Putting universal compulsory education into practice overstretches the financial and human capacities of many developing countries.

SOCIAL, GEOGRAPHICAL AND ETHNIC INEQUALITY
There are numerous countries in which ethnic minorities and indigenous population groups and children living in rural areas have substantially poorer educational opportunities than others. In the majority of developing countries, illiteracy rates in rural areas are twice to three times as high as in urban centres, and the rate of school enrolment is also substantially lower (Bruns et al., 2003). Moreover, children from poor families are distinctly less likely to have access to basic education than children from well-off families (Filmer and Pritchett, 1999; UNFPA, 2002). The reasons for this are varied: children are often called upon to contribute to supporting the family, and school learning teaches them few skills which might be considered relevant. The difficulties of travelling to school, the fees and other costs associated with school attendance make access to formal education all the more difficult. Social deprivation of ethnic minorities and indigenous population groups is frequently linked with regional disparities. Indigenous population groups, who usually live in remote, mountainous and poorer regions, barely have access to educational facilities (Psacharopoulos and Patrinos, 1994; Watkins, 2000). Moreover, the culture of indigenous population groups may not be acknowl-

edged by the public education system, and may even be suppressed.

DISCRIMINATION AGAINST GIRLS
According to the most recent estimates by UNICEF, 65 million girls worldwide do not go to school (UNICEF, 2004). One in five girls of primary school age is thus deprived of the opportunity to learn to read and write (UNDP, 2003c). There are also wide regional disparities: South and West Asia show the greatest differentials in the school enrolment rates of boys and girls, followed by the Arab states and sub-Saharan Africa, whereas in Latin America and the Caribbean, Central Asia, East Asia and the Pacific, boys and girls are enrolled in almost equal numbers (UNESCO, 2003b). In most countries where there are sizeable disparities in primary education, these only become more acute at secondary level, whereas elsewhere they diminish or even reverse (Box 3.2-5). Unless considerable additional efforts are made, women are still likely to account for two-thirds of all illiterate people in 2015 (Fig. 3.2-13).

Girls without basic education are particularly at risk from poverty, violence, child labour and prostitution. They marry earlier, more frequently die from complications of pregnancy, have more children and are at increased risk of HIV/AIDS (UNICEF, 2004). Realizing their human right to education not only improves girls' quality of life as individuals, but generates substantial social benefits. Women who have attended school are more likely than others to enable their children to go to school (UNDP 2003c). These women also act as multipliers in respect of other aspects of poverty reduction, because as well as caring for children, women are usually the members of the household responsible for food preparation, health and hygiene.

Box 3.2-5

Secondary and tertiary education

The rate of school attendance at secondary level varies greatly from region to region: in 26 developing countries, the majority of them in sub-Saharan Africa, fewer than 30 per cent of the relevant age-group attend secondary school. In Latin America and the countries of Central and Eastern Europe, the school attendance rate is close to 90 per cent. The number of students in tertiary education worldwide has risen from an estimated 69 million in 1990 to 88 million (1997), with growth of 50 per cent registered in developing countries. While women make up the majority of students in most countries of Central and Eastern Europe, Latin America and the Caribbean, there are only two-thirds as many female as male students in the Asia-Pacific region, and women are very underrepresented in sub-Saharan Africa.

Source: UNESCO, 2003b

3.2.4.3
Lack of education and environmental change

The interactions between education and the environment are more difficult to pinpoint than those between education and other dimensions of poverty. Environmental change has no direct effect on education, but intensifies the need for education and places particular demands upon curriculum content and learning objectives. Knowledge transfer concerning good management of a changing environment, or indeed the capacity and opportunity to acquire such knowledge, is one way of reducing the individual's vulnerability to environmental change.

But adaptive capacity is not the only outcome of education. As one of the prerequisites for participation in political processes, education also gives people a chance to protect themselves effectively against threatened environmental change. A lack of education – and hence an inadequate understanding of the ecological consequences of human actions – can harm the environment. Education guides people towards a systematic understanding of the connections between the natural world and personal lifestyles. It fosters learning skills and strengthens the motivation to continue learning. This in turn is a vital prerequisite for the capacity to take up innovations, e.g. environmentally sound technologies, and to develop them further.

Even so, more educated people do not automatically take care of the environment. The opposite can also be true. The economic development of some societies, which is normally associated with a higher level of education, can actually increase pressure on the environment. While this is primarily attributable to scale effects produced by economic growth and changed patterns of production and consumption, the dissemination of 'modern' knowledge is certainly capable of bringing about negative environmental impacts. This can be the case if there is no strategic alignment with the guiding vision of sustainable development, for example, or if local and indigenous knowledge is neglected or suppressed which can result in the loss of methods and practices of sustainable husbandry.

To ensure that education contributes not only to poverty reduction but also to the whole of sustainable development, education work must incorporate two additional elements. Firstly, the facts about the environment must be taught, and an understanding

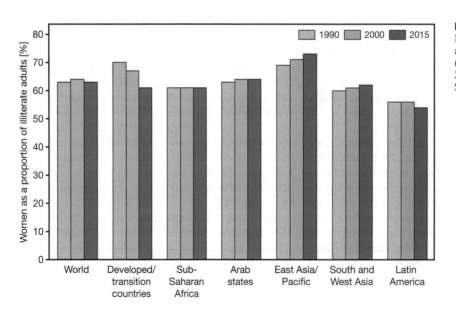

Figure 3.2-13
Proportion of illiterate adults who are women (1990, 2000 and forecast for 2015).
Source: UNESCO, 2003b

conveyed of the interplay between human action and environmental impacts, along with a stronger sense of responsibility. Secondly, it is necessary to foster local and indigenous knowledge, that is, traditional knowledge and cultural pluralism. Accordingly, basic education means more than the teaching of reading, writing and arithmetic. It must also satisfy fundamental learning needs, i.e. the basic knowledge and skills that people need if they are to improve their living conditions. Basic education should put people in a position to understand and contribute to shaping the development of the society they belong to.

These insights were neglected in development cooperation for decades, and are only gradually starting to take hold. At the World Conference on Education for All in Jomtien in 1990, an appropriately wide-ranging concept of education was formulated. It envisions basic education as a route towards the full development of human potential, which spans four dimensions: learning to know; learning to do; learning to live together; learning to be. Thus learning opportunities are milestones on the route towards sustainable development and peaceful coexistence (UNESCO, 2002; Box 3.2-6). The Decade of Education for Sustainable Development, proclaimed by the United Nations General Assembly (2005–2014) and coordinated by UNESCO, bears out this philosophy. Its purpose is to promote education as the foundation for a sustainable society, and the integration of sustainable development into all phases of the education system.

3.2.4.4
International goals on education

In 1990 at the first UN World Conference on Education for All, the international community agreed that by the year 2000, all children should be provided with access to basic education. Despite a number of improvements in the following years, many are still denied the human right to education as enshrined in the Universal Declaration of Human Rights (Art. 26), the UN Convention on the Rights of the Child (Art. 28) and the International Pact on Economic, Social and Cultural Rights (the Social Pact). This applies particularly to girls and women. In view of these overall results, the global community renewed its goal in the year 2000: under an international action plan, the Dakar Framework for Action, governments are committed to halving the number of illiterate people worldwide by the year 2015. Children in every country will be given the opportunity to complete their primary schooling. Women and girls should have equal opportunities in basic and further education.

Box 3.2-6

Declaration of the World Conference on Education for All, Jomtien, Thailand, 1990 (Art. 1)

'Every person – child, youth and adult – shall be able to benefit from educational opportunities designed to meet their basic learning needs. These needs comprise both essential learning tools (such as literacy, oral expression, numeracy, and problem solving) and the basic learning content (such as knowledge, skills, values, and attitudes) required by human beings to be able to survive, to develop their full capacities, to live and work in dignity, to participate fully in development, to improve the quality of their lives, to make informed decisions, and to continue learning. The scope of basic learning needs and how they should be met varies with individual countries and cultures, and inevitably, changes with the passage of time.'

Source: UNESCO, 2002

The last two targets were also incorporated into the Millennium Development Goals (Section 2.1):

- *MDG 2, target 3:* Ensure that, by 2015, children everywhere, boys and girls alike, will be able to complete a full course of primary schooling.
- *MDG 3, target 4:* Eliminate gender disparity in primary and secondary education, preferably by 2005, and in all levels of education no later than 2015.

Without a change of policy, there are prospects of achieving the MDGs in the field of education in some countries, primarily in Latin America and the Caribbean, but not worldwide (Fig. 3.2-14):

- In order to achieve the goal of basic education for all by 2015, additional school places for 156 million children would have to be created in the next decade, of which 40 million should be in South Asia and 23 million in the Arab states. In sub-Saharan Africa, some 88 million additional school places are necessary by 2015, which would mean a doubling of the school enrolment rate from its 1990s level. However, for some African countries, this would mean a tenfold increase in their school enrolment rates (Baaden, 2002). UNESCO takes the view that by 2015 there will still be 76 million children of compulsory school age without access to basic education (Section 3.2.4.2).
- Around 50 developing countries will not achieve the envisioned goal of equality for girls and boys in primary and secondary education by the year 2015.

Similarly, the goal under the Dakar Framework for Action of halving the number of illiterates by 2015 will not be achieved. As shown in Section 3.2.4.2

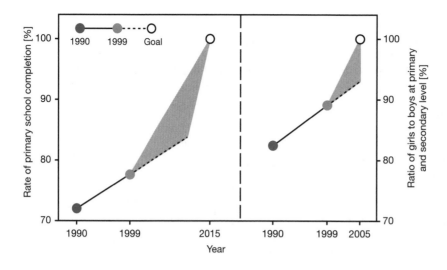

Figure 3.2-14
Recorded rates of primary
school completion and ratio
of girls to boys at primary
and secondary school level.
The trend has also been
extrapolated, showing the
divergence from MDGs 2
and 3.
Source: World Bank, 2004c

above, between 1990 and 2015 their number will only
have fallen from 879 million to 799 million, while in
South and West Asia and the Arab countries it will
actually rise (UNESCO, 2003b).

The development goals of creating jobs for young
people and improving access to information and communication technologies (MDG 8) are also closely
linked with education:

- *Target 16:* In cooperation with developing countries, develop and implement strategies for decent
  and productive work for youth.
- *Target 18:* In cooperation with the private sector,
  make available the benefits of new technologies,
  especially information and communications.

Progress in achieving these two targets can only be
monitored with great difficulty, however. Besides the
quantitative goals, it is important in both developing
and industrialized countries to pay greater attention
to the quality of education and its focus on the acquisition of skills for participation; in other words, the
ability to contribute to civil society.

3.2.5
Lack of social capital and societal stability

3.2.5.1
Stabilizing social cohesion

The living conditions and economic opportunities of
the poor are not determined solely by factors on the
individual level, such as health, education, income
and assets, but also by social capital. Over the past
few decades, development policy has turned the main
focus of its attention from material capital (primarily infrastructure) to human capital (investment in

education) and finally to good governance. By now,
social capital is viewed as an important resource for
prosperity and the well-being of individuals, private
households, communities and whole societies (Wissenschaftliche Arbeitsgruppe, 2000).

Despite the persistence of varying definitions,
social capital is generally understood as the totality of
social patterns of behaviour and formal and informal
networks in a society which serve to stabilize its long-
term cohesion (Wissenschaftliche Arbeitsgruppe,
2000). Likewise, it is a generally accepted view that
social capital strengthens a society's cultural identity
and promotes participation and non-violent conflict
resolution. Social networks also raise economic productivity, because mutual trust and common values
reduce transaction costs and increase anticipatory
certainty (Coleman, 1990; Putnam et al., 1993). As
part of its Social Capital Initiative, the World Bank
found abundant confirmation of the developmental
relevance of the concept, and developed standardized assessment methods (Grootaert and van Bastelaer, 2001).

Within a multidimensional concept of social capital, several distinct aspects can be identified. One of
these relates to the intensity and density of social networks. The term 'bonding social capital' can be used
to refer to the close ties among a relatively homogeneous group of people, for example family, friends,
the village or the ethnic group. In this context, operating on the basis of trust, reliability and reciprocity is
key to solidarity and social security. 'Bridging social
capital' refers to less powerful network structures
which enable interaction across divisions within society. This may be the case in a religious community if it
embraces different socio-economic or ethnic group-
ings. Finally, 'linking social capital' is the means by
which the individual or group is integrated into the

official institutional fabric of a society. On this basis, formal social institutions such as legal systems and political participation interrelate closely with the values and norms of informal social relationships, and jointly determine the extent of social stability and participation.

Social capital thus describes the diverse networks of relationships which make up civil society and shape its relationship with the state and the market. The process character of social capital is important; although it does not become depleted from use, it requires constant servicing to be maintained and enhanced.

A further distinction concerns the form in which social capital is manifested. In its structural dimension, social capital is manifested in the form of defined roles, generally accepted rules and clearly defined networks (e.g. a sports club). These facilitate the exchange of information, collective activities and decisions on the pursuit of common goals. In its cognitive form, it is reflected in common norms, values, attitudes, world views and trust, aspects which are important for the forging of interpersonal relationships but not so tied to a specific purpose (e.g. a circle of friends; Uphoff, 2000).

Social capital exhibits characteristics of a public good and is associated with positive externalities. For example, neighbourhood associations not only benefit their members but contribute to wider social stability and increased prosperity. However, social capital can also have negative effects and heighten conflicts, e.g. if public institutions and markets are controlled by groups with familial or ethnic ties. Similarly, drug cartels and violent gangs are holders of social capital. In such cases, the members of the relevant association profit from the social network, but it is damaging to society as a whole (Woolcock and Narayan, 2000). Negative consequences can also be seen in traditional societies when social norms pose an obstruction to modernization because individuals are not permitted to gain benefits at the expense of the collective (Gsänger, 2001).

The present report confines itself to the positive functions of social networks and uses social capital in a normative sense. It concerns itself with the specific contribution made by social networks to poverty reduction, participation, social stability and crisis prevention, combined with the conservation of local and global ecosystems. The social capital organized in non-governmental organizations (NGOs), among other institutions, gives the people of a community the ability and competence to shape and influence their living environment to suit their own needs and well-being. It is a particular function and strength of NGOs to activate social capital (Section 4.3.3).

3.2.5.2
Social capital, societal stability and poverty

Empirical studies available to date on countries with different income levels show that it is possible, though difficult, to measure the influence of social capital on individual incomes, macro-economic productivity and public sector performance (Box 3.2-7; Grootaert and van Bastelaer, 2001). The majority of these studies in developing countries have so far concentrated on households, villages and individual communities. Findings on the micro level suggest the conclusion that the individual welfare effect of social capital must be rated as equally or even more important than the contribution of human capital and material capital. The wealth elasticities for Bolivia, Burkina Faso and Indonesia, for example, are comparable for social capital and human capital (Table 3.2-6). The wealth elasticity figures mean the following: a 1 per cent increase in human capital generates a 0.18 per cent rise in prosperity in Bolivia, for instance; a similar change in social capital leads to a 0.13 per cent improvement in that country.

In development policy, social capital is a parameter of strategic importance because it exerts a positive influence on all three dimensions at the centre of the global poverty reduction strategy: economic opportunities, political participation and security (World Bank, 2000). In developing countries, social capital is the preferred class of asset for poor people ('Social capital is the wealth of the poor'). They can acquire it by working and dedicating their time, whereas the rich pay for their social capital. As a result, social capital is more evenly distributed between rich and poor than land or material capital (Collier, 1998).

This is rational and effective behaviour on the part of the poor, because the degree of poverty decreases as social capital grows (Grootaert, 2001). This effect is explained by the exchange of knowledge and information in social networks, and collective risk mitigation by pooling different types of income. Furthermore, social capital encourages asset formation of the poor, makes it easier for them to access loans, and improves their access to social services (Knack, 1999).

Development projects reveal the close connection between social capital and participation. For example the efficiency of local water supply systems in Indonesia depends on the cooperation capabilities of the population concerned and the opportunities they are given to participate (Isham and Kähkönen, 1999). Where tight social networks exist, people get involved in shared planning and monitoring processes and identify with the project, which makes it possible to deter freeriding by illegal users.

Box 3.2-7

Measuring social capital

Since it is not possible to measure social capital directly, it is necessary to use substitute indicators for quantitative studies (Table 3.2-5). This is comparable with the methodological problems of measuring human capital, where years of education and training and years in work are frequently used as informative alternative measures. Usually structural aspects of social capital are used for purposes of quantification. The choice of suitable indicators depends upon the sector of society, the region and culture. For example, membership of an association is a relevant scale in Indonesia, Kenya and the Andean countries, but not in India or Russia where informal networks are dominant. Other relevant aspects may be participation in events and decision-making, trust in other people and institutions, and support for norms like reciprocity and solidarity. For larger groups, contact with other organizations and government institutions play an important role in the measurement of social capital. Despite this diversity of indicators, there are nevertheless consistencies which enable cross-cultural comparisons.

Sources: Grootaert, 2001; Krishna and Schrader, 2000

Social capital	Indicators
Horizontal integration	Number/types of local organizations, degrees of organization, degree of ethnic or economic homogeneity of social structures, degree of self-organization, confidence in politics and trade unions, donation and transfer rate, dependency in old age, etc.
Civil society and political arena	Indices of civil liberties, indices for political and economic discrimination, corruption, state efficiency, decentrality of political decisions, measures of political stability, electoral abstinence, acts of political violence.
Social integration	Social mobility, measure of social tension, ethnic and social fragmentation, strikes, murder and suicide rate, crime rate, divorce rate, youth unemployment, rate of lone parenthood, etc.
Legal stability and quality of administration	Accessibility of the administration, independence of the judiciary, risk of expropriation and nationalization, contract certainty vis-à-vis the state, contracting costs.

Table 3.2-5
Indicators for social capital.
Source: nach Grootaert, 1998

SOCIAL CAPITAL AND GENDER

Given their prominent role in caring for children, the sick and the elderly, and their social exclusion in many societies, women make a special contribution to the creation of informal social capital. Under certain conditions this can be converted into formalized structures. For example, the community kitchens movement organized by women in Peru forged widespread networks and thus gave rise to new forms of political representation of interests, from the local to the national level (World Bank, 2000).

The Grameen Bank's microfinance programme in Bangladesh, viewed worldwide as a model of good practice, achieved impressive rates of repayment. Its success lay in activating women's existing social capital and customary mutual assistance (van Bastalaer, 1999). Men usually have better means of accessing formal networks and institutions. They can abuse this privilege to exclude women from the benefits of collective activities. In a case study on the rehabilitation of coal mining areas in India, for example, it was shown that once people split into groups, this increased the marginalization of disadvantaged groups and worsened the social exclusion of women (Pantoja, 2000; Box 3.2-8).

3.2.5.3
Situation and trends

The traditional forms of social capital (family, village community, ethnic group, religion), which have been of crucial importance to underpinning the livelihoods of the poor in many developing countries, are increasingly coming under pressure from processes of internal modernization within society and processes of globalization. A major factor in the disintegration of traditional solidarity-based communities is the grow-

Table 3.2-6
Individual welfare elasticities. The welfare indicator used was consumer expenditure at household level. * Additive index for Bolivia, otherwise multiplicative index
Source: Grootaert, 2001

	Bolivia	Burkina Faso	Indonesia
Social capital index*	0.13	0.09	0.12
Human capital	0.18	0.07	0.16

Box 3.2-8

The Gender Empowerment Measure

This measure developed by UNDP captures differences between the sexes in three areas: political participation, economic participation and control of economic resources. In each of these areas, the relative involvement of each gender is determined. To assess political participation, the figures used are the proportions of male and female members of parliament. Participation in the economy is rated according to the proportion of female executives and specialists. Control of economic resources is determined from the estimated income of women and men. Finally a mean value is calculated.

In a society with complete equality between men and women, this index would be equal to 1. The Scandinavian countries come closest, attaining a figure of up to 0.90. In a great number of countries, the value is significantly below 0.5, and falls as low as 0.12 in Yemen and 0.22 in Bangladesh.

Source: UNDP, 2003c

ing migration into cities. In the megacities, the vulnerability of the poor is rising because of a shortage of employment opportunities and a lack of social security systems (BMZ, 1999b). In response, new forms of social capital frequently emerge through self-organization of the population in urban settlements. They aim on the one hand to counteract risks (forced resettlement, crime) and on the other hand to create development opportunities and to meet social and cultural needs (education, health, community-based savings and insurance schemes). In rural regions too, other forms of social capital are increasingly emerging. These include bodies representing indigenous groups, credit cooperatives, networks of landless people, and associations of small farmers, demanding political participation and becoming more influential because they are integrated into global civil society networks (e.g. the World Social Forum).

3.2.5.4
Social capital, societal stability and the environment

The existence of social capital plays a demonstrable role in the collective use of natural resources. For example, a study on river basin management systems in India revealed that informal networks, defined allocation of roles, solidarity and mutual trust have very positive impacts (Krishna and Uphoff, 1999). Accordingly, the successful management of natural resources by local communities calls for a basic minimum of social capital. Similarly, such capital deter-

mines the adaptability of groups and local communities in the event of environmental disasters and other risks: it reduces their vulnerability, allows better risk management and broadens the range of alternative courses of action (ADB et al., 2003).

3.2.5.5
International goals on social capital and societal stability

For practical purposes, goals connected with social capital and social stability relate to the micro level, and as such they complement the objective of good governance contained within the Millennium Development Goals. The fundamental principle must be for the population of a country to be equipped or enabled to sustain effective informal safety nets, such as the extended family and the village community, or formal social insurance schemes. To reduce a society's vulnerability, political measures should be geared towards strengthening and not impairing the social capital of that society. This includes compliance with internationally recognized standards such as the Universal Declaration of Human Rights, the Civil Pact and the Social Pact, and the Conventions on the Rights of the Child, the Rights of Women, and Labour Standards.

3.3
Environmental change and poverty

Poverty, in its various dimensions, can be caused or amplified by global environmental changes. By 'global environmental changes', WBGU means those changes that modify substantially, sometimes irreversibly, the character of the Earth System and therefore influence appreciably, be it directly or indirectly, natural life-support systems for a large part of humanity. In extreme cases, such changes trigger environmentally-induced population displacement (Box 3.3-1). Relevant processes can affect global systems, such as in the case of climate change. Or the effect can be cumulative, as in the case of the mounting degradation of soils, freshwater and ecosystems, and the accumulation of persistent hazardous chemicals. Global environmental changes can have both natural and anthropogenic causes (WBGU, 1993).

In its reports, WBGU concentrates on anthropogenic global environmental changes, often characterized by their high speed in contrast to natural changes. This speed overstretches the adaptive capacity and remedial mechanisms of the Earth System. WBGU considers the following global environmental issues

Box 3.3-1

Environmentally-induced population displacement: The disaster of the future?

Observations confirm a fundamental experience: Migration is driven by push factors and pull factors. Push factors that move or force people to leave their home (village, city, region, country) are conditions at the place of origin that are intolerable to these people or are perceived by them to endanger their very survival. Natural disasters, land and water scarcity, unemployment and a lack of prospects in life, social discrimination, intra- or inter-state wars and political oppression are the main causes of such displacement. That this displacement is impelled or forced distinguishes it from more or less voluntary migration. In this context, wars are often linked with famines, the manifest violence of dictatorships with the structural violence of living conditions incompatible with human dignity.

Migration pressure from poor and conflict-prone regions can be a result of conflicts arising due to the marginalization of larger groups or the distribution of scarce resources. However, migration does not proceed according to some 'law of nature' as in a system of communicating tubes, nor does it follow the 'greatest gradient' as in a slide on an inclined plane from poor to rich regions. Similarly, the interpretations of the 'new exodus' explaining this in terms of a demographic surplus in poor countries with the highest levels of population growth fail, firstly, to take into account the fact that poor groups are scarcely able to migrate internationally because they lack the resources, and, secondly, underestimate the effective checks that have been set up in the meantime on the borders of the potential destination countries.

Environmental crises are now emerging as a driving force behind migration movements whose anticipated dimensions threaten to outstrip all other causes of displacement and migration. Estimates range up to hundreds of millions of people; this is several times more than the number of war refugees. According to the World Water Commission, in 1999 there were for the first time more environmental refugees (namely 25 million) than war refugees. The Commission expects this figure to double by the year 2010. UNEP estimates the number of environmental refugees at 20 to 24 million. It needs to be taken into account, however, when considering all numbers, estimates and predictions of migration movements, that the concepts and data used can be indeterminate. Under the definition in international law established by the 1951 Geneva Convention on Refugees only such persons are 'true' refugees who have left their countries of origin out of fear of political persecution. In mid-2004 the UN High Commission for Refugees counted

only about 17 million people as belonging to this group. There are, however, at least the same number of internally displaced persons, who, while being in a 'refugee-like' situation, have not crossed the borders of a state. For instance, in the Democratic Republic of Congo several million internally displaced persons are currently straying through their own country.

The International Organization for Migration estimates the current number of international migrants no longer living in their country of origin to total about 175 million. The great majority of these are people in the grey zone of 'irregular migration', who lack documents. Political parlance uses the stigmatizing term 'economic refugees' to refer to these people – yet they can scarcely be distinguished from 'environmental refugees', for environmental degradation generates economic misery.

Environmental refugees are people who leave the area in which they have traditionally settled or lived because natural or human-induced environmental crises have made their lives far more difficult or have even threatened their very survival. Desertification destroys natural life-support systems permanently, and is thus the main long-term cause of environmentally-induced displacement. Desertification itself has several underlying causes:
– the overexploitation of soils, above all due to population pressure,
– disturbances of the regional water balance due to overuse of water reserves and changes in regional climate,
– human-induced global climatic changes, which impact particularly upon arid zones.
135 million people are at risk due to advancing desertification alone. This is amplified by global and regional climate change, but is also exacerbated by local over-utilization of arable and pasture land and by the deforestation of entire regions. There is a fatal link between under-development, poverty and environmental degradation – a Sahel Syndrome that generates population displacement. Poverty amplified by environmental degradation is the cause, people fleeing environmental degradation and economic misery is the effect. This in turn can lead to conflict over increasingly scarce resources, with a potential to escalate into violence. It is consequently essential to not only conceive of environmental and development policy as an integrated whole, but also to take into consideration the security risks presented by environmentally conditioned conflicts. The 2003 World Development Report presented a strategic roadmap: the core elements of long-term global environment and development policy must be the reduction of poverty, the mitigation of climate change, the conservation of soil and water resources and the preservation of biological diversity.

Source: Nuscheler, 2004

to be particularly relevant to the poverty-environment nexus:
– Climate change (Section 3.3.1),
– Water scarcity and pollution (Section 3.3.2),
– Soil degradation (Section 3.3.3),
– Loss of biological diversity and resources (Section 3.3.4),
– Air pollution and toxic substances (Section 3.3.5).
In many instances, there are amplifying interactions among the various global environmental changes.

This is why it is impossible to analyse, or resolve, the issues in isolation. WBGU has already treated many of these interactions in depth in its report on institutions (2001a). Table 3.3-1 provides an overview of key interactions among the environmental changes discussed in the present report.

The following sections explore the linkages among the various dimensions of poverty and the global environmental changes noted above. The analysis shall examine, on the one hand, the relevance of pov-

Table 3.3-1
Key interactions among global environmental changes.
Source: WBGU

Impact of ▸ / upon ▾	Climate change	Water scarcity and pollution	Soil degradation	Loss of biological diversity and resources	Air pollution and toxic substances
Climate change	–	–	Loss of CO_2 sequestration, albedo increase	Loss of CO_2 sequestration, albedo change	Regional and global climate change caused by aerosols and trace gases
Water scarcity and pollution	Changed quantities and patterns of precipitation, desertification	–	Changed local hydrological balance, contaminant and sediment accumulation	Changes in the local hydrological balance caused e.g. by deforestation	Contamination of water resources caused e.g. by mercury from mining, or by pesticides
Soil degradation	Desertification, consequences of changes in precipitation	Salinization	–	Increased erosion caused by loss of vegetation cover	Soil contamination by heavy metals and organic substances
Loss of biological diversity and resources	Shifting biome boundaries, coral bleaching	Ecosystem degradation and conversion, species loss	Ecosystem degradation, species loss, harvest losses	–	Inputs of contaminants and nutrients to natural ecosystems
Air pollution and toxic substances	–	–	Dust loading of air caused by wind erosion	Reduced filtration of air	–

erty as a cause of environmental degradation. It shall further examine the impacts of global environmental changes upon poor groups, and upon efforts to reduce poverty.

3.3.1
Climate change

3.3.1.1
Climate change and its causes

Over the 20th century the global average near-surface air temperature has increased by 0.6±0.2°C. The global average sea level has risen by 10–20cm over the same period. The Intergovernmental Panel on Climate Change (IPCC) anticipates a further temperature increase by 1.4–5.8°C and a further sea-level rise between 9 and 88cm over the period from 1990 to 2100, depending upon humankind's behaviour (IPCC, 2001a). In terms of poverty impacts, the observed and projected local changes are of paramount importance; these vary greatly from region to region. Projections for such local changes are more uncertain than statements on the development of average global parameters. Key observed and projected changes in regional climate parameters include (IPCC, 2001a):
- *Changes in the average climatic conditions of a region:* It is highly probable that the quantity of precipitation at mid- and high latitudes and in the inner tropics has increased over the 20th century, while it declined in the greater part of the northern subtropics. Projections for the 21st century indicate that this trend will continue. The central parts of the continents will experience an above-average increase in temperature. This will cause greater evaporation that often cannot be compensated by increased precipitation, with the result that soils dry out to a greater extent in these regions, and water availability declines. This will affect in particular those regions in which precipitation is expected to decline in the future, such as the arid and semi-arid regions of Asia and Africa.
- *Changes in climate variability and in the frequency and severity of extreme events:* An increased incidence of drought in parts of Africa and Asia has been observed over the past decades. It is considered very likely that there will be an increased occurrence of heat waves over land in almost all parts of the world, and more frequent intense precipitation events in many regions. An increased risk of drought and of flooding in connection with El Niño events is also likely.

Rapid climate change has a predominantly negative impact upon almost all environmental domains. For example, it leads to reduced water availability, advancing soil degradation and to the loss of biological diversity (Sections 3.3.2 to 3.3.5).

Humankind influences the climate above all through its use of fossil fuels, through industrial production, land-use changes and agriculture. The long-lived greenhouse gases created in these processes alter the Earth's radiation budget and thus lead to a warming. The anthropogenic processes also cause short-lived aerosols to enter the atmosphere, which, depending upon their composition and the specific site at which they are released, can have a cooling or warming effect. Concentrations of the most important long-lived greenhouse gases have risen greatly since the onset of industrialization. Carbon dioxide levels in the air, for instance, have risen by somewhat more than 30 per cent, and have now reached 379 parts per million by volume (ppmv). CO_2 contributes 60 per cent of the radiative forcing caused by long-lived greenhouse gases, methane (CH_4) 20 per cent and nitrous oxide (N_2O) 6 per cent. Environmental problems that are initially local in nature, such as deforestation and soil degradation, also influence greenhouse gas sources and sinks. They change the reflective properties of the land surface and the levels of evaporation, thus triggering further climatic changes.

Prompted by a proposal made by Brazil that states should commit to emissions reductions in accordance with their respective contributions to global warming, several preliminary study findings are available that assess the contributions made by various country groups to the average global temperature increase caused by emissions of CO_2, CH_4 and N_2O over the period from 1890 to 2000. The studies indicate a contribution of 39–47 per cent by the OECD, 13–17 per cent by eastern Europe and the former Soviet Union, 22–29 per cent by Asia and 14–21 per cent by Africa / Latin America / Middle East (UNFCCC, 2002b).

No quantitative assessments of the climate impacts caused by poor people are available. However, the analysis of key anthropogenic greenhouse gas sources provided in the following suggests that poor people contribute little to current emissions. Material poverty often prevents behaviour harmful to the climate. Emissions from land-use changes are an important exception.

LAND-USE CHANGES

About 10–30 per cent of all anthropogenic CO_2 emissions are attributed to land-use changes, mainly deforestation in the tropics. Fire clearance additionally emits CH_4 (approx. 7–16 per cent of anthropogenic emissions; IPCC, 2001a). The net rate of forest loss in the tropics over the period from 1990 to 2000 is estimated at 8.4 million hectares per year; of this, the greater part was converted to permanent agriculturally utilized land (FAO, 2001a). One important reason for this is the need to feed a growing population (FAO, 2003a). However, according to Lambin et al. (2001) poverty and population growth

are not the main immediate cause of the destruction of tropical forests, but rather the economic incentives, which in turn depend upon political factors and infrastructure (Section 3.3.4.1). Illegal logging and a lack of education also lead to unsustainable silvicultural and agricultural practices and greater levels of clearance. State-sponsored resettlement projects (e.g. Transmigrasi in Indonesia) and the privatization of forest areas (e.g. in Chile) are examples of policies that are leading or have led to increased emissions from land-use changes. In dry years, vegetation fires can get out of control. Page et al. (2002) estimate that the CO_2 emissions from the month-long forest fires that occurred in Indonesia during the 1997/98 El Niño event totalled 0.81–2.57Gt carbon, which corresponds to 13–40 per cent of the annual CO_2 emission from the use of fossil energy sources. This was triggered by clearance fires laid by farmers, private-sector companies and state organizations to prepare arable land. Due to the drought, some got out of control, inflaming, in addition to the vegetation, the underlying meter-thick peat layers. Tropical peat-bogs are an important carbon reservoir; they are made susceptible to fires by draining and deforestation.

AGRICULTURE

Agriculture is a principal source of the greenhouse gases methane (CH_4) and nitrous oxide (N_2O). CH_4 is formed mainly in rice cultivation and in cattle farming. Due to the great importance of the agricultural sector in developing countries, their relative contribution to global CH_4 and N_2O emissions is greater than their contribution to CO_2 emissions. In 1995 the developing countries emitted 1.5 times as much methane as the industrialized countries (WRI, 2003). Nonetheless, the per-capita emissions of industrialized countries are still twice those of developing countries. South-East Asia is of particular relevance in this context, being responsible for about half of global anthropogenic CH_4 emissions, mainly due to wet rice cultivation (WRI, 1996).

The rise in global atmospheric CH_4 abundance has slowed continuously in recent years and there are indications that the atmospheric concentration may have stabilized, meaning that the strength of the sinks corresponds to that of the sources (Dlugokencky et al., 2003). As it is not yet possible to draw up a global CH_4 balance with any sufficient certainty, the role of methane in the future development of the climate system remains uncertain.

N_2O presents a similar picture: Here agriculturally utilized soils are clearly the strongest anthropogenic source. In 1995 the developing countries contributed 1.6 times as much to anthropogenic emissions as the industrialized countries did (WRI, 2003). As is the case for CO_2 emissions, it also needs to be noted for agricultural N_2O emissions that emissions from agriculture in poor countries are not automatically emissions by poor people. N_2O emissions require ownership of land or cattle, which is precisely what the poor lack.

<small>USE OF FOSSIL ENERGY CARRIERS</small>

The utilization of fossil energy carriers is the main source of anthropogenic greenhouse gases – accountable for about three-quarters of all anthropogenic CO_2 emissions and also for a substantial proportion (20–33 per cent) of anthropogenic CH_4 emissions (IPCC, 2001a). The World Bank lists annual per-capita CO_2 emissions from the use of fossil energy carriers and from cement production, the latter being far less relevant, as a key indicator of the development status of a country. In 1999 per-capita emissions in industrialized countries figured 10.8t, while in developing countries they averaged only 1.8t (WRI, 2003). The total emissions of industrialized countries were still 77 per cent higher than those of developing countries in that year. However, developing-country emissions had already risen by 37 per cent from 1990 to 1999, and a further rise is highly probable. Within the poor countries, the bulk of CO_2 emissions is caused by a small upper class; the contribution made by poor people to these emissions is slight, as they only benefit to a small degree from fossil-generated energy.

3.3.1.2
Poverty impacts of climate change

While climate change is a global phenomenon and problem, the adverse effects upon poor people and poor countries are particularly severe because these depend more strongly upon natural resources and are less able to adapt to climatic variations and extreme weather. Within the poor countries, in turn, the poorest people are the most vulnerable. This connection runs like a red thread through IPCC's Third Assessment Report (IPCC, 2001b). The following discussion presents only some representative linkages.

<small>CLIMATE CHANGE, FOOD SECURITY AND WATER AVAILABILITY</small>

Agriculture is particularly vulnerable to climatic changes. Factors playing a role here include, in particular, changed temperatures, water availability, the spread of plant and animal diseases, but also the fertilization effect resulting from increased CO_2 concentrations in the atmosphere. The issue is of great economic importance to poor countries. While in the year 2000 only 3 per cent of GDP was still generated in the agricultural sector in Europe, the proportion in sub-Saharan Africa, with the exception of

South Africa, was much higher (reaching 59 per cent in Guinea-Bissau; WRI, 2003).

It is probable that cereal yields in tropical and subtropical developing countries will already start to decline when the global mean temperature rises by 1.0–1.7°C compared to the pre-industrial level (WBGU, 2003). In higher-medium latitudes, a decline in yields is only expected after a greater rise in annual average temperatures by several degrees Celsius. Climate change will therefore not necessarily jeopardize food security at the global level. It will however cause an increased dependence of the poorer tropical and subtropical countries upon food imports. This will further amplify North-South disparities in food security.

A further threat will be presented to food security over the medium term by an increase in weather extremes, which is considered likely. Many studies on food security fail to take this aspect into account. Even today, climate variability (such as year-on-year changes in precipitation) in sub-Saharan Africa, South Asia and large parts of other developing countries has a key impact on the productivity of arable farming. Drought, in particular, leads to disastrous collapses of yields in these countries (FAO, 2003a; Section 3.3.2).

In many African and Asian countries a considerable proportion of protein needs is met by fisheries (Section 3.3.4.2). Rising water temperatures, droughts and changing ocean currents can impact negatively upon fish stocks and thus lead to food shortages (IPCC, 2001b). A noteworthy aspect in this connection is the bleaching of coral reefs and the associated loss of fishing grounds, which must already be expected to occur increasingly as a result of a global temperature rise of less than 1°C above the pre-industrial value (WBGU, 2003). Furthermore, a rising sea level can lead to the salinization and loss of arable areas and potable water supplies, presenting a vital threat to small island states in particular.

<small>CLIMATE CHANGE AND HEALTH</small>

Climate change generates direct health hazards through an increase in maximum temperatures and thus more intensive and more frequent heat waves. These cause cardiovascular and respiratory diseases in parts of the population, affecting above all older and ill people and the urban poor. The most recent example is the heat wave that occurred in the summer of 2003 in Europe, claiming more than 20,000 lives – mainly in the cities. Munich Re counts that event among the ten most devastating natural disasters of the year, exceeded only by the earthquake in Iran (Münchner Rück, 2003).

The spread of vector-borne infectious diseases such as malaria depends greatly upon precipitation and temperature conditions. It is thus highly sensitive to climatic changes. IPCC expects a growing number of people to be exposed to these diseases. There is still debate on whether observed climate change is already affecting the spread of diseases such as malaria (Thomas, 2004). The advance of malaria into new regions in which people have not yet been able to develop immunity causes particularly severe or even fatal courses of the disease. Similarly, weather extremes can be a direct cause of death and injury, can favour the development of epidemics and can devastate health infrastructure.

The extent of health hazards depends greatly upon the adaptive capacity of a specific society. The health impacts of a climatic change are particularly severe for those groups who have limited access to resources and technologies and whose infrastructure and institutions have a low degree of adaptive capacity, i.e. the poor (WHO, 2002).

A study by the World Health Organization on the health hazards presented by climate change in the year 2000 compared to the baseline scenario of the period from 1961 to 1990 examined four threats: malaria, undernourishment, diarrhoea and floods. The study found the largest disease burden in sub-Saharan Africa and South Asia. The overall burden is estimated at 5.5 million DALYs (Disability-Adjusted Life Years) of which only 8,000 DALYs or 0.15 per cent are assigned to the industrialized countries (Campbell-Lendrum et al., 2003). DALYs are a measure of the loss of healthy or productive life years (WHO, 2002).

Extreme events
A very strong increase in weather- and climate-related disasters has been observed in the 20th century. According to Brooks and Adger (2003) the greatest risk of suffering damage due to weather extremes during the past 30 years arose in developing countries, and among these particularly in small island states. It is difficult to quantify the contribution of climate change to the observed rise in damage caused by extreme events, and it is impossible to attribute individual disasters to climate change. Nonetheless, the effects of present extreme events can indeed be viewed as a pattern indicating the effects of a future intensification of such events, which is considered likely by IPCC (2001a).

Over the past decade (1992–2001) about 2,000 million people were affected by environmental disasters, 98 per cent of these by weather-related disasters. Flood disasters alone affected 1,200 million people in Asia across this period. Of the 78,000 people killed by weather-related disasters, 58 per cent lived in the least developed countries, and a further 39 per

cent in countries with medium levels of development (IFRC, 2002).

Poor countries often do not have the early warning systems and emergency services needed to warn the population in time of impending floods and storms or to evacuate them. Poor people are more vulnerable to natural disasters because they live in locations exposed to a greater level of hazard, have less protection, and command over less reserves and insurances. Economic misery often forces people to settle in hazardous locations – this applies quite particularly to the urban poor. Even today, tropical storms have a devastating effect in densely populated poor regions. For instance, Hurricane Mitch in October 1998 caused the proportion of the poor in the population of Honduras to rise from 63.1 per cent in March 1998 to 65.9 per cent in March 1999. 35,000 houses were destroyed and 50,000 damaged, of which most were located in flat coastal areas and on the banks of rivers. The proportion of houses affected figured 10 per cent for the poorer half of the population, and was thus higher than the average for the overall population (IMF, 2001). The wind speeds and precipitation intensities of tropical cyclones have not yet been found to have increased. However, this is considered probable in the future in some regions (IPCC, 2001a).

3.3.1.3
Guard rails for climate protection: The WBGU climate window

WBGU is convinced that, in order to avert dangerous climatic changes, it is imperative to comply with the 'climate guard rail' of a maximum rise in global mean temperature by 2°C relative to pre-industrial levels (WBGU, 2003; Section 2.3.5). As a secondary limit, the global long-term mean rate of warming should not exceed 0.2°C per decade. Even if global warming is kept within this 'climate window', many undesirable consequences will occur, particularly in developing countries. The present warming by 0.6°C relative to pre-industrial levels does not yet overstep this guard rail, but without resolute action its transgression must be expected.

3.3.1.4
Conclusions

Human-induced climate change is a global phenomenon. It is both acute and long-term. Its causes and effects are separate in time and often also in space. People who earn and own little are not in a position to emit great amounts of greenhouse gases – yet poor people are hit hardest by the impacts of climate change. Climate change will thus exacerbate poverty; poverty reduction, in turn, could accelerate climate change. However, the scenarios developed by IPCC, which assess future greenhouse gas emissions for a range of different global development pathways, do not show any clear link in this respect. Future high per-capita incomes with low disparities among regions lead to both high-emission and low-emission scenarios.

The aim must be to reduce the vulnerability of poor people to a changing climate and to substantially reduce worldwide greenhouse gas emissions without compromising the goal of eradicating poverty. WBGU considers a stabilization of the CO_2 concentration in the atmosphere below 450ppm to be essential in order to obey the 'climate guard rail' (WBGU, 2003). This will only be possible if, over the medium term, all states limit their greenhouse gas emissions and conserve their carbon reservoirs. WBGU has already set out in previous reports the prospects for a global transformation of energy systems that both permits CO_2 stabilization and promotes poverty reduction (WBGU, 2003, 2004).

3.3.2
Water scarcity and pollution

3.3.2.1
Causes of threats to global water resources

GLOBAL WATER CYCLE AND WATER RESOURCES
Water is an irreplaceable resource. The water cycle – defined as the entirety of water flows and water reservoirs in the form of ice, liquid, or gas – is fundamental to the Earth's energy balance and thus to the climate and life on Earth. The cycle is driven by solar energy which causes the water to evaporate on the ocean and land surfaces. This water then condenses and precipitates, often after extended transport. Human activity affects almost all sections of the global water cycle. It changes the evapotranspiration (through forest clearing, afforestation, agriculture, etc.), flow regimes, groundwater table and sea level. Indirectly, human activity even influences cloud formation via the emission of aerosols and their gaseous precursors (Krüger and Graßl, 2002).

Freshwater constitutes only 2.5 per cent of worldwide water reserves. The overwhelming part of it exists as glaciers, permanent snow layers and deep groundwater reservoirs, so that only less than 1 per cent of the freshwater can potentially be used (UNEP, 2002b). The main threats to the water resource for humans are:

- *Water pollution:* The contamination of surface water and groundwater reservoirs with chemicals and microorganisms.
- *Water scarcity:* The change of run-off regimes and the change (mostly lowering) of the groundwater table (UNESCO, 2003a).
- *Global climate change* with consequences such as redistribution of precipitation, rising sea levels, change in the CO_2 absorption of the oceans, and increase of extreme precipitation events (Stolberg et al., 2003; Palmer and Räisänen, 2002; Section 3.3.1).

There are numerous internal and external feedback paths between anthropogenic impairment of the water cycle and the environmental resources of the atmosphere, soils and the biosphere (WBGU, 1998a). Frequently, water crises can be traced back to a failure of state control, and thus to crises in governance (UNESCO, 2003a).

A region is in a state of high water-related criticality (susceptibility of a region or its population to crises) if water scarcity coincides with a low problem-solving capacity of the population (WBGU, 1998a). The critical regions include all arid and semiarid regions, and thus large parts of China and India. These regions are also among the poorest in the world. It is striking, however, that large parts of Africa, Latin America and South-East Asia have a low index of criticality despite belonging to the poor regions. Here, water scarcity is not expected in the medium term (Beese, 2004). This provides a first indication of where the international community and multilateral actors, such as the newly created United Nations Subcommittee on Water Resources or the EU Water Facility, ought to combat water scarcity.

WATER POLLUTION IN DEVELOPING COUNTRIES
About 90 per cent of sewage in developing countries enters water bodies untreated (Johnson et al., 2001). Every day, a total of 2 million tonnes of solid municipal waste is 'disposed of' into water bodies. For example, all rivers in Asia that flow through major cities are heavily polluted. Apart from mismanagement, water pollution is mainly caused by a lack of state resources, which means that no funds are available to build basic sanitary facilities and drinking water treatment plants. The discharge of pollutants leads to a shortage of high-quality drinking water in downstream regions and cities.

Other sources of water pollution are point or nonpoint discharges of industrial waste, oil products and agricultural chemicals (UNEP, 2002b). Inland waters in developing countries are severely affected in this respect, too, as they lack sufficient infrastructure for waste management and wastewater treatment (UNESCO, 2003a).

WATER SCARCITY AND FOOD SECURITY

Water is elemental to food security: it permits agriculture and, in the form of clean drinking water, is essential for a healthy life. Apart from weather-related disasters such as droughts, where extreme water shortages can cause large crop losses, water scarcity in agriculture arises primarily from overuse of water resources. The triggers of this overuse are inappropriate agricultural practices resulting from poor income and lack of education on the one hand, and on the other hand mismanagement of large water infrastructure projects such as river regulation, dams or canals. Inappropriate irrigation methods lead to salinization of large areas. The groundwater table is lowered, erosion washes away fertile fine particles and the soils' water retention declines (Section 3.3.3).

Water scarcity occurs particularly in areas with low precipitation, marginal soils and high population pressure, where too little food is produced, infrastructure such as a functioning market structure and reliable roads are missing and a failure of the state is the norm (Scherr, 2003). Production and distribution problems create hunger and undernourishment that in turn lead to intensified, ill-adapted farming and thus to increased pressure on water resources. This feedback loop has to be broken.

FRESHWATER LOSS AS A RESULT OF BAD AGRICULTURAL PRACTICE

Irrigated agriculture produces about 40 per cent of the global harvest on 20 per cent of the cultivated land (UNEP, 2002b). 75 per cent of the irrigated areas are in developing countries. Due to the use of inefficient technologies, however, only about 45 per cent of the freshwater used for irrigation eventually reaches the plant (Cai and Rosegrant, 2003). Even if the water reaches the plant, it often only benefits inadequately from the water due to poor irrigation practices. The 1995 water productivity of rice in numerous countries of sub-Saharan Africa was only 0.1kg per cubic metre of water, but up to 0.6kg per cubic metre in China, Egypt and Venezuela (Cai and Rosegrant, 2003). Insufficient knowledge of the interrelationships of water quantity and agricultural productivity and the limits of water availability are some of the reasons for inefficient agricultural irrigation practices. In addition, these may cause considerable loss of land due to salinization (Section 3.3.3). Education and information may have a significant impact here at low cost. If the forecasts for 2030 should prove to be correct and the current trend in South Asia, North Africa and the Middle East continues, it is feared that usage of the water reserves will exceed 40 per cent, a benchmark seen as critical (Beese, 2004).

3.3.2.2
Poverty impacts of water scarcity and pollution

Poor people suffer particularly hard from the effects of the water crisis. Water scarcity, low water quality and unhygienic or non-existent sanitary facilities jeopardize the health, food security, standard of living and educational opportunities of the poor.

WATER SCARCITY AND INCOME POVERTY

A third of the world's population lives in countries with moderate to high water stress, i.e. where water use exceeds water supply by 10 per cent (UNEP, 2002b). Adequate access to water is a basic requirement for secure livelihoods, in particular for developing countries whose economies depend heavily on agricultural production. In India, poverty correlates directly with agricultural productivity, which in turn depends on water for irrigation (Singh, 2003). Even if this statement is not universally transferable, water scarcity always implies yield losses and hence loss of material income for smallholders.

Water as a resource is distributed very unevenly, just as is the land resource (World Bank, 2003d). An analysis of per-capita water usage in relation to income (Figure 3.3-1) reveals large differences among countries. Among developing countries, water withdrawal varies between 28m^3 per person and year for Nigeria and 916m^3 per person and year for Iran (Gleick, 2000; World Bank, 2003d). Industrialized countries, however, exhibit the largest variation. Although the global statistic is only an estimate, it is evident that the transition countries of Central Asia have by far the highest per-capita usage worldwide. The reason is the widespread and inefficient irrigated agriculture, predominantly in cotton production (Section 5.2.2).

Not only water scarcity is a problem for many of the poor, but also the price of drinking water. In large cities of developing countries, the poor have to spend up to 10 per cent of their income to buy clean drinking water, in particular in suburbs without infrastructure. It therefore seems appropriate to favour the poor population by allocating water at controlled reduced prices, as is already being done in South Africa.

INADEQUATE ACCESS TO DRINKING WATER AND SANITATION

Access to safe drinking water and sanitation for the majority of the population is currently not guaranteed in most developing countries: 1,200 million people have no access to clean drinking water and 2,600 million people have no access to basic hygienic sanitary facilities (Table 3.3-2; WHO and UNICEF, 2004).

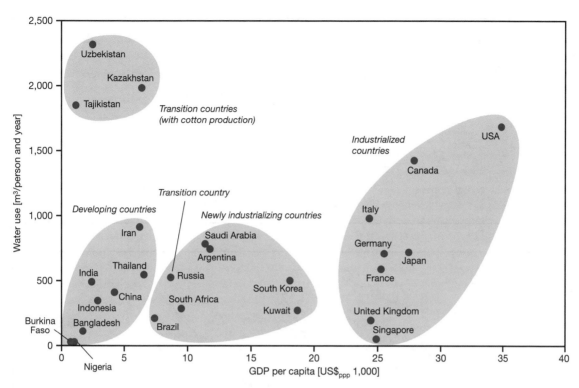

Figure 3.3-1
Per capita gross domestic product in 2001 and per capita water use in 2000. Water for agricultural irrigation makes the greatest contribution to the high values. Rain water for rain-fed agriculture is not included. ppp = Purchasing Power Parity.
Source: Own figures based on Gleick, 2000; World Bank, 2003d

Supplying the household with water remains the task of women and girls in many developing countries (Lenton and Wright, 2004). The time and energy spent on this task is lacking for other tasks or school education. The long distances to water sources or sanitation present considerable risks to women and girls. The low water quality to which the family is exposed harbours significant health risks and has a negative influence on the children's chances of survival. All of these restrictions combine to reduce the time available for women to spend on productive, income-generating tasks.

The MDG Target 10 states the aim of reducing the proportion of people without access to clean drinking water by half by 2015 compared to the base year 1990. At the WSSD in 2002, this aim was broadened to include access to adequate sanitation, mainly as a result of an EU initiative (Fig. 3.3-2).

The progress made so far in improving worldwide access to clean drinking water gives cause for optimism. Between 1990 and 2002, 1,100 million additional people gained access to improved drinking water, so that 83 per cent of the world's population now has an improved water supply. If this trend continues, the Target 10 on drinking water could be achieved (WHO and UNICEF, 2004). The region with the greatest improvements was South Asia. Sub-

Saharan Africa, on the other hand, will have to substantially increase its efforts despite making remarkable progress. Access to sanitation improved from 49 per cent of the world's population in 1990 to 58 per cent in 2002. The WSSD goal will presumably not be met globally, in spite of good progress, achieved particularly in East Asia (WHO and UNICEF, 2004).

Table 3.3-2
Proportion of urban and rural populations with access to clean drinking water and sanitation.
Source: UNESCO, 2003a

	Clean drinking water		Sanitation	
	Urban [%]	Rural [%]	Urban [%]	Rural [%]
Middle East and North Africa	97	72	92	53
Sub-Saharan Africa	77	39	70	35
East Asia and Pacific	95	58	77	20
Latin America and Caribbean	88	42	82	44
World	90	62	79	25

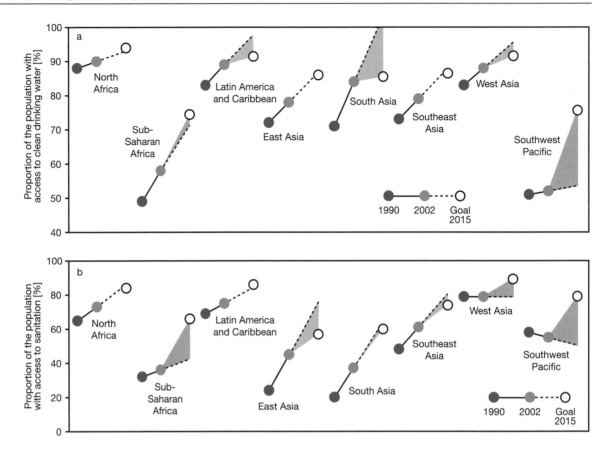

Figure 3.3-2a, b
Status and trends of the MDG target 10 to reduce by half the proportion of people without access to safe drinking water (a) and of the WSSD goal to reduce by half the number of people without access to sanitation facilities (b).
Source: UNFPA, 2003

THE EFFECT OF RIVER REGULATION AND RIVER
FRAGMENTATION ON THE FIGHT AGAINST POVERTY
60 cent of the world's 227 largest rivers are heavily fragmented by dams, flow regulation, and canals, *inter alia* causing damage to aquatic ecosystems. In some regions, this increases poverty, as water quality and quantity decrease downstream, reducing the fertility of the flood plains (UNESCO, 2003a). Some large rivers, such as the Yellow River in China, do not always reach the ocean. The construction of dams is usually accompanied by huge social and environmental problems, so that the advantages to be gained by these schemes are often not justified (WBGU, 1998a; WCD, 2000).

By 1998, the Aral Sea had lost 75 per cent of its original water quantity. This shrinkage was caused primarily by the diversion and canalization of the Amu Darya and Syr Darya rivers, whose water is used for intensive irrigated agriculture, in particular for cotton production. The original goal of some large-scale projects in semi-arid regions was to enable intensive agricultural production and thus to provide income for hitherto very poor regions, but the

opposite effect is often achieved. Poverty around the Aral Sea became so widespread that people were forced to leave the area (WBGU, 1998a).

Small-scale hydro-electric power plants make it possible to supply electricity to poor rural areas around the world. If the supply is adequate, water makes decentralized industrial development and energy use possible. This is another reason why arid and semi-arid regions are amongst the regions with the lowest rate of industrialization and the highest proportion of poor people globally.

WATER SCARCITY AS A POTENTIAL TRIGGER OF
CONFLICTS
The question of security is increasingly debated in the context of the water crisis (Gleick, 2000; Sullivan, 2002). Experience shows that cooperation is more likely than aggression in transboundary river catchments, in spite of the conflict potential associated with water scarcity and water pollution. An analysis covering a 50-year period revealed that 1,200 solution-oriented talks had been held between countries about such river catchments, as opposed to only 500

conflict-laden international negotiations, and that there were no formal wars (UNESCO, 2003a).

Disputes regarding water, however, have the potential to aggravate conflicts and complicate the maintenance of peace, as has become evident in the Middle East. Scarce water resources or their unjust distribution can also harm the internal stability of a country and lead to increased friction between local users. This may lead to violent conflict or migration of the local population (Box 3.3-1), which may cause significant internal and international migration pressure. Once again, poor people are affected first.

The severity of conflicts over water use is bound to increase as the pressure on the remaining water resources rises and more people are potentially affected by water crises (WBGU, 1998a). There are numerous regional procedures for addressing water problems cooperatively, but their effect is often reduced by failure to reach agreement on fair water allocation, unsatisfactory implementation of policies, lack of enforcement and lack of mechanisms for resolving disputes. Recent considerations focus on common use of the benefits associated with the water rather than the use of the water itself (UNESCO, 2003a).

3.3.2.3
Guard rails for water protection

In previous reports, WBGU has formulated 'guard rails' for conservation of water resources (WBGU, 1998a, 2003b):

- The functional capacity of freshwater ecosystems must be safeguarded as a prerequisite for sustainable development. The annual (ground) water withdrawal in a catchment must not exceed the rate of regeneration (WBGU, 1998a). If the water table falls below a critical level, the authorities must limit water withdrawals or allocated water rights.
- All internationally protected freshwater ecosystems must be conserved in their entirety (e.g. Ramsar wetlands and World Heritage sites). In line with the protection of land, about 10 to 20 per cent of inland bodies of water, including their catchments, should be reserved for conservation (WBGU, 2004; Section 3.3.4.4). The formal protection of other, globally important habitats dominated by freshwater should thus be supported within the framework of a global network of protected areas (WBGU, 1998a).
- To safeguard water quality, contamination with substances must not exceed the water's capacity for self-purification. For this purpose, quality tar-

gets should be set based on the precautionary principle.

3.3.2.4
Conclusions

The connection between water scarcity and poverty has been known for a long time. So far, however, it has not been possible to establish a coherent policy to overcome this negative interdependency. The conservation and sustainable use of water as a scarce but renewable resource should be an integral part of the fight against poverty. A great effort must be made not only to achieve the MDGs on drinking water and sanitation, but also to meet the Johannesburg goal of establishing integrated plans for water resource management and efficient water use by 2005 (Section 2.1).

In this context, it needs to be kept in mind that water initiatives and projects rarely have the same effect for both genders. Water management should therefore cater in particular for the requirements of women, who should be included in decisions on development and control of the infrastructure.

3.3.3
Soil degradation

3.3.3.1
Causes and extent

Soils are a valuable resource, non-renewable in the short term and difficult to restore after degradation. They are of crucial importance in the production of food for a growing world population. The growing demand increases the pressure on land use for food production. Inappropriate or overly intensive use leads to degradation. The extraction of mineral resources can also result in soil degradation. Soil degradation means a deterioration of the biological, chemical and physical properties of the soil, in particular through soil erosion (caused by water, wind or other natural processes), nutrient leaching, loss of organic matter, acidification or salinization (GTZ, 1994). The deterioration affects both agricultural land and the remaining natural vegetation, as new land is brought into use to replace almost every hectare of degraded land, which in turn is subject to the degradation process. WBGU has presented a comprehensive analysis of this issue (WBGU, 1994).

The increasing erosion and salinization of agricultural areas results in hitherto agriculturally unused areas, most commonly forest, being brought into cul-

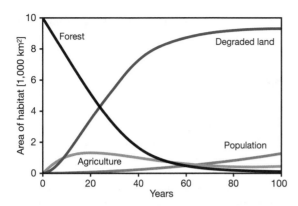

Figure 3.3-3
Transient dynamics following the settlement of 50 people in a 10,000km² tropical rain forest area. The original forest declines while the agricultural area and the amount of degraded land increase. The latter slowly regenerates into forest.
Source: Dobson et al., 1997

tivation. According to various estimates, 28 to 37 per cent of the global land area is currently used agriculturally. This value is almost constant, as a certain area is abandoned due to degradation and new (larger) areas are cleared at another site to compensate (Figure 3.3-3). A third of the temperate and tropical forests and a quarter of the grasslands have already been converted to agricultural use – a process that continues most notably in developing countries. Cities also spread at the expense of hitherto unused ecosystems, in particular in regions with high agricultural productivity.

The poorest section of the rural population usually has access only to inferior soils, frequently former stands of forest. As a consequence, the poor abandon their low-yield land, clear more forests and use it as farmland (Section 3.3.4.1). The newly cultivated nutrient-poor land is in turn subject to degradation that results in onward migration of the poor onto new land (Barbier, 1997). In Central America, this cycle of poverty, population pressure and inappropriate policies has led to widespread degradation of natural resources. Deforestation and the spread of agricultural practices from the lowlands to upland regions have led to an increase in soil erosion (Paolisso et al., 1999). Ambiguous ownership and insufficient economic power for the implementation of soil conservation also play an important role in the clearing of forest areas for new agricultural land (Ananda and Herath, 2003).

Erosion and salinization are the most important types of soil degradation caused by agriculture in developing countries. They are explained in more detail below. Soil degradation also appears in other forms, including nutrient deficiency, aluminium tox-

icity, clay translocation and the formation of impermeable horizons.

SOIL EROSION
Soil erosion is an urgent environmental problem, in particular for developing countries. Twenty per cent of vegetation-covered land in developing countries is already degraded (Barbier, 1997). Every year, another 20 million hectares of land there are lost to erosion. Soil losses are particularly high in the humid tropics of Asia, where on average 138t erode per hectare and year (Ananda and Herath, 2003). Large areas of soil degradation are also found in the densely populated highlands of Burundi, Rwanda, Uganda, Kenya, the sub-humid Central American hill countries and the semi-arid valleys of the Andes, the hill countries at medium altitudes of Nepal, India and Pakistan and also on the slopes of southern China and South-East Asia (Ellis-Jones, 1999). These territories all suffer from extreme poverty. Extensive soil loss also occurs on the Chinese loess plateau. One third of China's territory is now affected by soil degradation; the degraded area is increasing by 2,460km² per year (Zhao et al., 2002). In African countries, soils are threatened by erosion in many areas. In the productive highlands of Ethiopia, the erosion rates average 42t per hectare and year, with peaks of up to 300t per hectare and year. In comparison: the mass of a 30cm thick soil layer that is typically turned by a plough amounts to 2,000–4,000t per hectare, depending on the soil density. However, soil erosion is not solely a problem in poor countries. It also occurs in industrialized countries of the temperate zone where intensive agriculture is practised.

Important causes of soil erosion are the intensification of tillage and plant cultivation on slopes without soil conservation measures. Better seed, irrigation and fertilizer that could prevent soil erosion can only be afforded by a minority of people. Due to fuel shortages, manure and agricultural residues are no longer used as natural fertilizer (Shiferaw and Holden, 1999). In South Asia, there is the additional problem of deforestation: high population density, low soil fertility and cultivation on less fertile land have led to deforestation and soil erosion in the mountainous country of the central Himalayas in Uttar Pradesh, India. The growing demand for food and cash has forced the mountain population to cultivate almost all available land, which in most cases causes the soil to erode (Rawat et al., 1996).

SALINIZATION
Salinization plays an important role, in particular in arid and semi-arid regions (WBGU, 1994). Apart from about 1,000 million hectares of naturally salinized areas worldwide, there are now about 77 million hec-

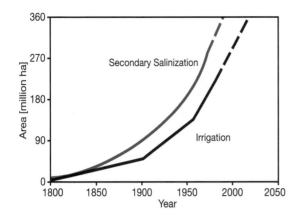

Figure 3.3-4
Global increase in irrigation and secondary salinization of soils.
Source: Lal et al., 1997

tares of anthropogenically salinized areas, 58 per cent of them irrigated agricultural areas. Throughout the course of human history, large areas of land have become salinized as a result of inappropriate irrigation methods, lack of drainage or primitive agricultural techniques. Worldwide, 20–30 per cent of irrigated areas are affected by salinization (Metternich and Zinck, 2003). Especially affected are areas in Argentina, Australia, China, Egypt, India, Iran, Iraq, Pakistan, Thailand, the CIS and the USA (Ghassemi et al., 1991). The process of progressive salinization runs parallel to the increase in irrigated areas, with a time lag of about 20 years (Fig. 3.3-4). The total extent of anthropogenically salinized areas exceeds that of irrigated areas (Lal et al., 1997). Figure 3.3-4 shows that the rate of soil salinization is continuously higher than the rate at which irrigated land is newly developed, i.e. an increasing amount of land must be brought into cultivation in order to keep up with salinization. From 1700 to 1984, irrigated areas over the entire world increased from 50,000 to 2,200,000km². During the same period, about 500,000km² were abandoned as a result of secondary salinization (Rozanov, 1990).

Salinization is not only caused by inappropriate irrigation, but also by rising water tables of saline groundwater aquifers, e.g. after clearing of land, as a result of dam construction in an area with saline groundwater, or the discharge of saline water from mining and industry into rivers. As the groundwater table rises to 2–3m below the soil surface, water starts to evaporate and rapid salinization begins (Ghassemi et al., 1991). There is also a connection between soil salinization and other degradation effects such as erosion, acidification and deterioration of the soil structure: where the vegetation dies as a result of high salt content and the penetration of water is reduced, this leads to erosion losses. Conversely, a loss of top-

soil through erosion can accelerate the salinization dynamics by exposing more saline subsoil (Feitz and Lundie, 2002).

3.3.3.2
Poverty impacts of soil degradation

All terrestrial ecosystems are literally based on the soil. A degraded soil, therefore, means lower fertility, loss of areas and/or reduced or altered biological diversity. These are all factors contributing to poverty (Bridges and Oldeman, 1999). If the world's population increases to about 9,000 million by 2050, with about 8,000 million living in developing countries, the current area under agricultural use will provide less than 0.1ha of land per person. Consequently, there is an urgent need to produce an adequate amount of food with a minimum amount of degradation (Lal, 2000).

Soil degradation has resulted in an average production loss of 13 per cent on arable land and 4 per cent on pasture during the last 50 years (Oldemann, 1998). There are significant natural local and regional differences. In general, developing countries are much more affected by soil degradation than industrialized countries, which often have deep young soils. Detailed studies for Argentina, Uruguay and Kenya based on forecast models show yield losses of between 25 and 50 per cent for the next 20 years (Mantel and van Engelen, 1997). For Africa, Lal (1995) calculated yield losses of 8 per cent over 20 years for water erosion alone. Where secondary salinization reduces the productivity of agricultural areas and triggers the creation of wasteland, farmers are often forced to migrate, as cultivation of agricultural crops is no longer possible (Ghassemi et al., 1991).

Apart from damage and yield loss in areas directly affected by erosion, more remote regions also suffer from modified sedimentation dynamics with siltation of water bodies, irregular drainage, problems with irrigation and water pollution. Hydro-electric power stations may also be affected by increasing sedimentation of eroded soil particles (Ananda and Herath, 2003). Such effects also promote poverty.

The extraction of minerals and its associated degradation has far-reaching effects on both the environment and the poor. Large-scale mining in particular leads to forced resettlement of the population, as the soils are no longer agriculturally usable over wide areas after extraction has finished. The mine workers' modest earnings often do not compensate for the health risks (mercury poisoning, risk of accidents in unsafe mines) and the environmental damage caused by the mining.

3.3.3.3
Adaptation – Possible countermeasures and their success

Soil conservation measures comprise different techniques depending on the cause of the degradation. The success of the methods applied also depends to a large extent on socio-economic factors such as the institutional setting, cultural circumstances, the perception of the problem and the economic viability of the measures chosen.

TECHNICAL SOLUTIONS
The threat to food security from soil erosion has led to change or adaptation of cultivation methods in some regions. In the mountainous regions of Nepal, for example, the state of the soils has actually improved in some areas, in spite of a growing population, as people have developed and applied effective management technologies to cope with the shortage of resources. Agricultural crops are being cultivated once again on flat terraces in order to minimize erosion. Sloped terraces have either been abandoned or improved. In order to reduce degradation and increase yields, agroforestry practices (a form of land use in tropical and subtropical countries that combines forestry, arable farming and/or grazing management on the same area) have been intensified. Furthermore, washouts have been prevented at the early stages, land at risk has been stabilized and water channels have been built. In addition, row planting, mulch, fertilizer, compost and green manure have been introduced to increase the soil fertility (Paudel and Thapa, 2001).

Even in the highlands of Peru, population growth does not necessarily lead to soil degradation. Limited resources may result in increased efficiency and sustainability of production. Traditional agricultural systems in particular, with sufficient fallow periods and resource-conserving rotation grazing, can reduce harvest losses from decreased soil fertility (Swinton and Quiroz, 2003).

Avoidance or remediation of salinization-related soil degradation is more difficult. In general, salinization is not irreversible (Dregne, 2002) and there are successful soil improvement projects using adapted irrigation, for example in Tunisia (Hachicha et al., 2000). However, implementation of soil improvement measures often requires extensive technical solutions or very large quantities of water. Methods for improving saline soils include, for example, flushing out excess salts from the topsoil into subsoil horizons, washing away saline crusts on the surface, biologically reducing the salt content in the topsoil by cultivating and harvesting salt-accumulating plants, and the combination of flushing and cultivation of

relatively salt-tolerant species (Qadir et al., 2000). In Australia, attempts were made to lower the groundwater table by cultivating deep-rooting hardy plants such as alfalfa or by adding various Atriplex species (goosefoot family), thus reducing the salinization risk from water rising through soil capillary action (Barrett-Lennard, 2002; Bathgate and Pannell, 2002). However, the cultivation or addition of deep-rooting plants is problematic: Firstly, there is the long-term risk of salt accumulation in the horizon penetrated by roots (Barrett-Lennard, 2002). Secondly, this method is economically unattractive since some of the agricultural area must be used for the permanent cultivation of deep-rooting plants and is therefore no longer available for cultivating other crops (Bathgate and Pannell, 2002). Because of these difficulties, Dehaan and Taylor (2002), for example, emphasize the importance of a monitoring system for the early detection of salinization, e.g. a remote monitoring system. This could fight salinization in its early stages through improved irrigation, drainage and agricultural practices.

EFFECT OF SOCIO-ECONOMIC FACTORS ON IMPLEMENTATION
In many developing countries, a poor household must weigh up the decision to improve currently available land against the option of abandoning it and migrating to other regions (Box 3.3-1). Economic factors play an important role in this decision. Agricultural producers in developing countries are often part of a semi-commercial rural economy. They produce in varying proportions for sale and their own consumption. A harvest which does not cover their minimum personal requirements leads to additional food costs, which can lead to hunger and malnourishment in extreme cases (Grepperud, 1997). The profitability of a particular soil conservation measure may thus decide whether a smallholder will continue to use it after an externally financed project comes to an end (Barbier, 1997).

In the long-term, measures only work if they reduce erosion or salinization and increase agricultural yields at the same time (Shiferaw and Holden, 1998, 1999). Overall, physical conservation measures (terraces, walls, ditches) result in a smaller increase in yield than, for example, agroforestry. Even in agroforestry, a profit for smallholders can often only be achieved after several years (Barbier, 1997). In the highlands of Ethiopia, for example, only low-cost measures such as grass strips have paid off for smallholders. In north Thailand, soil conservation methods were implemented successfully, leading not only to reduction of erosion, but also to an increase in soil fertility by improved cultivation techniques (Renaud et al., 1998). Philippine smallholders whose land is subject to torrential rain must weigh up the decreased risk of sudden harvest loss against the cost of soil conservation measures (Shively, 2001). Soil conservation measures are applied in cases where political measures reduce production losses, reimburse initial investment, or make loans available. In the short-term it can thus be sensible to support low-cost technologies that reduce erosion and increase yields after a short time, as these are most likely to be accepted by poor smallholders (Shiferaw and Holden, 2001).

The perception of the erosion problem plays an important role in the success of soil conservation measures. It depends directly on the location of the farms and on the smallholders' education. The perception of soil erosion as a problem is greater where smallholders suffer from water shortages. The will to apply new or improved conservation measures also depends to a large extent on the availability of fertilizer, one indicator for the existence of sufficient financial means. As farmers regard the shortage of water as being their greatest problem, soil conservation measures should provide solutions for this problem, too (Daba, 2003).

3.3.3.4
Guard rails for soil protection

Due to the importance of soil conservation measures for future food security, particularly in developing countries, there is an urgent need in many regions to develop measures – in cooperation with the local population – that conserve soils while simultaneously enhancing people's livelihoods.

The formulation of guard rails is a way of assessing agricultural practices with regard to their effect on soils and long-term soil conservation. In contrast to the Framework Convention on Climate Change and the Montreal Protocol on ozone, the Desertification Convention has not (yet) specified quantitative and verifiable reduction and conservation goals for a specific time period. WBGU regards the development of a core set of global indicators and guard rails as a high priority task. To define such a reference point, guard rails for global soil conservation must be established (WBGU, 1998a), i.e. specific values that, if exceeded, would lead to an irreversible environmental state that would threaten human existence. Schwertmann et al. (1987) defined a tolerance limit for anthropogenic soil degradation as follows: the natural yield potential should not be critically diminished over a time period of 300 to 500 years. Strictly speaking, the amount of eroded or otherwise degraded soil should not be permitted to exceed the amount of new soil being formed. This can, however, only be a long-term

objective, as soil formation takes place in geological timeframes.

Practical implementation of this guard rail has to differentiate between soil degradation through erosion and through salinization, the two biggest threats to soils. The tolerance limits for erosion damage are specific to soil types and determined by soil depth. The universal soil loss equation provides a way to formulate guard rails for degradation through erosion (Box 3.3-2). Using this universal equation, soil-specific tolerance limits can be worked out, predominantly determined by soil depth (Table 3.3-3).

As with soil erosion, the agricultural usability of soils threatened by salinization should be maintained over at least 300 to 500 years, i.e. during this time the salt concentration and composition should not increase above a level that common agricultural crops can still tolerate. When applying this guard rail to irrigated agricultural crops, care must be taken that the salt concentration of the soil solution does not exceed a certain level harmful to the individual crop. Care must also be taken to keep the ratio between sodium and other nutrients in the irrigation water below a certain level to avoid long-term soil degradation from topsoil siltation and reduced permeability. The Equivalence Factor EF of the irrigation water should be well below 1 (Box 3.3-3).

It is especially difficult to reverse salinization damage once it has occurred in regions with scarce water reserves. Artificial irrigation of agricultural areas should therefore be well planned. Salt transportation models as developed by Xu and Shao (2002) allow advance estimation of potential damage. Such models consider soil humidity, soil water flows, precipitation, evapotranspiration, surface runoff and surface properties and are coupled to land surface models.

3.3.3.5
Conclusions

Soils worldwide are threatened by degradation, in particular due to erosion processes and salinization, and are limited in their productivity. Twenty per cent of land covered by vegetation in developing countries is degraded due to soil erosion, and about 20 to 30 per cent of irrigated land worldwide is degraded due to salinization. The results are reduced soil fertility or a total loss of the affected areas, thus endangering food security and forcing people to migrate. Conservation measures such as terrace cultivation, increased agroforestry, etc. may be applied to reduce soil loss due to erosion. Soil conservation measures are particularly successful if they decrease the risk of erosion and simultaneously increase yields, thereby improving the economic situation of smallholders. In the

Box 3.3-2

Universal soil loss equation

After a long-term study of standardized plots of land to determine the soil loss in the USA, a set of erosion-causing factors was combined systematically into the universal soil loss equation:

$$A = R \cdot K \cdot L \cdot S \cdot C \cdot P$$

where
A: long-term average soil loss in tonnes per hectare and year
R: rainfall and surface runoff factor (a measure for location-specific erosion force of the precipitation)
K: soil erodibility factor
L: slope length factor (standard length: 22m)
S: slope gradient factor (standard gradient: 9 per cent)
C: vegetative cover and management factor (ratio of soil loss for arbitrary management compared to that during summer fallow)
P: factor for erosion control practice (ratio between loss/no loss in the case of erosion control measures)

The soil loss equation allows long-term loss to be calculated for a wide range of circumstances and allows prediction of the effect of changed conditions on erosion. This makes it possible to calculate whether the current loss exceeds the tolerance limit. The effect of erosion control measures can also be quantified. In the ideal case, the loss does not exceed soil formation, typically only a few tonnes per hectare and year in mid-latitudes.

Table 3.3-3
Tolerance limits of soil erosion for the temperate zone.
Source: Schwertmann et al., 1987

Tolerance limit [t/ha and year]	Soil depth	Depth [cm]
1	shallow	<30
3	moderately deep	30–60
7	deep	60–100
10	very deep	>100

TOLERANCE LIMITS
These limits specify the maximum number of tonnes of soil that may be lost annually from one hectare to maintain its productivity at the current level over 300 to 500 years. The shallower the soil, the smaller the losses must be in order that its yield potential is not impaired (Table 3.3-3).

Tolerance limits (tonnes per hectare and year) may also be calculated via the relationship between arable index or grassland index (yield index) and soil depth according to the following empirically determined equation:

$$\text{Tolerance limit} = (\text{arable or grassland index})/8$$

Arable or grassland indices are ratios that are used to compare the agricultural yields of different soils. They are therefore a measure of soil fertility.

Source: Schwertmann et al., 1987

case of salinization, improvement measures are difficult to implement and often require large amounts of water. Monitoring systems for early detection are important. Intact soils are particularly important for the poor in developing countries. As a consequence, guard rails for soil conservation ought to be formulated urgently: the natural yield potential of a soil should be maintained over a period of 300 to 500 years for both erosion and salinization processes.

3.3.4
Loss of biological diversity and resources

3.3.4.1
Biodiversity loss and its causes: The case of accelerating deforestation

Land clearance and the intensive human use of natural ecosystems over thousands of years have fundamentally altered the biosphere, with far-reaching consequences for biodiversity. Historically, the clearing of forests in the temperate zone increased the diversity of the landscape, and the resulting influx of species originally raised the level of biodiversity. With growing intensity of use, however, the impacts on biodiversity are now increasingly negative.

Unlike many regions in the temperate zone, the highest biodiversity in other zones is found in untouched vegetation, i.e. types of vegetation not affected by human extraction of natural resources (e.g. timber). In the tropics, anthropogenic vegetation tends to be species-poor. But there are also regions in the temperate zone, for example in Central Europe or Japan, where intensive human use is linked with a decline in biodiversity. Human interventions in the biosphere threaten not only the diversity of wild species but also the diversity of crop plant varieties, the latter being the result of human effort over the course of civilization. This limits the genetic basis for ongoing development of plant varieties, posing consequential risks for food security (FAO 1996). In the terrestrial environment, land-use change is probably the main catalyst for declining biodiversity, whereas in the marine environment, the overexploitation of the ocean's natural resources is a significant factor. The loss of biodiversity encompasses not only the extinction of species but also the genetic impoverishment of populations and the loss of natural ecosystems and their services to humankind (WBGU, 2001a).

Box 3.3-3

Harvest losses due to soil salinization

Salinization of soils inhibits plant growth. Above a certain salt concentration in soil solution, the growth of agricultural crops declines rapidly (Table 3.3-4). Usually, the electrical conductivity EC (reciprocal value of the electrical resistance, specified in Siemens) is specified as a measure for the salt tolerance of a plant, rather than the salt concentration. Beans, for example, are a crop with low salt tolerance. They show a yield loss of more than 50 per cent at a conductivity of 4mS per centimetre of soil layer, whereas more toler-

Table 3.3-4
Electrical conductivity of the soil solution and relative productivity of selected plants. NEL = no-effect level (conductivity at and below which a decline in fertility is no longer measurable).
Source: Scheffer and Schachtschabel, 1998

Plant	Relative productivity in per cent as a function of electrical conductivity [mS/cm]						NEL [mS/cm]
	1	4	8	12	15	24	
Beans	100	43	0				1.0
Oranges	100	63	0				1.7
Maize	100	84	54	24	3	0	1.8
Alfalfa	100	85	56	27	5	0	2.0
Rice	100	88	39	0			3.0
Dates	100	100	86	71	60	28	4.0
Sorghum	100	100	78	50	29	0	4.8
Wheat	100	100	86	57	36	0	6.0
Sugar beet	100	100	94	71	53	0	7.0
Barley	100	100	100	80	65	20	8.0

ant barley still produces 71 per cent of the maximum yield – even at 12mS per centimetre.

The conductivity of the soil solution should thus not exceed 4–8mS per centimetre depending on the crop. This corresponds to a salt concentration of 2.4 to 4.8g per litre. The following example clarifies the effect of irrigation on the sodium level in the soil solution: if one hectare in a semi-arid climate is irrigated with 10,000m^3 of river water with a sodium concentration of 24mg per litre and the water evaporates entirely from the soil and through the plants, 240kg of sodium remain in the soil each year. At a soil water content of 30 per cent, this translates into an annual sodium concentration increase in the soil solution of about 0.08g per litre. Depending on the original sodium content of the non-irrigated soil, this reaches the critical threshold of 2.4g per litre for many plants after no more than 30 years of irrigated agriculture. This state is reached correspondingly sooner if water with a higher salt concentration is used for irrigation. Only drainage can delay salinization, which is always a long-term threat in irrigated agriculture.

In addition to the salt's direct effect, a high sodium content leads to a break-up of aggregated soil particles and to a translocation of the clay particles into deeper layers. The resulting siltation of the topsoil leads to a reduced permeability for water, which hinders or prevents drainage and thus accelerates salinization. Another consequence is the susceptibility to erosion of dust-like soils. Since plant growth is reduced by both high salt levels in the soil solution and the siltation-induced decrease in soil permeability, Feitz and Lundie (2002) propose an equivalence factor EF for soil salinization. EF is the ratio between threshold conductivity (the conductivity above which crop damage occurs) and actual conductivity of the irrigation water. For EF<1, there is no danger of clay particles being dispersed. If the value is above 1, the danger of dispersion is increased. Multiplying this factor with the deposited salt quantity (salt concentration x irrigation volume) gives the salinization potential of an entire system. It accounts not only for the salt accumulation in the soil through EF, but also for the negative effects of siltation. The EF of the irrigation water must thus be well below 1 in order to avoid a drop in fertility from salinization.

According to estimates by Costanza et al. (1997) the value of global ecosystem services and products is approx. US$33,000,0000 million per year, in the same order of magnitude as global gross domestic product. Whatever the short-term economic benefits to be gained from the exploitation of ecosystems, in the long term, the resulting loss of biodiversity may be extremely harmful in economic terms. Now for the first time, in the Millennium Ecosystem Assessment, an effort is being made to gain a global overview of the consequences of anthropogenic changes on ecosystem services, and to develop options for better ecosystem management (MA, 2003).

The impacts of human activity on ecosystems and their productivity and biodiversity vary from one bioregion to another. In the temperate zone, losses of biodiversity relate chiefly to the increasing intensity of land use. In coniferous forests in northern latitudes, the primary impact of clearance is the loss of

important forest ecosystem services. For instance, the release of carbon from the vegetation and soil poses a grave problem in relation to the global climate. Often, however, such losses are not perceived as a problem because many of nature's services, such as carbon sequestration or flood protection, remain beyond the scope of economic valuations due to the difficulties of expressing their value in monetary terms (WBGU, 2001b).

In the tropical zone, the clearance of rainforests poses the greatest threat to biodiversity. In some cases where overexploitation of natural resources is observed, it is part of a strategy for development. In other cases, its sole purpose is to enrich an elite minority without regard for long-term national interests (Lambin et al., 2001). In the tropics, unlike the temperate zone, replacement with anthropogenic vegetation always results in loss of species. Road and dam construction and mining ventures open up previously inaccessible areas which are soon settled by marginalized population groups. In some cases this takes place within the structure of state-planned resettlement projects (e.g. Transmigrasi in Indonesia) while in others it is unregulated (e.g. Brazil). Poor settlers and mineral resource prospectors clear the forest by setting fires, transforming it into agricultural land or resource extraction areas. Within a few years, the soil is usually degraded, whereupon new areas have to be cleared for use (WBGU, 2001a). Alternatively, the cleared land may be used for extensive pastures, which generally belong to large landowners.

A striking example of these processes is the progressive deforestation of the Amazon Basin. In the years 2002 and 2003 almost 2.4 million ha of forest per year was cut down, usually in the wake of road and rail construction, electricity and gas supply schemes and followed by a sharp upturn in land speculation, livestock farming and soya production on land in the immediate environs (Laurance et al., 2004). Similar processes are under way in Central Africa and South-East Asia (e.g. Malaysia, Indonesia). Those who suffer most are the indigenous populations who still lead a traditional way of life, living in and from the primeval forest.

A major cause of overexploitation of forests is worldwide growth in demand for wood, particularly for industrial timber. For instance, China more than doubled its timber imports between 1997 and 2002 from 40.2 to 95.1 million m³, and is now the world's second largest importer of timber (Sun et al., 2004). The majority of China's timber imports come from Russia, Malaysia and Indonesia, but other sources of wood for export to China include the temperate forests of the United States, New Zealand and parts of Europe.

Patterns of destruction similar to those affecting forests are also occurring in other ecosystems. Coral reefs are under threat from dynamite and cyanide fishing (WBGU, 2001a). Mangroves, which play an important role in coastal protection and represent an important source of biological resources for the local population, are under threat from urban development, aquaculture and overuse by fisheries (Alongi, 2002).

Poverty is not regarded as the principal cause of rising deforestation and damage to ecosystems (Lambin et al., 2001). Nevertheless, local population groups living in extreme poverty are often forced into economic practices which have destructive impacts. For example, in Doi Inthanon National Park in the north of Thailand, unsustainable slash-and-burn agriculture by the Hmong and Karen peoples degraded 40 per cent of the national park area, causing local extinction of the tiger and many species of migratory birds. In this case, which is typical of tropical rainforests, the poverty of indigenous groups is a key factor in the threat to biodiversity, and hence in the destruction of resources which they themselves depend upon (Dearden et al., 1996). Similar examples are found in many national parks in the tropical zone (Africa: Hanks, 2001; the Philippines: Garrity et al., 2002). Other poverty-related threats to biodiversity are uncontrolled hunting for food (bushmeat), particularly in Africa (Barrett and Arcese, 1998), and trade in endangered species.

Local and indigenous communities on the margins of tropical rainforests who rely partly on the forest for their livelihoods can also play a significant part in the protection of these forests (Tomich et al., 1998). Molnar et al. (2004) estimate that 120 million ha of forest is managed by indigenous peoples and local communities to a conservation standard equivalent to that of major protected areas. A further 100 million ha are managed patchwork-fashion by long-established communities, which contributes to the conservation of biodiversity. Added to this are some 50 million ha on the margins of agricultural areas where people have settled only relatively recently, and adapt their economic activities to the conservation of biodiversity, as well as an area of some 100 million ha in which the local population make active efforts to maintain biodiversity and ecosystem functions (Molnar et al., 2004). The conservation efforts contributed in this way by local population groups with a deep-rooted attachment to their natural heritage can be valued at some US\$2,600 million.

3.3.4.2
Importance of biodiversity in developing countries and consequences of its loss for the poor

TERRESTRIAL ECOSYSTEMS
For rural communities in developing countries, natural ecosystems and their store of biodiversity take the place of supermarkets, builders' merchants, chemists' shops and pharmacies. Besides food, clean drinking water, fibrous materials and timber, they supply plant and animal genetic resources, traditional medicines, jewellery and sacred objects. By making use of various resources, the rural poor in particular can reduce their vulnerability. Up to 25 per cent of smallholders' income can result from the use of forest products (excluding timber) (Jenkins et al., 2004). In the Royal Chitwan National Park in the lowlands of Nepal, the local population use 32 forest species as wood for construction, 78 species as fuel wood, 172 species as animal feed and a further 89 non-woody plants for a variety of purposes (Stræde et al., 2002). Non-wood forest products are used in many households and often generate important additional income.

Traditional medicines play a central role in health care in many developing countries, where health care systems are inefficient or absent. 80 per cent of the population in developing countries are reliant on traditional plant-based medicines. A study in Bulamogi County in Uganda identified 229 plants from 68 different plant families being used for medicinal purposes, indicating that a huge number of species are used in the treatment of all manner of diseases (Tabuti et al., 2003). Two hundred years ago, a similar situation applied in Europe (WBGU, 2001a; Asche and Schulze, 1996).

The wealth of locally adapted, traditional crop plants used in food and agriculture has come about through breeding by indigenous and local communities over many generations. Today this precious hoard of genetic diversity is indispensable for the continuing development of modern varieties, and is the focus of efforts to conserve plant genetic resources. Local and indigenous communities play a major role in the conservation of these valuable resources *in situ*; in other words, by using them in agriculture (FAO, 1996)

In addition to plant biodiversity, the genetic diversity of livestock plays a key role for many poor people in rural regions. Livestock are a source of income, an insurance policy, a financial investment and a means of transport; they yield food, fertilizers, fibres, and so on. In the case of livestock too, local breeds are often better suited to meeting these varied requirements (Wollny, 2003). In semi-arid regions above all, the diversity of crop plants and animals is a crucial element in sustainable agriculture and environmental protection (Seely et al., 2003).

Further benefits accrue from the services provided by intact ecosystems: for the poor, very important factors are erosion protection, the regulation of pest populations and the presence of sufficient numbers of pollinators (e.g. bees, ants, bats). Last but not least, the conservation of biodiversity is especially important in cultural and spiritual terms for indigenous communities leading a traditional way of life (Posey, 1999).

Within ecosystems, there are strong dependencies and interactions between different components of the system, for instance between terrestrial and subterranean communities. The disappearance or advent of a plant species may have a beneficial or inhibitory effect on the system of decomposing organisms in the soil. Likewise, the loss of a particular fungus or part of the soil fauna may have a variety of impacts on terrestrial flora and fauna (Wardle et al., 2004). Because there are numerous such interactions, anthropogenic changes to biodiversity should always be viewed with caution.

Often people who live in close contact with nature have developed mechanisms for using natural ecosystems sustainably (WBGU, 2001a). If these traditional forms of management are lost, or if population growth and commercialization unavoidably intensify the pressure on biological resources, the resources in question will be overused and degraded, especially in semi-arid ecosystems. One example of this is pastoralism in the Sahel: the people have little if any cash and their wealth consists of natural resources, mainly their cattle herds. If these come to harm, the people descend into poverty (Sahel Syndrome, WBGU, 1996). Where traditional nomadism is impeded by political borders, national pasture lands will be subject to even more intensive use. The destruction of vegetation and the degradation of soils deplete the life-sustaining resource base, intensifying competition for the remaining resources. When resource scarcity is coupled with population growth, the potential for conflict looms large because poor national economies lack almost any means of addressing these issues (McNeely, 2003). Consequently, overuse of resources becomes self-perpetuating or the people migrate elsewhere.

The loss of biodiversity can therefore have far-reaching consequences for the lives of the rural poor. Once the available resources have been depleted due to increased pressure for use of natural ecosystems or through habitat loss, sustainable use of local biodiversity in keeping with traditional practices is no longer possible (Osemeobo, 2001). Overuse and biodiversity loss then become mutually reinforcing, which can trigger a 'spiral into poverty' whereby the capacity for self-sufficiency is eventually lost (Seely et al., 2003). Resource scarcity, such as a shortage of wood for fuel and building, depleted groundwater or soil erosion, sets in train feedback loops with further poverty, insecurity and environmental destruction (Solh et al., 2003). This ultimately accelerates migration to the slums of the big cities (Box 3.3-1).

MARINE ECOSYSTEMS
The biological resources of the oceans and inland waters are vital to the nutrition of rural populations in many developing countries. In these countries, subsistence fishery is common among people from poor social groups, who fish to meet their own needs or sell their catch in order to buy other staple foods with the income (Branch et al., 2002).

The principal problem in relation to the use of marine resources is overfishing (Pauly et al., 2002). Pressure on the fishing grounds has drastically increased due to rapid population growth, the collapse of traditional forms of use, an upsurge in demand from a cash-rich minority in the country in conjunction with growing demand in the global market, technical innovations, privatization and trade liberalization (Ibarra et al., 2000). Without political foresight and regulation, the rising volumes of catches and revenues from fish products lead to excessive use of resources. Where the decline in fish stocks threatens the livelihoods of poor fishers, they increasingly resort to harmful fishing methods (Glaesel, 2000). Even flawed development initiatives can trigger overfishing and lead to the disintegration of communities whose livelihoods are based on the fish trade (Walker, 2001). There are well known technical and legal methods for preventing overfishing, which are often already enshrined in law. Their implementation is frequently blocked, however, by corruption, political instability, and pressure from a lobby which is interested in short-term economic gains.

For developing countries, fishery around coral reefs is especially important, accounting for 25 per cent of their total catch (CORDIO, 1999). At the same time, reefs are among the habitats which are characteristically especially high in biodiversity. When yields are too low, the fishers resort to methods which are effective but harmful to the reefs (compressed air, dynamite, cyanide) and subsequently fish stocks decline still further (Amar et al., 1996). Another serious problem is the burning of mangrove forests to clear space for shrimp farming (e.g. in the Bay of Bengal). Whilst aquaculture is a way of boosting the local population's income in the short term, poor management often leads to unsustainable practices and to environmental degradation (pollution, acidification) and a return to poverty in the long term (Islam, 2003).

For many West African countries, marine resources in coastal regions – managed appropriately – are the only resources which can be used sustainably. Moreover, they provide an important source of protein. The fish catch in that region has risen from 60,000t in 1950 to more than 4.5 million t in the year 2000 (Alder and Sumaila, 2004). The bulk of the catch is exported to the EU, to Russia, Japan and China. Foreign fleets (including a number from EU member states) have secured access to many fishing grounds with bilateral fishing agreements. Because of corruption and inadequate means of control, on occasion this has given rise to illegal fishery activities (Alder and Sumaila, 2004), resulting in the overuse of marine resources. This is in conflict with economic and social objectives due to the detrimental impact on local fishers.

In many African countries, employment in the fishery sector declined, small coastal communities lost the basis of their livelihoods, and the fishers became even poorer than before. The revenues from the sale of fishery rights are not sufficient to provide the population with an adequate supply of affordable fish. Thus these agreements have major disadvantages for the poor local population. Marine biodiversity also suffers: when the overfishing of demer-

sal fish and invertebrates increased dramatically, this indicated that lower trophic levels were being fished because the higher levels were already depleted.

In the EU the problem has been known about for some time. A number of principles were established to strengthen coherence between EU development policy and fisheries policy. It remains to be seen whether they will be implemented and how they will affect subsistence fishing communities in places like West Africa. WBGU recommends that the German federal government should increase pressure within the EU to ensure that the rising demand for fish is not satisfied at the expense of the poor coastal population of West Africa. The main strand of this policy is the removal of subsidies for the fishing fleet, which are a major motivation for overuse (Porter, 2001) and amount to US\$14–20,000 million, depending on the method of estimation used (Milazzo, 1998; APEC, 2000). The example of Namibia shows that solutions to the problem of overfishing can certainly be found. The country has succeeded in developing an adequate model which combines sustainable fisheries and prosperity within the country with concessions for foreign fleets (Alder and Sumaila, 2004).

3.3.4.3
Conflicts and synergies between poverty reduction and biodiversity conservation

Despite the critical significance of biodiversity to the lives of the rural population, conflicts can easily arise between the conservation of biodiversity and the needs of the poor.

Local communities in the vicinity of protected areas often suffer considerable hardship because they no longer have access to resources (e.g. fruit, forest pasture) which they formerly used (Garrity et al., 2002). For example, South Africa's expansive wildlife reserves are difficult to reconcile with the pressing need for social and economic development to alleviate poverty if the poor reap little benefit from them. Often poor people were driven off the land, while big game became a threat for farmers around the edges of the parks (Wells, 1996). Here it is especially urgent to reconcile the conservation of natural resources with the mounting social and economic problems of the poor majority of the population (Picard, 2003).

This may be achieved through greater involvement of local communities (Hanks, 2001). If local communities have enhanced entitlements to their local biological resources and are able to exclude external actors from using them, there are much better prospects of success in establishing sustainable use. Key factors in this process are the provision of adult education and capacity building. It is extremely important for local populations in or on the margins of pro-tected areas to participate in decision making about their management, and to share in opportunities to earn income, e.g. from employment in nature conser-vation or tourism (Section 4.3.1.2).

If, as an example, local people increasingly gain for-est use rights, they are in a better position to market non-wood forest products. This form of use reduces the risk of descending into greater poverty but rarely constitutes a route out of poverty. Angelsen and Wunder (2003) also suggest that the local popula-tion should be able to use and process wood in order to improve their income situation. Bearing in mind the principle of conserving forests and their inherent biodiversity, however, proposals of this kind should be rejected, because even the selective use of single trees in tropical rainforests is linked to forest destruc-tion.

Assured property rights can simplify the proce-dure for providing payments to the local population for ecosystem services (biodiversity, water protec-tion, carbon sinks, recreation). This form of payment can also help to consolidate informal land rights for the poor. Moreover, payments for ecosystem services provide a secure income in the long-term, whereas earnings from the sale of non-wood forest products are subject to the vagaries of the market (Angelsen and Wunder, 2003). In Mexico, for example, where some 44 million ha of forest consists of collectively managed private land, a US$20 million fund was set up to guarantee the conservation and sustainable management of natural deciduous forests by granting the landowners US$30 per hectare per year (moun-tain forests: US$40). This is a way of combining con-servation of the forest ecosystem with poverty allevi-ation (Jenkins et al., 2004).

3.3.4.4
Guard rails for biosphere conservation

Because of the great importance of biodiversity to poor people's lives (Section 3.3.4.2), guard rails for the conservation of biodiversity are also effective in preventing or combating poverty. In its report on the conservation and use of the biosphere, the Council developed five biological imperatives which can be used as the basis for defining guard rails (WBGU, 2001a). These imperatives are compatible with the ecosystem approach which was developed by the Convention on Biological Diversity (CBD, 2000):
– Preserve the integrity of bioregions,
– Safeguard existing biological resources,
– Maintain biopotential for the future,
– Preserve the global natural heritage,

– Preserve the regulatory functions of the bio-sphere.

A GUARD RAIL FOR THE BIOSPHERE: PROTECT 10–20 PER CENT OF LAND AREA
The present state of knowledge does not yet allow for an exact, scientifically-based guard rail for bio-sphere conservation in terms of stating the exact pro-portion of land area that must be protected. Various approaches tend to arrive at similar figures, how-ever: 'conservation use' should be the priority land use form for 10–20 per cent of the Earth's land area (WBGU, 2001a). Such a worldwide system of pro-tected areas which is effectively managed and rep-resentative of the diversity of ecosystems (CBD, 2004a) can be considered as a guard rail, the crossing of which would be unacceptable to the global com-munity (WBGU, 2001a).

It is possible that the designation of protected areas may clash with the interests of local communi-ties if they are excluded from the regions concerned and no longer permitted to use them. Therefore the indigenous population should be involved in the man-agement of these protected areas and, where possi-ble, be permitted to use them in an environmentally sound manner, at least to some extent. The Council accords high priority to the consolidation and fur-ther development of the existing worldwide system of protected areas (WBGU, 2001a). Major deficits still exist regarding its overall representativeness and the effectiveness of its management.

A particular priority is conservation within 'bio-diversity hotspots', small areas containing unusually high concentrations of wild species (Mittermeier et al., 1999; Myers et al., 2000). Protection should be extended to those areas of special value in which undisturbed ecosystems still exist on a broad scale (e.g. tropical and boreal forests). For the sake of glo-bal food security, it is also important to preserve the 'gene centres' in which a great genetic diversity of crop plants or their wild relatives occur (Vavilov, 1926; Hammer, 1998). Similarly, 10–20 per cent of inland waters and their catchment areas should be reserved for nature conservation. There are particular short-comings in relation to the conservation of marine and coastal ecosystems (e.g. corals, mangroves, and the deep sea) which is an urgent priority.

The international community has agreed to estab-lish such a system of protected areas (CBD, 2004a). A positive sign is that in the last few years the number of protected areas and their area have risen signifi-cantly and currently cover approx. 11.5 per cent of the Earth's land area (WPC, 2003a). Yet many of these protected areas turn out to be 'paper parks', i.e. they are protected in law but local management is so inadequate that often it does not even succeed in preventing the overexploitation of biological resources (e.g. illegal logging, overfishing; Section 3.3.4.1).

INTEGRATING CONSERVATION AND LAND-USE

In the 80–90 per cent of land area which is not formally protected, sustainability limits should also not be exceeded (application of WBGU guidelines, WBGU 2000), nor should species conservation be neglected – for protected areas alone cannot halt biodiversity loss. It is particularly significant to establish interlinkages between protected areas and the surrounding landscape.

3.3.4.5
Conclusions

Overall, biosphere conservation is in acute crisis. It is a crisis which particularly affects the poor, whose daily lives are directly dependent upon ecosystem services. When steps are taken to conserve biodiversity, poverty can be intensified (by excluding access to local biological resources) or alleviated (through participation in revenues from nature conservation and tourism, and preservation of well-adapted, traditional ways of life and cultures). To conserve biodiversity successfully whilst combating poverty, two essential objectives must be set: prevent the feedback loop between poverty and biodiversity loss, and conserve and sustainably use biodiversity to safeguard the options it holds for the future.

Under the auspices of the Biodiversity Convention and at the World Summit on Sustainable Development, the global community agreed to achieve a significant reduction in the rate of biodiversity loss by 2010 as a contribution to poverty alleviation, among other objectives. A worldwide, representative and well managed system of protected areas covering 10–20 per cent of the Earth's land area (including river ecosystems and their catchments) is essential if the goal is to be achieved. Overall this may be considered as a guard rail (WBGU, 2001a). Major progress has been made in terms of the proportion of land area covered by protected areas, which currently stands at around 11.5 per cent (WPC, 2003a). However, there is much ground to be made up as regards their management: many of the protected areas are not succeeding in preventing destruction from taking place.

The protected area network is a necessary but by no means sufficient condition for the worldwide conservation of biodiversity. Further efforts must be made to mainstream nature conservation targets for the other 80–90 per cent of land. Achievement of the internationally agreed target by 2010 is in doubt, unless substantial political weight is thrown behind it at all levels.

3.3.5
Air pollution and toxic substances

Over the last century, and particularly over recent decades, numerous global environmental and health problems emerged as a result of anthropogenic emissions of noxious substances into the atmosphere. Greenhouse gases change the radiation balance of the Earth's atmosphere (Section 3.3.1). Acidifiers such as ammonia, nitrogen oxides (NO_X) and sulphur dioxide (SO_2) change the biosphere through acid rain with regional effects on soil quality and agriculture, as recently shown in China, for example. Precursor substances for tropospheric ozone such as carbon monoxide (CO), NO_X and volatile hydrocarbons have a negative impact on health (particularly in large cities) through direct toxic effects, and indirectly through the formation of ozone. Elevated surface ozone reduces agricultural yields, thereby reducing the income of the rural population. Production of substances that damage the stratospheric ozone layer has been discontinued in industrialized countries, but such substances continue to be used in some developing countries.

A further problem is the spread of toxic chemicals that can lead to regional health problems. Not least in developing countries, environmental policy increasingly focuses on suspended particulates from numerous sources. At times and regionally, such particulates can cause significant stress to humans and ecosystems. Poorer sections of population living near production plants are often especially affected.

3.3.5.1
Air pollution and toxic substances in developing countries

AIR POLLUTION IN CITIES

The main causes of air pollution are combustion of fossil fuels in vehicles and power plants, and industrial production. Natural sources such as vegetation fires or volcanic eruptions also contribute. Air pollution is now a problem in almost all countries, including developing countries. However, many studies and data refer to air pollution in industrialized countries.

The World Health Organization (WHO) and the United Nations Environment Programme (UNEP) list six main air pollutants, the concentration of which is monitored regularly (including developing countries): suspended matter or aerosols (particulate matter, PM), SO_2, lead, NO_X, CO and ozone (WHO, 2000; UNEP Chemicals, 2003). Apart from ozone, which is generated from precursor gases under the influence of solar radiation, these substances are directly released during the combustion of fossil energy carriers. In industrialized countries, strict environmental regulations have led to the use of technologies that produce lower emissions, particularly in the transport sector and in power plants. However, many developing countries are experiencing an increase in air pollutants, particularly in rapidly growing conurbations (Fenger, 1999). For example, it is estimated that, without further policy action, vehicle-kilometres in developing countries will increase by 2.5–4 per cent every year between 1990 and 2030 (Gorham, 2002). Unless vehicle technologies change, this means an associated increase in air pollutants.

The total concentration of all suspended particulates that the population of the largest cities is subjected to on average over the year tends to be highest in those countries with low per-capita energy consumption, i.e. in countries with low income (Gorham, 2002; Fig. 3.3-5).

Particles with a diameter of less than 10µm (PM_{10} particles) that can penetrate the lung are particularly hazardous. These small particles, and among them particularly soot, are associated with the formation of lung cancer and other heart and lung diseases (WHO, 2002). Soot originates from incomplete combustion. Recent findings indicate that the criticality of particles increases with decreasing size, so that the concentration of particles smaller than 2.5µm ($PM_{2.5}$) is increasingly regarded as an important indicator. $PM_{2.5}$ particles originate almost exclusively from combustion processes, either directly or indirectly. Particles from other sources such as cement production, min-

ing, etc. are usually larger than 2.5µm (Lvovsky et al., 2000).

The vast majority of anthropogenic SO_2 emissions originate from the combustion of sulphurous coal and (to a lesser degree) of fuel oil. Short-term effects of SO_2 include irritation of the mucous membranes and the upper respiratory tract. SO_2 adsorbed on the surface of suspended particulates can penetrate the lung. In larger doses, it can lead to respiratory distress and even death. In the atmosphere SO_2 is oxidized to sulphuric acid. Its deposition (usually via precipitation) contributes to the acidification of soils.

Air pollution due to lead largely originates from the combustion of leaded fuels in the transport sector. In industrialized countries utilization of leaded fuels has largely been discontinued. Approximately 85 per cent of the petrol sold worldwide is now unleaded. However, leaded petrol continues to be used in many developing countries, causing associated problems due to increasing road traffic, particularly in cities. Lead enters the human body (where it can ultimately be detected in the blood) mainly through the respiratory tract and via the intake of food. Low doses of lead over a long period of time can lead to increased blood pressure and reduced intelligence. High doses lead to anaemia, digestive problems, neurological damage, and kidney damage. 97 per cent of children with increased lead levels in the blood live in developing countries (WHO, 2002).

In many cities of developing countries other factors lead to further impairment of air quality. Inad-

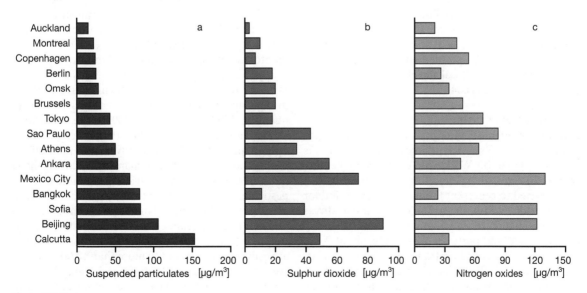

Figure 3.3-5a-c
Average annual air pollution (suspended particulates = a; SO_2 = b; NO_x = c) in selected cities. The WHO guidelines on air quality specify maximum concentration levels of 50 µg/m³ for SO_2 and 40 µg/m³ for NO_2. The data for suspended particulates refer to the year 1999, the other data were acquired between 1990 and 1998.
Source: WBGU, data after World Bank, 2003c

equate waste disposal often involves uncontrolled burning of waste in streets or on landfill sites, leading to toxic emissions. Further sources of dust pollution are construction sites and disused sites (UNDP et al., 2000). 646,000 deaths that occurred in the year 2000 in developing countries could be attributed to air pollution in cities. The figure for industrialized countries was 154,000 deaths (WHO, 2002).

Since the 1970s, the substances mentioned above and many other substances have been the subject of international, national and local clean air policies. However, measures for controlling air pollution and monitoring pollutant concentrations have only recently been introduced in some of the megacities in developing countries. One example is the recent reduction of SO_2 and ozone values in Mexico City (Molina and Molina, 2004).

ASIAN BROWN HAZE
Outdoor air pollution is not restricted to cities. The use of pesticides in agriculture, fires associated with large-scale forest clearance and soil erosion also have an impact on regional air quality and lead to associated health risks. A brown haze layer that often spreads across the whole of South and South-East Asia for months on end has become known as Asian Brown Haze. It consists mainly of sulphates, soot and organic substances originating from the utilization of fossil energy carriers (predominantly sulphurous coal) and from burning of biomass in rural regions. The main reason for the persistence of the brown haze is the long dry period during autumn and winter that is typical for this climatic zone. Unlike in moderate latitudes, the pollutants and aerosols suspended in the atmosphere are therefore not regularly washed out by rain (UNEP and C4, 2002). The haze may lead to the health problems discussed above, and can also contribute to local and global climate change (Krüger and Graßl, 2004).

INDOOR AIR POLLUTION
A further problem affecting poor sections of the population even more strongly than outdoor pollution is indoor air pollution. Worldwide, cooking and heating with solid fuels (dung, wood or agricultural waste) are assumed to represent the main source of indoor air pollution (WHO, 2002). The use of simple stoves leads to emission of air pollutants such as CO, NO_x, SO_2, benzene, and particles. Worldwide, about 2,400 million people depend on traditional fuels for heating and cooking (IEA, 2002). Fumes from these fuels can cause acute respiratory tract infections, chronic bronchitis, asthma and lung cancer (Section 3.3.5.2). The combustion of coal indoors causes similar problems, although the use of coal is less widespread.

Mineworkers and workers in the construction sector are subjected to microdust from quartz, coal or asbestos, the inhalation of which can cause cancer of the respiratory tract and other respiratory diseases. In many countries where control measures have been implemented the number of such diseases is gradually falling. No reliable figures are available for developing countries, nevertheless the problem has to be regarded as substantial (WHO, 2002).

TOXIC SUBSTANCES
A group of air pollutants and chemicals that is particularly harmful for the environment and for humans is referred to as POPs (persistent organic pollutants). POPs are synthetically produced organic substances that are toxic and long-lived. They can re-evaporate and spread over large distances in the air or in water, and they tend to accumulate in fatty tissue. Due to their persistence and mobility, POPs can spread globally. Because they are soluble in fat they have a tendency to accumulate in the food chain and can be passed on via breast milk. Humans take in POPs mainly through contaminated food. Such contamination can originate from air, water and soil pollution. POPs have a wide range of effects on human health, including acute poisoning and long-term damage. Some POPs are alleged to cause cancer or hormonal malfunctions.

The Stockholm Convention on Persistent Organic Pollutants came into force in 2004, with the initial aim of banning a group of chemicals referred to as the 'dirty dozen', including pesticides (aldrin, chlordane, DDT, dieldrin, endrin, heptachlor, hexachlorobenzene, mirex and toxaphene), industrial chemicals (PCB) as well as dioxins and furans. The latter have no commercial benefit. They are generated unintentionally in combustion and industrial production processes. Open fires for burning waste or biomass are thought to be a significant source of POPs in developing countries, although this is difficult to quantify (UNEP Chemicals, 2003). The Stockholm Convention allows for the fact that for some developing countries DDT is currently still the most effective method for fighting malaria. Moreover, many developing countries still have large quantities of old pesticide stockpiles (more than 20 per cent of which are POPs) that are stored under poor conditions and represent an immediate health risk for the population. For Botswana and Mali alone, these stockpiles are estimated to amount to more than 10,000t in each country (2000 figures, Goldman and Tran, 2002).

Mercury is a toxic heavy metal that can lead to neurological and kidney damage. As in the case of lead, poor sections of the population are affected particularly severely. One source of mercury release is the combustion of fossil energy carriers (particularly coal). In developing countries with inadequate workplace controls, workers in the mercury processing industry are at particular risk, as is the population living along rivers downstream of such plants (due to the intake of contaminated fish), and workers in gold mines (Goldman and Tran, 2002).

The OECD warns that risks associated with the production of chemicals will increase significantly if, as expected, a major shift of production occurs from industrialized to developing countries while health & safety and environmental standards remain weak in those countries (OECD, 2001). The Rotterdam Convention on Prior Informed Consent (PIC), which came into force in February 2004, deals with the export of chemicals. The PIC convention obliges exporting countries to transfer certain dangerous chemicals only after the importing country has been informed and has explicitly approved the transfer.

3.3.5.2
Poverty impacts

Air pollution and toxic substances mainly have a damaging effect on health, but they also influence nutrition and income.

HEALTH
Particularly obvious are the health effects of indoor air pollution. Poorer sections of the population are the worst affected. According to Bruce et al. (2002), it is estimated that approximately 2.5 million deaths in developing countries annually can be attributed to indoor air pollution. This figure corresponds to 4–5 per cent of all deaths. For the year 2000 the WHO (2002) estimates the number of deaths in developing countries due to fumes caused by the use of solid fuels as 1.6 million, 950,000 of which are female. Women and infants are usually subjected to contaminated indoor air for longer periods than men, because women spend more time indoors preparing meals. According to Smith et al. (2000), acute respiratory tract infections are the most common cause of child deaths in developing countries. Furthermore, statistics suggest that children whose mothers use solid fuels are born with a lower birth weight – similar to children of mothers who smoke (Bruce et al., 2002). The percentage of households using solid fuels is one of the indicators for attaining MDG 7 (environmental sustainability). Overall, there has been no change in this percentage (75 per cent) in developing countries between 1990 and 2000 (UN Statistics Division, 2003).

Outdoor air pollution, for example in cities, affects in the first instance the entire regional population. Yet here too the poor are often worse affected than more affluent sections of the population. The concentration of air pollutants not only depends on the quantity of emissions, but on the topography, climatic conditions, the time of day, and on reactions of pollutants with each other. The concentration usually decreases with increasing distance from the source: For example, approximately 10 per cent of the lead emitted from vehicles remains within a radius of 100m (Wijetilleke and Suhashini, 1995). How many and which people are affected by high pollutant concentrations also depends on the number of people living or working along main roads, for example road workers or street traders. Studies on schoolchildren in Bangladesh showed a correlation between increased lead concentrations in the blood and a low level of education of their parents, and with proximity of their residence to main roads (Kaiser et al., 2001). In typical residential areas of the urban poor, which are characterized by high population density and widespread utilization of solid fuels, indoor air pollution often also aggravates local outdoor air pollution (von Schirnding et al., 2002).

Data about the global distribution and associated health effects of POPs and other persistent toxic substances are sketchy. No comprehensive studies for developing countries have been carried out to date (UNEP Chemicals, 2003). From a synopsis of exemplary reports, a study commissioned by the World Bank (Goldman and Tran, 2002) concluded that the poor are often particularly badly affected by toxic substances. Extensive and improper application of pesticides in developing countries leads to numerous deaths and diseases, mainly among poor agricultural workers and their families. In poor countries, children in particular suffer from the negative influences of high doses of POPs. In 1997, for example, dioxin levels in the breast milk of women in cotton-growing regions of Kazakhstan were shown to be ten times the corresponding values in the USA (Solomon and Weiss, 2002).

NUTRITION AND INCOME
Air pollution and toxic substances can lead to reduced agricultural productivity and therefore have a negative effect on the nutrition situation and the income of the poor. Modelling studies have showed that Asian Brown Haze alone leads to a reduction in rice productivity by about 5–10 per cent due to a reduction in solar radiation reaching the ground (UNEP and C4, 2002). Increased surface ozone concentrations can also lead to reduced agricultural yield (Aunan et al., 2000).

3.3.5.3
Guard rails for protection of the atmosphere and for substances released to ecosystems

Exceedance of critical pollutant exposure levels for humans and ecosystems is not tolerable. The Council has not yet developed concrete quantitative guard rails for the protection of the atmosphere from air pollution or for substance inputs to ecosystems (e.g. nitrogen, effects of multiple substances). As an initial target for a quantitative guard rail, pollution levels should be no higher than those currently present in the EU (prior to EU expansion). It should be noted that the situation in Europe is by no means satisfactory for all pollutants. Nitrogen deposition, for example, is still too high. A definitive guard rail will have to be specified and implemented through national environmental standards and multilateral environmental agreements (WBGU, 2003).

3.3.5.4
Conclusions

Air pollution and toxic substances lead to significant health risks for the population in developing countries. There is evidence that poorer sections of the population are affected particularly badly. One of the main factors is indoor air pollution, which is often caused by poverty-related utilization of traditional fuels for cooking and heating. Consequently, the MDGs include utilization of solid fuels as one of the indicators for environmental sustainability. So far, the overall situation in developing countries has not improved. Three quarters of households still depend on traditional fuels.

Air pollution in cities is a significant problem, particularly in rapidly growing large and megacities of developing countries. Planning measures such as the development of mass transport systems and the introduction of emission control technologies appear promising. However, the growing number of motor vehicles continuously leads to new challenges. Outdoor air pollution and pollution from other toxic substances are not related to poverty. Their effect on the poor arises from the combination of rapid industrialization with poverty, which is often associated with inadequate knowledge of the risks and proper handling of the respective substances, and with inadequate safety regulations and institutional monitoring of such regulations.

In 2002 the WSSD agreed that by 2020 all chemicals should be used and produced in such a way that human health and the environment are protected from serious damage as far as possible. The Conventions described above are a step in the right direction. As a prerequisite for monitoring and assessing the health and environmental risks, there is an urgent need for action facilitating the systematic acquisition of data on toxic substances in developing countries.

3.4
The global setting: Key factors

The various poverty dimensions and environmental changes interact not only with each other (Sections 3.2 and 3.3), but are also influenced significantly by changes in global conditions. The interaction between demography, global economic trends and technological development, on the one hand, and poverty and the environment, on the other, will be analysed in the following sections.

3.4.1
Demographic development

3.4.1.1
Forecasts and factors

According to forecasts from the UN, IIASA and the U.S. Census Bureau, the world's population will increase from its present level of 6,300 million to around 9,000 million in 2050 (Lutz et al., 2001; UN Population Division, 2003a; U.S. Census Bureau, 2004). There is very little variation – around 200 million, i.e. roughly 2 per cent of the estimated figure – between the projections for this period.

The population projections beyond 2050 are by their very nature highly uncertain. For their projections on demographic development up to 2100, Lutz et al. (2001) therefore use a probabilistic approach which models fertility rates on the basis of specific assumptions. According to these estimates, there is a very high probability that the world's population will peak during the 21st century and then fall. The probability that this will occur by 2050 or 2100 is 20 per cent and 85 per cent respectively. The median projected population for 2100 is 8,400 million people (Fig. 3.4-1).

The decline in the fertility rate which underlies this slowing of population growth can be observed to a greater or lesser extent in all societies: Islamic countries (Iran, Bangladesh, Indonesia), poor countries (Bangladesh, Kenya) and countries with high illiteracy (Nigeria, Kenya) all show similarly strong trends in their falling birth rates.

Voluntary family planning programmes, such as those being delivered in Thailand, appear to be a key element in rapidly reducing fertility. Around half the

Figure 3.4-1
Median anticipated global
population figures (short
dashes) with confidence
intervals. The vertical line
in the centre marks the 95
per cent confidence interval
of the U.S. Census Bureau's
forecast for 2050. The long
dashes represent the UN's
mean estimate.
Source: Lutz et al., 2001

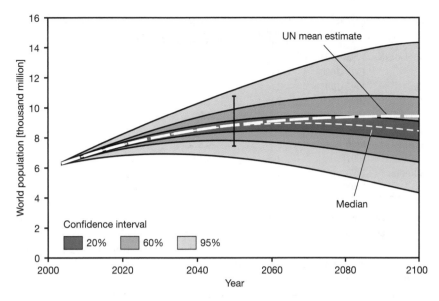

decrease in fertility rates between 1974 and 1994 can be attributed to pro-active family planning measures. The success of these programmes, which provide free access to contraception, can be explained as follows: in surveys, women in developing countries repeatedly state that they would prefer to have had fewer children than they actually have. Table 3.4-1 shows that the difference between desired family size and the actual number of births amounts to roughly one child. This gives rise over time to a consistent downward trend – the 'family planning gap' – in which desired family size decreases slightly (in India, for example, the figure fell from 2.6 to 2.1 children between 1992 and 1998), as does the number of children actually born (in India, the figure dropped from 3.4 to 2.8 over the same period).

Besides free access to family planning, other measures are highly significant in limiting population growth: they include education for girls, a decrease in infant mortality, equal rights for women, etc. However, the impact of these measures is felt over a far longer timeframe.

DIFFERENCES IN POPULATION GROWTH
- *Development status*: 99 per cent of global population growth between 2000 and 2050 will take place in the poor regions of the world (Fig. 3.4-2): China is the first developing country to have already completed the demographic transition, having stabilized its population over the long term.
- *Urban vs. rural:* Within 30 years, the global urban population will increase from below 3,000 million in 2000 to almost 5,000 million. 95 per cent of this growth will take place in the developing countries. In percentage terms, the rural population is likely to decrease. The megacities of the 1950s were mostly located in the industrialized countries. By

2015, the majority of the world's 15 largest cities will be located in developing countries (Leisinger, 1999), and will include Mumbai, Lagos and São Paulo.
- *Age structure:* As the birth rate declines, a population's mean age generally rises. That is why, by 2100 – according to the model developed by Lutz et al. (2001) – the average age of people in sub-Saharan Africa will actually be greater than that of today's Europeans. However, over the next 50 years, the age structure of the world's population will change deeply. The percentage of children under four years in the world's total population peaked at 14.5 per cent in 1955, with the figure falling to 10.2 per cent by 2000. At the same time, the proportion of people over 60 years of age rose from its lowest level of 8.1 per cent in 1960 to 10.0 per cent in 2000 (Cohen, 2003). With an ageing population, the dependency ratio – which is equal to the number of individuals aged below 15 or 65+ divided by the number of individuals of working age, i.e. the 15 to 65 age group – will shift greatly. Starting from a high dependency ratio, populations with a rapidly decreasing number of children will show an unusually low dependency ratio that lasts for around one generation (known as the 'demographic dividend'). After that, the dependency ratio starts to rise again, reflecting the growing number of older non-working individuals in the population (Birdsall et al., 2003).
- *Impact of HIV/AIDS:* All the projections mentioned take account of the impact of HIV/AIDS. In some sub-Saharan African countries in the mid 1990s, there was a reversal in the previously downward mortality trend (Garenne, 1996). Some estimates suggest that without the AIDS epidemic, the population of 38 severely affected African coun-

Country	Period	Desired number of births (=a)	Actual number of births (=b)	Unwanted fertility: Difference (=b–a)
Bangladesh	1993–1994	2.2	3.4	1.2
	1999–2000	2.2	3.3	1.1
India	1992–1993	2.6	3.4	0.8
	1998–1999	2.1	2.8	0.7
Indonesia	1991	2.5	3.0	0.5
	1997	2.4	2.8	0.4
Nepal	1996	2.9	4.6	1.7
	2001	2.5	4.1	1.6
Philippines	1993	2.9	4.1	1.2
	1998	2.7	3.7	1.0

Table 3.4-1
Difference between actual and desired number of births. The survey involved women between the ages of 15 and 49.
Source: UN Population Division, 2003c

tries would be 10 per cent greater by 2015 (UN Population Division, 2003b). The corresponding figures for five affected countries in Asia and eight Latin American and Caribbean countries are 1 per cent and 2 per cent respectively. However, based on current information, it would appear that the demographic impact of AIDS on the world's population is likely to be negligible.

The conclusions drawn in relation to these four points are naturally influenced by the various underlying hypotheses or scenario assumptions; however, these will not be discussed in detail in this report.

3.4.1.2
Demographic development and poverty

DEMOGRAPHIC DEVELOPMENT AND SOCIAL WELFARE
There is no consensus on the correlation between welfare and population size/demographic structure. However, all the literature highlights three key relationships:
1. A lower fertility rate is linked to higher social welfare. This correlation is well-documented, espe-

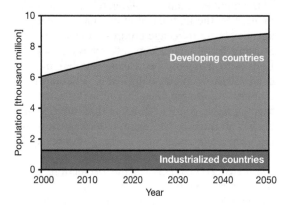

Figure 3.4-2
Demographic development in industrialized and developing countries. The developing countries here comprise Africa, Asia (excluding Japan), Latin America and Oceania.
Source: UN Population Division, 2003a

cially for the Asian growth states (Bloom and Canning, 2003). Lutz (1996) modelled the correlation between number of births, education and welfare. The welfare indicator consists of consumption variables (based on age groups) and production and environmental variables, with outdoor air pollution being used primarily in the latter case. Optimum welfare is achieved in the 'replacement reproduction' range (i.e. 2.04 children per woman), denoting a population which is stable and no longer increasing.
2. The process of building human capital is impeded by high fertility (Leisinger, 1999). This is best demonstrated for the health and education sectors, e.g. for the link between high fertility and high maternal/child mortality. In Peru, it has been shown that families invest less per child in schooling as the number of children increases (Birdsall et al., 2003).
3. In the demographic transition, strong fertility decline opens up a 'welfare window' for just one generation as a result of the beneficial ratio between productive and consumptive age groups (Kelley and Schmidt, 2001). This demographic effect becomes more pronounced as the population's education level rises (Lutz, 1996).

DEMOGRAPHIC DEVELOPMENT AND NUTRITION
Since the Second World War, the world's population has doubled while food production has increased threefold. As a result, mean per capita food supply has increased from 1925 to 2530kcal. However, since the start of the 1990s, per capita food production has risen more slowly and in several sub-Saharan African countries, it is actually declining (FAO, 2004). Food production must increase by 50 per cent by 2050 in order to maintain the current average quantity of food available per capita.

INCOME AND POPULATION GROWTH
At the International Conference on Population and Development in Cairo in 1994, the complex interdependencies between economic development, edu-

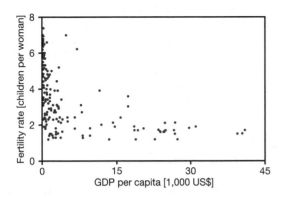

Figure 3.4-3
Correlation between fertility and income.
Source: WBGU

cation, the role of women, child mortality and population growth were explored. The key questions are these: in light of these factors, is significant development in the desired direction likely to occur? And what is the timeframe in which these factors are likely to curb population growth?

For the poorest countries, the correlation between income development and fertility is low (Fig. 3.4-3). The figure shows, firstly, the clear trend towards a medium-to-high number of births for low incomes, and a low number of births for high incomes. Secondly – and this is significant for policy recommendations – there is a very wide spread in the fertility rate, especially among poor countries. Whereas the fertility rate in countries with a per capita GDP of US$20,000 fluctuates only slightly around two children per woman, the countries with a per capita GDP of less than US$1000 show a broad spectrum of fertility rates ranging from 2 to 7.2 children per woman. It would therefore seem inadvisable to wait for prosperity to increase; instead, swift and effective measures should be taken to satisfy the demand for family planning services.

3.4.1.3
Demographic development and environment

The key question is whether there is an ecological ceiling on global population. This was raised long ago by Malthus (1798), who argued that the capacity of human beings to reproduce is greater than the capacity of agriculture to feed them. Any conclusions drawn about the Earth's 'carrying capacity' must take account of a wide range of variables, including assumptions about food production and distribution, technological development (e.g. genetically modified crops), soil quality and quantity, availability of water, and climate change. It is hardly surprising, then, that

there are currently no comprehensive models available that take adequate account of all the parameters mentioned.

Food is an important indicator of carrying capacity. Statistics on global averages conceal regional differences: in 64 out of 105 developing countries studied by FAO, per capita food production decreased between 1985 and 1995, while the population increased (Hinrichsen, 1997). In 1995, Africa produced 30 per cent less food than in 1967 (Hinrichsen, 1997). With such wide discrepancies between population growth and food production, it is hardly surprising that 840 million people in the world are undernourished and every year, 18 million people die from the effects of malnutrition.

WATER
Already, 54 per cent of the world's yearly total available freshwater is used by man. Assuming that per capita water consumption remains constant, this figure will increase to 70 per cent by 2025. Projections indicate that by 2050, 4,200 million people will live in countries in which the basic water demand of 50l per capita per day is not met (UNFPA, 2001). Indicators show that there is a downward trend in the quality of the available water supply, especially in developing countries, where 90–95 per cent of domestic wastewater and 70 per cent of industrial wastewater enters the drainage system untreated (UNFPA, 2001). Highly intensive agriculture is associated with groundwater pollution as a result of fertilizer and pesticide use. With high population growth expected in the developing countries until 2050, there will undoubtedly be attempts to intensify food production through the use of chemicals, which is very likely to result in rising toxicity levels in the water cycle.

CLIMATE
WBGU has shown that, within the 21st century, a transformation of energy systems which is compatible with the climate window, obeys other environmental guard rails (Section 3.3) and is environmentally and socially sustainable can be achieved (WBGU, 2004). This is based on the following demographic development scenario: the population will increase to 8,500 million by 2050 and then fall to 7,000 million by 2100. However, if the global population significantly exceeds this figure in 2100, it would be far more difficult to comply with the climate window. In that case, energy system efficiency must be increased, and renewable energy sources expanded, to a far greater extent than hitherto assumed. It remains to be seen whether this can be achieved via the global development currently anticipated for this period.

3.4.1.4
Conclusions

The WBGU recommends the adoption of pro-active, voluntary and supply-oriented family planning policies in order to close the 'family planning gap' illustrated in Table 3.4-1. On the one hand, effective family planning policy facilitates the mitigation of material poverty and improves other poverty dimensions such as education, health and nutrition. On the other, it encourages the conservation of environmental resources. Family planning policy should perform a catalysing, not a prescriptive function. This means that desired family size will be achieved rapidly through access to family planning services and information, thereby significantly accelerating the process of demographic transition. In this context, care must be taken that there is no conflict between spending on voluntary family planning and expenditure on HIV/AIDS programmes, even though both components fall within the conceptual framework of reproductive health.

3.4.2
Global economic trends

The situation of poor people in developing countries and the environmental situation depend not only on demographic development but also on the development of the global economy. However, it is extremely difficult to predict long-term economic trends. They are substantially influenced by factors such as technological progress (Section 3.4.3) and social and institutional changes whose trajectories are difficult to predict over longer periods of time. Two potential scenarios for the future will therefore be outlined below, each of which have a very different impact on poverty in developing countries, the environment, and the interaction between these two factors:
- *Development Pathway I – Global growth and convergence of national incomes:* In this scenario, there is steady growth in the global economy, with far higher rates of growth being achieved in developing countries than in the industrialized world. This leads to convergence of national per capita incomes. Open markets are the key feature of international economic relations. There are few restrictions in international trade. There is more direct investment, especially in low-income countries, and a rapid increase in know-how transfer. High productivity progress is achieved worldwide.
- *Development Pathway II – Uneven growth and marginalization:* High economic growth only takes place in a few regions which cultivate intensive trade and investment relations with each other but otherwise pursue a protectionist approach. The remaining regions and countries are partly excluded from these economic relations and the associated technology transfer, and become increasingly marginalized. At best, they achieve very low economic growth.

3.4.2.1
Economic growth and poverty

An economic catching-up process in an integrated world with high growth rates, as outlined in Development Pathway I, is the scenario which is most likely to contribute to poverty reduction. The prerequisite is that economic growth trickles down to the poor. Either their productivity and employment opportunities must directly increase or they must benefit, at least indirectly, from others' rising incomes. Economic growth generally generates higher government revenues. Such revenues can be spent on poverty reduction as well as on public investment in education, health and infrastructure, or on social transfers and subsidies.

Most empirical studies conclude that economic growth is a prerequisite for poverty reduction (UNCTAD, 2002). A study by the World Bank concludes that following the adoption of trade liberalization measures, the share of income going to the poorest 20 per cent of a country's population rises on average in step with the total income in the economy (Dollar and Kraay, 2001). Not all empirical studies share the view that growth automatically leads to a fall in income poverty. Although they accept that growth is a necessary prerequisite, they point out that growth itself is not enough to reduce poverty. If growth is to have a poverty-reducing impact, the poorest group must benefit to a disproportionately high degree from economic growth (Klasen, 2003). Yet in many countries, income inequality has remained almost unchanged in recent decades (Deininger and Squire, 1998). Very often, it is the workers who are employed in the formal sector in urban areas who benefit from higher growth. However, the majority of the poor live in rural regions and work in the informal sector (Ravallion, 2001).

Growth achieves the highest poverty-reducing impact in countries where there is initially a high level of literacy, low infant and child mortality, a relatively even distribution of property and a good infrastructure, which means that there is a broader basis for poorer demographic groups to participate in the economic process (Ravallion and Datt, 2002; Khan, 2002). Growth has a poverty-reducing impact primarily in countries which have managed to reduce population growth (Section 3.4.1). In many poorer countries, no discernible reduction in poverty has been achieved over the last five years despite high rates of growth, the reason being that population growth in these countries could not be offset by corresponding growth in the economy (UNCTAD, 2004a).

However, besides offering opportunities for growth, a world with a relatively high level of economic integration (Development Pathway I) poses a number of risks to economies which are becoming increasingly dependent on the world markets (Sections 4.2.13 and 4.3.4). These risks include the increasing probability that through no fault of their own, countries will be affected by economic crises in other nations or by international financial crises. In these situations, it is always the poor who suffer indirectly. Empirical studies also show that the regular fluctuations in world market prices may already be threatening the livelihoods of poor population groups that produce goods for export or depend on imported products. This is primarily because the poor generally have no savings to cushion temporary falls in income or rising costs (Section 4.2.13.1).

Economic growth can help to reduce income poverty. However, the extent to which the poor benefit from economic growth depends on a set of country-specific conditions, notably education, health, population growth, distribution and infrastructure. So even if the economy is growing, the state must continue to play a key role in combating poverty. Poor population groups' access to education, health and transport are as important as microcredit programmes and direct transfer payments in enabling the poor to share in the benefits of economic integration and growth (Bénabou, 1996; Ferreira, 1999; Atkinson, 1999).

3.4.2.2
Economic growth and environment

There is no simple and straightforward correlation between economic growth and environmental pollution. The Environmental Kuznets Curve (EKC) (Fig. 3.4-4), which has attracted considerable attention since the early 1990s (Grossman and Krueger, 1991; Shafik and Bandyopadhyay, 1992; Schubert et al., 2000), is an attempt to explain this relationship. Based primarily on empirical studies, there is assumed to be a correlation between environmental quality – measured against various indicators of environmental degradation – and per capita income. At lower income levels, environmental quality deteriorates and pollution increases in line with economic growth. However, according to the hypothesis, as per capita incomes continue to rise, environmental pollution levels out until it reaches a quantifiable peak.

From then on, there is a steady decoupling of pollution levels from economic growth. Indeed, once a specific income level is reached, environmental quality actually improves as the economy continues to grow (Vogel, 1999).

Although the typical EKC pattern can only be observed for a few pollutants, it has been expanded by a number of authors into a general relationship between environmental pollution and income (World Bank, 1992). The intuitive reason for this is that economic growth initially results in a deterioration of environmental quality as production, income and consumption increase, while other factors remain constant. Once a specific level of material prosperity has been reached, further rises in income go hand in hand with the general public's greater interest in environmental quality and, in many cases, an increased demand for 'environmentally compatible' products, prompting politicians and producers to adopt more stringent environmental standards. Moreover, the more prosperous nations generally have better-functioning legal and socio-economic institutions and technical and financial options, enabling them to enforce environmental protection laws more effectively than poorer countries.

The Environmental Kuznets Curve is sometimes used to justify 'wait and see' strategies in line with the 'grow first, clean up later' principle (Beckerman, 1992). However, this type of strategy is unsuitable when there is irreversible environmental damage such as species loss. What is more, the statistical analysis underpinning the EKC is far from sound. There are many counter-examples which make it clear that the assumed correlation does not apply to all countries with rising per capita incomes or to all types of environmental degradation (Stern, 2004). Furthermore, the correlations are far more complex than the

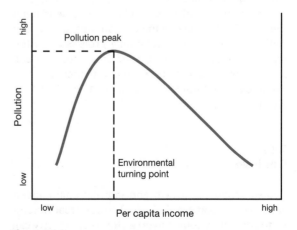

Figure 3.4-4
The Environmental Kuznets Curve: The relationship between absolute environmental pollution and per capita income.
Source: Michaelis, 2003

hypothesis suggests. The only generalized statement which can be made on the basis of recent empirical studies is that the concentration of pollutants is very likely to decrease once a medium income is reached, while emissions tend to increase steadily. Thus the concentration of some local pollutants in cities, notably air-borne particulates and lead, follows the EKC pattern (Lvovsky et al., 2000). However, pollutants also accumulate in the environment, so that even if emission levels fall as income rises, they can still cause increasing environmental damage. Examples are climate-relevant CO_2 emissions or the accumulation of urban waste (Stern, 2004).

And finally, a further factor to be considered is that encouraging targeted technology transfer can help to break the supposed 'logic' of the Kuznets Curve. The quicker clean-technology innovations – which are usually introduced first in high-income countries – are shared with other countries, the sooner emissions will fall in these countries too, largely irrespective of per capita income (Gallagher, 2003; Diesendorf, 2003).

The Environmental Kuznets Curve is not an automatic process. A key factor for its development is a pro-active environmental policy (Schubert et al., 2000; Michaelis, 2003). In medium- to high-income countries, environmental legislation plays the key role in reducing pollution. In this context, to achieve emissions reductions in developing countries, a policy which targets the pollution 'hotspots' and is based on market-oriented approaches is most likely to be successful. Better data and public pressure speed up the implementation of rigorous environmental policies (Dasgupta et al., 2002; Yandle et al., 2004). Another factor which is significant in decoupling economic growth from environmental degradation is the establishment of reliable and effective institutions, environmental information systems and education, functioning markets and, in particular, clean technologies (Section 3.4.3). Development cooperation activities can contribute to this decoupling process by fostering appropriate capacities, policy reforms, data collection, public education, and the diffusion of appropriate, clean technologies (Dasgupta et al., 2002; Yandle et al., 2004).

3.4.2.3
Conclusions

Global economic growth and international convergence (Development Pathway I) offer great potential to combat extreme poverty. However, poverty can only be abolished permanently if, at the same time, natural life-support systems are protected and maintained. This, in turn, can only take place if there is extensive decoupling of economic growth and environmental consumption (Section 3.4.3), in other words, if pro-active environmental policies are pursued and environmental externalities are internalized. Further global economic growth based on increases in industrial productivity and turnover, which were the hallmark of the 20th century economy, is unsustainable. Instead, a new direction must be pursued, based on innovative, low-input products which prioritize the benefits to consumers (e.g. an energy service instead of electricity; WBGU, 2004) and innovative production processes which make sparing use of resources.

Given that most of the requisite technologies are developed in industrialized countries, a technology transfer must take place without delay. In addition, development cooperation should focus on institutional capacity-building in the field of environmental protection and on supporting environmental education for the general public. However, it is possible that this type of environmentally compatible growth may not create enough jobs for unskilled or poorly skilled workers, a group which includes the majority of the poor. A strategy to decouple growth from environmental consumption must therefore be accompanied by additional measures to ensure that the poor also benefit from economic growth, not least through greatly improved access to education services and healthcare.

3.4.3
Technological development

Technological development must be viewed ambivalently in relation to poverty and environment. On the one hand, technological development and more intensive industrial production can alleviate material poverty, but on the other hand, increased rationalization of production may result in job losses for the less skilled, thus creating unemployment and poverty. Similarly, technological development can improve the supply of resources (e.g. drinking water) in the megacities in the developing countries, but it may also lead to over-use of natural resources. These examples show that technological development, environmental themes and poverty reduction must be seen as an entity in which maximum sustainability must be achieved.

3.4.3.1
Technological development and poverty

INFORMATION AND COMMUNICATION
TECHNOLOGIES

The spread of information and communication technologies (ICT) is progressing rapidly worldwide – in 1995, for example, there were 20 million Internet users, but today, this figure has increased more than thirty-fold. The success achieved by some companies and regions shows that ICT can make a significant contribution to economic development in developing countries as well (World Bank, 2003e; UNCTAD, 2003). The new technologies can also have a positive impact in the health sector and in relation to participation in social decision-making processes (Seibel et al., 1999; Pigato, 2001).

In recent years, many developing countries have been able to improve their technical infrastructure for these technologies, often by opening their telecoms markets to foreign investors. For example, Senegal, Bolivia and Bangladesh have successfully increased their very low density of telephone connections by 10–15 per cent per year over the course of a single decade. A growing number of small businesses are running telephone shops or Internet-cafés. This is encouraging mobile phone and Internet usage, although these positive developments are often confined to urban areas (UNDP, 2001a).

On the other hand, the advent of ICT can also widen disparities (digital divide). A number of countries are at risk of being decoupled from technological progress: around 70 per cent of all Internet users and 90 per cent of all Internet providers are based in the industrialized countries (UNCTAD, 2003). The digital divide arises not only between countries but also within societies. The average Internet user is young and male, with an above-average income (UNDP, 2001a; Primo, 2003). Can the opportunities afforded by ICT be utilized to promote economic and social development in developing countries? This will depend not only on technical availability but also on the political conditions and level of education in the society concerned. At present, even if they had access to it, the Internet is of very limited benefit to the poor. Most Internet content is incomprehensible (two-thirds of all websites are in English) or irrelevant to their lives (Painting and Wesseler, 2003; Seibold, 2004). Many developing countries have no opportunity to use modern ICT-based methods of knowledge transfer and education, and this state of affairs significantly impedes poverty reduction.

ENERGY SUPPLY

Alongside modern information and communication technologies, energy supply plays a key role in poverty reduction (WBGU, 2004). This applies not only to urban areas but also, and especially, to regions with low population density. More than 2,000 million people, primarily in the rural areas of Asia and Africa, have no access to modern energy services such as grid-connected electricity or liquid fuels (Box 3.2-1). In general, traditional biomass is used for cooking and heating. Besides the negative impacts of this usage on the natural environment, it also significantly impairs health: for example, each year, more people die from the effects of indoor air pollution than from malaria (WHO, 2002).

Due to a lack of electricity grids and poor electricity generating capacities, many energy services are not available in these regions. This obstructs the process of improving conditions, especially in relation to the poverty dimensions of education and health, and impedes the establishment of productive small businesses. The development of modern decentralized energy technologies can do much to improve this situation. Above all, local and regional electricity supply strategies based on renewables – especially solar energy – provide ideal solutions here: they offer universal availability of resources, high modularity and security of supply, while removing the need to transport electricity or fuels over long distances. Technological developments in the energy supply sector will therefore have a significant and positive impact on many poverty dimensions. With access to modern energy services, small businesses can generate additional income and thus reduce income and asset poverty. Safe drinking water and refrigerated storage of drugs improve health, while access to electronic media and electric light facilitate the education process. Improvements in living conditions in rural regions will also reduce the rural exodus.

TRANSPORT

Transport is another sector in which technological development has an impact on poverty dimensions. Mobility is a cross-cutting theme which affects many dimensions of poverty, e.g. geographical accessibility of health and education institutions, or transport to a place of work that safeguards income.

In order to combat poverty effectively, expanding the transport network must include developing an effective public transport system. Poverty-affected groups in particular can rarely afford individual mobility. One example of a well-integrated urban and transport policy is Curitiba, a Brazilian urbanized area with a population in excess of two million, which has developed an above-ground 'metro' system based on high-speed buses operating in reserved roadways. Its performance matches that of an underground rail system at a fraction of the cost (WI, 2004).

Due to the high costs of fuel imports for many developing countries, technological developments that promote locally deployable vehicles with low specific energy consumption can contribute significantly to increasing mobility. On the fuel side, technological developments to produce energy carriers based on biomass and solar energy would therefore be advantageous. Electric vehicles could also contribute to emissions-free mobility in urban areas based on a solar energy supply.

WATER SUPPLY

In the context of the water supply (drinking water and water for agricultural and industrial use) and wastewater management too, there is considerable interaction between technological development and poverty reduction. More than 1,000 million people around the world have no access to adequate and safe drinking water, and poorer population groups are worst affected (Section 3.3.2). In some cases, the supply infrastructure is lacking, while in others, water scarcity is a geophysical characteristic of the affected regions. In some instances, the available water is harmful to health due to poor wastewater management or contamination by industrial and agricultural residues.

As poor population groups are rarely connected to a central water treatment system, untreated waste often contaminates local drinking water supplies. Besides a better technical infrastructure combined with socially compatible pricing structures, progress on developing new technologies can also significantly improve health. For example, water treatment is often still carried out in highly complex and inflexible plants. In this case, more efficient methods of cleaning membranes using ultrasound techniques could result in far more flexible, decentralized sterilization and desalinization plants than exist under the current strategies. Appropriate technological developments could contribute substantially to achieving the WSSD goal of halving, by 2015, the proportion of people without sustainable access to safe drinking water (Section 3.3.2).

TECHNOLOGICAL LEAPFROGGING

When reviewing the technological development of countries and regions, it is important to consider, as a general principle, that traditional 'catch-up' development in the technology sector cannot always be viewed positively. In many cases, technological leapfrogging is preferable, enabling a country to bypass the interim stages of non-sustainable and wasteful economic management and adopt largely sustainable technologies right away. It is also important to note that investing in technologies which will soon become obsolete is not economical and rules out any prospect of leading the field in a sector. Examples of potential leapfrogging are:

- Establishing solar-powered desalinization plants instead of traditional systems powered by fossil fuels (suitable for North African coastal states, for example).
- Solar heating of energy-optimized buildings instead of traditional biomass use for heating buildings (e.g. in high-altitude mountain regions such as Tibet).
- Constructing cable-free communication systems (e.g. telephone and Internet), leapfrogging the conventional development stage via copper cable technology (suitable for worldwide use).
- Rural electrification with photovoltaic systems instead of motor-driven generator technology or grid expansion over large distances (suitable for sparsely populated regions in developing and newly industrializing countries, for example).

DEMATERIALIZING INDUSTRIAL DEVELOPMENT

Industrial production processes require material resources, cause waste and material flows, and manufacture products which must be disposed of or recycled when they have reached the end of their life. In terms of its physical inventory, the Earth is a closed system in which there are necessarily upper limits to the natural resources available for consumption. Economic growth, which is a prerequisite for poverty reduction in developing countries, is therefore subject to natural constraints in terms of materials throughput.

Because the massive consumption of materials by today's industrialized countries cannot be a model for global prosperity, technological development must contribute to a process of general dematerialization of economic growth over the medium term. This applies especially to industrialized countries, but also to newly industrializing and developing countries with increasingly dynamic economies. Economic growth should ideally be managed in such a way that the consumption of natural resources is decoupled from economic growth. Low input of materials, maximum recyclability with minimal energy input, and minimal waste generation must therefore become the core elements of production and processing strategies. Furthermore, technical services (e.g. mobility) must be delivered in ways which makes the most sparing use of resources. In this context, targeted technological development is essential and is thus a key prerequisite for sustainable poverty reduction through economic development in the Earth's closed system.

3.4.3.2
Technological development and environment

Technological developments not only have a poverty impact; they also impact on the natural environment. Via this pathway, environmental changes can be triggered which impact back on poverty dimensions (Section 3.2). Technological changes which increase growth may speed up the degradation of natural resources, but they may also indirectly safeguard their conservation. For example, global climate change is intensified by the increasing use of fossil fuels worldwide. A rapid shift in energy policy towards greater efficiency and carbon-neutral energy generation based on renewables is essential in order to mitigate climate change. Air pollution is largely the result of burning fossil fuels. Modern technologies which enable energy to be generated more cleanly and efficiently have a positive impact on the environment.

Improved modern technologies also allow more efficient water management across all sectors of society, thus reducing environmental impacts in this area. Erosion and salinization are the two key factors causing widespread soil degradation, but they can be reduced in part through the deployment of technological developments such as modern irrigation techniques.

3.4.3.3
Conclusions

To sum up, it is apparent that technological development can be an instrument for – not just an outcome of – development and poverty reduction. Leapfrogging and dematerialization are cross-cutting themes within the context of efforts to reduce poverty by means of technological developments that comply with sustainability criteria. WBGU recommends that policy settings and incentives be established, firstly, to promote technological development and diffusion to a greater extent and, secondly, to minimize polluting technologies and abate their impacts, while encouraging environmentally sound technological progress. Targeted technology development must be viewed as an element of poverty reduction and promoted accordingly.

3.5
New approaches towards an integrated analysis of regional vulnerability: Case studies on Burkina Faso and northeast Brazil

Chapter 3 offers a systems analysis of poverty and the environment. Section 3.1 contained a review of the different concepts of poverty and vulnerability, while Sections 3.2 and 3.3 presented the dimensions of poverty and environmental dimensions respectively, thereby setting out the overall context of interaction between poverty and the environment. The important role played by the most significant contextual factors of population, the global economy and technology within the poverty-environment nexus was detailed in a separate section (Section 3.4).

The point is now reached at which it would be appropriate to undertake a global, quantitative vulnerability analysis that brings together this wealth of information in a single model. However, the specific links between poverty, the environment and the various contextual factors that are subject to change due to processes of globalization depend largely on the region or society being looked at, such that a global vulnerability analysis would necessarily remain imprecise. Furthermore, such an analysis would almost certainly fail on account of the huge complexities involved as well as the lack of a reliable data base. What we introduce here instead is a new methodology by which a vulnerability analysis may be generated in the regional context. This methodology was developed in the course of producing an external report for WBGU (Petschel-Held et al., 2004) and can only be summarized briefly here. It will be illustrated using two case studies, one on Burkina Faso and the other on northeast Brazil. Given the current state of knowledge and data availability, however, the aim is not so much to arrive at concrete policy recommendations than to present the basic approach.

3.5.1
Conceptual fundamentals of the vulnerability analysis

The structure of the systems analysis of poverty and the environment can be expressed, using a system of linear equations, in the form of a mathematical analogy. This can be represented as a matrix operation:

$$\Delta s = V \cdot \Delta f$$

The vector Δs symbolizes the changes in the dimensions of poverty, that is in the variables of disease, undernourishment, income poverty, etc. as detailed in Section 3.2. The vector Δf contains the changes in the

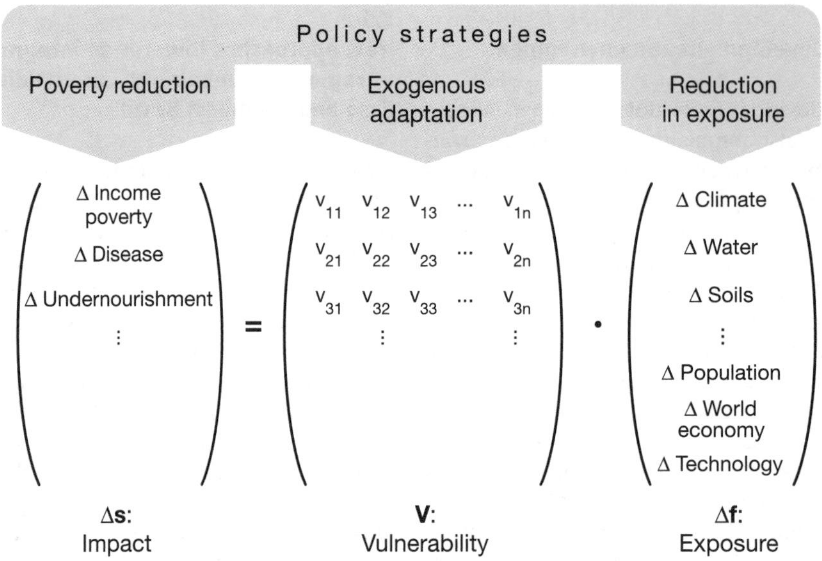

Figure 3.5-1
Matrix model of the systems analysis of poverty and the environment. Vector $\Delta\mathbf{s}$ of the dimensions of poverty (temporal changes in disease, undernourishment, etc.; Section 3.2), which is a result of multiplying the vector $\Delta\mathbf{f}$ by the vulnerability matrix $\mathbf{V}$ (middle), appears on the left. On the right is vector $\Delta\mathbf{f}$, which is made up of the change in the environmental variables being considered (climate change, change in soil degradation, etc., Section 3.3) and the changes in wider conditions (population growth, changes in the global economy, etc.; Section 3.4); the latter are included in the analysis by considering plausible paths of development. Policy strategies may be directed towards different elements of the equation.
Source: WBGU

driving forces. These are, on the one hand, changes in environmental variables $f_1, f_2, \dots, f_m$ such as climate change, the loss of biological diversity, water scarcity, etc. (Section 3.3) and, on the other, changes in societal circumstances ($f_{m+1}, f_{m+2}, \dots$) such as population development, global economic development, technology, etc. (Section 3.4).

The matrix $\mathbf{V}$ is a vulnerability matrix whose coefficients v_{ij} determine the degree of impact a specific environmental change will have on a specific dimension of poverty (Fig. 3.5-1). Each element in the vulnerability matrix therefore introduces a weighting by which the specific change in driver Δf_i contributes to the overall change in the relevant dimension of poverty. Thus, one element in the vector $\Delta\mathbf{s}$ – the change in the 'disease' dimension of poverty, for example – is calculated as follows:

$$\Delta \text{ disease} = v_{11} \cdot \Delta \text{ climate} + v_{12} \cdot \Delta \text{ water} +$$
$$v_{13} \cdot \Delta \text{ soils} + \dots + v_{16} \cdot \Delta \text{ population} +$$
$$v_{17} \cdot \Delta \text{ global economy} + \dots$$

The significance of the interactions within driving forces and within assets should not be underestimated. However, they are not the focus of attention in the model developed here. The model assumes that at any given moment in time, once these interactions have occurred within the vectors, only small changes in the driving forces (Δf_i) and their significance for the dimensions of poverty will be considered.

All the elements in the above equations can, as shown in Fig. 3.5-1, be changed by political strategies: A policy aimed at combating poverty begins directly with the relevant dimensions of poverty, e.g. in order to improve health care provision or to prevent an acute food crisis. This also involves strengthening people's capacity to cope with environmentally influenced adversities. Development policy has a broader focus and is directed, amongst other things, towards the coefficients of the vulnerability matrix. Thus, it also attempts to influence adaptation to environmental change (exogenous adaptation). By contrast, the main objective of environmental policy (and to some extent of development policy as well) is to prevent any deterioration in the environmental situation (reduction in exposure); in other words, it is directed towards the environmental elements of the vector $\Delta\mathbf{f}$. Other strategies, such as policy measures in relation to population, the economy and technology, are intended to improve the broader conditions. This conceptual categorization is necessarily rough and ready, as in practice, of course, it is neither feasible nor helpful to establish a strict division between different policy impacts.

The analysis is based on previous concepts of vulnerability that were developed in the context of research on global change (e.g. Turner II et al., 2003; Kasperson and Kasperson, 2001a). The terms impact, exposure, vulnerability, sensitivity and coping capacity are used here as follows:

- *Impact* refers to the effects of an exposure on a particular dimension of poverty, and therefore corresponds to Δs, the change in the vector s. Such an impact may be, for example, an increase in income poverty or in undernourishment. The impact is determined by exposure on the one hand and by vulnerability on the other: impact = vulnerability · exposure.

- *Exposure* refers to a specific disruption that acts on the system, such as a change in climatic conditions or in world market prices for agricultural exports. Exposure corresponds to Δf, that is, a change in the vector f.

- *Vulnerability* describes the link between an exposure and its impact. The greater the vulnerability, the greater the impact caused by a particular exposure. Vulnerability is calculated as a product of sensitivity and lack of coping capacity.

- *Sensitivity* is a component of vulnerability and describes the extent to which an exposure will act on a dimension of poverty when no explicit measures are taken to cope with it.

- *Coping capacity*, which is also a component of vulnerability, describes the ability of the groups or actors concerned to absorb dynamically the effects of an exposure by means of endogenous responses, e.g. income diversification or a change in production. What is being referred to here is endogenous adaptation. Exogenous adaptation, i.e. adaptation measures that go beyond the activities of individuals (e.g. national development programmes), are not explicitly included in the model analysis.

This simple model provides a good illustration of the structure of the vulnerability analysis. Nonetheless, it still needs to be further refined in order to be implemented in practice in regional case studies, particularly in order for the necessary feedback effects to be taken into account and also so that delayed responses can be incorporated. The formalism of the proposed method for undertaking a regional vulnerability analysis is shown in Box 3.5-1.

The aim of the vulnerability analysis presented here is to incorporate differentiation both with regard to dimensions of poverty and to environmental change on the one hand, as well as to facilitate a regionally differentiated analysis at subnational level on the other. Rather like the syndrome concept already proposed by WBGU in previous reports to serve as an instrument for looking at global change a differentiated way (WBGU, 1993, 1996, 1999), this approach can be used to develop a typology of regions using different vulnerability matrices.

The following sections present the new differentiated vulnerability analysis approach using two regions as examples, namely Burkina Faso and northeast Brazil. WBGU will give an indication of how the results of such an analysis might be used to assess policy measures aimed at reducing poverty. Given that the data available in the regions being looked at are inadequate and uncertain – particularly with regard to data on environmental change and the coping capacity of individuals, groups and the political system – the results of these analyses must be interpreted with the utmost caution.

3.5.2
Applying the vulnerability matrix

The aim of the vulnerability analysis is to assess the extent to which environmental change might affect specific dimensions of poverty. If vulnerability related to the specific dimensions of poverty is entered into a matrix as lines, and the dimensions of global environmental change as columns, this produces the vulnerability matrix. While Box 3.5-1 shows the systems analytical rationale for such a matrix, the focus here is on specifying the dimensions of poverty and the environment that are to be examined in the two case studies. Changes in the broader societal environment are not included in this example. The following dimensions of global environmental change are considered:
- climate change,
- shortage of drinking water,
- soil degradation,
- loss of biological diversity.

In the analysis of the two regions under consideration, we will look at the effects these four environmental changes have on five dimensions of poverty:
- *Income and asset poverty:* In both regions, crop and livestock farming are by far the biggest sources of income. Regional and global environmental changes thus have a significant impact on incomes in the region, especially through potential productivity losses in farming – whether this be due to climate change, shortage of drinking water, soil degradation or the loss of biological diversity.

- While *undernourishment* as a dimension of poverty is linked to income to a certain extent, there are also direct impacts of environmental changes on undernourishment, such as in the area of subsistence farming, for example. This is why we are looking especially at environmental impacts on subsistence farmers; however, a shortage of drinking water, for example, may also affect other farmers.

- *Lack of housing quality:* In both regions the rural poor population lives for the most part in traditional huts with wood-burning stoves. This type of accommodation is threatened by environmental change such as shifts in patterns of precipita-

Box 3.5-1

Differential vulnerability: Formal foundations

WBGU has repeatedly pointed out that global environmental change and its causes and consequences for the anthroposphere can only be understood within a systems analytical context (e.g. WBGU, 1993). In particular, it is important to take account of the close interactions between the environment and civilization. Leading to a new kind of procedure for assessing vulnerability, WBGU therefore, in a first step, proposes the following derivation and justification by means of a systems analysis.

On a regional scale, the processes of interaction between nature and the anthroposphere are embedded in global change, denoted in the following by F. The entirety of the dimensions of poverty (Section 3.2) will be termed as $\mathbf{s}$, a vector whose individual components $s_1, s_2, \dots, s_n$ denote the specific dimensions of poverty. Finally, regional environmental changes, i.e. including regional expressions of global change, will be denoted as $\mathbf{f}$, where the individual environmental changes (soil degradation, climate change, biodiversity loss, etc.) are represented by the components $f_1, f_2, \dots, f_m$. The ongoing assumption here is that global change translates first into regional environmental change and that this in turn has an impact on the specific dimensions of poverty. This can be written in formal terms as

$$s_i(t) = G_i[\mathbf{f}, \mathbf{s}](t) \qquad i = 1, 2, \dots n$$
$$f_i(t) = H_i[\mathbf{s}, \mathbf{f}, F](t) \qquad i = 1, 2, \dots m \qquad (1)$$

The square brackets indicate the presence of so-called functional equations, i.e. it is not the value of a figure in the brackets at a certain moment in time t that is decisive, but the entire stretch of time. This is to take account of the fact that the impacts of a change such as a drought may only be felt very much later on and may give rise to long term consequences.

In general terms, it is not possible to determine the functionals G and H completely. Therefore, the idea in the following is to use the general systems analytical description that formally describes the possible interactions between the different components of the regional human-environment-system, in order to find a way of developing a differential vulnerability analysis.

Differential vulnerability is intended to describe the changes in a dimension of poverty in relation to changes in an environmental dimension, such as soil quality, where the assumption is that all the other environmental dimensions remain unchanged. The linear approach chosen – which is valid as long as disruptions are not too great – makes it possible to determine an overall measure for the change in the dimensions of poverty by combining these individual vulnerabilities.

To do this, a reference dynamic $X^0 = (\mathbf{f}^0, \mathbf{s}^0, F^0)$ is introduced. A linear approximation can now be formulated for a development that is similar to this reference dynamic. This approximation is described by a matrix equation

$$\mathbf{s} - \mathbf{s}^0 = \underline{\mathbf{E}} \, (\mathbf{f} - \mathbf{f}^0) + \underline{\mathbf{C}} \, (\mathbf{s} - \mathbf{s}^0) \qquad (2)$$

using the elements

$$u_{ik,jl} = \left. \frac{\partial G_i}{\partial f_j(t_l)} \right|_{X^0(t_k)} \qquad (3)$$

and

$$b_{ik,jl} = \left. \frac{\partial G_i}{\partial s_j(t_l)} \right|_{X^0(t_k)} \qquad (4)$$

In forming the partial derivatives, it is necessary to pay attention to the functional characteristics of G. Equation (3) can now be reformulated to obtain an explicit expression for $\mathbf{s}$:

$$\mathbf{s} - \mathbf{s}^0 = (\mathbf{1} - \underline{\mathbf{C}})^{-1} \underline{\mathbf{E}} \, (\mathbf{f} - \mathbf{f}^0) = \underline{\mathbf{V}} \, (\mathbf{f} - \mathbf{f}^0) \qquad (5)$$

where $\mathbf{1}$ is the unit matrix in which the diagonal elements are set to 1 and all other elements are set to 0.

It is clear from this formal derivation that in the vicinity of a reference dynamic – in the so-called linear domain – the dimensions of poverty and the environment can be related to one another by a vulnerability matrix $\underline{\mathbf{V}}$. In this scheme, one single matrix element shows how a dimension of poverty changes at a particular point in time in relation to the reference if the environment changes or has changed at a particular – but not necessarily the same – point in time.

The matrix $\underline{\mathbf{V}}$ consists of two matrices $\underline{\mathbf{E}}$ and $\underline{\mathbf{C}}$. Here $\underline{\mathbf{E}}$ can be interpreted more as the direct sensitivity of the dimension of poverty in relation to environmental change, whereas the second matrix $\underline{\mathbf{C}}$ essentially makes a statement about the capacity to cope with changes in the dimensions of poverty.

Equation (5) thus shows that in the context of the linear approximation, sensitivities and coping capacity need to be linked by a multiplication function. In addition, the extent of the various environmental changes, i.e. $\mathbf{f} - \mathbf{f}^0$, which represents nothing else than the exposure, is crucial for calculating the actual change in s. As such, equation (5) reflects the different concepts of a 'classical' vulnerability assessment based on a systems analytical approach (Turner II et al., 2003):
– exposure is described by $\mathbf{f} - \mathbf{f}^0$;
– sensitivity is captured by the matrix $\underline{\mathbf{E}}$;
– and matrix $\underline{\mathbf{C}}$ describes endogenous coping capacity.
Since the operators G and H are not known, it is not possible to determine the matrices in accordance with the general rules in equations (3) and (4). Other methods have to be used to provide assessments of the matrix. Due to the specific data situation in each of the areas under study, a more pragmatic procedure based on indicators inevitably needs to be used, since the data base does not allow for an ideal multi-regression procedure.

Whereas in a multi-regression procedure the matrix elements would be derived from the data of the vectors $\mathbf{s} - \mathbf{s}^0$ and $\mathbf{f} - \mathbf{f}^0$ without any further assumptions, in the present procedure a large number of assumptions have to be made about the processes that contribute to the different matrix elements. The characters of these processes can be read off from rules (3) – (5) of the systems analysis-based determination of the matrix elements: assuming that all the other input data remain constant, it is necessary to ask which mechanisms may cause a variation in a specific piece of input data (in accordance with the columns of the matrix) to result in a change to a specific piece of output data (the rows of the matrix). In a second step, based on the specific process assumptions made in each case study and using the *ceteris-paribus* condition, an indication of the relevant matrix element can be attempted on the basis of statistical data, where a differentiation is made first between sensitivity and coping capacity, and the two resulting indicators are brought together in a subsequent step.

To give an example, the following shows the composition of the overall indicator (= matrix element) that links soil degradation with food security. This is described as follows:

To give an example, the following shows the composition of the overall indicator (= matrix element) that links soil degradation with food security. This is described as follows:

$$v_{ij} = (i_a + (1 - \underline{\mathbf{B}}) + S_{deg})\,((1 - I) + (1 - C) + d_m + (1 - l_\alpha))$$

The first factor represents sensitivity, while the second factor describes coping capacity. The individual standardized indicators are

i_a	agricultural income as a proportion of total income
$\underline{\mathbf{B}}$	subsistence level on staple food
S_{deg}	severity of soil degradation
I	total per capita income
C	total per capita livestock
d_m	distance from the nearest market
l_α	literacy rate of people over 15 years old

The assumptions on underlying processes that lead to the concrete composition of the matrix element are described in Section 3.5.3.

tion prompted by climate change. However, it is assumed that there is no vulnerability of the housing quality towards changes in the availability of drinking water or to soil degradation.

- *Disease* is a dimension of poverty affecting the rural poor population that may be caused by many direct environmental effects. These include, for example, drinking water shortages and pollution, which may lead to an increase in intestinal infections. These direct effects need to be taken into consideration in the matrix. In addition, a loss of biological diversity may lead to a loss of traditional medicinal plants.
- *Lack of education:* Environmental effects arise, for example, when additional labour is needed in order to cope with environmental change (e.g. a shortage of drinking water or firewood) and children are prevented from attending school as a result.

Thus, the vulnerability matrix in the examples initially consists of 4 x 5 = 20 elements, where the 'income-climate' element, for example, describes the potential change in income caused by climate change. Of these 20 matrix elements, however, only 17 will be analysed, as the vulnerability of health in relation to soil degradation and the vulnerabilities of housing quality in relation to drinking water scarcity or soil degradation are assumed to be negligible.

3.5.3
Case study: Vulnerability of food security to soil degradation in Burkina Faso

The following section sets out the procedure for determining the elements of matrix **V** for the specific case of Burkina Faso. This shows, using the example of the vulnerability in food security in relation to soil degradation, how to calculate a specific element in the vulnerability matrix.

Burkina Faso is situated in the Sahel region of West Africa. This region has a high level of natural variability with regard to precipitation. Soil degrada-

tion is widespread (Oldeman et al., 1991; Gray and Kevane, 2001; CONAGESE, 2002) and currently represents one of the most significant aspects of environmental change in this country. The causes of soil degradation are first and foremost inappropriate forms of land use along with deforestation. In view of the high proportion of the rural population that is directly dependent on farming, and given a high population growth, it is extremely unlikely that the pressure on soils will be reduced or food supply improved in the future (Section 3.2.3).

The first step is to establish an overall indicator for the matrix element food security-soil degradation for each province in Burkina Faso, on the basis of separate sets of indicators for sensitivity and coping capacity. Data available (e.g. the subsistence level on staple food among the population and levels of literacy) are standardized and used as indicators which eventually are used to calculate sensitivity and coping capacity. The mathematical rule for calculating the overall indicator for this matrix element from the different individual indicators is derived from assumptions about underlying processes developed on the basis of expert surveys, for example, and case study evaluations.

The interconnections described in the following thus do not represent the results of the vulnerability analysis, but are instead the hypotheses on which the analysis is based. The assumptions set out below were made in relation to sensitivity on the one hand and coping capacity on the other. They are to be understood as individually broken down parts of a whole context. Thus, the different impacts of high population density, for example, are captured separately so that the potential direct or indirect impact of high population density on soil damage is depicted implicitly in the sensitivity indicator 'severity of soil degradation', while the coping indicator 'population density' simultaneously reflects the fact that more workers are available to undertake soil protection on the other. No direct conclusions whatsoever can be drawn from either of these two separate effects to inform concrete policy measures. Only an overall analysis that includes consideration of the complex effects and side effects involved is capable of providing an indication of which measures might be suitable for influencing the situation. The choice of indicators is necessarily incomplete on account of data gaps. The assumptions that underlie them are quite rough and ready at this stage and need to be validated and refined in the course of further research.

ASSUMPTIONS FOR ESTABLISHING INDICATORS FOR SENSITIVITY

- Income from farming depends crucially on soil quality. It is therefore to be expected that especially in regions where the proportion of farming income in relation to overall income is high, a particularly high sensitivity will prevail in relation to soil degradation.
- The greater the severity of soil degradation, i.e. the more severely the soils in a region have already been damaged (such as by high livestock densities resulting from a high population figure), the smaller its buffering capacity will be in relation to further damage. As a result the soils will be more susceptible to ongoing degradation.
- The greatest sensitivity with regard to the production of staple food exists in provinces which on an average produce exactly the amount of food required locally. If less is produced on an average, sensitivity is reduced (e.g. provinces where no staple food is produced display no sensitivity); if more is produced on an average, sensitivity is likewise reduced, because in spite of soil degradation it might still be possible to produce surpluses, or else supplies may still be available from previous years.

ASSUMPTIONS FOR ESTABLISHING INDICATORS FOR COPING CAPACITY

- A high population density may improve coping capacity, since as a rule more workers are available and there is a greater potential for innovation with regard to soil protection measures.
- The shorter the distance to the nearest market, the easier it is to obtain food when soil degradation has led to a scarcity of food, thereby maintaining levels of supply of the basic necessities.
- The higher the per capita income, the more likely it is that a household will be in a position to compensate for the negative consequences of soil degradation or even to invest in soil protection measures. The latter may help in the long term to counter the negative effects that soil degradation has on levels of production.
- The larger the overall per capita livestock, the more likely it is that a household will be able to compensate for the negative effects of soil degradation by selling livestock in times of need. This does not contradict the fact that a high stock density per area may be a causal factor in soil degradation.

The next step is to link the individual indicators to one another in order to obtain an overall measure for the vulnerability of food security in relation to soil degradation. In this process, indicators on sensitivity are calculated in relation to one another in such a way that this corresponds to a logical 'OR', i.e. the individual processes are regarded as being equally relevant to sensitivity. The same procedure is followed for the coping capacity. Finally, the indicators for the sensitivity and coping capacity are linked to one another via a logical 'AND'. If there is high sensitivity and low coping capacity, then there is high vulnerability. A mathematical description of this overall indicator is given in Box 3.5-1.

This overall indicator for the element 'food security–soil degradation' in the vulnerability matrix was calculated for every province in Burkina Faso and represented in terms of regional distribution on a map (Fig. 3.5-2). As the map shows, the greatest vulnerability exists in the north of the country, followed by 'dispersed' regions in the east and the south. A number of factors are responsible for this, namely the soils that are already heavily degraded, the high proportion of the population directly dependent on farming, and the overall picture of a middle to low income range. By contrast, the provinces that have more of an urban character are only vulnerable to a small extent, something that can be traced to the low level of dependency on agricultural income. The uncertainties associated with the overall indicator, which are a result of the uncertainties related to the individual indicators, reach values of ±9 per cent to ±24 per cent. The key indicators in the area of sensitivity are the already heavily degraded soils and the high proportion of the population that depends directly on farming, which seems plausible given the information supplied by experts. The coping capacity is constrained when per capita incomes are in the middle to low range.

By means of this method, then, it is possible to identify key indicators for specific links between poverty and the environment. However, it is not possible to derive any direct statement about possible coping strategies from such isolated analyses. Some examples of possible starting points for strategies are presented in Sections 3.5.5 and 3.5.6.

Figure 3.5-2
Burkina Faso case study: Overall indicator of the vulnerability of food security to soil degradation. This corresponds to one of the matrix elements v_{ij} in the vulnerability matrix. The vertical white bars indicate the relative error of the overall indicator, which ranges from ±9 per cent to ±24 per cent.
Source: Petschel-Held et al., 2004

3.5.4
Integrated vulnerabilities for Burkina Faso and northeast Brazil

Using the method for determining a matrix element, as described in the previous section, a set of complete and regionally adjusted vulnerability matrices were produced for Burkina Faso and northeast Brazil (Petschel-Held et al., 2004). In the following, we describe one way of looking at the results systematically and in an aggregated way, namely by comparing provinces using typical features of their vulnerability matrices.

A cluster analysis was used, which enables a classification of the provinces to be made according to the characteristics of their vulnerability matrices. The only given element in this is the desired number of clusters, not the classification criteria.

A cluster analysis of the 17 elements of the vulnerability matrix to which the indicators had been applied was undertaken for all the provinces (in the case of Burkina Faso) and municipalities (in the case of northeast Brazil) in order to find clusters with a similar vulnerability structure. It proved to be appropriate to form four clusters in each case study region. The features of the province cluster for Burkina Faso are shown in Table 3.5-1 and their regional distribu-

tion in Figure 3.5-3. They can be characterized as follows:
- Cluster 1 shows high vulnerabilities throughout. The six provinces included in this cluster are located mostly in the north and the central region of the country.
- Cluster 2 shows relatively high vulnerabilities for the 'income' and 'housing quality' dimensions of poverty, predominantly in relation to climate change and the loss of biological diversity. The provinces in this cluster are located mainly in the east and the south of the country.
- Cluster 3 shows medium-range vulnerabilities in relation to most aspects of environmental change, but somewhat lower vulnerabilities in relation to biodiversity losses. The provinces included in this cluster are located mainly in the central western region.
- Cluster 4 displays relatively low vulnerabilities throughout and encompasses, among others, the more urban provinces of Kadiogo (K) and Houet (H) and their surrounding areas.

The order of the clusters shown here corresponds to a decreasing number of dimensions of global environmental change to which the different provinces are highly vulnerable. Thus, for example, the provinces included in Cluster 1 are highly vulnerable in relation to all four aspects of environmental change,

Table 3.5-1
Burkina Faso case study: Relative values of the cluster centres of the four clusters within all 17 vulnerability dimensions. Abbreviations for environmental changes: C = climate, W = drinking water, S = soil, D = biodiversity. The symbols (+, 0, -) were allocated according to the location of the cluster centre, after an equidistant division into three intervals between the smallest and the largest cluster centre: The cluster centre is in the lower third (-), the middle third (0) or the upper third (+).
Source: Petschel-Held et al., 2004

Asset	Income				Food				Housing		Health			Education			
Environmental dimension	C	W	S	D	C	W	S	D	C	D	C	W	D	C	W	S	D
Cluster 1	+	+	+	+	+	+	+	+	+	+	+	+	+	+	+	+	+
Cluster 2	+	0	0	+	+	0	0	0	+	+	0	0	0	0	–	0	+
Cluster 3	0	0	0	0	0	0	0	–	0	–	0	0	0	0	0	0	0
Cluster 4	–	–	–	–	–	–	–	–	–	–	–	–	–	–	–	–	–

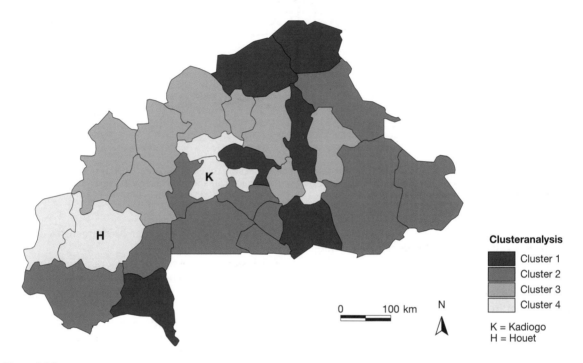

Figure 3.5-3
Burkina Faso case study: Cluster analysis of vulnerabilities. The clusters describe, in rising order, provinces with decreasing vulnerability to environmental change. Whereas the provinces in cluster 1 display a high vulnerability to all aspects of environmental change, the provinces in cluster 4 show barely any vulnerability at all.
Source: Petschel-Held et al., 2004

whereas the provinces in Cluster 4 are least vulnerable to any of the environmental dimensions.

The features of the clusters found for the municipalities of northeast Brazil (Table 3.5-2, Fig. 3.5-4) can be characterized as follows:

- Cluster 1 shows relatively high vulnerabilities throughout. The relevant municipalities are located principally in Piauí and Ceará.
- Cluster 2 mainly shows relatively high vulnerabilities for the 'food security', 'health' and 'education' dimensions of poverty in relation to the influences of climate change and water scarcity. Municipalities in the south of Piauí, in large parts of Ceará

and in the west of Pernambuco display this characteristic in particular.

- Cluster 3 records an especially high vulnerability to climate change and loss of biological diversity. The municipalities show a relatively high vulnerability for health, whereas income, housing quality and education are minimally vulnerable to these aspects of environmental change. These municipalities are located above all in Pernambuco and are also widely distributed in the north of Ceará and Piauí.
- Cluster 4 displays relatively low vulnerabilities throughout and includes, amongst other areas,

Table 3.5-2
Case study of northeast Brazil: Relative values of the cluster centres of the four clusters within all 17 vulnerability dimensions.
Abbreviations for environmental changes: C = climate, W = drinking water, S = soil, D = biodiversity. The symbols (+, 0, -) were
allocated according to the location of the cluster centre, after an equidistant division into three intervals between the smallest
and the largest cluster centre: The cluster centre is in the lower third (-), the middle third (0) or the upper third (+).
Source: Petschel-Held et al., 2004

Asset *Environmental dimension*	Income				Food				Housing		Health			Education			
	C	W	S	D	C	W	S	D	C	D	C	W	D	C	W	S	D
Cluster 1	+	+	+	+	+	+	+	+	+	+	+	+	+	+	+	+	+
Cluster 2	0	+	0	0	+	+	0	0	+	0	+	+	+	+	+	0	0
Cluster 3	0	0	0	-	0	0	0	0	-	-	+	0	+	0	0	0	-
Cluster 4	-	-	-	-	-	-	-	-	-	-	-	-	-	-	-	-	-

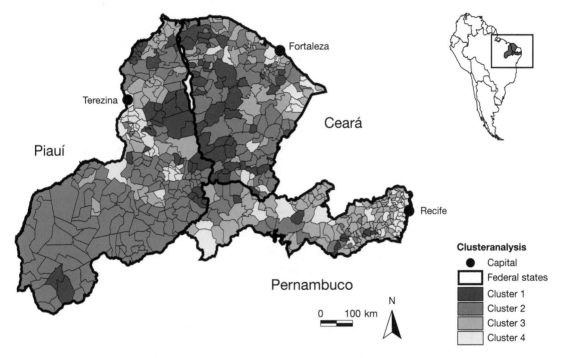

Figure 3.5-4
Case study of northeast Brazil: Cluster analysis of vulnerabilities. As in Figure 3.5-3, the clusters here also describe, in rising
order, municipalities with decreasing vulnerabilities to environmental change.
Source: Petschel-Held et al., 2004

the more urban municipalities and the coastal regions.

Here, too, the clusters are listed according to the decreasing number of dimensions of global environmental change in relation to which the different municipalities are highly vulnerable. Thus, the municipalities in Cluster 1 are highly vulnerable in relation to all four aspects of environmental change, whereas the municipalities in Cluster 4 are again least vulnerable in relation to any of the environmental changes.

The comparison of the results of the vulnerability studies in Burkina Faso with northeast Brazil shows that in both regions there are administrative units in which all the dimensions of poverty are highly vul-

nerable or barely vulnerable in relation to all the dimensions of global environmental change. Furthermore, units can be identified in which the vulnerability of specific dimensions of poverty are particularly relevant in relation to specific aspects of environmental change.

3.5.5
Developing strategies to reduce vulnerability

One important objective of the vulnerability analysis developed here is to derive starting points for strategies to reduce vulnerability.

The methodology presented in the following aims to show how priorities can be derived for the purpose of developing potential strategies. The first step involves identifying the most important key indicators that point to the main causes of vulnerability. The procedure for this will be presented using the example of a vulnerability analysis in relation to water scarcity in Burkina Faso. The basic assumptions are:

- The relative numerical value of an indicator within a matrix element corresponds to the relative significance of the process assumed to underlie it for this specific vulnerability. In a comparison of different standardized indicators, therefore, the largest will be viewed as the primary indicator for a matrix element. The primary indicator provides an indication of how best to set priorities when developing strategies to reduce vulnerability.
- The subsequent indicators with lower values provide further starting points that need to be taken into account.

In order to acquire information on which to base the strategies, then, it is necessary first to determine the primary indicators. Just as in the case of determining the individual elements of the vulnerability matrix (Section 3.5.3), the indicators for sensitivity and coping capacity will be looked at separately.

By way of an example, let us begin first by determining the primary sensitivity indicator for one column of the vulnerability matrix. The column chosen was the one in the Burkina Faso case study which describes vulnerability in relation to water scarcity. It is then possible to specify which indicators predominantly contribute to vulnerability in relation to water scarcity for every province of the country. This entails implementing the following steps:

1. Determining the relevant primary sensitivity indicator for each individual matrix element of the column concerned. This will be the largest of the sensitivity indicators in that matrix element. Due to uncertainties in the data relevant to the indicators, the primary indicator cannot usually be determined unambiguously, so that the probability of it actually being the primary indicator is also given.
2. Averaging the probabilities with respect to whether each sensitivity indicator is the primary one gives an average probability for this indicator being the primary one for the entire column.
3. The indicator with the highest average probability is categorized as the primary one for the entire column and is thus regarded as the indicator that is

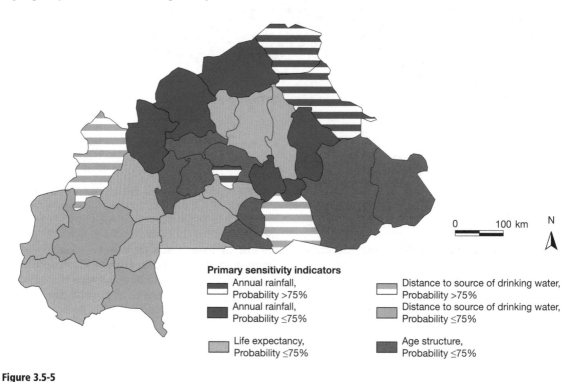

Primary sensitivity indicators

- Annual rainfall, Probability >75%
- Annual rainfall, Probability ≤75%
- Life expectancy, Probability ≤75%
- Distance to source of drinking water, Probability >75%
- Distance to source of drinking water, Probability ≤75%
- Age structure, Probability ≤75%

Figure 3.5-5
Burkina Faso case study: Evaluation of a column of the vulnerability matrix using water scarcity as an example. The map shows the regional distribution of primary sensitivity indicators of vulnerability to water scarcity in Burkina Faso. The colour shows the indicator and the hatching the relevant probability that the sensitivity indicator concerned is the primary one (≤75 per cent without hatching; >75 per cent with hatching). In most regions the probability for the primacy of the indicator is less than 75 per cent (see text). Only in the extreme north of the country is the average annual rainfall clearly the primary indicator.
Source: Petschel-Held et al., 2004

most significant for sensitivity in relation to water scarcity.

The primary indicators for sensitivity in relation to water scarcity are shown in Figure 3.5-5, along with their probability of being the primary ones. The provinces are each given the colour of the primary indicator. The hatching indicates the value of the probability: Those primary indicators that attain less than 75 per cent probability are represented by full shading, while the probabilities above 75 per cent are shown in stripes.

Sensitivity to water scarcity in the north of Burkina Faso is thus determined primarily by the mean annual rainfall (Fig. 3.5-5). In the southwest of the country, the main factors are the accessibility of sources of drinking water as well as the average life expectancy at birth, which is used as an indicator for the state of nourishment and general health of the population. In the east it is the age structure of the population above all which is the key indicator. It is striking that the probability of each sensitivity indicator being the primary one is usually less than 75 per cent, so that the subsequent indicators are potentially very significant in these regions as well. Only in the extreme north of the country does the mean annual rainfall appear as a primary indicator, with a probability of more than 75 per cent, which reflects the regional influence of the climate on sensitivity in relation to water scarcity. The procedure outlined here for determining the primary sensitivity indicators in relation to water scarcity can be used analogously to establish the primary indicators of coping capacity.

In order to establish some starting points for potential strategies, the indicators that have been identified as primary need to be interpreted. If an indicator turns out to be the primary one, then it will have a significant influence on sensitivity or coping capacity. The low probabilities for the primacy of the indicators in most provinces in the example above show that usually more than one indicator is significant here. Strategies aimed at reducing sensitivity in relation to water scarcity should therefore not address the primary indicator exclusively, but should take the subsidiary indicators into consideration in equal measure. For example, a strategy aimed at reducing sensitivity in relation to low rainfall in the northwest of the country alone, or at implementing health care measures to influence life expectancy and age structures in the east, would not be able to reduce sensitivity effectively. Taking also the secondary or higher indicators into account can help to identify further necessary strategies.

This analytical method can identify important starting points specific to a region for reducing sensitivity or raising coping capacity and thus lowering overall vulnerability. In order to work out strategies for the links between poverty and the environment, further aspects need to be taken into consideration, such as the direct or indirect impacts of potential measures on environmental change. The procedure introduced here may therefore provide some important indications of which locally suitable measures can be expected to have the greatest effects. These indications, however, must be complemented by further information and checked against the specialist knowledge of actors familiar with the local situation.

3.5.6
Reducing vulnerability: Starting points for Burkina Faso and northeast Brazil

In Section 3.5.2 we presented a model for deriving the relevant primary sensitivity indicator and the coping indicator for vulnerability in relation to a specific environmental change (in this case water scarcity) in every province of the two regions. In the following, this method will be extended in order to obtain an aggregated picture of the most important causes of vulnerability, one that is related to all provinces and all environmental changes. This will be done using the examples of the vulnerability matrices for the provinces of Burkina Faso and the municipalities of northeast Brazil.

The first step is to determine the primary sensitivity indicator and coping indicator for each of the environmental dimensions for every province (Burkina Faso) and municipality (northeast Brazil), as described in Section 3.5.5. The relative frequency with which each combination of the primary sensitivity and coping indicator occurs will be established from these primary indicators. Tables 3.5-3 (Burkina Faso) and 3.5-4 (northeast Brazil) show the relative frequencies for the most important combinations of indicators. The sensitivity indicators are listed in lines, while the columns correspond to the coping indicators. The 8 per cent figure in the upper left-hand corner of Table 3.5-3 means, for example, that in 8 per cent of cases (one case here is the vulnerability in a province in relation to a specific environmental change) the literacy rate is the primary coping indicator and the proportion of agricultural income is the primary sensitivity indicator. The 60 per cent figure in the lower right-hand corner means that the combinations of primary indicators listed in the table cover 60 per cent of all cases.

Literacy emerges as the dominant coping indicator for Burkina Faso, which limits people's coping capacity in relation to environmental change. Due to the high significance of oral traditions and the multilingualism of the country, however, no immediate and

Table 3.5-3
Burkina Faso case study: Combination of the primary sensitivity and coping indicators. The figures show the relative frequency of co-occurrence in any one province.
Source: Petschel-Held et al., 2004

Sensitivity indicators \ Coping indicators	Literacy rate [%]	Income [%]	Population density [%]	Total [%]
Income from agriculture as a proportion of total income	8	7	7	22
Use of firewood	6	8	–	14
Average annual rainfall	10	2	–	12
Condition of soil	4	6	2	12
Total	28	23	9	60

Table 3.5-4
Case study of northeast Brazil: Combination of the primary sensitivity and coping indicators. The figures show the relative frequency of co-occurrence in any one province.
Source: Petschel-Held et al., 2004

Sensitivity indicators \ Coping indicators	Income [%]	Cattle stocks [%]	Literacy rate [%]	Total [%]
Average annual rainfall	13	8	6	27
Soil depth	5	6	2	13
Average planting of basic foodstuffs	6	4	3	13
Proportion of workers employed in agriculture	4	1	2	7
Total	28	19	13	60

potentially over-hasty conclusions should be drawn from this analysis with regard to policy measures.

The combinations of the most frequent primary sensitivity and coping indicators for northeast Brazil are collated in Table 3.5-4, analogously to Table 3.5-3. Of the sensitivity indicators, the one that is of particular significance is the mean annual rainfall, which comes out at 27 per cent when all the combinations shown in the table are counted up. Of the coping indicators, income (28 per cent) plays the most important role. On this basis, the combination of both indicators has the highest relative significance and applies to 13 per cent of the cases.

On account of the kind of methodology used here and the limitations posed by the lack of data, amongst other things, these initial results need to be interpreted with care and with specialist expertise specific to the region. For example, there may be a case where important indicators can only be identified to a limited extent or not at all, simply because the indicator in question is only used in a few of the matrix elements, and that therefore relevant starting points for potential strategies for reducing vulnerability are likewise hard to identify. If the indicator in question had a high significance in these particular elements, important points might be missed. A similar kind of underestimation might occur with geo-

graphical under-representation, i.e. the significance of an indicator is underestimated for the country as a whole, even though it is of particular relevance to specific regions.

3.5.7
Outlook

The method presented here represents a new approach to vulnerability analysis. Indeed, the case studies on Burkina Faso and northeast Brazil already provide some interesting pointers towards findings that can inform policy. However, further research is needed in order to get from this approach to an operational method. This example of how the concept can be applied has shown that the ideal way of proceeding by means of a multi-regression analysis was not possible on account of the available data. This kind of vulnerability analysis makes considerable demands on the data base (Petschel-Held et al., 2004). Given this situation, the following recommendations for research are particularly urgent:

- *Improvement of data bases:* There is a considerable need for spatially and temporally highly resolved socio-economic and regional data for the environmental and poverty dimensions analysed.

Data collection programmes need to be homogenized and standardized in order to facilitate comparisons between different regions and different points in time.

- *Additional mathematical models:* In order to integrate certain aspects of the whole system more effectively, models that are already available for agricultural yield and other ecosystem services are just as helpful for describing and assessing coping strategies as are the actor-oriented models that are in the process of being developed. Such models can help to determine some of the matrix elements directly, using conjugated models.

- *Validation:* The quantitative data and the assumptions about the processes need to be validated by means of qualitative social scientific research. One way of doing this would be to seek collaboration with (local) research groups that have already implemented vulnerability analyses for specific regions in the context of international and interdisciplinary projects. This would make it possible to forge a link between the formal mathematical context of the concept presented here and what are usually qualitative methods for such vulnerability analyses. The results would thereby gain considerably greater explanatory power, making them of greater use to decision makers.

3.6
Implementing, financing and advancing international goals

The departure point for Chapter 3 was the proposition that poverty is critically influenced by global environmental change, with the consequence that global sustainability policies will only work if they take account of the interactions between poverty (Section 3.2) and environmental change (Section 3.3) – or between poverty reduction and environmental policy. Consideration must also be given to the global setting (Section 3.4), for instance the effects of worldwide demographic change, economic development and technological development. The case studies on Burkina Faso and northeast Brazil in Section 3.5 demonstrated how poverty dimensions, environmental change, the global setting and vulnerabilities can be integrated in a single model and analysed together. Models of this kind can help to ensure that well-targeted sustainability policies are identified at regional level.

By stipulating the goals in the Millennium Declaration and the WSSD Plan of Implementation, the global community has made a commitment to view and implement environment and development policy as an integrated whole. This should invigorate efforts to tackle such problems as income poverty, hunger, gender inequality, lack of education, poor healthcare provision, inadequate water supply and environmental degradation. Furthermore, targets were set for reducing debt, increasing development inputs, expanding fair world trade and transferring technologies to developing countries (Section 2.1). Following Agenda 21, the goals in the Millennium Declaration and the WSSD Plan of Implementation are further milestones along the route towards global poverty reduction and global environmental protection. They have brought the world's nations and governments significantly closer to a common understanding of the acute challenges posed by global change, and of the steps that must be taken if problems of development are to be overcome. They are complemented by goals set within the framework of multilateral environmental agreements.

3.6.1
State of implementation

INTERNATIONAL GOALS ON POVERTY REDUCTION
As Section 3.2 shows, progress towards achieving the Millennium Development Goals (MDGs) has been mixed. While some regions have made great strides, others have had setbacks. The report on progress for 2004 by the Secretary-General of the United Nations states that the developing countries fall into three groups (UN, 2004a; Table 3.6-1). The first group, which includes most countries in Asia and North Africa, is largely on track to halve income poverty and achieve the social goals. The second group, mainly consisting of countries in western Asia, Latin America and the Caribbean, have made good progress on certain goals such as education but have been less successful in combating income poverty. The third group, predominantly comprising countries in sub-Saharan Africa and the least developed countries (LDCs) in other regions, has so far recorded little progress. Some of these countries have even slipped back from previous levels of achievement. The World Bank stills sees the goal of halving the proportion of the world's population living in extreme poverty (on a per capita income of less than US$1 per day) as feasible (Section 3.2.1; World Bank, 2003b). At the same time, the 2003 Human Development Report contains the alarming fact that 54 countries are poorer at the start of the 21st century (measured in terms of per capita GDP) than in the year 1990 (UNDP, 2003c). In view of the underinvestment in basic social services, UNDP warns: 'Without extraordinary efforts, there is a real risk that international leaders will be setting the same targets a generation from now.' (UNDP, 2003c).

Table 3.6-1

Progress in meeting the Millennium Development Goals in developing countries, by region. Population of Africa as of 2002, other continents and regions as of 2003. Violet: goal met or on track. White: slow progress but not on track to meet goal by 2015. Grey: no change or negative change since 1990.
Source: after UN, 2004a

Region	Africa		Asia				Oceania	Latin America and Caribbean	Commonwealth of Independent States (former republics of the Soviet Union)	
Population (million)	840		3,738				8	536	281	
	Northern	Sub-Sahara	East	South-eastern	Southern	Western			Europe	Asia
ERADICATE EXTREME POVERTY AND HUNGER (GOAL 1)										
Reduce extreme poverty by half	on track	high, no change	met	on track	on track	increase	–	low, minimal improvement	increase	increase
Reduce hunger by half	on track	very high, no change	on track	on track	progress but lagging	increase	moderate, no change	on track	low, no change	increase
ACHIEVE UNIVERSAL PRIMARY EDUCATION (GOAL 2)										
Universal primary schooling	on track	progress but lagging	on track	lagging	progress but lagging	high, no change	progress but lagging	on track	decline	on track
PROMOTE GENDER EQUALITY AND EMPOWER WOMEN (GOAL 3)										
Equal girls' enrolment in primary school	on track	progress but lagging	met	on track	progress but lagging	progress but lagging	on track	on track	met	on track
Equal girls' enrolment in secondary school	met	no significant change	–	met	no significant change	no significant change	progress but lagging	on track	met	met
Literacy parity between young women and men	lagging	lagging	met	met	lagging	lagging	lagging	met	met	met
Women's equal representation in national parliaments	progress but lagging	progress but lagging	decline	progress but lagging	very low, some progress	very low, no change	progress but lagging	progress but lagging	recent progress	decline
REDUCE CHILD MORTALITY (GOAL 4)										
Reduce mortality of under five-year-olds by two thirds	on track	very high, no change	progress but lagging	on track	progress but lagging	moderate, no change	moderate, no change	on track	low, no change	increase
Measles immunization	on track	low, no change	–	on track	progress but lagging	on track	decline	met	met	met
IMPROVE MATERNAL HEALTH (GOAL 5)										
Reduce maternal mortality by three quarters	moderate level	very high level	low level	high level	very high level	moderate level	high level	moderate level	low level	low level
COMBAT HIV/AIDS, MALARIA AND OTHER DISEASES (GOAL 6)										
Halt and reverse spread of HIV/AIDS	–	stable	increase	stable	increase	–	increase	stable	increase	increase
Halt and reverse spread of malaria	low risk	high risk	moderate risk	moderate risk	moderate risk	low risk	low risk	moderate risk	low risk	low risk

ENSURE ENVIRONMENTAL SUSTAINABILITY (GOAL 7)

Reverse loss of forests	*less than 1% forest*	decline	met	decline	small decline	*less than 1% forest*	decline	decline (except Caribbean)	met	met
Halve proportion without improved drinking water in urban areas	met	no change	decline in access	high access but no change	met	met	high access but no change	met	met	met
Halve proportion without improved drinking water in rural areas	high access but little change	progress but lagging	progress but lagging	progress but lagging	on track	progress but lagging	low access, no change	progress but lagging	high access but limited change	high access but limited change
Halve proportion without sanitation in urban areas	on track	low access, no change	progress but lagging	on track	on track	met	high access but no change	high access but no change	high access no change	high access but no change
Halve proportion without sanitation in rural areas	progress but lagging	no significant change	progress but lagging	progress but lagging	progress but lagging	no significant change	no significant change	progress but lagging	no significant change	no significant change

As regards the evaluation of progress towards the MDGs, the general remark must be made that for most of the goals, data is only available for the period up to 2002 and is not complete for all countries. National monitoring reports on the nature and extent of progress towards the goals have only been completed by 73 developing countries so far (UN, 2004b). Moreover, most trend projections take 1990 as the baseline year so that they largely reflect progress made before the MDGs were agreed and the relevant policies were developed. Relying on such old data to predict future trends may result in unduly pessimistic forecasts.

INTERNATIONAL GOALS ON ENVIRONMENTAL PROTECTION

As a result of Russia's decision to ratify the Kyoto Protocol, it will enter into force in February 2005. WBGU has made it clear, however, that even successful implementation of the Kyoto Protocol can only be an initial milestone on the way towards a sustainable climate policy. In order to prevent dangerous anthropogenic climate change, WBGU considers it essential to halt the rise in the atmospheric concentration of CO_2 and to stabilize it at a level below 450ppm (WBGU, 2003, 2004). The present average concentration of CO_2 is around 376ppm and is rising by around 1.5ppm per year on average. There is no sign of any slowdown in this rising trend.

In the year 2025, one in four of the world's population will be living in a country affected by water scarcity. The growth of urbanization, changes in lifestyles and, to some extent, the changing climate will continue to raise the utilization pressure on local water resources. Whereas good progress has been made on access to clean drinking water in southern Asia and Latin America, the situation in sub-Saharan Africa is taking far too long to improve (Section 3.3.2).

Worldwide, soils are threatened by degradation and in many cases their productivity is already restricted. 20 per cent of soils in developing countries are affected by erosion. Another 20–30 per cent of irrigated croplands are affected by salinization (Section 3.3.3). Despite this situation and the unaltered trends, so far no international goals exist for combating soil degradation.

Increasing the area of land designated for nature conservation to 11.5 per cent of total land area was an important advance towards implementing the agreed international goals to conserve biodiversity. However there is still much ground to be made up as regards the management of protected areas and the integration of nature conservation targets in the management of other land (Section 3.3.4).

Despite progress in a few megacities, urban air pollution in developing countries is still a major problem and one which continues to grow in some locations. The progress made with indoor air pollution in some localities between 1990 and 2000 contrasts with a deteriorating situation in other regions. Thus, in developing countries, three-quarters of all households on average are so poor that they still depend on the use of traditional fuels. Owing to the lack of data, no clear statement can be made about trends in the area of toxic substances. Based on the POPs and PIC Conventions which recently came into force, progress can be anticipated, however (Section 3.3.5).

In summary, WBGU notes that on the environment dimensions, too, the implementation status of international goals is anything but satisfactory. On the whole, what has been achieved falls short of the targeted objectives. Global sustainability is and remains a vision. Further efforts to mobilize additional financial resources and to advance the international goals are an absolute necessity.

3.6.2
Financing requirements for selected policy fields

Adequate funds are an important prerequisite for the accomplishment of international environmental and poverty-related goals in the medium and long term. They cannot and should not be mustered only by those countries in which concrete measures are being taken for global sustainability. International transfers are necessary, essentially from industrialized countries to developing countries. The level of international financing required exceeds the amounts currently being provided from private and public sources for poverty reduction and international environmental protection. This results in an additional international financing requirement, referred to here as an international financing gap. On the basis of selected studies, the following section attempts to gauge the size of this financing gap with regard to meeting the international goals for specific fields relating to poverty or the environment (Table 3.6-2).

3.6.2.1
Methodological issues

Any estimate of the additional financing requirements can only be a very rough approximation, on account of unavailable or poor data, problems in issue classification, methodological differences in establishing the individual financing requirements, a disproportionately high degree of uncertainty about future developments, and sometimes varied and imprecisely applied definitions of costs and spending. For example, there is often an assumption of good governance and efficient use of funds despite the fact that supportive political and institutional conditions are not yet in place. This would require spending which is not included in estimates of the additional resources required. Thus the real financing gap may be greater than the statistics indicate.

Furthermore, the assumptions made about global economic development, the level of future economic growth within countries or the participation of the poor in macro-economic income growth are often very optimistic. For this reason, too, the real financing requirement and hence the international financing gap are often underestimated. Counterbalancing this, major positive synergies – as well as certain negative effects – operate both within and between the two areas of poverty and the environment. WBGU takes the view that overall, these synergies act to reduce the international financing requirement, even if it is not possible to assess the scale of such effects based on the available data. WBGU sees a considerable need for further research in respect of data collection and particularly in respect of quantifying the synergy effects within and between the fields of poverty reduction and environmental protection (Chapter 6).

Finally, mention should be made of the often imprecise definitions used for costs, spending and investment in the various estimates of the international financing gap. For example, clear distinctions are not always drawn between national and individual economic costs, between costs and spending, between private and public spending, and between the total necessary financing and the amount needed in international contributions. Furthermore, the baseline year for estimates is not always clear from the studies. For these reasons, details from different studies can only be compared with one another with great difficulty, if at all (Vandemoortle and Roy, 2004).

The few overall estimates found in the literature (Section 3.6.2.4) are either out of date or relate solely to the achievement of the MDGs and take insufficient account of the environmental sphere: climate change mitigation, in particular, is generally omitted. Owing to these methodological problems, it is currently impossible to state with precision the annual additional funding transfers necessary to achieve the international targets, based on an analysis of the literature. WBGU nevertheless endeavours to identify at least the order of magnitude of the financial challenge posed by the poverty and environment dimensions described in Sections 3.2 and 3.3, and – if possible – to illustrate it with reference to the range of estimates from the literature.

The original statistics from selected studies for individual poverty and environment dimensions are collated in Table 3.6-2. If no references can be found for the additional or total international financing requirement, alternative provisional figures are cited: the total financing requirement in developing countries (met out of developing countries' budgets and international transfers) or the total global financing requirement (without subdividing spending by groups of countries).

Table 3.6-2
Additional financing requirement for poverty reduction and environmental protection. Survey of the results of selected studies. Where not otherwise stated, this concerns the additional (public) funding required. Where a study only gives figures for the total funding required (current expenditure plus additional spending required), this is indicated with an asterisk*. No adjustments are made for synergies between the dimensions. The methodological problems are discussed in Section 3.6.2.1. The Millennium Development Goals (MDGs) are set out in Section 2.1.3. Dates before figures mean that figures are only available for the stated year.
Source: see column at right of table; compiled by WBGU

Purpose	Additional international financing requirement (transfers from ICs to DCs) [US$1,000 million per year]	Total additional financing requirement in developing countries (transfers from ICs *and* own input by DCs) [US$1,000 million per year]	Worldwide additional financing require-ment [US$1,000 million per year]	Source
INCOME POVERTY				
Direct income transfers to the poor to eliminate extreme income poverty		40		UNDP, 1997
Halving income poverty (MDG 1)	54–62 at least 20			Devarajan et al., 2002 UN, 2001b
DISEASE				
Achieving all MDG health targets	20–25			Devarajan et al., 2002
Reducing child mortality (MDG 4)		7.5		The Bellagio Child Survival Study Group, 2003
Financing modern methods of contraception		11*		AGI and UNFPA, 2004
Halting and reversing the spread of HIV/AIDS (MDG 6)		2007: at least 10 7–10*?		UNAIDS, 2004 UN, 2001b
Treating tuberculosis in 83 developing countries (no reference to MDGs)		2007: 0.5 2015: 1		Commission on Macroeconomics and Health, 2001
Preventing and treating malaria in 83 developing countries		2007: 2.5 2015: 4		Commission on Macroeconomics and Health, 2001
UNDERNOURISHMENT				
Halving the proportion of hungry people (MDG 1)	16			FAO, 2003c
LACK OF EDUCATION				
Universal primary education (MDG 2)	9 5–7 10–30 10	33–38*		UN, 2001b Bruns et al., 2003 Devarajan et al., 2002 UN, 2004c
(Range from studies by UNICEF, UNESCO, Oxfam, World Bank)		7–15		Birdsall et al., 2004
Gender parity in education (MDG 3)	3			UN, 2001b
Universal primary education (MDG 2) and gender parity in education (MDG 3)		5.6		UNESCO, 2004
SOIL DEGRADATION				
Soil rehabilitation in arid zones over 20 years			11*	Dregne and Chou, 1992
AIR POLLUTION AND TOXIC SUBSTANCES				
Indoor air pollution: providing 3,000 million people with 'healthy indoor air' over 12 years)		2.5*		Warwick and Doig, 2004

Purpose	Additional international financing requirement (transfers from ICs to DCs) [US$1,000 million per year]	Total additional financing requirement in developing countries (transfers from ICs *and* own input by DCs) [US$1,000 million per year]	Worldwide additional financing requirement [US$1,000 million per year]	Source
WATER SCARCITY AND POLLUTION				
Halving the proportion of people without access to safe drinking water and sanitation (MDG 7)		6.7		UN Millennium Project, 2004a
		10		Winpenny, 2003
		10–30		UNESCO, 2003a
(incl. sewerage systems and wastewater treatment for urban populations)		49		Averous, 2002
Investment in the water sector up to 2025 (Vision 2025), *total*		max. 100–110		WWC, 2000
Drinking water and sanitation systems		45		Cosgrove and Rijsberman, 2000; WWC, 2000
Drinking water		0		Winpenny, 2003
Sanitation systems		16		Winpenny, 2003
Significant improvement in the lives of 100 million slum dwellers by 2020 (MDG 7)	4			UN, 2001b
LOSS OF BIOLOGICAL DIVERSITY AND RESOURCES				
Worldwide representative system of protected areas			12–21.5	James et al., 1999, 2001
			25	WPC, 2003a
Threatened forest ecosystems in developing countries		19.6		World Bank, 2002b
Effective worldwide protected areas programme			38.5	Balmford et al., 2003
Conservation of biodiversity in valuable utilized ecosystems outside protected areas (49 without agriculture, 290 with agriculture)			290* (very tentative)	James et al., 1999, 2001
MULTISECTORAL ESTIMATES				
Provision of basic social services	10			UNDP, 1997
Achievement of the MDGs	40–70			Devarajan et al., 2002
	50			UN, 2001b
	0.46% of donor countries' GNI*			UN Millennium Project, 2004b
(Average 2005–2007)	94			UN Millennium Project, 2004c
(Average 2013–2015)	126			
Agenda 21 (1993–2000)	125*			BMU, 1997
CLIMATE CHANGE	NO MEANINGFUL ESTIMATES OF (PUBLIC) FINANCING REQUIREMENT			
Long-term costs of achieving a stabilization target of 450ppm CO_2			0.7–1.5% of global GDP (equivalent in 2003 to: 250–540*)	WBGU, 2003
Long-term average losses of global GDP resulting from reduction measures to achieve a stabilization target of 450ppm CO_2, calculated for the year 2050			1–4% of global GDP (equivalent in 2003 to: 360–1,440*)	IPCC, 2001c

3.6.2.2
Poverty dimensions

INCOME POVERTY

To halve income poverty by 2015 (MDG 1a) will require additional annual official development assistance (ODA) funding of US$20,000–62,000 million according to different estimates (Table 3.6-2). These amounts are not enough to eradicate income poverty altogether, however. To do so, transfers would have to be continued beyond 2015. Unless other poverty dimensions show improvement, it is highly likely that an additional funding larger than that needed until 2015 will be necessary in order to lift the other half of the world's poor above the poverty line. Purely hypothetically, if a global system of social security payments were established to eradicate extreme income poverty (less than US$1 per day; Section 3.2-1), the total financing requirement for such an initiative in developing countries would amount to an estimated US$40,000 million per year on a simple mathematical estimate (UNDP, 1997).

DISEASE

Many of the estimates are based on individual MDG targets such as those for HIV/AIDS, child and maternal mortality, etc. (Table 3.6-2). One exception is the World Bank, which estimates that the additional ODA requirement in order to achieve all the health targets is some US$20,000–25,000 million per year (Devajaran et al., 2002).

UNDERNOURISHMENT

According to FAO estimates, additional government spending of US$24,000 million per year is required to achieve the World Food Summit and Millennium Declaration goal of halving the proportion of hungry people in the world by 2015 (FAO, 2003c). To do this would require spending of US$8,500 million per year by the affected countries and US$15,500 million per year in ODA from the industrialized countries. In total the FAO recommends a doubling of annual ODA for rural and agricultural development from US$8,000 million (1999) to US$16,000 million. This is where positive synergies between spending to combat different dimensions of poverty become particularly apparent: for instance, the Zedillo Report comes to the conclusion that the halving of income poverty will halve hunger worldwide, and vice versa (UN, 2001b).

LACK OF EDUCATION

According to MDG 2 all children worldwide should have the opportunity to complete primary school. Almost all estimates of the necessary additional ODA payments are in the range US$5,000–15,000 million per year. A World Bank study assumes an annual figure of up to US$30,000 million, however (Devarajan et al., 2002).

3.6.2.3
Environment dimensions

CLIMATE CHANGE

The international financing requirement for the mitigation of climate change is heavily dependent on the target stabilization level for greenhouse gases, opportunities for global cost optimization (for instance, through emissions trading), the allocation of emission rights and general features of global development as characterized in the IPCC scenarios. Moreover, the time frames in question here extend far beyond the MDG target year of 2015. Hence the lack of reliable details on the financing requirement, not to mention the international financing gap, comes as little surprise.

It is therefore necessary to rely on estimated costs, which are generally modelled as losses of economic growth or per-capita consumption. Normally the development of global GDP including climate change mitigation is compared with the development of GDP in a reference scenario without climate change mitigation. With a stabilization target of 450ppm CO_2 the IPCC (2001c) calculates that GDP could be 1–4 per cent lower in the year 2050 depending on the scenario. However this does not take into account the possibility of CO_2 sequestration, nor the impacts of ambitious emissions targets as a stimulus for technological change. In more recent model studies which allow for more dynamic technological developments, there is a tendency to arrive at lower costs. In its 2003 special report, WBGU shows that given favourable conditions (low population growth, strong economic growth, convergence of world regions, dynamic technological development, etc.) stabilization at between 450 and 400ppm CO_2 is possible. This would result in an average reduction of only 0.7 per cent of GDP between 2000 and 2100, with the maximum reduction in GDP in the year 2050 being lower than 1.5 per cent (WBGU, 2004). A third scenario results in an average reduction in global GDP of 1.5 per cent. For all scenarios, a global distribution of emissions rights was assumed, in accordance with the 'Contraction and Convergence' approach.

Model calculations of climate-related damage yield such a wide range of results that WBGU does not venture any estimate here of the global cost of damages that would remain in the event of CO_2 stabilization. One reference for the losses already caused by climate change originates from Munich Re. According to them, the explosion in losses from weather-related disasters in the last three decades can be attributed, in part, to inappropriate local-level behaviour such as building in floodplains, but this does not explain all the damages.

Nevertheless it is undeniable that the potential costs of damage can be significantly reduced by regional adaptation measures. Estimates of the costs of adaptation measures are not available in globally aggregated form as yet, but tend to be limited to particular regions and sectors, e.g. with reference to coastal protection in selected countries.

WATER SCARCITY AND POLLUTION
Most estimates of the investment requirement in the water sector refer to an expansion of existing infrastructure. The greater number of the studies deal with the investment that appears necessary to achieve the goals of the 'World Water Vision' up to 2025 on drinking water and sanitation systems, irrigation, industrial effluents, wastewater treatment, water resources and environmental management (WWC, 2000). The World Water Council puts the additional worldwide financing requirement at max. US$100,000–110,000 million per year. To achieve the 2025 objectives in the field of sanitation and drinking water supply alone, an extra US$45,000 million per year would have to be mustered (WWC, 2000; Cosgrove and Rijsberman, 2000).

The additional annual resources needed to achieve the less ambitious MDG 7 of halving the proportion of people in developing countries without access to drinking water and sanitation by 2015 are estimated variously at US$6,700 million (UN Millennium Project, 2004a) to US$10,000 million (Winpenny, 2003). In a different estimate, the additional cost for drinking water supply alone is taken to be US$10,000–30,000 million per year (UNESCO, 2003a). With the addition of sewerage systems and wastewater treatment in cities, the necessary additional funding is put at US$49,000 million per year (Averous, 2002; Winpenny, 2003).

SOIL DEGRADATION
When considering the financing requirement to combat soil degradation, a distinction must be made between prevention costs and rehabilitation costs. The rehabilitation of soils presupposes that further degradation can be prevented – particularly erosion and salinization – and aims to restore the value of degraded land (Section 3.3.3). For all arid zones worldwide, the annual financing requirement for the rehabilitation of soils is estimated at US$$_{1990}$11,000 million per year over 20 years (Table 3.6-2). The necessary annual spending (2001–2015) to halt desertification, which only accounts for a part of worldwide soil degradation, is estimated at US$6,000–18,000 million (World Bank, 2002b).

BIODIVERSITY LOSS
The few available estimates stating the additional financing required for a worldwide, representative system of protected areas are in the region of US$12,000–38,500 million per year. The most recent figure cited by the World Parks Congress is US$25,000 million per year (WPC, 2003c; Table 3.6-2). The proportions of this to be mustered from internal and from external spending, i.e. international transfers, are not itemized. There is a scientific consensus that the protected area system alone is not enough to achieve the conservation of biodiversity (Section 3.3.4), and that supplementary measures must be introduced to integrate nature conservation goals into land use practices in other areas. A first rough classification by James et al. (1999, 2001) puts the total financing requirement for this at around US$290,000 million per year.

AIR POLLUTION AND TOXIC SUBSTANCES
No estimates are available on the international financing requirement to achieve the goals of the POPs Convention, nor the expected overall costs. Warwick and Doig (2004) state that 3,000 million people use solid fuels (including coal) and estimate the amount needed to protect them from harmful indoor air pollution at US$2,500 million per year over a 12-year period.

3.6.2.4
Appraising overall requirements

Few aggregated figures are to be found in the literature on the financing of sustainable development. In Agenda 21 the total ODA funding required for implementation for the period 1993–2000 was estimated at US$125,000 million per year. Assuming an efficient and effective deployment of funds, UNDP (1997) considers additional public expenditure of US$40,000 million per year sufficient to ensure basic social care in developing countries. Three-quarters of these resources could be found by the developing countries through budget restructuring, while the remaining US$10,000 million should be financed by international transfers. To achieve all the Millennium Goals, according to Devarajan et al. (2002) and UN (2001b) additional transfers of US$40,000–70,000 million per year from the industrialized countries will be needed. The Task Force on Poverty and Economic Development set up for the UN Millennium Project (2004b) estimates that a doubling of the present ODA to 0.46 per cent of the GNI of donor countries is necessary to achieve this.

The draft of the as yet published final report of the UN Millennium Project chaired by Jeffrey Sachs suggests that ODA funding will have to rise to US_{2005}156,000 million from 2005 to 2007 (0.53 per cent of GNI in industrialized countries) and to US_{2005}188,000 million from 2013 to 2015 in order to attain the MDGs (UN Millennium Project, 2004c). Based on the absolute level of current ODA payments, this would result in an ODA financing gap of US$94,000 million in the first period and US$126,000 million in the second period.

Table 3.6-2 summarizes the various figures for the additional international financing requirement, or the costs of achieving the goals, citing the source in each case. Once again it is evident that the estimates to be found in the literature for individual dimensions differ considerably. The data from this evaluation of the literature are taken up in Section 5.6.3, where they form the basis for assessing whether implementation of the international sustainable development targets can be financed.

3.6.3
Advancing international goals

The international goals in relation to sustainability cannot be achieved unless extraordinary efforts are made. Additional financial resources must be mobilized. Even the international goals themselves have certain shortcomings, however. For instance, the Millennium Development Goals fall short in environmental terms, even though the Millennium Declaration expressly affirms respect for nature as a value and fundamental principle. Essentially the goals barely take account of the interactions between poverty dimensions and global environmental change. The resolutions of the WSSD have done little to alter this (Section 2.1.4). In the following section, WBGU therefore highlights shortcomings of the international goals on poverty reduction and environmental policy, and recommends suitable additions to these goals.

FOCUSING ON STRUCTURAL CAUSES
The MDGs and the Johannesburg goals tend to address the symptoms of global crisis rather than the deeper structural causes of poverty and environmental destruction. This applies not only to the power structures and socio-economic disparities within society, but also to international relationships of dominance and global economic mechanisms. It is conspicuous and, in the light of a globalized world economy, unjustified that so little attention is given to the patterns of production and consumption in industrialized countries and their adverse effects on the social and economic conditions in poorer countries.

INTEGRATING HUMAN RIGHTS
Both the MDGs and the Johannesburg goals are not systematically cross-referenced with internationally recognized human rights standards (for instance, the Universal Declaration of Human Rights, the Civil and Social Covenants, the Convention on the Rights of the Child, the Convention on the Rights of Women) although their material substance is directly related. In contrast, WBGU views the universal realization of human rights and labour rights conventions as a key condition of sustainable poverty reduction.

PUTTING PARTICIPATION OF THE POOR ON THE AGENDA
The international goals contain relatively few statements on enabling and empowering the poor to participate with equal rights in political, economic, social and cultural processes. A key aspect in poverty reduction, however, is the access of the poor to goods and services provided by the ecosystems in their own territories. In this context, it is important that they have a say in decisions on relevant utilization and management strategies. Other issues to be placed on the agenda are transparency and accountability of the public sector, and the necessary structural changes to realize equal rights and living conditions for women and men.

TAKING ACCOUNT OF INTERACTIONS AND CONFLICTS BETWEEN GOAL DIMENSIONS
Poverty and environment dimensions are tightly coupled. Hence it is impossible to tackle and solve these problems by working on separate goal dimensions in isolation. This may even give rise to conflicts of objectives. In the long term, development policy will not be successful if the environment dimensions are disregarded. Equally, the isolated pursuit of environmental goals without considering the impacts on the living conditions of poor people has poor prospects of success. What is needed is an integrated approach as WBGU has repeatedly called for in its reports (WBGU, 2001b).

This necessitates further reinforcement of existing assessment, coordination and integration functions on the global institutional level. Assessment must build upon input from scientists and research-based policy advisors, who should be in a position to undertake cross-sectoral analysis and develop suitable recommendations (Section 4.3.4). In Chapter 5 of this report, recommendations are made for improving the coordination and integration functions.

EXTENDING THE TIME HORIZON

An anticipatory style of policy must be adopted to counter the long-term impacts of global environmental change. This is clearly exemplified by the case of climate change mitigation: what WBGU dubbed the 'long-term reduction profile' extends over several decades (WBGU, 1998b). Even if the need to transform energy systems for greater sustainability is addressed with the utmost vigour, in 15 years the necessary adaptations of energy systems will still be in their infancy (WBGU, 2004). A similar case can be made with regard to biodiversity loss. Natural ecosystems which are destroyed today can trigger species losses which only become evident many years or decades later. Reversibility in natural ecosystems must even be measured in centuries or millennia. Hence, an appropriate time horizon for the study of global environmental change would extend to the middle of the century. Likewise, in relation to the socio-economic goals, the realization of a full-scale sustainability strategy will take until long after the year 2015. By contrast, all the MDGs and Johannesburg goals relate to target dates before 2020 (Section 2.1). Therefore these goals can only be first significant milestones on a longer route towards sustainable development. WBGU recommends long-term in-process review and refinement of the goals at world conferences at regular intervals.

REFINING ENVIRONMENTAL GOALS

In the long term, poverty reduction can only be successful if natural resources are conserved as life-support systems. Global environmental change is of major and growing importance for the poor due to their vulnerability. It is thus a necessary though not a sufficient condition for broad-scale poverty reduction to halt global environmental degradation by complying with ecological guard rails (Section 3.3). The consequences of violating the guard rails weigh considerably more heavily upon developing countries and especially their poor populations, because of their increased vulnerability, than on industrialized countries. However, it is important to note that even adhering to the ecological guard rails cannot guarantee that all regions will be protected from far-reaching consequences (Section 2.3.1).

These facts are not made explicit in the Millennium Development Goals. Coverage of the environmental dimension of sustainability is beset with inadequacies and omissions. Environmental problems such as climate change which will increasingly have life-threatening impacts, particularly for poor people, are not given sufficient prominence. The heavy focus on socio-political shortcomings promotes the illusion that poverty reduction can be achieved in isolation from the condition of natural life-support systems. Target 9 listed under environmental Goal 7 remains sweeping and abstract ('Integrate the principles of sustainable development (...), reverse the loss of environmental resources') and does not adequately reflect the current environmental debate and the approaches deemed most effective (Table 2.1-1). The associated indicators do not permit meaningful conclusions on the requisite measures and success of implementation, because they are drawn relatively arbitrarily from an array of relevant crises. Moreover, unlike the poverty reduction goals, no measurable criteria or deadlines have been specified for this target.

These shortcomings have already been discussed at the WSSD. Admittedly, the resolutions passed at that summit add important environmental policy dimensions to the list of MDG targets and are geared towards the implementation of global sustainable development (Section 2.1.4). In their analytical substance, the Johannesburg Declaration and the accompanying Plan of Implementation do take account of the systemic interactions between poverty reduction and preservation of the global ecological balance. Nevertheless, the goals and indicators derived from them are not adequate. WBGU believes that a more distinct framing of the environmental goal dimension of sustainability, together with the adoption of indicators better able to capture trends, is an international policy objective of the highest priority.

A good political opportunity to strengthen the environmental dimension of the MDGs is provided by the UN conference to review progress with the international development goals, the Millennium Summit 2000+5 in September 2005. Taking the guard rail concept as a basis, WBGU's thematic reports, its analysis of the various environment dimensions and its associated recommendations (Section 3.3) give concrete pointers on which ecological goals the international community should aim for on the different environment dimensions.

Even though from the viewpoint of WBGU the Millennium Development Goals exhibit distinct shortcomings, they should be understood – in combination with the resolutions of the WSSD – as a first step towards a consensual global sustainability strategy, and their momentum should be utilized. The present report provides the necessary reference points and guidelines. A key prerequisite for the effectiveness of international efforts is that state action should be coherent on all levels. This applies to collaboration among different ministries and actors over the design of country-level programmes, as well as to multilateral and transnational regimes and policy processes.

Linkages among international environment and development policy spheres 4

4.1
The new setting of global politics

The conditions under which the international community can act to overcome the global environmental and development crisis have changed radically in recent years. The key factors responsible for this change are as follows:

1. *Globalization:* The collapse of the bipolar world order since the end of the 1980s has accelerated the dissolution of the boundaries between economic spaces. Information, goods, capital and financial flows are increasingly evading national control, while comparable rules governing transnational transactions do not (yet) exist. Technological progress in the information and communications industry and the transport sector is a significant force driving the integration of actors, regions and systems. Even the industrialized nations cannot evade the ensuing interdependencies and mutual vulnerabilities within the 'World Risk Society' (Ulrich Beck); this applies as much to the globalization of insecurity through international terrorism as it does to instability in the financial markets or the impacts of climate change. However, the capacities of societies and political systems to cope with these transnational challenges vary substantially. Globalization heightens the differential vulnerability of demographic groups and countries (Section 3.1.2).

2. *The North-South power divide:* Since the start of the 21st century, the negotiating power of the Group of 77 and China (G77/China) on contentious global economic issues has been greatly weakened by internal conflicts of interest. Furthermore, this group of states, now comprising 132 developing countries, either has no representation at all or is under-represented or has very limited negotiating powers in the international organizations in which key global policy and economic decisions are adopted:

   - In the Boards of Directors of the IMF and World Bank, the OECD countries – the numerical minority in these bodies – control most of the votes, which are weighted according to the number of shares held. The developing, newly industrializing and transition countries, which account for 89 per cent of the world's population, have just 38 per cent of the total votes.
   - In the UN Security Council, China is one of the privileged permanent members which have the right to veto any decision, but the major regions of the world – Latin America, Africa and Asia (excluding China) – are only represented as non-permanent members with lesser status, which are elected via a rotation procedure. Within a matter of decades, India, already a nuclear power, will overtake China as the world's most populous country. Both countries are already political and military heavyweights.
   - In the WTO, all members are formally granted equal rights, but despite the requirement for decisions to be adopted by consensus, key decisions are reached through informal bargaining among the major global economic actors. Many developing countries lack the analytical and negotiating capacities needed to deal with the complex WTO rules, and are therefore scarcely capable of exploiting the opportunities afforded by the multilateral rules to enhance their own prosperity.

   However, various movements have now emerged to challenge the dominance of the OECD countries in international organizations and negotiations. The Group of 21 (G21) – an alliance of 21 major developing and newly industrializing countries formed at the WTO Ministerial Conference in the Mexican city of Cancún – successfully vetoed the OECD countries' attempt to assert their interests on key topics under negotiation, although the alliance's position also led to deadlock over the issue of farm subsidies, which are seen as highly detrimental to development.

3. *The developing countries' negotiating power in international environmental policy:* Contrasting sharply with the weak position of the Group of 77 and China in the global power hierarchy and

in negotiations on North-South trade relations, the developing countries have gained substantial influence over negotiations on global environmental policy, which has become a new arena in the North-South conflict (Sachs, 1993). In this policy field, the South can impose conditions on the North because the North is reliant on the South's cooperation on many environmental issues: 'The developing countries' newly acquired negotiating power in global environmental policy is not directly based on their economic or, indeed, military potential but on their opportunity, due to the functioning of the global ecological system, to damage the environment in the industrialized countries, either intentionally or as a result of failings on the part of the state' (Biermann, 1998).

The developing countries' increased negotiating power in the global environmental policy field does not only have positive implications for sustainability policy, however. The elites in these countries are often dependent on increased resource consumption and regard environmental protection as a luxury which only the wealthy countries can afford. They claim the right to exploit their abundant natural resources (such as tropical forests and marine economic zones) and oppose the new 'eco-imperialism' which, in their view, is simply an attempt to restrict their sovereign rights over their natural resources under the pretext of protecting the global environment. It was the OPEC countries which exerted their geostrategic influence as suppliers of a scarce resource in order to block moves to reconfigure global energy systems, with Saudi Arabia, the leading power within OPEC, throwing its weight behind the US Government's strategy rejecting the Kyoto Protocol. The CIS states – some of which belong to the Middle Eastern 'energy ellipse', but all of which face major adaptation and poverty problems – have also shown little interest in any 'greening' of the patterns of production and consumption. Many developing countries – notably those with the greatest influence in the international political and economic arena – are applying the brakes rather than driving forward policies geared towards sustainability. They have opted in favour of this role because they give primacy to economic growth and have yet to fully accept the correlations between poverty and environmental degradation. Any hope that the South could 'go green' in tandem with its economic development, as has occurred at least to some extent in the North due to the shift towards post-materialist values, is an illusion (Jänicke, 1998).

4. *Failed states and anarchic tendencies:* Since the end of the Cold War, the global political situation has not become more peaceful; on the contrary, it is now more turbulent and conflict-ridden. Although the number of inter-state wars has decreased, numerous ethnic and political conflicts have broken out. War and conflict have a major and adverse impact on countries' ranking in UNDP's Human Development Index and, according to FAO, are the cause of half the famines in Africa (FAO, 2003b). In a rising number of African countries, legal and administrative structures have collapsed, along with the state's monopoly of force, leaving a power vacuum in which warlords have been able to establish repressive regimes. This group of failed states poses a security and development problem by destabilizing entire regions, impeding the development of at least a partly ordered economic and social life and undermining any viable development cooperation. But they have also become an environmental problem because the warlords and their militias, but also the governments, ruthlessly exploit the natural resource base for their own enrichment and for weapons procurement. The international community has so far been reluctant to intervene with preventive and, if necessary, repressive measures to restore peace and thus create the conditions for development.

These trends must be taken into account in the following analysis of key international policy processes and institutions operating in the fields of environmental protection and poverty reduction.

4.2
Assessment of key policy processes and institutions

This chapter will explore international policy processes in the fields of environment and development on a comparative basis. The intention is not to provide a comprehensive overview of all the relevant policy processes or actors but to focus on processes and actors which play a key role in the nexus between environmental policy and poverty eradication. It also discusses the WTO and the IMF – two institutions whose primary purpose is not poverty reduction or environmental protection but whose activities nonetheless substantially influence the prospects for successful global development and environmental policy.

Each section starts with a brief description of the specific policy processes and actors. This is followed by a qualitative assessment of the impacts of these processes on poverty reduction and global environmental problems. The questions whether, and how, environmental protection measures also have positive effects on poverty reduction and whether successes in poverty reduction can trigger improvements in the environmental field will also be explored.

The analysis of poverty reduction policies is based on the dimensions of poverty discussed in Section 3.2 above and the associated international goals. Similarly, the analysis of environmental impacts is based on the environmental aspects explored in Section 3.3 and the associated environmental guard rails. The overall assessment identifies the policy processes which are especially suitable for environmental protection and poverty reduction. The aim is also to illustrate the conditions under which individual policy processes can be especially effective in combating poverty or addressing global environmental problems and to determine whether positive synergies can be generated between the two policy areas. Finally, various policy processes will also be examined in terms of their financial resources, enabling a judgement to be made on whether reinforcing these policy processes is desirable and/or feasible.

4.2.1
Framework Convention on Climate Change

4.2.1.1
Purpose and goals

The United Nations Framework Convention on Climate Change (UNFCCC) was signed by 154 countries at the UN Conference on Environment and Development in 1992. It entered into force on 21 March 1994 and by May 2004, had been signed or ratified by 189 countries. The ultimate objective of the Convention is the stabilization of greenhouse gas concentrations in the atmosphere at a level that would prevent dangerous anthropogenic interference with the climate system. Such a level should be achieved within a time-frame sufficient to allow ecosystems to adapt naturally to climate change, to ensure that food production is not threatened and to enable economic development to proceed in a sustainable manner (Article 2 UNFCCC). In accordance with the principle of common but differentiated responsibilities, the industrialized countries pledge to take the lead in combating climate change and the adverse effects thereof (Article 3 (1) UNFCCC).

The Convention makes several references to poverty. For example, the Preamble states that 'responses to climate change should be coordinated with social and economic development in an integrated manner with a view to avoiding adverse impacts on the latter, taking into full account the legitimate priority needs of developing countries for the achievement

of sustained economic growth and the eradication of poverty'. Article 4 (7) addresses this priority: in relation to the implementation of commitments, it is fully taken into account that 'economic and social development and poverty eradication are the first and overriding priorities' of the developing countries.

THE KYOTO PROTOCOL

The Kyoto Protocol, adopted at the Third Session of the Conference of the Parties to the UN Framework Convention on Climate Change (COP 3) in December 1997, sets binding numerical targets for the limitation and reduction of greenhouse gas emissions – carbon dioxide, methane, nitrous oxide, hydrofluorocarbons, perfluorocarbons and sulphur hexafluoride – for the industrialized and transition countries during the period 2008-2012. No numerical targets for the reduction of emissions were set for the developing countries, but they are required to report on their emissions. By September 2004, the Kyoto Protocol had been ratified by 125 countries and was thus recognized as binding. For the Protocol to enter into force, it must be ratified by 55 Parties to the Convention, incorporating as many industrialized countries as accounted in total for at least 55 per cent of the total carbon dioxide emissions for 1990 of Annex I countries (Article 25 (1)). Following Russia's decision to ratify the Kyoto Protocol, it entered into force on 16 February 2005. The EU adopted a separate decision to introduce an emissions trading scheme irrespective of the status of the Kyoto Protocol. The EU Member States thus have the opportunity to grant limited recognition to credits from the project-based Kyoto instruments, i.e. the Clean Development Mechanism (CDM) and Joint Implementation (JI).

4.2.1.2
Effect upon the nexus of poverty and climate change

The goals of the Framework Convention on Climate Change are both to prevent future climate change and to adapt to climate change. As the poorer countries will be particularly hard hit by the predicted impacts of climate change (Section 3.3.1), and since climate change is also likely to exacerbate poverty, policies aimed at preventing climate change will have a positive impact on eradicating poverty. However, this is a long-term correlation, and the positive impacts are to be expected only over a period of several decades. An immediate benefit to the developing countries may arise through the combination of emissions prevention and sustainable development, as envisaged in the Kyoto Protocol in relation to CDM. However, measures which assist the developing countries to adapt to climate change will also become increasingly important.

Preventing climate change

Poverty reduction in the developing countries is generally accompanied by a rise in per capita energy and resource use and therefore also an increase in greenhouse gas emissions. The Climate Change Convention and the Kyoto Protocol take account of this correlation in that emission limitation and reduction targets have only been agreed for the industrialized countries to date. However, in order to achieve the ultimate objective of the UNFCCC – namely to prevent dangerous anthropogenic interference with the climate system – economic development in all countries must be decoupled from the emission of greenhouse gases over the medium term. The UNFCCC therefore regulates support for the transfer of 'climate-friendly' technologies to the developing countries, along with human and institutional capacity-building to tackle climate-relevant emissions.

Clean Development Mechanism

Article 12 (2) of the Kyoto Protocol defines the purpose of the Clean Development Mechanism: to assist the developing countries in achieving sustainable development and in contributing to the ultimate objective of the UNFCCC, and to assist the industrialized countries in achieving compliance with their quantified emission limitation and reduction commitments. The CDM offers private investors incentives to carry out greenhouse gas reduction projects in developing countries. The investors benefit from certified emission reductions which they can use as a contribution to fulfil their domestic emission reduction commitments. Alternatively, the certificates may be traded in an emissions trading scheme. The CDM thus offers the opportunity to mobilize additional funds for developing countries, especially in the field of renewables and energy efficiency.

Ideally, the relevant projects in the specific host country should promote sustainable development, e.g. by reducing water or air pollution or by creating jobs. The decision whether a CDM project can be classified as sustainable is entirely a matter for the host country (Ott, 2001), whose priorities therefore determine whether CDM projects will be targeted towards poverty reduction or, alternatively, towards other aspects of sustainable development. However, the developing countries' scope for action largely depends on the supply situation. If CDM projects are in short supply, developing countries could step back from their aim of gaining development benefit from projects so as not to jeopardize potential investment (McGuigan et al., 2002).

For the developing countries, CDM offers an opportunity to raise funds and promote sustainable development. For the industrialized countries, on the other hand, it is a way of complying with emission reduction commitments at low cost. It is likely, therefore, that investors from the industrialized countries will favour projects which hold out the promise of maximum emission reductions at minimal cost. These are not necessarily projects which should be prioritized from a sustainable development perspective (Austin et al., 1999). For example, afforestation projects based on fast-growing, monocultural tree plantations may be problematical (WBGU, 2001a; OECD, 2002a). Analyses of CDM projects currently being planned show that the number of small-scale projects in the field of renewables and energy efficiency is declining while the number of large-scale end-of-pipe projects is rising. These projects typically reduce the proportion of greenhouse gases such as CH_4 or HFC emitted by industrial plants, but have few direct economic, social or environmental benefits contributing to sustainable development (Ellis et al., 2004). Studies also indicate that without further conditionalities, the majority of projects will be carried out in those developing countries which already attract the lion's share of foreign direct investment (Michaelowa et al., 2003) or those with significantly increasing emissions that are therefore offering considerable potential for avoiding emissions (Troni et al., 2002). This largely excludes the poorest countries.

The type of CDM projects being carried out and therefore their potential to foster poverty reduction can be influenced by pooling investments within designated funds. The World Bank, for example, has launched the Community Development Carbon Fund which focuses on small-scale projects in poor rural communities in the developing countries. The CDM evaluation procedure ensures the projects' environmental relevance, while a further CDCF-specific evaluation verifies their impact on poverty reduction. At the same time, transaction costs are reduced and the risks spread, thus giving smaller investors access to the CDM as well. Other opportunities are afforded by investors' voluntary commitments to specific standards, such as the Gold Standard launched by the World Wildlife Fund, which certifies CDM projects fulfilling a list of specific sustainability criteria (WWF, 2004).

Investors are responsible for financing the additional costs of CDM projects against a reference project which does not involve emissions reduction. These additional costs must be covered by the certified emission reductions whose value, in turn, largely depends on their tradability and therefore on the Kyoto Protocol's entry into force and/or the number of participating states. Following a vote in the European Parliament in April 2004, European companies will be able to count credits from CDM projects towards their obligations under the EU's emissions trading scheme, which will also influence the demand for CDM projects. However, the option of hosting CDM projects is only available to countries which have ratified the Kyoto Protocol. To date (July 2004), just 23 out of 47 LDCs have ratified the Protocol.

MAINTAINING CARBON STOCKS

At present, the Kyoto Protocol does not provide any incentives to conserve the natural carbon stocks of terrestrial ecosystems, such as primary forests, wetlands and grasslands, in the developing countries. WBGU considers that such incentives are required and, in previous reports, has called for the introduction of a relevant additional protocol. This should define commitments relating to the conservation of these natural carbon stocks and offer economic incentives to encourage a shift away from destructive land use (WBGU, 2003). The conservation and sustainable use of these ecosystems would benefit poor people and indigenous communities, which rely on them as natural life-support systems (Section 3.3.4). Furthermore, in the resource-rich developing countries, tradable non utilization commitment certificates could help to reduce poverty (Section 5.6). The protection of ecosystems also accords with the principles of the Convention on Biological Diversity (CBD), so negotiations on an additional protocol must tie in with the objectives of the CBD (Section 4.2.2). Measures to combat desertification, e.g. by preventing erosion, also help to conserve natural carbon stocks in soil, so here too, synergies can be anticipated and generated between the UNCCD (Section 4.2.3) and UNFCCC. Cooperation between the various Conventions is therefore appropriate and useful.

ADAPTING TO CLIMATE CHANGE

The impacts of present and future climate change vary considerably from region to region, so the design of potential adaptation measures must also vary. The Third Assessment Report produced by the IPCC summarizes the current state of knowledge about the regional manifestations of climate change and thus offers a basis on which to develop national adaptation strategies (IPCC, 2001a, b). For almost all the poor countries, this will necessitate reforms in the agricultural and water management sectors, for example. Many of these countries will also have to adopt measures to protect against storm damage, flooding and soil erosion. Many measures one can think of (e.g. improved water management, protecting coastlines by mangrove planting, better safety of buildings to

protect against storm damage, establishment of early warning systems) reduce poor communities' overall vulnerability to environmental changes and natural disasters. In other words, they are no-regret measures which will promote sustainable development irrespective of climate change (ADB et al., 2003). Adaptation to the impacts of climate change should therefore become an integral component of national development strategies.

Although the need for adaptation to climate change is mentioned in many parts of the Convention, attention has only recently started to focus on practical implementation and financing, largely as a result of pressure from the developing countries.

4.2.1.3
Financing

Article 4 of the UNFCCC states that the industrialized countries and other developed Annex II countries shall provide new and additional financial resources for the developing countries in complying with their obligations (preparation of country reports, etc.) and for the development and enhancement of their capacities and technologies for adaptation to and prevention of climate change. The Global Environment Facility (GEF) operates as the financial mechanism of the UNFCCC and other multilateral environmental agreements. From 1991 to 2002, GEF allocated some US$1,500 million in grants to climate change projects; this funding has leveraged an additional US$5,000 million in cofinancing contributions from the private sector (Section 4.2.8). Most of these financial resources were allocated to projects aimed at mitigating climate change (UNFCCC, 2002a). The GEF has established four Operational Programs in the field of climate protection:
1. Removal of Barriers to Energy Efficiency and Energy Conservation,
2. Promoting the Adoption of Renewable Energy by Removing Barriers and Reducing Implementation Costs,
3. Reducing the Long-Term Costs of Low Greenhouse Gas Emitting Energy Technologies,
4. Promoting Environmentally Sustainable Transport.

At the Seventh Session of the Conference of the Parties to the Climate Change Convention (COP 7) in Marrakesh in 2001, the launch of three new funds was agreed, two to be funded by voluntary contributions from the parties to the UNFCCC, and the third operating within the Kyoto Protocol.
- The *Special Climate Change Fund* was set up to assist developing countries to implement programmes and measures that are complemen-

tary to those funded by GEF. In accordance with the decision adopted at the Ninth Session of the Conference of the Parties (COP 9) in Milan in 2003, adaptation activities to address the adverse impacts of climate change have top priority for funding. Technology transfer and capacity-building for technology transfer are identified as priority areas (UNFCCC, 2003). A decision on two other areas identified at Marrakesh in 2001 (firstly, energy, transport, industry, agriculture, forestry and waste management, and, secondly, activities to assist developing countries in diversifying their economies) is anticipated at the Tenth Session of the Conference of the Parties (COP 10) in December 2004. The financial scope of the fund is unclear at present.

- The *Least Developed Countries Fund* is designed specifically to assist the poorest countries (LDCs). It provides support for the preparation of National Adaptation Programmes of Action (NAPAs) by the LDCs and is advised by a Least Developed Countries Expert Group. The NAPAs are short documents in which the LDCs outline the adaptation measures that are most urgently required. The NAPAs shall be designed in a way which facilitates the integration of adaptation strategies into existing national and international development programmes and strategies and other policies (UNFCCC, 2002a). A large number of NAPAs is currently in preparation. In April 2004, the pledged contributions to the Fund stood at US$35 million in total, with contributions paid amounting to US$16.5 million. Germany has pledged US$15 million in total, with US$3 million already paid, making it the largest donor (GEF, 2004b).

- The *Kyoto Protocol Adaptation Fund* is to support the implementation of concrete adaptation projects and programmes in developing countries which are parties to the Kyoto Protocol. The Fund will be financed from a 2 per cent share of the proceeds on CDM projects, to be supplemented by voluntary contributions from the parties to the Kyoto Protocol. The financial scope of the Fund therefore largely depends on the development of the CDM market and is still unclear at this stage.

Furthermore, in the business plan for GEF's financial period 2005–2007, a sum of US$50 million is earmarked for a new strategic priority, namely the operationalization of adaptation measures (GEF, 2004a).

4.2.1.4
Assessment

For the energy sector, the UNFCCC provides an appropriate framework and, in principle, suitable instruments to encourage sustainable development and, associated with that, poverty reduction in the developing countries. However, special incentives are required to ensure that the poorest countries and population groups also benefit from this. In contrast, the UNFCCC at present does not give adequate support to sustainable development in the forestry and agricultural sectors even though these sectors account for a substantial proportion of greenhouse gas emissions produced in the developing countries. Strategies for adaptation to unavoidable climatic changes have only recently become the focus of debate, so it is still too early for any assessment to be made. However, it is already apparent that the financial instruments planned to date (adaptation funds) are quite inadequate in scale to address the problem.

4.2.1.5
Recommendations

- It is essential to decouple economic development in industrialized and transformation countries – and, as soon as possible, in developing countries – from the emission of greenhouse gases. This issue should become a stronger focus of debate and be adopted as an objective. This will require research as well as the political will to implement appropriate measures across all departments of government.

- Regarding the further development of the rules governing the allocation of financial resources from the SCCF, LDCF and Kyoto Protocol Adaptation Fund, the German government should work pro-actively to ensure that synergies are utilized to a greater extent for the benefit of poverty reduction.

- The resources available to the adaptation funds should be increased and their financial base secured. To this end, the Council has already recommended that a state's relative contribution to the funding required to offset climate damage and facilitate adaptation to climate change should match its own relative contribution to global warming (WBGU, 2003).

- A Compensation Fund should be established in order to enable countries particularly affected by climate change to gain compensation for climate related damages (Section 5.6.3.3).

- The German government should provide support for measures and initiatives which create incentives for more investment in those countries and regions which are especially affected by poverty, as well as for poverty-relevant projects within the CDM framework. The certification of projects which promote compliance with specific quality standards (e.g. the WWF Gold Standard) or funds – such as the World Bank's CDCF – which pool investment and support poverty-relevant projects offer opportunities in this context. However, it is still too early, at this stage, to make a firm assessment of the CDCF.

- Not only adaptation to, but prevention of, climate change should be integral elements of bi- and multilateral development policy. Here, horizontal integration (mainstreaming) is required, which means that at all levels and stages of development projects and programmes, their impacts on the objectives of the UNFCCC and on capacities to adapt to unavoidable climate change must be monitored, considered and evaluated.

- Internationally binding rules on the conservation of natural carbon stocks should be adopted, also taking account of the aims and objectives of the Convention on Biological Diversity and the needs of local communities. These rules should give special priority to protecting the areas home to indigenous communities.

4.2.2
Convention on Biological Diversity

4.2.2.1
Purpose and goals

The Convention on Biological Diversity (Biodiversity Convention – CBD), which was adopted at the Rio Conference and entered into force in 1993, is an expression of an integrative approach: the CBD emphasizes the connection between conservation and use of biodiversity and attempts to balance the interests of North and South. Industrialized countries have an interest in access to genetic resources and in conservation of biological diversity, not only in their own countries, but in developing countries too. Developing countries, which are rich in biodiversity, should be able to derive benefits from the use of their biodiversity and genetic resources, and, via technical and financial assistance, be enabled to improve nature conservation. The Convention does not set out concrete, quantitative goals or commitments. By formulating concepts, goals and principles, it primarily attempts to establish a framework for common understanding concerning management of the biosphere (WBGU, 2001a). It can be supplemented by protocols that are binding under international law, in which commitments are set out in more concrete terms (e.g. the Biosafety Protocol).

The objectives of the Convention are (1) the conservation of biodiversity, (2) the sustainable use of its components, and (3) the fair and equitable sharing of the benefits arising out of the utilization of genetic resources (Art. 1). The Convention has now gained almost universal acceptance, with only Andorra, Brunei, the Vatican, Iraq, Somalia, East Timor and the USA (the latter due to fundamental political reservations) having declined to ratify it to date.

In order to differentiate among the general provisions, the Convention develops programmes of work, voluntary guidelines and supplementary protocols that are binding under international law, and whose implementation is supported via the Global Environment Facility (GEF) (Section 4.2.8). One focus is its work on different types of ecosystem (drylands, forests, marine and coastal ecosystems, inland waters, agricultural ecosystems, etc.). Recommendations are developed concerning, among other things, conservation and sustainable use tailored to each ecosystem. Of particular importance is the overarching conceptual work of the CBD, e.g. the development of the ecosystem approach, which includes principles for managing ecosystems and their biodiversity.

In addition, the CBD undertakes studies addressing cross-cutting issues of relevance to all thematic areas (access to genetic resources and benefit-sharing, biological diversity and tourism, invasive alien species, traditional knowledge, indicators, protected areas, etc.). Proposals and guidelines for action are developed to address these issues, which can then serve as the basis for developing national legislation and programmes. These guidelines, which are initially voluntary, are intended to be put to the test via practical implementation by the Parties to the Convention before being translated into binding regulations under international law.

With the Cartagena Protocol on Biosafety, the step towards establishing regulations that are legally binding has already been taken concerning the important issue of the safe transfer, handling and use of living modified organisms. The Protocol focuses primarily on the import and export of genetically modified seed, food and feed, and issues relating to the safe handling of genetically modified plants, identification and liability. The Protocol entered into effect in September 2003 and has now been ratified by 87 countries.

At the World Summit on Sustainable Development (WSSD) in 2002, the position of the CBD as the key international regime on the biosphere was explicitly confirmed. Likewise, the 2010 target adopted in the strategic plan of the Convention at the 6th Conference of the Parties (CBD, 2002a) was included in the Johannesburg Plan of Implementation. In it, the international community declared its support for the goal of the 'achievement by 2010 of a significant reduction in the current rate of loss of biological diversity'. As a result of the resolution on the establishment of an international regime on access to genetic resources and on benefit-sharing within the framework of the CBD, this issue has been high on the agenda again since Johannesburg (Section 4.2.2.3).

4.2.2.2
Poverty as a theme in the CBD process

WBGU has set out comprehensive recommendations on the CBD in its previous reports (WBGU, 2001a). In this section, we will deal only with the connection between poverty and biodiversity. For many people, securing biodiversity is a prerequisite for sustainable development and poverty reduction. In particular, poor rural population groups in developing countries depend on using biodiversity (Section 3.3.4). The Convention thus operates in an area of conflict between environment and development priorities.

Poverty alleviation is not, however, one of the primary, concrete objectives of the CBD. Although the close link between biological diversity and development is mentioned in the preamble to the Biodiversity Convention, neither poverty reduction nor sustainable development are given any prominence in other sections of the Convention. Even in the Bonn Guidelines regulating access to genetic resources and benefit-sharing, poverty alleviation only crops up in the general objectives, and not in the concrete operational sections (CBD, 2002b), although in this case the potential positive impact on poverty reduction is obvious (Stoll, 2004; Section 4.2.2.3).

The text of the Convention states twice (in the Preamble and in Art. 20, paragraph 4) that 'economic and social development and poverty eradication are the first and overriding priorities of developing countries'. Therefore, in the event of any conflict over objectives, the priorities of the developing countries lie firmly on the side of economic and social development.

In contrast, the Strategic Plan for the Convention clearly affirms that conservation of biological diversity contributes to poverty alleviation (CBD, 2002a): 'biological diversity provides goods and services that underpin sustainable development in many important ways, thus contributing to poverty alleviation. First, it supports the ecosystem functions essential for life on Earth, such as the provision of fresh water, soil conservation and climate stability. Second, it provides products such as food, medicines and materials for industry. Finally, biodiversity is at the heart of many cultural values.' The strategic 2010 goal mentioned above is also seen as contributing to poverty reduction (CBD, 2002a).

The stance of the Convention as regards poverty reduction is thus ambivalent. On the one hand, conservation and sustainable use of biological diversity and its close link with poverty reduction and sustainable development crops up again and again at the highest level, in the preambles and lists of objectives in resolutions of the Conferences of the Parties to the Convention. In concrete proposals for action, on the other hand, poverty reduction only plays a subordinate role.

Of the many issues covered by the Convention, the following section will focus on examining one priority issue that is of considerable significance for the nexus of nature conservation and poverty reduction, and is currently the subject of international debate.

4.2.2.3
Focus: Access to genetic resources, benefit-sharing and the use of traditional knowledge

WBGU has already discussed in depth the great significance of genetic resources for industry and agriculture (WBGU, 2001a). The CBD has set new standards by linking access to genetic resources with benefit-sharing (ABS). States (not landowners) have rights of disposal over genetic resources, and access to these resources requires the approval of the country of origin and must take place according to pre-agreed terms and conditions (WBGU, 1995; Henne, 1998).

Access to plant genetic resources for food and agriculture has been subject to separate international regulations since the entry into force of the International Treaty on Plant Genetic Resources for Food and Agriculture in 2004 (Stoll, 2004; Section 4.2.4.2).

The expected outcome of the ABS regulations of the CBD is that negotiating ABS contracts between applicants for access in industrialized countries and the countries of origin, and thereby harnessing the economic value of biological diversity, will on the one hand create positive incentives to protect biodiversity and, on the other, generate income for developing countries. The distribution of this income within the developing countries is still an open question, however.

Initial pilot projects engendered hopes of being able to establish methods of prospecting for biological material for industrial purposes (bioprospecting) that would be compatible with CBD rules, in other words, that would bring financial resources and knowledge to developing countries and provide companies in developed countries with access to the desired genetic resources. The actual outcome, however, has fallen far short of expectations (Stoll, 2004). For example, the much-cited agreement between

Merck and INBio (WBGU, 1995) has so far generated no new products. No other agreements of such major significance have been concluded (Dalton, 2004b), and only a few successful cases of individual ABS contracts are known (Henne et al., 2003). In addition, even though the CBD has been in existence for more than ten years, there are still deficits as regards its implementation: there have been repeated cases of genetic resources being utilized without the consent of the country of origin ('biopiracy').

This disappointing overall outcome is at least in part due to the fact that, in order for ABS contracts to be successful, a number of important conditions must be met:

- There must be reliable demand for genetic resources.
- Unless prices for genetic resources are attractive, ABS contracts will not be able to exert any significant financing effects.
- Clear and practicable international and national rules are crucial in order to create positive incentives for fair ABS contracts and cut transaction costs. These rules must be verifiable and not easy to circumvent.

DEMAND FOR GENETIC RESOURCES

Agricultural research is just as dependent on genetic resources for developing new and improved crop varieties (Section 4.2.5) as the chemical or pharmaceutical industry (WBGU, 1999). Naturally occurring substances or their derivatives account for just under one-third (Proksch, 2004) of global annual turnover on the pharmaceuticals market (approx. US$400,000 million; Labrador, 2003). 42 per cent of the 25 most successful medicines world-wide are naturally occurring substances or derived from them (ten Kate and Laird, 1999). Naturally occurring substances also play an important role in the discovery of new chemical structures. They are comparable to blueprints, serving as the starting point for further work to optimize their chemical structure, which, after considerable investment and laborious testing, can then lead to new medicines. The use of traditional knowledge is likewise important for modern research into active substances, although this should not be overestimated (Proksch, 2004).

In the period 1981–2002, naturally occurring substances and their derivatives accounted for 38 per cent of new anti-cancer agents developed; in the case of anti-bacterial agents the share was as high as 78 per cent (Newman et al., 2003). The potential of naturally occurring substances as sources of future active substances is also thought to be considerable: microbial ecology, marine ecosystems, tropical biotopes (coral reefs, rainforests) and extreme natural environments in particular are seen as possible locations where new chemical structures might be discovered (Proksch, 2004). In principle, this potential is an important motivating factor for protecting natural ecosystems from destruction (WBGU, 2001a). On the other hand, however, the quantities of sample material required for experimentation and analysis, or indeed for actual therapeutic use, may be so great that collection in the wild is no longer sustainable and the ecosystem is thus put at risk (WBGU, 2001a; Proksch, 2004).

Demand is curbed by the fact that there are indeed alternatives for industry other than gathering naturally occurring substances from their natural ecosystems in developing countries. On the one hand, access is still freely available to 'old' biological substance banks and gene banks in developed countries (botanical and zoological gardens, museums, collections, etc.) established prior to the entry into force of the CBD. Considerable use is certainly made of this possibility (Stoll, 2000). Moreover, due to the lack of control mechanisms, it is possible to acquire genetic resources in ways that are incompatible with the Convention ('biopiracy') without much risk. In addition, there are synthetic procedures that can be used successfully without recourse to naturally occurring substances. In some cases, research into naturally occurring substances is regarded as too expensive, too slow and too problematic to keep pace with these modern methods (ten Kate and Laird, 1999). Nowadays it is mainly small, specialized firms that are involved in bioprospecting for naturally occurring substances, while research into these substances by many major biotechnology firms has been cut back in recent years (Newman et al., 2003; Dalton, 2004b). This trend could rapidly be reversed, however, by new successes in research into naturally occurring substances (ten Kate and Laird, 1999).

FINANCIAL IMPACT

Assessing the possible financial impact of ABS contracts presents some difficulty. A successful drug can produce an annual turnover of several thousand million US$, but the likelihood of a particular sample providing the starting point for a success on this scale is extremely slight. The majority of R&D expenditure is incurred only after a new, active chemical lead compound has been identified, and this compound does not generally match the original, naturally occurring substance, but is derived from it. Calculating the 'fair' share of a sample taken from a natural ecosystem in a product's success is exceedingly difficult. Since genetic resources are right at the beginning of the value chain and thus have something of the nature of 'raw materials', observers reckon that the pharmaceutical companies will be reluctant to pay much for them (Soete, 2003). The few ABS contracts that do exist provide for payments in the region of 1–5 per cent of product sales. Even in the case of a successful product, the financial flows generated in this way would not come anywhere close to providing an adequate incentive for conserving natural ecosystems or combating poverty (Henne et al., 2003; Section 3.4).

An important reason for these seemingly low figures is the fact that the balance of information and negotiating power between the contracting parties in ABS contracts is weighted against the provider (Stoll, 2004). Consequently, discussions are taking place in one group of developing countries with a view to establishing a resource cartel, which, in conjunction with a common regime for access and benefit-sharing, would be able to command higher prices for genetic resources (Group of Like-Minded Megadiverse Countries, 2003; Vogel, 1994). However, a cartel of this sort would not necessarily guarantee success, because the new genetic resources acquired through bioprospecting are at least partially substitutable. If the asking price rises, the incentive for the demander to find alternatives also increases.

If a larger share of the research were transferred to developing countries, the financial effects for developing countries would be enhanced. In such a case, not only genetic raw materials, but also high-value intermediate products (extracts, screening products) would be exported (Reid et al., 1993). Moreover, joint research projects with scientists on the ground have both direct and indirect positive effects in terms of biodiversity conservation (Coley et al., 2003). In order to eliminate the imbalance in negotiating power and promote high-quality products, capacity building of individuals, institutions and communities in developing countries in the area of access and benefit-sharing (e.g. legal know-how, developing biotechnological competence) is crucial.

INTERNATIONAL AND NATIONAL RULES
The current situation is marked by legal uncertainty and mistrust (Stoll, 2000). Developing countries are demanding an end to unlicensed utilization of their genetic resources. Companies and researchers from developed countries complain that their work is being impeded by new administrative hurdles (Dalton, 2004a; Pethiyagoda, 2004). There is a lack of transparent, practicable and verifiable rules (Stoll, 2004).

The non-legally binding Bonn Guidelines negotiated in the framework of the Convention are an important step towards promoting translation of the CBD into national law – countries' efforts in this regard continue to be disappointing – and providing advice on drafting ABS contracts. Without waiting for these Guidelines to be implemented and exert an impact, at the World Summit on Sustainable Devel-

opment (WSSD) the international community took the next step in the direction of establishing binding rules under international law with surprising speed, calling for countries to negotiate an international regime on ABS within the framework of the CBD.

In doing this, it will be particularly important to minimize existing shortcomings with regard to verification and identify instruments that enable verification in the user countries too (Barber et al., 2003; Stoll, 2004). Some shortcomings are unlikely to be overcome; for example, it would be next to impossible to apply the CBD rules retroactively to cover access to the great quantities of genetic resources removed from countries before the Convention entered into force and now fill the gene banks and botanical gardens of the developed countries (Henne, 1998; IUCN, 2004). This huge loophole alone makes it exceedingly difficult for countries of origin to prove unauthorized utilization of genetic resources.

A number of instruments are under discussion with a view to reducing loopholes like this. One example is the proposed international certificate of provenance for genetic resources, which would serve as proof of origin and proof that their acquisition complied legally with the provisions of the CBD. Another proposal suggests making the presentation of such a certificate a condition for issuing a patent. Whether proposals of this sort are consistent with existing international law (WIPO, WTO/TRIPS), however, is a matter of some controversy (Ho, 2003; WIPO, 2003).

WBGU recommends using the opportunities provided by the negotiations on the international regime for ABS to eliminate existing shortcomings with regard to implementation and verification. In the context of these negotiations, the German government should support measures to improve verification in user countries. Appropriate instruments, various forms of which are currently under discussion in the international arena, should be tested to assess their consistency, effectiveness and feasibility.

EFFECTIVENESS IN TERMS OF POVERTY REDUCTION
If these conditions are met, and if flows of funds on a considerable scale were generated as a result of ABS contracts, the question of how the revenues obtained should be used in developing countries remains open; the CBD makes no provision that ties these resources to nature conservation or poverty reduction measures (Stoll, 2004).

In extreme cases, the financial flows could even contribute directly to the destruction of natural resources in developing countries, for example if the money were used to promote dubious infrastructure projects in natural ecosystems. Good governance in the sense of sustainable development is therefore a vitally important prerequisite for ensuring that the benefits are used to promote conservation of natural ecosystems and poverty reduction at local level.

Although the CBD is not an instrument for poverty reduction, there are certainly win-win situations that can be achieved by coupling protection of natural ecosystems and poverty reduction (Section 3.3.4). The local level is crucial in this regard. The chances of success are particularly good if local and indigenous communities possess traditional knowledge and this is utilized in accordance with the provisions of the CBD. As these social groups are often marginalized, revenue from the use of their knowledge can bring about a direct improvement in their living conditions. At the same time, this would also have the desirable effect of enhancing the status of the achievements and capabilities of groups living traditional lifestyles.

It is imperative that national legislation and ABS contracts are drafted in such a way as to exclude deployment of any monetary benefits in a manner that destroys natural resources. They should be deployed first and foremost in a manner that promotes both conservation of biological diversity and poverty reduction on the ground. Strengthening the entitlements of indigenous and local communities could also improve chances of success. Traditional knowledge is often directly connected with the use of particular genetic resources. It might be possible to reinforce positive effects at local level if, in addition, the state's rights of disposal over the genetic resources concerned in the local area were also transferred to the local communities in such cases. Bundling rights in this way could enhance incentives to protect biological diversity and at the same time, as a result of the revenues generated, mitigate pressure to overexploit local ecosystems. Research should be undertaken to explore these linkages further.

The German government should continue to back projects that promote capacity building and integration of the CBD goals in national legislation. In doing so, opportunities for linking nature conservation and poverty reduction should be thoroughly explored.

CONCLUSIONS

There are opportunities to create positive effects for poverty reduction via sustainable use of genetic resources on the ground. By improving the local revenue situation, pressure to exploit semi-natural ecosystems is reduced, while incentives and financing for biodiversity conservation are increased. The current situation, however, does not warrant high hopes of any rapid or substantial flows of money, so the financial effects of ABS contracts should not be relied upon when planning either nature conservation or poverty reduction measures. Nevertheless, WBGU believes that there is potential in the medium to long

term, provided the conditions referred to above are created.

4.2.2.4
Poverty, protected areas and sustainable tourism

Poverty can pose a threat to protected areas if it forces the population to overexploit these areas (WPC, 2003b). Protecting natural ecosystems generally entails imposing restrictions on use and access, which often deny indigenous and local communities access to traditional natural resources. A share in the income generated as a result of nature conservation, however, can also alleviate poverty among the local population, for example, if there is an increase in tourism or if payments are made for ecosystem-related services (e.g. ensuring water availability or maintaining a clean water supply by means of forests; Angelsen and Wunder, 2003).

Tourism is one of the biggest and fastest-growing sectors in the world. Sustainable tourism in natural ecosystems is also developing vigorously and becoming increasingly important as a source of income for poverty reduction. A good example of this is Costa Rica, where sustainable tourism on the basis of a functioning system of protected areas has now become an important source of foreign exchange earnings (Costa Rica, 2001).

Tourism can provide opportunities for the management of protected areas and for local communities. In this regard, it is not only the economic benefits that are important for local economy (jobs, strengthening local markets), but also the indirect effects resulting from the enhanced status of the cultural and natural heritage in the eyes of both visitors and local residents. If tourism is to be sustainable, however, it must be extremely carefully planned and implemented, because in the case of sensitive areas or species (e.g. tigers) even minimal impact can result in major damage. In extreme cases, destruction of the cultural landscape and exclusion of local communities from the biological resources of a protected area can actually exacerbate poverty (WPC, 2003b). The IUCN has published useful guidelines for sustainable tourism in protected areas (Eagles et al., 2002).

It cannot therefore be taken for granted that eco-tourism will have a positive impact on poverty reduction. There are examples where the local communities themselves have barely benefited at all, even from major flows of eco-tourists (e.g. in the Royal Chitwan National Park in Nepal; Bosselmann et al., 1999). If, however, there is a desire to achieve a positive local impact and appropriate measures are put in place to promote this, then success is possible (e.g.

the Annapurna Conservation Area Project, likewise in Nepal; Gurung and Coursey, 1994).

The CBD Programme of Work on Protected Areas calls upon the Parties to the Convention to integrate nature conservation into their poverty reduction strategies, and to use the revenues from nature conservation for poverty reduction measures. In this regard, conservation of natural resources must of course continue to be given priority to ensure that total protection in core areas is maintained and networks are established linking protected areas with the surrounding landscape (CBD, 2004a).

Among the goals listed in the voluntary Guidelines on Biodiversity and Tourism Development drafted within the framework of the CBD, there is a call for revenues and employment opportunities generated as a result of tourism to be used for poverty reduction in order to minimize threats to biodiversity from indigenous and local communities (CBD, 2004b). Improving the entitlements of local communities will play an important role in this regard. Much will now depend on how these guidelines are implemented in practice.

4.2.2.5
Assessment: Applying guard rails and policy goals

The CBD is now recognized as the key policy instrument for the biosphere (WSSD, 2002; WPC, 2003a). The Convention has chalked up some successes: the adoption of the Biosafety Protocol represents the successful achievement of an international, consensus-commanding, legally binding regulation on a highly controversial issue. It serves as an important reference point for discourse within countries, since it sets out principles and concepts that provide signposts for implementation on the ground. GEF provides financial resources that can be used to promote the drafting of national strategies and action plans and to tackle implementation of these in concrete projects.

The now near-complete compliance with the WBGU guard rail on protected areas (Section 3.3.4) is a major success. Today, 11.5 per cent of the total terrestrial area has been designated a protected area (WPC, 2003a). The Convention has certainly played a part in this positive development. However, the management of many protected areas and linkages with the surrounding landscape are still utterly inadequate. In addition, protection of marine areas and inland waters is lagging behind considerably. The new CBD Programme of Work on Protected Areas provides a good basis for the further development of the protected areas network; now, it needs to be implemented. Loss of biodiversity cannot be halted

by protected areas alone, however. Nature conservation must also be made an important criterion for the 80–90 per cent of the areas that are not protected. Integrated approaches (e.g. bioregional management; WBGU, 2001a) continue to receive far too little attention.

Despite these efforts, biodiversity loss continues unabated. Implementation of the CBD at both national and regional level must still be considered unsatisfactory. The political will to give the internationally agreed rules the clout they need on the ground is lacking, particularly where they conflict with other policy objectives (e.g. land use, settlement policy; WBGU, 2001c). This happens in Europe too, for example concerning implementation of the Habitats Directive: in cases where there are conflicting interests, economic considerations often take precedence.

It would be hard to overstate the significance of the 2010 target agreed at the WSSD (to significantly reduce the rate of loss of biodiversity by 2010) for the CBD: it has given the Convention fresh impetus. This impetus must now be utilized to generate the political will to improve implementation of the Convention, as otherwise it will not be possible to achieve the 2010 target.

4.2.2.6
Financing

Conservation of biodiversity as a global good is in the interests of the whole of humankind, whereas the costs of conservation and the costs of abstaining from destructive utilization in the country concerned are incurred locally (WBGU, 2002). For this reason, international compensation payments are needed in order to motivate developing countries to abstain from exploiting local natural ecosystems. This applies especially to areas that are, or are intended to be, part of a global system of protected areas. These payments must also reach communities on the ground, however, if they are to contribute to poverty reduction and create incentives for nature conservation.

In 2003 GEF spent approximately US$150 million, equivalent to 27 per cent of its budget, on biodiversity projects (GEF, 2003a), with financing of protected areas being a priority (CBD, 2003). Overall annual expenditure on this area is in the region of US$6,500 million (Balmford et al., 2002). WBGU, in contrast, has estimated the annual costs of putting in place an effective system of protected areas covering 15 per cent of the global land area at around US$27,500 million (WBGU, 2001a). The World Parks Congress put the figure required annually over the next 30 years for a comprehensive global system at US$20,000–

30,000 million (WPC, 2003b), whereas current budgets only cover about 20 per cent of the costs. Overall, estimates of the funding shortfall affecting the protected areas system range between US$12,500 and 38,500 million annually (Sections 3.6, 5.6). The funding gap for integration of nature conservation objectives into land use outside protected areas is very difficult to estimate, but may well exceed this by a factor of 10 (James et al., 1999, 2001).

Closing this gap by means of additional funds from public budgets must be considered unrealistic. Investigation of the opportunities offered by ABS contracts for financing mutually reinforcing measures for nature conservation and poverty reduction (Section 4.2.2.3) has shown that they are unable to make a significant contribution in the short and medium term. Instead, fresh consideration should be given to two instruments already recommended by WBGU:

- *Non utilization commitment certificates:* A global system of tradeable non utilization commitment certificates would commit wealthy countries to provide developing countries with compensation for conserving natural ecosystems. In doing so they would be paying for the benefits of the global protected areas system – the conservation of valuable biodiversity for humankind – and thus shouldering a portion of the opportunity costs arising for developing countries as a result of abstaining from destructive forms of utilization (e.g. clearing of tropical forests). If protected carbon stocks were also taken into account in this process, then it is conceivable that a synergy effect and a financial effect with climate protection could be created (UNFCCC; WBGU, 2003). WBGU has pointed out that world-wide implementation of such a system is not feasible in the short term (WBGU, 2002). WBGU emphasizes the need for research on these new instruments and reaffirms its recommendation that this concept should be brought into the international policy debate with greater vigour – for example in the case of pilot projects relating to the Biodiversity Convention.
- *Restructuring subsidies:* Closing the funding gap appears in a different light if one compares the annual funding gap of US$12,500–38,500 million for protected areas with global government agricultural subsidies: around US$311,000 million (IFPRI, 2003) are spent annually on support for agriculture (Sections 3.6 and 5.6). If these subsidies were dismantled perceptibly, a significant funding contribution could be made towards establishing a world-wide system of protected areas.

4.2.2.7
Summary of recommendations

In the Biodiversity Convention, the issue of poverty currently plays more of a role in programmatic proclamations and less at operational level in concrete recommendations, not to mention legal commitments. Without shifting the priorities of the Convention from biodiversity to poverty reduction, increased efforts should be made to make the most of opportunities to create win-win situations (Section 5.4.2). WBGU's recommendations can be summarized as follows:

- *Access to genetic resources and benefit-sharing:* Even though the present situation does not warrant high hopes of any rapid or considerable flows of funds, conditions for successful ABS contracts should be improved. The opportunities provided by negotiating an international ABS regime should be utilized to eliminate existing shortcomings with regard to implementation and verification. The instruments proposed to tackle this should be tested for their consistency, effectiveness and feasibility. Promotion of research in developing countries and capacity building to eliminate the imbalance in negotiating power could likewise improve the chances of success for ABS projects.
- *Financing of protected areas:* The protected areas network, sustainable tourism and fair regulations on benefit-sharing all depend on adequate financing. For protected areas alone, the estimated annual funding gap runs into tens of thousands of millions. WBGU considers it possible to close this gap if environmentally damaging subsidies are abolished and a portion of the funds thus saved is used for biodiversity conservation (Section 5.6). However, innovative concepts such as tradeable non utilization commitment certificates should be promoted in order to open up new opportunities for finance-generating effects, at least in the long term. In this regard there are interesting possibilities to create synergies with climate protection (WBGU, 2003).

4.2.3
United Nations Convention to Combat Desertification

4.2.3.1
Purpose and goals

Of the three Conventions launched by the Earth Summit in Rio de Janeiro, the one most concerned with development policy is the 'United Nations Convention to Combat Desertification in countries experiencing serious drought and/or desertification, particularly in Africa' – UNCCD. Poverty reduction is an explicit goal of the UNCCD alongside resource conservation in arid zones. The Convention was negotiated as a result of pressure from developing countries. It came into force in 1996 and has so far been ratified by 190 countries (Pilardeaux, 1997).

The goal of the UNCCD is to combat desertification and mitigate the effects of drought, especially in Africa. It provides for measures to be put in place to this end, supported by international cooperation and partnership arrangements, in the framework of an integrated approach. To achieve these objectives, long-term, integrated strategies were agreed that focus simultaneously on improved agricultural productivity and rehabilitation, conservation and sustainable management of land and water resources. The aim of this was to improve living conditions, in particular at the community level.

In Article 1 of the UNCCD, desertification is defined as land degradation in arid, semi-arid and dry sub-humid areas resulting from various factors, including climatic variations and human activities. The term 'land' is used to refer to the terrestrial bioproductive system (e.g. soil, vegetation) and the ecological and hydrological processes that operate within the system. Correspondingly, the term 'land degradation' means human-induced reduction or loss of the biological or economic productivity of rain-fed cropland, irrigated cropland, or range, pasture, forest and woodlands resulting from processes such as soil erosion, deterioration of the properties of the soil, and long-term loss of natural vegetation.

4.2.3.2
UNCCD and poverty reduction

In the preamble to the UNCCD, reference is made to the fact that desertification and drought affect sustainable development through their interrelationships with problems such as poverty, poor health and nutrition, lack of food security, and those arising from migration, displacement of persons and demographic dynamics. For poor people, who rely mainly on arable farming and livestock keeping for a living, desertification and drought represent an insidious and in extreme cases a direct threat to their livelihood, and can lead to famine and emigration (Box 3.3-1). Current estimates put the number of people directly affected by desertification at around 250 million (UNCCD, 2004). Media images of the great Sahelian droughts in the early 1970s publicized the problem worldwide. The connection between

desertification and poverty was given corresponding expression in the concept of the UNCCD.

For example, in Article 4 (c) of the UNCCD the Parties to the Convention commit to integrating strategies for poverty eradication into efforts to combat desertification and mitigate the effects of drought. In Article 10 (4) of the Convention, which deals with National Action Programmes (NAPs) to combat desertification, the Parties to the Convention agree to set priorities for strengthening national policy aimed at poverty eradication and ensuring food security. Such priority fields include, for example, the promotion of alternative livelihoods and improvement of the national economic environment. Further areas of action to be included in the NAPs are demographic dynamics, sustainable resource management, sustainable agriculture, energy supply and strengthening monitoring capabilities and capacity building.

In Article 17 of the UNCCD, which is concerned with research and development, the Parties undertake to take into account in their scientific activities the relationship between poverty, migration caused by environmental factors and desertification.

Article 20 (7) of the Convention lays down that developed country Parties must support developing countries affected by desertification in their efforts to implement the Convention by transfers of financial resources and technology. In fulfilling their obligations under the Convention, the developed country Parties should take into account that social and economic development and poverty eradication are the first priorities of affected developing country Parties.

4.2.3.3
Resource conservation and poverty reduction in National Action Programmes

After six Conferences of the Parties, the building of the institutions of the UNCCD is regarded as largely complete. The implementation phase has begun. 57 countries have so far drawn up National Action Programmes to Combat Desertification (as of May 2004), and now the next task is implementing these on the ground. To support this, there are sub-regional and regional action programmes. These action programmes set out approaches for integrated solutions. How effectively these are implemented, however, depends primarily on the affected countries' readiness to undertake reforms and create an appropriate organizational framework. This realization was one outcome of the first session of the Committee for the Review of the Implementation of the Convention (CRIC) at regional level in 2002. Overall, implementation of the Convention to date in a number of

Table 4.2-1
Priority areas of action for
implementing UNCCD
goals.
Source: WBGU based on
UNCCD, 2003

Resource conservation measures	Poverty reduction measures	Measures relating to *both* resource conservation *and* poverty reduction
Sustainable land use, including sustainable management of water and land resources	Developing early warning systems for food security and drought forecasting	Developing sustainable agriculture
Sustainable use of pasture		Dissemination of modern and renewable energy technologies
Establishing reforestation/ afforestation programmes and soil conservation measures		
Desertification monitoring and assessment		

countries has shown that the UNCCD contributes to enhancing the efficiency and effectiveness of measures to combat desertification (BMZ, 2003a).

An evaluation of the National Reports submitted by the Parties to the UNCCD shows clearly that resource conservation and poverty eradication have been made priority areas in the context of National Action Programmes (Table 4.2-1). On the one hand, the UNCCD exerts an influence on the incidence and persistence of absolute poverty resulting from environmental factors by promoting measures to conserve natural resources. At the same time, it helps to counteract poverty-induced overexploitation of resources by promoting poverty-reducing measures (see Section 3.3.3 for details of interaction effects).

4.2.3.4
Integrating efforts to combat desertification and mitigate the effects of drought within poverty reduction strategies

One of the goals of the UNCCD is to integrate efforts to combat desertification and the effects of drought into affected countries' Poverty Reduction Strategies (PRS – see Section 4.2.10). However, it is striking that, on the political agenda of these countries, desertification is often not given the same weight as under the terms of the Convention.

A glance through the Poverty Reduction Strategy Papers (PRSPs) of Burkina Faso, Mali, Mauritania and Niger reveals clearly that desertification has not been identified as a primary causative factor in poverty and is therefore not designated an important area of action (Holtz, 2003). The interactions between desertification and poverty are not fully discussed as a central theme. Neither the economic significance of desertification and its effects on poor sections of the population, nor the trend of increasing resource degradation are dealt with in the PRSPs of these four countries, all of which are particularly hard hit by desertification and drought.

Another indication of the lack of coherence in tackling environmental and poverty issues in the poverty reduction strategies of some countries is to be found in the Country Strategy Papers (CSPs). The CSPs set out guidelines for cooperation on development policy between the countries of Africa, the Caribbean and the Pacific (ACP) and the EU (Section 4.2.11). With the adoption of its new development policy guidelines in 2000 and its strategy for the integration of environmental considerations into EU development policy in 2001, the EU encouraged the ACP countries to integrate poverty reduction and environmental protection into the formulation of their policies. The countries in question have relatively ample scope to do this. Evaluation of the CSPs for Burkina Faso, Ethiopia, Mali, Namibia, Niger, Senegal and Tanzania revealed that consideration was given 'more or less' to desertification (Holtz, 2003), but that the connection between poverty and environmental degradation was hardly mentioned. Combating desertification and the effects of drought is not considered a priority in these countries' CSPs, despite the fact that these countries are severely affected by desertification and drought. This may be due in part to the fact that other donors are active in this area, or to the fact that these UNCCD goals are covered indirectly via other areas of action such as rural development or food security. The desired mobilization of additional financial resources for implementing the UNCCD in the countries in question has not been successful. This is presumably also due to inadequate integration of the goals of the Convention into the CSPs (Holtz, 2003).

Despite the rather low priority given to desertification control in the PRSPs, there is agreement in almost all of the affected countries as regards the significance of integrating this area of policy into the planning of the national poverty reduction strategy, and it is considered a priority for their successful implementation. The sessions of the Committee for the Review of the Implementation of the Convention at regional level demonstrate this. At the same time, the need for integration of environmental considerations into PRSPs has also been acknowledged on the donors' side, and in Germany Gesellschaft für Technische Zusammenarbeit (GTZ – German Technical Cooperation) has been commissioned to investigate options for integrating environmental considerations into national planning processes (BMZ, 2002a). In China and Central Asia, pilot projects are being planned that simultaneously aim to tackle desertification control and poverty reduction (BMZ, 2002a).

4.2.3.5
Synergies between desertification control, climate protection and biodiversity conservation

The UNCCD Secretariat, together with the Secretariats of the UNFCCC and the CBD, has established a Joint Liaison Group aimed at developing joint working programmes, workshops and consultation forums. The objective is to reinforce institutional links between the Conventions and other relevant institutions, to drive forward cooperation at the operational level, develop joint policies and coordinate support for national initiatives. This top-down approach, however, has not proved very successful (BMZ, 2003a). Each environmental Convention has established its own implementation pathway without any discernible common action. A more promising approach, therefore, would be to promote practical collaboration on projects on the ground and coordination to fulfil the numerous reporting obligations of the individual countries (Section 5.3.5). For example, Germany is supporting a project in Mauritania aimed at jointly implementing the UNCCD and the CBD (BMZ, 2002a).

4.2.3.6
Financing

The budget of the UNCCD Secretariat for the two-year period 2004/5 amounts to US$17 million. The UNCCD is financed by regular contributions from countries that are Parties to the Convention, and by voluntary donations. In addition to its regular contributions (2003: €713,000), Germany, as host country of the UNCCD Secretariat, which is based in Bonn and employs a staff of 43 (2003), makes a voluntary contribution of around €511,300 annually towards the core budget of the Secretariat. In addition, Germany contributes a further €511,300 annually to help fund conferences organized by the Secretariat.

Projects to combat desertification are financed through bilateral and multilateral cooperation mechanisms that were already in existence prior to the UNCCD negotiations, and more recently also via GEF. In addition, there is also the Global Mechanism of the UNCCD (which has a staff of 10 and is man-

aged jointly by the International Fund for Agricultural Development (IFAD), UNDP and the World Bank). The role of the Global Mechanism (annual budget approximately US$3 million) is to advise the countries affected by desertification on mobilizing appropriate resources and to foster partnerships.

MULTILATERAL DONORS
Between 1990 and 1998, the World Bank implemented around 160 projects in the field of desertification control and land management in dry areas. Current credit volume in this field totals around US$9,000 million. These funds are supplemented by cofinancing, resulting in a total of around US$18,000 million (BMZ, 2002a). In addition, the World Bank has also made available a total of US$3.75 million (2001–2004) for the elaboration of National Action Programmes under the UNCCD.

Since 2002, land degradation (especially desertification and deforestation) has been included as a focal area of GEF. This has made GEF a funding mechanism of the UNCCD (GEF, 2003b). Prior to this, projects aimed at combating desertification could only receive support if they were concerned with one of the other focal areas of GEF (e.g. climate protection or conservation of biodiversity). During the 2nd GEF project phase alone, some US$278 million flowed into projects aimed at desertification control, forest and soil conservation (related to biodiversity, water or climate; BMZ, 2002a). Between 1991 and 1999, a total of US$350 million has been channelled into projects primarily aimed at forest conservation and desertification control (GEF, 2004c). A distinct advantage of having a separate focal area within the GEF mechanism is that countries can now receive support to fulfil their reporting obligations.

The EU is also an important donor: in the period 1990–1999, the EU supported projects aimed at combating desertification, reforestation, soil conservation and water management to the tune of more than €1,000 million (BMZ, 2002a).

FINANCING BY GERMAN DEVELOPMENT
COOPERATION
Combating desertification has been a priority area of support in Germany's bilateral development cooperation since as far back as the mid-1980s (Box 4.2-1). Around 250 projects are currently under way that have combating desertification as their primary or secondary aim (BMZ, 2003b). Their total funding volume is in the region of €1,500 million. In regional terms, the projects are distributed as follows: Africa (60 per cent), followed by Asia (25 per cent) and Latin America (15 per cent). In addition, BMZ provides support for regional projects in Africa (€4.5 million since 1995), Asia (€1.5 million since 2002)

Box 4.2-1

Resource-saving farming project in Burkina Faso

Efforts to combat desertification have been a part of bilateral and multilateral development cooperation since the 1980s, quite independent of the UNCCD, which came into force in 1996. One example is the PATECORE project in Burkina Faso, which began in 1988 and was visited by WBGU members in the course of a study tour in February 2004. PATECORE stands for Projet d'Aménagement des Terroirs et de Conservation des Ressources dans le Plateau Central. The project is being managed as a collaborative initiative of GTZ/KfW/DED until 2006. The primary development objective of PATECORE is to help to secure the nutritional subsistence of agricultural producers and promote sustainable use of resources.

The project region in the Central Plateau covers a total area of 63,000km², and is home to around 4 million people, with a population density of 63 inhabitants per square kilometre. The agricultural area totals around 1.5 million ha, equivalent to about 50 per cent of the national agricultural area. As a result of the PATECORE project, around 60,000ha of land have already been protected from soil erosion. There is a demand on the part of the population for erosion protection as well as soil and water conservation measures for an estimated additional 500,000ha.

The job of PATECORE is to erect dry-stone walls in areas vulnerable to erosion in order to reduce the speed of rainwater run-off. This helps to limit soil erosion and increase infiltration of rainwater into the soil. Collection and breaking of stones for building these walls is carried out communally by the village, while transportation by truck is organized by PATECORE. It takes around 50m³ of stone to provide dry-stone walls for 1 hectare of arable land; this is equivalent to 10 truck-loads, or 50t of stone. A team of 150 workers can complete wall-building work on one hectare in a day.

The primary focus of the current phase of the project is on strengthening management capacities among the rural population with regard to resource-saving farming methods and techniques for rehabilitation and sustainable use of resources. PATECORE currently works with more than 450 villages. Around 3,000 farmers have been specially trained

to act as local advisors to pass on knowledge and provide support on the ground to more than 800 groups of farmers (or around 100,000 direct beneficiaries of PATECORE) in the different areas of activity covered by the project. In addition, more than 100 plant nurseries have been established. Participation in PATECORE is open to all interested villages in the project region.

The 800-plus groups of farmers that collaborate with PATECORE are organized into 40 interest groups that are increasingly taking over planning and implementation responsibilities. Direct access to PATECORE for beneficiaries of the project has been facilitated by the establishment of eight field offices.

Each field office serves 500–1,000ha annually; in terms of implementation, each field office is a standardized module with uniform process sequences, quality and performance standards. Transportation services are provided by around 75 private haulage contractors. The activities of PATECORE staff in this context are limited to training, logistics and quality control. The 'doers' are the farmers themselves, and they provide a combined total of more than a million person days. This is equivalent to 4,500 year-round jobs.

Improved water infiltration of the land (up to 100 litres more water per cubic metre) increases agricultural production; degraded soils can gradually be reclaimed; erosion protection speeds up the introduction of more intensive fertilizer management, and the vegetation as a whole benefits as a result of the rise in the groundwater table. In short, a clear increase in agricultural carrying capacity has been achieved by means of ensuring sustainable productivity of the land used.

The economic analysis is equally positive: as a result of soil and water conservation measures, millet yield has increased by an average of 250kg per ha (equivalent to CFA25,000 per year; CFA is the currency of the African franc zone). In terms of the external funding of CFA80,000 per ha, the investment will have paid for itself in four years. In terms of farmers' work input (CFA75,000 per ha), the investment will have paid for itself in three years (balance sheet for 1ha = CFA155,233 ~ €237; external 1ha = CFA80,244 ~ €122; farmer 1ha = CFA75,000 ~ €115). Overall, PATECORE has evolved into a competence centre that is in the vanguard of soil and water conservation measures.

Source: GTZ Burkina Faso

and Latin America (€1 million since 2003) (BMZ, 2003c). These regional projects are aimed at promoting cross-border cooperation to implement the goals of the UNCCD through pilot projects and best practice.

4.2.3.7
Assessment

It has now been eight years since the UNCCD entered into force, and its strengths and weaknesses are beginning to crystallize out more clearly. The UNCCD has made a significant contribution to taking the decades-old issue of combating desertification beyond Africa and turning it into a global policy area

(Pilardeaux, 2003a). At the same time, the UNCCD has helped to strengthen civil society participation. Moreover, the development of National Action Programmes has created a common framework for combating desertification, which is particularly helpful for the poorest developing countries. In particular, this has fostered the development of institutions and strategies for combating desertification in the countries affected, with the Convention providing a structural 'blueprint'. For example, in most countries, national Focal Points have been set up. In many countries, NAPs have now been drawn up, and the Global Mechanism has created an information service on funding opportunities that is open to all countries.

The UNCCD has also brought about a change in people's understanding of the causes of desertification and how to combat it: the connection between desertification and poverty was first established as a result of the UNCED process and the UNCCD. Prior to this, combating desertification was largely seen as a technical matter. Ultimately, the UNCCD also promotes the interests of the developing countries, as it is considered the 'development convention' of the three Rio conventions. It is unclear whether the UNCCD was able to increase mobilization of financial resources overall, but there has been a clear increase in a number of individual cases.

There are also a number of serious problems in the UNCCD process, however. A key problem continues to be the differences in opinion regarding its regulatory depth and the role of the Secretariat (Pilardeaux, 2003a). Many developing countries perceive the Convention as an instrument for financing or implementation with an extensive global network of organizational structures, and they see its Secretariat as a kind of implementing agency. The majority of the donor countries, on the other hand, take the view that the UNCCD merely provides a framework for national implementation and they refer to the principle of subsidiarity. In their view, the process of implementation should largely be the task of the countries themselves, especially by integrating desertification control and poverty reduction into national policies. This call for mainstreaming, however, is not being heeded by the industrialized countries themselves, especially if one considers the lack of coherence that exists between trade policy, agricultural policy and development policy. Agricultural development can be hindered, for example, by inadequate access to developed-country markets (Section 5.1.2).

These differences in opinion mean that the transaction costs of the UNCCD are very high. In many instances, a considerable proportion of the resources is spent on events relating to negotiations and less on actual implementation of the Convention on the ground. As a result, there is a danger that the already low status accorded to the Convention in donor countries will decline even further (Pilardeaux, 2003a). There have already been warning signals, such as the decision of the USA to consider its contributions to the UNCCD as voluntary donations from now on, and the fact that other countries too are considering making their contributions to desertification control on a bilateral basis.

4.2.3.8
Recommendations

- *Agree quantitative goals for soil conservation:* The UNCCD has no quantitative and verifiable targets for reduction or conservation over a given period comparable to the emissions targets under the UNFCCC or the biodiversity targets under the CBD. An important reference parameter for setting goals of this sort is to develop global guard rails, in other words, to set ceilings for soil degradation (Section 3.3.3.4). Agreeing protection goals on this basis would provide a yardstick for assessing the effectiveness of measures undertaken and create pressure to succeed. This would be likely to bring about a distinct increase in effectiveness, and the Convention's importance as a global institution for soil conservation would increase significantly.
- *Improve the knowledge base through regular status reports:* The UNCCD has no independent scientific policy advisory service of the sort provided by the IPCC in the case of the Climate Convention. Regular status reports would assist with monitoring the impact of UNCCD measures. WBGU therefore recommends setting up an Intergovernmental Panel on Land and Soils (IPLS), into which existing national scientific networks such as DesertNet (Germany) or the Comité Scientifique Français de la Désertification (France) could be integrated.
- *Improve integration of sustainable land use into relevant policy areas:* Sustainable land use should be more closely integrated into relevant areas of national policy such as poverty reduction strategies, sustainability strategies or action programmes on climate protection and biodiversity conservation. Mainstreaming in this way would greatly enhance the leverage effect of the UNCCD.
- *Enhance the role of local authorities:* The principle of subsidiarity should be given greater emphasis when implementing the goals of the UNCCD, and therefore the importance of the role of local authorities should be correspondingly enhanced. Problems on the ground can best be resolved by practical linking of environmental protection and poverty reduction at local level, because those affected can exert a direct influence on the process and weigh up conflicting goals. Use of the UNCCD as a strategic framework for such measures at local level remains limited at present.
- *Join separate implementation pathways:* Efforts to implement the different environmental conventions and national development strategies should be streamlined in a consistent and coherent way in the countries concerned in order to improve

the effectiveness and the impact of the resources deployed. Hitherto, there have been too many disparate implementation pathways, often running concurrently. Integrated measures at local level could form practical fields of action.

- *Improve coordination of EU donors:* To enable more effective use of the limited resources available for combating desertification, better coordination among donors is needed. Efforts to do this have already begun. Now the focus needs to be on pushing forward coordination in the context of the EU. Donor coordination here also refers to ensuring coherence between the different policy areas (e.g. economic policy, environment policy and poverty reduction policy).

4.2.4
Food and Agriculture Organization

4.2.4.1
Purpose and goals

The Food and Agriculture Organization of the United Nations (FAO) was founded as a specialized agency in 1945. According to its Constitution (Preamble, Art. I), its goals are to raise levels of nutrition and standards of living, secure improvements in the production and distribution of agricultural products, better the condition of rural populations, contribute to an expanding global economy and help to fight hunger in the world. To achieve these goals, FAO exercises the following fundamental functions:

- collecting, analysing and disseminating information on agriculture, forestry, fisheries, and food
- promoting and recommending international and national action for agricultural development, e.g. research, improving methods of agricultural production, improving the processing and marketing of agricultural products
- providing advice and support to the member states.

Today, FAO has 187 member states. The general assembly of the member states, the FAO Conference, convened every two years, is the supreme governing body of FAO and has exclusive control of the organization's budget. The Council (49 member states) is the body that governs the organization between Conference sessions. It is assisted by eight Standing Committees on World Food Security, Fisheries, Forestry, Commodity Problems, Agriculture, Constitutional and Legal Matters, a Finance Committee and a Programme Committee. At intervals of two years, between FAO Conferences, regional conferences are held; in recent years, environmental issues have figured increasingly on the agenda. There are no formal participation rights for non-governmental organizations (NGOs). The Director-General and the Secretariat of FAO are based in Rome, and the number of staff now totals just under 3,500 (2002–2003) (in 1994 there were around 4,800 staff). FAO has resources of its own that it can allocate to projects in the context of its Technical Cooperation Programme (Section 4.2.4.3).

The current activities of FAO are reflected in the Programme of Work that is approved every two years by the FAO Conference in a package along with the Budget. There are specific programmes on agricultural production, food and agriculture policy and social development, fisheries, forestry and sustainable development (FAO, 2003a). FAO also has extensive databases, notably on global agriculture and nutrition, and on the state of natural resources such as land, forests and fisheries. These are often the only data available and therefore form an important basis for policy decisions. For example, a report on forests produced in the year 2000, despite areas of uncertainty, became an important basis for decision-making in the negotiations on the Kyoto Protocol. FAO is also a leader in the field of setting norms and standards for agriculture, forestry and fisheries.

THE STRATEGIC FRAMEWORK 2000–2015
In 1999, the member states of FAO approved a Strategic Framework for the period 2000–2015, in which five key strategies or areas for action were agreed upon (FAO, 2004):
1. Reducing food insecurity and rural poverty
2. Ensuring enabling policy and regulatory frameworks for food, agriculture, fisheries and forestry
3. Creating sustainable increases in the supply and availability of agricultural, fisheries and forestry products
4. Conserving and enhancing sustainable use of the natural resource base
5. Generating knowledge of food and agriculture, fisheries and forestry.

To assist with the practical implementation of these strategies, 16 priorities were established, creating a structure for integrated, interdisciplinary cooperation. These include biodiversity, biotechnology, climate change, ecosystem management, emergency assistance, nutrition for urban areas, gender issues, global issues, organic agriculture, spatial information management, sustainable livelihoods and trade agreements. The objective of this new Strategic Framework is to establish a common long-term basis for FAO member states so that future challenges can be dealt with more effectively.

4.2.4.2
Mainstreaming resource conservation and poverty reduction

Since its inception, FAO's concept of development has changed markedly. In its early years as a specialized agency, it was still focused primarily on promoting agriculture as a support for urban industrial development (providing food for urban areas and freeing up labour). From the mid-1960s the 'Green Revolution' aimed at increasing agricultural production and promoting rural development using technical and process innovations. Some of these innovations came out of the CGIAR network (Box 4.2-2). Although the Green Revolution brought considerable increases in productivity, its successes were mainly limited to the irrigation areas of Asia. Its socio-economic effects are also controversial; in many cases, existing disparities tended to be exacerbated (Bohle, 1998; WBGU, 1998a). Moreover, instances of environmental degradation, and especially salinization, as a delayed effect of the irrigation technology deployed, have become increasingly prevalent (Section 3.3.3). Since the World Food Summit in 1996, therefore, the buzz-word has been the 'New Green Revolution', a term referring most notably to the use of biotechnology in agriculture.

As a parallel development, since the United Nations Conference on Environment and Development (UNCED) in 1992, the concept of sustainable agriculture has become established within FAO.

The basis for this was the DenBosch Declaration of 1991, in which the FAO Council resolved to include sustainability criteria in all of FAO's programmes and activities. This declaration also formed the basis for drafting Chapter 14 of Agenda 21, 'Promoting sustainable agriculture and rural development' (Buntzel, 1995).

As part of the sweeping reform process undertaken in the 1990s, the Sustainable Development Department of FAO was set up in 1995. Its work focuses on four areas:
1. Sustainable livelihoods, people's participation and mainstreaming of gender and population issues into all relevant policy areas
2. Agrarian transformation and institutional reform
3. Research, extension, education and communication
4. Natural resource monitoring and management.

Its aim is to integrate the concept of sustainability into all of FAO's activities. This Department also coordinates FAO's follow-up to the UNCED Conference. FAO is further concerned with the conservation and sustainable use of fish stocks. In 1995 it initiated the adoption of a Code of Conduct for Responsible Fisheries (Unser, 1997). In the field of forestry, following the failure to conclude a Forest Convention, the adoption of the non-legally binding statement of principles on forests (the 'Forest Principles') at the UNCED Conference in 1992 led to FAO taking on important new implementation functions.

Box 4.2-2
Consultative Group on International Agricultural Research

The Consultative Group on International Agricultural Research (CGIAR), established in 1971, is an informal association of 48 public and private donors that support a network of 16 international agricultural research centres. Alongside FAO, cosponsors of CGIAR include the World Bank, UNDP and UNEP. As a rule, a Vice-President of the World Bank serves as chairman of the group. The CGIAR Secretariat is also located in Washington. The task of CGIAR is to promote the development of sustainable agriculture in developing countries through research. The issues pursued by the international research centres are increasing agricultural productivity, protecting the natural environment, improving the policy framework and promoting agricultural research in developing countries. In the food and agriculture sector, these centres host the most important gene banks in the world, which are indispensable for the development of genetic material for new crop varieties. Their structure and character are highly varied. While some focus on specific crop species, e.g. CIMMYT in Mexico (maize, wheat) and IRRI in the Philippines (rice), others focus on particular types of area, e.g. ICARDA in Syria

(drylands). The approaches they take as regards the connection between environment and poverty are equally varied.

In CGIAR's first decade (1971–1980), the centres concentrated on increasing production. Highest priority was given to research on cereals (wheat, rice, maize). The research portfolio was soon broadened, however, to include cassava, chickpeas, sorghum, potatoes and millet. In the second decade (1981–1990), sustainable food production to improve the nutritional level of the poor became the primary research objective of CGIAR. In the early 1990s, CGIAR entered a period of crisis after being reproached for operating inefficiently. Several donor countries drastically reduced their contributions. In 1994 it was decided to redefine the functions and objectives of CGIAR, revise its research agenda and create greater openness and transparency. In the years that followed, the involvement of developing countries in CGIAR has increased enormously. Poverty reduction was made a central objective of CGIAR, and participation rights for non-governmental organizations were strengthened. Since then, conflicts have arisen repeatedly, for instance in November 2002 over the failure of the Mexico-based international research centre for maize and wheat (CIMMYT) to take action against contamination by genetic engineering experiments of Mexico's region of origin for maize biodiversity.

Sources: Stoll, 2004; Grain, 2004; BMELF, 1995

The current activities of FAO in the field of sustainable development are reflected in its specific programme of work on that theme. Within this framework, attention is given to follow-up to the UNCED, the WSSD, the World Food Summit and the Conferences of the Parties to the UNCCD, the CBD and the UNFCCC (Section 4.2). As a specialized agency of the United Nations, FAO is required to translate United Nations resolutions into its own activities. Another task of the Programme is mainstreaming gender equity into all FAO activities. It also addresses the impact of HIV/AIDS on the nutrition situation. Other areas of work include preparing geographical information systems for land use planning. The first ever Soil Map of the World was drawn up as part of this programme (Unser, 1997).

At the WSSD, FAO and the CGIAR Research Centres initiated the Global Crop Diversity Trust, a body whose purpose is to support the conservation of crop diversity to ensure food security. The Trust sees its work as a contribution to achieving the Millennium Development Goals. The aim of the Trust is to provide long-term support and financing for seed and gene banks throughout the world. Part of this involves protecting valuable collections and ensuring their conservation in the long term. Core funding of US$260 million and other additional resources are to be raised for conservation of the most important gene banks. US$45 million have already been committed (The Global Crop Diversity Trust, 2004).

Despite these changes in structure and content towards sustainability, even today FAO still lacks any binding and comprehensive definition of sustainability suited to assessing operative projects. Although FAO has been promoting concepts such as integrated plant protection, integrated plant nutrition and organic farming for some time now, there is no code of conduct aimed at reducing the use of plant protection products and biocides. The primary focus remains merely to ensure that such products are used safely.

In 1985, the FAO Conference adopted a Code of Conduct on the Distribution and Use of Pesticides, which was updated in late 2002 as a consequence of the influence of the PIC Convention that has since entered into force. In an ever more closely interconnected world, the International Plant Protection Convention (IPPC) is also gaining importance. Hosted by FAO, the Convention is aimed at preventing the spread and introduction of pests of plants and plant products. The Convention sets standards for international trade and is intended to protect indigenous plant stocks and biological diversity.

Another topic that has arisen as a result of the debate on sustainability is the disparity between North and South as regards nutrition – undernour-ishment and hunger in developing countries and malnourishment in industrialized countries. These issues have recently become a focus of attention within FAO. FAO and WHO plan to engage in closer cooperation in this area. The demand for land connected with high meat consumption, however, does not yet play any discernible part in considerations concerning scarcity factors for food security.

In the context of the sustainability debate, FAO's stance on biotechnology has attracted public criticism in recent times. For example, more than 650 NGOs criticized in the strongest terms (Grain, 2004) the FAO report entitled 'Agricultural Biotechnology: Meeting the Needs of the Poor' published in 2004. In an open letter, they accused FAO of drawing up the report without involving civil society or smallholder farmers' associations. Criticism is levelled particularly at what the NGOs see as a biased technological focus coupled with neglect of issues of access and distribution of food. According to the open letter, the lessons from the Green Revolution have not been learned; instead, a belief in the all-embracing effects of diffusion of technological innovations continues to predominate, and especially a belief in the potential offered by genetic engineering. The development of *golden rice* is one example of this conflict (Section 3.2.3). In his response, the Director-General of FAO emphasized, among other things, that biotechnology is only one component of food production.

INTERNATIONAL TREATY ON PLANT GENETIC RESOURCES FOR FOOD AND AGRICULTURE

In the 1980s, a debate developed within FAO that centred around concerns that cultivation of homogeneous high-yielding varieties in fields could erode wild stocks and traditional forms of farming, thereby resulting in the loss of important genetic material for future breeding purposes, especially the material of wild landraces or hitherto little-studied material. As a consequence of this, FAO adopted a non-legally binding Undertaking on Plant Genetic Resources for Food and Agriculture, in which, among other things, issues relating to *in situ* and *ex situ* conservation are addressed (WBGU, 2001a). The great significance of this agreement lies in its declaration that genetic resources for food and agriculture are the common heritage of mankind. Soon after, however, additional resolutions were drafted that once again excluded certain plant material from this 'common heritage'; first, material protected under statutory provisions for the protection of new varieties of plant was excluded, and the exclusion was later extended to cover material in plant breeders' nurseries (Stoll, 2004).

The attempt thus made to regulate the conservation and use of plant genetic resources for food and agriculture at international level was overtaken by various developments. On the one hand, the principle of the sovereign rights of nations over their genetic resources was enshrined in the Convention on Biological Diversity, which linked this to the sharing of the benefits arising from their use (Section 4.2.2). On the other, the development of genetic engineering and its use in breeding and developing crop plants enabled the introduction of patents in some areas. Initially, patenting of certain methods and processes of plant breeding involving genetic engineering became possible. Patents were subsequently also issued for genetically modified plants for particular agricultural uses, and for individual genes.

The key aspect of this broadening of intellectual property rights in the field of agriculture, breeding and propagation is that patent law does not contain any special provisions regulating cultivation of saved harvested seed. This means that every time propagation takes place subsequently, the approval of the patent holder is required, and this is generally tied to payment of a fee (Stoll, 2004). Moreover, patent protection largely determines access to the protected material by third parties for breeding purposes. In addition, the conclusion of the WTO Agreement on Trade-Related Aspects of Intellectual Property Rights (TRIPS Agreement) has resulted in much tougher protection of intellectual property in international terms. The confluence of these developments resulted in re-negotiation of the Undertaking. These negotiations culminated in the International Treaty on Plant Genetic Resources for Food and Agriculture that came into effect in 2004.

Development of private rights over plant genetic resources for food and agriculture continues. From the point of view of poverty reduction, the most important aspect of this concerns forms of subsistence agriculture (farmers' rights). For subsistence farmers in developing countries, unhindered access to plant genetic material for seed multiplication (conserving harvested seed for planting), for varietal maintenance and development, and for exchange within farming communities is vitally important. In the case of genetically modified plants, access is impeded by tougher enforcement of regulations protecting new varieties, or even by patent law and the associated licence costs. Farming communities that live and work in traditional structures often simply do not have the necessary financial resources (Stoll, 2004). For this reason, before promoting high-yielding, modern varieties subject to variety protection provisions or protected by patent, it is important to consider carefully whether the advantages outweigh the socio-economic consequences. Particular caution should be exercised when considering varieties where the re-use or exchange of harvested seed is prevented either by law or in actual fact (Terminator technology).

THE RIGHT TO FOOD

Since the mid-1990s, there has been ongoing debate concerning recognition of a rights-based approach (Section 3.1.1) to food security in the policy of FAO, an approach advocated especially by the international non-governmental organization Food First Information and Action Network (FIAN). The aim is to orientate FAO more towards poverty eradication. This debate was continued at the World Food Summit in 1996, where it was officially agreed to translate the right to food into concrete voluntary guidelines. These guidelines did not constitute a legally binding instrument under international law, but they did provide a framework that made it easier to assess the conduct of governments and international organizations beyond the United Nations with regard to food security (Pilardeaux, 2003b). Concrete rules for implementing the right to food, which is recognized in principle under international law, have hitherto been lacking. In the best-case scenario, with a view to ensuring coherence in global governance, such rules should also include the policy of the Bretton Woods institutions, the WTO and the private sector. This could be expected to contribute significantly to achieving the MDG on food security (Section 2.1). Further progress was made with this initiative in 2002, when the World Food Summit+5 called upon FAO to set up an Intergovernmental Working Group to develop guidelines for the realization of the right to food in the context of national policy and to report to the United Nations Committee on World Food Security. The working group convened for the first time in March 2003, and is expected to present its results within two years.

4.2.4.3
Financing

FAO has a biennial programme budget that totalled around US$850 million in the period 2004–2005. Germany is the third biggest contributor after the USA and Japan, making an annual payment to FAO of around US$30 million. Alongside this, the German Ministry for Consumer Protection, Food and Agriculture runs bilateral projects with FAO. Up to US$10 million in funding will be made available for these projects in 2005.

FAO estimates the total additional financing required annually up to 2015 to implement the Millennium Development Goal on food security at US$24,000 million, US$16,000 million of which is to come from the industrialized countries (Pilardeaux,

2003b; Section 3.6.2.2). According to FAO, these additional resources are to be mustered through increased official development assistance in the field of agriculture and rural development, contributions from affected countries, and loans.

4.2.4.4
Assessment

When assessing the role of FAO, the competing competences of the United Nations system must be taken into account. As a specialized agency of the UN, FAO is obliged to comply with the recommendations of the UN General Assembly. These are binding upon FAO. The World Food Programme, established in 1961 for the purpose of providing multilateral food aid, is a joint institution of the UN and FAO. The International Fund for Agricultural Development (IFAD; Box 4.2-3) was set up outside of FAO but using FAO structures, rather like UNDP and the World Bank (Buntzel, 1995). Formally, CGIAR is also independent of FAO.

Donors have exploited these overlaps in areas of responsibility, playing them off against each other. For example, in the mid-1990s, the USA in practice distanced itself from its membership of FAO and instead supported the World Food Programme and CGIAR. Behind the non-payment of the US contributions there were substantive conflicts, such as whether plant genetic resources represent a common resource or are subject to national sovereignty, or whether international food aid should be provided largely from industrialized countries' surplus stocks or involve other groups of countries. In this dispute, the stance taken by FAO was sympathetic to the developing countries (Buntzel, 1995). In the context of the WTO agriculture negotiations, FAO has made a valuable contribution with its 27 country case studies, and as regards agricultural trade issues in particular it has provided a useful counterpoint to the WTO in development policy terms.

4.2.4.5
Recommendations

- *Checking and ensuring the transparency of data gathering in reporting countries:* FAO data are compiled on the basis of reports from individual countries. These are often the only data available in the field of food and agriculture. The quality of these data, however, is inconsistent and often unclear. At the same time, these data form the main basis for policy decisions. In order to enhance clarity with regard to data quality, FAO should strive to ensure checking of data gathering in the individual countries.
- *Developing and applying sustainability criteria:* In its follow-up to UNCED, FAO set up a department and a work programme on sustainable development. Nevertheless, a binding and comprehensive definition of sustainability that could also be used to evaluate operative projects is still lacking. WBGU therefore advocates developing concrete and practicable sustainability criteria for FAO. Germany should support this in the context of its FAO membership.
- *Developing a user-oriented focus:* The majority of the world's farmers, and thus the largest target group of FAO, are subsistence farmers. FAO's strong orientation towards technical matters and its shortcomings in terms of social integration of farmer-led projects are also due to the lack of involvement of farmers in developing and implementing FAO projects. WBGU therefore recommends improving FAO's user-oriented focus by establishing participation rights for farmers.
- *Focusing on disparities in consumption patterns:* Existing North-South disparities in terms of nutrition – undernourishment and hunger in developing countries, and malnourishment in industrialized countries – are not being given adequate consideration as a central issue within FAO. As a rule, only population growth is taken into consideration as a scarcity factor, while the role of e.g. high demand for land associated with high meat con-

---

Box 4.2-3

International Fund for Agricultural Development

The International Fund for Agricultural Development (IFAD) was founded as a specialized UN agency in 1976 on the recommendation of the 1974 World Food Summit. The purpose of IFAD is to provide funds on preferential terms in the form of loans and grants, particularly for projects aimed at increasing food production and improving the nutrition situation of the rural poor.

The Fund is financed via membership contributions. Projects are often financed jointly with other financial institutions, such as institutions in the World Bank group or regional development banks. Planning, implementation and monitoring of projects is often entrusted to FAO as well as to these institutions. Between 1978 and 2003, IFAD disbursed some US$7,700 million in loans and US$35.4 million in grants for project financing (628 projects in 115 countries). IFAD currently has a staff of around 300.

Sources: BMELF, 1995; Unser, 1997; Stokke and Thommessen, 2003

sumption is ignored. Disparities in consumption patterns should be included in a strategy for global food security.

4.2.5
World Health Organization

4.2.5.1
Purpose and goals

The World Health Organization (WHO) was founded in 1948 as a specialized agency of the United Nations, and has its headquarters in Geneva. Its supreme governing body is the World Health Assembly, comprising representatives of all 192 Member States, which elects the 32-member Executive Board and the Director-General. With its six regional offices, WHO operates globally, leading and coordinating international cooperation in the field of health, and developing norms and standards, for example as the basis for international agreements. In addition, WHO advises governments on the design of health care systems. In doing so, it pursues four strategic objectives:
1. to reduce mortality, morbidity and disability in all population groups (Health for All);
2. to promote healthy lifestyles and reduce health risk factors, with environmental risk factors being high on the list of priorities;
3. to develop effective health care systems;
4. to involve the health sector in developing social, economic and environmental policy.

WHO implements this strategy primarily with a view to solving the following health problems:
– malaria, tuberculosis and HIV/AIDS (acting together with UNAIDS),
– cardiovascular disorders and diabetes,
– smoking,
– mental illness,
– reproductive health,
– local and global environmental risk factors.

The regional offices support the countries in their respective regions with specific programmes in the areas of environment and health. WHO headquarters focuses primarily on risk analysis, UV radiation and biodiversity in this area. The Regional Office for Europe, together with the European Centre for Environment and Health, maintains comprehensive technical facilities (offices in Rome and Bonn). The Bonn office covers the area of urban environment and health, and its areas of activity include air quality, housing and the housing environment, noise, and information systems and indicators. The office in Rome focuses on the health consequences of cli-

mate change and develops appropriate strategies for adapting to it.

4.2.5.2
Integrating health promotion, environmental policy and poverty reduction

WHO's strategic priorities encompass the health-related Millennium Development Goals. The work of the Commission on Macroeconomics and Health (WHO, 2001) promoted international acceptance of health as a prerequisite for economic growth and development. This realization led to consistent inclusion of the health dimension in strategies to eradicate poverty, such as the Poverty Reduction Strategy Papers (Box 4.2-4; Section 4.2.10).

For decades, through publications and at conferences, WHO has presented in great detail the importance of environmental influences as determinants of health. In the World Health Report 2002, environment-related health risk factors feature prominently. With the support of the World Bank, WHO has introduced a universal measure for loss of health and quality of life: the burden of disease, expressed in Disability Adjusted Life Years (DALYs; World Bank, 1993). One unit represents the loss of one year lived in a state of health. DALYs represent the years of healthy life lost as a result of premature death, acute and chronic diseases and disability. WHO has applied this approach rigorously to assess health risks arising from changes in the environment. The outcome: worldwide, around 26 per cent of the global burden of disease is attributable to environmental factors (WHO, 2002; Section 3.2.2). Socially disadvantaged population groups and the poor suffer particularly from the effects of global environmental change. This is clearly evident, for example, in the case of indoor air pollution due to cooking and heating using biomass, or the greater vulnerability of poor people to natural disasters (Corvalan et al., 1999). Mindful of the health consequences of global environmental change, WHO is directing efforts to define and implement efficient precautionary measures and multisectoral strategies (Box 4.2-5).

4.2.5.3
Financing

The Member States of WHO have committed themselves to paying a contribution in accordance with their financial position and population size. These contributions are channelled into the regular budget, which is approved biennially. The regular budget for 2002–2003 totalled US$856 million. Since this

Box 4.2-4

WHO and Poverty Reduction Strategy Papers

Poverty Reduction Strategy Papers (PRSPs) are a key instrument for poverty reduction (Section 4.2.10). A study by WHO investigated the extent to which PRSPs had included the health dimension of poverty and established the connection between social and economic development and improved health status. To assess this, the PRSPs from 21 countries dating from between 2000 and 2002 were examined with a view to answering the following questions:

- Is the link between poverty reduction and improved health addressed as a central theme?
- Is priority being given to promoting the health of the poorest?
- Are goals, resources and monitoring of strategies consistent with each other?

The outcome of the study was that, in all of the PRSPs, health is considered as a dimension of poverty. Improving health in general and that of the most vulnerable population groups in particular is given prominence in all cases. In the majority of the PRSPs, however, the conceptual links between poverty and health are expressed in terms that are too general and too proclamatory. Even in their analysis of the existing state of affairs, only very few of the PRSPs present data disaggregated by income or population group.

Table 4.2-2 shows that most countries favour health strategies that implicitly benefit the poor, focusing especially on water, nutrition programmes and combating infectious diseases. While the strategic focus is the right one, it is rarely supported by data or appropriate indicators, with the result that it is almost impossible to assess whether the goals set are being achieved. Moreover, in many cases the indicators are not consistent with those used in the reports on progress towards achieving the MDGs.

The resources allocated to the health sector in PRSPs vary considerably, from 5 per cent (Yemen) to 36 per cent (Burkina Faso). Although this puts them, without exception, above the share allocated to this sector in the countries' national budgets (an average of 2 per cent), WHO considers these resources inadequate to achieve the Millennium Development Goals.

WHO emphasizes the need for targeted deployment of health strategies in the fight against poverty. It therefore calls for:

- measures and indicators specifically aimed at poor population groups,
- monitoring that is consistent with goals,
- better focusing of resources on the key areas of water, nutrition and control of infection and
- establishing links with other sectors that are relevant for health, such as education, agriculture, transport and energy.

Source: WHO, 2001

Table 4.2-2
Health sector priorities from the PRSPs of 21 countries, and their implementation.
Source: WHO, 2004a

Health problem	Discussed in PSRP data	Data disaggregated according to poverty	Pro-poor strategies	Indicators available	Poverty-disaggregated monitoring
Infectious diseases	21	2	10	15	1
Maternal health	21	5	10	21	1
Child health	21	7	13	21	2
Water, sanitation	21	13	17	19	11
Strengthening health services for poor people	20	4	9	3	1
HIV/AIDS	17	7	7	13	3
Nutrition	16	6	9	12	3
Financial obstacles	15	1	12	3	–

budget has been frozen for years, WHO is only able to perform its burgeoning duties thanks to so-called extrabudgetary contributions. In 1990 these contributions exceeded the regular budget for the first time (Vaughan et al., 1996). Of the US$1,130 million in voluntary contributions received in the period 2002/03, 68 per cent were provided by Member States (Table 4.2-3), while the remainder came from private donors and foundations. Top of the list in terms of extraordinary donations in 2003 was Britain, with US$187 million. Germany donated just US$11 million (WHO, 2004b), putting it in 17th place. Together with other resources, WHO had total funds of US$2,240 million

at its disposal in the budgetary period 2002/3 (WHO, 2003).

4.2.5.4
WBGU recommendations

Health is a key element in overcoming poverty and a prerequisite for sustainable development. The health of poor population groups in particular is put in jeopardy by many facets of global environmental change. Credit is due to WHO for having highlighted these connections in a timely and consistent fashion. Nevertheless, WHO has neither the financial

Box 4.2-5

Healthy Cities Initiative: Linking policy on poverty, environment and health

The Healthy Cities Initiative was launched in 1987 by WHO with the aim of improving health and quality of life in municipalities and towns. The initiative is based on the principles of equality, participation, inter-sectoral cooperation and sustainable development. Both the private sector and the public sector are involved in the initiative in the areas of town planning, transport, traffic, environment and lifestyles. Initially piloted in 11 cities, the initiative now encompasses more than 1,000 Healthy Cities projects world-wide.

The Healthy Cities Initiative includes, for example, priority programmes on traffic accidents, disabled transport users, building more cycle paths, reducing vehicle emissions and intervening in key areas to ensure provision to the poor of e.g. water and energy. A survey of Healthy Cities projects in developing countries showed that understanding of the links between environment and health has been improved, considerable resources have been mobilized and effective inter-sectoral cooperation has been achieved at both national and international level.

Source: Harpham et al., 2001

nor the human resources to be effective in developing strategies and implementing them together with its Member States. WBGU therefore recommends strengthening WHO's capacities and political clout. For one thing, this should include substantive German involvement, especially by sending more German experts to WHO headquarters and offices dealing with environmental issues.

In addition, to enhance cooperation with WHO, WBGU recommends improving consultation among the ministries for health, environment and economic cooperation. Another option worth considering might be to organize an international conference jointly with WHO in Germany on the subject of

'Health, Poverty and the Environment'. Such a conference should be given a high profile like the 2004 International Conference for Renewable Energies in Bonn, for example.

In addition, Germany should increase its extrabudgetary contribution to WHO. This would enable the German government to exert more influence than hitherto on the setting of objectives, staffing and planning of work within WHO.

4.2.6
The United Nations development and environment programmes

The UN Development Programme (UNDP) and the UN Environment Programme (UNEP) are the two key players within the United Nations dedicated to poverty eradication and environmental protection respectively. The following section explores the scope these programmes have to fulfil their mandate. It further examines the extent to which they take account of the interrelationships between environment and poverty, and aim towards a coherent sustainability policy.

4.2.6.1
United Nations Development Programme

INSTITUTIONALIZING 'DEVELOPMENT' WITHIN THE UNITED NATIONS
The decision to set up the United Nations Development Programme (UNDP) was made in the 1960s. This new Programme was intended to facilitate and enhance the effectiveness of financing, overall planning and coordination of the various programmes for technical cooperation within the UN. Headquartered in New York, UNDP is subject to the authority of the Economic and Social Council (ECOSOC), one of the principal organs of the United Nations.

Country	Ranking	Fixed contributions (regular budget) [US$ million]	Country	Ranking	Extrabudgetary contributions [US$ million]
USA	1	166	UK	1	187
Japan	2	160	USA	2	164
Germany	3	81	Norway	3	80
France	4	54	Netherlands	4	79
UK	5	41	Canada	5	74
Italy	6	41	Japan	6	29
			...	...	...
			Germany	13	11

Table 4.2-3
Fixed and voluntary contributions in WHO financing by country, 2002–2003.
Source: WHO, 2004b, c

The UNDP Administrator is appointed by the UN Secretary-General.

Although even today it does not constitute a specialized agency of the UN, UNDP has evolved into the largest UN organization for technical cooperation, with 195 Member States, activities in 166 countries and offices in more than 130 countries. UNDP and the United Nations Population Fund (UNFPA) share an Executive Board comprising representatives from 36 Member States, who are elected by ECOSOC for a term of three years. Regional quotas ensure that developing countries have a voting majority. In practice, however, decisions are generally made by consensus. Among other things, the Executive Board decides on UNDP programmes in individual countries and supervises disbursements from the UN Population Fund.

The UNDP Administrator supervises the work of several thousand employees, the majority of whom work in field offices. UNDP also chairs the United Nations Development Group established in 1997 as part of Kofi Annan's reform agenda to improve coordination of development activities within the UN system. In addition, the Executive Board of UNDP and UNFPA is responsible for a number of other UN entities that are engaged in the development sector, including the UN Capital Development Fund, the UN Development Fund for Women, the UN Sudano-Sahelian Office and the United Nations Volunteers programme.

UNDP's position within the UN system

When considering the position of UNDP within the UN system, the importance of its network of country offices cannot be overstated. Each country office is managed by a Resident Representative of UNDP, who in most cases also functions as the highest UN representative and de facto UN ambassador in this country, and coordinates all UN agencies operating in the country. UNDP thus has far greater influence than one would expect of a subordinate body of the Economic and Social Council. This does not mean, however, that its role is unquestioned by other UN organizations keen to protect their turf – especially by specialized agencies that also deal with development policy, such as FAO (Section 4.2.4), UNIDO or UNESCO.

Poverty reduction is an integral part of UNDP's mission to promote 'sustainable human development'. The World Bank, however, shares this mandate and perceives itself as the lead agency in the intergovernmental arena (Section 4.2.9), which gives rise to conflicts of interest and rivalries. The World Bank developed the instrument of Poverty Reduction Strategy Papers (PRSPs) (Section 4.2.10). UNDP is involved in drawing up such PRSPs in around 60 countries (UNDP, 2001b). Although the PRSP initiative of the World Bank and the IMF impinges on UNDP projects at country level, its impact on UNDP activities has not yet been subject to systematic assessment. UNDP itself has criticized PRSPs for being a revamped version of structural adjustment conditionalities (UNDP, 2001b) and seeks to avoid being associated more closely with this instrument in order to preserve its good reputation with developing countries (Biermann and Bauer, 2004b). Another explanation may be rivalry between the World Bank, UNDP and other organizations (Eberlei and Siebold, 2002).

Mainstreaming environmental issues

While UNDP gave little consideration to environmental issues during the first few decades of its existence, more attention was focused on the environment as a consequence of Agenda 21 (Timoshenko and Berman, 1996). The UNDP Administrator at the time, Gustav Speth, placed the environment high on his agenda, advocating the creation of an international environmental organization as a counterweight to the World Trade Organization (Biermann and Simonis, 2000). UNDP, along with the World Bank and UNEP, was made an implementing agency of the Global Environment Facility (GEF) (Section 4.2.8). A similar role is played by UNDP in the Multilateral Fund of the Montreal Protocol on Substances that Deplete the Ozone Layer (Biermann, 1997). In addition, UNDP produces a biennial report on World Resources together with UNEP, the World Bank and the World Resources Institute, (WRI, 2003). Since the change of UNDP Administrator in 1999, however, environmental concerns have receded in importance compared to other issues such as crisis prevention and recovery. There were even discussions on whether UNDP should renounce its environment responsibilities altogether in order to free up resources for poverty reduction and development policy. No such radical steps were taken in the end (Biermann and Bauer, 2004a). Instead, the environment – along with energy – is now one of UNDP's five priority areas. US$298 million, in other words 16 per cent of the organization's annual budget, was channelled into this area in 2002 (UNDP, 2004e). The focal themes are sustainability strategies, water management, sustainable energy, soil conservation, conservation of biological diversity and national/sectoral policies to control POPs and ozone-depleting substances. Together with the European Commission, moreover, UNDP has launched the Poverty and Environment Initiative, which is aimed at formulating practicable recommendations to address environmental problems in poor countries.

FINANCING

In 2003, the budget of UNDP was US$3,200 million (UNDP, 2004c). The regular budget is made up of voluntary contributions from governments, which hampers long-term planning. After the 'Rio boom', government contributions declined. Over the last decade, the regular budget of UNDP fell from US$1,100 million in 1990 to US$634 million in the year 2000. Since then, it has increased again slightly, totalling US$769 million in 2003 (UNDP, 2004c). UNDP has been able to compensate partially for this shortfall in its core financing via other sources of funding. These grew considerably over the course of the 1990s – from US$268 million in 1991 to US$2,200 million in 2002 – and now account for more than three-quarters of total expenditure (UNDP, 2001c, 2003a; Klingebiel, 2000). These resources, however, which derive from programme cofinancing, trust funds and cost-sharing by recipient countries, can be a double-edged sword. They give the organization added financial impetus, but they do not lend themselves to forward planning, and they give governments greater say regarding how resources are used – a trend that has been criticized as a bilateralization of UNDP (Klingebiel, 2000).

85–90 per cent of UNDP inputs go to the least developed countries (Box 3.1-1). In contrast to World Bank loans, UNDP grants do not have to be repaid, which makes them particularly attractive. Moreover, developing countries appreciate the comparatively high degree of participation afforded to them, for example through round-table discussions or decentralized communication via country representatives.

ASSESSMENT

Rigid structures and the growing strength of other sectorally specialized UN organizations resulted in a fall in acceptance and contributions in the 1990s. After the incumbent UNDP Administrator, Marc Malloch Brown, took office in 1999, UNDP underwent fundamental reform that involved strengthening UNDP focus on particular issues, decentralizing its structures, streamlining procedures and an overhaul of staffing. The reform has already led to increased acceptance of UNDP in partner countries and by other UN entities, and a rise in donor contributions. According to an independent survey of respondents including governments, NGOs, enterprises and other development agencies, 87 per cent now consider UNDP a useful organization (UNDP, 2002). UNDP has responded to continued external pressure and made clear improvements in its evaluation work. Moreover, the Administrator has introduced a framework of results-based planning and performance management instruments aimed at helping to improve the organizational performance of UNDP (UNDP, 2003a). In addition, a series of institutional and substantive reforms have been undertaken, such as decentralization by establishing sub-regional and regional centres. At the same time, through their coordination and advisory role, these centres are intended to drive forward the transformation of UNDP into a globally networked knowledge organization and provider of policy support services (UNDP, 2004d).

Governments of developing countries in particular acknowledge the efforts of UNDP to implement concepts such as participation and ownership consistently, in contrast to the World Bank and the IMF. In this regard, the round-table mechanism implemented at country level, for example, has been acknowledged as a useful instrument (Klingebiel, 2000). At the same time, thanks to its extensive organizational network, UNDP is particularly well placed to support international goals through capacity building at country level (Engberg-Pedersen and Jorgensen, 1997).

UNDP has also made considerable impact on international development discourse by the introduction of its Human Development Index (HDI). Its annual 'Human Development Report', first published in 1990, has become a standard reference text for the development community worldwide. However, the recommendations of the Human Development Report are not necessarily reflected in the activities of UNDP, as they often lack support in the organization's governing bodies (Klingebiel, 2000). In addition, UNDP's work on global public goods has attracted much attention (Kaul et al., 1999, 2003). Likewise, however, in the practical work of UNDP to date there is little evidence of this concept, which among other things highlights the linkages between global environmental protection and poverty eradication policy (UNDP, 2004d).

In the context of the reform programme launched by UN Secretary-General Kofi Annan, progress has been made as regards involving UNDP in the system-wide UN agenda for sustainable development. In WBGU's opinion, the Member States should reinforce UNDP as a counter-weight to the World Bank and support the Programme in its conceptual work on global public goods.

4.2.6.2
United Nations Environment Programme

INSTITUTIONALIZING 'ENVIRONMENT' WITHIN THE UNITED NATIONS

Following the UN Conference on the Human Environment in Stockholm in 1972, the UN General Assembly decided to create an Environment Programme (UNEP) with a secretariat located in Nairobi, Kenya. This was the first and, to date, only time that a major UN institution has chosen to site its headquarters in a developing country. Like UNDP, UNEP is obliged to report to the General Assembly via ECOSOC. Its Executive Director is appointed by the UN Secretary-General. The programme is governed by a Governing Council composed of 58 members based on regional quotas. Here too, developing countries have a voting majority, and again decisions are generally made by consensus. The many similar institutional characteristics notwithstanding, the United Nations programmes for development and environment differ markedly in terms of size and scope, as well as in terms of their de facto position within the UN system.

The UNEP Secretariat currently employs 456 professional officers (UNEP, 2004a), in other words, around a quarter of the staff of UNDP. Around half of UNEP staff work in the organization's regional offices (in Bahrain for West Asia, Bangkok for Asia and the Pacific, Geneva for Europe, Mexico City for Latin America, and Nairobi for Africa), and four liaison offices: at UN headquarters in New York, at the seat of the European Union in Brussels, at the seat of the African Union in Addis Ababa and at the seat of the Arab League in Cairo.

UNEP's POSITION WITHIN THE UN SYSTEM

UNEP has a peculiar position within the UN system. On the one hand, it is expected to be the guiding force for all United Nations activities relating to the environment; it has no powerful rival organizations with similar mandates, as is the case with UNDP. On the other hand, it has remained a small and formally rather low-ranking body that struggles to coordinate an increasingly fragmented policy arena. The most recent attempt to strengthen coordination via the UNEP-led Environmental Management Group appears so far to have met with little success.

Time and again, governments have expressed their commitment to strengthen UNEP financially and institutionally (e.g. Nairobi Declaration, 1997; Malmö Declaration, 2000), but have so far failed to live up to these declarations. A case in point is the introduction of universal membership. This proposal has been discussed several times without success at sessions of the UNEP Governing Council; it was not addressed at the WSSD (UNEP, 2002a) and the debate has been adjourned again until the 23rd session of the Governing Council in 2005. Opponents of the idea are anxious that UNEP might thereby be transformed into a specialized UN agency (IISD, 2004). Although UNEP has achieved a degree of de facto 'upgrading' by successfully institutionalizing the Global Ministerial Environment Forum, it nevertheless remains in a weak position compared to other UN agencies.

MAINSTREAMING POVERTY REDUCTION

UNEP is confronted by a situation in which the environmental issues that are closely related to poverty reduction and have traditionally been a domain of UNEP have effectively been outsourced to the secretariats of the multilateral environmental agreements. This has been the case, for example, with the issues of climate change and desertification following the introduction of the UNFCCC and UNCCD (Section 4.2.1 and 4.2.3; Chasek and Corell, 2002; Busch, 2004). As regards the issue of biological diversity, the Secretariat of the CBD, although formally under the administration of UNEP, operates largely independently from its base in Montreal (Section 4.2.2). The closest links between UNEP activities and poverty reduction are thus to found in its work on water, sanitation and human settlements. However, these issues are also part of the focus of organizations such as UNDP and UN HABITAT, which are sometimes reluctant to allow the global perspective of UNEP interfere with their work on the ground (Biermann and Bauer, 2004b).

Unlike UNDP, UNEP is primarily responsible for awareness-raising and policy development at global and regional level, rather than for implementation. In conceptual terms, the UNEP Secretariat has always affirmed the close links between poverty reduction and environmental policy. With the limited resources at its disposal, however, UNEP is unable to implement its concepts at the operational level (Biermann and Bauer, 2004a).

FINANCING

The regular budget of the UN finances the UNEP Secretariat in Nairobi, including 43 posts (UNEP, 2004a). In a manner similar to the situation at UNDP, both the amount and the share of resources have declined since the early 1990s: from US$6.2 million in 1991 (6.8 per cent of the total budget) to US$4.7 million in 2003 (3.9 per cent of the total budget; UNEP, 2004a). For programme activities, the primary source of funding is a separate Environment Fund, administered by the UNEP Secretariat and replenished by voluntary contributions from governments. This Fund holds an average of US$50 million in funds per year, giving a cumulative total of around US$1,000 million in its first two decades. Following the decline in contributions to the Environment Fund in the 1990s, current figures not only show a reversal in this trend (US$52.5 million in 2003, after 44 million in 2001), but also a broadening of the member-state donor base. In 2003, a record number of 123 governments contributed to the Environment Fund, after 92 in 2002 and an average of 74 in earlier years (UNEP, 2004a). The current positive trend can be partially attributed to the indicative scale of voluntary contributions introduced in 2002 – although financially powerful donors such as Japan or the USA do not participate in this (IISD, 2004). It remains to be seen whether governments will maintain this level of support.

Since 1994, UNEP, together with UNDP and the World Bank, also advises on project disbursements via the Global Environment Facility (Section 4.2.8). The major share of GEF resources, however, flows into projects of the two big development agencies. In addition, the share of extrabudgetary resources allocated to the numerous trust funds of the environmental conventions, and earmarked contributions for specific project activities, have increased in recent years. For example, the trust funds of the conventions provide for 89 posts at the UNEP Secretariat (UNEP, 2004a). Moreover, as a recent development, governments are now able to enter into partnership agreements with UNEP to enhance the management of priority issues – four countries have so far provided resources totalling US$38 million over three years for specific programme activities (UNEP, 2004c).

Overall, therefore, the budget of UNEP is considerably smaller than that of UNDP because UNEP is not meant to be a funding or implementing agency. However, in view of the broad scope of the organization's mandate, UNEP's meagre financial and human resource base has been the subject of repeated criticism (see e.g. Imber, 1996; Wapner, 2003). It is noteworthy that the financial resources of the 'leading global environmental authority', as it was described by governments at the 19th session of the UNEP Governing Council in the 1997 Nairobi Declaration, are more modest than the budgets of many environment ministries and some of the larger environmental NGOs (French, 1995).

ASSESSMENT OF UNEP

Mindful of the cross-cutting nature of the issues involved, UNEP was created more than three decades ago as a small programme for 'catalytic' action. In view of the continuing increase in environmental problems and massive deficits in the implementation of global environmental policy, it is clear today that UNEP, in its present institutional form, is unconvincing and its capacity inadequate. As a result, the overall credibility of international environmental policy is suffering. The fact is that the ambitious goals of the world conferences in Rio de Janeiro and Johannesburg cannot be achieved if international environmental protection is given the weakest organizational form within the UN system by comparison to international trade and social policy.

In view of its limited mandate, and especially its lack of resources and political clout, UNEP's standing as an organization is remarkably good. The Programme, whose reputation had been poor in the years subsequent to the Rio summit, was given fresh impetus in 1998 by the appointment of a new Executive Director, Klaus Töpfer, former Chairman of the Commission on Sustainable Development. Töpfer has been lauded around the world for restoring UNEP's authority as the leading agency in the environmental field and for improving the efficiency of the UNEP Secretariat, developments that are also reflected in the increase in financial contributions. UNEP has initiated a number of multilateral environmental agreements. These include the Vienna Convention on the Protection of the Ozone Layer, a whole set of conventions on regional seas, and the Rio conventions on biological diversity, climate change and desertification. Most recently, UNEP has been given credit, among other things, for the successful negotiation of the Convention on Persistent Organic Pollutants (POPs). Although many of the issues dealt with by these agreements, notably the Rio conventions, are not directly related to poverty reduction, they are nevertheless of paramount importance for developing countries because they touch on issues of social or economic development.

UNEP has been actively engaged in promoting inter-agency cooperation in the environmental field, both to enhance its own influence and to integrate environmental perspectives into policies in other areas and into the work of other bodies (Bauer, 2001). Such joint programme development includes partnerships with specialized UN agencies such as the World Meteorological Organization, the International Maritime Organization and WHO, smaller UN agencies such as the United Nations Centre for Human Settlements (HABITAT), hybrid organizations such as the World Conservation Union (IUCN) or expert bodies like the IPCC. Moreover, UNEP has been widely lauded for its role in monitoring and assessing the state of the global environment. The Programme hosts the Global Environmental Monitoring System and since 1997 has published regular Global Environment Outlook reports (UNEP, 2002b). Governments expect UNEP to further strengthen the scientific basis of its monitoring, assessment and early warning activities, although opinions diverge regarding how this should be achieved.

4.2.6.3
UNDP-UNEP coordination and cooperation

Following UNCED in 1992, all UN organizations found themselves facing the demand 'to strengthen cooperation and coordination on environment and development in the United Nations system' (Agenda 21, Chapter 38, Para 8(c)). While for UNEP this demand meant incorporating more comprehensively the goals of socially and economically sustainable development, it required UNDP to integrate environmental perspectives into its activities (Timoshenko and Berman, 1996). In addition, all international organizations were required to orient their activities more strongly towards the overarching goal of poverty reduction. Implementing the integrative concept of sustainable development, however, has proved difficult in view of the historically-grown lack of coordination of development and environmental activities within the UN. Initiatives by UNEP to link development and environmental policies in the run-up to UNCED met with a reluctant response on the part of development organizations, including UNDP (Biermann and Bauer, 2004a).

In order to improve cooperation and coordination on environmental and development policies, the Commission on Sustainable Development was established in Rio de Janeiro in 1992 (CSD; Section 4.2.7). Since the creation of the CSD, environmental concerns have indeed been addressed to a greater extent by UNDP, but effective coordination at policy and project level remains the exception (Biermann and Bauer, 2004a). At the time of the CSD's inception, there were concerns that the Commission would further undermine the status and authority of an already weak UNEP instead of strengthening system-wide coordination (e.g. Henry, 1996; Elliott, 2005). UNEP has succeeded in asserting its central position in international environment policy – particularly since the introduction of the Global Ministerial Environment Forum in 2000. However, the actions of the United Nations in the sustainable development sphere continue to be characterized by lack of overall coordination (Section 4.4).

4.2.6.4
Recommendations

CREATION OF AN UN ENVIRONMENT ORGANIZATION

Given the fragmentation of the international institutional framework of environmental governance and the weak position of UNEP, WBGU advises upgrading the Programme to an United Nations Environment Organization. This proposal was already set out by WBGU in 2001 as part of its vision for the reorganization of global environmental governance into a new 'Earth Alliance' (WBGU, 2001). Support for the creation of such an organization has been growing in the scientific community and among decision-makers alike (Bauer and Biermann, 2004). In 2001, the United Nations set up a working group to systematically assess existing institutional weaknesses, identify future needs and consider feasible options for reform. The current view of the majority of governments appears to be that founding a new UN organization for environmental policy is an option that warrants consideration, but not in the short term (UNEP GC, 2002; Para. 12). The French government took the initiative again in 2003, putting forward a new proposal to transform UNEP into a specialized agency of the UN (UNEO). This proposal is also supported by Germany and the Council of Europe. An international working group comprising 26 countries and the EU Commission has been set up to formulate a plan by 2005.

In WBGU's view, an international environment organization in the form of a new specialized UN agency would contribute significantly to upgrading environment issues within the UN family, and to ensuring better coordination in the environmental field. The existing network of more than 500 international agreements and institutions on the various environmental issues is fragmented and lacks coherence. More effective protection of the natural environment requires more cogent linking of environmental issues with the underlying economic and social questions at all levels of environmental governance. Without an overarching structure or organization that takes on leadership functions, this cannot be done. Any institutional reform should, however, retain the strengths of the existing decentralized system. The fragmentation and autonomy of the multilateral environmental agreements, which have proved highly innovative over the past 30 years, should only be limited if and when they become an obstacle to progress in environmental policy. A sensible step towards establishing coherence within the decentralized governance system would be to formulate a joint memorandum of understanding on principles (Section 2.3 and 5.3).

An international environmental organization does not have to promote development *per se*, as is the mandate of UNDP. In WBGU's view, however, it must ensure that poverty reduction and economic development in poor countries are given due consideration in global environmental policy, and that the latter complies with the criterion of globally equitable burden-sharing. This will also help considerably to overcome the scepticism of developing countries as regards creating a stronger environmental organization. The following aspects in particular should be given careful consideration when establishing a UNEO:

- The first task will be to define the organization's mandate: should the organization cover all environmental problems, or only – like the Global Environmental Organization proposed by some (GEO; Esty and Ivanova, 2001) – so-called global environmental issues? The terms 'global environmental issues' or 'global commons' are difficult to define in a legal-political context. Forests, for example, are often considered a global common because of their environmental functions in the Earth System, but the majority of developing countries would object to any sovereignty restrictions in this area. It is not surprising that the epithet 'global' has not been used to denote an international institution – with the exception of the Global Environment Facility, which expressly excludes local problems and has attracted criticism from developing countries as a result (Section 4.2.8). At present, UNEP addresses all forms of environmental problems, from the local to the global level. The creation of a GEO would either entail the restriction of the universal mandate, or it would require the establishment of a parallel international organization to deal with local environmental issues. A number of successful local and regional UNEP programmes like the Regional Seas Programme would fall entirely outside the scope of such a GEO. It is not unlikely that this development would lead to a split: on the one hand, there would be a strong 'global' environment organization with world-wide reach, considerable financial resources and the support of industrialized countries, addressing the issues of immediate concern to these countries, such as climate change, loss of biodiversity or depletion of the ozone layer; on the other, meanwhile, there would be a weak, if not altogether non-existent international mechanism for the local environmental problems of developing countries, ranging from water pollution to indoor air pollution (Biermann, 2002). This is hardly likely to be acceptable to developing countries and would ultimately do little good for the environment.

- Attempts to reconcile environment and development within an international environmental organization must also address the concerns of developing countries that a new international organization could be given a mandate to impose sanctions on members, either directly or through linkages with the trade regime. Some commentators in industrialized countries do indeed support the idea of an international environmental organization explicitly with reference to the WTO experience, notably with its rules on monitoring compliance. These rules allow WTO members to bring alleged infringements of the trade agreements before a dispute settlement body, whose decisions are binding. For an international environmental organization, however, such procedures seem problematic. WTO members are at the same time parties to multilateral trade agreements, while this will presumably not be the case with the membership of an international environmental organization. Although ratification of a set of environmental agreements could be made compulsory for new members of an international environmental organization, this might hinder many countries from joining the organization (Biermann, 2002).

- An international environmental organization would not receive the support of the developing countries or be able to address environmental and development issues in a coherent manner unless its decision-making procedures afford sufficient control both to industrialized and developing countries regarding the outcome of negotiations and the future evolution of the organization. A strong organization only seems feasible, therefore, with a double-weighted majority system comparable to that introduced for the Montreal Protocol since 1990 (Biermann, 2000). In this system, decisions require the assent of two-thirds of the members, which must include a simple majority of both developing and industrialized countries. This system of North-South parity in decision-making represents a third way between the one-country-one-vote formula of the UN General Assembly, which grants developing countries an inbuilt majority, and the one-dollar-one-vote system of the World Bank and the International Monetary Fund, which favours the interests of the major industrialized countries. Decision-making mechanisms based on North-South parity could help to ensure that an international environmental organization does not become a mechanism for curtailing the development prospects of poor countries, for example by enforcing expensive industrialized-country environmental standards in poorer developing countries that have other priorities and more pressing needs due to their limited resources (Biermann, 2002).

- Lastly, an international environmental organization must not fall short of the compromises made in Rio de Janeiro in 1992. The constituting treaty of an international environmental organization must encompass more than merely environmental provisions, and above all it must address development concerns. Thus, for example, principles such as the right to development, the sovereign right over natural resources within a country's jurisdiction, or the principle of common but differentiated responsibilities and capabilities, need to be enshrined in the constituting act of such an organization.

Since negotiation and approval of a new, specialized UN agency will take more than just a few years, parallel efforts should be made to drive forward smaller reforms. For example, since 2000 the Global Ministerial Environment Forum has been meeting annually as the ministerial arm of the regular UNEP Governing Council or, in the intervening years, in the framework of an extraordinary session of the Governing Council. Such regular meetings of member states' environment ministers should be used to promote international cooperation to a greater extent. Moreover, the Forum should be able to make recommendations to other UN entities with environmental activities. Additional goals must include stabilizing the financial resources of UNEP and extending membership of the UNEP Governing Council/ Global Ministerial Environment Forum to all UN Member States, a move which Germany's government already supports. In addition, efforts should be made to promote the involvement of private-sector players (multinational enterprises, pressure groups and NGOs) in the consultative mechanisms and dialogue processes of international environmental policy. Cooperation among governmental and non-governmental players from the local to the global level is a key condition for successful global environmental governance.

IMPROVING COOPERATION BETWEEN UNEP AND UNDP

In order to improve coherence and cooperation between UNDP and UNEP (or a possible future international environmental organization), WBGU advises that further efforts be made at various levels.

Such cooperation should be improved first at the leadership level. For example, the recently established Environment Management Group should be strengthened to better coordinate the environment-related activities of UN agencies and their policy objectives under the wider sustainable development agenda. The Group has so far been little more than another talking shop.

Cooperation could also be improved at the administrative level by means of management reforms. For example, environment programmes could be explicitly linked to PRSPs (as a kind of 'integrated development assessment'), and findings from environmental assessments of development projects could be applied more rigorously. Moreover, improved interagency communication should at least help to prevent 'turf wars' between organizations. A Memorandum of Understanding addressing the potential and the mutual benefits of such closer cooperation is currently being negotiated between UNEP and UNDP. Among other things, it is expected to answer the question of whether and how UNEP might benefit from closer cooperation at country level by utilizing the world-wide infrastructure of UNDP. More extensive environmental activities in developing countries at some point require specialized expertise on

the ground. UNEP should therefore be allowed to develop operational programmes, a route that UNEP already appears to be embarking on, for example on energy efficiency, management of river catchments or prevention of air pollution. These programmes, however, should tie in with UNDP's existing network of field offices. This could also be a means of giving UNEP a stronger role with regard to implementation of projects on the ground arising out of its GEF portfolio, projects which in any case require closer cooperation with UNDP and the World Bank.

Finally, to improve coordination and cooperation between UNDP and UNEP and other UN agencies involved in the environment and development arena, the UN Commission on Sustainable Development must be given a prominent role.

4.2.7
United Nations Commission on Sustainable Development

4.2.7.1
Purpose and goals

The CSD, which was brought into existence by a Resolution adopted in 1992 by the General Assembly of the United Nations, is responsible for monitoring, coordinating and implementing Agenda 21, the Programme for the Further Implementation of Agenda 21 and the Johannesburg Plan of Implementation. Since 1993, the Commission has been meeting once a year, for two weeks, at UN Headquarters in New York; preparatory meetings and intersessional activities also take place. The CSD is a functional commission of ECOSOC and has 53 rotating members, organized on a regional basis; however, all UN States may participate in the meetings. In addition to national delegations and Ministers, representatives of civil society and the private sector also participate in the meetings. The Commission does not have any funds of its own.

After discussions at the WSSD, agreement was reached on a new approach and a programme of work for the period to 2017, with the aim of revitalizing the Commission. Henceforth, major thematic clusters will be addressed in a series of two-year cycles. The first year's review session will evaluate progress made on implementation and the second year's policy session will draw conclusions and translate these into political action. Between three and six linked themes are addressed in each cycle; consideration of these themes also covers cross-cutting issues such as health, poverty eradication and the means of implementation (see Table 4.2-4).

Cycle	Thematic cluster	Cross-cutting issues
2004/2005	Water, sanitation, human settlements	• Poverty eradication
2006/2007	Energy for sustainable development, industrial development, air pollution/atmosphere, climate change	• Changing unsustainable patterns of consumption and production
2008/2009	Agriculture, rural development, land, drought, desertification, Africa	• Protecting and managing the natural resource base of economic and social development
2010/2011	Transport, chemicals, waste management, mining, a ten-year framework of programmes on sustainable consumption and production patterns	• Sustainable development in a globalizing world • Health and sustainable development
2012/2013	Forests, biodiversity, biotechnology, tourism, mountains	• Small island developing states • Africa • Other regional alternatives
2014/2015	Oceans and seas, marine resources, small island developing states, disaster management and vulnerability	• Means of implementation • Institutional framework for sustainable development
2016/2017	Overall appraisal – Agenda 21 – Programme of Further Implementation of Agenda 21 – Johannesburg Plan of Implementation	• Gender equality • Education

Table 4.2-4
The CSD's programme of work for the period from 2004 to 2017. The cross-cutting issues are to be addressed in all two-year cycles.
Source: UN DESA, 2004

CSD members agreed that, in the first cycle (2004/05), the themes of water, sanitation and human settlements should be tackled. The second cycle (2006/07) will cover energy, climate change, air pollution and industrial development.

4.2.7.2
Assessment

Within the UN system, the CSD is the central institution for the consideration of sustainable development. It is the first and the only UN body to consistently address the issues of environment and development in interaction. The CSD raises issues which are either not discussed at all or not covered sufficiently by other international UN forums, thus providing a platform for these issues. Examples of these include sustainable consumption and production patterns and energy. The Commission also plays an important role in increasing an awareness that environmental policy must not be made at the expense of development issues. It is no coincidence that the chair chose 'Environment for Development' as the session's motto in 2004.

A very broad mandate and programme of work have made the Commission's work difficult. Agenda 21 covers well over 100 themes. The focus on major themes, as foreseen in the new programme of work, is therefore likely to improve the effectiveness of the institution. As the CSD is an intergovernmental body, responsibility ultimately lies with the members. If the members are not prepared to move on a particular issue and cannot agree on the line to take, the

Commission will achieve little. It should, however, be noted that the CSD is not a forum for negotiating international agreements or financial obligations, but a soft law forum for the joint development of approaches to resolving global problems. The review sessions provide an opportunity to avoid wrangling about abstract notions and therefore a chance for open dialogue, which can then be used in the policy sessions as a basis for initiating and supporting negotiation processes.

The Commission's purpose is to ensure that sustainable development issues are given consideration within the United Nations system and to coordinate the United Nations' activities in the areas of environment and development. However, the Commission is not able to adequately perform this function: the CSD is faced with the difficult task of exercising an influential leadership role from a relatively lowly position in the institutional hierarchy. Decisions of the CSD must be accepted by ECOSOC, which is considered to be a weak, relatively ineffective body, then brought before the General Assembly. The CSD can make policy recommendations, but scarcely has any decision making authority over other UN bodies such as UNEP or GEF. Insufficient effort is made to bring the processes which run parallel to the CSD, such as the work on an integrated and coordinated follow-up of the major UN conferences under the aegis of ECOSOC, into line with the CSD's outcomes. Yet the CSD does make efforts to influence the activities of other organizations. This can be seen in its recommendation that the Global Environment Facility move toward an improved consultative status of NGOs, in its call to the WTO to pay greater heed to environmental requirements and in the invitation it extended to the Convention on Biological Diversity to cooperate on drawing up guidelines for sustainable tourism (Stephan, 2001).

The Commission plays a pioneer role in bringing civil society into the UN system. Representatives of NGOs and business are included in national delegations. They are given the opportunity to participate not only in formal meetings but also in informal negotiations. In addition, they may organize side-events, make statements, etc. The Commission's development of innovative participation mechanisms for civil society in 1998 paved the way for the preparations for and progress of the WSSD. In contrast to other UN forums, the CSD involves civil society by addressing nine major groups: youth, women, trade unions, the scientific and technological communities, non-governmental organizations, local authorities, indigenous people, farmers and business (Chapters 24–32 of Agenda 21). This approach has been welcomed by NGOs; they have recommended that it be adopted by other UN bodies. Nevertheless, this range of participants will need to be broadened in future: other interest groups such as representatives of education and training establishments, senior citizens, the media and faith communities are also asking to be acknowledged in this way.

Since the WSSD, the CSD has also played the role of contact point for the Partnerships for Sustainable Development. In its review sessions, the Commission will discuss the contribution made by these voluntary, multi-stakeholder initiatives to implementing Agenda 21 and to the Johannesburg Plan of Implementation. Partnerships fairs and learning centres, to be organized alongside the meetings, will support these initiatives. They are seen as making an important contribution to the realization of sustainable development. The CSD emphasizes that the partnerships can only complement, not substitute governmental obligations. Another requirement is that the partnerships are formed in line with certain criteria and guidelines (Bali Guiding Principles, General Assembly Resolution A/RES/56/76 of 11 December 2001). By means of a database, in which 291 partnerships had been recorded (September 2004), the Commission intends on the one hand to facilitate the international sharing of experience and knowledge, and on the other hand help individual initiatives present themselves and thus attract new partners and donors (UN, 2004e).

The CSD also has an important function in national reporting. As early as 1995, the CSD agreed a methodology for creating a set of indicators of sustainable development, to be used as the basis for annual reporting (Fues, 1998). However, the process has been faltering for several years. To the chagrin of many NGOs, the members have so far been unable to agree on binding reporting obligations. Many developing countries fear that financial support could become dependent on progress made in implementing Agenda 21. Often, they already find it difficult to fulfil their international reporting responsibilities, without any extra tasks being added by the CSD. It is therefore proposed that voluntary reports on national developments be drawn up every two years. In many cases, alternative reports submitted by NGOs also provide information about the status of implementation in the individual countries.

The work of the Commission on Sustainable Development is heavily restricted by the fact that political decisions are made elsewhere: within the other UN organizations, at Conventions, in the Bretton Woods Institutions and at the WTO. Of necessity, the considerable policy making efforts of both governments and non-governmental participants are sharply focussed on these bodies. Indeed – in contrast to the multifaceted nature of sustainability – the makeup of almost all government delegations, especially to the high-level segment of the annual CSD meeting, is almost exclusively determined by the environment and development ministries, while other ministries (such as finance and economy) actually take key decisions setting the overall course of sustainability policy. Apart from those directly involved, other relevant ministries barely acknowledge the CSD's decisions, nor do parliaments. Their practical implementation into national policy is accorded a similarly low priority. For reasons of cost, many developing countries also almost exclusively delegate representatives of their UN offices in New York to the CSD meetings. These offices deal with matters from a heavily foreign policy-biased perspective and have only a vague notion of the specialist subjects involved. Against this backdrop, the fact that the preparatory meetings, which had previously always been held in New York, have been replaced by regional forums in review years, is very welcome. This provides an opportunity to bring the internal UN negotiation process, which many developing countries can no longer fathom, down from global level where the players are less diverse. It has become clear from the follow-up processes to world conferences how productive the regional stage can be in supplementing global processes.

Possibly the greatest obstacle to the success of the CSD's work is the conflict of interest between environmental and development issues. 'Agenda 21 and the CSD will only lead to sustainable, equitable and clean development if we can overcome the North-South divide' (I. Razali, President of the UN General Assembly, 1997). The developing countries complain that environmental issues and the northern perspective dominate discussion at the CSD. In their view, questions of financial resources and the transfer of technology raised by Agenda 21 have been neglected. In contrast, the industrialized countries are demanding good governance and the efficient management of resources in recipient countries. Although the CSD was established in order to monitor and follow up the implementation of Agenda 21, it has often been used to renegotiate decisions, sometimes due to an ignorance of the results of previous negotiations (UNU, 2002).

4.2.7.3
Recommendations

- The Ministerial Segment should continue to be opened by the UN Secretary-General, as first occurred in 2004, in order to generate more interest in the CSD.
- A key issue in the work of the CSD is how to translate the momentum and outcome of the discussions which emerge during the review session into ambitious political acts the following year. The first step towards achieving this would be to bring the periods of office for both the Chair and the Bureau into line with the two-year cycle.
- A more far-reaching proposal is that of transferring the position of Chair of the CSD to a prominent personality, one who is trusted and respected in both environmental and development policy circles. The UN High Commissioner for Human Rights could act as a model for this. Ideally, in addition to the theme-based work required, the Chair would be in a position to improve cooperation and coherence in the United Nations system – especially when mediating the conflicts of interest between UNEP and UNDP and other organizations working in the area of sustainable development. This proposal would not overcome the general lack of coordination, but its implementation is feasible and it could contribute to the consistent implementation of both Agenda 21 and the Johannesburg Plan of Implementation.
- In order to ensure that the work of the CSD and other relevant UN bodies is tied more closely together, the activities of the Working Group on Sustainable Development of the United Nations Chief Executives Board for Coordination should be brought into line with the CSD's ten-year programme of work.
- In order to achieve better integration of social and environmental aspects into other policy areas, not only environment and development ministers, but also economy, finance and energy ministers should

be involved in the high-level segment of the Commission's meetings.

4.2.8
Global Environment Facility

4.2.8.1
Purpose and goals

The Global Environment Facility (GEF) was established in 1992. It currently has 176 member states (as of September 2004). Its objective is to provide financial support to developing and transition countries to help in their implementation of global environmental policies. GEF focuses on the protection of biodiversity, the climate, international waters, the ozone layer, the fight against desertification and the management of persistent organic pollutants.

GEF is financed through funds from 32 donor countries, which provided US$6,000 million during the first decade of its existence. For the period 2002–2006 financial support up to US$3,000 million has been pledged for GEF.

GEF gives financial support to developing countries by taking on the incremental costs of a project, provided that the project generates a benefit for the global environment in one of GEF's focal areas. However, uncertainty remains in the interpretation of the concept of incremental costs. According to the basic principle, GEF only takes on those project costs that are incurred from those measures that protect the global environment. In this sense, incremental costs are those investments that change a project from one that creates a national benefit (such as power generation) into one that creates a global benefit (GEF, 1996; Young, 2002). If, for example, a developing or transition country decides to build a solar energy system rather than a coal-fired power station, it can apply to GEF for funds to cover the incremental costs that it incurs in implementing the environmentally more sustainable alternative. Since the identification of incremental costs can in practice be very complicated, the GEF Council has asked its Secretariat and the implementing agencies to develop clearer guidelines to simplify the process (Brühl, 2004).

4.2.8.2
Structure

The World Bank, UNDP and UNEP are GEF's implementing agencies. The GEF Council, which meets biannually, is responsible for developing, adopting and evaluating GEF programmes and priority areas.

It consists of representatives from 16 developing, 14 industrial and two transition countries. Decisions are made, if possible, by consensus.

The Assembly is the highest body in GEF. It is made up of representatives of all GEF member states and of the three implementing agencies. It meets every three years. Its task is to oversee the work of GEF and to submit proposals for improvement, based on existing assessments. Decisions are taken by consensus.

Since May 1995 five NGO representatives have been able to participate in the debates of the Assembly, but they do not hold voting rights. A further five NGO representatives can follow the debates in adjacent rooms via video links. NGOs decide among themselves which organizations receive these exclusive participation rights (Brühl, 2003). NGOs are also involved in the development, implementation and assessment of GEF projects.

4.2.8.3
Project approval practices

The proposal as well as approval of a GEF project follows a process that has been set by the GEF Council and begins with a proposal by the recipient country. Either a government or a non-governmental actor can present a project idea. At this stage the initial points of contact are the respective national focal points, which assess whether the project idea complies with GEF regulations. This process reflects the principle of ownership that lies at the core of the GEF process: applicants will represent and implement a project with greater commitment if they view it as 'theirs'.

As the second step, one of the three implementing agencies assesses the project idea for consistency with the objectives of GEF and, if necessary, revises it in collaboration with the national focal point, before the applicant develops it into a concrete proposal. The Executive GEF Operations Committee then assesses the proposal to determine whether it will be presented to the GEF Council for discussion, or whether it will be returned for further revision. Proposals that have been assessed positively are revised further by the implementing agency that was involved in the development of the original idea. The final version is then presented to the head of GEF, who assesses it and recommends the final acceptance or rejection to the GEF Council. Proposals that have been accepted are then assessed for their financial framework and are passed on to the implementing agencies, which are ultimately responsible for the monitoring of the project.

Given that a proposal has to comply with the criteria of the GEF Council as well as those of the implementing agencies, a very long time can pass from the original idea to the completed proposal. It also takes several months before the various GEF bodies have decided on a proposal. This means that in the case of medium-sized projects (approximately US$50,000 to 1 million) approximately five years can pass from the original idea to the final decision (NRO Interventions, 2003). NGOs have also criticized that the proposal process is very complicated and difficult to follow from the outside. This strongly limits the opportunity for civil society actors to submit proposals to GEF.

GEF projects are carried out by one of the implementing agencies or, since May 1999, by one of the regional development banks (AfDB, ADB, EBRD, IBD), FAO (Section 4.2.4), IFAD (Box 4.2-1) or the United Nations Industrial Development Organization (UNIDO). In this way GEF pursues not only its objective of focussing purely on project financing, but, more importantly, aims to contribute to a stronger overall integration of environmental policy in the development policy agenda. The image of the Trojan horse has been used to symbolize GEF's role in this context: it is expected that through this the World Bank and UNDP will increasingly make their own contributions to environmental policy (Bichsel and Horta, 1998). GEF itself describes this the mainstreaming of environmental issues. A comparison with other institutions shows that such integration is sensible: GEF receives only a small fraction of the funds that are available to the World Bank. These funds on their own are not sufficient to fund global environmental policies. There is also the additional aim that pledging GEF funds will lead to further investments in a specific project, for example from other countries or from conservation NGOs. This mobilization of additional funds is described as cofinancing. This type of financing currently represents approximately three times the level of GEF funding.

The majority of projects, with a share of approximately 23 per cent, is financed in Asia, followed by Latin America (17 per cent) and Africa (15 per cent). The European transition countries have so far received a share of approximately 12 per cent. A further share of approximately 33 per cent has been allocated to transnational and global projects.

The World Bank implements more than half of all GEF projects (approximately US$3,300 million), followed by UNDP (approximately US$2,000 million). UNEP projects amount to US$540 million. It is noticeable that at present the participation of regional development banks, as well as of FAO and UNIDO, is almost negligible.

4.2.8.4
GEF and poverty reduction

GEF's primary focus is on the protection of the global environment and, in particular, on the absorption of incremental costs. GEF emphasizes that global environmental protection is an essential part of the effort to reduce poverty and to increase living standards (GEF, 2002c): on the one hand, poverty should be reduced to protect the environment, while, on the other hand, it is the poor in particular who suffer from the effects of environmental degradation, which in turn curtails their opportunities (GEF, 2000, 2002c). However, GEF places explicit responsibility for poverty reduction with other actors (especially those in governmental development cooperation).

GEF policy has changed in past years towards placing importance on capacity building. A joint inquiry by GEF and UNDP concluded that currently almost 96 per cent of all projects contain elements of capacity building (GEF and UNDP, 2000), while in the pilot phase this was the case in approximately 58 per cent of all projects. Capacity building most frequently serves the development of technical expertise, followed by information dissemination or the development of networks. GEF focuses on capacity building not so much as an objective in itself, but uses it as a means to improve programme implementation (Brühl, 2004).

At first sight the high share of capacity building measures in GEF projects appears promising, since such measures have a long-term positive impact on poverty reduction. However, GEF projects have short timelines, and follow-up financing is not guaranteed. For example, projects in the area of biodiversity last between two and five years (Wells, 1994).

The objective of poverty reduction is also integrated into GEF's strategic planning: GEF's activities should not be in conflict with national and regional initiatives, should aim for sustainability, reduce vulnerability and should complement traditional forms of development cooperation. They should also enable other institutions to respond to global environmental problems. Negative impacts and repercussions between the environmental spheres should, if possible, be avoided (GEF, 2002b).

4.2.8.5
Problems and criticisms

Proposing a project to GEF is a drawn-out and complicated process, because it involves a multitude of actors. Given the urgency of so many environmental challenges, the five-year time span that is needed to move medium-sized projects from the initial idea to actual implementation appears too long. There is often a lack of transparency and simple processes. This can have a deterrent effect for some groups, so that proposals that could originate from the 'bottom up' are not even submitted in the first instance.

There are currently discussions on a performance-based funding system, initiated by the United States. This system is designed to make the process of allocating funds simple, transparent, pragmatic, cost-effective and steered by the countries themselves. The aim is to create equal opportunities in accessing GEF resources for all recipient countries (GEF, 2003a). However, under the proposed system funds would be allocated at the beginning of a replenishment round, with each country receiving a specific share that would be determined not so much by environmental criteria, but rather by governance indicators. This could mean that countries with comparatively less developed institutions would no longer receive support from GEF, even though, from the perspective of global environmental protection, the opposite would be sensible and desirable. The internal debate on a performance-based funding system is still ongoing.

The generally short duration of GEF financing is a further problem. Since GEF wants to give support particularly to innovative projects, follow-up financing is not always guaranteed. This puts into question not only the environmental benefit; increasing the duration of project financing would also be sensible to help support longer-term capacity building. However, GEF can rarely make long-term commitments: it can allocate its funds for periods of only four years following each replenishment round, and it does not know the level of funding that it will be allocated in the following round. This forces GEF to develop different scenarios for potential longer-term projects. Guaranteeing at least a part of the funding for a longer time span would therefore be desirable.

A common point of criticism focuses on the current position and procedures of the GEF Secretariat. Given that its staff is paid by the World Bank, and that it is located in World Bank offices, there is a concern that it is influenced too strongly by that institution. Because of this concern it has been suggested that the Secretariat should be strengthened, so that it will be able better to coordinate the work of the participating actors and to work more closely with the recipient countries in order to support them in developing their own ideas for projects (GEF, 2002a).

The lack of cooperation between the implementing agencies has been criticized since GEF's pilot phase. Because of conflicts between the World Bank on one side, and the UN organizations on the other, about the funding and implementation of projects, the original hope that synergistic effects could be created through the cooperation between these organizations was not realized. For this reason the three organizations no longer advise jointly on projects. Instead, the Secretariat now negotiates individually on a bilateral basis between the institutions and the recipient country.

The concept of global benefit poses a fundamental problem. While this benefit appears obvious in some projects, it is difficult to identify in others. For example, it is argued that the fight against desertification benefits climate protection. However, while such a benefit for the global climate is conceivable, it is difficult to quantify. It is often a matter of definition whether an environmental problem is a global or a national problem (Horta, 1998). There has been criticism that the focal areas which GEF considers to be of global importance are primarily a reflection of the views of industrialized countries, while the environmental problems on which developing countries place priority, such as urbanization or access to freshwater, are addressed only to a limited extent or not at all (Klingebiel, 1993).

While project ideas should be generated in a 'bottom up' process whenever possible, in practice this is only rarely the case. In reality local actors are hardly integrated into the process. There are national focal points that take the initial decision on whether to accept a project idea, but generally they consist only of a contact person in a government department. It even happens that the implementing agencies suggest projects to GEF, which are then accepted by the recipient country without the involvement of the population. Occasionally there are even popular protests against GEF projects.

An example of this is the Ecodevelopment Project in the Indian Nagarhole National Park. The aim was to utilize the Park, which had been established in 1974, more systematically and to improve its use for tourism. To support this, environmental education projects and visitor centres were to be established, and neighbouring villages were to be connected to potential sources of income in the Park. However, at the first GEF Assembly in New Delhi (1998) indigenous communities from the region complained about the project: they had been partly displaced from their land, and the construction of a fence had deprived them of access to the basis of their livelihoods. GEF funds had been used mainly to buy expensive equipment such as four-wheel drive vehicles, surveillance cameras and so on, while no funds remained for the development of alternative sources of income (Young and Makoni, 2001). The focal points, at least in their current set-up, therefore do not seem in a position to guarantee the implementation of the bottom-up approach.

In reaction to the criticism of its top-down approach, in 1992 GEF introduced the Small Grant Programme for the financing of projects with a value of up to US$50,000. Civil society actors can apply for funds up to this limit. Furthermore, the recipient countries themselves make the decision through steering committees that have been set up for this purpose, and which consist of government members, NGO representatives, scientists and national UNDP representatives. Approximately 1 per cent of GEF funds are distributed through the Small Grant Programme.

4.2.8.6
Recommendations for action

GEF should continue to focus its work on the protection of the environment. To widen its mandate to include poverty reduction would not be advisable. A clear focus helps in building the necessary structures and in developing expertise. In addition, given that GEF projects are embedded within the programmes of the implementing agencies, if those agencies would actually implement their sustainability agenda (Sections 4.2.6 and 4.2.9), the principle of sustainability would be reflected in all GEF projects. Having said that, projects should be assessed for potential negative poverty impacts as a rule and, if necessary, be revised, and positive synergies should be incorporated. As long as GEF holds fewer funds than its remit requires, additional assessment criteria besides the contribution to global environmental protection have to be applied. WBGU believes that a suitable criterion for choosing between projects with the same environmental contribution would be their respective contribution to poverty reduction. This would create a win-win situation for the objectives of environmental protection and poverty reduction.

A further strengthening of the GEF Secretariat would be desirable in view of the problems that have been discussed. This would yield several advantages: for one, it would be able to cooperate more closely with the recipient countries within the framework of the Country Support Teams that have been envisaged. Similar to the Small Grant Programme, this could also simplify and significantly shorten the proposal process. In addition, it would give civil society in recipient countries a stronger sense of involvement in the process. In this context thought should be given as to whether, in the medium term, Country Support Teams might not wholly replace the focal points. This seems advisable for several reasons: given that in their current configuration focal points generally consist of only one staff member in a government department, bottlenecks can easily occur when it comes to selecting project ideas. To add to this, the process is not very transparent, as neither the GEF Secretariat nor the implementing agencies are informed about which proposals are moved to the next stage and about the reasons behind those decisions. This means that cases of preferential treatment cannot be excluded. Using Country Support Teams as a standard practice could mitigate these disadvantages while retaining the bottom-up approach and would have the additional advantage of shortening the proposal process.

The current proposal for a performance-based funding system should be revised. GEF should develop its activities in line with global environmental considerations and should not make its support dependent primarily on the quality of a country's institutions. In this regard it seems more sensible to utilize the assistance directed at developing capacities to bring about positive structural changes, rather than to deny support outright.

It would also be desirable to develop a precise definition of global environmental projects. This could address the suspicion that GEF merely implements projects that are in the interest of its donors.

The organization also requires additional funds. Global environmental protection is currently one of the most urgent tasks as well as an important investment in the future. This is in the interest of both donor as well as recipient countries.

4.2.9
The World Bank Group

The World Bank Group is part of the UN family, but operates autonomously. The Group is made up of five legally and financially independent agencies:
- International Bank for Reconstruction and Development (IBRD),
- International Development Agency (IDA),
- International Finance Corporation (IFC),
- Multilateral Investment Guarantee Agency (MIGA), and
- International Centre for Settlement of Investment Disputes (ICSID).

The World Bank Group, together with UNEP and UNDP, is further involved in the administration of GEF (Section 4.2.8).

IBRD and IDA are jointly referred to as the World Bank. IBRD grants loans at market rates to middle income and poorer countries with good credit records, while IDA is responsible for low income countries (LICs). IDA funds are allocated in the form of either grants or loans with favourable terms.

IBRD was founded in 1944. Membership of the International Monetary Fund (Section 4.2.13.2) is one of the prerequisites for IBRD membership. IBRD currently has 184 member states that underwrite the funding of IBRD according to the level of their national income. The level of member states' contributions also determines their voting powers within IBRD. The United States holds the largest share of votes (16.4 per cent), followed by Japan (7.9 per cent), Germany (4.5 per cent), Great Britain (4.3 per cent) and France (4.3 per cent). IBRD raises funds on international capital markets to finance its loans to developing countries. Due to its AAA rating, IBRD is able to raise funds with very favourable terms, which it can pass on to those member states that would not be able to raise funds on international financial markets, or would only be able to do so with very onerous terms.

IDA was founded in 1960 as a 'development assistance' agency and now counts 164 members. Membership of IBRD is a prerequisite for membership of IDA. IDA loans are financed through special deposits from wealthier member states, repayments and profit transfers from IBRD. The United States holds the dominant share of voting rights (14.3 per cent). Germany holds a 7 per cent share.

IFC grants credit to the private sector, while MIGA supports foreign direct investment in developing countries by providing guarantees.

4.2.9.1
Purpose and goals

According to its statutes, the principal task of IBRD is to encourage investments in support of economic growth. IDA complements the tasks of IBRD by providing, with special consideration of the conditions in less developed regions, long-term support for their economic development.

Poverty reduction and sustainable development, while not explicitly stated in the World Bank's statutes, have nevertheless been part of its stated objectives since the 1990s. The World Bank, like other international organizations, has committed itself to aligning its activities with the MDGs (Section 2.3.1). Over the past years its understanding of poverty has evolved from a purely economic to a multidimensional perspective (World Bank, 2001b; Section 3.1.1).

For almost two decades the World Bank has been highlighting environmental problems as an important theme. The impetus for this came largely through pressure from NGOs, the US Congress and the media (Le Pestre, 1995; Kolk, 1996) and was reflected institutionally in the formation of an environmental department in 1987. In 2001 the World Bank published for the first time a comprehensive environmental strategy (World Bank, 2001a), which now serves as the basis for cooperation with developing countries in the environmental sphere. The World Bank recognizes explicitly the importance of the environment in following a sustainable development path, and acknowledges the close link to other development concerns such as poverty. However, as has been criticized by, among others, the Extractive Industries Review (EIR, 2003), this realization has so far not been applied sufficiently (Section 4.2.9.5).

4.2.9.2
The World Bank's importance

The World Bank is the most important institution in the sphere of international development. It funds a large share of development cooperation and sets the development policy agenda that guides other bilateral and multilateral donors. In the 2004 financial year the World Bank issued loans amounting to a total of US$20,000 million, of which US$11,000 million was disbursed through IBRD and US$9,000 million through IDA. Through the use of loan conditions it also exercises a significant influence on the economic and social policies of recipient countries (conditionality). The World Bank is now involved in a range of sectors in more than 100 developing countries (Fig. 4.2-1). Loans issued by the World Bank, as well as by IFC and guarantees provided by MIGA, are also often a prerequisite for the involvement of commercial banks in the recipient countries.

4.2.9.3
Programme lending

The World Bank has been issuing loans tied to economic policy and institutional conditions since the beginning of the 1980s. These loans are summarized under the umbrella terms of structural adjustment loans or structural adjustment programmes. Sectoral adjustment loans, which provide financial assistance to individual sectors of the economy (such as agriculture, education, energy and mining), form part of this class of loans. Following a revision of internal guidelines for the disbursement of programme-tied loans (OP/BP 8.60), these loans are now referred to as development policy lending. However, there has been little change in the fundamental nature of these loans (Michaelis, 2003). Even if conditions are relaxed in the future, programme lending will continue to exert a significant influence on a country's policy development. Although loans in this class were intended to account for not more than 25 per cent of all loans, this threshold has been exceeded every year since the 1997 financial year (Fig. 4.2-2). For the 2005 and 2006 financial years, loans in this class are projected at one-third of all loans (World Bank, 2004d).

The conditions tied to these loans can be summarized broadly under the terms structural adjustment (in its narrower sense) and stabilization. While World Bank programmes contain measures in both areas, this analysis will focus on structural adjustment and its impact on poverty and the environment. Stabilization is the main task of IMF (Section 4.2.13.2). Both organizations cooperate closely in the area of programme lending. The disbursement of a structural or sectoral adjustment loan by the World Bank to a developing country is also dependent on either

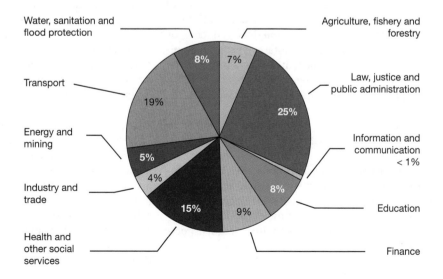

Figure 4.2-1
Loan disbursement by IBRD and IDA by sectors in the 2004 financial year. Shares of total loan disbursement of US$20,000 million.
Source: after World Bank, 2004g

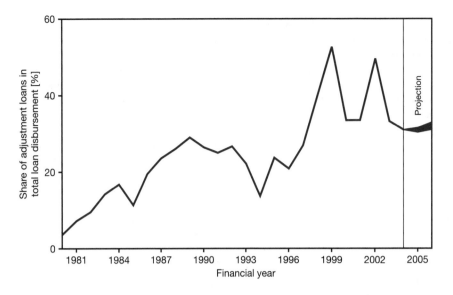

Figure 4.2-2
Share of adjustment loans in
total loan disbursement by
IBRD and IDA.
Source: World Bank,
2004d, g

the disbursement of a loan by IMF, or at least IMF's agreement to the World Bank's loan. The change in loan class terminology has not led to a change in this requirement.

The objective of structural adjustment, in its narrower sense, is to ensure the operability of market mechanisms, and especially of price mechanisms. The intention is to enable the efficient allocation of resources and, through this, to promote economic growth. The diverse range of measures can be divided into three areas:

- *Privatization:* privatization or reform of state-owned enterprises and sectors, such as energy and water supply, marketing boards, credit and banking systems, education and health.
- *Market liberalization:* measures to liberalize foreign trade and to deregulate national product, financial and factor markets. This includes price liberalization, a reduction in quantitative restrictions and support for private sector initiatives. There are also measures aimed at reducing or restructuring the role of the state in economic policy-making to one where it works alongside the market, primarily in a regulatory capacity, but also as a partner, catalyst and moderator (World Bank, 1997; Kulessa, 1999).
- *Institutional reforms:* in particular, measures to create efficiently functioning markets and administrations.

Over the past years loan conditions have been widened to include additional institutional as well as social and ecological criteria. The question remains whether inclusion of these criteria is sufficient to reduce poverty effectively and to address environmental aspects adequately.

STRUCTURAL ADJUSTMENT AND POVERTY
REDUCTION

When the World Bank introduced structural adjustment programmes it assumed that they would make a long-term contribution to poverty reduction by boosting economic growth (the so-called trickle-down effect; Section 3.4.2). However, some of the structural adjustment measures that aimed to increase efficiency have led to heightened poverty and inequality, at least in the short term:

- Increases in efficiency in the public sector and reductions in subsidies in the private sector have resulted in higher unemployment. This has affected the poor not so much directly, but certainly indirectly.
- Reductions in subsidies for basic goods have led to a relative worsening of the economic position of – among others – poor farmers and consumers.
- The education and health sectors are also affected by general budget cuts (which are part of stabilization packages; Section 4.2.13.2). This usually also affects the poor.
- Contrary to general expectations, in countries with very unequal patterns of land distribution and many large landowners small farmers have not been able to profit from the general rises in producer prices that followed in the wake of liberalization measures (Kulessa, 1998a).

Structural adjustment programmes have also neglected questions of gender equality. Since women are responsible for raising children, frequently work in farming and food preparation, look after the elderly and control household budgets, they are affected more significantly than men by cuts in social expenditure budgets that have occurred in many countries (Zack-Williams, 2000).

As early as the late 1980s the World Bank recognized the poverty-increasing effects of its structural adjustment programmes and introduced some compensatory social measures. In cooperation with other multilateral and bilateral donors it has:

– introduced social funds for the poor sectors of the population that are particularly affected by the adjustment process,
– integrated social buffering measures into its programmes (such as loans and special retraining programmes for public sector employees who are made redundant).

However, because of the chosen demand-led approach and insufficient financing, the success of these compensatory measures has been limited: many of these measures did not reach the poorest sectors of the population (Kulessa, 1998a; Michaelis, 2003).

Since 1999 programmes for the poorest countries have been developed on the basis of PRSPs (Section 4.2.10). This is designed to take greater account of the country-specific poverty situation within the framework of adjustment programmes. IBRD continues to issue loans to poorer countries with good credit records as well as middle-income countries on the basis of programmes that it designs itself, even though poverty represents a significant problem in many of those countries (such as Brazil, Section 4.2.9.6).

STRUCTURAL ADJUSTMENT, ENVIRONMENTAL PROTECTION AND POVERTY

Environmental protection is not an explicit objective of structural adjustment loans. However, a study by WWF initiated a debate about the impact of structural adjustment programmes on the environment (Reed, 1992). This, and studies that followed, were based largely on individual cases and country case studies. The lack of studies with findings that can be generalized is due to insufficient data and methodological difficulties. However, there is no doubt that structural adjustment measures have an impact on the natural environment in the medium to long term (Gueorguieva and Bolt, 2003). Among the positive effects are:

• A reduction in environmentally damaging agricultural subsidies, such as those for pesticides, fertilizers and energy, can reduce the use of these inputs and encourage an efficient use of scarce environmental resources.
• Economic stability improves the predictability of economic activity, and thus can foster the responsible use of resources (Section 4.2.13.2).
• Higher living standards can result in growing demand for improvements in the quality of the environment, and technological progress enables a more efficient use of resources (Section 3.4.2).

The following limitations or negative effects can be identified:

• Economic policy frameworks are not sufficient to ensure the conservation of natural resources and the environment.
• Trade liberalization and other structural adjustment measures can increase the exploitation of natural resources (Section 4.2.13.1).
• The targeted promotion of cash crops for export can lead to the degradation of agricultural land and to increasing deforestation.
• Cuts in public finances can lead to a reduction in the funds that are available especially for sensitive policy areas such as the environment and poverty reduction.

It is not possible to determine the net effect of the measures that are stipulated by the World Bank as loan conditions (Battikha, 2003; Michaelis, 2003). The World Bank has recognized that the impact of macroeconomic and sectoral economic policies on the environment is significantly stronger than that of project-specific investments and has therefore introduced additional measures. However, the environmental strategy that it pursues in connection with its structural adjustment programmes has so far lacked focus. It consists of different components or levels that range from environmental assessments and national environmental action plans to measures that are directly integrated into structural adjustment programmes.

Environmental assessments are only used in projects and sectoral adjustment programmes, but not generally in structural adjustment programmes. According to the new guidelines for development policy lending, all future programme lending should take systematic account of social and environmental aspects (World Bank, 2004d). However, so far, the process that has been proposed to support this is not very transparent, and the guidelines are not stringent enough to ensure that environmental aspects will be taken into consideration in practice.

Up to now national environmental action plans have been part of Country Assistance Strategies (CAS). The World Bank uses CAS to lay out its strategy for the recipient country for the following three years. Since 1999 the World Bank has been producing it's Assistance Strategies on the basis of PRSPs (Section 4.2.10), but only for countries that have applied for debt relief or wish to receive an IDA loan. Since the late 1980s the development of national environmental action plans has been a prerequisite for granting loans.

There have only been a few general studies so far, largely produced by the World Bank itself, on the assessment of poverty and environmental aspects in CAS. In 2000 and 2001 it carried out a self-assessment on the consideration of environmental aspects and their links to poverty in CAS (Shyamsundar and Hamilton, 2000; Shyamsundar et al., 2001). According to this self-assessment, success has been achieved at least in the identification of environmental issues and in environmental policy reforms. While there has also been progress in the analysis of the link between environmental and poverty aspects, there nevertheless remains – as the World Bank has itself acknowledged – a significant need for improvement (Belle et al., 2002; World Bank, 2003b). The multifaceted interplay between poverty and the environment has so far been reflected insufficiently in CAS. A critical observation is that the evaluation of CAS is carried out by means of a relative performance ranking (with the 'best' CAS in each section receiving the highest mark), rather than by an absolute ranking against a best-practice ideal.

Assessments of the current state of implementation can only be made on the basis of individual cases, since there are no comprehensive studies on this topic. Because of this, the impact of structural adjustment programmes on poverty and the environment will be analysed in more detail through a country case study and a sector case study (Sections 4.2.9.5 and 4.2.9.6).

4.2.9.4
Project lending

Project lending is an important component of financial cooperation between bilateral and multilateral donors. In contrast to programme lending, project lending refers to the financing of development projects that can be clearly defined in terms of time as well as technical and economic aspects.

The World Bank is an important actor in this sphere as well. It pursues the objective of developing the physical and social infrastructure that is necessary for poverty reduction and sustainable development through the use of investment loans. These days this includes a very broad range of projects (World Bank, 2001b):

- reduction of urban poverty (such as the construction of new housing with private enterprise involvement),
- rural development (such as the formalization of ownership rights to create greater security for small farmers),
- improvement in water supply and sanitation,
- improvement in the management of natural resources (training programmes in sustainable forest management and sustainable agriculture),
- post-conflict rehabilitation (such as the reintegration of soldiers into society);

- education (such as the promotion of girls' education)
- health (such as the establishment of rural clinics and training of medical personnel).

WBGU welcomes such projects in principle. However, many of the projects in which the World Bank has been involved have been criticized strongly from a social as well as an ecological perspective. Dam projects are a striking example: while big dams can make an important contribution to economic development, in the past the World Bank has frequently neglected the social and ecological aspects of such major projects (WBGU, 1998a; WCD, 2000; WBGU, 2004). In particular, poor people and future generations often have to pay a high share of the social (particularly in the form of forced resettlements) and environmental costs, without receiving proportionate economic benefits from such projects (WCD, 2000).

Not least due to public criticism, the World Bank withdrew temporarily from the financing of new dam projects, and concentrated on supporting the modernization and safety of existing dams (World Bank, 2000). However, it recently announced that it intends to become involved again in the development of big dams by following a high-risk/high-reward strategy (World Bank, 2004b). So far, however, it has not integrated social and ecological aspects sufficiently into its operational policies (Environmental Defense et al., 2003).

The World Commission on Dams has developed recommendations for the planning and implementation of such projects (WCD, 2000). The World Bank has endorsed the basic principles (equity, sustainability, efficiency, participatory decision-making, accountability) and the strategic priorities of the Commission, but it has expressed reservations with regard to the specific guidelines. Based on the comparison with its own safeguards, the World Bank has reservations about, for example, the possibility of a right of veto for affected and indigenous communities, as this could be counter to the interests of the whole society. In addition, the recommended multi-level negotiations for project preparation are considered impractical (World Bank, 2004b). While these concerns are understandable in part, they should not lead the World Bank to neglect the search for more socially and ecologically sound project alternatives, which could consist, for example, in the bundling of several small projects.

In many cases, analysis of the sustainability of dam projects is still hampered by a lack of basic ecological, social and project-specific data. Therefore there is a need to increase investment in an improved scientific database in the coming years (WBGU, 2004). In cases where a sustainability analysis is (so far) not possible due to the lack of reliable data, the precautionary principle should apply (von Bieberstein Koch-Weser, 2002). In addition, an environmental and social impact assessment should be completed before a decision about a project is made. Affected sectors of the population should be involved in the planning and, in the case of resettlements, should be compensated adequately. WBGU recommends that, as a global guard rail, 10–20 per cent of each different type of riverine ecosystem, including catchment areas, be given conservation status (Section 3.3.6; WBGU, 2004).

WBGU is critical of an unpublished World Bank strategy paper, which was planned to be implemented from July 2004, about its support for middle-income countries: in order to increase its support for infrastructure projects in these countries, to avoid prolonged and cost-intensive assessments and to be able to issue loans more quickly, the World Bank intends to transfer responsibility for the social and ecological guidelines to the respective governments (IRN, 2004). As a first step, it was intended that, in the 2004 financial year, the conditions in three pilot countries would be assessed and certified against the World Bank's guidelines, in order then to implement pilot projects in the 2005 financial year. WBGU advises discontinuing this strategy, as the necessary ex-post reviews would be prolonged and cost intensive. The World Bank should carry ecological and social responsibility for its large projects through its own strict impact assessments.

4.2.9.5
Case study: Mining, oil and gas extraction

THE ROLE OF THE WORLD BANK
Mining, oil and gas extraction play an important role in the economies of more than 50 developing countries and have always represented an important field of activity for the World Bank Group. The promotion of resource extraction can lead to increases in tax and foreign currency revenues, debt repayments, production yields, the creation of new jobs, the development of infrastructure and the introduction of enterprise-based social programmes. Some developing countries have extensive deposits of mineral resources, oil or gas, whose extraction is potentially attractive to private investors. In many cases political instability deters businesses from making investments. The World Bank Group has supported the development of this sector through structural and sectoral adjustment programmes, with the objective of securing better governance, improved entitlements and wider investor guarantees. In addition, it also provides direct project support (EIR, 2003).

In this sector the World Bank Group works not only with governments, but also with industry, civil society and other interest groups. However, the role of IBRD and IDA has changed in the past decades. While in the 1960s through to the early 1980s they concentrated on supporting the development and extraction of raw materials, in the 1980s the focus shifted to sectoral policy reform and the privatization of state-owned enterprises. In the 1990s, the emphasis lay on building capacities and developing the private sector.

Today the work of the World Bank concentrates on sectoral reforms, developing capacities, rehabilitation and on reducing the social and environmental impact of mining and oil and gas extraction (EIR, 2003). The size of loans that were issued for mining and oil extraction in the last decade has fluctuated considerably and, due to changes in World Bank priorities as well as industrial trends, has undergone an overall reduction. The development and extraction of mineral raw materials is increasingly left to the private sector, since it can carry out this task more efficiently. As a result, the involvement of IFC and MIGA in this sector has increased (Fig. 4.2-3). This development has so far contributed little to poverty reduction and sustainable development.

EXTRACTIVE SECTOR, POVERTY REDUCTION AND ENVIRONMENTAL PROTECTION
In the past only few resource-rich developing countries were successful in reducing poverty and achieving long-term economic growth through prudent management and distribution policies. The Operations Evaluation Department of the World Bank has determined that, between 1990 and 1999, there was a negative correlation between dependency on mining, oil and gas extraction and economic growth for all loan recipient countries. These countries are even less likely to achieve the Millennium Development Goals than other developing countries (OED et al., 2003).

In 2001 the World Bank asked an expert commission under the chairmanship of the former Indonesian Environment Minister, Emil Salim, to produce a study about its activities in the extractive sector. This Extractive Industries Review (EIR) was published in December 2003. EIR analysed the economic, social and ecological impacts of sectoral adjustment programmes and projects in the mining, oil and gas extraction sector in Peru, Tanzania and Indonesia over the period from 1990 to 2002. From a macroeconomic perspective the development of the extractive sector was only partly successful for the countries under assessment (Mainhardt-Gibbs, 2003). The World Bank recognized that the development of this sector is linked with significant negative social and

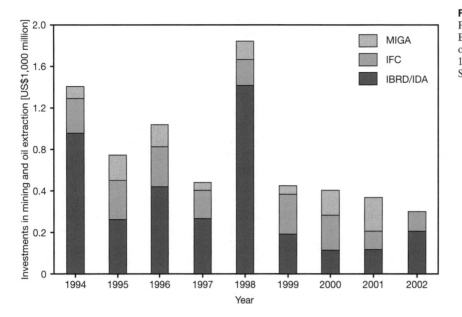

Figure 4.2-3
Participation of the World
Bank Group in mining and
oil extraction, financial years
1994–2002.
Source: EIR, 2003

ecological consequences and initiated additional measures to compensate for these consequences. However, these measures were not sufficient.

- Income poverty was not reduced in these countries.
- Profits from mining, oil and gas extraction were rarely transferred to the affected communities.
- Investment in mining, oil and gas extraction, which was made possible through structural adjustment programmes, led to significant social unrest in the countries studied. This had a negative impact on the investment climate, which led to either the freezing of investments or their withdrawal.
- Mining, oil and gas extraction often takes place in socially and ecologically vulnerable areas. New opportunities for direct investment and technological advances have made access to such areas easier. Concessions in the extractive sector often overlap with settlement areas for indigenous communities and nature conservation areas.
- The marginal improvements in environmental protection that can be attributed to World Bank efforts were not sufficient to compensate for the degradation caused by increased exploration and extraction of raw materials.
- The development of the extractive sector increases the demand for electricity. In some cases, power stations, largely fired by oil or coal, were built to improve the supply of energy. This led to an increase in air pollution (Mainhardt-Gibbs, 2003).

CONCLUSION
When economic, social and ecological aspects are considered equally, sectoral and structural adjustment programmes that have supported the devel-

opment of the extractive sector cannot be judged to have been sustainable. This is particularly true of the projects supported. The emphasis on the economic dimension of development is too pronounced. The World Bank and IMF have concentrated on reforms that support investor-friendly policies and institutions, while appropriate policies and institutions that benefit the poor and the environment were not sufficiently fostered (Mainhardt-Gibbs, 2003).

EIR (2003) recommends that the World Bank should only support mining, oil and gas extraction if this sector can contribute to poverty reduction through sustainable development. The conclusions for structural and sectoral adjustment programmes are as follows:

- There should be an analysis of the social and ecological aspects of programme lending with the aim of creating incentives for the private sector.
- Social and ecological accountability should be introduced to accompany the liberalization and privatization of investments.
- In order to ensure that the poor benefit, and that the natural environment receives greater protection, the institutional capacities of a country should be strengthened before the extractive sector is developed.
- The development of mining, oil and gas extraction should generate added value for the whole national economy. It should stimulate other sectors of the economy and not just simply increase exports (Mainhardt-Gibbs, 2003).
- The World Bank should introduce a mechanism to monitor good governance, poverty reduction and environmental performance.

IFC and MIGA should examine closely the country's political system and the likely impact of projects. Projects should only be supported if governments are able to cope with the social and ecological challenges. The activities of the World Bank should be coordinated in CAS processes. In addition, the World Bank should reassess its strategy for the energy sector and end its support for coal extraction immediately, and for oil extraction by 2008. The funds that are released as a result should be invested in renewable energies, emission control, clean technologies, improved energy efficiency and storage technologies to mitigate greenhouse gas emissions (EIR, 2003). In this context WBGU welcomes in principle the announcement made by the World Bank at the 2004 International Conference for Renewable Energies that it intends to increase its spending on renewables and energy efficiency at an average annual rate of 20 per cent over the next five years. This means that from 2010 onwards it will provide US$200 million annually for this sector. However, the announced level of funding is much lower than that recommended by the Extractive Industries Review. Given the size of the problem and its current share in World Bank expenditure of only 6 per cent, more ambitious expenditure targets for renewables and energy efficiency would be appropriate. In the medium term the World Bank should mainly fund renewable energies.

4.2.9.6
Case study: Brazil

Brazil is particularly suited as a case study for World Bank programmes and projects in middle-income countries because of the serious nature of the challenges it faces in relation to poverty reduction and environmental degradation. The Operations Evaluation Department of the World Bank has assessed its cooperation with Brazil over the period from 1990 to 2002 (OED, 2004).

THE SETTING
In Brazil the 1980s were referred to as the 'lost decade': the country suffered, as did many other Latin American countries, from high inflation and low rates of economic growth. Real per-capita incomes fell between 1980 and 1990, and the share of the population living in extreme income poverty rose from 16.5 to 19 per cent, and from 36 to 42 per cent in the northeast of the country. Income disparities grew, and, especially in the northeast, social indicators barely improved. Positive developments were only discernible in 1994 with the Plano Real of the Brazilian government. Economic stabilization contributed to a decrease in poverty and enabled the government

to formulate a development agenda with clear objectives for education and other sectors.

MAIN ELEMENTS OF THE WORLD BANK'S STRATEGY
• The World Bank's main objective for Brazil was to reduce poverty through economic growth.
• The strategy placed emphasis on the poor northeast and on measures that were aiming at tackling poverty at its roots. The focus was on education and health. The share of World Bank loans in this sector increased from 5 per cent in the 1980s to approximately 20 per cent between 1990 and 2002. In addition, the World Bank boosted its investments in the provision of basic services and assets for the poor (water, sanitation, electricity supply in rural areas, land).
• The growth component of the strategy supported the decentralization and privatization of infrastructure through technical cooperation in the regulatory sphere and through selective loan allocation.
• The share of environmental projects in total loans disbursed was increased in the 1990s from 0.9 to 6.2 per cent, of which 60 per cent were allocated to sustainable forest management, 10 per cent to reducing industrial pollution and 30 per cent to water management.
• In the late 1990s the World Bank increasingly issued programme loans in order to support the government in its stabilization and reform efforts. Between 1990 and 2002 the share of structural adjustment loans in total loan disbursement rose from 6 per cent in the 1980s to 26 per cent. The main objectives were fiscal and financial reforms as well as social security (Table 4.2-5).

MAIN OUTCOMES OF THE WORLD BANK'S WORK
The World Bank's own Operations Evaluation Department assessed the Bank's 1990–2002 strategy for Brazil largely positively. The shift towards social sectors and the focus on north-eastern Brazil and on more intensive structural adjustments at the end of the 1990s were justified. Economic crises linked with inflation could have had a negative impact on the poor. The support for social sectors was maintained during the disbursement of adjustment and technical support loans.

Income poverty has remained a grave problem, although its national rate has fallen from 40.7 (1990) to 33.6 per cent (2000). There is still a very high degree of income inequality: the Gini index (Box 3.2-3), which was 61.6 in 1990, was reduced only negligibly to 59.6 in 2000 (Table 4.2-6).

Almost half of the loans that were issued were directed at the non-monetary dimensions of poverty. Satisfactory results were achieved in this regard: the

Sectors	Share of all loans [%]		Share of investment loans [%]
	1980–1989	1990–2002	1990–2002
AGRICULTURE	32.5	13.4	18.1
Rural Development/ Poverty	11.4	10.1	13.6
Other	21.1	3.3	4.5
EDUCATION	2.0	11.7	15.9
ENVIRONMENT	0.9	6.2	8.5
FINANCIAL SECTOR AND PRIVATE SECTOR	12.7	8.9	4.9
HEALTH	2.8	6.9	9.4
INFRASTRUCTURE	43.4	28.7	34.9
Transport	13.0	16.5	22.4
– urban	3.8	7.4	10.0
– other	9.2	9.2	12.4
Energy	21.0	5.8	3.8
Water and sanitation	9.5	6.4	8.6
PUBLIC SECTOR MANAGEMENT	0.2	11.0	3.8
SOCIALE SECURITY	0.0	9.9	0.1
URBAN DEVELOPMENT	5.4	3.2	4.3
SHARE OF ADJUSTMENT LOANS	6.8	26.4	–

Table 4.2-5
Sectoral composition of World Bank loans to Brazil in 1980–2002.
Source: OED et al., 2003

primary education enrolment rate rose from 84 to 96 per cent nationally, and from 72 to 93 per cent in the northeast. The enrolment rate for secondary education has remained low. The quality of primary and secondary education is inadequate especially in the northeast of the country. Illiteracy among teenagers fell from 9.8 to 4.2 per cent nationally, and from 22.7 to 9.6 per cent in the northeast. The World Bank has created appropriate infrastructures, supplied educational materials and strengthened public education ministries. It has also introduced information and evaluation systems for primary education as well as minimum operating standards in all schools. The World Bank has contributed to a reduction in infant mortality, which fell from 48 to 29 per 1,000 live births nationally, and from 73 to 44 per 1,000 live births in the northeast. Other health indicators, such as life expectancy, the prevalence of infectious diseases and the provision of health infrastructures, have also improved. However, the maternal death rate is still high.

The World Bank has contributed to an improvement in basic infrastructures for the poor through projects aimed at rural poverty reduction, water supply, sanitation and urban transport. However, there is still a shortage in sufficiently qualified medical personnel. In addition, access to sanitation is still inadequate and results in the pollution of urban river systems and an inadequate quality of water supplies (Table 4.2-6).

Between 1990 and 1992 the World Bank played an important role in developing environmental institutions and supporting the Brazilian government across a range of environmental policy challenges. Although the country's environmental indicators still lag far behind those of wealthy economies, they have nevertheless improved in the last decade. While annual deforestation rates have remained high, they have fallen from 20,300km² per year in the 1980s to 16,800km² per year in the 1990s. Protected areas have grown from 2.4 to 6.5 per cent of the country's total size, and pollution in big cities such as São Paulo has decreased. Average CO_2 emissions have risen from 1.4t to 1.6t per capita in the past two decades, but are below the Latin American average of 2.4t per capita.

Overall Brazil has made progress in implementing the MDGs. It seems likely that many targets will be achieved by 2015, but increased efforts will still need to be directed towards some (improve maternal health provision, combat AIDS and tuberculosis, ensure access to safe water in rural areas). The collection of data on undernourishment has to be improved. The World Bank unfortunately did not include in its analysis target 11 of MDG 7, which relates to improvements in the lives of slum dwellers. This analysis would have been particularly relevant to Brazil (Table 4.2-7).

Table 4.2-6
Poverty and social indicators in Brazil (1980–2000).
Source: World Bank, 2004a

	1980	1990	2000
POVERTY RATE (HOUSEHOLDS IN %)			
all	40.0	40.7	33.6
Northeast	66.8	68.6	57.4
Rural Northeast	–	84.9	72.6
EXTREME POVERTY RATE (HOUSEHOLDS IN %)			
all	16.6	19.1	14.6
Northeast	36.2	41.8	30.0
GINI INDEX			
all	58.4	61.6	59.6
DISTRIBUTION OF AVERAGE INCOME (10% OF THE WEALTHIEST. 40% OF THE POOREST)			
all	21.5	26.7	23.6
ADULT ILLITERACY RATE (% OF POPULATION AGED 15 AND ABOVE)			
all	22.8	18.7	12.4
Northeast	41.6	36.4	24.3
YOUTH ILLITERACY RATE (% OF POPULATION AGED 15 TO 24)			
all	12.0	9.8	4.2
Northeast	27.0	22.7	9.6
NET RATE OF SCHOOL ENROLEMENT. PRIMARY EDUCATION (% OF POPULATION)			
all	80.1	83.8	95.4
Northeast	69.1	72.0	92.8
AIDS PREVALENCE (PER 10,000 PEOPLE)			
all	–	0.6	1.0
MALARIA PREVALENCE (PER 1,000 PEOPLE)			
all	14.0	32.7	30.3
LIFE EXPECTANCY AT BIRTH (YEARS)			
all	62.6	65.6	68.6
CHILD MORTALITY (PER 1,000 BIRTHS)			
all	79.2	48.0	29.6
Northeast	112.8	72.9	44.2
ACCESS TO ELECTRICITY (% OF HOUSEHOLDS)			
all	74.9	87.5	96.0
Northeast	50.8	70.5	89.4
Rural Northeast	12.6	35.4	66.5
ACCESS TO IMPROVED WATER SOURCES (% OF HOUSEHOLDS)			
all	60.7	74.2	87.3
Northeast	30.8	43.3	67.0
Rural Northeast	4.9	10.6	22.8
ACCESS TO SANITATION (% OF HOUSEHOLDS)			
all	51.3	63.2	71.3
Northeast	30.9	43.2	54.2
HOUSEHOLDS WITH REFRIGERATORS (%)			
all	56.6	70.6	85.1
Northeast	28.7	41.5	64.9
Rural Northeast	5.9	14.5	33.9

Table 4.2-7
Progress made by Brazil in achieving MDGs 1–7. Progress made towards Target 11 was not analysed.
Source: World Bank, 2004a

Goals/Targets	Progress made by Brazil
MDG 1: ERADICATE EXTREME POVERTY AND HUNGER	
1. Halve, between 1990 and 2015, the proportion of people whose income is less than a dollar a day.	Halve, between 1990 and 2015, the proportion of people who suffer from hunger. The proportion of people below this poverty line has fallen from 19.1% in 1990 to 14.3% in 2000. According to World Bank calculations, a further reduction by 2015 to 9.5% or below requires an average economic growth rate of 3%.
2. Halve, between 1990 and 2015, the proportion of people who suffer from hunger.	Child undernourishment fell by 30% between 1990 and 1996. In 1996 the rates of undernourishment were 10.5% (height) and 5.7% (weight). While this reduction reveals progress towards achieving the target, there is a lack of up-to-date reliable data.
MDG 2: ACHIEVE UNIVERSAL PRIMARY EDUCATION	
3. Ensure that, by 2015, children everywhere – boys and girls alike – will be able to complete a full course of primary schooling.	The youth illiteracy rate has fallen to 4.2%, and net enrolment rates at primary level have risen to 95.4%. This makes it likely that everyone will complete primary school education.
MDG 3: PROMOTE GENDER EQUALITY AND EMPOWER WOMEN	
4. Eliminate gender disparity in primary and secondary education, preferably by 2005, and in all levels of education no later than 2015.	In the 1990s the educational indicators for girls/women improved faster than those for boys/men and in 2000 were slightly higher. The Goal was achieved, and it is likely that the result will be maintained until 2015.
MDG 4: REDUCE CHILD MORTALITY	
5. Reduce by two-thirds, between 1990 and 2015, the under-five mortality rate.	The under-five mortality rate fell from 60‰ in 1990 to 37‰ in 1999. A further reduction to 20‰ is very likely.
MDG 5: IMPROVE MATERNAL HEALTH	
6. Reduce by three-quarters, between 1990 and 2015, the maternal mortality ratio.	Many indicators linked to this, such as antenatal and gynaecological examinations in the public health system, have improved. However, the maternal mortality ratio is high in comparison to other middle-income countries. Achieving this Goal is possible, but this will require increased efforts.
MDG 6: COMBAT HIV/AIDS, MALARIA AND OTHER DISEASES	
7. Have halted by 2015 and begun to reverse the spread of HIV/AIDS.	The number of AIDS infections has fallen from 12.7‰ in 1995 to 10.33‰. There are signs that the pandemic has stabilized on the whole. However, some regions show an increase in transmission. This requires closer surveillance and control.
8. Have halted by 2015 and begun to reverse the incidence of malaria and other major diseases.	The incidence of malaria was stabilized, and, despite some temporary setbacks, it was possible to reverse the negative trend in relation to the size of population. Success in reversing the trend by 2015 is likely. The spread of tuberculosis has increased, but controlling this disease is possible.
MDG 7: ENSURE ENVIRONMENTAL SUSTAINABILITY	
9. Integrate the principles of sustainable development into country policies and programmes, and reverse the loss of environmental resources.	The Brazilian development agenda and the multi-year development programme embraces the principles of sustainable development.
10. Halve by 2015 the proportion of people without sustainable access to safe drinking water and sanitation.	The share of households with access to safe water has increased from 74.2% in 1990 to 87.3% in 2001. The aggregated Goal was achieved. There is a need for further efforts in order also to achieve the Goal in relation to rural areas.

CONCLUSION

- World Bank loans have contributed to progress in poverty reduction as well as environmental protection in Brazil. However, it will scarcely be possible to eradicate poverty in Brazil in the foreseeable future.
- The World Bank should promote more strongly enrolment in secondary schools and the quality of school education.
- While the focus on illnesses that affect the poor in particular has been successful, it is not sufficient. A public health structure that allows the poor greater access and reduces maternal death rates has to be created, and reproductive health measures should be promoted.
- In the environmental sphere, there is still a lack of reliable analysis of the private and social costs and benefits of deforestation. The World Bank has to increase its share of environmental expenditure, especially if environmental policy is approached as part of the effort to reduce poverty. Integrated water management systems should also be promoted.

The World Bank should analyse its strategy for potential synergies as well as conflicts between objectives. It should also make explicit the links between poverty and environmental protection. There continues to be a need for a consistent strategy on this issue.

4.2.9.7
Recommendations

- The World Bank should pursue a consistent sustainability strategy – in the sense of development that will be economically, socially and ecologically sustainable in the future – to achieve its declared aim of poverty reduction. Principles relating to a consistent consideration of social and ecological aspects of programme lending need to be articulated more explicitly. Strategic and procedural considerations should be tied into CAS processes and should be linked into individual programmes and initiatives through environmental assessments. The German government should exercise its influence within the World Bank to advance these activities.
- Programme lending measures should be examined, on a country-specific basis, for potential conflicts as well as synergies between the objectives of poverty reduction and sustainable development. Structural adjustment should not be limited to the economic sphere and should be linked closely with social and economic considerations. Particular attention should be given to the linkages between poverty and environmental issues.

- There is also a need for action on the part of IFC and MIGA, whose loan conditions influence the decisions on loan issuance made by large banks. For example, the current revision of the IFC safeguards and the Pollution Prevention and Abatement Handbooks should, apart from refining them further, concentrate more firmly on the link between poverty and the environment.
- World Bank programmes and projects should pay greater attention to the position of women.
- PRSP processes should also be initiated in the countries that receive structural adjustment loans from IBRD, since these countries also face pressing poverty problems. In middle-income countries, too, poverty can only be reduced effectively through a consistent strategy that is supported by the countries and does not place its sole emphasis on economic development.
- The World Bank should push more strongly for the implementation of political measures on the part of the loan recipient countries. There is a need for a policy of conditionality that promotes development goals and is aligned consistently with sustainability principles.
- WBGU supports the call made by the Extractive Industries Review (EIR, 2003) to cease support for oil and coal extraction (WBGU, 2004). In addition, significantly more funds than those announced at the 2004 International Conference for Renewable Energies have to be invested in the promotion of renewables and energy efficiency.
- WBGU urges the German government to persist in its efforts to change the allocation of voting rights within the World Bank and to strengthen the position of developing countries within the institution.

4.2.10
Poverty Reduction Strategy Papers

Developing countries produce Poverty Reduction Strategy Papers (PRSPs) in participatory processes. Since 1999 the World Bank, IMF as well as the G7 countries have required these national strategies as a prerequisite for granting debt relief and for disbursing additional funds at favourable terms. Fifty-five countries are part of the poverty reduction strategy (PRS) effort; a slight majority of these countries are in sub-Saharan Africa. The PRS process stipulates a multi-step approach in the beginning, before it evolves into a periodic policy cycle. At the beginning, the governments of the countries develop a draft strategy – the interim PRSP. This document does not require the consultation of civil society and can be kept relatively short and general. Countries that are included in the debt relief initiative for Heavily Indebted Poor Countries (HIPC) can then already receive some initial debt relief on the basis of such a draft. In addition, or if a country is not part of the HIPC initiative, concessionary multilateral donor funds are disbursed. In particular, this is the case for loans made by the World Bank's subsidiary organization IDA as well as funds that are allocated by IMF under the framework of the newly established Poverty Reduction and Growth Facility. Several bilateral donors have also stated their political willingness to make new bilateral commitments to development cooperation conditional on the presentation of an Interim PRSP, and ultimately a full PRSP.

Following the submission of the interim PRSP, a full PRSP has to be produced with the involvement of relevant social actors, such as enterprise associations, unions, churches and NGOs. Out of the group of 55 countries, 35 have so far completed this step (Table 4.2-8). The full PRSP has to include a comprehensive poverty analysis, which outlines poverty reduction strategies and includes information on implementation, monitoring and evaluation.

After three years there should, ideally, be a review or continuation. This means that PRSPs are not intended to be one-off policy papers and therefore should not be assessed as such. They should become steering tools for medium-term poverty reduction in the poorest countries and should stimulate among domestic stakeholders a continuous debate on the best ways to achieve this. Such a debate should become the basis for the countries involved taking greater ownership of the policies that affect them.

Since the introduction of the PRS approach there has been a significant increase in the participation of society in the development of the poverty reduction strategies. Social actors have played an active role in more than 35 countries that have so far produced full PRSPs. In some countries the process created for the first time a dialogue between the government and social actors. The most comprehensive study to date on the introduction of the PRS process has identified many shortcomings and weaknesses in the first phase of the PRS processes in relation to the aim of increasing countries' sense of ownership. However, the study is nevertheless optimistic that these processes can contribute to markedly improved poverty reduction efforts (Booth, 2003).

Despite overall positive assessments, all the studies highlight weaknesses in the PRS processes:
- In many countries the participatory processes suffer from significant organizational and technical shortcomings, which lead to considerable time pressures and poor information provision for participants.
- It is questionable whether socially representative participation has actually been achieved: the processes largely took place in the capitals. They favoured NGOs with full-time personnel, while grassroots organizations, indigenous and women's groups were placed at a disadvantage. The poor have not been involved.
- Many of the participatory processes developed on an *ad hoc* basis. They were mostly organized as consultations, and less as exercises in cooperation. The dialogue was rarely institutionalized, a notable exception being Uganda.
- National parliaments participated in only a few cases (Eberlei and Henn, 2003). In some instances parliaments did not even participate in those countries whose constitutions explicitly require their involvement in strategic decisions.
- Implementation of the results of the participatory processes into concrete results was undertaken in many different ways and has left many civil society actors questioning the power of participation.
- Despite the existence of national participatory processes, the content of the strategy papers continued to be influenced strongly by IMF, the World Bank and other donors (Cling, 2003).

At the same time, one should not underestimate the opportunities that are offered by the PRS processes, which have become apparent a few years after the introduction of the approach:
- Poverty reduction is presently high on the agendas of many developing and donor countries alike. This is the first time that there has been such a concerted effort. The German government has also repeatedly expressed its support for the PRS approach and aims to promote it through its development cooperation measures. It also intends to develop its country-specific policies in line with the relevant PRSPs.
- PRSPs are not a set of static policy principles, but rather documents that reflect the political cycle. PRSPs should be revised more frequently than only every three years: annual progress reports also provide opportunities to reflect on the experiences made during implementation. If the PRS policy cycle is integrated into a participatory monitoring process, it can develop into a learning process for wider society that supports longer-term poverty reduction.
- The participatory processes that are part of the PRS effort strengthen the position of civil society actors. This can increase the transparency of political processes and the accountability of governments. The beginnings of such developments are clearly recognizable (Eberlei and Führmann, 2004).

Table 4.2-8
Country-specific treatment of links between environment and poverty in PRSPs. Evaluation scheme:
0=no discussion, 1=marginal discussion, 2=significant discussion.
Source: Eberlei, 2004 (after Bojö and Reddy, 2003; World Bank, 2001c)

Country (month/year of current PRSP)	*Dependence on natural resources:* Impact of nutrition on income situation, and similar	*Environment and health:* Impact of air and water pollution on health	*Vulnerability:* Susceptibility to climatic changes (floods, drought, storms)	*Property rights and entitlements:* Access to natural resources, such as land and water
Albania (11/2001)	0	1	1	2: forests, fields
Armenia (2003)	1: fishery, energy	1: soil and water pollution	1: earthquakes, aridity	1
Azerbaijan (2003)	2: nutrition	2	1	0
Benin (12/2002)		1		
Bolivia (3/2001)	2: nutrition	2: breeding grounds for transmitters of diseases	2	2
Burkina Faso (5/2000)	2: nutrition	0	1: quantity of-rainfalls	1: land-use rights
Cambodia (12/2002)	2: water	1	2: floods	0
Cameroon (4/2003)	0	0	0	0
Chad (6/2003)	2: nutrition	1	2: droughts	1: water use
Ethiopia (7/2002)	2: nutrition	1	2: droughts	2: overexploitation
Georgia (6/2003)	1	1	2	0
Ghana (2/2003)	1	0	0	2: fee systems for water, forests
Guinea (1/2002)	2: nutrition	0	1	2: forest use rights, controlled exploitation
Guyana (11/2001)	2: nutrition	1	2: floods	2: overexploitation
Honduras (8/2001)	2: nutrition, air	2: disease/morbidity due to air pollution	2: hurricanes, natural disasters	2: overexploitation
Kyrgyzstan (12/2002)	0	1	0	0
Madagascar (7/2003)	2: nutrition	0	0	0
Malawi (4/2002)	2: nutrition, energy	1	0	2: soil and water use
Mali (5/2002)	2: nutrition, energy	1	2: droughts, pests	0
Mauretania (12/2000)	2: nutrition, energy	1	2: climatic variability	0
Mongolia (7/2003)	2: nutrition, energy	1	2: steppe fires, droughts, storms, floods	1: conflicts over grazing rights
Mozambique (4/2001)	2: nutrition, energy	1	2: floods, droughts	1
Nepal (5/2003)	0	0	0	0
Nicaragua (7/2001)	2: nutrition	2	2: droughts, storms, volcanic eruptions, earthquakes, fires, El Niño, floods	1: land-use rights
Niger (1/2002)	2: nutrition, energy, house construction	1	2: droughts	0
Rwanda (6/2002)	2: nutrition	1	1: rainfall	0
Senegal (2002)	1: nutrition	0	0	1: forest and water use
Sri Lanka (12/2002)	1	2: air and water pollution	0	2: forest and water use
Tajikistan (6/2002)	1	0	0	0
Tanzania (10/2000)	2: nutrition, energy	1	1: droughts	0
Uganda (3/2000)	1	1	0	0
Vietnam (5/2002)	2: food security, employment	0	2	0
Yemen (5/2002)	1: nutrition, water	1	1: aridity	0
Zambia (3/2002)	2: nutrition	0	1: rainfall	1

- The approach offers the opportunity to demand the implementation of poverty reduction strategies in all policy spheres, for example in budgetary policy.

4.2.10.1
Involving environmental actors in PRS processes

An analysis of the full PRSPs that were produced by 35 countries has illustrated that, in the PRS processes that have been completed up to now, actors that represent sustainable development or conservation issues have so far remained significantly underinvolved. References to environmental actors, such as environmental government ministries, environmental committees in parliaments or NGOs, can be found in only very few sections on participatory processes. The multiple weaknesses of the processes of developing and implementing PRSPs are particularly pronounced in the case of environmental actors (Eberlei, 2004).

Countries generally involved all government departments in the preparation process. The limited references to environmental ministries reflect the weak position of these sectoral ministries in many of the poorest countries. This is similarly true for environmental associations and NGOs, whose influence in those countries is limited. The fact that in many cases PRSPs were understood purely as social policy instruments provides a further explanation of the limited involvement of environmental actors in PRS processes. In many countries with well developed civil societies, environmental actors generally concentrate on specific environmental issues, such as on the environmental impact of dam construction. Heidbrink and Paulus (2000) have argued that 'so far there have only been initial steps towards moving the discussion on the National Strategies for Sustainable Development away from the environmental policy sphere'. However, the opposite is also true for PRSPs: political actors that focus on environmental issues have so far barely acknowledged the relevance of PRSPs to their own concerns. Some countries' PRS documents refer to the broad involvement of social actors in the development of environmental strategies; however, it is not clear whether these actors were also included in the PRS consultations.

4.2.10.2
Links between environment and poverty in PRSPs

In the early phase of the PRS processes there were concerns that the environmental dimension of development would be completely excluded (Heidbrink

and Paulus, 2000). By now environmental aspects are partially integrated: environmental factors are identified as a source of poverty, and, vice versa, poverty is recognized as a cause of environmental pressure and degradation. Numerous Participatory Poverty Assessments (PPAs) have also illustrated that the poor are fully aware of the links between environmental aspects and poverty. In their poverty analyses, 20 of the 35 countries that have been assessed have emphasized dependence on natural resources as an important, or even systemic factor that will need to be reduced through their poverty reduction strategies. Ensuring food security is the most important concern in this context.

The PRSP produced by Ethiopia is a good example of this: it identifies systematically the relationships between food availability and environmental risks and, in doing so, highlights the link to the vulnerability of the population, whose livelihoods are extremely dependent on environmental factors. The Ethiopian PRSP has a strong impact because it portrays this relationship not as an immutable fate that has been assigned by nature, but rather uses its analysis of the dependency on natural resources as a basis for concrete environmental policies in the areas of rural development and early-warning systems.

The impact of air and water pollution on disease is also a subject of discussion in many countries, albeit often only on a superficial level. While the issue of water pollution is on the agendas of many countries, air pollution, if mentioned at all, is only discussed in the margins. The poverty reduction strategy developed by Honduras provides a positive departure from this trend: a comprehensive analysis of air pollution, including its causes (such as an increase in the number of vehicles, industrial plants without environmental filters) and effects, such as respiratory diseases, is accompanied by a coordinated strategy aimed at reducing this form of environmental pollution.

More than two-thirds of the PRSPs emphasize the vulnerability of the poor and the impact that environmental factors have on the success of poverty reduction strategies. The problems posed by droughts as well as insufficient rainfalls, which prevent adequate harvests, are highlighted repeatedly. On the other hand, strong rainfalls, which can cause floods, pose a recurrent threat in some countries.

Besides natural disasters, anthropogenic environmental changes are identified less frequently as a cause of poverty. Some PRSPs identify limited access rights to natural resources, above all to land, forests or water, as a problem for the poor. On the other hand, there is hardly any mention of the influence of governmental policy upon the environment-poverty nexus (Eberlei, 2004).

4.2.10.3
Integrating environmental aspects within poverty reduction strategies

Environmentally relevant aspects play a visible role in the strategic approaches to poverty reduction. The need for sustainability is recognized in almost all countries that have developed poverty reduction strategies. A serious analysis of the problem has been undertaken by 14 countries. However, there is not a single persuasively presented strategy that includes clearly defined and integrated concepts as part of a policy aimed at sustainability. In several poverty reduction strategies there is also a conceptual confusion of the different dimensions of sustainability: for example, there are references to sustainable growth, which does not refer to an environmentally sound path of development, but rather describes a trajectory of sustained growth. Some countries also use the concept of sustainable livelihoods, which includes, or could include environmental aspects, but is generally interpreted from a predominantly economic perspective. Almost all countries that have developed poverty reduction strategies neglect the issue of environmental sustainability.

Many countries include environmental elements in their poverty reduction strategies. With the exception of Nepal, each country that has developed a poverty reduction strategy has integrated at least some environmentally relevant aspects into their strategies. Efforts to improve the quality of water are most frequent: the poverty reduction strategies identify access to safe drinking water and availability of proper sanitation as key issues. The pollution of water systems and the consequences for fishing are highlighted as important by a number of countries.

Attention is also given to soil erosion and desertification, as well as deforestation, which in some cases is connected to the soil theme. First steps to address this form of environmental degradation can be found in 26 of the 35 poverty reduction strategies, but in most cases these proposals are modest or rather general. Yet, some countries also provide convincing approaches: for example, Honduras provides a comprehensive analysis of the causes of deforestation. Overall, however, the issue of soil erosion, which is of great importance in many of the poorest countries, is not dealt with adequately (Holtz, 2003), and issues such as air pollution, loss of biodiversity or climate change are barely addressed.

4.2.10.4
Conflicts between poverty reduction and environmental policy approaches

Poverty reduction strategies show gaps not only with regard to issues linked to environmental sustainability. Gaps are also apparent in the discussion of the fundamental approach of all poverty reduction strategies aiming to reduce poverty through economic growth (pro-poor growth). There is rarely an explanation as to how economic growth is meant to help the poor, and the potential conflicts between the objectives of economic growth and environmental sustainability are not discussed. On the one hand, this could be due to the fact that the poverty reduction strategies provide a clear reflection of the old conflict between development and environmental sustainability. In the case of most governments the latter receives little more than lip service: instead, development is the priority. On the other hand, IMF and the World Bank do not require anything more detailed in their evaluations of documents and processes. Critical authors (such as Jerve, 2002) therefore view the PRS approach as merely the old neo-liberal development paradigm, which does not attach sufficient importance to environmental dimensions. There are many discussions on whether poverty reduction strategies do in fact represent national programmes, or whether actually they are dominated by donors. As far as the environmental dimension is concerned, there seems to be an alliance between donors and the governments of the South to accord primacy to economic growth.

This basic tendency is also evident in individual aspects of economic strategy, for example in energy policy. In a few cases, however, there are also positive examples that demonstrate the opposite, such as Armenia's consideration of energy efficiency and renewables in the development of its strategy, or Mozambique's intention to strengthen the solar energy sector. Inconsistencies between documents are apparent in particular in the field of energy policy. References to the links between environment and poverty that are contained in the poverty analyses are rarely taken up in the sections on strategy (Eberlei, 2004).

In some countries the tourism sector at least provides an exception from the rule according to which environmental and economic aspects are not linked convincingly in poverty reduction strategies. The development of this sector is approached as part of a poverty reduction strategy, and there are signs that the importance of a well-managed and protected environment as a competitive advantage and important production factor is being recognized.

4.2.10.5
Implementing environmentally relevant aspects of poverty reduction strategies

Although the implementation of poverty reduction strategies has by now begun in the majority of the countries that have developed such strategies, the process has been dragging more than had been expected. Implementation has been documented in progress reports in only a dozen countries, and a lack of expert personnel means that the production of high-quality reports is beyond the capacities of many countries. As a result, it is only possible to provide an interim assessment at this stage. Such an assessment shows that environmentally relevant aspects can be found in many countries' policies, implementation plans and budget preparations that describe the implementation of PRSPs in more detail. However, while countries such as Albania, Honduras, Cambodia and Mozambique give detailed accounts of their plans, most countries have provided this information at only a very basic level.

Some countries are already carrying out specific environmental projects or programmes to which the poverty reduction strategies refer, or the implementation of which is thematically linked to the implementation of the poverty reduction strategies. To the extent that an analysis of poverty reduction strategy documents can show, no new programmes with specific relevance to the environment were introduced to support poverty reduction strategies. Rather, they are either projects that are already underway, or projects whose start happened to coincide with the conclusion of poverty reduction strategies.

Some countries have explicitly included environmentally relevant aspects in the information they provide on the PRS monitoring systems. This is a further sign of a political willingness to implement these aspects. Bolivia, Burkina Faso and Mozambique, which have provided comparatively comprehensive information, should be highlighted as positive examples in this regard. While these countries list standards, tools and indicators for goals and to some extent even for targets, the information provided by most countries, if available at all, is again only superficial. Approximately 40 per cent of the full PRSPs use indicators that refer to the environmental aspects of the UN Millennium Development Goals (Bojö and Reddy, 2003).

Information on the evaluation and reformulation of the strategy, which should take place three years after the presentation of the full PRSP, can barely be found. Progress can be detected in the treatment of environmentally relevant aspects from the interim versions of the poverty reduction strategies that were produced at the start, to the full PRSPs, and finally

the progress reports. The degree of complexity as well as the quality of the discussion of environmental aspects has improved in the 12 countries that have presented progress reports. These reports also provide the only information about which of the environmentally relevant aspects of the strategy were actually tackled.

There are no signs that the international actors who are pushing the PRS agenda pay increased attention to the implementation of environmentally relevant aspects in poverty reduction strategies. For example, the key report by IMF and the World Bank on the progress in the PRS approach (2003) does not place any coherent emphasis on the link between poverty and the environment: individual aspects, such as clean water, receive only marginal mention, and controversial questions, such as energy issues, are approached exclusively from economic perspectives (e.g. energy supply as a prerequisite for investment). Establishing links between poverty and environmental aspects is largely viewed as a distraction, because it is feared that this would overcomplicate poverty reduction strategies. In addition, the dividing of the relevant pieces of work between, and even within individual donor agencies has resulted in parallel work on different strategic approaches. It is not recognized that environmental policy can support poverty reduction.

4.2.10.6
Case study: Burkina Faso

Development and content of the PRSP
Burkina Faso is one of the pioneers in the field of poverty reduction strategies. The country already presented its full PRSP in May 2000, that is, only a few months after the introduction of the new approach. IMF and the World Bank accepted the report shortly afterwards. In doing so, the donor community rewarded the country's government for the comparatively strong focus on poverty. The Letter of Intent for Sustainable Human Development, which had been passed in 1995, served as the basis for the PRS consultations. The process was steered by an inter-ministerial committee, which was divided into four working groups, including the working group on Natural Resources Management. However, representatives from civil society were not involved in these working groups and were consulted only superficially at national and regional level in a series of workshops. The description of the participatory processes mentions at one point the 'Comprehensive Framework for Consultations between NGOs and Associations on Environment and Development', which also deals with environmental issues. However,

it remains unclear whether this framework played a role in the PRS process.

The consultative process for the development of the PRSP began in November 1999 and took place within a few weeks. While the documents mention the participation of unions, cooperatives, human rights organizations, other development NGOs, churches, the media and different grassroots organization, environmental activists have criticized the consultation process: according to them, the National Action Plan to Combat Desertification (NAP), which already existed before the poverty reduction strategy was produced, was ignored in the development of the strategy, even though 50,000 people had been consulted during the development of the NAP. This is not surprising, given that many countries did not even refer back to the widely existing action plans for poverty reduction that had been produced in the follow-up process to the 1995 Copenhagen World Social Summit.

The poverty analysis that is part of Burkina Faso's PRSP establishes a general link between the environment and the degree of poverty. According to the analysis, the poor perceive an inhospitable natural environment as a factor that exacerbates poverty. While the PRSP refers to the letter of intent mentioned above and uses the concept of sustainable development repeatedly in this context, it does not consider environmental aspects in its economic growth strategy.

The PRSP analyses how the vulnerability of agriculture to environmental influences could be limited. Soil erosion and irrigation are cited as the key issues. Since 1984 the Government has been working to address the issue of population growth and to ensure access to land for the poor. Potential issues of conflict, such as the growing competition for fertile land as a result of the commercialization of agriculture, are excluded from the analysis.

The experiences made in Burkina Faso during implementation are slightly better documented than in other countries, since there are already three progress reports. The 2001 report highlights the budget funds that were used specifically for environmental protection measures, while the 2002 report mentions the formation of dedicated environmental sections within government ministries. There is also information on a programme, which started in 2001, that is aimed at stopping soil erosion. In addition, since 2001 a new technical system that can influence rainfalls artificially (SAAGA) has been installed. Finally, an Environmental Plan for Sustainable Development has been announced.

EVALUATION AND FURTHER DEVELOPMENT OF THE PRSP

In April 2003 Burkina Faso began the process of evaluating and developing further its poverty reduction strategy. The intention is that this will result in a second-generation PRSP. A summary progress report was published in December 2003. This report refers to the period 2000–2002 and serves as the basis for formulating a new strategy. It provides information on how many of the funds that were freed up as a result of debt relief were used by respective government ministries: less than half a percent of these funds were allocated to the policy area for which the Ministry for the Environment and Water is responsible. While it should be assumed that other government ministries could also contribute to the financing of environmental sustainability, the low percentage allocated to the environment and water ministry nevertheless indicates that these issues do not receive high political priority.

The establishment of the National Observatory on Poverty and Sustainable Human Development (ONAPAD) can, however, be judged positively. This institution is expected to monitor the PRS implementation process and to assess its performance. ONAPAD has introduced a set of indicators including, among others, several designed to measure changes in the environmental sphere and the management of natural resources.

The report also judges the Integrated Soil Fertility Management Plans programme, which began in 2001, to have been a success. The goal of digging 50,000 manure pits was attained. Within the framework of a national agricultural congress it was agreed with farmers to prepare up to 200,000 manure pits in 2003 and 2004.

The report also celebrates the SAAGA programme as a success: the technology prolonged the 2002 rainy period, and agricultural production was increased significantly as a result. There is also, however, some scepticism about the programme.

The Government makes an overall positive assessment but also states, without providing further detail: 'Experience in PRSP implementation during the period under review has indicated that the priority program should be extended to sectors as sanitation, environment, the fight against desertification, rural electrification, promotion of small scale mining, and promotion of small and medium scale industries and enterprises, which will have a clear impact on poverty' (GoBF, 2003).

Here there are self-critical reflections in the midst of the many positive messages, but they are not elaborated upon further. The predominantly positive evaluation of the integration of environmental aspects in Burkina Faso's poverty reduction strategy is also largely shared by the few assessments that focus on the link between reduction strategies and environmental aspects. Compared with many other PRS countries, Burkina Faso has made serious efforts to integrate environmental aspects into the poverty reduction strategy.

4.2.10.7
Assessment and recommendations

In the five years since its introduction the PRS approach has become a central political planning tool in more than 50 developing countries. Implementation of the strategies has begun on a broad front, albeit much more slowly than had been expected by IMF and the World Bank.

In the 35 countries that have produced full PRSPs there are signs that the theme of environmental sustainability in its many various dimensions does play a role in the strategies. The reciprocal links between poverty reduction and environmental protection are now recognized in many countries and are reflected to some extent in the political strategies.

The different degree of emphasis that has been placed on environmental aspects is not surprising, given that poverty reduction strategies are the responsibility of individual countries. It is possible to determine approximate categories (Table 4.2.8): in six to eight countries environmental aspects have been integrated to a significant extent into the strategy documents. A further 15 countries have reflected environmental aspects in their strategies, but not systematically and consistently. Eleven countries have at best incorporated environmental sustainability in only some individual aspects.

The involvement of environmental actors in the participatory PRS processes is not satisfactory. Only a few countries have involved expert ministries and environmental NGOs in a meaningful way. Actors from the social policy sphere have dominated the participatory process, which has resulted in an emphasis in particular on the education and health sectors. The basic principles laid out in the PRSPs have been influenced not only through the participatory processes, but also to a significant extent by the interaction between governments and external actors, in particular IMF and the World Bank. Within the donor community economically oriented actors had, and continue to have, a strong influence on poverty reduction strategies, while neither national nor international environmental actors have been involved in a meaningful way in PRS processes.

This is also reflected in the approaches, objectives and programmatic messages: for example, the health sector, which is a frequent focus of poverty reduction

strategies, provides many overlaps with environmental issues. Curative health policy approaches, however, dominate, while too little attention is paid to the environmental causes of diseases. This is to some extent also due to an inadequate linking of poverty analyses with poverty reduction strategies: it is not uncommon for both strands of work to have been developed by different expert teams and to have remained unconnected. Agricultural policy objectives and messages – another important focus of poverty reduction strategies – also provide obvious overlaps with environmental issues. Nevertheless, while countries that face significant problems of soil erosion and desertification have addressed these aspects, they have generally done so only from a perspective that views the environment as a factor of production. Little reference has been made to the environmental impact of population growth.

PRSPs generally do not highlight conflicts between different objectives: only a few PRSPs provide convincing accounts of the impact of economic growth strategies on poverty reduction, while the effects of the strategies on the environmental sustainability of development processes are left completely out of the analyses.

There is still little that can be said about the implementation of the environmental strategies of PRSPs. On the one hand, the implementation of most PRSPs began only a relatively short time ago. On the other hand, there is also a lack of information, as, so far, only one-third of the countries that produced full PRSPs have presented progress reports. There has been a significant qualitative improvement in how environmental aspects have been addressed in five of the 12 progress reports that have already been presented.

The discussion has moved the focus towards potential reforms that would be suited to give environmental aspects more space and weight in poverty reduction strategies:

• Processes are more important than documents: greater attention should be paid to involving environmental actors throughout the entire PRS cycle. This requires the governments of developing countries to listen more to their own ministries that deal with environmental issues and to integrate environmental NGOs into the processes more consciously than has so far been the case. The task for such NGOs in PRS countries is to participate actively in PRS processes by presenting concrete proposals for poverty analyses and poverty reduction strategies. The international partners of the governments as well as of the environmental NGOs should pay greater attention to the participatory processes and offer more support to their partners. Greater focus on the involvement of parliaments is imperative. There is an overall need to promote the institutionalization of participation within PRS processes.

- The link between the environmental dimension in poverty analyses and political strategies has to be strengthened. Explicit analyses of the causes, which identify above all the human causes of environmental degradation, have to be integrated into poverty reduction strategies and used as the basis for strategic objectives. The logical gaps that are frequently found between analyses and strategic approaches to eliminating or reducing the problems call for improved capacities among governments and NGOs.

- The evaluation of poverty reduction strategies has to place more emphasis on environmental sustainability. This presents a challenge for donors, in particular IMF and the World Bank, for which the environmental dimensions of poverty reduction are secondary to the economic and social dimensions. The task for donors and governments in PRS countries is to establish meaningful links between these dimensions and not to shy away from addressing conflicts between objectives. The Joint Staff Assessments of IMF and World Bank should consider environmental aspects more systematically than they have done so far. The annual progress reports of IMF and World Bank could also pay systematic attention to environmental aspects.

- The coherence of strategic planning tools must be strengthened. The parallel existence of different programmes and many sectoral and thematic strategic approaches as well as donor-focussed strategy documents (CAS, PRGF, etc.) is too taxing for all participants. A strict and consistent focus on the UN Millennium Goals, as is already being carried out by some countries, would offer a feasible framework for the integration of poverty reduction and environmental sustainability.

- The debate on pro-poor growth has only just started and must not be limited to the question of how the poor can profit – in the sense of obtaining a share of income – from economic growth. The question of how growth strategies affect sustainable development in the poorest countries, including the environmental dimensions, also has to be addressed more strongly from a conceptual perspective.

- The PRS monitoring systems are not just technical tools, but also have political relevance: the question of which indicators are used, which data are collected and who has access to this data must not be left to statisticians. The principle of participation also has to be applied in this context. It is, moreover, the task of international experts in the donor organizations to develop and propose relevant indicators that capture developments in the environment-poverty nexus.

The analysis of poverty reduction strategies leaves no doubt that, if these strategies are to be successful, more attention will have to be paid to the environmental dimension of development in the poorest countries. However, poverty reduction strategies also illustrate that neither the governments nor the majority of civil society actors in the poorest countries accord high importance to the protection of the environment. The belief that, in the case of conflicts between objectives, the reduction particularly of absolute poverty should take primacy over the longer-term perspective of environmental sustainability continues to dominate in the South, as it does in the North.

4.2.11
The European Union as development policy actor

As a result of its Common Commercial Policy, the European Union (EU) has become the world's largest trading power, influencing the design of the global economy and economic North-South relations. As a union of states that includes four members of the G8 group, it carries substantial weight in international negotiations on the environment. Furthermore, it constitutes the largest source of Official Development Assistance (ODA) worldwide. Depending on the fluctuating contributions made by the US and Japan, the EU provides a good half of international ODA. The lion's share of 80 per cent of the EU's overall contributions is, however, generated through bilateral ODA payments made by its member states.

European development policy in the narrower sense therefore only refers to inputs administered and devised by the European Commission, amounting to about 11 per cent of overall international ODA. These 'actions in external relations' are, again, to be divided into those financed out of the general EU budget, and those administered by the European Development Fund (EDF). The latter is financed through obligatory contributions made by the EU member states and is used for the exclusive benefit of the ACP states, currently numbering 77 states in Africa (48), the Caribbean (15) and the Pacific (14). The EEC/EC has been establishing special commercial and political relations with these states in treaties since 1975: The four Lomé Conventions and, since 2000, the Cotonou Agreement. By stylizing these special relations as a model for partnership and the EDF as Europe's Marshall Plan, the EU put itself under high pressure to perform and justify its actions. Article 130, EC Treaty, establishes the basic principles for

EU development policy. They became known as the three C's:

- *Complementarity:* The EU's development policy shall be complementary to the policies pursued by the member states. It is remarkable that the treaty emphasizes bilateralism in development policy, despite aiming at greater Europeanization of many other policy fields.
- *Coordination:* Article 130 (X) of the Maastricht Treaty (1992) explicitly requests the member states to coordinate their policies on development. Even the Treaty of Amsterdam, which aimed to strengthen the Common Foreign and Security Policy (CFSP), did not abolish the nation state's independence in development policy, despite the integration of the same within the CFSP project.
- *Coherence:* Article 130 (V) obliges the EU to take account of the political objectives of development cooperation in all decisions which affect developing countries. This coherence principle allows the institutions of the European Union great flexibility. However, the mainstreaming of development policy objectives in other policies remains insufficient in a great number of areas. In some policy areas, the coherence principle is violated. This applies particularly to the Common Agricultural Policy which, due to its partly protectionist nature, counteracts the objectives of development policies.

European development policy incorporates the following programmes, which also include transition countries:

- The consolidation of trade relations and cooperation with states in Central and Eastern Europe (CEE) and the former Soviet states forming the CIS is to narrow the divide between western and eastern Europe. The PHARE programme for the CEE states and the TACIS programme (Technical Assistance for the Commonwealth of Independent States) have been equipped with considerable funds. PHARE was complemented in 1999 by two further programmes in preparation for EU accession: ISPA (Instrument for Structural Policies for Pre-Accession) and SAPARD (Special Accession Programme for Agricultural and Rural Development).
- The CARDS programme (Community Assistance for Restructuring, Democracy and Stabilisation) is the EU's main instrument for the promotion and stabilization of the Balkan states, which World Bank statistics categorize as developing countries. According to the EU Commission, the volume of these programmes exceeded that of the EDF in 2002 (Table 4.2-9).
- The consolidation of trade relations and cooperation with the Mediterranean and neighbouring

Table 4.2-9
EU external assistance (2002).
Source: European Commission, 2003

Programmes/Regions	Commitments [€ million]	Payments [€ million]
PHARE	1,683	1,101
ISPA	1,109	398
TACIS	444	395
SAPARD	555	124
Food aid	506	417
Humanitarian aid	520	474
Asia	575	454
Latin America	333	182
Sub-Saharan Africa	124	119
Mediterranean	633	705
Middle East	151	138
Balkans	821	749
Overall	*8,438*	*6,052*
EDF	1,768	1,853
General budget + EDF	10,206	7,905

countries, promoted by the Barcelona Declaration in 1995, also pursues a security policy goal: To prevent the growth of fundamentalist movements and migration pressures. The objective of the Barcelona Declaration is the establishment of a Euro-Mediterranean free-trade area by 2010. At the same time, the EU is, with substantial resources, promoting the peace process in the Middle East, with a special commitment to the Palestinian autonomous areas.

- The extension of trade relations and cooperation with regional economic communities (ASEAN, MERCOSUR and the San-José countries in Central America) and with important countries in Asia and Latin America underscores the EU's interest in worldwide cooperation.

The EU furthermore contributes substantial food aid out of its surplus stocks, and disaster and refugee aid which is organized by ECHO – the European Commission's Humanitarian Aid Department founded in 1992. EU food and disaster aid, financed out of the EU budget, accounts for more than half of EDF funds allocated for long-term structural assistance. The portion of food aid, a controversial development policy issue, which amounted to one-third of total EU assistance in the 1980s, was reduced to 7 per cent in 2002. Criticism by NGOs and the European Parliament has thus made an impact.

After the end of the Cold War, the EU reoriented its development cooperation from South to East and into the Mediterranean. The reasons for this shift were obvious. The destabilization of these regions represented an immediate security risk unequalled by more distant poverty and crisis areas. It was furthermore feared that substantial differences in wealth would lead to large migration movements. While regional assistance programmes directed at neighbouring buffer zones were massively increased, the portion allocated to the EDF out of the EU's total 'external assistance' budget decreased from more than 50 per cent to less than 20 per cent. Among the top 20 recipients of assistance are ten Latin American countries followed by India and Bangladesh. At the same time, African countries that mostly belong to the group of the poorest developing countries fell behind.

The integration of the Development Council in the General Affairs and External Relations Council, decided by the Seville European Council (2002), signifies the strategic embedding of development policy in the Common Foreign and Security Policy. While serving EU geo-political interest, this may result in the devaluation of development policy as an independent policy area.

4.2.11.1
From Lomé to Cotonou: Trade and aid

On France's insistence, the association of the former French colonies was already established in the founding treaties of the EEC. When Great Britain joined the EEC, former British colonies in Africa, the Caribbean and the South Pacific joined the group of aspiring countries. The first two association conventions, signed in 1964/69 in Yaoundé, Cameroon, were followed by the four Lomé Conventions, signed in the capital of Togo. The first three Lomé Conventions covered five-year periods, the last Convention (1990–1999) was effective for ten years. While their contents were modified each time to reflect the outcomes of tough negotiations, the following core elements were maintained:

- The EEC/EU granted non-reciprocal trade preferences, allowing all industrial goods from ACP countries tariff-free access to European consumer markets without demanding a corresponding treatment. The value of this allowance was, however, more symbolic than practical as few ACP countries were able to export competitive industrial products. For many countries, special trading protocols on beef, bananas, sugar and rum were of greater importance. They guaranteed prices that, at times, exceeded world market prices considerably.
- The stabilization of export receipts – not prices – of 46 agricultural products (STABEX) and seven mineral resources (SYSMIN) has been regarded as exemplary. STABEX, which was financed out of the EDF, gave funds to offset losses when export

earnings of ACP countries fell below their average earnings of the previous four years. Losses had to reach a given percentage and the country in question had to depend on the export of particular raw materials to a certain degree.

The stabilization of export receipts appeared to provide more advantages than the stabilization of prices as it could also offset losses resulting from breaks in production, e.g. through natural disasters. Moreover, this approach did not remove the price-formation mechanisms of supply and demand. Nevertheless, critics argued that STABEX hindered diversification of production and export structures.

For the poorest ACP states, the financial help of the EDF has always been more important than the STABEX and SYSMIN funds as its conditions for allocation were, and still are, very favourable: 97 per cent of its assistance payments are allocated in the form of non-repayable grants. Its budget has consequently been the subject of repeated disputes during negotiations of the convention, especially because it had to be divided between a growing number of eligible countries.

The EDF, which was also used to fund STABEX and SYSMIN, is not financed out of the EU budget but through contributions made by the Union's member states. It is therefore vulnerable with respect to quota negotiations and excluded from the European Parliament's budgetary control and supervision by the anti-corruption authority. The EDF has occasionally been celebrated as Europe's Marshall Plan. Its limited budget does not, however, justify this claim.

The ACP states' disappointment over the limited advantages gained through their special trade relationship with the EC/EU mounted. Their portion of the world market had halved in two decades. Their share of exports into the EU had, due to their inability to improve their competitiveness, also diminished. The preferential trade treatment had furthermore not contributed to reducing the concentration of ACP exports upon a small number of raw materials (Wolf, 1996).

Within the EU, growing criticism was directed at the bureaucratic and inefficient management of the EDF and at a project policy that even failed to call off promised funds. After the expiration of Lomé IV (1999), €10,000 million were still in the pipeline of promised funds that had not been implemented into projects. Remainders of the sixth EDF (1985–1990) were, for example, only called off in 2002. The limited success achieved in important policy areas, e.g. the fight against poverty, the protection of the environment, and human rights policy, was met with even more severe criticism (Kappel, 1999). The construction of 'cathedrals in the desert' has been criticized in many reports, one of them dating back as far as 1982, as well as in the European Parliament. The EDF became a virtual byword for inefficiency, bureaucratic inertia and lack of transparency and targeting.

4.2.11.2
The Cotonou Agreement

Following years of controversial negotiations between the EU and the ACP countries, the Cotonou Agreement was signed on 23 June 2000 in the capital of Benin. Its ratification by all EU member states was, however, delayed by two years. The new agreement is to run for a period of 20 years. It changed the basis of the EU's trade and development policies with the 77 ACP states.

Changes in the area of trade cooperation demonstrate the end of 25 years of EU development policy as initiated by the Lomé Convention in 1975. According to the EU Commission, a highly protected powerhouse of trade is to change into a less protected and competitive market. The non-reciprocal trade preferences have been declared incompatible with WTO rules, which are based on the principle of a free market. WTO-compatible trade arrangements are to substitute them and a new trading arrangement is to be negotiated by 2007 during a transitory period. In the meantime, a WTO waiver is requested. At the same time, STABEX and SYSMIN shall be gradually abolished.

Within the agreement, the EU confirms its intention to prepare the smooth integration of competitively-weak ACP countries into the world economy, to strengthen regional economic communities and to enter into regional agreements with them. In 2001, the EU adopted the 'Everything But Arms' initiative to benefit the 49 Least Developed Countries (LDCs), which include 39 ACP countries. It granted duty-free access from 2004 to all LDC exports, with the exception of bananas, sugar and rice. More significant was, however, the EU delegation's willingness and intention to gradually reduce its agricultural protectionism, especially its export subsidies counter-productive in development policy terms. This new stance was declared by the EU delegation at the WTO negotiations in July/August 2004, following the failed round of negotiations in the Mexican city of Cancún. However, concrete and binding arrangements, which have to overcome massive resistance by national agrarian lobbies, have yet to be made.

The Cotonou Agreement made any assistance from the European Development Fund conditional on the implementation of basic human rights, democratic principles and good governance. According to EU usage, the latter refers especially to the rule of law and to measures taken against corruption, which is common in many ACP countries (Conzelmann, 2003). It is above all this political dimension of the Cotonou Agreement which has been considered as marking a point of departure to new shores in EU development policy (Schmidt, 2002). On the one hand, the EU promised preferential treatment for countries implementing democratic reforms and making development efforts. On the other hand, it threatened regimes unwilling to reform with sanctions.

The agreement also envisages greater participation of non-state actors in development cooperation. Private companies are to be involved in the process of planning and financing projects while NGOs are to support the mobilization of civil self-help organizations. The European Parliament remains, however, excluded from decision-making processes on the EDF budget, and also the new country and regional programmes. The latter are to achieve greater efficiency and more accurate targeting through regional and country-specific measures.

4.2.11.3
Administrative reforms for improved coherence

The EU Commission, which had been reorganized in 1999, also responded to the massive criticism of its ponderous procedures for granting and processing assistance by making administrative and procedural reforms. However, fragmentation of competence within the EU Commission, especially between the Development Directorate-General (DG Development) and the Europe Aid Cooperation Office, established in 2001, continues to cause considerable loss of time and also causes interdepartmental friction. Furthermore, separate directorates-general shape development policies for important areas like trade, environment and agriculture. Their objectives are in many cases incompatible. Even the newly established Quality Support Group, whose purpose is to coordinate the activities of different directorates-general with regard to external relations and to achieve overall coherence, struggles to find sufficient common ground for competing departmental interests. The Development Assistance Committee of the OECD (OECD DAC, 2002) carried out a detailed analysis of administrative weaknesses and friction in the EU Commission's development policy decision-making process, highlighting the failure to fulfil the principles of coordination and coherence. The upgrading of the role of EU delegations in recipient countries demonstrates that progress has been made in the centralized and bureaucratic decision-making process. For example, the process of designing Country Strategy Papers (CSPs) shows a connection to the PRSPs that is not limited to their title.

4.2.11.4
The primacy of poverty reduction: Stated but unfulfilled

Article 19 of the Cotonou Agreement establishes the reduction of poverty as a central objective of ACP-EC cooperation. A joint declaration on 10 November 2000 by the Council of Ministers and the EU Commission emphasized: 'Community development policy is based on the principle of sustainable, equitable and participatory human and social development. […] The central objective must be poverty reduction and ultimately its eradication.' The draft of the EU constitution commits itself in one of its first Articles to the universal eradication of poverty. Its chapter on development policy reaffirms this objective. At the same time, the Council of Ministers and the EU Commission committed themselves in several declarations to the MDGs and pledged to make an important contribution to their achievement. One can certainly talk of a programmatic 'millennium shift' in European development policy.

However, if the EU wants to fulfil the objectives of these declarations and self-imposed obligations it will also need to make considerable changes in the operation of its development policy. Several studies and evaluations produced by the DAC and by NGO networks have shown that the EU performs badly in comparison with many bilateral donors with regard to investment in basic social services (VENRO, 2002). According to DAC statistics, in 2000 the EDF invested only 4 per cent of its payments in basic education, 2 per cent in basic health services and 3 per cent in water provision and sewage disposal. The portion of EU aid delivered to the poorest developing countries during the term of Lomé IV (1990–1999) decreased from 70 per cent (1990) to 38 per cent (2000). Another evaluation of the new European development policy conducted by Alliance 2015 (2004), an affiliation of European NGOs, gives a harsh verdict on the question of the EU's contribution to the achievement of the MDGs: 'There is a large discrepancy between policy and implementation, between theory and reality, between rhetoric and results.' However, the criticism expressed in the report is supported by statistics that differ considerably from those used by the DAC. Nevertheless, it confirms the low social priority of EU assistance. Plans for the ninth EDF, which were initiated in 2001, show a stronger emphasis on basic social services.

Funding of the EDF is to be only slightly increased to €13,500 million between 2000 and 2007. This amount is to be distributed among 77 countries. The fund can therefore not be expected to perform better than it did with the help of financial injections amounting to nearly US$50,000 million over a quarter of a century. However, rather than pinning their hopes on the EDF to achieve sustainable reduction of poverty, development strategists are focusing on the promotion of ACP countries' competitiveness and greater integration into the world market and also on incentives for private investors. Hence, the Cotonou Agreement introduced an investment facility to stimulate private investment. The EU Commission coordinates Country Strategy Papers with the World Bank and likewise assumes that trade and direct investment will greatly promote development. Many ACP states exporting only raw materials and thus unattractive to private investors view this as insufficient. They want external financial aid.

The EU's success in overcoming its widely criticized lack of efficiency in development cooperation depends largely on reform of its own decision-making and administrative structures, and on the 25 member states' willingness to concede it more competence in coordinating development policies for individual countries. Bilateral cooperation still accounts for 80 per cent of the overall assistance provided by the EU. Europe Aid, the new department established in 2001, has still to prove it can speed up the flow of funds without becoming a gigantic and correspondingly expensive bureaucracy. There are experienced implementing organizations within the member states that can also implement EU projects with the assistance of development policy instructions from Brussels. Stronger competition would put German implementing organizations – especially GTZ and KfW, which have a national monopoly – under pressure to become more competitive and thus efficient.

4.2.11.5
The interplay between environmental degradation and poverty: Perceived but yet to be acted on

The EU Commission participated in the evaluation of the policy paper on 'Linking poverty reduction and environmental management' presented to the WSSD by several international development organizations. In 2003, it presented a draft declaration containing a strategy and an action plan to mainstream climate change issues in development cooperation activities (COM(03)85). Article 32 of the Cotonou Agreement declares environmental protection and sustainable utilization of natural resources to be central objectives of cooperation with ACP treaty states. It calls upon all treaty partners to 'mainstream environmental sustainability into all aspects of development cooperation and support programmes and projects implemented by the various actors.' Sustainable development is therefore defined as a cross-sector task and is placed high up on the development policy agenda of the EU.

The EU Commission's 2003 annual report on EC development policy and external assistance in 2002 delivered a convincing rationale for linking environmental protection with the fight against poverty: 'There is a growing international consensus on the links between poverty and the environment. In fact, environmental problems are an important cause of poverty and generally hit the poor hardest. However, the poorest often contribute significantly to environmental degradation due to a lack of alternatives. Loss of agricultural land, shrinking forests, diminishing supplies of clean water, dwindling fish stocks, and the threat of growing social and ecological vulnerability as a result of climate change and decreasing biological diversity have the most severe impacts in the developing world where most of the poor live. Better environmental management is therefore essential to long-term poverty reduction.'

However, implementing this realization in actual programmes has so far only been rudimentary. The EU Commission itself draws the following conclusion in its 2003 annual report: 'A review of 60 Country Strategy Papers undertaken in 2002 highlights the fact that environmental issues are not yet consistently addressed'. A more detailed review of these CSPs shows that this self-criticism in fact plays down the lack of consistency between strategic considerations and operational action. Only a few country strategies defined environmental protection as a programming priority. A list of areas focused on in the CSPs finalized in 2002 for ACP countries does not even include environmental protection as an independent category (Table 4.2-10).

However, in the Regional Strategy Papers for ACP states, the management of natural resources has a 9.3 per cent share of allocations. 57 per cent of funds are allocated to the promotion of economic integration and trade and 31 per cent to transport and communication. When analysing these numbers, one has to be aware that the EU's strengthened commitment since the WSSD to water supply and the promotion of renewable energies can be seen as part of the cross-sector theme of sustainable development. Nevertheless, the CSPs show there is an urgent need for the EU to speed up the implementation of its strategy papers.

While criticizing the environment policy implementation deficit in the EU's development programmes, the Union's pioneering role in negotiations on international and regional environmental regimes – especially in the area of climate protection – must

Table 4.2-10
Programming priorities in the Country Strategy Papers for ACP countries.
Source: European Commission, 2003

Area of concentration	Share of planned resources for ACP countries [%]
Transport	30
Support for macroeconomic policies and fight against poverty	23
Capacity building/promotion of institutions	11
Education and health	9
Food security and rural development	9
Water supply/sanitation	7

not be overlooked. This is, however, counteracted by a form of trade protectionism that not only has harmful effects on the development opportunities of poor countries, but can also lead to environmental degradation. For example, fisheries agreements with Western African countries benefit highly subsidized fishing fleets from EU countries, which not only decimate fish stocks in western African coastal areas, but also deprive numerous coastal fishing communities in the area of their most important source of income and jeopardize the local population's protein supply (Section 3.3.4.2). Agricultural protectionism and large subsidies causing environmental degradation are both responsible for inconsistencies in EU environmental policy.

4.2.11.6
Conclusions and recommendations

European development policy's lack of success and the inefficiency of the EDF have been widely criticized, especially by the European Parliament and NGOs. In particular, criticism was directed at the marginal focus on poverty of EDF projects and insufficient coherence between trade, environment and development policy. Nevertheless, WBGU urges stronger Europeanization of the individual development policies of EU member states for the following reasons:
• The EU could and should pursue its development policy objectives with far greater efficiency if it had a more unified development policy instead of 25 individual, poorly coordinated, and at times even competing development policies which are only complemented by a small common segment. It has to concentrate its efforts especially on Africa, as it also bears a historic responsibility for the prob-

lems of that continent. Better coordination means that the EU and its member states should sectorally do what they are best at. The EU should concentrate on cross-border programmes.

- Europeanization does not mean the establishment of a new super bureaucracy but the strengthening of the political coordination and governance role of the EU Commission under the parliamentary control of the European Parliament. This also means that the EDF would be integrated in the EU budget and thus be subject to parliamentary control. Europeanization of development policy also means that executive directors representing EU member countries in multilateral development banks, who wield a great deal of voting power, come to more agreement amongst themselves, one possible effect of this being to establish a counterbalance to the US.
- If the EU is serious about developing a truly common foreign and security policy, a development policy that includes policies for worldwide peace and preventive security measures represents an important strategic element of this European project. It has to be integrated into coherent policies on external relations, security, human rights and the environment as well as into the important and already common trade policy.
- With its successful history of integration and its model of a social and ecological market economy, the EU has more to offer than the limited EDF. It should use its comparative advantage as an interface for integration more effectively to promote regional projects of cooperation and integration which will form part of the future in a regionalized world.
- To claim a guiding role in the sphere of environmental and development policy, the EU has to overcome the contradictions to its own principle of coherence. It has to do its 'homework' so that this coherence principle becomes embedded in its own policy and decision-making processes. It is not enough to play a progressive role in international negotiations on the environment if, at the same time, EU agricultural, trade and development policies neglect principles of sustainability.

Initially, the EU must direct its development policy more resolutely towards the MDGs and, secondly, draw operational conclusions from its recognition of the link between environmental degradation and poverty. These two policy areas exhibit considerable weaknesses in implementation and a lack of credibility. The EU represents the biggest source of ODA and thus carries considerable weight in international development policy. However, it still lacks a formative profile, which it could gain by increasing the focus of its development policy on poverty and ecology.

4.2.12
Germany

In this section, WBGU analyses the German government's poverty reduction policies in relation to global environmental protection. It considers the global dimension of the National Strategy for Sustainable Development, the Programme of Action 2015 for poverty reduction, bilateral development cooperation, and foreign trade policy.

4.2.12.1
National Strategy for Sustainable Development

The starting point for this analysis of German government policy is the National Strategy for Sustainable Development, which was adopted by the Federal Cabinet in April 2002 (Bundesregierung, 2002). The core of the Strategy is the guiding vision of sustainable development, described under four headings: intergenerational equity, quality of life, social cohesion, and international responsibility. The Strategy dedicates an entire chapter, entitled 'Taking Global Responsibility', to this latter dimension, with the focus on reducing poverty and promoting development, and on global environmental and resource protection.

The environment-poverty nexus is expressly stated to be the basis for a German global strategy for sustainable development. The federal government acknowledges that the impacts of global environmental change are distributed unequally and are 'a threat to people's foundations of life, especially in the South'. Elsewhere, the text is even more explicit: 'Environment and development form a unit. An integrated approach should link the fight against poverty with regard for human rights, economic development, environmental protection, and responsible action by governments'.

Two out of a total of 21 indicators, which define targets and serve as a means of monitoring progress, are dedicated to international responsibility; these are development assistance (ODA as a proportion of GNI) and EU imports from developing countries. The quantitative targets formulated for these international indicators are far less ambitious than those defined for other areas. Most of the targets contained in the National Strategy for Sustainable Development cover the period to 2010 or even 2020, but the ODA/GNI target is restricted to the voluntary commitment undertaken at the Monterrey Conference in spring 2002, when Germany pledged to increase ODA/GNI to 0.33 per cent by 2006. No target at all is set for the second indicator, i.e. EU imports from developing countries.

The international dimension is absent from the priority fields of action, which target practical measures to implement sustainable development. Instead, the chapter on 'Taking Global Responsibility' adopts a more programmatic approach, with the main focus on poverty reduction and international structural reform. The integration of the environment-poverty nexus is addressed at various points here, e.g. in relation to cooperation with trade and industry on the introduction of voluntary environmental and social quality labels and codes of conduct, or with regard to the implementation of the OECD Guidelines for Multinational Enterprises, which include environmental principles. The Strategy proposes the launch by Germany of a funding programme to cover the areas of organic farming, forestry certification, fair trade, and BMZ's Round Table on Environmental and Social Standards.

The federal government also calls for greater integration of environmental and social criteria in international trade and investment regimes, financial organizations and financial services. It designates the conservation and sustainable use of forests, clean energy systems, water supply, and sustainable water resources management as further priorities for the poverty-environment nexus. The only pilot project in this field of action is aimed at combating world hunger through sustainable, site-appropriate land use, with lead responsibility lying with BMZ and GTZ.

The federal government plans to review and develop the National Strategy for Sustainable Development on an ongoing basis. Its first progress report was presented in autumn 2004 (Bundesregierung, 2004). An implementation report will be published regularly every two years thereafter. The State Secretaries' Committee for Sustainable Development has put four focal points, one for each field of action, on the agenda for the current legislative term (to 2006): tapping the potential of older people, reducing land consumption, developing a new energy supply structure, and fostering alternative fuels. Only the last two have a global dimension, namely in relation to international climate protection.

The current key indicators for the International Responsibility chapter exhibit a slight upward trend in ODA/GNI – although with ODA/GNI amounting to just 0.28 per cent in 2003, there is still considerable ground to make up to achieve the 2006 target of 0.33 per cent. By contrast, progress on the second indicator (EU imports from developing countries) has actually been retrograde. There are plans to announce, in the 2006 progress report, that two further fields of action

will be included in the Strategy: biological diversity, including the international dimension, and sustainable financial policy (Bundesregierung, 2004).

In its assessment of Germany's National Strategy for Sustainable Development and the consultation paper on the first progress report, WBGU draws the following conclusions.

- At programmatic/conceptual level, the federal government's National Strategy for Sustainable Development does justice to the strategic objective of linking global environmental policy with poverty reduction. The priorities set for development cooperation – protecting resources and ecosystems, especially forests, soil, water and wetlands that are vital to safeguard the livelihoods of the poor – are welcome. The promotion of renewable energies, especially in off-grid areas, and the comprehensive support for environmental and social standards also point in the right direction.

- A further plus point is that other government ministries and departments are assigned responsibility for integrating the poverty-environment nexus into Germany's external relations, e.g. in the context of foreign direct investment and export credit guarantees.

- The federal government largely restricts its focus to describing existing programmes. No new accents are set. The failure to make a rigorous case for the poverty relevance of international environmental measures is also unsatisfactory. The Strategy for Sustainable Development does not set any quantitative targets for official development assistance on the environment-poverty nexus.

- *Intra*generational equity, as a core element of sustainable development, is neglected. The consultation paper on the first progress report does not explicitly address the issue of Germany's relations with developing countries. In light of Germany's major role in the global economy, it would be appropriate, in WBGU's view, for one of the future priority areas of action to be clearly dedicated to the poverty-environment nexus from a global perspective.

- WBGU endorses the frequent demand for the Johannesburg goals to be incorporated into the National Strategy for Sustainable Development (DNR et al., 2004). Regrettably, the German Council for Sustainable Development has failed to highlight the general lack of focus on the international dimension in the further development of the Sustainability Strategy (RNE, 2004). The 'Challenger Report' by Bode (2003), which was commissioned by the German Council for Sustainable Development, focusses solely on the poverty-security nexus without exploring the environmental dimension of German foreign policy.

- WBGU endorses the German Council for Sustainable Development's call for sustainable production and consumption patterns and lifestyles to be included in the Strategy, as these impact directly on the livelihoods of people in poor countries.
- WBGU shares the concerns of the German Council for Sustainable Development regarding the export of obsolete industrial plants and other goods which, in the home country, often exceed the limit values for emissions and consume a great deal of energy. Outmoded technologies also do nothing to improve the developing countries' competitiveness.

4.2.12.2
Programme of Action 2015 for poverty reduction

The federal government adopted its Programme of Action 2015 (Aktionsprogramm 2015 – AP 2015; BMZ, 2001a) in April 2001. This document, which is designed to facilitate implementation of the United Nations Millennium Declaration, is binding on all government departments (Section 2.1). In the AP 2015, the federal government distills the multifaceted Millennium Development Goals down to a single objective: halving absolute poverty. It ignores the other areas, such as the environmental policy objectives contained in MDG 7.

In the AP 2015, the environmental dimension is dealt with in the sixth out of ten priority areas for federal government action. It is based on a multidimensional concept of poverty that includes lack of access to natural resources. The AP 2015 argues that living in poverty, in turn, often forces people to exploit fragile ecosystems to a point beyond repair. For example, the insufficient supplies of energy available to poor people lead to increased deforestation and thus to a loss of natural resources such as biodiversity. Energy efficiency and renewables are identified as major sectoral priorities to break the negative causal chain.

The impacts of climate change on the poor and the lack of access to safe drinking water and sanitation are also addressed as key elements in the poverty-environment nexus. The AP 2015 voices a warning about the negative environmental impacts of the dynamic growth witnessed in East Asia – an example of misguided development strategies which, while able to achieve progress on poverty reduction over the short term, will lead to a loss of prosperity in the long run.

In its first progress report, published one year after the programme's adoption, BMZ (2002b) reports on the initial steps taken. It identifies the following key

activities in the environmental sector (Priority Area of Action 6):
- Supporting international processes relating to the poverty-environment nexus (e.g. WSSD, Bonn Guidelines on Access and Benefit Sharing, Programme of Work on Forest Biological Diversity within the framework of the Convention on Biological Diversity);
- Integrated bilateral assistance, e.g. advising on the Bonn Guidelines (strengthening traditional/indigenous knowledge on the protection of biodiversity), completion of the BMZ sector concept 'Forest Conservation and Sustainable Use' and – in cooperation with the business community – the preparation of a code of conduct for the coffee industry.

In March 2004, the second progress report was published. Unlike its predecessor, this was based on a collaborative effort involving all the federal government ministries (BMZ, 2004b). Familiar priorities defined in the report include protection against natural disasters, sustainable water supplies and sanitation, sustainable energy supplies, and environmental and social standards. However, it does not report systematically on the implementation of the measures announced in the Programme of Action.

In its evaluation of the AP 2015, WBGU underlines the positive signal sent out by the adoption of a programme to reduce global poverty that is binding on the entire federal government. However, it criticizes the fact that the report focusses solely on one, albeit the key, Millennium Development Goal in the social policy field. In the interests of promoting systematic integration of the environment-poverty nexus, equal precedence should be given to the environmental aspects of MDG 7; otherwise, there is no hope of achieving the poverty reduction target.

The publication of two progress reports to date can be viewed as a sign of the political will to achieve the targets set out in the AP 2015. In WBGU's view, however, what is lacking are innovative accents and binding targets, also for the poverty-environment nexus. The implementation plan announced for early 2002, which supposedly defines practical steps for the various fields of action and the lead actors for each field, is still awaited (GKKE, 2004; OECD DAC, 2001).

4.2.12.3
Development cooperation priorities

Since 2000, German development cooperation has focussed on sectoral priority areas agreed with each partner country. Development cooperation in the field of environmental policy now operates under the heading: 'Environmental policy, protection and sustainable use of natural resources (combating desertification, preserving soil fertility, sustainable forest management, biodiversity)'. As a further measure to increase effectiveness, BMZ is currently restricting its activities to just 70 cooperation countries (Priority Partner Countries, with a maximum of three priority areas, and Partner Countries, with the focus on just one priority area). An environmental priority has been agreed with 26 countries.

Using BMZ's statistical system, it is possible to identify the bilateral projects which have both environmental and poverty impacts. BMZ distinguishes between the following types of assistance relating to poverty and environment (Table 4.2-11):

SHA: Self-help-oriented poverty alleviation;

SUA: Other direct poverty alleviation, especially basic social services;

MSA: Cross-cutting poverty alleviation at macro and sector level;

UR2: Environmental and resource protection as a primary objective;

UR1: Environmental and resource protection as a secondary objective.

BMZ has granted its poverty reduction 'quality seal' to varying proportions of its activities. However – due to the lack of clarity in the classification criteria – the data from BMZ and the OECD's Development Assistance Committee vary significantly; the DAC has repeatedly criticized the low priority given to social issues in German development coopera-

Table 4.2-11
Projects in bilateral technical (TC) and financial (FC) cooperation.
Source: BMZ, 2004b

Year	Actual commitments	Share of annual total TC + FC
	[€ million]	[%]
SELF-HELP-ORIENTED POVERTY ALLEVIATION PROJECTS (SHA)		
2000	183.10	28.3
2001	211.40	24.7
2002	261.54	31.5
2003	298.45	34.9
PROJECTS WITH ENVIRONMENTAL AND RESOURCE PROTECTION AS A PRIMARY OBJECTIVE (UR2)		
2000	532.72	39.1
2001	449.88	27.6
2002	498.34	30.4
2003	394.94	23.9
PROJECTS WHICH INTEGRATE POVERTY AND ENVIRONMENTAL GOALS (SHA AND UR2)		
2000	67.81	10.9
2001	113.49	12.9
2002	60.09	7.6
2003	78.30	9.9

tion. BMZ's own data also reveal a steady decrease in investment in two key sectors – primary education and basic health services – even though Germany has signed up to the Global Campaign for Education and, at the G8 Summit in Kananaskis, pledged to do its utmost to guarantee universal primary education by 2015. The planning data for 2004 also reveal a downward trend for the priority area of environmental and resource protection: commitments fell from 24 per cent of the total the previous year to 21 per cent (BMZ, 2003b).

As regards the integration of these two objectives into BMZ's policies (projects which fulfil both the SHA and UR2 criteria), no clear trend can be determined. After peaking at €113 million in 2001, clear decreases could be observed in subsequent years. WBGU recommends the regular publication of this type of information in future. To date, the information produced by BMZ on the key areas of German development cooperation has tended to be sparse.

Tropical forests are one of five priority areas for which informal quantitative criteria have been adopted by BMZ's political leadership. The other priority areas are: HIV/AIDS, primary education, renewable energies, and energy efficiency. In 2002, a figure of €131.50 million was pledged for tropical forest conservation. This amounts to approximately one-quarter of total funding for environmental and resource protection and around 9 per cent of total technical cooperation (TC) and financial cooperation (FC) commitments (BMZ, 2003c). The previous annual target of DM300 million has now been reduced to €125 million. A further reduction to €100 million is impending in the framework planning for 2005. WBGU is critical of these cuts in a field of action which is of strategic importance for the poverty-environment nexus, since 90 per cent of the world's people living in absolute poverty are dependent on forests and forest products (World Bank, 2003d). The DAC has also voiced criticism of the status of tropical forest conservation within BMZ.

A positive example of the programmatic and conceptual linkage between the poverty and environmental agendas is the BMZ sector concept 'Forest Conservation and Sustainable Development', adopted in 2002, which BMZ developed in close cooperation with NGOs (BMZ 2002c). The concept's strategic approach links forest conservation and sustainable use by poor and indigenous communities.

Projects aimed at conserving biodiversity are an important priority in Germany development cooperation (DC) at the interface between poverty and environment. The aim is to take systematic account of local communities' interests in protected areas, both for their own use and for income generation, and involve them in the management of these areas. This approach seeks to reconcile conservation and utilization interests, and to foster benefit-sharing (Section 4.2.2). Yet financial commitments for this area in German DC have fallen dramatically in recent years. From 1992 to 1997, €50–80 million were made available annually through bilateral TC and FC, peaking at €110 million in 1995 (BMZ, 2004a). Since 1998, new commitments have levelled out at a far low figure of €10–40 million, signalling the lower political priority now given to this field of work. Actual disbursements on biodiversity projects to implement previous decisions have steadily risen, however, exceeding €70 million in 2003.

WBGU supports the DC approach, which is based on close linkage between protecting biological diversity and reducing poverty. Environmental targets can only be achieved if the poor are involved in concepts for the sustainable use of resources and ecosystems in and around protected areas. The federal government should be guided by this basic principle when engaged in international negotiations (Section 4.2.2).

BMZ views the development of a sustainable energy supply as key to tackling the poverty-environment nexus. In 2002, funding for energy efficiency and renewable energies was increased, which BMZ describes as a successful step in implementing the decisions adopted at the WSSD. At Johannesburg, Chancellor Schröder announced the launch of a programme to promote renewable energies and energy efficiency within the DC framework, with the allocation of €100 million annually for each of these two areas for a five-year period (2003–2007). The low figures planned for 2003 and 2004 contrast starkly with this announcement (Table 4.2-12). As an additional measure, the Chancellor announced at renewables 2004 in Bonn in June 2004 that the federal government, in cooperation with the KfW Group, would be setting up a special fund for renewable energies and energy efficiency, totalling up to €500 million. Starting in 2005, for a period of five years, the fund will provide public and parastatal institutions, banks and

even private individuals with reduced interest loans for investment in developing countries.

BMZ's commitment as the largest contributor to the LDC Fund established within the UNFCCC framework is to be welcomed. The Fund is intended to assist the poorest countries to develop national strategies for adaptation to the unavoidable impacts of climate change. A figure of €15 million has been pledged so far, with €3 million actually disbursed to date. BMZ's response to a further adaptation fund (Special Climate Change Fund) has been restrained, largely because the OPEC countries predominate with their demand for compensation for abandoning oil production.

The debt relief measures adopted by Germany have also had a positive impact on the environment-poverty nexus. At UNCED in 1992, former Chancellor Helmut Kohl extended debt conversion for developing countries to environmental projects as well; in the 2001 budget, a total of DM210 million was earmarked for bilateral debt conversion, with 20–50 per cent being available for environmental, poverty reduction and education measures (BMZ, 2001b).

A further positive point is that since 1997, up to 25 per cent of bilateral financial cooperation for environmental and resource conservation projects and other specific measures (e.g. improving women's social status, self-help-oriented poverty alleviation) can be paid out in non-repayable grants to countries that would otherwise only receive loans. The KfW Group allocated around 21 per cent of new FC commitments to this type of project in 2001 (BMZ, no year).

4.2.12.4
Poverty and environmental standards for foreign trade promotion and the activities of German companies abroad

The issue of reforming the system of foreign trade promotion through export credit guarantees in order to bring it into line with environmental and poverty-

Table 4.2-12
BMZ's technical cooperation (TC) and financial cooperation (FC) projects in the field of energy generation and supply. Source: BMZ, 2003a, b

	Actual figure for 2002		Target for 2003		Target for 2004	
	Funding [€ million]	Share of total TC and FC [%]	Funding [€ million]	Share of total TC and FC [%]	Funding [€ million]	Share of total TC and FC [%]
Energy generation and supply	182.3	11.8	72.0	5.0	160.8	11.9
Of this, renewable energies	135.9	8.8	48.5	3.4	90.8	6.7

relevant criteria has featured on the federal government's agenda since 1998. A tangible outcome was achieved in April 2001 with the adoption of 'Guidelines for the inclusion of environmental, social and development policy criteria in the federation's provision of credit guarantee services' (Schaper, 2004a). However, NGOs believe that this reform, although announced, has yet to be implemented (Urgewald et al., 2003). They criticize both the inadequacy of the Guidelines and the continued practice of granting export credit guarantees to dubious projects. They also call for a social impact assessment to be carried out to measure compliance with human rights and labour standards. Within the government coalition, the Guidelines are also considered to be too weak to achieve environmental and development policy objectives. The 2002 coalition agreement therefore calls for transparency in export credit guarantee decisions, compliance with World Bank standards, and monitoring of human rights violations.

The OECD's Development Assistance Committee also identifies a need for independent analysis of the Guidelines' implementation to date, in order to enhance the credibility of government policy in this area (OECD DAC, 2001). Since 1998, the OECD's Working Party on Export Credits and Credit Guarantees has been discussing Common Approaches on Environment and Officially Supported Export Credits, with the aim of harmonizing national environmental standards for export credit agencies. In December 2003, this body adopted a set of standards for the first time, which were supported by all member countries. To date, national implementation in Germany has taken place in accordance with the 2001 Guidelines. It is debatable, however, whether the current Guidelines are sufficient to meet the requirements of the Common Approaches, especially as regards the rules on transparency. A review of the national Guidelines, which is taking place in other OECD member countries at present, would ensure that the Common Approaches are implemented on a comprehensive basis and would also offer the opportunity to correct the weaknesses identified in the current Guidelines, notably the lack of clarity on exemptions for the nuclear industry, for example.

Alongside the discussion about environmental compatibility of funded projects, a further issue now being considered is how export credit agencies can encourage exports of renewable energy technologies. At international level, UNEP's Division of Technology in Paris is coordinating this discussion process, while in Germany, the Federal Environment Ministry, the German Institute for Economic Research, and the NGO Germanwatch have initiated a dialogue. Here, improved terms could, and should, help to implement the federal government's public and international commitment to renewable energies in foreign trade promotion as well. What is required is a general overhaul of the terms and conditions governing the granting of export credits and an agreement that comparable framework conditions will be adopted for renewable energies (Schaper, 2004b).

German companies' export activities are also subject to multilateral rules which include social and environmental standards. Within the context of the OECD's Guidelines for Multinational Enterprises (Section 4.3.5), Germany, along with the other participating states, has committed to set up a National Contact Point with responsibility for implementing the Guidelines and handling complaints and enquiries. However, apart from offering a mediation and conciliation procedure, these National Contact Points (NCPs) have no power to impose sanctions on offending companies. The principle of transparency enshrined in the OECD Guidelines should be used to expand the NCPs' scope for action. More transparency could ensure, for example, that the NCPs would be required to justify why certain credit transactions, according to their interpretation of the OECD Guidelines, do not represent an 'investment commitment'. Here too, more transparency could enhance the credibility of government policy.

In Germany, the NCP was set up within the Federal Ministry of Economics and Labour. An associated working group was also established, involving industry, trade unions and NGOs. The scope of the Guidelines is proving to be a contentious issue, e.g. as regards the inclusion of commercial transactions. NGOs criticize the federal government's position, which they claim is based on a 'narrow interpretation of the Guidelines'. Moreover, they demand that export and investment guarantees should only be granted if the applicant companies undertake to comply with the Guidelines (Heydenreich, 2003).

In January 2001, as part of its preparations for the WSSD, the Federal Environment Ministry initiated a dialogue on the theme of 'Environment and Foreign Direct Investment (FDI)', involving trade and industry, the trade unions and NGOs (Feldt and Martens, 2003). The aim was to develop – on the basis of consensus – environmental guidelines for German investment abroad and to present these guidelines in Johannesburg together with models of best practice from German companies. In May 2003, a draft compromise paper was presented which contains commitments to the precautionary and polluter-pays principles, consumer protection measures and access to information for the affected local population. More far-reaching concepts for sustainability guidelines presented by the NGOs, as well as practical demands for environmental protection and external monitoring of progress, met with opposition from trade and industry. Instead, it was merely agreed that a joint working group would be established on the basis of parity as the contact point for complaints. The NGOs made their endorsement of the compromise conditional on the guidelines being viewed purely as an interim step towards more far-reaching international rules for transnational corporations – whereupon the Federation of German Industries refused to sign the document. The German Association of the Chemical Industries, on the other hand, signalled that it was prepared to endorse the deal. The Federal Ministry of Economics and Labour had walked out of the process earlier due to what it described as the overemphasis on reporting obligations and monitoring of corporate activities.

The commitment of the federal government, especially the Federal Foreign Office and the BMZ, to promote the UN Global Compact has helped to achieve positive poverty and environmental impacts in German companies' overseas activities (Section 4.3.5). The central elements of this initiative, which was launched by UN Secretary-General Kofi Annan, are respect for human rights, ILO core labour standards, and appropriate consideration of environmental aspects on the part of the private sector (Hamm, 2002).

4.2.12.5
Recommendations

- WBGU recommends that the federal government present an implementation plan for its Programme of Action 2015 as soon as possible, in order to concretize the abstract goals of poverty reduction through the adoption of practical targets and voluntary commitments. This would also make it clear that the objectives set out in the AP 2015 cannot be achieved with falling investment in basic social services.
- WBGU welcomes BMZ's commitment to climate issues, especially capacity-building in partner countries on adaptation to unavoidable climate change. It encourages BMZ to intensify its work and funding activities in this area, e.g. through the LDC Fund set up within the UNFCCC framework.
- WBGU endorses the federal government's intention to promote the poverty-environment nexus in the GEF and the PRSP process sponsored by the World Bank and IMF. The prerequisite, in this context, is that the poverty-environment nexus must be addressed more systematically by BMZ and the German development agencies.
- WGBU calls for the financial resources allocated to the conservation of tropical forests, tradition-

ally a priority in German DC, to be restored to the previous level of €150 million at the very least. The BMZ sector concept 'Forest Conservation and Sustainable Use', which was developed in conjunction with NGOs, should become one of the binding criteria in decisions on the granting of Hermes credit guarantees. WBGU also recommends the introduction of quantitative criteria in the annual framework planning of bilateral technical and financial cooperation in the fields of biological diversity and desertification, which offer favourable conditions for linkage between poverty and environmental objectives.

- WBGU calls upon the federal government to implement the Common Approaches, adopted by the OECD's Working Party on Export Credits and Credit Guarantees, within the framework of new national guidelines and to interpret them as stringently as possible. In particular, the granting of credit guarantees should always be conditional on the publication of environmental information. WBGU also supports the DAC's call for an independent monitoring system to be introduced for the implementation of the German government's 'Guidelines for the inclusion of environmental, social and development policy criteria in the federation's provision of credit guarantee services'.

4.2.13
The global economy: Policy processes

Neither poverty reduction nor global environmental protection forms part of the core mandate of the World Trade Organization or the International Monetary Fund. Nonetheless, both organizations greatly influence not only the development of international trade relations and hence the world economy (Section 3.4.2), but also global poverty reduction and environmental policy. Like macroeconomic stabilization policy – a core area of IMF's activities – the trade policy principles and measures which are the subject of the WTO Agreements have tangible impacts on the poor and the natural environment.

4.2.13.1
Trade liberalization and the World Trade Organization

TASKS
The precursor of the World Trade Organization (WTO) is the General Agreement on Tariffs and Trade, which was signed in 1947 (GATT 1947) and deals with trade in goods. The World Trade Organization was created on 1 January 1995 as part of the entry

into force of the agreements concluded under the last GATT round, i.e. the Uruguay Round of trade negotiations. With 148 member countries and 25 nations currently engaged in accession negotiations, WTO is, in essence, a global organization. WTO administers GATT 1994 and the other WTO Agreements, offers a forum for negotiations, and has established a fairly efficient dispute settlement mechanism. In addition, the WTO secretariat publishes reports on the trade policies being pursued by the individual WTO members. According to the Preamble of the 'Agreement Establishing the World Trade Organization', WTO's purpose is to ensure that relations in the field of trade and economic endeavour are conducted with a view to raising standards of living, ensuring full employment, and expanding the production and trade in goods and services, as well as integrating the developing countries into world trade, while allowing for the optimal use of the world's resources in accordance with the objective of sustainable development. In practice, however, other objectives defined in the Preamble are overriding (Kulessa, 1998b): the substantial reduction of tariffs and other barriers to trade, the elimination of discriminatory treatment in international trade relations, and developing a more viable and durable multilateral trading system. WTO is therefore geared towards the liberalization and promotion of trade in goods (GATT 1994) and services (GATS). There is also the TRIPS Agreement, which, in essence, aims to 'universalize' the industrialized countries' legal standards for the protection of intellectual property rights, e.g. patents and copyright.

TRADE LIBERALIZATION AND POVERTY
- *Poverty-reducing impacts:* Three separate channels can be distinguished through which trade liberalization and trade promotion can reduce poverty (Kulessa and Oschinski, 2004): growth impacts, wage and employment impacts, and direct price and sales quantity impacts.
  1. If trade leads to higher economic growth, i.e. an increase in national income, this can help reduce poverty through the 'trickle-down effect' (Section 3.4.2). Trade can promote growth through a variety of factors: export revenue can be used to pay for imports (inputs and capital goods) that increase production and may be more readily available as a result of import liberalization. Trade also leads to specialization and facilitates economies of scale. Furthermore, trade increases competitive pressure, thereby creating incentives to adopt more efficient production techniques and to generate innovations. And finally, trade encourages the spread of knowledge and technologies.

  2. Wages and employment can have a poverty-reducing impact if countries specialize in the production of those goods which offer them comparative advantages. As poorer countries often have low skilled workers and abundant natural resources, they can gear their trade towards the production of labour-intensive and agricultural products and mineral resources. This triggers the expansion of sectors which also offer employment to the poor.
  3. Prices and sales quantities have a direct poverty-reducing impact because trade liberalization increases sales of labour-intensive and agricultural products. Furthermore, consumer goods and intermediate products which are imported or compete with imports become cheaper through the removal of trade barriers. The poor benefit directly if they are consumers of these goods.
- *Impacts which impede development and worsen poverty:* For many developing countries, specializing in the export of agricultural products, mineral resources or fossil fuels can also become a poverty trap. The primary goods sector offers little potential for innovation, contributes very little to the training and development of the workforce, often has working conditions which are harmful to health, and offers no long-term growth potential due to a minimal increase in demand (Kappel, 2003; Sachs, 2000). A static comparative advantage thus becomes a dynamic disadvantage. Furthermore, falling prices for imported goods are generally accompanied by rising prices for exports, which means that the poor suffer if they are net consumers, rather than producers, of export goods. Dependence on cash crops or other export products can worsen the situation of the poorest population groups who have no social security or assets to cushion the impact of the dramatic price falls that are typical of the cyclical price fluctuations on the world's agricultural and commodities markets. And finally, if domestic production is squeezed by imports and general competitive pressure, the result may be higher unemployment in the short to medium term; at the very least, the poor suffer indirectly and more people fall below the poverty line. Thus the positive growth impact of trade liberalization is a contentious issue in the debate among economic scientists (Rodrik, 2001).
- *Empirical findings:* The majority of empirical studies conclude that foreign trade, at least over the long term, helps to generate economic growth, also in developing countries. It is largely undisputed in empirical terms that growth is a necessary, although not the sufficient, condition for poverty reduction (UNCTAD, 2002; UNDP,

2003b; Kulessa and Oschinski, 2004; Section 3.4.2). Studies on wage and employment impacts conclude that trade liberalization, especially in the rural sector, helps to reduce poverty. However, this positive outcome depends primarily on the distribution of land and assets, access to education and healthcare, and the speed of trade liberalization. Countries such as South Korea or Vietnam – where land and assets are distributed more equitably, poor people's access to education and healthcare is facilitated and foreign trade has been liberalized on a progressive basis – have achieved positive poverty impacts (Ravallion, 1990; Litwin, 1998; ILO, 2001). However, the empirical findings on the direct poverty impacts of prices and sales quantities reveal a rather more mixed picture. Although the poor have certainly benefited from cheaper imports, they have been disproportionately and adversely affected by fluctuations in the prices of export products (Rao, 1998; Easterly and Kraay, 1999; Bannister and Thugge, 2001). Here too, it is apparent that without product diversification and additional complementary measures such as access to training and technology, social security systems and credit markets, trade liberalization can exacerbate poverty (Deininger and Okidi, 2002).

TRADE LIBERALIZATION AND ENVIRONMENT

The effects of trade promotion and liberalization on the environment can be captured in various analytical categories (OECD, 1994; Rao, 2000). Scale effects and the qualitative effects of demand essentially capture those environmental impacts that are associated with (trade-induced) economic growth (Section 3.4.2). Scale effects also include the trade-related increase in international transport flows, whereby the overall environmental impact depends on the parallel restructuring of national transport flows and the modes of transport concerned. Furthermore, trade facilitates technological progress, which – depending on the technology concerned – may have a positive or a negative impact on the environment.

Moreover, international trade has structural and product effects. The environmental effects of the international division of labour vary according to the nature and extent of the environmental impacts which increase as export-based industries expand or decrease as sectors competing with imports shrink. If poor countries specialize in the production of primary goods – which is likely, in view of the high availability of labour in these countries, and their relatively poor financial and human capital – this can result in serious over-exploitation of natural resources. The key issue in terms of structural effects is that of which sectors are shrinking or expanding, and which pro-

duction methods (manufacturing technologies, filter systems, etc.) are being used. Here, international trade offers the opportunity for cleaner technologies to be deployed worldwide, although there is also a risk that technologies which are relatively harmful to the environment, including outdated industrial plants imported from industrialized countries, will be used in developing countries.

The environment is also affected by consumption-related structural and product effects. On the one hand, products which have less impact on the environment squeeze out environmentally harmful goods; on the other hand, trade encourages the worldwide distribution of goods whose use and consumption significantly increase environmental stress. Locational effects also come into play. If, for example, the adoption of environmental standards creates export disadvantages, or if investors view low environmental standards as relevant to their investment decisions, this – especially in a free trade environment – can lead to the abolition of environmental standards worldwide (race to the bottom) or, at least, may paralyse environmental policy (Kulessa and Schwaab, 1998).

The diversity of trade-related environmental effects makes it impossible to draw any theoretical or analytical conclusions about the overall environmental impact of trade. Nonetheless, it is apparent that trade *per se* does not destroy the environment; indeed, it has the potential to relieve environmental stresses.

EMPIRICAL FINDINGS

Empirical studies show that besides scale effects (Section 3.4.2), (trade-induced) specialization plays a key role in determining the environmental situation (Suri and Chapman, 1998). Whereas it has been possible to reduce environmental impacts in industrialized countries by specializing in services and introducing stricter standards, a rise in pollutant emissions has occurred in the rapidly developing economies of South East Asia and Latin America in particular, where export promotion and trade liberalization, among other things, have greatly increased manufacturing industry's share of GDP. However, pollutant emissions in sectors protected by protectionist measures are sometimes higher than in industries which are subject to free trade (Lucas et al., 1992).

For developing countries which specialize in primary goods, there are incentives to over-exploit the land and engage in deforestation for agricultural purposes, especially after a worsening of the terms of trade (Anderson and Blackhurst, 1992; Box 4.2-6). Besides trade, political and social factors are key. For example, farm subsidies, monopolistic market structures, insecure ownership rights, public debt and pop-

Box 4.2-6

Trade liberalization and sustainable development

The United Nations Environment Programme has recently published a series of empirical sector studies on the impacts of trade liberalization. The following sectors and countries were investigated: shrimp farming (Bangladesh), mining (Chile), the automotive industry (India), forestry (Philippines, Tanzania), rice (Vietnam), the water sector (Romania), bananas (Ecuador), cotton (China), fisheries (Uganda, Argentina, Senegal), cocoa and rubber (Nigeria).

The scale effects resulting from trade liberalization have generally had a negative environmental impact. In Bangladesh, increased investment in shrimp farming resulted in the over-exploitation of natural resources. The deforestation of mangroves to create space for new shrimp farms caused soil erosion and salinization of wide areas of cropland, leading to crop failures and a rise in unemployment.

In Chile, too, trade liberalization initially led to a decline in environmental quality as a result of higher investment in mining. The transfer of improved technologies has offset these impacts over the medium term, however, ultimately resulting in positive improvements in environmental standards.

In India's automotive industry, trade liberalization measures led to an increase in imports, more intensive competition and therefore lower vehicle prices. In New Delhi alone, the number of registered vehicles rose by 136 per cent from 1988 to 1998. Motor vehicles account for around 67 per cent of pollutant emissions in New Delhi, which has a very high level of air pollution.

In Uganda, trade liberalization generated increased investment in the fisheries sector. The value of exports from this sector rose from US$1.3 million to US$45 million between 1990 and 1996. The industry employed around 1 million people in total. However, the strong growth had negative environmental impacts, notably overfishing and a rise in pollutant emissions from the fish-processing industry. This resulted in higher water and air pollution, accompanied by a loss of biodiversity.

Overall, the studies indicate that unless flanking measures are adopted, trade liberalization tends to have negative environmental impacts. The authors therefore consider it necessary to create incentives for environmental awareness-raising through policy action. The Philippines and Romania are cited as positive examples. In both cases, the costs of environmental pollution are borne by the industries concerned. This has encouraged the use of modern, clean technologies, thus mitigating the adverse environmental impacts of growth.

In relation to poverty reduction, the studies' conclusions were ambivalent. While the poor have certainly benefited from liberalization, as in Chile, Uganda and India, pollutant emissions and the loss of biodiversity have increased poverty. In Bangladesh and Uganda, for example, many farmers were adversely affected by soil erosion, salinization and deforestation and often became unemployed.

Sources: UNEP, 1999, 2002c, 2003

---

ulation growth all encourage the overexploitation of natural resources (Rao, 2000).

There is no empirical evidence to support the 'race to the bottom' theory, partly because companies base their investment decisions on other factors. Indeed, surveys of high-value-added companies have revealed that a low level of local environmental stress is regarded as a locational advantage (Schwaab and Busch, 1999). The experience of various newly industrializing countries certainly belies any suggestion that a general 'race to the bottom' is occurring. In China, Brazil and Mexico, for example, pollutant emissions have decreased since the 1980s, while a clear increase in foreign investment has occurred over the same period (Dasgupta et al., 2002).

FREE TRADE PRINCIPLES AND GLOBAL ENVIRONMENTAL POLICY

The WTO rules generally permit trade restrictions that are necessary to protect the environment. Nonetheless, conflicts of interest sometimes occur between the international trade regime, on the one hand, and protection of the environment, on the other. In essence, this is caused by two issue areas:

- *Production process standards*: Together with the most-favoured-nation principle for goods and service, the principle of equivalence in relation to 'like products', whether manufactured at home or abroad, is one of the core principles in the international trade system. The concept of equivalence is based on product qualities, irrespective of the way in which the product is produced. That means that e.g. goods produced using environmentally harmful manufacturing techniques cannot be treated less favourably, in trade policy terms, than those produced in an environmentally sound process, provided that they are 'like products' in all other respects. Over recent years, however, there has been a growing trend to interpret the WTO Agreements in such a way as to justify import restrictions for 'like products' manufactured in an environmentally unsustainable way, provided that these restrictions are deemed necessary for a member country to avert clear and tangible transboundary environmental damage or protect shared natural resources. This applies especially if the trade-restricting country can justify its position on the basis of international agreements which protect the environment or natural resources. One example is the report published by WTO's Appellate Body in 1998, which related to a US restriction on the import of shrimps caught in turtle-unfriendly nets (WTO Document WT/DS58/AB/R). An explicit ruling is still awaited, however.

- *Precautionary principle*: In the WTO Agreement on Sanitary and Phytosanitary Measures (SPS) and the WTO Agreement on Technical Barriers to Trade, WTO members have agreed that product standards for imported goods which are established with the intention of protecting the environment or consumers must satisfy other criteria besides equivalence and the most-favoured-nation principle. The standards must either be based on international norms or there must be a proven scientific need for them. The burden of proof lies with the trade-restricting party, which must demonstrate that the product harms the environment. Although there is the option of temporarily adopting standards as a precautionary measure in cases of obvious uncertainty as to the harmful nature of a product, the application of the SPS Agreement to date has tended to restrict the scope for precautionary policies.

International environmental agreements

Around 20 international environmental agreements regulate environmentally harmful trade flows. Trade restrictions are provided for in various conventions on the protection of animals and species, the Montreal Protocol on Substances that Deplete the Ozone Layer, the Basel Convention on the Control of Transboundary Movements of Hazardous Wastes and Their Disposal, the Rotterdam Convention on the Prior Informed Consent (PIC) Procedure for Certain Hazardous Chemicals and Pesticides in International Trade, the Cartagena Protocol on Biosafety, and the Stockholm Convention on Persistent Organic Pollutants. In some respects, the Kyoto Protocol on climate protection can also be regarded as one such agreement, although the proposed emissions trading scheme does not fall within the purview of the WTO rules (WBGU, 2004).

The WTO Committee on Trade and Environment has focussed on the issue of multilateral environmental agreements for many years. The use of trade restrictions against countries which have not signed up to a particular environmental agreement but are WTO members is viewed as especially problematical. Decisions by WTO's dispute settlement mechanism indicate that considerable importance is attached to multilateral environmental agreements. To avoid uncertainty and inter-state conflicts, however, the overriding precedence of multilateral environmental agreements must be explicitly enshrined in the WTO rules; this would make the imposition of multilateral trade restrictions permissible (WBGU, 2001b).

Environmental themes at the Doha Development Round

At the WTO Ministerial Conference in Doha, Qatar, in November 2001, WTO agreed to launch its first round of comprehensive trade negotiations. Besides the relationship between multilateral environmental agreements and GATT/WTO, the agenda for the Doha Round included various other environmentally relevant issues:
- The effects of environmental standards on market access,
- Ecolabels,
- TRIPS Agreement and the Convention on Biological Diversity, especially rules on plant variety protection,
- Reduction of fisheries subsidies,
- Tariff cuts/tariff freedom for environmental products (technologies and services),
- Support for developing countries in assessing the environmental impact of trade policy measures and agreements.

Unlike poverty reduction, however, environmental protection is not a central theme in the current negotiating round. Indeed, in the hope that trade will have a poverty impact, the Doha Round has been labelled a 'development round'. However, the talks were broken off in autumn 2003 because the developing countries took the view that the market liberalization measures proposed by the industrialized countries were too limited to warrant any further import liberalization by the developing countries in return. The talks were formally resumed in August 2004 after the industrialized countries, and especially the EU, signalled their willingness to undertake further reductions in their agricultural protectionism. The aim is to conclude the Doha Round by the end of 2005.

THE INDUSTRIALIZED COUNTRIES' TRADE POLICY

Trade in industrial products
The industrialized countries have steadily reduced their average tariff rate from 40 per cent (1945) to below 4 per cent (1995). Although most developing countries are granted preferential treatment by the industrialized countries, on closer inspection, it becomes apparent that the tariff policy operated by the industrialized countries – and, indeed, by many developing countries – is skewed against goods from developing countries.

For example, the tariff burden on processed goods from developing countries amounts to around 3.4 per cent, compared with 0.8 per cent on goods from high-income countries (Hertel and Martin, 2000). The average tariff burden imposed by the industrialized countries is still highest in those sectors of greatest interest to the poorer developing countries: textiles/clothing (8.4 per cent) and leather/rubber/shoes (5.5 per cent). Admittedly, after the conclusion of the last GATT 1947 round in 1994, it was agreed to liberalize world trade in textiles and clothing, but the high average and peak tariff rates have remained largely unaffected. Besides peak tariffs on labour-intensive low-tech products, a key feature of the tariff structure of the Quad economies (EU, Japan, Canada and the USA) is that the highest tariff burden affects semi-finished products, especially the categories of greatest relevance to the poorer developing countries (Fig. 4.2-4).

A study by IMF and the World Bank attempts to convert the real burden of tariffs and import quantity restrictions into tariff equivalents. It reveals that on average, the lower the income of the exporting country, the higher the import restrictions imposed by the industrialized countries (IMF and World Bank, 2002). If this trend continues after the end of the Doha Round, the economically prosperous countries will lose all credibility in the war on poverty.

Agricultural trade
In developing countries, more than one-quarter of GDP is generated in the agricultural sector, and around half the population depends on agriculture for their economic survival. By contrast, agriculture accounts for a relatively low share of their exports, amounting to 13 per cent on average, although this figure rises to one-fifth for Africa and one-quarter for Latin America, with agriculture accounting for more than half the exports of around 20 low-income countries. By contrast, agriculture's share of the industrialized countries' export trade is surprisingly high. Although agriculture accounts for just 2–3 per cent of the industrialized countries' GDP, it totals 9 per cent of exports. The EU is the source of more than 40

per cent and North America of almost 20 per cent of all agricultural exports (WTO, 2002).

There are various reasons for this imbalance: extremely high average and peak tariff rates, 'classic' tariff escalations, and the export subsidies paid by the industrialized countries. The total farm and food subsidies paid by the OECD countries are estimated at around US$350,000 million per year (Section 5.6.3.2). Farmers in industrialized countries receive subsidies equivalent to 130–150 per cent of the world market price (IMF and World Bank, 2002). Surpluses are sold on the world market at up to 75 per cent less than the costs of production (agricultural dumping). The recently agreed abolition of all export subsidies and more far-reaching reductions of all production-boosting farm subsidies are a step in the right direction in terms of opening up better development opportunities for the poorer countries. However, as agreed back in 1993 at the conclusion of the Uruguay Round and recently reaffirmed, cushioning measures must be adopted and financed in order to benefit the LDCs. Otherwise, in many LDCs which are net food importers, the price increases which will result from the abolition of subsidies will have serious social consequences and will exacerbate poverty.

Trade restrictions for the poor?
Most industrialized countries grant special tariff concessions on goods from poorer countries. In Europe, the EU's 'Everything But Arms' (EBA) initiative is a notable example. Goods from LDCs enjoy tariff- and duty-free market access, although this will apply to bananas only from 2006 and to sugar and rice from July and September 2009 respectively. Furthermore, the rules of origin are excessively tough and the EU reserves the right to reintroduce import restrictions if adaptation problems arise. If the Triad economies

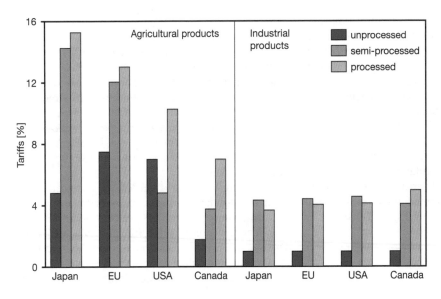

Figure 4.2-4
Average unweighted tariffs on agricultural and industrial products.
Source: IMF and World Bank, 2002

(EU, Japan and USA) were to open their product markets to the LDCs with no restrictions, it is calculated that this would generate additional export revenue for the LDCs amounting to US$2,000–3,000 million over the medium term (Hoekman et al., 2002). The current revenue generated for the Triad economies from tariffs on goods from developing countries is estimated to exceed US$10,000 million – equivalent to around one-fifth of their ODA spending.

Trade liberalization and revenue
Various studies attempt to estimate the global income growth which could be generated for all countries through the greatest possible liberalization of world trade. Conclusions vary between US$85,000–620,000 million annually, with one-quarter to half accruing to the developing countries (Anderson et al., 2001; World Bank, 2002a). Even if only the industrialized countries eliminated all their tariffs and quotas, impressive results could be achieved. Anderson et al. (2001) estimate the income effect to be in the region of US$43,000 million per year, while according to IMF (IMF and World Bank, 2002), the prosperity dividend resulting from full unilateral liberalization of the trade in textiles and clothing would amount to US$24,000 million annually. In the Doha Declaration, all the WTO members committed to free market access for goods from the LDCs. If the industrialized countries, at least, implemented this in full, the LDCs would benefit from an estimated 3–11 per cent in additional export revenue (UNCTAD, 2002; Hoekman et al., 2002), and sub-Saharan Africa's economy would grow by an extra percentage point annually (Ianchovichina et al., 2001; Anderson et al., 2001).

APPROACHES TO GIVE SPECIAL ACCOUNT TO THE POVERTY AND ENVIRONMENTAL EFFECTS OF TRADE LIBERALIZATION

Development Box for agricultural trade
The proposal to establish a Development Box (a negotiating package with proposals to improve policy instruments for farm trade) was initially presented by a group of like-minded countries within WTO, comprising Pakistan, Kenya, the Dominican Republic, Cuba, Honduras, Haiti, Nicaragua, Uganda, Zimbabwe, Sri Lanka and El Salvador. India put forward a similar proposal entitled Food Security Box. The governments of these countries are concerned that the unrestricted liberalization of farm trade could jeopardize food security and the livelihoods of small farmers in developing countries. They consider that their agricultural sectors are under threat from free market access for market-dominant Western corporations. They argue that local producers are often unable to compete with these transnational corpo-

rations (Green and Priyadarshi, 2001). Against this background, the group calls for countries with scarce resources and significant food security problems to be exempted from trade liberalization. In particular, the developing countries should be empowered to safeguard jobs in rural regions, protect small farmers from cheap imports, and expand their food production, especially basic foods (Murphy and Suppan, 2003). The key elements of a Development Box should enable developing countries, despite the general liberalization of the agricultural sector, to impose or increase tariffs on crops which promote food security ('food security crops'):
- Unrestricted promotion of 'food security crops' from the public purse. In this context, it should be noted that this includes not only food crops but also crops whose cultivation involves a significant proportion of the rural population. Food security should therefore be understood as potential access to food.
- Exemptions should be granted for subsidies with which developing countries fund the transport of basic foods into regions suffering from food scarcity.

The purpose of a Development Box should be to integrate poverty reduction and development policy components into the WTO framework. This aim is welcome in principle. However, the following problems can be identified in relation to the current WTO negotiations (von Braun et al., 2002). First of all, it must be clarified which countries would genuinely be entitled to participate. Furthermore, the term 'food security' must be defined as precisely as possible. The existence of a Development Box is also likely to entail higher development cooperation costs for the industrialized countries in order to support especially the poorest countries through transfers to the rural poor. A further problem arises if industrialized countries use the introduction of a Development Box to negotiate protection clauses for their own vulnerable groups. Although it is essential to give special consideration to the livelihoods of the poorest and most vulnerable groups in the context of increasing trade liberalization, it must be ensured that the introduction of a Development Box is not used by economic interest groups to operate a form of protectionism which impedes general development prospects and becomes a burden on the poor.

Sustainability Impact Assessments for trade agreements
In recent years, Sustainability Impact Assessments (SIAs) have been increasingly undertaken for trade agreements, with the EU a pioneer in this area. The EU commissions such assessments in order to appraise the sustainability impacts of proposed trade agree-

ments. The key indicators are real income, income inequality, literacy, health, environmental quality and biodiversity (CID, 2003; Santarius et al., 2003). The aim is to base future trade agreements on the findings of the SIAs in order to introduce a sustainability component into world trade. The SIA takes place in three stages (George and Kirkpatrick, 2003). Firstly, using literature and case studies, economic models and chain analyses, the sustainability aspects of potential trade agreements are summarized in a preliminary assessment. This is appraised by experts and interest groups, who provide comments before the final assessment is made. This forms the basis for the EU's negotiating position.

While the EU's attempt to incorporate sustainability principles more fully into international trade relations is welcomed by many states and NGOs, some measure of criticism is being voiced about its current implementation. Firstly, it is argued that the assessments commissioned by the EU are interest-driven. It is claimed, for example, that to date, the assessments have not called for any change in EU trade policy, but only in the policies being pursued by its trade partners (CID, 2003). A further criticism is that the comments and suggestions put forward by interest groups from developing countries have not been adequately considered so far. The overall process should be made more transparent (WWF, 2002). The introduction of SIAs in the WTO framework could help to enhance sustainability in world trade. However, if the EU persists with its current approach, which it adopted as the basis for its negotiating position in Cancún, this tool could lose credibility.

CONCLUSIONS
In principle, trade liberalization does not conflict with a coherent global environmental and poverty reduction policy. Indeed, it can become a driver of an economic policy which destabilizes the vested interests of elites, well-organized interest groups and the industrialized countries in order to benefit larger sections of the population and the developing countries. However, neither the free trade principle nor the other GATT principles should become dogma. For example, far more importance should be attached to the precautionary principle and there should be an unequivocal consensus that multilateral environmental agreements take precedence over the WTO Agreements. Measures and standards agreed within the framework of the multilateral environmental agreements must not be jeopardized by decisions made by WTO's dispute settlement mechanism. The same applies to international social standards, e.g. ILO standards, and other measures adopted by the International Labour Organization.

The relatively recent practice of carrying out SIAs when planning trade agreements should continue. However, in this context, countries should review their own trade policies more carefully and the SIAs should be standardized over the medium term. The publication of SIA reports prior to the conclusion of negotiations increases the opportunities for parliaments and civil society to bring influence to bear and greatly improves the prospects of achieving consistent sustainability policies.

Industrialized and newly industrializing countries should open their markets to products from the developing countries to the greatest possible extent. They should completely abolish production-boosting farm subsidies and stop the practice of agricultural dumping. In return, the developing countries should be expected to make trade policy concessions which are directly aimed at reducing poverty and protecting the global environment. This includes facilitating market access for goods which are used and consumed by the poor or applying zero tariffs to environmental technologies such as solar technology, an issue which is already under discussion.

4.2.13.2
International Monetary Fund

TASKS
The International Monetary Fund (IMF) was founded in 1944 at the same time as the World Bank. Its task is to promote stability in the international currency and financial systems, to foster economic growth and international trade and to provide temporary financial assistance to member states to help ease balance of payments difficulties (IMF, 2003). In accordance with these objectives, IMF monitors the economic policies of its, by now, 184 member states, grants loans to countries with balance of payments difficulties and provides technical assistance. Loans are mostly made to developing or newly industrializing countries that do not receive any commercial loans. In return, the country commits itself to implement a number of economic policy measures that are aimed at eliminating the sources of its balance of payment difficulties and at fostering economic growth (conditionality). In contrast to World Bank loans, which have medium to long-term maturities, IMF loans are made with the explicit purpose of providing short-term bridging assistance. However, successive loans are often disbursed, so that the comparison with World Bank loans becomes rather relative, even more so since IMF has also been granting medium to longer-term loans for some time, for example within the framework of the Poverty Reduction and Growth Facility. According to its mandate, IMF is responsible for

stabilization, while the World Bank focuses on structural adjustment (Section 4.2.9). In reality, however, there are many areas these days where the two overlap (Michaelis, 2003).

MACROECONOMIC STABILIZATION AND POVERTY REDUCTION

The macroeconomic stabilization of an economy can be divided into an external and an internal part. External stabilization primarily consists of reducing balance of payment deficits, while internal stabilization focuses mainly on controlling inflation and balancing the budget. Stability is a basic prerequisite for future economic growth and thus also for lasting poverty reduction (Section 3.4.2). However, internal stabilization is often linked with a short-term reduction in growth and even a fall in output. If this economic contraction trickles down to the poor, the initial impact of stabilization is to increase poverty. In addition, the reduction of public sector deficits often occurs at the expense of poor sectors of the population. On the other hand, they gain directly from stabilizing prices as they do not hold durable or foreign assets and therefore suffer particularly from high rates of inflation.

Fiscal and monetary instruments
IMF recommends primarily restrictive measures to achieve stabilization, such as cuts in public expenditure, in particular reductions in subsidies, public sector salary cuts and redundancies as well as the consolidation of state enterprises. Cuts normally occur in all sectors, and therefore also in the services that are provided for the benefit of the poor. In addition, IMF advises increases in tax revenues, which generally means increases in consumer taxes, which are much more common in developing countries than income taxes, which are more challenging to administer. Rising consumer taxes affect the poor sectors of the population particularly negatively, because of their relatively higher consumption rate (regressive taxation effect). Even if the poorest do not have access to the services that have been cut and do not pay taxes, they are nevertheless affected indirectly by the general impact of economic contraction (Kulessa, 1998a). For example, if the incomes of the consumers of goods that are produced by, or through the participation of, the poor fall, the situation of the poor is worsened, and deteriorates further due to increasing competition in the informal sector and a rise in crime. Restrictive monetary policies, such as an increase in the real rate of interest, have similar effects: while the poor often do not have access to the formal credit market and therefore do not feel the impact of interest rate rises directly, they can be affected nevertheless indirectly as a result of recession induced by a change in monetary policy.

Although the poor are particularly vulnerable during the stabilization process, IMF has only taken care for the past few years that the budget share of basic social programme expenditures does at least not have to be reduced. However, this does not rule out a decline in the actual level of these expenditures.

Exchange rate policy
Currency devaluation as part of the stabilization process is aimed at improving the current account balance and at stimulating economic growth, as it makes foreign goods more expensive on the domestic market, while domestically produced goods become cheaper on the world market. With all other conditions unchanged, the result is a rise in the volume of exports and a fall in the volume of imports. This results in an increase in output, to the extent that this is inherently possible. This can have the effect of reducing poverty, provided that either the poor produce those goods that have replaced the goods that were previously exported or imported, or they find employment in those sectors. However, this is counterbalanced by poverty-increasing effects, if the poor, or the sectors in which they are likely to be employed, are net consumers of the goods that have now become more expensive.

Liberalization of financial and product markets
Since the 1990s at the latest, IMF has been pushing measures that extend beyond a policy of short-term stabilization. These include the integration and liberalization of financial markets – measures that are expected to foster economic growth in developing countries. However, it has not been possible to demonstrate this effect empirically (Prasad et al., 2003). Rather, it is likely that the premature liberalization of financial markets, which in only a few cases was supported by suitable institutional frameworks (such as a functioning financial regulatory and supervisory system), actually fuelled the development of balance of payment crises. Financial crises increase poverty, as, among others, the experiences from the 1997/98 South-East Asian crisis have shown. IMF now also emphasizes the importance of supporting institutional measures (Aninat, 2000). Nevertheless, it retains the principle of financial market liberalization, albeit in a now more gradual form.

Export promotion, import liberalization as well as the general deregulation of product markets are also part of IMF's set of conditions. These policies have a noticeable impact on both poverty and the environment (Section 4.2.9 and 4.2.13.1).

Poverty Reduction and Growth Facility
In 1999, as part of the HIPC debt relief initiative, IMF renamed the Enhanced Structural Adjustment Facility as Poverty Reduction and Growth Facility (PRGF). The PRGF grants longer-term loans, which are aimed at building structures, to countries that have prepared a PRSP. However, up to now there has been no evidence that this process has made a significant contribution to poverty reduction (Section 4.2.10).

STABILIZATION AND ENVIRONMENTAL PROTECTION
Economic instability is characterized by high unemployment, hyperinflation and extreme uncertainty. This makes it more difficult to deal sensitively with the environment and to implement effective environmental policies. Economic stability, on the other hand, can contribute to the protection of the environment. However, it is not possible to generalize about the environmental impact of stabilization and its associated measures.

Measures that are aimed at balancing the public budget can have directly positive effects on the environment, if environmentally harmful subsidies, such as those for coal or petrol, are cut, or if newly introduced or increased taxes, such as a mineral oil tax, lead to a reduction in environmental pollution. However, citing the lack of adequately functioning institutions in most developing countries, IMF has argued that explicitly correcting market prices to reflect external costs is problematic (IWF, 2000).

Measures that are designed to promote exports can often have directly negative environmental effects. Since many developing countries export primary goods (from forestry, agriculture, fishing, mining), non-sustainable exploitation of natural resources can arise (Section 4.2.13.1). Overexploitation of resources, which is driven by the pressure to earn export revenues, can be exacerbated by perverse supply responses: if the price for a raw material falls, possibly because several developing countries happen to have increased their exports in accordance with IMF and World Bank recommendations, the producers of that raw material, faced with a lack of alternative income sources, increase production. This results in a further drop in prices (UNCTAD, 2003) and further intensifies the destruction of natural resources.

While IMF does not deny that its programmes can exacerbate ecological problems, it does not take responsibility for this: instead, it argues that institutional weaknesses, poor governance and inadequate environmental policies in the recipient countries lie at the heart of the problem. While these shortcomings have to be addressed, IMF believes that this is beyond its remit, and that it therefore does not have

specialist expertise to develop functioning environmental institutions. Other international organizations should therefore be approached (IWF, 2000). As a logical consequence of this view, two years ago IMF initiated a process to delineate tasks better and also to coordinate them more effectively: IMF should, in essence, focus on the economic stability of its members, while the World Bank should take the lead on sustainable development (Schneider, 2002). Accordingly, IMF aims to reduce the number of its loan conditions. It is not clear whether, in doing so, it simply wants to evade the debate on the ecological and social effects of its stabilization policy, or whether it is prepared to let external experts on sustainability participate in the development of stabilization programmes.

ACTORS
The policy agenda of IMF is largely determined by the industrialized countries. Voting rights are essentially calculated according to a country's deposits (quotas), which largely reflect the economic power of that country. The United States (17.4 per cent), Japan (6.15 per cent), Germany (6.01 per cent), France (4.96 per cent) and Great Britain (4.96 per cent) exercise the biggest influence. There are at least discussions to reform the allocation of voting rights in favour of developing countries. NGOs (Section 4.3.3) have so far hardly played a role in the structures of decision-making, although there are first signs of a dialogue with civil society.

CONCLUSION
Internal and external economic stability can contribute to lasting poverty reduction and, in principle, can also foster environmental protection. Nevertheless, in reality the stabilization measures that are imposed by IMF often have, at least in the short to medium term, effects which increase poverty and which are detrimental to the environment. Stabilization policies therefore need to be developed more sensitively, and measures need to be tailored more closely to the country and issues at hand. For example, expenditures on basic and educational services should not be cut under any circumstances and should, if possible, be restructured in favour of the poor. Stabilization measures that result in temporary economic contraction should be counterbalanced as much as possible. Harmful subsidies in particular should be cut back, and environmental aspects should be given special consideration in the event of tax increases. In addition, increases in taxation should not be supported if they place a direct or indirect burden on the poor. Instead, IMF should collaborate closely with the World Bank and other UN organizations to ensure

that the taxation system is changed so that it becomes more socially equitable.

There are different ways to achieve economic stability. The challenge is to find the route that is most compatible, particularly in the short to medium term, with the objectives of poverty reduction and environmental protection. Refocusing IMF's remit on its core tasks – stabilization and monitoring the fiscal, monetary and exchange rate policies of its members – would help align its stabilization policy with environmental and poverty-reduction goals.

The Meltzer Report also supported the idea of focussing IMF's remit on its core tasks, albeit for partly different reasons (Meltzer, 2000). Such refocusing should also alter the balance of power between IMF and other UN organizations. In this context it is important to develop and enforce sustainability requirements as prerequisite for the conditions of stabilization programmes. The task of orienting IMF towards environmental protection and poverty reduction and of identifying and assessing the potential trade-offs between IMF's objectives could be allocated to an overarching mechanism, such as a Council on Global Development and Environment (Section 5.3.1.1).

4.3
Socio-political obstacles to sustainable policies and the role of interest groups

The analysis of key political processes and institutions in the field of development and the environment has made clear what role international policy processes and actors play in reducing poverty and environmental problems around the world. However, it should not be overlooked that there are fundamental socio-political obstacles which stand in the way of sustainable development and which must be overcome (Section 4.3.1). These include a lack of long-term thinking and action as well as the tendency towards monocausal explanatory models and approaches based only on subaspects of the respective problems. The necessary political change is also hindered by a materialistically based understanding of prosperity coupled with unsustainable patterns of consumption and production. To what extent these barriers can be overcome depends quite considerably on the behaviour of social groups (Section 4.3.2). As far as global policy is concerned, special interest attaches to non-governmental organizations (Section 4.3.3), transnational corporations (Section 4.3.4) and the international scientific community (Section 4.3.5).

4.3.1
Overcoming socio-political obstacles

SHORT-SIGHTEDNESS

One of the greatest obstacles to sustainable development is a mode of behaviour which results from a short-term or blinkered perspective that fails to take long-term impacts, side effects and complex interactions into consideration. This concerns equally the decisions taken by consumers or producers, patterns of social behaviour, and policies tailored to election periods. Such short-sighted actions may have a variety of causes, including an ignorance of the specific interrelationships, a disregard for future needs, insufficient consideration of external effects and lack of a sense of responsibility combined with the free-rider problem.

However, short-sighted behaviour is sometimes also the consequence of practical constraints. For example, poor people in developing countries often have no option but to overuse natural resources (soils, forests, etc.) or to endanger their health (such as through the traditional use of biomass for cooking and heating) because they have no sustainable alternatives at their disposal (Section 3.3). Countries which are short on financial resources and human capital may not be in a position, for instance, to set up a functioning water treatment system or to establish renewable energy systems, although they are perfectly well aware of the detrimental impacts of their actions on the environment.

Finally, political decision-makers throughout the world are interested above all in short-term success so as to be re-elected or so as to serve directly the interests of those groups close to them. As a consequence, they shy away from policy measures such as in the field of environmental protection, because, in the short term, such measures would lead to material losses and would therefore cost both support and votes, even though, in the medium to long term, they would result in incomparably greater benefits. The situation is similar when it comes to the fight against poverty: short-term palliatives are often given priority over those measures which would be more effective in the long term; fast economic growth takes precedence over sustainable economic development.

A MATERIALISTICALLY BASED UNDERSTANDING OF PROSPERITY

The current consumption of natural resources in the industrialized countries is approximately three times as high as in the developing countries (Gillwald, 1996), which justifiably aspire to the same standards of prosperity. However, if the industrialized world persists in a materialistically based understanding of prosperity, and if the rest of the world aspires to the same, then the vision of a globally increasing and internationally converging prosperity will lead to environmental collapse and therefore, ultimately, to the worsening of poverty around the world. The goal of prosperity for all can thus become an obstacle to sustainable development. Efforts to establish a different understanding of prosperity are concerned with decoupling economic growth from environmental pollution, but also address, in particular, the distribution of resources and development opportunities between North and South. There is a need, firstly, for different methods of production and, secondly, for a change in consumer habits and lifestyles. The 'western' lifestyle cannot be extended to all and is not sustainable (Reusswig et al., 2002; Venetoulis et al., 2004; Worldwatch Institute, 2004), and it is above all the citizens of the industrialized countries who are duty-bound to change their patterns of consumption. Yet also in the developing countries, people must critically examine their understanding of prosperity as well as their production and consumption habits. Certainly, the prime focus is on those who are more prosperous and on 'modern' lifestyles, but importance attaches also to poor people and to traditional production and consumption habits (Box 4.3-1; Reusswig et al., 2002).

TOWARDS SOCIAL CHANGE

A precondition for sustainable development is that, above all, the people of the industrialized world and the more prosperous citizens of the developing and newly industrializing countries modify their habits and their understanding of what prosperity means. This is where education and information play a pivotal role. An important starting point at the international level is the UN Decade of Education for Sustainable Development (2005–2014) under the aegis of UNESCO, which is being accompanied in Germany by the national committee on 'Learning Sustainability'. In addition, the federal and regional governments of Germany have since 1999 been funding a programme entitled 'Education for Sustainable Development' – BLK 21. The educational institutions of the industrialized countries are called upon to refocus their existing educational programmes with a view to holistic, interdisciplinary approaches which take account of cultural and regional peculiarities. Key importance attaches to the promotion of knowledge, skills, lifestyles and values which facilitate the creation of a sustainable future. There is also a need to develop in all members of society an awareness and understanding of the interrelationships between the individual issues of sustainable development within society and to make individuals better able to assume responsibility for a sustainable future.

Addressed already by the 1987 Brundtland Report, the issue of the need for change in consump-

> **Box 4.3-1**
>
> **Example of unsustainable traditional lifestyles: Millet beer in Burkina Faso**
>
> In certain ethnic groups in Burkina Faso, such as the Bwaba, millet beer (dolo) has played an important role since time immemorial. Dolo is drunk at every celebration and meeting; traditional life cannot be imagined without it. The production of millet beer is a multi-stage process which involves non-stop boiling for 36 hours. This requires considerable quantities of firewood, which is collected by the women. Just for the production of dolo in the town of Nouna (around 20,000 inhabitants), the 150 dolo bars burn 72,000m³ of wood every year, i.e. around 3.5m³ of wood per inhabitant. Consequently, the brewing of dolo contributes considerably to deforestation and therefore to the destruction of the environment.
>
> Dolo represents a three-fold health risk and thus increases poverty: alcohol damage with the known consequences of liver damage; exposure of women and children to smoke during the lengthy boiling process; infectious diseases, such as hepatitis A and amoebic dysentery, owing to poor hygiene during production and storage of the beer, which is not preserved.
>
> Dolo also poses a threat to the food supply, because its production requires considerable quantities of millet. The production of dolo accounts for 50kg of grain per head per year, i.e. approximately one-quarter of the minimum annual requirement of grain for food. In Nouna alone, this amounts to 730t of millet per year. Dolo is drunk mainly by men, thereby depriving especially the women and children of food.

tion and production was taken up once again at the WSSD with the 10-year work programme for sustainable consumption and production. Entirely in accordance with their 'common but differentiated responsibilities', the industrialized countries are called upon to switch to sustainable consumption patterns and to support the developing countries in finding alternative paths to prosperity (Chapter 4 of Agenda 21; Johannesburg Plan of Implementation). In addition to educational policy, the proposed fields of action include, for example, the strengthening of corporate responsibility and the provision of better information to consumers.

However, appeals and educational work are not sufficient. A further indispensable element is a functioning market which is provided by government with a consistent, sustainability-oriented framework that lays down targets and standards in addition to requiring the internalization of external environmental costs. Furthermore, government-applied misincentives (such as environmentally damaging subsidies and tax benefits) must be removed and measures taken to directly promote environmentally sound practices and technological advances (Section 5.1). These are preconditions for novel, resource-extensive production methods and innovative products involving low levels of material input, whose focus is on the utility provided to the consumer (such as energy service instead of power consumption). Efforts in the fields of eco-efficiency, closed-loop materials management, integrated product policy, life-cycle analysis, environment labelling and Fair Trade schemes need to be stepped up. Public contract award and procurement agencies should serve as role models in the implementation of sustainable patterns of consumption. When being updated, national sustainability reports should include sustainable consumption/lifestyles as a theme in its own right, but also as a cross-cutting issue in other themes. Greater emphasis should in particular be given, also in Germany, to reducing the consumption of land, to increasing energy and raw-material productivity and to shifting transport from road to rail.

4.3.2
Taking poverty reduction and environmental protection into account in policy making

Poverty reduction and environmental policy call for national reforms whose implementation directly or indirectly affects the interests of various groups within society. Whether these groups are in a position to assist or impede the process of change will depend in large degree on the extent to which they are able to articulate their interests and gain recognition for them at the political level. The more homogeneous the interests of the members are, the more easily and successfully they can be pursued (Olson, 1998). Liberal states founded on the rule of law, whose self-image embraces the concept of pluralism, explicitly recognize the interests of groups. In many cases, the legislature is reliant on the participation of lobby groups to provide it with information. However, there is a risk when there are no effective institutions capable of balancing out the interests of groups. Where states lack workable 'ground rules' and institutions for preventing the disproportionate concentration of political and economic power, it is possible for small, yet well organized interest groups to exert excessive influence on the political decision-making process (Olson, 1998). This can result in disparities of distribution in favour of certain interest groups and in a loss of the legitimacy of pluralism.

In developing countries, the economic, political and military elites are often closely interconnected or even to a large extent identical. Particularly in so-called weak or failing states, governments contribute considerably to the erosion of the state's authority and basis of legitimacy by misusing its institutions and resources for personal enrichment or in order to serve the interests of minority groups (Debiel, 2003). Such minority interests within governments and administrations frequently impact on the success of reforms. Governments attempt to satisfy the interests of their clientele to the greatest extent possible, because they are dependent on their support. The poorest people in a country seldom belong to such a clientele; on the contrary, poor people often have no voice whatsoever in political decision-making processes (World Bank, 2003d). As a consequence, the cutbacks undertaken, for example, as part of stabilization programmes (Section 4.2.13.2) tend to be made predominantly in those areas where the least resistance is expected, i.e. at the expense of the rural poor rather than, say, at the expense of the urban population. There are similar examples in the field of trade policy (Section 4.2.13.1). Liberalization tends to be focused on imports of those products whose availability and lower price are in the interests of influential, and usually more prosperous, groups within society, and on exports from those industries which are in the possession of elites. The administration is all the more likely to press ahead with reforms if it anticipates that this will extend its influence and budgets.

There are various reasons for the fact that, to date, poor population groups, particularly in developing countries, have had little opportunity to have their interests addressed: on the one hand, they form a group with relatively heterogeneous interests; on the other hand, they frequently have no possibility to organize themselves because they lack not only rights and the material prerequisites, but often also education. This is true above all of women, inhabitants of rural areas and indigenous communities (Section 3.1.1). Consequently, poor people are dependent on other better-organized and more influential groups who corepresent the interests of the poor. Some parties, trade unions, churches and NGOs take it upon themselves to perform this representative role and thereby make valuable contributions. Conversely, such groups sometimes pursue their own interests which are not conducive to the fight against poverty (Lindbeck and Snower, 2001; Section 4.3.3).

As a fundamental principle, the participation opportunities available to disadvantaged social groups must be increased (Shams, 1991). A decisive factor in the empowerment of disadvantaged groups is the improvement of their educational situation and their self-organization, so that they are able to represent their interests more effectively and gain better access to entitlements and property rights. Outside support should be given to reform efforts aimed at promoting the rule of law and the stability of the law as well as at decentralization, local development and the combating of corruption (Section 5.5).

Governments in industrialized countries often have a greater interest in the conservation of global public environmental goods than in the reduction of poverty in developing countries. This can partly be explained by the fact that they believe they are more likely to win over voters with environmental protection measures than with the combating of poverty, because the electorate sees itself more directly affected by environmental problems than by the living conditions of people in other parts of the world. Certainly, this is true more of local environmental problems in the industrialized countries than of global changes in the environment. Yet not only local environmental protection, but also, and in particular, global environmental protection are able to provide domestic industries with direct and concrete sales opportunities (e.g. for environmental protection technologies). Conversely, the combating of poverty can only be expected in the long term, if at all, to provide increased opportunities for exports. Moreover, support in the industrialized world for the economic development of poor countries soon comes up against its limits (dictated by interest groups) once domestic industries and jobs appear under threat, for example with regard to the removal of barriers to the importation of products from developing countries.

Nor is global environmental protection an issue that is considered decisive with regard to electoral success. The improvement and long-term maintenance of environmental quality are hindered by the freerider problem. Environmental protection is essentially a public good from which individual voters will benefit regardless of whether they are willing to pay the associated costs (Volkert, 1998). Finally, in view of the fact that parliamentary terms last for between four and five years, governments have comparatively little motivation to represent long-term interests or to embark on costly reforms whose success, if any, will only be felt over the long term. Consequently, sustainability strategies receive less attention than short-term measures and objectives.

Whether and to what extent the existing political and institutional framework makes it possible to pursue a policy of sustainability depends also on what incentives there are for politically competing interest groups to argue in favour of sustainable development. At the international level, it is above all the NGOs (Section 4.3.3) and the transnational corporations (Section 4.3.4) which have the potential to act both as the driver of and also as a brake on sustainable development. In addition, science plays an important role as a provider of impetus (Section 4.3.5).

4.3.3
Non-governmental organizations

Civil society is just as vague a construct as the heterogeneous 'NGO scene', to which the concept is frequently shortened. It remains difficult to find definitions to reduce the organizational features, activities and self-conceptions of NGOs to a common and undisputed denominator. The liberal theory of state and society categorizes NGOs as a 'third sector' between state and market which performs a stopgap function at once desired and promoted by the state. A different school of thought sees NGOs as an emancipatory counterforce to the world of government and industry which seeks to wrest autonomous fields of action from the state and to put profit-oriented industry under the pressure of legitimation with regard to the social and environmental common good. In this sense, NGOs are an organizational and motive force of social capital (Section 3.2.5). This is also how NGOs are understood in this report.

The advancing process of globalization is conducive to the transnational organization of civil society. Internationally active NGOs see themselves as guardians of globalization, especially those NGOs which are engaged in the field of international environmental, human-rights and development policy. They are regarded as the 'new International' in world politics, as the 'world's environmental conscience' (Willets, 1996) and as constructional elements of global governance (Fues and Hamm, 2001). Political scientists are already diagnosing a shift of power away from the world of governments to the 'social world' of civil society.

UNDERESTIMATED OR OVERESTIMATED?
The assessments of increasingly international NGOs vary between romanticization and contempt. These different judgments result not least from the scenery and symbolism of international negotiations and consultation processes. Most international organizations involve NGOs in their work, for example in dialogue forums, and also support them financially. In UN organizations, NGOs have long since held a consultation status acknowledged by ECOSOC. NGOs are no longer pushed off into anterooms or side rooms, but are in some cases even incorporated into government delegations. Governments and international organizations 'tap' the expertise of increasingly specialized NGOs and at the same time 'embrace' them. In return, NGOs are afforded access to 'domination knowledge', are able to influence discussions and agendas and win public attention. Civil society actors are involved at all levels of political action. In Germany for example, they have driven forward the implementation of Local Agenda 21,

they have successfully pushed for the establishment of Sustainability or Future Councils at the regional and federal levels, and they have acquired influence in global negotiations.

4.3.3.1
Roles and functions of NGOs

STRENGTHS OF NGOS

- NGOs 'disrupt' the established routines of politics and, through their increasingly skilful media work, they constitute a counterforce. They act as society's feelers, address neglected issues and do politics a useful service through the early detection of socio-political problems and conflicts.
- NGOs also confront the world of practical constraints with ideals which, while often being removed from day-to-day political business, are still capable of providing the latter with normative direction. NGOs have a focus which reaches beyond the short time horizon of election dates and they submit proposals which are tabooed by the political leaderships (Section 4.4.1). This is true not only of unpopular development policies, but also of environmental and human-rights policies. NGOs owe their popularity, among other things, to the weaknesses of representative institutions and to the loss of trust in political parties.
- NGOs make a fundamental contribution to realizing a society's social and moral capital. They demonstrate that, apart from individualization, there is also a need for creative common activity and international solidarity.
- Finally, NGO networks, which are increasingly organized on a transnational basis, form the organizational core of an emerging international civil society and global opposition to concentrations of power in world politics and the world economy (Kössler and Melber, 1993). NGOs expose untransparent power cartels which, in the process of globalization, are increasingly freeing themselves from democratic control. NGOs enforce a modicum of publicity and transparency. Although their role as the 'guardians of globalization' (Walk and Brunnengräber, 2000) cannot replace the control of democratically elected parliaments, they can urge and enable the elected representatives to perform their control functions more effectively.

WEAKNESSES OF NGOS

Some NGOs tend towards media-effective and spectacular actions which, however, do not always hit the target and are sometimes even misguided. Yet, above all, many NGOs concern themselves with often quite specific problem areas in which they develop considerable expertise while, however, failing to take account of the impact on other problem areas. They, too, therefore, fall prey to the short-sightedness of which they are wont to accuse politicians. Their success is based not least on the privilege, unlike in the case of governments, of not having to worry about the resolution of conflicting goals. A different form of short-sightedness can be discerned in various charitable NGOs, some of which are very strongly supported by donations, but which focus on the alleviation of symptoms while failing to exert direct influence on policy processes. Conversely, other NGOs tend towards a high-minded sense of morality, which has given them the image of 'do-gooders' who are remote from reality. It is here that NGOs have learned that they will only be respected as partners in dialogue through their professionalism and expertise. However, they then run the risk of becoming too caught up in politics.

NGOs, therefore, generally face a number of existential dilemmas. The less they wish only to protest and the more they focus on cooperative lobbying with governmental institutions, the greater is the risk of their losing autonomy and public credibility in their role as guardians and, ultimately, of their being functionalized as an extension of the state. Finally, the large number of NGOs which have sprung up all over the world since the 1980s obscures the fact that only few of them can afford to maintain large numbers of staff, to engage in 'conference tourism' and to carry out professional PR and lobbying work. Smaller, more grassroots-based organizations which are extensively dependent on volunteers scarcely find access to the forecourts of power. All the same, their work comes closest to what Jürgen Habermas sees as the quintessence of civil society: namely the 'independent, self-organized and frequently spontaneous association of citizens to achieve non-profit goals'.

THE PROBLEM OF DEMOCRACY AND LEGITIMACY

With their increasing professionalization, there is the risk that NGOs may lose touch with reality and forfeit their claim to represent grass-roots democracy. Some demand from them that which others criticize them for: the willingness and ability to engage in conflict or dialogue with the powerful. Only few manage this balancing act between competing requirements. Consequently, the fiercest criticism comes not from outside, but from within. Particularly the large NGOs have a problem with democracy in respect of their internal organization, and this is something which is not consistent with their claim to be especially close to the grass-roots. The fact that NGOs enjoy high levels of acceptance in opinion polls does not of itself confer upon them any democratic legitimacy, particularly as donors hardly have any influence on the selection of officials. The myth of democratic grass-roots organizations committed exclusively to noble objectives is, therefore, in need of correction.

In contrast to NGOs, interest groups such as trade unions or business associations stress their internal democratic structures as well as the fact that they are financed and controlled by their members. Yet they, too, as they seek to influence political decisions in a state dominated and penetrated by interest groups, must face the question of their legitimacy, a question which is being asked ever more accusingly of NGOs. If the lobbying of industry associations on behalf of minority interests is accepted as a legitimate tool in a pluralistic democracy, then NGOs cannot be denied the same legitimacy. The participation of civil society, combined with their contribution to the political culture of pluralism, endows NGOs, from the viewpoint of democratic theory, with a basis of legitimacy, although, from the viewpoint of constitutional law, they have no democratic mandate. A further important argument in support of their legitimacy is delivered by experiences from the field of environmental policy (Brunnengräber et al., 2001). Environment ministers emphasize that the public pressure from environmental organizations helps them to carry through an active environmental policy in the face of opposition from other departments and industrial interest groups. NGOs can, therefore, lay claim to legitimacy if they are successful in persuading society that they are the promoters of civil involvement and are needed as a counterweight to powerful interest groups, while seeing themselves not as a substitute for, but as a complement to, democratically legitimized institutions.

4.3.3.2
NGOs before global environmental challenges

Environmental NGOs organized themselves on a transnational basis at a very early stage. With reference to the example of climate change, it can be demonstrated how NGOs became the driving force behind a consistent global policy on climate and sustainability (Walk and Brunnengräber, 2000; Brühl, 2003). They acted in some cases as experts, seeking to influence the scientific and political discourse, and in other cases as lobbyists with the traditional repertoire of pressure politics, and in yet other cases as moralists with the image of the 'world's environmental conscience'.

Also in Germany, the environmental and development lobbies initially each pursued their own specific environmental and development policy goals, but, at the latest after the Earth Summit in Rio de Janeiro, they discovered their interdependencies. One example in Germany was the 'Sustainable Germany' study. Other examples are the conciliar process of 'Justice, Peace and the Integrity of Creation', which has been in existence since the 1970s, and the German NGO Forum on Environment and Development. At the NGO level, therefore, there is quite a long history of the joint conception of environmental and development policy.

4.3.3.3
NGOs in development cooperation: Bearers of exaggerated hopes?

The development lobby of civil society has long since become an accepted player. The World Bank, many UN organizations, the EU Commission and the national development agencies regularly invite NGOs to consultations and (partially) finance many of their activities. The World Bank has had an NGO Committee since 1981; the OECD describes NGOs as 'pillars of development', and the UN has invited them to world conferences which, precisely because of NGO involvement, have been turned into spectacular media events. Alternative NGO socio-political forums now receive no less public attention than, say, the World Economic Forums in Davos.

National and international development agencies need the cooperation potential of NGOs in the South if they wish to activate civil society's potential for self-help, and they need the mobilization and promotion potential of NGOs in the North. For example, studies have discovered that NGOs enjoy far greater respect and trust than governmental development agencies. They are considered the committed standard bearers of policies which are less influenced by commercial and foreign-policy interests.

The activities of NGOs are as manifold and diverse as their forms of organization and founding principles. Many are torn between concrete project work in developing countries and solidarity-generating work in their own country. The major relief organizations attempt both. Some NGOs concentrate entirely on development policy education and on dialogue with decision-makers. They, too, thus perform an important advocacy function, although, despite some success stories, their influence on governmental and international decision-making bodies should not be overestimated.

ADVANTAGES OF NGOS ON LOCATION
Governmental development agencies channel some of their project resources into the South through NGOs. This is because NGOs offer advantages over governmental implementing organizations: they are better at reaching the respective target groups than

government programmes, or programmes which are negotiated by international financial organizations and administered by governments (Fisher, 1998). They are, or are capable of finding, partners who are familiar with the local conditions. This applies in particular to religious relief organizations with their global partner networks. NGOs are sooner able to organize the self-help, participation and empowerment of the poor, because self-help that is organized by government bodies is a contradiction in itself, especially when it is directed against existing power structures. Furthermore, NGOs have lower administrative and personnel costs than governmental implementing organizations or profit-oriented consultants.

GROWING CRITICISM OF NGOs

In the meantime, there are growing numbers not only of scandals in relation to wrecked governmental development cooperation, but also of reports on failed NGO projects and questionable activities. Dozens of scientific publications have criticized the uncontrolled proliferation of NGOs and have come up with the concept of 'NGO plague'. Indeed, in many capitals NGOs are treading on each other's toes in their attempts to help themselves to the overflowing chalice of foreign aid. Some critics now even call into question almost all the advantages of NGOs (Glagow, 1992; Edwards and Hulme, 1996). While not every criticism is justified, it is certainly problematic when NGOs 'persist in their comfortable, but ultimately irrelevant niche of petty projectitis' (Eberlei and Siebold, 2002). This is not true of the major religious relief organizations or of the political foundations, whose activities certainly do achieve structure-forming impacts. However, their status is disputed owing to their proximity to public-law institutions.

NGOs IN THE SOUTH: ORGANIZATIONAL ELEMENTS OF PARTICIPATORY DEVELOPMENT

In the 1980s there was an observable boom of diverse kinds of NGOs in many regions. The reasons lay, firstly, in a growing resistance to the arrogance and corruption of state bureaucracies – and in some cases also in their failure to improve living conditions – and, secondly, in the efforts undertaken by external governmental and private lenders to find partner organizations which were as close to the grass-roots level as possible.

In terms of their size, degree of organization, areas of activity, ideology and objectives, the NGOs in the South are no less heterogeneous than their partners in the North. When some 30,000 NGOs are counted in a country such as Kenya, for example, one must first of all ask what different kinds of NGOs there are:

- The nationally organized, larger NGOs, which act as procurers and distributors of money from the North for certain project areas. They are often fund-raising agencies which know how to formulate funding applications in a manner such as to convince potential donors.
- The numerous local self-help groups, which organize themselves in order to avert certain threats (such as the construction of a dam) or to enforce socio-political demands (such as the supply of drinking water).
- Human rights organizations, women's and environmental associations, which seek the redress of unacceptable states of affairs in social and political areas.
- Organizations which attempt to change social conditions and political power structures through the mobilization of counterforces. Their organizers are especially frequently threatened by state repression.

There are very different assessments of these activities. Some see them as true instruments of participation and as the organizational nuclei of social capital. Others see the risks which emanate from a 'globally organized hunt' by lenders in the North for access to NGOs in the South. It is known for unemployed academics to set up NGOs with the sole purpose of obtaining funds from the North. Externally sponsored NGOs are often more attractive as employers than public administrations and industry, with the consequence that the latter come off second-best when it comes to competing for well trained employees. It is also known for some governments or politicians to go through the pretence of setting up NGOs in order to accommodate the policies of the industrialized countries, which tend to favour non-governmental partners. Instead of eliminating the corruption of state bureaucracies, this creates new channels of corruption. These aberrations must not be overlooked and they require that funding organizations should have sound local and organizational knowledge. Nevertheless, if 'genuine development' can only come from the bottom, then self-help groups, however organized, are indispensable.

4.3.3.4
Conclusion: Overextended but nonetheless essential

Despite having some negative aspects, NGOs in the North and in the South are the driving force behind sustainability policies. However, they are under an unrealistic pressure of expectations. They cannot act as substitutes for the environmental and development policies of governments, but can merely complement those governments and put them under constant pressure to implement what has been promised in many official declarations of intent. Therefore, the 'domestic work' of NGOs in the North is at least as important as their project work in the South. NGOs are stimulating organizational elements in Public Private Partnerships and, precisely because of their critical involvement, they are essential. In the sphere of international politics, NGOs act as the world's social and environmental conscience. They play the role of 'guardians of globalization' in many different ways, in some cases through violent protest. This is illustrative of the tense relationship that exists between their lobbying work, which may include a measured amount of cooperation with the state, and their desired profile as a protest movement (Altvater and Brunnengräber, 2002). Within societies they constitute motive forces of social capital whose potential has also been identified by the World Bank as an asset with regard to environmental and development policy (Section 3.2.5).

4.3.4
Transnational corporations

4.3.4.1
Definition and review

Depending on the definition used, there are, according to data from the World Investment Report of UNCTAD (2004b), 20,000 or even 60,000 transnational corporations (TNCs). According to a minimum definition, a corporation is transnational if it is active in more than two countries and if its foreign sales account for at least one-quarter of its total sales. The number of such TNCs has doubled since 1995, with the number of their suppliers rising to 800,000. Together they employ around 125 million people. Out of the top 100 TNCs, 93 have their headquarters in the industrialized core zones: 43 in the EU, 35 in the USA and 15 in Japan. In a comparison of countries by gross domestic product and TNCs by sales, the top 100 entities comprise 50 countries and 50 corporations. Consequently, the sales of these globally active corporations are higher than the gross domestic products of many developing countries.

A large proportion of international capital movements takes place within the Triad of North America-EU-Eastern Asia. This is also where over two-thirds of direct foreign investment are made. Such investment underwent astronomical growth from just under US$60,000 million at the beginning of the 1980s to over US$1,100,000 million in 2000. The origins and destinations of transnational capital flows

are extremely unevenly distributed: around 90 per cent of the sums invested came from Western corporations, with just under 30 per cent going to newly industrializing and developing countries (UNCTAD, 2004b). The lion's share of direct investment flowed into a dozen newly industrializing countries in the Far East and Latin America, of which the major proportion (fluctuating around 40 per cent) went alone to China. In the coastal regions of that country, this massive influx of foreign capital has led to the creation of a 'super newly industrializing country' with the futuristic symbols of a world economic power in the making. On the other hand, of the US$143,000 million in direct foreign investment which flowed into the South and East in 2002, just US$4,000 million reached the 49 least developed countries (World Bank, 2003f). The losers in this global competition for investment were Africa, South Asia and parts of the CIS region. The reason for the direction of the capital flows is obvious: where the political risks are high and, frequently, the preconditions for profitable investment, such as a qualified workforce and a good infrastructure, are lacking, there is little investment.

4.3.4.2
The role of transnational corporations in globalization

TNCs are the main actors in the private sector and the trailblazers in the globalization process. They account for no less than 40 per cent of world trade in the form of intracorporate trade. This share is growing on account of their globally dispersed production plants, and this growth is being accelerated by the liberalization of trade. TNCs seek out the lowest-cost business locations and are able to change location with relative ease, whereas the affected countries can be hard hit by the comings and goings of foreign companies. The negotiating power of TNCs has grown, while that of countries and trade unions has been weakened (Messner, 1998). The problem applies not so much to countries at the centre of foreign investment such as China, South Africa or Brazil, where a functioning state is able to enforce the conditions required for investment, but above all to small and weak economies. If, in such countries, individual foreign-owned corporations acquire control over the mines or plantations, this leads to the creation of monopolies capable of exercising not only great economic but also political power. At many levels of political action, therefore, there are attempts to subject TNCs to the primacy of the political process. Because they are globally active, this calls for global rules and regulations.

The International Labour Organization (ILO), as the guardian of its internationally binding core labour standards, has demonstrated in many studies that working conditions especially in various 'world market factories' of the duty-free Special Economic Zones do not comply with ILO standards. Often, elementary workers' rights and labour protection standards are refused. The 2001 Annual Report of Amnesty International concluded that the growing economic pressure now caused in all societies by globalization represents a systemic threat to human rights. On the other hand, many studies show that foreign companies normally pay higher wages, provide better training, guarantee better working conditions and are more likely to respect the rights of trade unions than domestic companies. To that extent, they make a positive contribution to development.

TNCs are perceived by the public more as a brake on global sustainable development than as a driving force behind it. They are held responsible for a large number of environmental scandals, for example in the petroleum and mining industries. They are accused of destroying fragile ecosystems and of polluting air and water, while the timber industry is accused of looting the tropical rainforests and the tourism industry of spoiling beaches. Environmental organizations often accuse 'dirty industries' of avoiding the more stringent environmental protection regulations in their countries of origin and of exploiting the laxer, non-existing or (under pressure of competition) non-applied environmental legislation in developing and transition countries. These accusations, however, can be empirically substantiated only for few industries.

4.3.4.3
Corporate social and environmental responsibility

Also within industry, there is currently a debate over what responsibility the private sector should bear for the fight against poverty, the enforcement of human rights and environmental protection – above and beyond compliance with locally valid legislation. One group of economic actors takes the viewpoint that their sole concern should be to pursue their legitimate business interests and that they are not responsible for the achieving of ethical or humanitarian goals. In contrast to this standpoint, many corporations explicitly acknowledge their Corporate Social Responsibility, which includes the respecting of human rights (Braun, 2001). Since the world conferences of the 1990s, there has been growing support for this position. Business organizations such as the World Business Council for Sustainable Development and the Sustainable Development Forum of German Industry are working hard to gain the support of their own members.

There are also numerous trade unions and NGOs which call for industry to play an active role in helping to establish a global regulative framework with social and environmental guard rails. Since the mid-1990s, within the context of the debate on globalization, the campaigns conducted by human-rights, development and environmental groups have intensified the pressure on individual corporations and business associations to submit to codes of conduct which are applicable at all levels of the global value-added chain (Messner, 2004). A 1998 study counted as many as 215 such codes of conduct which were focused above all on compliance with the key ILO standards (ILO, 1998). An OECD study from 1999 which examined 182 codes of conduct made a distinction between four types of code: firstly, those which require companies to engage in fair business practices; secondly, those which require compliance with the existing laws; thirdly, those which require companies to provide fair working conditions; and, fourthly, those which require consideration to be given to the environment (Köpke, 2000).

There are many different codes of conduct for TNCs, including national, intracorporate and sectoral codes. One of the typical features of such codes is their voluntary character, which, within the meaning of international law, establishes at best a 'soft law', the binding character of which, however, increases as more corporations accept the rules of the code. These codes involve ethical guidelines which lay down voluntary standards of corporate social and environmental conduct. NGOs, on the other hand, call for the external verification of corporate business practices as an intermediate stage on the way to legally binding international rules and regulations of the kind which had already been demanded – albeit in vain – in the 1970s by UNCTAD during the debate on a New World Economic Order. NGOs have no confidence in voluntary codes (Kerkow et al., 2003).

As far as end consumers are concerned, increasing importance is being attached in many industrialized countries to externally audited labels of quality which guarantee compliance with certain environmental and social standards. These labels create transparency with regard to the social and environmental production conditions and product characteristics and widen the freedom of consumers by, for example, bringing into shops products which do not involve child labour (e.g. Rugmark carpets) or products for which producers receive prices above the world market level (e.g. Transfair coffee). However, owing to significant price differences in relation to conventional products and because of limited marketing efforts, both organic foods and fairly-traded products have so far failed to escape from their niche status.

In the field of social standards, the ILO Conventions – alongside international human rights agreements – constitute the key benchmark. The social human rights codified therein are intended to humanize the process of globalization. However, their regulatory force is weak although many agreements have been ratified by the majority of countries. An important step with regard to enhancing the status of ILO rules and regulations was the focus on so-called core labour standards: banning of forced and child labour; elimination of gender-specific discrimination as well as the elementary rights to freedom of association and coalition and to collective bargaining. However, there continue to be large gaps in numerous contracting states with regard to the implementation of the agreements. Not all industrialized and developing countries have ratified the underlying conventions.

In the countries of the South, there are varying assessments of social and environmental standards for transnational corporations. Governments and industry, considering them to be primarily a form of hidden protectionism on the part of industrialized countries in order to stop TNCs from investing abroad and thereby to reduce capital flows into developing countries, express heavy opposition. On the other hand, the forces of civil society emphasize the potential of such standards with regard to poverty alleviation and sustainable development and maintain that this potential is especially great when, at the same time, suitable measures are taken, say, in the social field (e.g. alternatives for child workers and their families). Both positions must be taken seriously. However, the accusation of protectionism will not weigh too heavily as long as the external requirements do not go beyond the internationally agreed core labour standards and as long as violations are punished not unilaterally by the TNC's home country, but through an international regulatory mechanism. As far as environmental standards – particularly process standards – are concerned, there are no internationally agreed core standards comparable with the ILO standards. An initial starting point is provided by voluntary undertakings on the part of TNCs as well as by the OECD guidelines, compliance with which should be ensured.

4.3.4.4
Voluntary undertakings: OECD guidelines and UN Global Compact

A framework for corporate social and environmental responsibility is established by international rules and regulations which, although based on the voluntary principle, lay claim to global and cross-sectoral validity. Signed by 30 OECD countries and by three Latin American countries (Argentina, Brazil and Chile) in the summer of 2000, the OECD Guidelines for Multinational Enterprises extended the guidelines adopted as early as 1976 and significantly raised the standards (DGB-Bildungswerk, 2003; Heydenreich, 2003). The OECD guidelines, which are addressed at all TNCs with headquarters in one of the signatory states, make reference to international agreements such as the conventions on human rights and labour law, are based on the model of sustainable development and the precautionary principle, and explicitly require enterprises to combat corruption. The debate is now focused on the question of how to improve the effectiveness of the guidelines (Section 4.2.12.4) and how to call 'black sheep' to account.

Surprisingly enough on the merits, the UN Global Compact proposed by UN Secretary-General Kofi Annan at the World Economic Forum in Davos in 1999 received more international publicity than the OECD guidelines. The UN Global Compact is directed primarily at the global players of the business world, whom it seeks to win over through the principle of voluntary self-obligation. Participating TNCs undertake to report on the Internet on their compliance with the agreement to respect social, environmental and human-rights standards. However, they are not required to submit to an independent reporting system. This is the crucial flaw which has brought the Global Compact more criticism than praise, because it can be misused for no-cost image promotion. The concern of the UN Secretary-General is to establish a 'new partnership' between the United Nations and the private sector. However, it is doubtful whether, by adopting such an accommodating line, he can persuade TNCs to engage in sound social and environmental practices unless they have other motivations for doing so (Paul, 2001).

Also of interest in the area of international self-obligation are the Equator Principles, which came into being on the basis of a joint initiative by banks and NGOs. Similarly to the OECD's Common Approaches, this voluntary undertaking on the part of banks engaged in the field of international project funding is based on the environmental standards of the International Finance Corporation, which is part of the World Bank Group (Section 4.2.9). The Equator Principles are both applicable to export credit agencies, as is demonstrated by their adoption by Denmark's Eksport Kredit Fonden, and are also suitable as a model for voluntary self-obligation on the part of other branches of industry. However, the principles are critically assessed by NGOs, particularly with regard to their verifiability.

Without effective campaign pressure from NGOs, voluntary codes of conduct – such as the Global Compact and the OECD guidelines – can have only limited effect. Indeed, without that pressure, many of the voluntary undertakings entered into by business associations and individual corporations, as well as the processes of dialogue between government, industry and NGOs, would not have come about in the first place.

4.3.4.5
Conclusions: Concepts for moving reform ahead

A multiplicity of reform concepts for the creation of effective corporate social and environmental standards, particularly for globally active corporations, is currently on the agenda. These concepts are on different planes of action: some relate to the further development of seals of quality for consumers while others call for governments to exert influence as regards the introduction and monitoring of voluntary codes of conduct. And, finally, there are voices from international NGOs calling for internationally binding conventions for TNCs. WBGU supports the position, held also by the German Parliament's Study Commission on Globalization of the World Economy, that the soft law of voluntary self-obligation should be gradually transformed into binding international law.

In its Green Paper entitled 'Promoting a European Framework for Corporate Social Responsibility', the European Commission (2001) advocated the creation of a seal of quality for social responsibility. This might lead – similarly to the successfully introduced labelling scheme for organic farming – to the adoption of an EU-wide standard for social process and product dimensions, including fair conditions of exchange with developing countries. Consumers, presently unsettled by a multiplicity of competing initiatives, would thus be provided with a point of orientation. The German Study Commission on Globalization of the World Economy has called for a stronger regulatory role of governmental bodies by supporting the European Parliament's demand for the establishment of a European monitoring agency for the codes of conduct of European TNCs (German Bundestag, 2002).

The area of legally binding rules and regulations is currently dominated by two initiatives. Firstly, the UN Human Rights Commission is seeking a separate way of obliging TNCs to comply with fundamental human rights and to adopt UN standards for the human-rights responsibilities of transnational corporations and private industry. The innovative character of the process lies in the fact that the standards address enterprises directly, whereas interna-tional agreements have to date usually been directed at governments. A subcommission has presented an ambitious draft proposal which has met with support from many NGOs. Whether this proposal will find a majority in the full commission is currently uncertain (Strohscheidt and Hamm, 2003).

Secondly, a broad alliance of forces from civil society is lobbying for a binding international convention on corporate responsibility which lays down ethical standards for economic practices. The Plan of Implementation from the Johannesburg World Summit partially took up this demand and acknowledged for the first time in a UN document the principle of corporate social and environmental responsibility (Fues and Messner, 2003). However, in view of the great opposition from governments in North and South to an internationally binding convention, the realization of this proposal lies in the distant future. Until that time, TNCs will be suspected of acting more as a brake on global sustainability policies than as the driving force behind them.

4.3.5
Science: Impulses for sustainability policy

In many areas, today's world is not functioning or developing sustainably. Numerous scientific disciplines, often organized in major international research programmes, have delivered the pieces of the jigsaw necessary for arriving at this overall finding. Thus, especially in the environmental field, science has acted as an important driver behind the essential political processes. Probably the best-known example of the identification of an environmental threat and the translation of research results into an international agreement is the ozone regime. In 1974 the damage to the Earth's ozone layer caused by emissions of CFCs was discovered. Just 13 years later – comparatively quickly by the standards of international negotiations – the Montreal Protocol was adopted (WBGU, 2001c). Yet also the Framework Convention on Climate Change adopted at the 1992 Conference on Environment and Development in Rio de Janeiro would never have come about without the preparatory work of the IPCC; and Agenda 21 would never have been adopted at that conference without the submission of the ICSU paper entitled 'Ascent 21'.

However, scientists can also have a negative influence on the political process if they misuse a one-sided scientific interpretation of the facts in the interests of an ideological bias, guided primarily by economic interests. Although the peer review system is capable of restricting the extent of such misuse within the scientific community, it can counteract the reflection of eccentric opinions in the public domain only to a limited extent. The publication of a balanced opinion in such cases would, in Germany for example, also be the task of the major research organizations. A German Academy of the Sciences, the establishment of which has long been debated, would have an important part to play in the public presentation of scientific findings.

Science is capable in countless areas of devising, and offering to society, solutions to the problems associated with sustainable development. WBGU considers it essential to establish an issue- and action-focused branch of research concerned with clashes of interests, conflicts of objectives and the problem of acting under uncertainty. This can only be done through inter- and transdisciplinary research integrating natural and social sciences in order to tackle the problems of global change.

4.3.5.1
Sustainability science

A decisive impetus for resolving the problems of global change comes from the major international research programmes IGBP, WCRP, IHDP and Diversitas. WBGU has presented these programmes in detail and acknowledged their value while at the same time calling for an integrative scientific approach to the solution of global problems (WBGU, 1996). However, it was also made clear that basic research is an indispensable culture medium for such interdisciplinary work. Integrative research is not possible without deep rooting in individual disciplines.

At the Open Science Conference in Amsterdam in 2001, the four above-mentioned programmes joined forces to form the Earth System Science Partnership (ESSP) and, as their first joint activity, programmes were set up on the carbon cycle, nutrition, water and health. These integrative approaches, which address the dynamic and non-linear interactions between nature and society, characterize an entirely new research paradigm referred to as 'sustainability science'. The new paradigm differs from the conventional one in terms of its structure, methodologies and contents:

- Natural and social sciences are interlinked from the outset in a transdisciplinary approach.
- The issues addressed are problem-oriented, with the objective of generating and applying knowledge to aid the decision-making process for sustainable development.
- Social groups are involved in the research in a new form of cooperation.
- The core processes of global change are analysed and integrated on all scales, from global to local.
- The processes are modelled qualitatively and quantitatively, depending on the requirements and possibilities.

Kates et al. (2000) have compiled a set of key questions for sustainability science which are intended to supplement the issues addressed by the existing global change programmes. They are directed above all at the fundamental character of human-environment relations and at the options available to society for steering a sustainable course (Box 4.3-2).

The WBGU report on global change research particularly emphasized the problem-solving process (WBGU, 1996). Global environmental problems are often of a long-term nature, which results in difficulties with regard to diagnosis and prognosis. Furthermore, they are significantly more complex than other issues, which has an impact on the political consensus-building process and on the choice of instruments.

Box 4.3-2

Core questions of sustainability science

1. How can the dynamic interactions between nature and society – including lags and inertia – be better incorporated in emerging models and conceptualizations that integrate the Earth system, human development, and sustainability?
2. How are long-term trends in environment and development, including consumption and population, reshaping nature-society interactions in ways relevant to sustainability?
3. What determines the vulnerability or resilience of the nature-society system in particular kinds of places and for particular types of ecosystems and human livelihoods?

4. Can scientifically meaningful 'limits' or 'boundaries' be defined that would provide effective warning of conditions beyond which the nature-society systems incur a significantly increased risk of serious degradation?
5. What systems of incentive structures – including markets, rules, norms and scientific information – can most effectively improve social capacity to guide interactions between nature and society toward more sustainable trajectories?
6. How can today's operational systems for monitoring and reporting on environmental and social conditions be integrated or extended to provide more useful guidance for efforts to navigate a transition toward sustainability?
7. How can today's relatively independent activities of research planning, monitoring, assessment, and decision support be better integrated into systems for adaptive management and societal learning?

Sources: Kates et al., 2000

Finally, the conflicts of goals are also especially difficult to resolve on account of their international character, as a consequence of differences in culture, religion and, above all, development status of the countries involved. The following elements in the problem-solving process must be addressed by research:

- Securing the data pool: Reliable observation systems for data collection are an indispensable basis for problem identification.

- Decision-oriented treatment of issues: Environmental issues must be identified, explained and predicted, so that options for political decision-making processes can be demonstrated.

- Guiding vision, identification and goals: The guiding vision of sustainable development must be made operable. To this end, WBGU has developed its guard rail approach (Section 2.3.5).

- Global governance: The further development of the UN system and the stronger anchoring of environmental policy within the UN must be accompanied by research (Chapter 6).

- Optimization of global environmental policy: The effectiveness of environmental regimes must be analysed and evaluated.

- Implementation of international agreements: The verification of measures and the use of sanctions have been little researched.

4.3.5.2
A new pact between society and science

In the second half of the 20th century, a remarkably stable social pact developed between science and society: society invested heavily in basic research on the assumption that the results of the research would lead to higher economic growth and greater national security. This pact must now be renewed and extended (UNESCO, 1999; ICSU et al., 2002). Under this new contract, science should undertake to devote a growing share of its R&D agenda to the social goals of sustainable development. In return, society should undertake to provide appropriate funding for this agenda. For the practical implementation of this contract, ICSU et al. (2002) propose the following steps:

- *Boosting the supply and demand sides of science and technology:* Enhancing the demand side requires a considerable expansion of public and political knowledge about the nature and extent of the necessary challenges to be faced in the transition towards sustainability. At the same time, it is necessary to convince society that science and technology are capable of offering solutions. This calls for partnerships with key social groups such as private industry and civil society. Science must communicate its findings and potentials in

a very much stronger and more accessible form; nor should it turn its back on modern marketing methods. Moreover, indigenous and traditional knowledge should play a greater role.

- *Thinking beyond business as usual:* In order to become an attractive partner for society, science needs to add new directions to its traditional approaches. R&D priorities must be set in such a way that science and technology deliver solutions to the most important sustainability problems. The problems must also be formulated by society and not just by scientists. The findings should be available not only to governments or powerful groups, but to all members of society.

- *Focusing on exemplary socio-ecological systems:* The most important dynamic interactions between nature and society take place in certain places and at certain times. Science must be embedded in these specific realities. It will be a great challenge to develop approaches which meaningfully transfer research findings to other places and social systems.

- *Combining credibility with legitimacy:* If knowledge is to effectively promote sustainable development, it must not be geared towards the peer reviewer. Rather, knowledge must be so dependable and credible that it can serve as the basis for political action, i.e. it must be relevant and of the highest quality for decision-makers. Furthermore, knowledge must be ethically defensible in its choice of means and in its dealings with the persons concerned. The balance between credibility, quality and legitimacy constitutes a great challenge with regard to the form given to those institutions that are to carry out research and development, assessments and decision-making assistance.

Science thus has an important role to play in civil society in the implementation of sustainable development: conscious of its responsibility, it is a trailblazer towards solutions. Of course, it also retains its original function: science identifies potential new problems and attempts to predict possible future events. In doing so, it must make clear where its findings are uncertain and it must explain to decision-makers the necessity to act under uncertainty. These insights must be intelligibly formulated and must be conveyed to those with political responsibility and also to the public so as to engender corresponding awareness. This is ultimately also the central function of governmental scientific advisory bodies.

4.3.5.3
Scientific policy advice

WBGU has already demonstrated in earlier reports that knowledge is one of the keys to overcoming the challenges of global change, but that, to date, it has been insufficiently used (WBGU, 1999, 2001a). Owing to the complexity of global problems, science must undertake considerable efforts to make its findings intelligible and usable for the bodies that steer policy, and for civil society. However, independent scientific advice must also be promoted and requested by politicians.

WBGU sees great deficits in scientific advice, especially at those international institutions concerned with environmental and development policy. And yet the Intergovernmental Panel on Climate Change (IPCC), which was set up in 1988 by WMO and UNEP, provides a highly successful model for such bodies. Even though IPCC executive summaries are edited line by line by government representatives and there is therefore the risk that they will be rendered politically opportune, the IPCC's full reports capture a broad international scientific consensus on the state of the climate system. The foundation for political agreements was thus laid (WBGU, 2001b).

WBGU has repeatedly recommended the establishment of further panels modelled on the IPCC, particularly panels to support the environmental conventions (WBGU, 1999, 2000, 2001a). As presented in Section 3.3, soil protection, the conservation and sustainable use of biological diversity as well as access to modern forms of energy are key areas in the fight against poverty. WBGU reaffirms its proposals from earlier reports:

*   *Intergovernmental Panel on Biological Diversity – IPBD:* The Convention on Biological Diversity requires the continuous provision of scientific advice which summarizes and evaluates the numerous local activities. This panel could provide ongoing follow-up for individual projects such as the Global Biodiversity Assessment and the Millennium Ecosystem Assessment and could derive recommendations for action from such reviews (WBGU, 2001a).
*   *Intergovernmental Panel on Land and Soils – IPLS:* The Convention to Combat Desertification has no independent scientific advisory body so far. In addition to providing advice on desertification issues, the panel should in the long term set up a structure to continuously monitor and assess the changes in soil (WBGU, 2001b).

Proposed by UNEP and also considered by the EU, the establishment of a further panel, the Intergovernmental Panel on Global Environmental Change (IGEC), appears, from a present perspective, to have

a very extensive field of work. WBGU feels that priority should be given initially to the provision of advice on the environmental compartments of biodiversity as well as land and soils. However, IGEC could have an important role to play in coordinating IPCC, IPBD and IPLS with regard to issues relating to two or more conventions.

Two further bodies highly relevant in relation to poverty reduction are not directly linked to conventions, but are necessary for creating a dependable level of knowledge:

*   *Intergovernmental Panel on Sustainable Energy – IPSE:* The World Energy Assessment, published in 2000, should also be continuously followed up in a scientific advisory body. There is a need here for maximum possible regional representation. Scientists from developing countries should be specifically supported and involved (WBGU, 2004).
*   *Risk Assessment Panel:* This panel should act as a hub for systematically collating and assessing the existing national risk identifications and evaluations. It should concentrate less on analysing the identified environmental problems and more on the early identification of new risks in connection with global change (WBGU, 1999).

In addition, the establishment of an international panel on poverty and disparities should be examined; such a panel might possibly be supported by IHDP and UNDP (Section 5.3.6).

4.3.5.4
Conclusions

Science can act as an important provider of impetus towards sustainability policies by collecting, analysing and assessing data and by using those data to derive options for the political decision-makers. Sustainability science, which is becoming newly established and employs an integrated approach, should therefore be expanded and its national and international self-organization should be promoted. In addition, the bridge between science and politics should be strengthened through the establishment of intergovernmental advisory bodies. There are large deficits with regard to scientific policy advice in the EU. In the field of the environment and sustainable development, although numerous European environment councils have merged within the loose network of the EEAC (European Environment and Sustainable Development Advisory Councils), the EU-coordinated provision of advice takes place on a rather *ad hoc* basis and is not oriented towards the long-term problems.

In Germany, the standing of science in the process of the elaboration and implementation of national sustainability strategy should be significantly raised. Science is not an interest group in the usual sense, but has a special role to play as the provider of basic knowledge for orientation and action.

4.4
Résumé: Challenges in shaping the institutional framework

4.4.1
The international setting has changed

The changed setting in which international policy processes are shaped determines the success or failure of the processes and institutional arrangements set out in Chapter 4. WBGU has identified three paramount aspects of this setting:

1. To avert the crises that globalization is widely feared to cause, it needs to be channeled in regulatory frameworks.
2. In view of the constantly changing setting, international trade and financial policy, as well as development and environment policy, must operate as global structural policy seeking to alter both internal and international structures.
3. Similarly, the risks arising from global change can only be managed if countries create binding multilateral regimes and institutions to deal with them.

4.4.1.1
Global governance

A principle adopted by the German Bundestag's Study Commission on Globalization states that: 'When the economy goes global, policy must follow suit.' The preservation of global public goods requires us to think and act globally. The concept of global governance is based on various types and levels of international coordination and cooperation. The rapid proliferation of international organizations and multilateral regimes attests to the need for such cooperation. These regimes translate the will to cooperate into binding frameworks on a regional or global scale. In the context of the regimes, countries undertake to tackle shared problems in order to prevent global public 'bads'. Even superpowers agree to be bound by certain, selected regimes which regulate matters that they cannot resolve on their own and that are vital for their own well-being.

However, global governance is not just an intergovernmental matter, implemented exclusively by countries and international organizations. Under the heading of global governance, both governmen-

tal and non-governmental stakeholders are active on levels ranging from local to global. This is because, in today's complex world, countries can no longer expect to resolve problems in diplomatic isolation. The world conferences organized by the United Nations in the 1990s played a key role in formulating joint perspectives on and approaches to solving pressing global problems. These conferences and the associated follow-up processes have proved their worth as innovative, learning-based policy arenas tackling global change. They have been correctly identified as the foundries where global governance is forged (Fues and Hamm, 2001). These arenas embody a transnational model of governance of a new quality. Their model is better suited than the conventional intergovernmental decision making approach to tackling the growing complexity of transboundary interconnections.

The new, powerful global players include transnational corporations (Section 4.3.4), but also NGOs, which are organized on an increasingly international basis (Section 4.3.3). New global policy networks and Public Private Partnership structures are also forming, providing a means by which countries, international organizations, companies and NGOs can find solutions to the problems they face. These new structures include the World Commission on Dams and global funds such as the Global Health Fund, where private companies and foundations work alongside countries in a funding capacity and sometimes also initiate and broker agreements.

4.4.1.2
Global structural policy

Alongside the globalization debate and discussions about global governance, a new concept has emerged: global structural policy. It allocates a new role and priority to development and environmental policy:

- Global structural policy aims to create international conditions which provide better development opportunities for poorer countries. International development policy must therefore, in addition to implementing projects and programmes, also aim to modify national and international structures.
- Global structural policy asks that funding be concentrated on areas where global issues are at stake, especially reducing poverty, halting environmental degradation and maintaining peace. The challenge for constructive North-South policy lies in understanding that even the countries on the fringes of international policy making and the 'ailing' participants in the world economy must be considered as partners, whose cooperation is required if

many of the global and regional problems are to be resolved.

- Global structural policy means branching out from the one-way street which runs North to South. It requires even industrialized countries and populations to concede that they share responsibility for development and environmental problems, even in areas of the world which may seem far removed, and accept that they may feel the effects of these problems.

Development policy will only be able to fulfil its ever-expanding list of responsibilities if it is taken as a cross-cutting task, on a par with foreign and security policy, trade and financial policy, environmental and agricultural policy and human rights policy, forming part of a coherent overall policy framework. This requirement for coherence applies in equal measure to environmental policy.

4.4.1.3
Multilateralism

One of the guiding principles in the final declaration of the World Summit on Sustainable Development (WSSD) is that the future of sustainable global development lies in multilateralism, and that multilateralism is fundamental to the successful handling of environmental and development crises. The reason why the declaration makes this demand of the international community is clear: both gaining control of global risks and preserving global public goods require cooperation between countries, binding regulatory frameworks within which countries can act in the global arena and institutions to make rules and monitor their enforcement.

Multilateralism is already a feature of many approaches and policy areas, but needs to develop further. The answer to the question put by Yehezkel Dror (1995) in a report to the Club of Rome, namely 'Can the earth still be governed?' is: 'the earth can no longer be governed with the conventional methods and tools'. Multilateralism promises to be better at solving problems than the more traditional bilateral approach or the unilateralism of the present US government – as illustrated by its resistance to inclusion in multilateral frameworks such as the Kyoto Protocol. The global political dilemma, which also exerts a major influence on international development and environmental policy, is that without the cooperation of the most powerful players, global regimes either fail to emerge or have only a limited effect. Without global regimes there can be no sustainable development.

4.4.2
The existing institutional architecture lacks efficiency and enforcement capability

Since the United Nations was established, an institutional architecture has grown up to deal with global poverty and environmental issues. While poverty reduction was an early addition to the UN's agenda, environmental protection was a relatively late arrival, being added due to the impetus from the first international environmental conference in Stockholm in 1972 (see Section 2.1). By the time the Brundtland Report was published in 1987, it had been accepted that these two policy areas must be linked in the interests of sustainable development. This process received a boost and considerable extra emphasis from the pioneering 1992 United Nations Conference on Environment and Development (UNCED) and the establishment of a whole raft of institutional innovations (CSD, UNFCCC, CBD, UNCCD and the Rio Principles, see Section 4.2). At UNCED, private stakeholders and non-governmental organizations became an established part of international environment and development policy. However, the key question is whether the existing institutional architecture, which continues to branch out in different directions, is able to manage present and future problems, or whether it will require more effective and robust structures in order to do so. Administrative reforms are also required, with the aim of achieving increased internal efficiency and effectiveness, accelerated negotiation and decision making processes and more rigorous cost management at all organizational levels.

Analysis in Sections 4.1 to 4.3 of this report has shown that, although the existing institutional architecture provides a suitable framework within which the problems described in Chapter 3 may be solved, it is too weak to solve them within a reasonable time frame. It has become abundantly clear that the policy processes investigated play key roles in setting the agenda, raising awareness and establishing the conceptual framework for individual policy areas. However, there is often a lack of coordination and implementation.

For instance, no body within the UN has overarching responsibility for the sustainable use of freshwater. Yet many institutions have mainstreamed the issue. A consensus has now been established within the international community on the sustainable use of freshwater (at World Water Forums, in the MDGs and the CSD). The implementation of this consensus view is not coordinated across institutions. There is no body to monitor that, say, the World Bank adheres to the consensus position in its policies. Nor is there any overarching regulatory body to deal with conflicts of interest, such as those that arise when the World Bank supports major dam projects.

One problem which applies to all areas and arises time and time again is the lack of enforcement capability within the UN. The United Nations Environment Programme (UNEP), which has rendered great services despite a lack of financial and human resources, cannot respond adequately to global environmental risks (see Section 4.2.6.2). The United Nations Development Programme (UNDP; Section 4.2.6.3) only has access to around one twentieth of the funds which the World Bank Group (Section 4.2.9) can employ. At the same time the World Bank and IMF are not sufficiently incorporated into the UN. Following the last half century, in which development and environmental crises have become an increasingly acute threat, the United Nations requires a complete overhaul if it is to escape the same unfortunate fate as the League of Nations.

Implementation on the ground is also inadequate. That is why the WSSD revolved around implementation and the political will to move from negotiation to action. However, the particular focus on voluntary partnership initiatives has only brought about limited progress. Treaties which are binding in international law, such as the Rio Conventions, set the global framework for successful implementation, heighten awareness of the issues involved and generate political will. Political will is in turn a decisive factor in creating opportunities for successful implementation at local and regional levels. Success in implementation is therefore determined primarily by governments. The main deficits lie with those governments and in the lack of willingness among industrialized nations to provide sufficient financial and technical support for the relevant programmes.

Most policy processes are related to both environment and poverty. It is now clear that conflicts of interest and of objectives can usually be resolved. Thus the conservation of biological diversity *and* the sustainable use of its components are given equal weight under the CBD. In many cases, progress has been made towards integrating the two policy areas. The World Bank produced an environmental strategy in 2001, many countries developed sustainability strategies in the run-up to the WSSD and the OECD's Development Assistance Committee (DAC) has taken up the issue of coherence.

As its founders intended, and as its treaty texts stipulate, the UN is a forum for coordination and cooperation. However, expectations of the UN generally prove to be excessively high and unachievable, as its Member States are not prepared to grant it either the powers or the financial resources required for effective problem solving. Contrary to its Charter, the UN has been marginalized in decisions of war and peace; even in international development and environmental policy, it only plays a major role as a forum for generating discussion and initiatives. The important decisions are mainly made in forums where the OECD countries – due to the capital they contribute – have the final say on policy (the World Bank, IMF, etc.). The UN system is also characterized by 'a complex, indistinct structure, which could be seen as a network of very loosely coupled institutions, acting independently of one another either in principle or in practice. The optimum balance between a centralized coordination and control of programme content and the regional-decentralized implementation of programmes has yet to be found. This is true for the work the subsidiary organs carry out for the General Assembly and for ECOSOC as well as the specialized agencies' work with one another and for the UN system as a whole.' (Hüfner, 2000).

Nevertheless, the UN's role as a forum for generating initiatives and discussions should not be underestimated: environmental protection, which was a relatively late addition to the UN system (it did not feature in the initial stages), has earned a permanent place in the international community. The forums in which environmental protection is included range from UNEP to binding agreements in international law such as the Rio Conventions. They further include forums such as the CSD. Poverty reduction is firmly anchored in the UN system through UNDP and through specialized agencies such as FAO or WHO. An integrated approach to problem solving, as flows from the concept of sustainability, has been taken up by the United Nations. WBGU therefore believes that one of the preconditions for successful poverty reduction and environmental policy making has been fulfilled.

4.4.3
Trade and economic policies lack commitment to sustainability goals

Chapter 4 explored the extent to which WTO and IMF and the principles of trade liberalization and macroeconomic stabilization that underpin them can act as either a brake or an accelerator on a policy focused on poverty reduction and environmental protection. It emerged that trade liberalization does not fundamentally conflict with a coherent global environmental and poverty reduction policy. There is, however, a need to reform many aspects of the GATT/WTO. The precautionary principles from environmental and consumer protection policy must be applied, multilateral environmental agreements need to be given explicit priority and the interests of the economically poor countries should be taken more explicitly into account. It is well known that the IMF's stabilization terms can have the effect of increasing poverty and degrading the environment, at least in the short to medium term. However, the fact that no consequences have been drawn from this brings WGBU to argue strongly that this stabilization policy be more carefully designed and that the measures imposed be tailored more closely to the countries and issues involved. Sustainability audits are recommendable for both trade agreements and IMF programmes.

A further problem to emerge from the analysis of policy processes is that much of the international community has yet to realize that it must follow a new path towards development. In particular, the idea of decoupling economic growth from natural resource consumption is not sufficiently well embedded in poverty reduction and environmental strategies. The strategic option of leapfrogging stages in technological development has not been given sufficient thought by international environmental and poverty reduction actors, although there are many cases which illustrate how this approach can succeed.

Reducing poverty and protecting the environment: Recommendations for integrated policies

5

At the start of the 21st century, the international community faces major challenges: human intervention in the natural environment is already jeopardizing livelihoods in many regions of the world. Unless countermeasures are adopted, such interventions will have an even more life-threatening impact in future. Poor groups, particularly women and children, are especially vulnerable to these environmental changes. Economic development is essential to improve the living conditions of the poor in developing countries. However, the industrialized countries' model of development, which is based on intensive resource consumption and an acceptance of the associated environmental degradation, is not a suitable model for emulation. It cannot be maintained by the industrialized countries or replicated by the developing countries, for the following reasons:

- Simply on account of the limited fossil reserves, the fossil energy pathway is not open to developing countries.
- Over-exploitation of renewable resources such as water, timber or fish is jeopardizing the natural life-support systems used by human communities and is undermining the bases of human livelihoods.
- The present economic system causes dangerous global climatic changes, degrades natural ecosystems and resources, widens existing disparities, and thus inflicts major damage on the fabric of society. It therefore undermines poverty reduction efforts and impedes sustainable development.
- Moreover, the biogeographical potential – especially of sensitive soils – in many developing countries militates against catch-up development at the expense of the natural ecosystems. The destructive exploitation of natural resources and forest clearance cause irreversible losses of biological diversity more rapidly in the tropics than in Central Europe.

In order to fight poverty and protect the environment worldwide, the systematic dovetailing of poverty reduction and global environmental protection is essential. This is the only way to fulfil the guiding vision of sustainable development forged at Rio in 1992. Given that the problems facing the world are intensifying, the policy processes and institutions analysed in Chapter 4 are becoming increasingly inadequate as a means of implementing the international community's agreed objectives (Section 3.6).

Now more than ever, there is a need to forge alliances between the industrialized and developing countries in order to address the environment-poverty nexus effectively. Both sides must face up to their responsibilities and honour their commitments in order to guarantee peaceful international development.

Since they are responsible for a substantial proportion of global environmental changes and in view of their economic and technological capacities, the industrialized countries have an obligation to develop a new concept of prosperity and an economic system which makes more sparing use of resources. They must also share the appropriate technologies with the developing countries and show a willingness to provide financial and technology transfers to poor countries in order to preserve the natural environment and combat poverty. Besides their ethical responsibility, sustainable development is in the industrialized countries' own interest as well – for in the Earth System, long-range geophysical, biochemical and civilizational effects ensure that damage can not remain local. The resource consumption associated with the industrialized countries' traditional model of prosperity not only overtaxes the environment; it also undermines the developing countries' prospects for the future. To avert this in the long term it is essential that the industrialized countries start the process by changing their production and consumption patterns. As recognized in the Rio principle of common but differentiated responsibility, it is the consumer societies which offer the greatest scope to ease the pressures on the world's natural resource base.

For their part, the developing countries must establish domestic political conditions which are conducive to good governance. Global governance and the support provided by the wealthy countries cannot achieve successful outcomes unless there is government accountability, the separation of powers, legal certainty for citizens and enterprises, and respect for human rights. This in turn means that people from all social groups must have opportunities for participation. More intensive promotion of education and access to healthcare are prerequisites for this process. To ensure that development does not take place at the expense of the environment, it is essential to implement, in parallel, a strategy aimed at decoupling economic growth from environmental pollution. The developing countries also have an obligation to abolish environmentally harmful subsidies, to establish environmental standards, reduce tariffs on environmental protection goods and, as far as possible, take the first steps towards an environmentally oriented system of taxes. Environmental protection must be viewed as a worthwhile investment for the future. As part of this process, the private sector must not only be regarded as the object of public environmental policy, but must also be a partner in developing a more socially equitable and environmentally sound economy.

In this chapter, WBGU makes recommendations on ways of moving closer to the sustainability goal:
- Policy coherence must be established in the fields of environment and development (Section 5.1).
- Mutually reinforcing dynamics must be created between environmental and development policies (Rio strategies) (Section 5.2).
- International law must be strengthened, and coordination and cooperation within the framework of international organizations and multilateral regimes must be expanded (global governance; Section 5.3).
- Good governance must be promoted as a key prerequisite for successful environmental and development policies (Section 5.4).
- International agreements must be implemented effectively and efficiently at national and regional level (Section 5.5).
- The financing of environmental and development policy must be safeguarded through new and existing mechanisms (Section 5.6).

5.1
Linking environment and development policy

Due to the predictable and serious impacts of environmental changes on the livelihoods of poor groups in the developing countries, further human intervention in the natural environment must be avoided and adaptation measures intensified. WBGU's core hypothesis is this: an effective environmental policy is the prerequisite for development in the poor countries (Section 2.2.1). There must be closer linkage between environmental and poverty reduction

policies and the environment-poverty nexus must be embedded more effectively as a cross-cutting theme at domestic political level. WBGU presents options for a more integrated policy which can act as an important lever in poverty reduction and environmental protection.

5.1.1
Providing compensation for environmental destruction and channelling liability

Industrialized countries are responsible for the major share of emissions of long-lived trace gases and modifications to natural biogeochemical cycles which trigger global environmental changes such as climate change. Very often, however, it is the developing countries which are most severely affected by the negative impacts. The payment of compensation for environmental damage would take account of this fact. In particular, compensation should be paid to developing countries for the climate-related damage caused since the problem was identified (Fig. 5.1-1). This includes an obligation to pay compensation for future emissions. Compensation payments are therefore not only a financing mechanism; they also create incentives for emissions avoidance.

Instruments such as charges for the use of global common goods or non utilization obligation payments promote the internalization of external effects and thus improve the operability of the markets. They also send out a signal that the industrialized countries are honouring their special responsibilities. At the same time, they could help reduce the vulnerability of poor people in developing countries and thus fight poverty. Over the long term, this type of transfer will have positive effects for all concerned, even though it may increase the burdens faced by the industrialized countries in the short term. If these payments are used by the developing countries primarily for environmental protection and poverty reduction, positive synergies can be created.

HOLDING STATES LIABLE IN LINE WITH THE 'POLLUTER PAYS' PRINCIPLE
WBGU recommends that states be obliged to pay appropriate compensation for climate damage in line with their contribution to global warming, taking 1990 as a baseline year for the calculation of their emissions. This should primarily be done through the funding of remedial and adaptation measures in the developing countries affected. The existing adaptation funds are under-resourced and their long-term future is not secure. The introduction of 'climate liability' could overcome this problem. Charges for the use of international airspace and waters could make

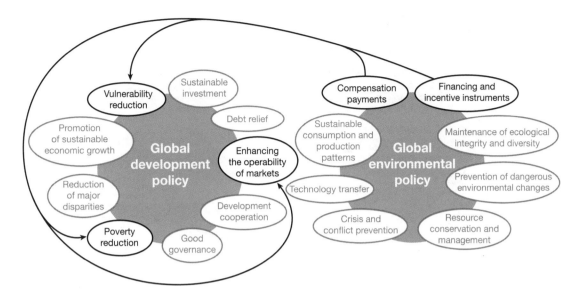

Figure 5.1-1
Coupling by 'Providing compensation for environmental destruction and channelling liability'. Countries causing transboundary environmental damage – usually the industrialized countries – must pay compensation to the countries, generally in the developing world, which are most severely affected by the adverse effects. New financial instruments are required for this purpose. This not only promotes the internalization of external effects and thus improves the operability of the markets; provided that these instruments are deployed in a targeted way in the developing countries, they also help reduce poverty and vulnerability.
Source: WBGU

a contribution here (WBGU, 2002). These charges have the potential to generate revenue amounting to ten times the current volume of funding available to the GEF. Payments for obligations to abstain from the destructive use of natural resources could also be used to generate funding (WBGU, 2002). These instruments and their potential contribution to the financing of development are discussed in Section 5.6.

HOLDING PRIVATE ENTERPRISES LIABLE FOR THE ENVIRONMENTAL DAMAGE THEY CAUSE
Enterprises which cause environmental damage through their exploitation of natural resources or other environmentally harmful activities must – in line with the 'polluter pays' principle – face liability under civil law. This must apply both to local companies and transnational corporations. Appropriate regulations must be established in national and international law. The inadequate sectoral environmental liability regimes which already exist at international level (e.g. in the law of the sea or in relation to transboundary movements of hazardous wastes) should be reinforced and extended to other environmental media (e.g. transboundary freshwater regimes). The focus must be on strict (absolute) liability; the object of protection should be the environment *per se*, irrespective of ownership status and economic value. The ongoing efforts to conclude cross-

sectoral international agreements on environmental liability in civil law should also continue.

5.1.2
Aligning the world economy more closely with social and environmental principles

For the world economy, a framework must be established which promotes sustainable development, especially in the developing countries. In order to grant the developing countries' products free access to the industrialized countries' markets, tariffs and subsidies must be abolished. This is an important step in enhancing the operability of the (world) markets and opens up revenue and growth opportunities for poor countries. Debt relief is a key prerequisite for sustainable development and can also encourage economic growth. To ensure that the poor benefit from – and can contribute to – growth, a range of measures are required to boost their opportunities for participation in the institutional/political, social and economic spheres. Furthermore, sustainable investment by companies from the industrialized countries can help to foster sustainable economic growth in the developing countries and facilitate resource conservation and management (Fig. 5.1-2).

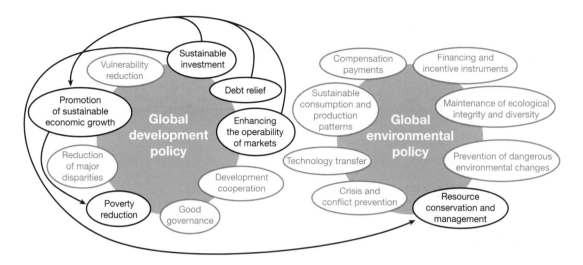

Figure 5.1-2
Coupling by 'Aligning the world economy more closely with social and environmental principles'. Debt relief and the
establishment of functioning markets through the abolition of subsidies and tariff and non-tariff barriers to trade, especially
in the primary sector, can – in conjunction with sustainable investment – help to promote sustainable economic growth.
By increasingly decoupling economic growth from resource consumption through sustainable investment, better resource
conservation and management can be achieved.
Source: WBGU

USING INTERNATIONAL TRADE AS A LEVER
Germany should intensify its efforts within the EU
and multilateral organizations such as the World
Trade Organization (WTO) to ensure that the developing countries' products are granted free access to
the industrialized countries' markets. Industrialized
and newly industrializing countries should open up
their markets to products from developing countries
as far as possible, abolish agricultural subsidies which
distort competition and immediately end the practice
of agricultural dumping. This includes aligning the
EU's fisheries agreements with developing countries
with environmental and social principles and phasing
out the subsidies paid to the EU Member States' fishing fleets. The only trade policy concessions which
should be demanded from the developing countries
in return are those which have a direct and beneficial impact on poverty reduction and global environmental protection, e.g. easier market access for goods
required by the poor, or zero tariffs on goods whose
use eases environmental pressure (such as solar technology). The negotiations in the Doha Round were
resumed in August 2004 because the EU, in particular, declared its willingness to undertake more far-
reaching measures to end its agricultural protectionism. The Doha negotiations, which are intended
to flesh out the trade liberalization process and are
likely to continue to the end of 2005 at the very least,
offer a useful opportunity to use trade as a 'lever' for
the benefit of the developing countries.

ENVIRONMENTAL AGREEMENTS MUST TAKE
PRECEDENCE OVER THE WTO'S FREE TRADE RULES
Within the WTO, the environmental precautionary principle should be given far higher priority, and
there should be an explicit recognition that multilateral environmental agreements take precedence
over WTO agreements. An appropriate addition to
the exemptions contained in the GATT/WTO treaties could ensure, for example, that programmes and
standards adopted under international environmental conventions are not challenged by any decision
taken within the WTO's dispute settlement mechanism. The international trade regime and the efforts
to protect the environment and promote sustainable
development must be mutually reinforcing. Cooperation between the WTO and UNEP should be intensified. The German federal government should continue to lobby pro-actively for these objectives at the
WTO negotiations. WBGU also recommends that
Sustainability Impact Assessments (SIAs) be developed further as a mechanism to measure the environmental quality of proposed trade agreements and
that appropriate SIA standards be adopted at international level (Section 4.2.13.1).

INTRODUCING A SUSTAINABILITY OBLIGATION FOR
THE IMF
A stable world economy is a key prerequisite for sustainable poverty reduction and environmental protection. In the past, the stabilization policies and programmes sponsored by the International Monetary

Fund have often contributed to an increase in poverty and environmental degradation over the short to medium term. In future, these negative impacts should be better anticipated and taken into account in the development of programme conditions. WBGU also recommends that the IMF's activities be restricted to its core competence, i.e. stabilizing economies (Section 4.2.13.2). In the long term, WBGU recommends the establishment of a new lead UN agency (Council on Global Development and Environment, Section 5.3), which would focus the IMF's activities towards the guiding vision of sustainable development.

INSTITUTIONALIZING ENVIRONMENTAL AND SOCIAL STANDARDS

In many emerging markets, private capital transfers now exceed the funding provided through official development assistance (ODA) many times over (Section 5.6). It is therefore becoming increasingly important to adopt more binding environmental and social codes of conduct at institutional level for multinational corporations and the private banking sector and establish similar codes for state export guarantee schemes as well.

- WBGU recommends that the German federal government continue to work actively for the implementation of the OECD Guidelines for Multinational Enterprises (Section 4.2.12). A system to monitor compliance with codes of conduct should also be set up at EU level. The establishment of a monitoring agency has been supported by the German Bundestag's Study Commission on Globalization of the World Economy (Enquete-Kommission, 2002) and also called for by the European Parliament. Voluntary commitments are an important interim measure, but should be incorporated progressively into binding international law (Section 4.3.5).
- Minimum standards should also be introduced for exports of used industrial goods which do not meet current environmental standards. The global trade in these goods (e.g. used motor vehicles) currently amounts to €150,000 million annually (RNE, 2003). Foreign trade policy rarely focuses on the environmental impacts of these exports. The global market for used goods is largely unregulated; monitoring of the application of WTO rules in this area is inadequate and few efforts have been made to assess whether these rules need to be reinforced (RNE, 2003).
- The German 'Guidelines for the Inclusion of Environmental, Social and Development Policy Criteria in the Federation's Provision of Credit Guarantee Services' should be revised and brought into line with the Common Approaches adopted by the OECD's Working Party on Export Credits and Credit Guarantees in December 2003; they should also be incorporated into the terms and conditions for export credits. An independent monitoring system should further be established, as called for by the OECD's Development Assistance Committee (Section 4.2.12). The granting of export credit guarantees by Euler Hermes Kreditversicherungs-AG should take place in accordance with the OECD's Common Approaches to promote the use of renewable energies (Section 4.2.12).

5.1.3
Fostering local environmental protection as a precondition to poverty reduction

Preserving the integrity of the local environment, preventing dangerous environmental changes, and conserving and managing resources in line with sustainability criteria are key prerequisites for poverty reduction. The vulnerability of poor rural communities is closely linked to the functionality of local ecosystems. For example, Tropical Storm Jeanne would not have caused such devastation in Haiti in September 2004 had it not been for the massive deforestation of the island. So the adoption of measures – such as bioregional management (WBGU, 2001a) – to preserve ecosystem services not only helps solve many problems (supply of goods made from natural products, water resources management, soil protection); it also helps avert crises, thereby contributing to a reduction in vulnerability and combating poverty (Fig. 5.1-3). Environmental damage also has a highly adverse impact on the urban poor, who suffer from the health impacts of air pollution, toxic waste or contaminated water. Here, what is needed, above all, is a reduction in air pollution and other toxic loads through appropriate waste management, sanitation and transportation systems. Limit values for harmful substances must be introduced, monitored and enforced as well; setting health and environmental standards is essential in this context.

- *Climate protection:* WBGU recommends that the German federal government work actively for an international commitment on the preservation of carbon stocks in terrestrial ecosystems (e.g. primary forests, wetlands, grasslands), perhaps in the form of a protocol to the United Nations Framework Convention on Climate Change (UNFCCC). In this context, an international system of tradable non utilization obligations could be established (WBGU, 2003). This type of agreement would enable the costs of protecting local ecosystems that afford global benefits to be distributed equitably among the international community (Section 4.2.2.1).

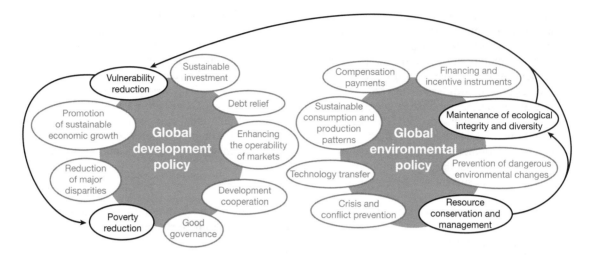

Figure 5.1-3
Coupling by 'Fostering local environmental protection as a precondition to poverty reduction'. The preservation of ecosystem services through improved resource conservation and appropriate resource management and the preservation of environmental integrity and diversity is a key prerequisite in minimizing the vulnerability of poor groups to environmental changes and natural disasters. This makes an indirect contribution to eliminating absolute poverty.
Source: WBGU

- *Preventing water scarcity and water pollution:* The commitment undertaken at the WSSD in Johannesburg for each country to develop integrated water resources management and water efficiency plans by 2005 must be vigorously pursued. For the purposes of implementation, international funding should be pooled and deployed, as a priority, in the least developed countries, in the most water-poor areas and in regions where there is a high prevalence of water-borne diseases. Access to clean drinking water should be recognized as a fundamental right under binding international law.

- *Conservation and sustainable use of natural ecosystems:* Bioregional strategies (integrating conservation and use at regional and local level; WBGU, 2001a) offer the opportunity – provided that good governance is in place – to enhance local and indigenous communities' entitlements to local ecosystem services and promote sustainable management methods (Section 3.3.4.3). This includes improving local communities' participation in the management of conservation areas. Projects which link sustainable ecosystem use with benefits at local level (e.g. sustainable tourism, access to genetic resources, benefit-sharing; Section 3.3.4) should be promoted as priorities. WBGU is critical of the cuts in federal budget funding for tropical forest conservation, as this is a key area in relation to the poverty-environment nexus (Section 4.2.12).

- *Soil protection:* The scale and extent of the regional 'hotspots' where soil loss is occurring as a result of erosion or salinization are well-known. Very often, the worst-affected regions are those used for intensive agriculture, whose role in food security now and in future is key. Overall, physical protection measures are less effective than changes to cultivation systems, e.g. the introduction of agroforestry. In the short term, it may be helpful to promote low-cost technologies which offer rapid benefits to poor farmers. Wherever there is potential for leapfrogging, this should be exploited. Salinization is a particularly serious problem as it is extremely costly to reverse. WBGU therefore calls for the establishment of a global monitoring system for the early detection of salinization.

- *Reducing air pollution:* To reduce indoor air pollution, it is essential to encourage the replacement of traditional biomass with modern fuels. To this end, WBGU has already proposed that pilot projects be launched which aim to establish a distributed energy supply, e.g. using biogenic liquefied petroleum gas (WBGU, 2004). To improve urban air quality, support should be provided to long-term projects for integrated transport planning; these projects must take greater account of environmental and health impacts as well as social and economic factors. Measures which can achieve positive outcomes very quickly, such as conversion to lead-free petrol, should be introduced as a matter of urgency. With support from the industrialized countries, the institutional framework for the adoption of standards for vehicle and industrial emissions, together with an appropriate monitoring structure, must be established.

5.1.4
Reducing vulnerability through adaptation

People with adequate entitlements, such as access to education and healthcare, are better able to cope with environmentally related pressures. Improving basic social services should therefore be given higher priority in development cooperation. In poor countries with high rates of population growth, measures should be taken to satisfy the demand for family planning services. In addition, programmes aimed at conserving and managing natural resources, especially soils, must be a key focus of efforts to reduce vulnerability (Fig. 5.1-4).

SAFEGUARDING THE CAPACITY FOR POLICY ACTION
The poverty reduction strategies currently being pursued must be adapted in anticipation of the likely regional impacts of global environmental changes. There must be better linkage between poverty reduction strategies such as the Poverty Reduction Strategy Papers (PRSPs) and ongoing planning processes, e.g. the National Action Programmes on Desertification and other national environmental action programmes (Section 4.2.4). WBGU endorses the German federal government's intention to promote the poverty-environment nexus in the GEF, the PRSPs of the World Bank and the IMF. The prerequisite is that poverty reduction and environmental strategies are integrated more systematically into the structures of the German Development Ministry (BMZ) and the German implementing organizations (GTZ, KfW, DED,

etc.; cf. Section 4.2.10). WBGU recommends that a new priority area be established in development cooperation, i.e. 'adaptation to anticipated global environmental changes'. Greater importance should also be attached to the policy field of resource conservation as an integral component of a development cooperation approach targeted at mitigating environmental crisis. In addition to these conceptual developments, the UN Millennium Development Goals need to place a stronger emphasis on environmental sustainability (Sections 3.6 and 5.3.4).

REDUCING RISKS AND VULNERABILITY THROUGH
DEVELOPMENT COOPERATION
- It is not just natural disasters themselves that obstruct development or reverse the progress made; the scale of a disaster and the damage caused are also affected by conceptual weaknesses in development work (UNDP, 2004a). In order to address these deficits, WBGU recommends the inclusion of disaster risk management in the preparation of the Poverty Reduction Strategy Papers (PRSPs), greater integration of disaster preparedness into the German federal government's Programme of Action 2015, the incorporation of disaster mitigation into the implementation of the UN Millennium Development Goals (MDGs), and the inclusion of disaster risk management in poverty reduction programmes. WBGU also recommends that disaster prevention be made a new sectoral priority in development cooperation and that adequate funding be provided.

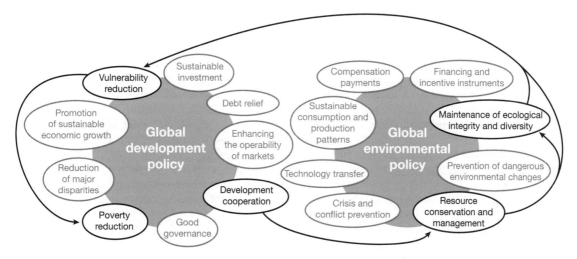

Figure 5.1-4
Coupling by 'Reducing vulnerability through adaptation'. Resource conservation and management programmes undertaken within the framework of development cooperation – e.g. reforestation, sustainable water resources management or soil amelioration projects – reduce poor communities' vulnerability to environmental changes. For example, biological diversity helps to prevent pest outbreaks, ground vegetation helps to ward off desertification and contributes to water storage, and hillside forests prevent mudslides from occurring after heavy rain.
Source: WBGU

- In the developing countries, agriculture is extremely important for poor groups, and especially for women, as they produce most of their food themselves. Any change in climatic conditions or increased frequency of weather extremes can therefore have a direct impact on poor people's livelihoods. An agricultural system which is robust enough to withstand global environmental changes must fulfil the following criteria: it must promote a diversity of cultivation systems and plant species (also in order to cushion the impacts of climate-induced blights and infestations), it must be able to cope with the stresses caused by drought, intense heat or salinization, and it must take account of the needs and problems of highly vulnerable small-scale producers at all stages of planning and implementation. The funding programmes established within the framework of development cooperation must also take appropriate account of women's key role in safeguarding families' and communities' livelihoods.

- Promoting environmentally relevant spatial planning as part of development cooperation is strategically important, especially in terms of boosting the coping capacities of developing countries in response to – often insidious – environmental changes. Among other things, the development and enforcement of effective environmental laws, the production of national environmental statistics, and policy coherence play a key role in this context. WBGU recommends that national environmental planning in the developing countries focus to a greater extent on these long-term effects. This is the only way to ensure that the necessary systemic changes, e.g. in agriculture, are undertaken in good time. In this context, WBGU recommends that the training and advisory activities carried out by German human resources and organizational development institutions focus more on the issues of vulnerability to global environmental changes and opportunities for prevention and adaptation.

ESTABLISHING RISK PREVENTION INSTITUTIONS

- Risk and vulnerability assessments are urgently needed in the planning of risk prevention schemes. An international risk and vulnerability assessment programme should therefore be established, whose task would be to develop 'disaster risk indices' to identify priorities for financial resource deployment based on cost-benefit analysis. A key prerequisite is the definition of internationally accepted standards for risk and vulnerability assessments.

- Environmental changes can lead to harvest losses and thus directly threaten the livelihoods of poor groups. At the G8 Summit in 2003, it was agreed

that the introduction of insurance against hunger would be explored as an option. In addition, the international community should adopt measures to guard against the hardships caused by natural disasters. Efficient financial instruments such as weather derivatives or disaster loans could be considered to overcome the hardships not covered by insurance or from other sources. Furthermore, the World Bank and World Food Programme should have access to index-linked derivatives on the international financial markets in order to avert famines (Section 5.6.3.3). In light of the predictions being made by environmental researchers, WBGU takes the view that the introduction of such safeguards is likely to become increasingly important. However, the launch of these mechanisms should not absolve governments of their responsibilities.

- In addition to the successful micro-credit schemes already introduced (e.g. Grameen Bank; Section 5.6.3.3), the launch of micro insurance schemes for the purpose of risk spreading in the event of individual hardship (e.g. illness) should also be considered as an element of risk management. These micro schemes should be integrated into existing banking and insurance systems to a greater extent and additional funding provided for them.

5.1.5
Protecting the environment by reducing poverty

The significance of poverty's adverse effects on the natural environment is often overestimated – prosperity and industrialization play a far greater role in causing environmental change (Section 3.3). Nonetheless, the poor are often forced to over-exploit the natural resources which generally form the basis of their livelihoods as no other income sources are available to them. Combating poverty through better provision of basic services (infrastructure, basic social services), enhanced rights of participation and entitlements, especially for women, along with better income-generation opportunities can reduce the pressure on local ecosystems and thus help conserve resources and preserve environmental integrity and diversity (Fig. 5.1-5). This applies not only to poverty in rural regions but also to the long-range impacts of cities on the surrounding ecosystems.

PERMANENT DEBT RELIEF

Further debt relief is essential to promote economic development in developing countries. In order to assist countries which cannot achieve this development from their own resources, the HIPC Initiative should be reformed and expanded to include heav-

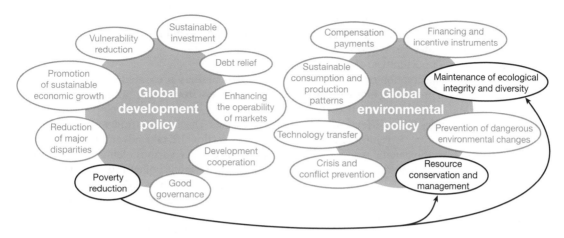

Figure 5.1-5
Coupling by 'Protecting the environment by reducing poverty'. Better provision of basic services (infrastructure, basic social services), enhanced rights of participation and entitlements, along with better income-generation opportunities for the rural poor can reduce the pressure on local ecosystems and thus help *conserve resources* and *preserve environmental integrity and diversity*. This applies not only to poverty in rural regions but also to the long-range impacts of cities on the surrounding ecosystems.
Source: WBGU

ily indebted middle-income countries. However, the expansion of debt relief cannot take place at the expense of other development financing: debt relief should not be factored into ODA, which is what often happens at present. The linkage between debt relief and the submission of a PRSP is welcome in principle, although there must be a greater focus, in the PRSPs, on environmental aspects and their correlation with poverty. The poor must be given the opportunity to escape the poverty trap without over-exploiting the natural environment. The PRSPs should offer a holistic strategy that empowers the developing countries to embark upon an environmentally compatible development pathway without increasing their current debt or taking on new debt (Section 4.2.4). A key prerequisite, in this context, is good governance – i.e. legal stability, an efficient public administration, and government accountability – in the partner countries (Section 5.5). WBGU welcomes the British government's announcement in September 2004 to cancel more of the developing countries' debts, and urges the German federal government to follow suit.

PRSPs WITH INTEGRATED ENVIRONMENTAL
TARGETS – A PREREQUISITE FOR DEBT RELIEF
Heavily indebted poor countries benefit from debt relief under the HIPC Initiative if they submit a Poverty Reduction Strategy Paper (Section 4.2.10). In future, the PRSPs should include a national environmental strategy and should also give greater priority to measures addressing poverty dimensions such as lack of education, disease, malnutrition and social exclusion. The concept of granting debt relief

in exchange for environmental programmes dates back to the debt crisis in the 1980s. These 'debt-for-nature swaps' proved contentious, however – not least because the debt reduction was often marginal at best. There was also a concern that debts which had already been written off would be reactivated and that countries' commitment to their own environmental policies would decrease as a result of the environmental programmes that were a condition of debt relief. These criticisms would be mitigated by PRSPs that give greater priority to environmental aspects: debt relief would have a far more significant impact and would be based on a holistic, longer-term development strategy which would be controlled and implemented by the country itself.

STRENGTHENING LOCAL COMMUNITIES'
ENTITLEMENTS AND PROPERTY RIGHTS
Income-generation measures, functioning social security systems and more equitable distribution and legal recognition of local and indigenous communities' property rights in relation to land, water or biological resources are extremely important in reducing poverty. Entitlements to ecosystem services should also be improved at local level, and there should be better participation by local and indigenous communities in decisions on biological resources (e.g. in the framework of a bioregional management approach; WBGU, 2001a; Section 3.3.4). Appropriate framework conditions (e.g. good governance, secure entitlements, avoidance of renewed concentration of rights in the hands of a few stakeholders) can help lessen the negative incentives which encourage over-exploi-

tation of sensitive ecosystems. The participation of local and indigenous communities in decision-making on the management of conservation areas and in income-generation opportunities, e.g. through employment in nature conservation or tourism, also enhances the prospects of preserving biological diversity (Sections 3.3.4 and 4.2.2). In this context, it must be ascertained whether the positive effects of the use of traditional knowledge can be reinforced if state power of disposition over the genetic resources concerned is transferred to the local communities.

IMPROVING CONDITIONS IN URBAN SLUMS
Local air pollution, contaminated drinking water and health hazards resulting from a lack of sanitation and waste disposal are the key environmental problems facing poor urban areas. The causes include inadequate infrastructure, uncontrolled settlement growth, partly as a result of rural-urban migration, and obsolete technologies in the transport sector. Strategies for sustainable urban development, integrated development plans for urban slums and the introduction of low-emission engines can all help to reduce poverty and prevent environmental damage. WBGU endorses the German federal government's commitment to improving the living conditions of around 100 million slum-dwellers (Programme of Action 2015) and recommends that the Programme focus especially on water supply, sanitation and energy issues.

OVERCOMING ENERGY POVERTY
The linkage between energy poverty, over-exploitation of resources and health risks was described in detail by WBGU in its energy report (2003b), which demonstrated that the introduction of modern forms of energy is a key innovation in the context of poverty reduction (Box 3.2-1). Overcoming energy poverty on a sustainable basis is therefore a core element not only of development but also environmental policy measures. The International Conference for Renewable Energies which took place in Bonn in 2004 achieved major progress in this area. The German federal government should give targeted encouragement and support to those developing countries which have not yet launched projects for the expansion of renewables. The German federal government should deploy some of the €500 million designated for the promotion of renewables in the developing countries (for a five-year period from 2005) for this purpose as well.

5.2
Rio strategies: Examples of self-reinforcing dynamics

The opportunities presented in Section 5.1 to link individual environmental and development policy fields can be used to develop integrated holistic strategies. These 'Rio strategies', which are introduced in Section 2.2, take advantage of positive feedbacks between the various elements of environmental and development policy, thus creating coherence between individual measures and enhancing their effectiveness. In the following sections, two examples on very different scales are presented. Section 5.2.1 describes a global strategy whose environmental 'starting point' is climate protection. Section 5.2.2 focuses on cotton cultivation in the Sahel and sets out a strategy with a regional focus, which nonetheless requires international cooperation.

5.2.1
A Rio strategy for climate protection

A Rio strategy for an integrated approach to human-induced climate change must contain both preventive and remedial elements. These must be coordinated such that all measures are mutually reinforcing. This is the only way to create positive feedbacks; in other words, actors can achieve far greater effectiveness through their concerted efforts than through individual measures. Self-reinforcing dynamics can emerge. This can be viewed as a reversal of the syndromes outlined by WBGU in previous reports (WBGU, 1996, 1998a). In the interests of clarity, the preventive and remedial elements of the holistic strategy will be presented separately at first. The strategy presented here is not intended to question the need for emissions reductions in the industrialized countries. On the contrary: they are an essential prerequisite for climate protection. WBGU has made comprehensive recommendations on this issue in other reports (WBGU, 2003, 2004).

PREVENTIVE MEASURES
The model for the preventive element of the overall strategy is based on a dynamic investment strategy (Fig. 5.2-1). The underlying hypothesis is that increased investment in sustainable, low-emission technologies in the developing countries can be used to stimulate environmentally sound economic growth, which will ultimately help reduce poverty while preventing human-induced climate change. This can only be achieved if a form of growth that is based on the increasingly intensive use of conventional technologies and therefore leads to higher emissions of

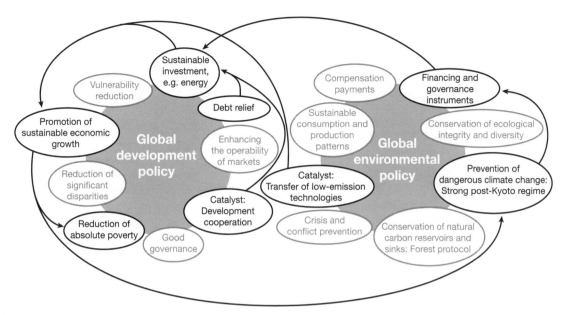

Figure 5.2-1
The preventive chapter of the climate strategy. In order to prevent dangerous climate change, a robust post-Kyoto regime
provides for more intensive investment to generate sustainable economic growth in developing countries. By means of
leapfrogging, an emissions-intensive development pathway is avoided.
Source: WBGU

climate-relevant gases is explicitly avoided. At the
same time, it must be ensured that growth dividends
are used to combat poverty (Section 5.1.1). The catalysts, i.e. the amplifying elements which determine
the direction of the dynamic investment strategy, are
therefore development cooperation and the transfer
of low-emission technologies.

A robust climate regime is required in which the
parties to the UNFCCC agree on specific climate protection targets and measures beyond the first commitment period of the Kyoto Protocol; this regime
must take on important steering functions as well as
mobilize financial resources. In order to prevent dangerous human-induced climate change, a clear reduction in global greenhouse gas emissions is required in
a process which must involve the developing countries as well, but without jeopardizing the goal of
global poverty reduction. The climate regime must
therefore ensure that the developing countries are
provided with increased financial resources to support sustainable development.

This can take place, firstly, through incentives for
private investment to promote global access to sustainable technologies (especially in renewable energies). Here, the further development of the Clean
Development Mechanism (CDM), with a greater
focus on sustainable development in the target countries, would be useful. Other important financial and
steering instruments are compensation and states'
and companies' liability for the emissions they cause.

Corresponding recommendations are set out in Section 5.1.1.

On the other hand, the transfer of emissions-
reducing or low-emissions technologies should take
place both within the climate regime (e.g. with support from the GEF) and on a bilateral basis in such
a way as to simultaneously promote sustainable
economic growth. Technology transfer must not be
restricted to exports of final products and systems. In
parallel, there must be a focus on knowledge transfer
and investments aimed at enhancing the quality of
local production. Transfer in the energy supply field
should strengthen the focus on ending energy poverty, and technologies in the transport sector must be
tailored to the needs of poor groups.

Development actors, especially the World Bank,
must incorporate climate policy objectives in their
programmes and strategies. Preventive climate protection must not be restricted to individual development projects or programmes but must be viewed as
a cross-cutting theme in development cooperation,
especially in economic development. This means that
development cooperation must refrain from investing in non-sustainable technologies. As called for in
the Extractive Industries Review (EIR, 2003), the
World Bank in particular should phase out its support for coal and oil production and allocate even
more of its resources than announced at renewables
2004 in Bonn towards promoting renewables (Section 4.2.9). Better cooperation among development
actors is also essential, with improved coordination

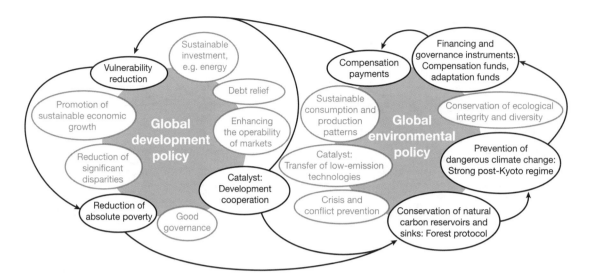

Figure 5.2-2
The remedial chapter of the climate strategy. The international community faces up to its responsibility for human-induced climate change and pays appropriate sums to affected poor countries as compensation for, and to promote adaptation to, climate change. In return, these countries refrain from damaging natural carbon reservoirs and thus make a contribution to climate protection.
Source: WBGU

of EU development cooperation being the first step in this context (Section 5.5).

In the event of future conflicts arising between the interests of the WTO and the UNFCCC, the UNFCCC should take precedence (Section 4.3.6). Foreign trade policy must also prioritize the export of sustainable technologies, and more intensive efforts must be made to implement the OECD Guidelines for Multinational Enterprises (Sections 4.2.12 and 4.3.5). The German State Secretaries' Committee for Sustainable Development is a suitable forum in which to resolve goal conflicts between economic development and emissions avoidance in Germany. At international level, the financial institutions and regional development banks must review their funding allocation mechanisms in light of the UNFCCC objectives. As a long-term vision, a new lead agency – the Council on Global Development and Environment – should be established within the UN system to take over coordination in this area.

The key prerequisites, on the part of the developing countries, are good governance (Section 5.2) and the willingness to pursue a sustainable climate protection and development strategy. Conditional debt relief offers the industrialized countries a way of creating an incentive for the developing countries and offering them the financial opportunities to move away from emissions-intensive development pathways (Section 5.3.5).

REMEDIAL MEASURES
The remedial part of the overall strategy (Fig. 5.2-2) consists of two elements. Firstly, it must reduce poor groups' vulnerability to the adverse effects of climate change. Secondly, it must protect natural carbon stocks from poverty-induced degradation.

A sound financial basis must be established for new financial instruments within the climate regime (adaptation funds, compensation fund and reinsurance mechanisms). These instruments must not be reliant on voluntary contributions; instead, in line with the 'polluter pays' principle, countries should be obliged to pay appropriate sums in accordance with their contribution to climate change (Section 4.2.2.1). In this way, states will help to increase investment, e.g. in disaster preparedness, health systems or agricultural and forest management planning, in order to reduce the vulnerability of poor groups to climate change. A further source of funding is the introduction of charges for the use of airspace and international waters (Section 5.2.1).

The measures must be shaped in such a way that they help to reduce poverty while easing poverty-induced pressure on ecosystems. This can only be achieved if economic growth generates additional poverty reduction impetus. Appropriately configured interaction between the two parts of the strategy is required here. Both the preventive and the remedial elements of the climate strategy require close cooperation between development policy actors, the climate regime and world trade institutions. This cannot be

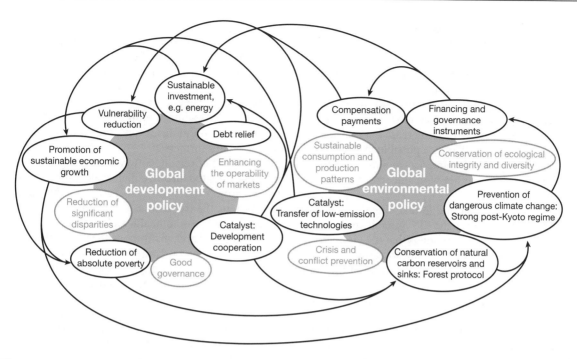

Figure 5.2-3
A holistic strategy to integrate climate protection and poverty reduction (Summary of Figures 5.2-1 and 5.2-1). Climate and development actors coordinate their programmes in order to create the greatest possible synergies and generate self-reinforcing dynamics.
Source: WBGU

achieved without more intensive commitment from the developing countries' governments. The development policy actors now view and treat adaptation to climate change as an important cross-cutting theme. This approach must be supported and developed further. However, equal priority must also be given to preventing climate change. For the poorest countries, this means that preserving ecosystems and avoiding climate-relevant land use changes must be integrated to a greater extent as a cross-cutting theme in development policy strategies.

To ensure the success of the overall strategy, it is essential to adopt an international agreement on the conservation of natural carbon sinks and reservoirs (CBD forest protocol: WBGU, 1995, 2000; UNFCCC carbon stocks protocol: WBGU, 2003). This must focus on climate protection issues, conservation of biodiversity and the interests of the local communities, including indigenous peoples. This means, for example, identifying alternative sources of income for poor groups so that they no longer need to over-exploit local ecosystems. WBGU has presented various recommendations on this issue (WBGU, 2001a, 2002).

IMPLEMENTING THE OVERALL STRATEGY
To sum up, WBGU makes five core recommendations for a strategy which integrates climate protection and poverty reduction:

- Further development of a robust climate regime beyond the first commitment period of the Kyoto Protocol, including effective funding mechanisms;
- Integration of poverty reduction into technology transfer;
- Greater integration of climate protection into development cooperation;
- Securing and increasing funding for adaptation and compensation within the UNFCCC framework;
- An international agreement on the conservation of carbon stocks, especially forests.

To ensure that the overall strategy functions effectively (Fig. 5.2-3), human-induced climate change should not be viewed as a sectoral problem to be resolved by environmental policy actors; instead, it must feature prominently on the international agenda as a cross-cutting theme. Furthermore, the strategy can only be successful if all stakeholders gear their actions within their particular sphere of competence towards the overall strategy. The priority is not to initiate new investments or activities which specifically focus on the prevention of, and adaptation to, climate change, but to steer existing investment flows and development policy activities in a way which supports the UNFCCC's objectives and poverty reduction simultaneously.

One risk to the success of the strategy is that a form of economic growth may be stimulated that results in higher global emissions, thereby exacerbating climate change and ultimately undermining poverty reduction. Short-term increases in emissions in selected countries, which are possible in line with the Contraction and Convergence model endorsed by WGBU, do not conflict with the strategy, however (WBGU, 2003).

Poverty reduction and global climate protection will be key themes at the G8 Summit in July 2005. WBGU therefore recommends that the German federal government propose a holistic strategy for climate protection and poverty reduction at this Summit.

The high-level conference agreed by the UN General Assembly and scheduled for September 2005 will review the fulfilment of the Millennium Development Goals (MDGs). It therefore offers an opportunity to give fresh impetus to the further development of the international institutional arrangements for poverty reduction and climate protection. In particular, the conference should address the hitherto inadequate treatment of climate issues and identify ways of dealing with this problem more effectively. There will be scope for scientific input at side events at both the review conference and the G8 Summit.

5.2.2
A Rio strategy for cotton cultivation in the Sahel region

There are currently three major cotton-exporting regions in the world: the USA, which accounts for around 50 per cent of global exports, the Sahel countries in francophone Africa, and Central Asia. The 1.5 million African cotton farmers produce 15 per cent of global cotton exports and generate around US$1,500 million revenue annually. This figure is fairly high compared with the US$2,000 million allocated to this region in ODA each year, but is far lower than the US$4,000 million in subsidies paid by the United States to its 25,000 cotton farmers over the same period. The subsidies paid by China and the EU also contribute to the distortion of competition on the world cotton market (Peltzer, 2004).

As cotton cultivation is a form of land use which has many adverse environmental impacts, but is nonetheless an important source of income for the poor Sahel region and its farmers, cotton cultivation would appear to be an suitable candidate for a Rio strategy (Fig. 5.2-4). In the African countries' case,

this strategy should start with development cooperation. The French government has provided support in the Sahel region for the establishment of state-owned and, more recently, private enterprises which work together with the cotton farmers, e.g. through cooperatives. They provide seed, fertilizers, agrochemicals and technical support as well as road maintenance. This promotes forms of technology transfer which benefit farmers.

In the Sahel region, cotton is not irrigated but is mainly cultivated through small-scale rainfed agriculture in crop rotation with food crops. In this cultivation system, the frequent use of often persistent pesticides poses a risk to health and biological diversity. The cotton research institutions therefore play a key role in deploying integrated plant protection methods to reduce the use of agro-chemicals and slow the emergence of resistant pests and diseases (Peltzer, 2004). Organic cotton farming, which is already being successfully undertaken in Turkey, could be especially effective in preserving environmental integrity and diversity. The promotion and targeted use of natural predators of cotton pests, along with seed treatment to avoid fungal infection and increase germination rates, could reduce pesticide use. In the Sahel region, the customary small-scale rotation of cotton with food crops such as maize, sorghum or peanuts plays a key role in securing the population densities of suitable predators for biological pest control. Green manuring and fallow periods can help protect soils over the longer term by preventing soil degradation (resource conservation). Both the conservation of biodiversity through mixed cropping and the prevention of soil degradation reduce cotton farmers' vulnerability by improving the prospects for sustainable agriculture in existing croplands and reducing pesticide-related risks to farmers' health. This in turn helps to reduce poverty – and with less poverty, there is a greater willingness to manage natural resources sustainably.

The economic element of the cotton strategy focuses especially on increasing the operability of markets. The abolition of subsidies for US, European and Chinese producers is a key prerequisite in this context. The USA in particular, at the WTO negotiations, must be urged to phase out its cotton subsidies. The EU's reform efforts in this field must be implemented speedily and further expanded. If subsidies are abolished, African cotton farmers will be able to achieve higher prices on the world markets – and the markets' operability will increase. Assuming that world market prices increase by 10–20 per cent, this would generate additional income of US$250–500 million annually for the Sahel region's cotton-producing countries (Peltzer, 2004). As small farmers are the primary actors in cotton cultivation (cultiva-

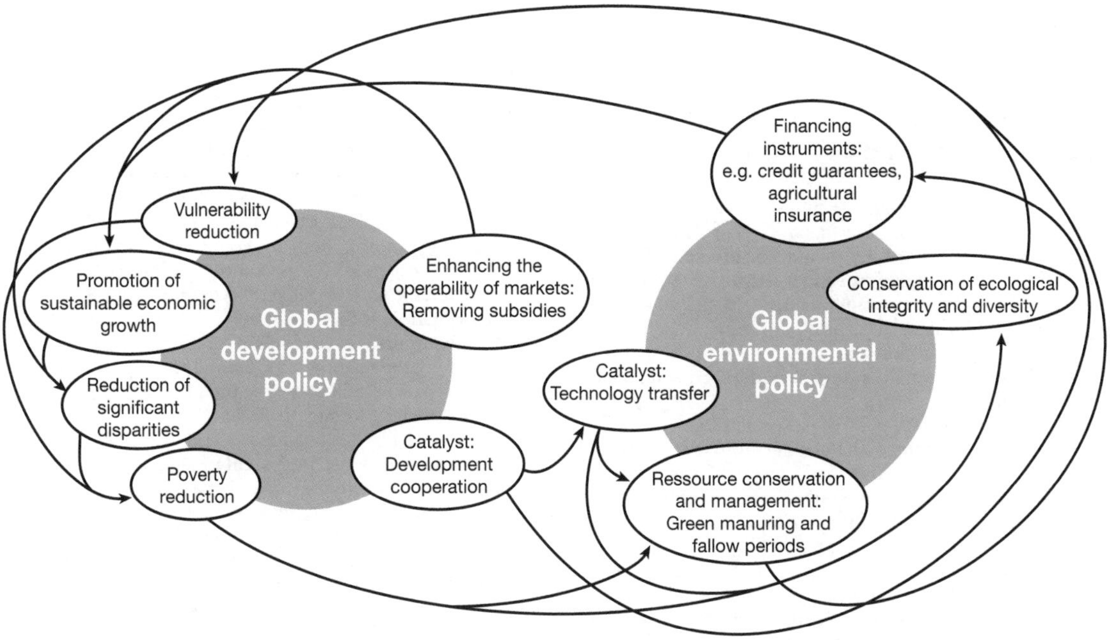

Figure 5.2-4
A Rio strategy for cotton cultivation. Through development cooperation geared towards sustainable cotton cultivation, combined with the transfer of appropriate technologies and the abolition of cotton subsidies by the industrialized countries, sustainable economic growth in the Sahel countries can be encouraged. This narrows North-South disparities and reduces poverty and vulnerability.
Source: WBGU

tion areas ranging between 1 and 5 ha), an increase in the price of raw cotton would directly reduce poverty. Sustainable economic growth can also narrow the disparities between North and South, thereby reducing poverty. Credit guarantees and agricultural insurance could have a positive impact as funding instruments here.

In addition, development cooperation, such as that taking place between the EU and some African countries, could help promote the diversification of production and technological innovation in the cotton-growing regions (technology transfer). This reduces the vulnerability arising from dependence on a single crop. As the cotton associations and research institutions promote integrated cultivation with food crops and provide fertilizers for this purpose, cotton cultivation can make an indirect contribution to food security and thus reduce vulnerability to famine. A diversified export structure and local processing of cotton could further promote economic growth in these countries.

The most important recommendation, in the context of this strategy, is the abolition of the cotton subsidies paid by the USA and Europe. The WTO Framework Agreement of July 2004 is both imprecise and inadequate in relation to cotton. In WGBU's view, the introduction of clear and binding measures to abolish subsidies is essential. Development coop-

eration and technology transfer play a key role as catalysts for the Rio strategy on cotton cultivation in the Sahel region as well as in the climate protection strategy discussed above. Development actors have a special responsibility in relation to the implementation of these strategies at local level.

5.3
Global governance: Reforming the multilateral institutional architecture

WGBU concurs with the German government's stated position and the consensus declarations made at various world conferences that the major challenges from environment and development issues can only be addressed by means of global regimes and fully-functional international organizations, i.e. global governance. This paradigm means on the one hand strengthening international law (Box 5.3-1) and on the other intensifying multilateral cooperation. This does not imply any further proliferation within the already bewildering array of organizations and programmes, but instead – and this is particularly relevant to the United Nations system – a better coordination and coherence between them (Chapter 4). The profiles and remits of the individual institutions must be more clearly defined and delineated, as there

Box 5.3-1

Translating the principles of sustainable development into action

In international negotiations, there is widespread agreement on a whole series of 'sustainability' or 'Rio' principles (Section 2.3). Most worthy of note in the context of this report are the ideas of: protecting natural life-support systems; observing the principle of integration (which lends particular importance to aspects of equity, and therefore to reconciling environmental concerns with poverty reduction); the proportionality principle and ensuring an institutional framework.

However, realization of these principles is hampered both by the indeterminacy of the obligations that arise therefrom under international law, and by a widespread lack of precision. It is difficult to operationalize the principles; they thus need to be translated into concrete terms. The extent to which it is possible to operationalize these principles in the form of rules for application to real-world issues is limited, however. Their potential is confined to providing guidelines and interpretation rules which will be relevant to the future development of regulatory frameworks and to the interpretation of existing obligations. Nonetheless, in order to clarify the normative role they play, it is necessary to agree that the sustainability principles are indeed binding in international law, in the sense of guidelines which represent fundamentally binding obligations and must therefore be considered. WGBU recommends that the German government argue this case at international level. When drafting its arguments, the government should use existing texts, especially the Rio documents, as a basis and also employ formulations from other treaties which have received widespread international support. This would take the wind out of the sails of any sceptics. In view of the overarching significance of the principles in question, it would be best to present them to the UN General Assembly in the aim of obtaining a resolution on the issue. Such a resolution could cite the main sustainability principles and acknowledge the role they play as normative guard rails – a procedure which was used for the Universal Declaration of Human Rights. A further, closely connected initiative would have the principles formulated when framework agreements are being negotiated; supplementary obligations could then be established on the basis of these agreements. This procedure was applied in the case of the Framework Convention on Climate Change.

However, it is also clear that mainstreaming and reinforcing the legal recognition of the above-mentioned principles is not enough. Initially, the role of these principles cannot extend beyond that of guidelines, as is the case when a purpose of state is determined in a national context, or as is the case with the basic obligation to cooperate under the UN Charter. Further efforts are necessary to translate the above principles into action. WGBU sees a need on two levels:

1. Firstly, the principles should be observed when international treaties are being drafted in the areas of environment and development, and translated into real terms in the relevant area. This will lead to a more pronounced internalization of the principles and should thus also increase the weight which the basic ideas behind the principles can bring to bear. For example, in the area of climate protection, the precautionary principle should apply when concrete obligations to reduce emissions are established. It is therefore recommended that the German government seek, when preparing for negotiations and during the negotiations themselves, opportunities to operationalize and concretize the principles, and that it submits corresponding proposals.

2. Secondly, as regards compliance and procedure, the aim should be to increase the extent of legal regulation: one major problem with the implementation of international law in general and international environmental law in particular is that, once obligations have been created, only in exceptional cases is it possible to monitor them effectively, especially when it comes to the independent settlement of disputes. Were this aspect of the regimes established under international law to be strengthened, one might expect the above-mentioned principles to be more successful, especially in environmental and development law. The experience of the European Union demonstrates exactly that: the European Court of Justice has applied environmental law principles when determining the jurisdiction of the Community legislator (viewing the principles as binding in substance, yet open to be construed broadly) as well as when more closely restricting Member States' scope for action and when interpreting secondary legislation. Alongside the part played by tribunals/courts and other, similar means of reaching a settlement, those forms of procedure and bodies that reinforce the implementation of treaty obligations should be promoted. For instance, the increased involvement of NGOs in reporting procedures could be considered.

WGBU therefore recommends that, when drafting international treaties, the government work towards creating judicial or quasi-judicial (i.e. independent) compliance and enforcement mechanisms, such as penalties. Importantly, these would be beyond the influence of the treaty signatories; the signatories would be obliged to comply with them. It is true that resistance can be expected from some countries, as a loss of sovereignty is at stake. However, experience in the area of human rights shows that sustained pressure can indeed bring success, especially with regard to regulations that are restricted to certain sectors. It is also possible to take specific concerns into account when drafting such mechanisms in detail, for example when defining who has standing to sue.

---

is overlap in the mandates of all too many organizations, programmes and funds, which makes for both a loss of efficiency and high costs. These bodies' acceptance among the general public worldwide suffers as a result, as does the willingness of states to reinforce multilateral institutions and equip them with additional powers and funds.

The global problems that lie before the international community do not simply require repairs to the existing structures, they require a new global governance architecture. Its focus must lie on how to improve the coordination of tasks and activities within the complex and diffuse UN structure and thus optimize the system's performance. The UN Secretary-General stated on 2 September 2003 in a report to the General Assembly: 'The question that inevitably arises is whether it is sufficient to exhort States and individuals to more enlightened attitudes and greater efforts, or whether a radical reform of our international institutions is also needed. My own view is that Member States need at least to take a hard look at the existing 'architecture' of international institutions and to ask themselves whether it is adequate for the tasks we have before us [...] I believe that we now need to go beyond those useful but essentially managerial changes and to pose some more fundamental questions, not just about the way decisions are implemented, but about the adequacy or efficiency of the bodies whose task it is to take those decisions' (UN, 2003).

WGBU shares the view that a complete overhaul of the international institutional system is required. The slow-moving UN supertanker must be better equipped to steer a course through global politics. At the same time, it must become an institutional backbone for a global partnership on environment and development, operating according to the principles enshrined in the UN Charter. This would not imply any weakening of the international financial institutions or the WTO. What it does imply is that these institutions are more closely tied into a coherent global governance architecture, under the political leadership of the United Nations. Whether or not the UN system can handle this root-and-branch reform depends on the willingness of the UN apparatus and in particular of the 191 UN Member States and the cartel of five permanent UN Security Council members, since this Council can block any structural reforms. Germany is not (yet) a member, but is in a position to initiate key reforms now within the European Union. The German government, which has often stated a wish to strengthen the United Nations, should bring action and initiative to this reform process.

Many proposals have been made for reform of the multilateral political architecture in general and the UN system in particular (Commission on Global Governance, 1995; The Independent Working Group on the Future of the United Nations, 1995; UN, 1997, 2002b; UNU, 2002). A High-level Panel on Threats, Challenges and Change, convened by the Secretary-General, is due to report at the end of 2004.

WGBU has proposed a step-by-step reform of the funding, research and coordinating institutions in the environmental sector in the framework of an Earth Alliance (WBGU, 2001b). The following recommendations refer to these proposals, while also taking them one stage further in the aim of achieving a more coherent environment and development policy at international level. WGBU believes these

points must form the basis for the reforms of the UN system:

- In order to guarantee a greater degree of coherence in environment and development policy within the UN system, the UN's Specialized Agencies, Programmes and Funds and the international financial institutions must be better attuned to one another (Section 5.3.1).
- The more decisions are transferred from within the remit of nation states into the global arena, the more necessary it becomes to improve the representation of voices previously excluded from the international institutions (Section 5.3.2).
- Environmental policy must be clearly upgraded within the UN; it must be accorded the same rank as security and economic policy (Section 5.3.3).
- The environmental targets and indicators contained in the Millennium Development Goals (MDGs) must be reinforced if the interaction between poverty and the environment is to be adequately considered by donor and partner countries and international institutions (Section 5.3.4).
- The Rio conventions represent an important building block for global environmental policy. In order to avoid conflicts between the aims of these conventions, they must be better coordinated with one another (Section 5.3.5).
- In order to predict and identify global environment and development problems and indicate possible courses of action, research-based policy advice needs strengthening (Section 5.3.6).

However, reform of the global institutional framework will only be successful if further criteria are met: the handling of global issues by multilateral institutions requires both good governance in the partner countries (Section 5.4) and coherent policy and the consistent implementation of international agreements at regional and national levels (Section 5.5). Last but not least, finance must also be secured (Section 5.6).

5.3.1
Ensuring coherence of environment and development policy within the UN system

5.3.1.1
The vision: Transforming ECOSOC into a Council on Global Development and Environment

Environment and development issues are the keys to the future of humanity. They should rank just as highly in the UN system as security issues. A reform commensurate with the pressures arising from these issues will in WBGU's view have to include the creation of a new, overarching authority as part of the UN system. Only with such a paramount structure or organization, with a lead function, can the much-maligned lack of coherence in the international institutional system be reduced and the ability of the international community to realize sustainability goals be strengthened. WGBU therefore recommends that a Council on Global Development and Environment be created in the long term. This Council should set the strategic policy agenda and coordinate the activities of all multilateral organizations in the areas of environment and development, including international financial institutions, aligning such activities with the guiding vision of sustainable development.

WGBU recommends that the Economic and Social Council of the United Nations (ECOSOC) be absorbed into the new Council. Although it is one of the six principal organs in the UN system, ECOSOC is largely subordinate to the General Assembly, which appoints ECOSOC's 54 members, each for a three-year term. It is not merely the central advisory body on international economic, development and social issues: under the UN Charter, ECOSOC is also required to coordinate UN activities. However, it has proven incapable of exercising its allotted coordination function. One reason was the proliferation of specialized programmes which emerged in the 1960s and 1970s at the insistence of the developing countries, which have represented a majority in the UN General Assembly since the main wave of decolonization. The factor which has been decisive in its shadowy existence is the lack of willingness among OECD countries to grant the 'non-paying' majority of countries a more heavyweight role or even a supervisory role vis-à-vis the international financial institutions which the OECD nations dominate.

A Council on Global Development and Environment spawned by ECOSOC would not only be in a position to ensure that environment and poverty were given sufficient priority within the UN system, but could also overcome the *de facto* slide of the international financial institutions away from the UN system. However, this would only be possible if decisions taken by the new Council were more binding than current decisions taken by ECOSOC, including beyond the immediate circle of UN institutions. The Council would thus exercise political leadership. It should not intervene in the day-to-day running of the international financial institutions, but could make decisions setting the course for development and environmental policy. The establishment of a Council of this type would require a precise analysis of how it is to be embedded in the UN system from both a policy and a legal viewpoint.

WGBU would expect more from this type of institutional integration of development and environ-

mental policy, which is in line with the Rio imperative, than it would from the division of ECOSOC into an economic council and a social council in line with the proposal made by the Independent Working Group on the Future of the United Nations (1995), or indeed from upgrading ECOSOC to form an Economic Security Council, as proposed by the Commission on Global Governance (1995) and supported by the Zedillo panel (UN, 2001b) and the Commission on the Social Dimensions of Globalization (2004). WGBU recommends that the decision making process in the new Council be based on the proposal made by the Commission on Global Governance. According to this proposal, the Council should be made up of 11 permanent members from the major industrialized and developing countries and 11 additional representatives of the world's regions, chosen in rotation. The proposal on voting procedures contrasts with the rules which currently apply to the UN Security Council, and sets the tone for this reform. According to the proposal, the permanent members will not have a right of veto. Decisions will not only require an overall majority of votes, but also majorities of both industrialized and developing countries.

Establishing a new Council in line with WBGU's proposal would require an amendment to the UN Charter. Reform of this nature could therefore only be achieved in the medium term. Therefore, in order to avoid wasting precious time, WGBU suggests a step-by-step reform as described below, which can most probably be realized with less resistance and more quickly.

5.3.1.2
Enhancing coordination and coherence within the UN system

USING THE UN CHIEF EXECUTIVES BOARD FOR COORDINATION
As coordination within and between the Member States in the UN system is insufficient, interinstitutional coordination plays an important role. The Administrative Committee on Coordination (ACC), established for this purpose as early as 1946, was ineffective as the Specialized Agencies and Programmes largely led an independent existence, enabled and supported by their own Governing Boards and budgets. Thus no coherence emerged between sectoral policies. In 2001, ACC was reformed and renamed the UN Chief Executives Board for Coordination (CEB). CEB, which reports to ECOSOC, is chaired by the UN Secretary-General. CEB comprises 27 member organizations, including Specialized Agencies, Funds and Programmes as well as the WTO, IAEA and the Bretton Woods institutions. It

is too soon to assess its influence and successes. However, it should be noted that CEB's authority derives from its members' positions as Directors-General of the organizations involved. This is both a strength and a weakness, as the heads of the Specialized Agencies are only responsible to their own steering committees and, where any conflict occurs, will represent their own organizations' interests (Göthel, 2002).

As the proposed new Council on Global Development and Environment will not be established in the foreseeable future, CEB is currently the most important coordinating body within the UN system. It should therefore set itself a challenging agenda, with a willingness to consider overriding policy objectives. The UN Secretary-General should continue to chair CEB energetically and in person.

UPGRADING THE UN COMMISSION ON
SUSTAINABLE DEVELOPMENT
The UN Commission on Sustainable Development (CSD) is the one and only UN body in which the themes of environment and development are consistently treated as being interdependent. It provides an intergovernmental forum for developing joint approaches to global problems and monitors national implementation. Within the UN system, it is responsible for ensuring that sustainable development issues are considered and activities in the areas of environment and development coordinated. It has so far been unable to perform the latter task satisfactorily, due to its weak institutional position. In WBGU's view, the Commission should be enhanced by being chaired permanently by a high-ranking figure. The UN High Commissioner for Human Rights could be the model for this. Ideally, the role would be positioned so that, besides undertaking thematic work, the Chair could improve coordination and coherence within the UN system – especially between organizations working on sustainable development. A proposal of this nature could not remedy the general lack of coordination, but could be realized and could lead to a more coherent implementation of both Agenda 21 and the Johannesburg Plan of Implementation. In order to ensure a better alignment of CSD's work with that of other relevant bodies within the UN, the work of the High Level Committee on Programmes on sustainable development under CEB should be aligned with CSD's ten-year programme of work (Section 4.2.7).

5.3.2
Widening participation in international institutions

The future power of the UN system to shape events will depend not only on its improved effectiveness (output legitimacy), but also on increased participation and representation (input legitimacy).

This requires on the one hand the involvement of private stakeholders (NGOs, companies and interest groups) in consultation mechanisms and dialogue processes. In this regard, the World Commission on Dams provides a good example to follow. Global governance is not exclusively an intergovernmental matter, but instead relies on cooperation between state and non-state actors at all levels, from local to global. The recent report of the Cardoso panel provides valuable indications of how civil society can be involved to a greater extent in the work which takes place within the UN system (UN, 2004d).

On the other hand, improving representation means, among other things, increasing the involvement of developing countries in multilateral decision making fora. This is especially true of the powerful financial organizations (IMF, World Bank) and the regional development banks, which are currently dominated by the OECD countries. This disparity in power currently prevents a global environment and development partnership being established, yet such a partnership is indispensable if the world is to resolve its environment and development problems. WGBU therefore welcomes the German government's initiative, which aims to alter the distribution of voting rights in the decision making committees of both the World Bank (Section 4.2.9) and the IMF (Section 4.2.13.2). The North-South parity already practised within the GEF and the Montreal Protocol on Substances that Deplete the Ozone Layer could, in the medium term, constitute a model of a partnership-based decision making structure for international organizations which has firmer foundations in equality.

5.3.3
Upgrading environmental policy within the UN system

WGBU reiterates its oft-repeated recommendation, now supported by the governments of several countries, including Germany, that UNEP be converted to an international environmental organization with the status of a UN specialized agency under international law (Section 4.2.6; WBGU, 2001b). The network of over 500 international agreements and institutions on various environmental issues is scattered and inconsistent. To effectively maintain and protect the natural environment, better links at all levels of environmental policy are required between environmental issues and the underlying economic and social questions. This will not be achieved without an overarching structure or lead organization. Yet any institutional reform should maintain the existing strengths in the decentralized system. The fragmentation and autonomy of multilateral environmental agreements (MEAs), which have proved highly innovative over the past 30 years, should only be restricted if and when they hamper progress in environmental policy. An international environmental organization need not foster development as such, as this is within UNDP's remit. However, WGBU notes that such an organization must guarantee that the issues of combating poverty and promoting economic development in the poorer countries are considered by global environmental policy and that such policy abides by an equitable global sharing of burdens. Developing countries should be included in the decision making process, for example by means of double-weighted majorities and North-South parity. This would also make a significant contribution to overcoming the developing countries' scepticism about a strong environmental organization.

Alongside this, a number of smaller steps need to be taken towards reform. The Global Ministerial Environment Forum has met every year since 2000 as a ministerial segment of the regular UNEP Governing Council or, in years when the Council does not meet, in the context of a special session of the Council. This type of regular meeting of environment ministers from the member states should be used to a greater extent to promote international cooperation on environmental matters. The Forum should also be able to make recommendations to other UN bodies that undertake environmental activity. Further steps include stabilizing UNEP's financial resources and expanding the membership of the UNEP Governing Council/Global Ministerial Environment Forum to include all UN Member States.

5.3.4
Strengthening the environmental component of the Millennium Development Goals

The Millennium Development Goals (MDGs) are milestones along the road towards the successful reduction of global poverty. With these Goals, heads of state and government have for the first time committed themselves to precisely defined aims and a fixed timetable. However, the strong focus on socio-political deficits creates an illusion that poverty reduction can be considered separately from the

state of natural life-support systems. WGBU therefore recommends that the environmental policy objectives set forth in the MDGs be reinforced and coupled with meaningful indicators. A cross-sectoral, integrated approach should be strengthened in order to avoid conflicts between environmental and poverty reduction objectives and improve coherence. In addition to this, the timescale for the Goals should be extended (Section 3.6.3). A useful political opportunity for this will arise at the UN Conference to review the progress made in achieving the MDGs, the 'Millennium Summit 2000+5' in September 2005.

5.3.5
Intensifying cooperation among the Rio conventions

In many cases, the goals and implementation strategies in the three Rio conventions UNFCCC, UNCCD and CBD are complementary. For example, conserving forests helps reduce pressure on soils and contributes to climate protection. Conversely, successful climate protection prevents further desertification and loss of biodiversity. Some climate protection measures, however, may also lead to a loss of biodiversity. The generation of renewable energy from biomass or the creation of carbon sinks are two instances of activities where objectives can conflict. Cooperation both between the Rio conventions and within the particular areas they address has so far been unsatisfactory. Even within biodiversity policy, the many specialized conventions – with a few exceptions such as CBD and the Ramsar Convention – operate side by side but independently of one another. This restricts the effectiveness of international biodiversity policy (Vorhies, 1999; WBGU, 2001a).

Often, the way forward is to develop joint strategies within the framework of the conventions and bring together at national level strands of implementation that had previously been largely separate. However, increased cooperation such as this must not serve, as some developing countries fear it will, as a pretext for cutting the funding provided by industrialized nations, such as that allocated to GEF. The German government should further help to ensure consistency of policymaking by integrating the Rio conventions into development cooperation, as proposed by the OECD (OECD, 2002a). In general terms, public awareness of the fact that global environmental problems impose restrictions on development opportunities should be increased. Equally, the goals of the Rio conventions should be integrated into other policy areas such as economic or agricultural policy, they should be considered to a greater extent in national planning processes and responsibility for implementing them should be mainstreamed in all sectors, not just within environment ministries, which are normally weak in developing countries.

Cooperation between the Rio conventions is especially crucial in cases where aims conflict. Thus, for example, the question of managing ecosystems to maintain carbon stocks and store CO_2 is very important for both the UNFCCC and the CBD (WBGU, 1998b, 2003a). During negotiations, it is difficult to focus attention on these interface issues and the potential for win-win situations to emerge. Cooperation is not always sought, especially where the goal conflict is clearly apparent. This is due less to a lack of information than to the difference in interests emerging from the differing perspectives of the various conventions. Mutual information sharing such as the right to speak at the various conferences of the parties and the exchange of papers, which already occurs, is not sufficient in this respect. The Joint Liaison Group of the three Rio convention secretariats is a good place to begin addressing these issues. It will have to demonstrate that it is not only in a position to identify win-win situations, but also to highlight conflicting objectives. Joint thematic working groups under the various conventions, established on an equal footing, could constitute an additional tool with which to communicate the conflicting interests and propose solutions to the relevant conferences of the parties.

In some unregulated areas of international environmental policy, civil society forums have emerged and cooperation with UN organizations has been established, leading to considerable progress in the international recognition and handling of specific environmental issues. The aims of sustainable water management, for example, have gained sufficient exposure through activities both within the UN framework (MDGs, the first World Water Development Report in 2003) and at the World Water Council for the international community to have already effectively approved a basis for implementing sustainable water policy. Due to its strong focus on implementation, the usefulness of this approach as an innovative form of problem-solving within the international community warrants closer examination.

5.3.6
Improving scientific policy advice

Knowledge and evaluation are the keys to sustainable policies. In order to identify and predict global environment and development issues and identify possible courses of action, research-based policy advice must be strengthened. By the time damage on a global scale can be definitively proven, it could be too late to effectively counteract it. Policy making must therefore act against a backdrop of uncertainty. In order to reduce that uncertainty, science must identify risks early and flag up the possible courses of action (Section 4.3.5). WGBU therefore reaffirms the recommendations made in its previous report (2001a):

- *Improve the knowledge base by means of regular assessment reports:* No independent scientific policy advice, such as IPCC successfully gives UNFCCC, is provided to UNCCD or CBD. Regular assessment reports would be a means of establishing and demonstrating an international knowledge base, which could then form the basis for political decisions and agreements. WBGU therefore recommends that an Intergovernmental Panel on Biodiversity be established (IPBD: Section 4.3.5.3; WBGU, 2001a, b), as well as an Intergovernmental Panel on Land and Soils (IPLS: Section 4.3.5.3; WBGU, 2001b), as in both areas, although international regimes exist, there is no institutionalized independent advisory mechanism. In the future, an Intergovernmental Panel on Global Environmental Change (IGEC) could be established to coordinate interaction between IPCC, IPBD and IPLS. The establishment of an International Panel on Poverty and Disparities should also be examined; this might be funded by IHDP and UNDP. For research into agriculture and development, the International Assessment of Agricultural Science and Technology for Development (IAASTD), established in 2004, represents an intergovernmental committee structured on the IPCC model.

- *Set up an Earth Council:* As the paramount advisory authority for the evaluation of environmental issues, WGBU proposes that an independent body be set up to indicate in good time where especially dangerous developments are occurring. As a body with outstanding ethical and intellectual authority, it should also draw up the normative basis for global sustainability policy, in the form of guard rails (WBGU, 2001b).

- *Reinforce the data base:* The collection of both socio-economic and natural science data is patchy in most developing countries. It is therefore very difficult to recognize trends and make predictions. Yet comprehensive monitoring is the very basis for decisions on measures and for the review of their effectiveness. Numerous international agreements oblige member states to produce progress reports. Many developing countries lack the capacity to meet this requirement. The industrialized nations are therefore called upon to provide support for establishing national data collection institutions and the associated monitoring stations, as well as for training the necessary experts. Only then will developing countries be able to meet their various reporting obligations (Chapter 6).

5.3.7
Advancing environment and development policy as global structural policy

'Traditional' development projects, aimed at the sustainable management of resources on the ground, can only make a limited contribution to sustainable societal development. They are indispensable in terms of providing practical solutions, but do not bring about any changes in the framework conditions. Yet development policy needs to aim first and foremost at altering national and international structures. Without an enabling setting within the developing countries, development processes can make little headway and projects fail as soon as the donors withdraw. The shift which began in the 1990s towards seeing development policy as a form of global structural policy – and pursuing it as such – must be sustained. The same is true of environmental policy: international cooperation pursuing environmentally sustainable development should neither be viewed as predominantly an intergovernmental affair nor restricted to the realm of national governments.

On the one hand, global structural policy is a process by which national policy is shaped by the interaction of government, the economy and civil society. On the other hand, these actors' input is required for global structural policy to realize transboundary solutions. The strategies it employs not only include enabling developing countries to play an active part in global political processes, but also tackling structural adjustments and correcting wrong turns taken in the industrialized nations. Global structural policy must provide firm answers as to how global environmental and poverty reduction policy stands in relation to changes within the industrialized nations and as to how conflicts can be resolved. It must be made a pivotal element of global structural policy to demonstrate and convince those concerned that short-term losses arising from necessary reforms in the industrialized countries will deliver long-term gains to them.

5.4
Implementing international agreements

Global governance requires both an effective institutional architecture at global level (Section 5.3) and the implementation of global decisions at local level. Agreements binding in international law, such as the Rio conventions, provide a framework for success-ful implementation, for raising awareness and for generating political will. However, implementation can only succeed if it is understood that the national and local stakeholders provide the true driving force behind this process. Unfortunately, the transition from drafting and adopting global programmes of action to implementing them on the ground through regional and national programmes is usually unsatisfactory. This implementation gap, which is widening in step with the growing number of global agreements, urgently needs more attention from the international community.

The negotiation and implementation of the many programmes of action always comes unstuck at the same points: the developing countries keep citing the requirement for funding and the industrialized nations' responsibility to provide new, additional funding. The industrialized nations keep pointing to their ongoing activities in the area of development cooperation and the need for an effective and efficient use of resources, stating that this is not just a question of financial resources but a question of the individual countries creating conditions conducive to development, in other words: good governance. These arguments often go round in circles, leaving implementation not much further forward.

Generating collective political will is the key to successfully implementing multilateral agreements. The major world conferences have provided and continue to provide an opportunity to achieve this. In this respect, the importance of the international renewable energy conference 'renewables 2004' as a forum at which concrete projects can be announced in front of the international community should not be underestimated. However, implementation cannot be left to state actors alone. Only by involving civil society can implementation move forward to any significant extent.

WGBU outlines below how conditions conducive to the successful implementation of policies can be created in specific areas:

AGREE QUANTITATIVE TARGETS
It is possible to set concrete, quantitative and time-bound targets along the lines of the MDGs in individual policy areas. While the Convention on Biological Diversity (CBD) has already adopted this approach, no such concrete, quantitative and time-bound targets have yet been established for other policy processes such as the Convention to Combat Desertification (UNCCD). Setting such targets makes the subsequent review of processes and their impacts significantly easier and should therefore be introduced in all areas of poverty reduction and environmental policy.

DEVELOP AND APPLY SETS OF INDICATORS

Measuring the success or failure of implementation measures is crucial to any assessment of the status quo or the extent to which international targets have been attained; it also helps improve tools and strategies. Quantifying success in this way is an essential prerequisite for the industrialized nations' commitment to development policy. Regular monitoring of the impacts of measures at local level using appropriate sets of indicators is something which is often called for, but is still not being fully implemented.

BRING REPORTING SYSTEMS UNDER ONE ROOF

Many developing countries that lack strong administrative structures and specialist personnel are overwhelmed by a multitude of reporting responsibilities. It is therefore frequently stated that reporting obligations to international institutions, which even in industrialized nations take a disproportionate amount of human resources to administer, should be brought under one roof. This is not easy to achieve. Making national reporting conditional on consultation among the major international players (the World Bank, UNDP, conventions, etc.) would significantly slow down all the processes involved. Yet countries' reporting obligations are an important tool in promoting implementation and checking effectiveness. Efficiency problems will not be resolved easily. A start could be made by adopting sets of indicators that are as similar as possible – this could speed up national reporting. Unification of reporting obligations has the best chance of success where processes are closely related (CBD, Ramsar and CITES). The industrialized nations should help the developing countries by means of increased capacity building.

MERGE THE SEPARATE IMPLEMENTATION PATHWAYS OF ENVIRONMENTAL CONVENTIONS

The implementation pathways of environmental conventions, national sustainability strategies or programmes of action for poverty reduction often run parallel to one another but are not sufficiently coordinated. Implementation should therefore be streamlined consistently and coherently, so as to improve the effectiveness and impact of the resources deployed. Integrated measures at local level can promote this goal. A practical merging of environmental protection and poverty reduction within a bioregion or at community level can often deliver the best solution to local problems, as the parties affected can take direct action and can reconcile conflicts of interest.

INVOLVE CIVIL SOCIETY

Involving civil society in the decisions of global institutions fosters democracy and serves as an early indicator of areas of conflict. NGOs play an important monitoring role and make a significant contribution to generating political pressure, without which the will to act would only build up slowly. The local knowledge held by civil society is pivotal to implementation, as implementation is performed at local level. In this respect, the successful integration of NGOs into the UNCCD process can provide a model when international agreements are further developed or new ones are negotiated. Civil society should become more involved in this manner in the work of international organizations, such as the WTO (Section 4.3.2).

ADVANCE IMPLEMENTATION EVEN IN UNREGULATED AREAS

Even where an individual environmental issue area, such as water or forests, is not regulated by an international agreement, this must not lead to an impasse in implementation. For instance, the sustainable use of fresh water is not firmly anchored in the UN system, nor is responsibility for the issue clearly established. However, the World Water Council, which has close ties with UNESCO and no restrictions on membership, regularly holds global conferences on the issue. In many cases, discussions have made such progress and such a broad international consensus has been reached that a setting sufficient to support implementation has been established.

IMPROVE COORDINATION AMONG DONORS

Most ODA funds are still distributed under bilateral agreements. The UN Secretariat has calculated that a lack of coordination between donor countries' bilateral and multilateral development policies means approximately US$7,000 million is deployed inefficiently each year. Two organizations are working to improve the coordination of donor countries' development contributions, but have so far only achieved limited success as national interests have hampered their efforts:

- The OECD's Development Assistance Committee (DAC) attempts, by compiling statistics and monitoring donor countries, to contribute to compliance with the Monterrey international agreements and the Barcelona EU agreements, which state that at least 0.33 per cent of Gross National Income should be deployed for ODA by 2006. It also works towards improving the efficiency of development cooperation and focusing it more sharply on poverty reduction, as agreed at the 2002 Rome conference. DAC joined forces with the international financial institutions and the UN in establishing a Working Party on Aid Effectiveness and Donor Practices, the work of which is based on good practice guidelines already established by DAC members. Partner governments should take greater control of development cooperation and use it as an opportunity to implement national poverty reduction strategies (PRSPs). German development cooperation should therefore increasingly promote capacity building in partner countries, as this capacity is necessary in order to use the complicated tools of development cooperation and for the partner governments themselves to improve their coordination of these. In so doing, it should ensure that its actions increasingly complement those of other donors. The 2003 action plan for the harmonization of donor practices in German development cooperation, which aims at increased coordination with other donors as part of sectoral programmes and was intended to focus programmes of financial and technical cooperation more closely on PRSPs, is a step in the right direction. The German government should also campaign in international fora for improved donor coordination; one opportunity to do so will be the high-level forum organized by the DAC and the international financial institutions on progress made towards harmonization (Paris, March 2005) and the forthcoming UN conference to review the progress made in achieving the MDGs (autumn 2005).

- The Treaty on European Union only gives the European Commission a 'complementary' role in European development policy, which makes effective coordination and coherence difficult, even within the EU (Section 4.2.12). WGBU actively supports a strengthening of the European element in development policy and its dovetailing with the EU Common Foreign and Security Policy. This is particularly relevant to the priority region of sub-Saharan Africa, where stronger European Community development policy could achieve significantly more than the bilateral efforts of the EU Member States, which now number 25, in pursuit of their own national interests. The EU Member States should set priorities, agreed at the Council of Ministers, relating to countries and sectors; the European Commission should coordinate these and itself promote regional cooperation projects, preferably using the toolkit contained in the Cotonou Agreement.

MAINSTREAMING ENVIRONMENT AND
DEVELOPMENT POLICY GOALS

As the German Council of Environmental Advisors (SRU) also emphasizes, environmental policy needs to be understood in industrialized and developing countries alike as both a sphere in its own right and a cross-cutting policy area (SRU, 2004). Environmental aspects must be mainstreamed in all policy areas. Responsibility for many environment-related areas such as waste management, protection of the Earth's atmosphere, water supply and sanitation, agriculture and forestry, nature conservation and land use is not always assigned to environment ministries and departments. Environmental policy interests therefore compete with resource use interests in other spheres. Strategies for the sustainable use of resources should be mainstreamed in all sectors: in water and energy management, agriculture and forestry, trade and industry, in transport, in urban development and in tourism. In the international policy arena, the German government should seek to promote, in order to ensure coherence among policies, that trade, economic, security and foreign policy do not thwart development or environmental policy goals. With this in mind, the German government should, among other things:

- involve all the relevant departments when deciding on how to allocate its export credit guarantees by Euler Hermes Kreditversicherungs-AG and strengthen the role of the interministerial working group in this area,
- give the German Green Cabinet (Committee of State Secretaries for Sustainable Development) a higher public profile, in order to reinforce its key role in setting the agenda,
- ensure that the corresponding special committees of the German Bundestag cooperate more intensively.

WGBU believes the steps towards mainstreaming thus outlined, which would boost the implementation of international cooperation, to be suited to dovetailing environmental and poverty issues and thus narrowing the gap between the pledges made and their implementation.

5.5
Fostering good governance in developing countries

Most leading development theorists agree that neither the colonial legacy, the high rate of population growth nor the unfavourable climatic conditions provide a satisfactory explanation of the backslide in development in large parts of sub-Saharan Africa. Furthermore, neither more development cooperation nor a more equitable economic world order, even with comprehensive debt cancellations, would appear to be capable of solving the problem of poverty, with all its negative consequences. Since the beginning of the 1990s, the donor community in the West, with the World Bank to the fore, has been focussing on the lack of good governance as an important explanation.

Box 5.5-1

Gender equity in the struggle against poverty and environmental degradation

One of the central demands to emerge from both the Earth Summit in Rio de Janeiro in 1992 and the World Conference on Women in Beijing in 1995 was that women should be more closely involved in social and political decision-making processes: 'Empowerment of women and equality between women and men are prerequisites for achieving political, social, economic, cultural and environmental security among all peoples' (Beijing final document). However, in spite of a number of promising developments at the international level, women's and children's rights have suffered noticeable setbacks in certain countries, especially as a result of military conflicts and the growing influence of religious fundamentalist groups. While considerable progress has been made in terms of devising programmes to address the issue of environment and gender, the message from the world conferences has so far not found adequate expression in environmental and development policy or been put into practice sufficiently at country level. This is largely due to the fact that measures designed to address environmental issues and gender equality are often simply 'added on' to existing policies, without there being any fundamental structural change. However, incorporating justice between the sexes is a cross-cutting task that needs to be integrated into every activity and project at a structural level. The need for 'gender mainstreaming', as it is called, has been made a binding principle internationally (Beijing Platform of Action, EU Treaty of Amsterdam, DAC guidelines, etc.). Nonetheless, a great deal of uncertainty exists around how to put this concept into practice; indeed, the concept itself is subject to differing interpretations. Progress can only be made slowly, as gender issues generally reflect social patterns that are deeply rooted culturally and can only be transformed over the long term – that is, over a period of generations. In addition, the complex, multi-layered interconnections between environmental goals and the gender issue make practical progress even more difficult. In order to overcome these practical problems, there is not only a need to improve the quality of gender research in different, specific local contexts, but also to make the issue a more prominent part of the environmental and development policy agenda. One important starting point for this is the Millennium +5 Summit due to take place in 2005, at which participants will examine the extent to which the Millennium Declaration has been put into practice.

Women's practical expertise and innovativeness, fostered through networks and cooperatives, have been amply proven when it comes to protecting natural resources. An outstanding example of this is the Green Belt Movement in Kenya, initiated by recent Nobel Prize winner Wangari Maathai. National governments as well as organizations involved in international development should provide greater support for grassroots initiatives such as this. Many policy tools aimed at supporting women and girls already exist, e.g. the OECD/DAC Guidelines for Gender Equality; these must now be used to the full. Gender Impact Assessment – developed in Germany as an obligatory tool for testing legislative measures across all government departments and modelled strongly on Environmental Impact Assessment – should be implemented in other countries as well.

According to the World Bank, nothing is worth investing in more than the education of women and girls. Every girl that goes to school today is an ambassador for the changing nature of women's self-perception. Governments of both donor and partner countries are therefore called to invest more in fulfilling the Millennium Development Goal of promoting gender equality and empowering women.

Source: UNEP, 2004b

Good governance, a key term in development cooperation, means the rule of law, legal certainty for citizens and companies, the respect of fundamental human rights including improving women's position in society (Box 5.5-1), government accountability and a fight against corruption. Non-fulfilment of these conditions is a social and political problem in many countries, it frightens investors, is the source of frequent contraventions of national and international conservation programmes for forests or water and is often the reason why development assistance is misallocated. Global environmental and development policy is often thwarted by poor governance at local level. Having acknowledged this fact, WGBU suggests the following action be taken:

- It makes sense and is wholly legitimate for donor countries to link their development cooperation and assistance to a requirement that good governance be established (conditionality). Development cooperation should prioritize recipient countries that are prepared for reform and take positive action. These countries should also be granted money for their general budgets which has no conditions imposed on it by the donors and which the recipients can decide to use as they see fit (budgetary assistance). These countries should of course be subject to regular reviews. Furthermore, the principle of 'challenging and promoting' must be integrated into development cooperation to a greater extent.

- It is necessary to support international NGOs and national stakeholders in their attempts to uncover networks of corruption. The criminal prosecution and tax authorities in the OECD countries must ensure that bribery, used as a means of securing a contract, is not considered as a pardonable offence or even held to be a tax-deductible cost. Germany should ratify the new UN Convention against Corruption at the earliest opportunity.

- Fragile states with an underdeveloped political infrastructure need support in building both fully-functional administrative and legal structures (institution building) and environmental management systems (capacity building). Environmental regimes will be nothing but window dressing if states are not even in a position to fulfil their reporting responsibilities. This is an issue that needs to be taken up mainly by UN organizations such as UNDP and UNEP.

- What is more, there are security and humanitarian reasons why the international community cannot afford to write off as hopeless cases failing or collapsed states, in which government development cooperation can find no significant foothold. It must find ways and means of maintaining or restoring these states' monopoly on power as a prerequisite for peace, stability and development. The uncertainty which still reigns as to what should be done in such cases from the point of view of development and peacekeeping should not serve as an excuse to do nothing. Failing states should therefore continue to receive humanitarian aid and assistance with institution-building.

- It is therefore necessary to develop differential cross-country typologies or sets of performance indicators such as the BTI (Bertelsmann Transformation Index) to guide the differentiation of strategies and instruments. German development cooperation should act – as DFID has in the UK – to increase its capacity for scientific policy advice, thus enabling it to act on a more informed basis (Section 6.2.4).

5.6
Financing

The following section explores the question of how to mobilize the financial resources needed to implement international poverty reduction and environmental protection goals. It provides a synopsis of likely levels of required financing, and discusses different financing instruments and their potential contribution. It demonstrates that it is possible to close the financing gap.

5.6.1
Financing requirements

In Section 3.6.2, detailed information was presented about the estimated international financing requirements linked to poverty reduction and environmental protection. These estimates originate from several international studies and vary widely in some areas.

The different estimates for individual poverty or environment dimensions are aggregated here in a way that allows the size of the financing gaps for these dimensions to be estimated (Table 5.6-1). In this regard it has to be emphasized again that estimates of the financing gaps are problematic due to poor data quality, methodological difficulties and

uncertainties as well as disparate concepts of cost and expenditure (Section 3.6.2). There is an urgent need for further research to improve the assessment of financing requirements for poverty reduction and environmental protection (Section 6.2.6).

In order to determine the overall financing gap, the figures for individual poverty and environment dimensions are added together. Information on the financing gap must be interpreted with great caution due to data and methodology problems. There are several further reasons why a straightforward adding together of the figures in Table 5.6-1 does not produce an easily interpretable picture of the financing gap in international poverty reduction and environmental policies. On the one hand, attention needs to be paid to positive and negative synergies between measures directed towards individual poverty and environment dimensions. The estimates do not take synergies into account or do so only to a limited extent. WBGU assumes that, provided there is a meaningful integration of environmental and poverty reduction policies, cost-saving synergy effects dominate, so that the overall financing requirements are lower than the sum of the individual requirements.

On the other hand, achieving the goals also requires advance expenditures, and the estimates do not include these either. Finally, the fact that much of the data on the financing requirements for poverty reduction only refer to the fulfilment of the MDGs also has to be considered. WBGU believes that this focus is insufficient (Section 3.6.3). Policy measures that go beyond those included in the estimates therefore also have to be financed. This embraces aspects such as human rights and participation rights, which were neglected in the MDGs, and for which there are no quantitative estimates. The data provided in Table 5.6-1 should therefore be interpreted as the minimum, rather than the maximum amount required for worldwide poverty reduction and global environmental protection.

If, however, these critical aspects are set aside, and the issue of climate protection is excluded from the analysis for now, Table 5.6-1 shows that, for the international transfer from industrialized to developing countries, an annual requirement running in the lower hundreds of thousand millions is plausible. Even if the above mentioned additional policy measures are included, the requirements are very likely to be significantly below US$400,000 million. In view of the synergistic effects that, on balance, are likely to be positive, the gap could, with some probability, be significantly lower than US$200,000 million. Compared with worldwide military expenditures, which amounted to US$956,000 million in 2003 (SIPRI, 2004), the financing requirements for pov-

Table 5.6-1
Financing gap for international poverty reduction and environmental protection policies. Synopsis of selected estimates. The additional financing requirements are stated as a range (minimum-maximum from several sources or a single source) based on the data in Table 3.6-2. Table 3.6-2 cites the sources for these data. Due to missing data and the already relatively wide ranges, data were not adjusted for inflation. If no data on additional financing requirements are available, annual total costs are given and marked with *. Synergies between the dimensions are not reflected, with the exception of the World Bank's estimate on the total costs for achievement of all MDGs. The MDGs refer to the target year 2015. n. a. = not available. DCs = Developing Countries, ICs = Industrialized Countries
Source: Compilation by WBGU from Table 3.6-2

Purpose	Additional transfers from ICs to DCs (ODA) [US$ thousand million per year]	Additional transfers from ICs *and* own inputs by DCs [US$ thousand million per year]
INCOME POVERTY		
Reduce extreme poverty by half (MDG 1)	20–62	
DISEASE		
Achieve all MDG health targets	20–25	
UNDERNOURISHMENT		
Halve the proportion of undernourished people by 2015 (MDG 1)	16	
LACK OF EDUCATION		
Universal primary education (MDG 2)	5–30	
Gender equality in education (MDG 3)	3	
WATER SCARCITY		
Halve the proportion of people without access to safe drinking water (MDG 7)	n. a.	6.7–49
SOIL DEGRADATION		
Total costs of soil rehabilitation in arid zones	n. a.	max. 11*
AIR POLLUTION AND TOXIC SUBSTANCES		
Total costs for indoor air pollution	n.a.	max. 2.5*
By comparison: Achievement of all MDGs (World Bank, UN)	40–126	

	Worldwide costs [US$ thousand million per year]
LOSS OF BIOLOGICAL DIVERSITY AND RESOURCES	
Worldwide representative system of protected areas	12–40
Total costs outside protected areas *(very uncertain estimate)*	290*
CLIMATE CHANGE	
Long-term average losses of global GDP resulting from reduction measures to achieve a stabilization target of 450ppm CO_2, calculated for the year 2050	0.7–4% of global GDP

erty reduction and environmental protection do not appear extremely large.

On the basis of the data currently available, assessments of the requirements for international transfers in the area of biodiversity can only be made indirectly and with significant caveats. The amount of international transfers required for preventive climate protection is even more difficult to predict (Section 3.6.2.3). This is due to methodological difficulties, varying time horizons and the significant uncertainties that surround the next stages of the Kyoto Protocol process and the development of emissions in individual countries (Section 4.2.2). The total estimated costs of 0.7–4 per cent of global GDP until 2100 or 2200 that would result from pursuing policies in line with the climate guard rail scarcely permit conclusions about the necessary financial transfers from industrialized to developing countries. This is all the more so given that these estimates do not take the economic benefits of climate protection sufficiently into account.

WBGU nevertheless believes it justifiable to draw the conclusion, based on its own estimates of costs (WBGU, 2003, 2004), that the annual requirement for funds to be made available on an international level over the next decades for policies in the areas of global biodiversity and climate protection is unlikely to exceed one per cent of global GDP. It is highly likely that the average annual requirement over the entire twenty-first century will be significantly lower.

WBGU agrees with other assessments according to which current ODA funding of approximately US$70,000 million will need to at least be doubled in order to achieve the poverty targets that were agreed under the MDGs (Devajaran et al., 2002; UN, 2001b, 2004d). If the WSSD goals, the objectives of multilateral environmental agreements and the broadening of international goals suggested by WBGU (Section 3.6.3) are included, significantly larger financial transfers will be required.

The following section will compare the financing gap with examples of the costs incurred by inaction. This analysis underscores that it is worth mobilizing the global community to finance coherent poverty and environmental policies. Possible financing tools are then presented, and their potential for closing the financing gap is discussed. It is shown that there are sufficient private and public resources.

5.6.2
Costs of inaction

The financing requirements for global poverty reduction and environmental policies must be assessed against the benefits from such measures. Investments not only avoid costs that could result at a later stage from the degradation of environmental resources or a weakening of human capital. Rather, investments in poverty reduction indirectly strengthen the performance of economies. The following provides some examples in this regard:

- *Undernourishment*: The annual 'monetary benefit' of halving the proportion of undernourished people is estimated at US$120,000 million, as a result of a healthier and longer life for all those who have been lifted out of a state of undernourishment (FAO, 2003c).
- *Disease*: The World Health Organization has emphasized that investments in health care systems yield disproportionately positive developmental benefits, particularly for low-income countries. It has been estimated that annual investments in the region of US$66,000 million could result in a six times higher 'economic return' of US$360,000 million per year between 2015 and 2020 (WHO, 2004a).

- *Soil degradation and desertification*: The annual loss of income due to desertification has been estimated at a total of US$42,000 million (Dregne and Chou, 1992). The economic damage from desertification and soil degradation has been quantified at around 5–10 per cent of developing countries' GDP (Bishop and Allen, 1989; Pearce and Warford, 1994). However, regional estimates are probably more reliable: for South Asia the economic damage from soil degradation is estimated at US$10,000 million per year (Khor, no year). For the US and Australia the estimates are US$44,000 million (Pimentel et al., 1995) and US$750 million (Campbell, 1990) per year respectively.
- *Loss of biological diversity and resources*: Costanza et al. (1997) have estimated the total value of global ecosystem services at around US$33,000,000 million per year, which is in the same order of magnitude as global GDP. Balmford et al. (2002) have estimated the value of ecosystem products and services of an effective global system of protected areas at US$4,400,000–5,200,000 million per year. Just the value of artificial pollination of agricultural plants has been put at US$200,000 million per year (Richards, 1993). The costs of nature conservation are very variable and difficult to estimate (Section 3.6.2.3), but they are significantly higher than current expenditures (currently at around US$6,500 million per year) and much lower – at least by a factor of 100 – than the associated benefits (Balmford, 2003). The cost-benefit ratio is most favourable in tropical developing countries (Balmford et al., 2003).

These numbers are just examples. Significant aspects, such as the costs that result from inadequate climate policies or from losses in human capital, are completely excluded. If poverty reduction is not pursued worldwide in a manner linked with global environmental policy, such costs have to be interpreted as the benefits of integrated environmental and development policies. The above figures suggest that the benefits of global poverty reduction and environmental policy exceed significantly the additional international financing requirements that such a policy necessitates. It therefore makes sense to search for ways of mobilizing the requisite financial resources.

5.6.3
Tools and recommendations

5.6.3.1
Starting points for the mobilization of financial resources

Funds can be raised, on the one hand, by obtaining additional funds or redirecting funds that have already been raised. On the other hand, the financing gap can also be reduced by discontinuing existing policy measures that work counter to global poverty reduction or global environmental policies. For example, the dismantling of environmentally harmful subsidies and trade barriers particularly against developing countries can make a significant contribution to poverty reduction and environmental protection.

The financial potential that can be tapped indirectly if such counterproductive measures are eliminated stems from several effects:

- Damage that would result if the measures (such as environmentally harmful subsidies) were retained is avoided, thus freeing up expenditures that would have been used to mitigate or adapt to the damage.
- The removal of measures (such as market access barriers in industrialized countries for goods from developing countries) opens up sources of income and development opportunities for many developing countries. On the one hand, this increases the funds that developing countries themselves can invest in policies to achieve sustainability. On the other hand, provided that there is pro-poor trade and pro-poor growth, poverty will decrease, as will expenditure to combat poverty.
- The removal of counterproductive measures (such as protectionism) will also result in industrialized countries, over the medium to long-term at the latest, in higher economic growth and thus absolute improvements in countries' financial position. This becomes even more apparent in relation to costly measures such as subsidies. Their dismantling would free up considerably and directly the budgets of many industrialized nations as well as those of developing and newly industrializing countries and would create scope for expenditures that support sustainability.

5.6.3.2
Indirect mobilization

The dismantling of environmentally harmful subsidies can make a substantial contribution to global sustainable development. A total of approximately US$850,000 million in environmentally harmful subsidies are spent every year in the areas of agriculture, fossil fuels and nuclear power, road traffic, water systems, fishing and forestry (Myers and Kent, 2001). If only 20 per cent of these subsidies were dismantled, and half the money were invested in development and environmental policies, this would already make a significant contribution to the financing of global poverty reduction and environment policy.

The removal of trade barriers will result in gains in real incomes and will therefore contribute directly or indirectly to poverty reduction and environmental protection. According to different scenario estimates, a complete opening of the markets of industrialized countries for goods from developing countries would result in increases in incomes in developing countries of at least US$40,000 million per year (Section 4.2.13.1). According to a pro-poor scenario developed by the World Bank (World Bank, 2003e), in 2015 there would be static gains of US$20,000 million in the areas of agriculture and food and at least US$25,000 million in the area of processed goods. Other estimates put the annual growth in income at US$24,000 million if industrialized countries were to remove all trade barriers for textile imports alone (IMF and World Bank, 2002). For industrialized countries, the static gains from trade in agricultural and food products are estimated at up to US$64,000 million in 2015 (World Bank, 2003e). Worldwide liberalization in trade would result in multiple increases in income growth (Section 4.2.13.1).

According to IFPRI (2003), if OECD countries were to abolish their estimated US$350,000 million in annual subsidies in their agricultural and food sectors (OECD, 2004), developing countries could earn an additional US$60,800 million through trade. Poor developing countries, however, would profit little from this (Panagariya, 2004; Section 4.2.13.1).

5.6.3.3
Direct mobilization: Private investment

FOREIGN DIRECT INVESTMENT
A first source of obtaining additional funds is the steering of foreign direct investment (FDI). In 2003, US$172,000 million flowed into developing countries as direct investments, of which the largest share came from industrialized countries (UNCTAD, 2004b). Almost a quarter of these flows were due to company mergers and takeovers that did not directly increase production and employment. Yet, if it were possible to direct only a share of the remaining funds towards projects that contribute to worldwide poverty reduction and global environmental protection, signifi-

cant progress would already be made towards the achievement of the global agenda. A correspondent widening of global sustainable FDI would achieve even more. WBGU recommends that industrialized countries support global sustainable FDI especially in poor developing countries through active support policies (such as tax preferences and the development and upgrading of suitable infrastructure as an advance service to newly establishing businesses, educational and health facilities) and by monitoring the use of such funds. For the time being, however, on a purely quantitative basis official development assistance (ODA) funds are likely to play a greater role than FDI, particularly in very poor developing countries. Public Private Partnership projects are important in this context.

Public Private Partnerships

Public Private Partnerships (PPPs) play an increasingly important role in the planning and financing of projects and programmes. This is due not least to the stagnation in levels of ODA funding in a context of increasing financing requirements to help achieve the MDGs. Examples include the Global Fund to Fight AIDS, Tuberculosis and Malaria and the Global Alliance for Vaccines and Immunization (GAVI). Governments, international organizations, foundations, businesses and wealthy private individuals provide the funding for these and other global funds. For example, the Melinda and Bill Gates Foundation, which has a capital base of US$27,000 million, has contributed US$750 million to the financing of GAVI.

The advantage of PPPs is that they offer the opportunity to mobilize additional private funds. The danger, however, is that, by providing large shares of the financing, the private sector gains significant influence over the projects of the fund, which can come into conflict with the steering role of public organizations, such as the WHO. In this context critics have referred to 'highjacked' UN organizations, meaning above all the WHO, which has many PPPs in its sphere of operations (Diekwisch, 2002). They are critical of the potential use of PPPs for commercial purposes and for raising businesses' public profiles. There is also the concern that governments could withdraw from their obligations to finance public tasks so that in effect no additional funding would be made available, funds merely being diverted instead.

WBGU supports the instrument of PPPs, as the major challenges of global environmental and development policies, such as full access for all to energy and drinking water, cannot be tackled without mobilizing private sources of finance. WBGU recommends, however, that public organizations use their involvement in PPP projects to ensure that public welfare takes precedence over business interests. Otherwise there is the danger that particularly the sectors of the poor that have limited purchasing power will not be targeted by PPPs. A new report to the Club of Rome argues for this ethical limitation to the privatization of public tasks.

Insurance and capital markets

The vulnerability of the poor to environmental risks such as harvest failures, floods, pests, etc. could be reduced through insurance schemes (World Bank, 2001b). This requires, on the one hand, efforts to develop financial infrastructures particularly in the least developed countries. On the other hand, it would also make sense to subsidize insurance premiums with the assistance of an international fund. WBGU recommends that financial infrastructures be developed more strongly than up to now with the assistance of ODA funds, and that at the same time efforts be made to promote the development of an international fund for sustainable individual insurance schemes. The insurance and financial sectors should be involved in such a fund alongside the governments of industrialized and newly industrializing countries (IMF and World Bank, 2004).

Resources for the financing of poverty reduction and environmental policy can also be raised directly from the capital markets. Apart from weather derivatives, which provide insurance against famines caused by weather conditions, catastrophe bonds should be considered. Investors in these bonds would receive financial yield if no natural catastrophes occur over a specific period of time in a clearly defined group of poor developing countries. If, however, catastrophes do occur, the interest payments are used to address those damages that are not covered by insurance payments. Such catastrophe bonds could be issued by, for example, governments or sustainability funds. Since investors take on the risk of a natural catastrophe occurring – something that humankind cannot control in the short term – in which event there are no returns, the yield in 'good times' would have to be higher than for investments that carry a risk that is either lower or more easily controllable. Particularly because of the wide spread of the risk, such bonds could make a significant contribution to reducing the vulnerability of the poor in developing countries. WBGU recommends that capital market products for promoting poverty reduction and environmental protection be developed further, and that their use be promoted at national and international level.

Civil society

In 2001 NGOs transferred approximately US$7,300 million of their own funds as well as donations to countries that receive ODA. Private development funds now account for almost 0.03 per cent of the GDP of DAC countries or more than 10 per cent of ODA (World Bank, 2004f). While the share of private donations in the financing of worldwide poverty reduction and global environmental policy is by all means remarkable, the financing potential is far from fully exploited. This is due, on the one hand, to the fact that only a few countries, such the US or the UK, have a culture of making donations. A further factor is that private donations are frequently made for the short term and to ease hardship in geographic proximity. Hence, long-term development and environmental projects can only mobilize few private donations. WBGU recommends that tax incentives for private donations for poverty reduction and environmental protection be strengthened, and that the establishment of foundations that aim to promote poverty reduction and environmental protection be made easier, and appropriate financial incentives be created. Such foundations, for example the Ford Foundation, the Rockefeller Foundation, Ted Turner's UN Foundation or the Bill & Melinda Gates Foundation, have significant funds. For example, the Ford Foundation, which, among other objectives, aims to reduce global poverty, has awarded more than US$12,000 million (currently approximately US$600 million per year) in the form of grants and loans since it started in 1936. The Bill & Melinda Gates Foundation, which was founded in 2000, had assets of US$25,000 million in 2003 and every year awards more than US$1,000 million (US$1,500 million in 2003; UN, 2004c; Belasquez and Malabed, 2002).

A further opportunity for mobilizing private donations is the establishment of a global lottery. According to a UN report (UN, 2004c), this could raise annual net revenues of approximately US$6,000 million. The United Nations, for example, could be the agency for such a lottery. The Technical Group on Innovative Financing Mechanisms (2004) has also suggested boosting the amount of private donations through the introduction of a credit card, with which the cardholder would show his or her support for the implementation of the MDGs. Credit card holders and banks would direct a percentage of the payments made with the card to measures aimed at reaching the MDGs or at financing global sustainability.

MICRO FINANCING

Micro financing is an increasingly important tool in poverty reduction, particularly in light of the insufficient provision of credit by formal financial institutions in developing countries. The particular characteristic of micro credits is the use of group liability instead of individual liability or assets as loan guarantees. This is important above all in countries where individual property is not available, or where property rights are unclear. The number of poor with access to micro credits rose from 7.6 million in 1997 to 26.8 million in 2001, of which 21 million were women. Particularly for women micro credits are an important means to escape poverty. Every year approximately 5 per cent of participants in micro financing programmes and their families free themselves from poverty (UNDP, 2003c; The Microcredit Summit Secretariat, 2002; Environment Department et al., 2002). Studies on the impact of micro credits in more than 24 countries have found significant increases in the level of household incomes. The Grameen Bank provides an impressive example of the positive impact of micro financing institutions: over a period of eight years, only 4 per cent of the poorest in Bangladesh were able to cross the poverty line without receiving credit services, while this was achieved by 48 per cent of the poorest that received credits from the Grameen Bank (Data Snapshots on Microfinance, 2004).

German development cooperation already supports micro financing. WBGU recommends that ODA funds be used to extend the development of micro financing systems. Apart from the provision of credit, emphasis should also be placed on building capacities. ODA funds that are used directly or indirectly in micro financing systems have a leverage effect, which ensures that a share of the financing requirements for poverty reduction and environmental protection identified above can be met. There are no reliable data on the share of the overall financing requirement that can be met through micro financing. Nonetheless, in view of the great importance of micro financing and small-scale projects for family groups, especially in poor developing countries, the significance of this financing source should not be underestimated.

5.6.3.4
Direct mobilization: State tools

OFFICIAL DEVELOPMENT ASSISTANCE

At first sight an increase in official development assistance (ODA), financed through general public budgets, seems an obvious source for financing poverty reduction and environmental protection targets in developing and newly industrializing countries. On the other hand, the volume of ODA is less than that of private net financial flows into developing countries (Figure 5.6-1). Particularly for the poorest developing countries, however, ODA is likely to remain one of the most important external sources for the foreseeable future, even if there is success in better harnessing and steering the potential of private financial

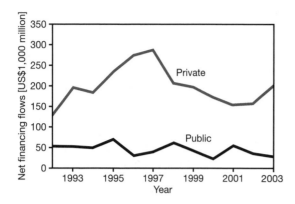

Figure 5.6-1
Private and public net financing flows to developing
countries from 1992 to 2003. Public financing flows include
development cooperation funds as well as loans.
Source: World Bank, 2004f

flows for poverty reduction in the developing world
and global environmental protection.

In the second half of the 1990s, ODA flows fell
from 0.34 per cent of the GNI of donor countries to
0.22 per cent in 2001. By now they have increased
again to 0.25 per cent, or US$68,500 million (OECD
DAC, 2004). Apart from direct international transfers, however, this figure also contains other spending, such as granting relief from debt repayments,
which is discussed in further detail below.

According to a World Bank estimate, on average 3
per cent of bilateral ODA and 5 per cent of multilateral ODA (Table 5.6-2) is directed towards projects
for environmental protection. This is equivalent to
approximately US$2,000 million per year and there-
fore remains far below the funding requirement for
public development cooperation in the environmental sphere that, in Agenda 21, were put at approximately US$100,000 million per year (1993–2000).

At the Monterrey Conference donors pledged to
increase ODA by 7 per cent per year in real terms by
2006. If this commitment is kept, ODA will increase

by approximately US$18,500 million to approxi-
mately US$77,000 million in 2006 (Development
Committee of the World Bank, 2004a). This would
raise the share of ODA to 0.29 per cent of GNI. This
increase, however, is far from sufficient for closing
the financing gap. WBGU believes that it is necessary
to develop a binding timeline for the fulfilment of the
0.7 per cent target. Given the urgency of the problems, it would be appropriate to aim for a target of
1 per cent in the longer term. Germany's announcement to allocate 0.33 per cent of GNI to ODA in 2006,
thereby increasing its amount of ODA from €5,700
million (2002) to €7,000 million, is a first step. As a
next step, WBGU has suggested a target of 0.5 per
cent of GDP by 2010 (WBGU, 2004).

INTERNATIONAL FINANCE FACILITY
The proposal by the UK to establish an International
Finance Facility (IFF) is a mechanism for mobilizing additional ODA funds. The objective of this facility would be to mobilize as quickly and fully as possible the long-term shortfall in financing, including
the commitments made at Monterrey. The mechanism is based on the concept of utilizing already now
future ODA commitments (the so-called frontload
mechanism). The participating countries make formal and irrevocable multi-annual commitments for
future ODA payments, and IFF issues corresponding
bonds on international capital markets. The repayment of bonds issued by the IFF is guaranteed by
the commitments made by the participating countries. The funds generated through the issue of bonds
flow through existing bilateral and multilateral channels into development financing and are earmarked
for specific purposes based on conditions set by the
donor countries. These conditions have to be aligned
with the IFF's overarching sustainable investment
principles. According to its own estimates, the IFF is
able to generate up to US$50,000 million per year in
additional ODA in the period of 2004 to 2015. This
mechanism therefore offers an opportunity to gen-

Table 5.6-2
Official development assistance for environmental projects.
Source: Development Committee of the World Bank, 2004b

Share of environmental projects	1990	1991	1992	1993	1994	1995	1996	1997	1998	1999	2000
Bilateral development cooperation [US$ million]	1,033	652	921	737	806	1,083	1,822	1,526	1,012	1,394	984
Multilateral development cooperation [US$ million]	657	604	1,683	368	1,942	822	744	812	1,439	590	962
Total development cooperation [US$ million]	1,690	1,256	2,604	1,105	2,748	1,905	2,566	2,338	2,451	1,984	1,946
Total development cooperation [% of GDP of bilateral donors]	0,010	0,007	0,014	0,006	0,013	0,008	0,011	0,011	0,011	0,008	0,008

erate the funds that are currently lacking to achieve the MDGs by 2015. It has to be considered, however, that the IFF transfers the burden of repayments onto future generations. From 2015 onwards, a share of ODA would have to be used to repay IFF commitments. The facility is to be dissolved in 2030 (Technical Group on Innovative Financing Mechanisms, 2004; IFF, 2004). WBGU welcomes the idea of the IFF, because it enables a short-term increase in ODA and holds donors countries more strongly to their commitments. WBGU points out, however, that the financing potential of this instrument will not be sufficient on its own. At least in the near future it will be necessary to maintain ODA at a high level.

DEBT RELIEF

While developing countries had debts of a total of US$72,000 million (less than 10 per cent of their GDP) in 1970, their debts now amount to US$2,527,000 million (37 per cent of their GDP; Pettifor and Greenhill, 2002). While the current value of the debt of the 37 developing countries that are classified as Heavily Indebted Poor Countries (HIPC) of US$55,000 million (IMF and World Bank, 2004) seems comparatively small, it is nevertheless not sustainable for these countries. Not only HIPC countries, but also other developing countries have to use far more funds for debt repayments than they receive in ODA (Table 5.6-3).

Relief from interest and capital repayments would release relatively large funds in developing countries, which could be used to finance sustainability programmes. A widening of the HIPC initiative to include high-debt middle-income countries, accompanied by a reform of the PRSP process, is advisable in principle, because high levels of external debt stand in the way of poverty reduction and environmental protection (Section 4.2.10). A blanket unconditional relief of a part of the debts of, for example, 10 to 20 per cent could in the first instance widen the scope for action for the indebted countries. For additional debt relief, however, it has to be ensured that the funds that no longer have to be repaid will really be channelled towards poverty reduction and environmental protection.

The upcoming G8 summit in July 2005 will address issues of poverty reduction and climate protection. In this context WBGU welcomes the announcement by the British government to grant further debt relief to developing countries. The German government should join this initiative, as debt reduction is essential for the economic development of poor countries.

The mechanism behind debt-for-nature swaps failed for various reasons (Hansen, 1989; Deacon and Murphy, 1997; Resor, 1997). Alongside the PRSP approach, a multilateral safeguarding mechanism that guarantees a sustainable use of the released funds would need to be found. Perhaps the approaches developed and discussed in connection with the CDM could serve as models. WBGU recommends that further research be undertaken on the concrete aspects of the exchange of debt repayments for poverty and environmental policies in and on the part of developing countries (Chapter 6). On the one hand, bilateral and multilateral as well as private creditors in particular would probably need to make a greater direct contribution to financing the debt swap. On the other hand, it is conceivable that various organizations and funds for global poverty reduction and environmental policy could participate.

USER CHARGES

In a special report WBGU has already recommended levying charges on the use of global common goods to help finance environmental protection measures (WBGU, 2002). For example, it appears expedient to levy user charges on aviation: this would result in emission-reducing effects and would also produce revenues that could be used for climate protection or measures to adapt to climate change, which is partly caused by aviation. It would be sensible to introduce such charges gradually. In the short to medium term, the likely revenues would therefore not be very high, but in the long term they could – with a globally applied system of charges – correspond to the share of climate damage that is caused by aviation. There are various possible forms of user charges for aviation. A charge that is linked to the use of aviation fuel, if introduced across the EU and charged at €0.05 per litre, could produce revenues of approximately €13,000 million to 21,000 million per year.

Table 5.6-3
Debt servicing and official development assistance in 2000.
Source: Pettifor and Greenhill, 2002

Region	Debt servicing [US$ thousand million]	ODA [US$ thousand million]	Debt servicing/ODA
East Asia and Pacific	88.2	8.5	10.4
Europe and Central Asia	51.8	10.9	4.8
Latin America and the Caribbean	144.3	5.0	28.9
Middle East and North Africa	20.5	4.6	4.5
South Asia	12.9	4.2	3.1
Sub-Saharan Africa	12.6	13.5	0.9

Similar to aviation, user charges could also be levied on the use of the oceans and seas by international shipping. WBGU favours levying an annual, ecologically differentiated charge that creates incentives to develop shipping along more environmentally friendly lines (WBGU, 2002). If, to start with, such a user charge is levied only in industrialized countries – but independent of flag state or shipping company – and if the charge is set at €0.5–1 per tonne deadweight carrying capacity of the vessel or per kW of propulsive power, the annual revenue would amount to approximately €360–720 million if the scheme were introduced across the EU (WBGU, 2002).

COMPENSATORY PAYMENTS AND NON UTILIZATION OBLIGATION PAYMENTS

In earlier reports WBGU already recommended non utilization obligation payments to help protect environmental resources whose preservation is a common concern and responsibility of humanity, but which are not global common goods in a strict sense (WBGU, 2001a, 2002). Goods of global value, such as biodiversity, should be protected through international compensatory payments that are made in return for abstaining from their damaging utilization in the host countries. This way countries pay for the internalized benefit that is generated for them by the preservation of a resource in another country. Host countries are compensated for the loss of income, such as from logging. At the same time, incentives for the preservation of the resource are created.

While this concept is being used in some countries in the areas of ecosystem and climate protection, it has so far hardly been used at international level. This is partly due to the risk of free-rider behaviour. Possibilities for implementation range from direct compensatory payments to efficiency-increasing tradeable non utilization obligations, such as commitment certificates (WBGU, 2001a; Kulessa and Ringel, 2003). It would already be a success if it were possible, as a first step, to reduce free riding to the extent that at least all high-income countries commit themselves to financing jointly a worldwide representative system of protected areas (Section 4.2.3). This would result in a burden of approximately US$20 to 30 per capita and year in high-income countries. The benefit that the population would experience as a result of the preservation of biodiversity is likely to be a multiple of this.

5.6.3.5
Direct mobilization: Climate protection instruments

CLEAN DEVELOPMENT MECHANISM

Estimates about the size of the Clean Development Mechanism (CDM) vary considerably (Section 4.2.1.2). It is probable, though, that by the end of the first Kyoto commitment period total investments in the region of US$1,000 million to 10,000 million will have been made (Michaelowa et al., 2003; Ellis et al., 2004). Using optimistic assumptions, which foresee, among other things, an early agreement on the eligibility of CDM emission reductions beyond 2012, a World Bank study estimates that a CDM investment volume of US$10,000 million per year could be achieved in 2010 (Haites, 2004). The CDM therefore has the potential to make a significant contribution to the financing of sustainable development in the near future. It has to be noted, however, that the CDM is mostly limited to those developing countries that already attract the bulk of foreign direct investment (WBGU, 2003). Moreover, CDM investments only constitute a fraction of the total required sector investments. In the energy sector, for example, these are estimated at US$192,000 million per year (IEA, 2003). WBGU recommends early agreement on the eligibility of CDM emission reductions in future periods so that investment flows in the current commitment period are not prejudiced. In addition, it should be examined whether CDM projects that not only reduce emissions but also make a contribution to sustainable development more generally could be promoted through greater eligibility in the trading of emission rights (WBGU, 2003). In the medium term, emission limitation obligations should also be introduced for developing countries. This, however, would mean that CDM projects would loose relevance (WBGU, 2003). Alternative sources of financing would then become all the more important.

EMISSIONS TRADING

In the first commitment period under the Kyoto Protocol, emissions trading has been limited to industrialized countries. If extended in the future to newly industrializing and developing countries, emissions trading would replace the CDM and could then result in considerable financial transfers to poorer countries. However, given that negotiations on future commitment periods have not yet begun, estimates of potential financial transfers generated by emissions trading can only be hypothetical. WBGU has proposed committing all countries to limit their emissions and participate in emissions trading in the future in line with the contraction and convergence approach (WBGU, 2004). According to model calculations by WBGU, emissions trading would result in cumulative transfer payments of US$8,000,000 million to 12,000,000 million from OECD and transition countries to developing countries in the period up to 2100. This corresponds to annual average transfers of US$84,000 million to 128,000 million – whereby actual annual transfers are subject to considerable variation over time. These payments would make a significant contribution towards meeting the costs of emission reductions in developing countries (WBGU, 2003). For the upcoming negotiations WBGU recommends pushing for a rapid integration of all countries in a regime based on contraction and convergence to help mobilize the necessary funds in this way.

FUNDS AND COMPENSATORY PAYMENTS

Up to now three funds for adaptation financing have been created within the climate regime (Section 4.2.2): the Special Climate Change Fund (SCCF), the Least Developed Countries Fund (LDC Fund) and the Kyoto Protocol Adaptation Fund. In addition to reliable and greater financing of the funds in a manner more in line with the polluter pays principle, WBGU recommends that the issue of liability, and therefore the instrument of compensatory payments, be integrated more firmly into the financing of global poverty reduction and environmental policy. For climate protection policies in particular, this means international payments made by emitters to countries to compensate for the net costs of climate change. Given the financing volume required for such compensation, all countries would have to make payment commitments based not only on their current greenhouse gas emissions, but at least also their cumulative emissions since 1990 (WBGU, 2003). In terms of practical implementation, a fund for the compensation of developing countries which is only financed by countries that have exceeded specific per capita emissions appears suitable. Present knowledge on future climate change is by no means clear cut, and it is therefore not possible to make definitive statements on the net damage that can be expected and its distribution. The design of the fund and the contribution per tonne CO_2 equivalent should therefore not be cast in stone. Rather, transparent rules should be agreed, so that commitments can be adjusted according to the development of damage and countries' economic capacity.

In view of the manifold problems associated with estimating and monetarizing climate-related damage and its regional distribution, and because of the uncertainty about the future emissions by individual countries, the appropriate level of international compensatory payments can only be stated with significant caveats. Using available calculations of the worldwide costs of climate change and the methodology of a very recent examination of compensatory payments in climate policy (Tol and Verhejen, 2004), WBGU holds the following to be justifiable: if worldwide emissions are brought to a level that remains within the WBGU climate guard rail, then, based on current knowledge, compensatory payments from OECD countries to developing countries of between 0.1 and 1 per cent of the OECD's overall GDP per year during this century are appropriate.

5.6.4
Poverty reduction and environmental protection policies are financeable

In view of the multitude of financing instruments discussed above, WBGU is convinced that it is possible to mobilize sufficient funds for global poverty reduction and environmental policy. However, to tap this potential it will be essential to reconfigure the policy setting and restructure expenditures. The annual additional financing requirement for international poverty reduction and environmental protection goals is likely to run in the lower hundreds of thousand millions.

The studies cited above suggest that the MDGs for poverty reduction can be reached by increasing current ODA funding two- to threefold. It needs to be recalled, however, that the MDGs are inadequate (Section 3.6.3). Inefficiencies in the use of funds can also not be excluded, and expenditures for preliminary activities that are necessary to implement the MDGs are difficult to estimate. WBGU therefore believes that a tripling of ODA funds is necessary. This, however, does not guarantee long-term poverty reduction. The suggested increase in ODA funds therefore has to be accompanied by a reorganization of the framework conditions of the world economy in favour of poverty reduction and environmental protection. In particular, the dismantling of subsidies, with which industrialized countries prevent products from developing countries from entering their own markets, holds a significant potential for savings. An important prerequisite for an increase in ODA funds is, however, the political willingness on the part of the international community, and above all the industrialized countries, to channel more financial resources than so far towards worldwide poverty reduction in interplay with global environmental policy.

For measures in the environmental sphere, that is above all for the implementation of multilateral environmental agreements, including all measures on climate change, a further increase in ODA is, however, not realistic. Financing based solely on the principle of economic performance (GDP) is not appropriate in any case. In this sphere, other financing instruments discussed above should be used, such as emissions trading or charges on the use of global public goods.

The mobilization of private resources can and should play a key role in financing poverty reduction and environmental protection. The challenge to governments is to create incentive structures that boost private-sector contributions.

In industrialized countries the political willingness to do more for poverty reduction and environmental protection is blocked by, among other things, the fact that industrialized countries will be faced with more costs than benefits in the short term. In the medium and long term, however, not only developing countries, but industrialized countries as well will benefit from poverty reduction and environmental protection. Industrialized countries can expect positive dividends in four respects:

- *Environmental dividend*: Due to the protection of global public goods, environmental damage and its costs will be reduced in industrialized countries as well.
- *Development dividend*: The worldwide reduction in poverty and environmental degradation creates markets and improves the climate for foreign direct investment in developing countries. The more successful the implementation of sustainable development goals in these countries, the less will be the need for financial transfers from industrialized countries.
- *Trade dividend*: The reduction of subsidies in industrialized countries results in an intensification of world trade. In the medium to long term industrialized countries will profit from this as well, not least because products can be imported more cheaply, and because of an increase in the demand for their products due to the worldwide increase in per capita incomes.
- *Security dividend*: The number of people fleeing poverty and environmental degradation is likely to drop if the natural bases of human livelihoods are preserved, and poverty is reduced effectively. Concerns in industrialized countries about unwanted immigration can thereby be allayed, and expenditures, for example for deterring measures, can be reduced. Moreover, better living conditions, enhanced social participation and stronger entitlements in developing countries will undercut the base for terrorism.

In summary, the conclusion is that international poverty reduction and environmental protection goals can be achieved. The necessary political will can be generated by communicating the benefits of such an approach to political actors and the wider public in industrialized countries.

Reducing poverty and protecting the environment: Research recommendations

6

In Chapter 5 WBGU proposed a number of measures aimed at tackling the environment-poverty nexus. The focus throughout is on establishing coherent links between the relevant policy fields and on devising key strategies both for preventing or mitigating the global problems and for adapting to unavoidable developments. In many cases, these measures involve action under uncertainty. This is the situation WBGU seeks to address with its recommendations for research, identifying a series of deficiencies in both knowledge frameworks (knowledge for orientation) and practical knowledge (knowledge for action), without thereby claiming to have set out a complete research programme.

While knowledge frameworks determine the extent to which non-sustainable trends and risks are able to be identified at an early stage, practical knowledge highlights the options available for risk assessment and policy design. Both varieties of knowledge are therefore indispensable in the process of developing policy decisions in the context of societal problem solving.

WBGU presents its recommendations against the background of current research developments; within this, the emergence of 'sustainability science' (Section 4.3.5) deserves special attention. Sustainability science is committed to North-South cooperation and to strengthening research capacity in the poorer countries, not least because it is important that the search for solutions should involve those who are especially affected by problems of the environment and poverty, both now and in the future.

The research needs established by WBGU regarding the environment-poverty nexus are also intended as a contribution towards implementing the German government's framework programme 'Research for Sustainability', set up in 2004. The research themes referred to are intended as a suggestion for potential priority funding areas of the framework programme. In addition, WBGU also wishes to put forward these recommendations by way of input to the designing of the EU's 7th Framework Programme (2006–2010).

6.1
Knowledge for orientation

6.1.1
Basic research: Basic knowledge for policy making

Any research process aimed at linking results from the natural and the social sciences in a meaningful way must be supported by basic research in the relevant disciplines. When it comes to poverty and environment, it is indispensable to carry out wide-ranging research in many different sectors: climate, atmosphere, hydrosphere, soils, biodiversity, health, population trends, migration, urbanization, economics, technology and society. WBGU (1996) has already made its position on research needs in some of these areas abundantly clear. Many of these areas of research are now organized in very successful international programmes, such as IGBP, IHDP, WCRP, Diversitas and the new Earth System Science Partnership. Further development of this network of international research ought to be given greater priority in German funding practice.

Absolute poverty is concentrated in specific regions. International projects, with their carefully coordinated research programmes, offer the possibility of harnessing national or EU funding to support collaborative research with developing countries in order to build the scientific capacity so urgently needed there; this must then be supported by the developing countries as well.

The process of acquiring knowledge is a difficult one in many relevant research sectors due to utterly inadequate data. Whether gleaned from remote sources, such as satellites, or from surveys conducted with individuals, empirical data constitute an indispensable part of research programmes. The process of data gathering requires financing, as does the development of robust data processing methods. Considerable deficiencies exist in socio-economic monitoring in particular. Transdisciplinary longitudinal data streams are essential. Research funding should therefore provide long-term support for the construction and maintenance of appropriate monitoring programmes, since it is not possible to achieve reliable results within short-term project funding cycles. In particular, measurement networks need to be designed in such a way that their structure guarantees a sufficient density of supporting sources for the relevant data. Theoretical foundations for this are available in principle (e.g. random sampling and approximation theory); however, they are not utilized enough in the planning of environmental measuring programmes. These instruments cannot be developed further unless models are calibrated and validated using measuring data (Section 3.5). WBGU recommends the following measures:

- *Funding should be provided for basic research on the poverty-environment nexus, with a special regional focus.* Project clusters should target a limited number of areas affected by poverty (e.g. West Africa, the Caucasus, South-East Asia). In addition to national funding, suitable windows should be created for this in the EU's 7th Framework Programme. The division of research funding at EU level into topics such as environment, health, etc. works against the integration of different sectors and disciplines called for here. The German government should use its influence to ensure that funding for sustainability science occurs in a transdisciplinary manner. In future project funding assessments, the issue of incorporation into internationally coordinated activities should be given higher priority.

- *Funding should be provided for social scientific theory building around the interaction between environment and development.* Extensive studies do exist in the field of development theory, although they emerged at a time when environmental issues were not yet high up on the international agenda. The first significant work carried out along these lines includes studies on the risk society. What is lacking, however, are theories dealing explicitly with environment and development that would thus assist in asking the right questions when it comes to analysing problems and looking for solutions.

- *Cooperation with developing countries should be sought in respect of training and research.* Funding for partnerships between German universities and research institutes and those in developing countries should be increased and carefully targeted. Switzerland, for example, has set up a national twelve-year North-South research programme for which €341 million are available in the first four years. This involves entering into research partnerships specifically with developing countries (Hurni et al., 2004). It is unrealistic, however, to call for partnerships with scientific institutes in poor countries without ensuring that long-term financial support is guaranteed. Therefore, long-term funding should be provided specifically for the infrastructure of selected partner institutions in poor countries, independently of project funding.

- *Postgraduate courses and graduate colleges should be established in developing countries in partnership with German universities.* This would enable young scientists from developing countries to be trained in the most effective way, close to where the problems exist, and to be included in joint research efforts.

- *Continuous, sustained funding should be channeled into data acquisition programmes aimed at gathering data in both the social and natural sciences.* This includes processing the data – including a test for consistency – for evaluation, developing models, and building adequate simulation capacity in the relevant projects.

6.1.2
Prognostic research: Reducing uncertainties and mapping the indeterminate

Shaping policy in the international context of environment and development is generally a matter of action under uncertainty. The circumstances and trends of global environmental change and its interaction with poverty have, in many cases, been insufficiently researched. At present, the most significant contributions towards improving prognostic capacity in the field of poverty and the environment are emerging out of international research programmes such as IGBP and IHDP or else from policy advice networks such as the IPCC. This has led to a situation in which scientific projections – particularly with regard to climate change – have been developed to a relatively great, if not sufficient, extent. In other issue areas, such as soil degradation and the loss of biological diversity, prognostic capacity is still weak in contrast. It is particularly sketchy in the socio-economic and health sectors. In order for practical policy in the sphere of poverty and environment to be designed with greater certainty and efficiency, appropriate research must be a central plank of international cooperation.

One important step towards improving the knowledge base is the Millennium Ecosystem Assessment, which analyses the current state of ecosystems, assesses their capacity for providing essential services and points towards practical options for implementing better management techniques. A similar international project could be aimed at socio-economic development trends, as in the sense of a Millennium

Globalization Assessment. In this context, WBGU would like to draw particular attention to the following research needs:

- *The largest and most important uncertainties should be 'mapped' and a clear distinction drawn between 'lack of knowledge' and 'indeterminability'.* Hardly any data have been gathered, for example, on what motivates poverty-driven migration. On the other hand, it appears fundamentally impossible to achieve a prognostic, mathematical description of the motivational dynamics of all the actors involved.
- *Targeted work should be undertaken to improve analytic and simulation procedures in relation to the most important uncertainties.* In particular, this means gathering additional data and devising higher-resolution models, where the positive effects on prognostic capacity are more than proportional. Such progress may generally be expected to occur more in the previously neglected field of socio-economic research on global change.
- *Funding should be provided for innovative approaches towards optimizing the acquisition of information from fuzzy, uncertain and vague knowledge.* Important techniques that have not been adequately utilized thus far include ensemble simulations, Monte Carlo procedures, Bayesian methods, fuzzy logic and possibility theory.
- *Approaches for analysing structural stability in complex systems and identifying robust intervention strategies should be developed further.* This stems from the insight that within the scope of poverty reduction and environmental policy lie 'islands of stability', where success can be achieved with relative certainty.

6.1.3
Research on guard rails and goals: Structuring the action space

For the purpose of rendering sustainable development operational, WBGU developed the principle of setting normative guard rails and goals (Section 2.3). Both these structural elements determine the scope for policy action and therefore also define the framing conditions for social and economic action. Guard rails are limits that may upon no account be exceeded or fallen short of. Goals are quantitative requirements that are to be achieved within a defined period of time. Indicators are indispensable for assessing the state of these values and the way they are developing; such indicators must be capable of displaying as accurately as possible how far away one is from the guard rails or goals. This can often be done only by combining parameters. Science must create the pre-

conditions for setting normative guard rails and goals with regard to basic human needs (food, health, minimum income, etc.) and the preservation of natural resources (soil, water, biological diversity, etc.). The following research efforts are of particular importance in this context:

- *To produce a summary account of critical threshold values in the biogeophysical components of the Earth System.* Exceeding or falling below such values in the key planetary parameters may lead to large-scale, abrupt and irreversible transition to new (generally harmful) environmental regimes. Thus, these limits are natural candidates for applying normative guard rails. The international scientific community began to identify these threshold values only a few years ago. This requires a research programme that should be supported mainly by process studies and computer simulations. Alongside these identification programmes, it is necessary to get a comprehensive campaign underway for monitoring the critical elements in the Earth System mentioned above. Examples of this include the intensive monitoring of North Atlantic deep water formation and of the Indian monsoon. In this context it is also necessary to improve early recognition of such regime change, for example by improving the way in which early signs are analysed and perceived.
- *To conduct research into socio-economic instabilities and transitional phases.* Abrupt transitions in social structures triggered, for example, by a combination of environmental and poverty-related stresses, can be even more dangerous than biogeophysical regime change. Research into the stress factors affecting vulnerable social structures is still very much in its beginnings.
- *To conduct scientific analysis of potential minimum standards for basic human needs and develop multi-criteria assessments of adverse socio-economic impacts* (i.e. taking into account all the dimensions of poverty; Section 3.5).
- *To investigate the problem of scale in relation to setting guard rails.* How many people have to be affected, how large do the regions affected have to be, how long does the damage have to last in order to count as violation of a guard rail? These questions reach into substantive areas of ethical debate and can only be addressed jointly by scientists and ethicists.

6.1.4
Systems research: Approaches and methods for holistic analysis

The linkages between poverty and the environment can be understood only through transdisciplinary research, given that the conditions determining the emergence, duration and impact of such linkages are highly varied and multilayered. This places considerable demands on those involved in developing and combining methods aimed at deriving appropriate strategies for achieving sustainable development. Scientific methods such as analytic models, case studies and qualitative surveys are often used in isolation, rather than as part of an interdisciplinary effort. Over the past few years, integrated systems analysis has made new inroads in this regard. For example, WBGU has pointed out ways of looking at the issue from a holistic standpoint, including the syndrome concept, the analytic concept of a 'Rio transmission' newly proposed in this report, and analysis of differential vulnerability. However, integrated systems analyses of the links between environment and development are still at the stage of being a methodological challenge, and ought to be developed further in a variety of different ways. In order to do this, WBGU recommends the following:

- *Research on poverty should be intensified with particular regard to environmental aspects.* A combination of modelling and empirical social research in transdisciplinary projects should be pursued when undertaking systematic study of the poverty-environment nexus.
- *Further detailed work should be carried out to develop the syndrome concept* (WBGU, 1996). This concept should be utilized more to identify generic opportunities for intervention (e.g. for breaking through the vicious circles surrounding the poverty-environment nexus).
- *Semi-quantitative and intermediary complex procedures should be tested and applied in analysing and synthesizing complicated problems.* One approach that might usefully be developed, for example, is qualitative differential calculus. Special attention should be given to viability theory with regard to controlling vulnerable systems within tolerable windows.
- *'Regional simulators' should be constructed and put into operation.* These are (semi-)quantitative integrated models for depicting the poverty-environment dynamic in especially important regions (e.g. north-eastern Brazil). A series of prototypes are currently being developed. The regional simulators can be used especially to stage 'virtual theatres' for decision makers.

6.2
Knowledge for action

6.2.1
Vulnerability research: Enhancing capacity to adapt to environmental change

It is poor people in developing countries above all who will be affected by the now inevitable consequences of global environmental change and of climate change in particular. In the context of these new problems surrounding poverty reduction, the question of how best to adapt and of how to widen poor people's scope for action is becoming increasingly important. Vulnerability analyses are required in order to address this question. It is only once current and future regional hotspots have been identified, along with the groups that are particularly vulnerable, that the preconditions for developing appropriate instruments of crisis prevention and crisis management can be created. Such vulnerability assessments should, in the view of WBGU, contain the following elements:

- *Identification of the social groups* that are vulnerable to global environmental change on the one hand and that are particularly relevant to adaptation and coping on the other. These may be the same groups, but not necessarily so. This depends in particular on the significance of social structures for the sensitivity of these groups.
- *Analyses and case studies of the influence of global environmental change on poor people's livelihoods* (Section 3.3). The impact of economic globalization as well as current processes of marginalization affecting specific population groups should also be taken into account here. Quantitative and qualitative methods of social research should be combined for this purpose. In view of their extensive experience, closer cooperation should ideally be sought with those involved in development research. An attempt should be made to devise comparative case studies that draw on common basic structures, so that general statements can be made following subsequent generalization. These structures may be based on an extensive review of existing vulnerability studies.
- *Scenarios of important development trends* that influence the sensitivity of social systems and their coping capacity. A differentiation should be made here in particular between dimensions of poverty (Section 3.2), social groups and different spatial levels. In addition, analyses are needed of the impacts of globalization on social groups, countries and specific groups of countries. The scenarios must enable researchers to identify which

external conditions are needed in order to achieve success. Options for improved adaptation to environmental change should also be worked out in the context of such scenario development. These analyses should be more exact than, for example, those in the 1999 Human Development Report or in the 2004 report by the World Commission on the Social Dimension of Globalization, and could take their lead from recent attempts to develop an integrated scenario, such as the Global Scenario Group or the Millennium Ecosystem Assessment.

- *Analyses of responses on the part of both societies and the natural environment*, and in particular the capacity of societies and social groups to cope with perturbations or to learn from them. In this regard it is important to identify and study especially critical thresholds and positive feedback loops. Here, too, greater cooperation between the development research and climate research communities is necessary in order, for example, to guarantee sustainability of development projects.
- *Studies on the determinants of poor people's vulnerability in relation to environmental change.*
- *Application to threats from global environmental change of the available expertise regarding factors that hinder adaptation to local environmental threats or extreme events.* It would be desirable to see research programmes and projects come into being that facilitate and vigorously promote such cooperation. This may occur through a form of cooperative financing by development organizations and research institutions, as in the Swiss programme North-South Mitigating Syndromes of Global Change.
- *Synoptic review of studies on vulnerability indices and how they may be identified, and of their analytic strengths and weaknesses; further development of research on indices and indicators.* A continuous process of longitudinal data collection is indispensable for this.

6.2.2
Research on socio-economic disparities: Identifying their relevance to problem-solving

Socio-economic disparities in the developing and newly industrializing countries are considerably greater than those in the OECD countries. The point at which an increase in these disparities becomes an obstacle to coping with environmental and development problems is reached when such an increase is linked with an increase in absolute poverty. What has not been adequately investigated so far, however, are the circumstances under which extreme disparities in terms of opportunities in life may hinder the capacity

of societies to deal with adversities. It is necessary to clarify, for example, at what point socio-economic disparities preclude good governance and to what extent social participation is constrained. WBGU recommends the following:

- *Analyses and country studies on the role of socio-economic disparities in coping with the consequences of global environmental change.*
- *More research on the links between income and asset distribution and environmental degradation.*
- *Intensification of research on the significance of land ownership rights (e.g. state, individual or community property) for economic development, poverty and land degradation.* This should include analyses and country studies on the impacts of different systems of assigning entitlements.
- *Analyses on the determinants of (large) socio-economic disparities.*
- *Analyses on North-South disparities in lifestyles and resource consumption, and how these might be influenced through international cooperation.* For example, how do expectations and reality prevent states from entering into cooperative problem-solving in relation to, say, climate change – which is caused above all by the North, and whose impacts are felt above all in the South? WBGU therefore recommends analyses on the role of North-South disparities in lifestyle (resource consumption) in combating the causes of global environmental change.
- *Analyses of the international and intranational distributive impacts of global sustainability policies in industrialized countries, geared towards finding solutions.* Greater efforts should be invested in developing and testing mechanisms for overcoming conflicts of interest that stand in the way of sustainable development.
- *Intensification of empirical studies on pro-poor growth and its practical implementation.* This also includes the role of trade and, therefore, research on pro-poor trade. This needs to be looked at more closely at the micro level. There should be an emphasis on empirical research and implementation strategies. Environmental issues should be integrated to a greater extent into these studies.

6.2.3
Technology research: Stimulating technological developments for poverty reduction

Technology development holds out a great potential to combat poverty in all its dimensions, while at the same time reducing environmental degradation. The German Research Ministry (BMBF) has set up a 'Research for Sustainability' programme that already contains many well-targeted approaches towards reducing poverty through technology development. Development cooperation actors should follow this lead, with targeted research on sustainable technology development, possibly adapted to specific regions. WBGU recommends giving special consideration to the following research areas in order to stimulate clean technology development for poverty reduction:

- *Sustainable industrial production processes and products:* The industrialized countries are characterized today by massive levels of energy and materials throughput. It will not be possible to emulate this model worldwide. As a general principle, it is essential to research development pathways on which economic growth can be decoupled from environmental degradation. Such decoupling must be achieved early on and with a high degree of certainty. This will require intensive research on sustainable industrial patterns of production. Keywords here include the dematerialization of production, the optimization of products in terms of their recyclability, the optimization of production processes in terms of their pollutant emissions, extending the service life of products, and minimizing the energy consumed to manufacture them. Research on 'environmental leapfrogging' merits particular attention, i.e. development pathways that bypass the unsustainable production technologies used by industrialized countries.

- *Energy supply*: Energy supply is a cross-cutting theme that impacts upon numerous poverty dimensions. Research on this theme needs to concentrate upon the regionally appropriate provision of renewable energies on the one hand, while also aiming to improve energy efficiency under the conditions prevailing in developing countries. Great importance attaches in this connection to the development of cost-effective energy-optimized 'solar buildings', including aspects of solar air-conditioning. Moreover, research should make a greater contribution to further reducing, by means of photovoltaics, the currently high costs of distributed energy supply. In rural regions, photovoltaic systems are already more cost-effective today than e.g. grid expansion or diesel generators. Technology development in this field should also lead to clean local production of components and systems.

- *Water supply:* Research on water supply and effluent disposal needs to address the following points: Further development of efficient irrigation techniques, development of energy-efficient technologies for potable water production from saline waters (sea and brackish water, but also water from overexploited wells), and the development

of technologies for the multiple use of water by means of closing cycles or making use of specific effluent streams. Research should concentrate on technologies that do not need extensive infrastructure. Here the linkages with distributed energy supply need to be taken into account, as all water treatment technologies require energy.

6.2.4
Development research: Designing development cooperation in the face of future environmental change

Although by no means new, the controversy over which policies and measures are most effective for reducing poverty is subject to intense debate among national and international development agencies. As the OECD and the World Bank, the Committee on Economic Cooperation and Development of the German Bundestag, NGOs and many development researchers (Stockmann, 1996) have repeatedly found, not enough empirical analyses exist regarding impacts and sustainability. Despite reports of success emanating from the development agencies, these have not been able to eliminate doubts about the effectiveness of development policy to date. Underlying the credibility gap in development cooperation is a gap in research and knowledge. This finding gives rise to the following research recommendations:

- *Independent evaluations:* By international standards, evaluation remains underdeveloped in German development cooperation. Internal evaluation reports produced by the BMZ and by implementing organizations, which are hardly accessible to the public, are no substitute for independent evaluation.

- *Coherence research:* Deficits in coordination between different actors and different levels of action along with deficits in coherence between policy areas relevant to the environment and to development place considerable constraints on the effectiveness of international development policy. Coherence research needs to work on producing systematic studies, related to specific regions and countries, on the consequences and the advantages and disadvantages of policies on trade, development and the environment. For example, comparative studies on coherence deficits in bilateral and multilateral development cooperation, organized by the European Association of Development Institutes, should be carried forward and extended via international participation (Stokke and Forster, 1999). In addition, a research project comparable to the UN Millennium Project, which carries out relevant research on the implementation of MDGs, should be initiated as quickly as possible at the European level, in order to close the research gap that exists in relation to the USA, which is also a leader in development studies.

- *Development studies:* As a result of staff cutbacks at universities and non-university research institutions, development studies in Germany have suffered a loss of international reputation and competitiveness in comparison with environmental sciences. Good quality development cooperation requires qualified scientific expertise, however, and this should be allocated more funding by the relevant ministries at national level (BMZ, BMBF and BMU), the finance ministries at regional state level and research funding institutions. Cooperation with research institutes in the developing world should also be stepped up. This can involve both capacity building and research collaboration. WBGU proposes, in addition, that scientific centres of excellence should be set up and funded, much along the lines of the British Department for International Development model; these centres could then play an appropriate role in international agenda setting.

- *Research on environmental refugees:* So far, neither environmental researchers nor migration researchers have undertaken systematic work on the growing number of environmental refugees. The quality of prognoses suffers above all from uncertain assumptions about the impacts of desertification and water scarcity. The challenge facing environmental and development researchers is to pool their knowledge about problem regions and to propose appropriate preventive measures for international development policy.

- *Research on failing states:* Whereas the causes of state failures and conflicts over resources have been researched in some detail, few studies exist on the harmful environmental impacts of state failure. There is insufficient research that might identify appropriate points of intervention for the international community and development organizations. The construction of development paths for these states would serve the purpose of identifying 'critical junctures' at which development begins to fail and where development policy could take effect. While development and foreign policy actors demand that science demonstrate practical expertise, in Germany they themselves fail to provide adequate resources for generating this expertise.

- *Interaction between environmental degradation and development opportunities:* The German Research Ministry (BMBF) should specify its framework research programme for sustainability in such a way that environmental and development researchers are required to engage in interdisciplinary collaboration. There continues to be a lack of empirically sound and theoretically systematized knowledge about the interactions between environmental destruction and societies' long-term development opportunities, as well as about the costs of environmental destruction and the funding requirements of promising global, regional and national counter strategies.

6.2.5
Institutional research: Shaping institutions for an enabling setting

Analyses of multilateral institutional structures for coping with global problems of poverty and the environment have shown that while potentially suitable structures do exist they are still too weak and ineffective. One challenge here is to channel globalization through regulatory mechanisms. Environmental and development policy too should be oriented towards structural change (global structural policy). In order to achieve this, research should be intensified in the following areas:

- *The political science and juridical aspects of according greater importance to environmental policy and meshing environmental and development policy at institutional level within the UN system should be examined in greater detail.* This is of particular relevance to the recommendation put forward by WBGU to merge ECOSOC into a Council on Global Development and Environment.

- The idea of *establishing a UN Environment Organization* has received fresh impetus through the initiative of French President Jacques Chirac in connection with the WSSD. Further research is required on the international process of negotiation and on the shape the organization might take, especially with regard to the following questions: How might a new international environmental organization contribute to greater efficiency, effectiveness and coherence in the UN system, and what new ideas for reforming the UN system does the establishment of such an institution suggest? What kind of financial resources would such an organization require? How can work on founding a UN Environment Organization and a parallel strengthening of UNEP create synergies? How should relationships to other environmental institutions and conventions be shaped?

- *The link between implementation of environmental agreements and actual improvements in the environment* has not been adequately researched. This applies especially to assessments of the effectiveness of international organizations dealing with global environmental change, including the convention secretariats and UNEP. Further research – both theoretical and based on experience and data sets – is necessary in this area.

- *Interplay of the PRSP approach of the World Bank and IMF with the projects and activities of other development actors.* A few studies exist on the role of specific organizations in the PRSP process, such as UNDP. Above and beyond this, however, further research is necessary in order to systematically capture and comprehensively assess the interconnections between PRSPs and relevant UN organizations, especially UNEP.

- *Free market incentive mechanisms* are crucial for stimulating sustainable development, whether it be in a national economy or in an organization. More practical research should be undertaken on this regarding how to design effective incentive structures, taking into account regional, cultural and socio-economic particularities.

- *The inability of complex institutional structures to develop and implement coherent strategies* constitutes a big management problem. This deficiency is especially serious when it comes to acting on issues of poverty and the environment because then the very existence of individuals, species and ecosystems is at stake. These management problems are frequently a result of institutional structures of communication and action: Just like democratic organizations, hierarchically structured organizations are prone – albeit in different ways – to external and internal perturbations. Therefore, complexity research based on systems theory, administrative science and organizational sociology should be driven forward and applied in practice to existing organizational structures. This context can only be researched in an interdisciplinary way, for example using the concept of multiscale networks or mean connectivity. The multilateral institutions gathered beneath the umbrella of the United Nations are particularly in need of such approaches to internal reorganization and improvements in external cooperation.

6.2.6
Research on financing: Identifying requirements and mapping out ways to meet them

In order to achieve the goals of international environment and development policy, there is a need not only to assess what financing is required for coping with environmental and development problems but also to clarify how that funding can be generated and put to use. Projections of funding needs have been prepared both for individual MDGs as well as for

sustainability policy as a whole (Agenda 21). What is lacking, however, is an assessment of financing requirements that has been prepared systematically and justified rigorously (Sections 3.6 and 5.6).

Over the past few years, a number of innovative financing mechanisms have been discussed, including charges on the use of global commons, compensation for not exploiting resources and an International Finance Facility, in addition to the traditional financing instruments of bilateral and multilateral cooperation. New funds have also been set up within the UNFCCC process. There is no systematic assessment of these various financing options either. Finally, there has been no assessment of the possibilities for generating funding by making changes in the wider setting, such as dismantling subsidies or making market access easier for developing countries. The different scales of magnitude in relation to public financing instruments need to be made clear. WBGU therefore recommends:

- *An assessment should be made of financing requirements for preserving natural life-support systems and combating absolute poverty.*

- *An assessment should be made of what proportion of expenditure on environmental protection is relevant to development, and what proportion of expenditure in development cooperation is relevant to the environment.* WBGU has identified a considerable need for research in this regard, both in respect of gathering data and, above all, of quantifying the synergy effects present within the fields of poverty reduction and environmental protection and between the two.

- *Research should be carried out on developing innovative financing instruments and applying them in practical contexts.*

- *An analysis should be undertaken of direct and indirect financing options,* including an estimation of the scales of magnitude involved.

- *Research should be carried out on national financing mechanisms for performance-linked infrastructure services in developing countries.* One priority should be to develop and analyse incentives financed by user contributions for the construction of environmentally sound energy and water supply systems in rural areas.

Environmental policy is a prerequisite for poverty reduction

Human intervention in the natural environment is already jeopardizing livelihoods, especially those of the poor, in many regions of the world. Unless countermeasures are adopted, environmental changes will have an even more life-threatening impact in future. While those who are responsible for global and transboundary environmental problems, such as climate change, are predominantly based in the industrialized countries, the vast majority of those affected live in the developing world. Poor groups are especially vulnerable to environmental changes as these people are more exposed to risks which threaten their survival (disease, hunger, harvest losses, etc.) and have very few coping and adaptive capacities. This must be the starting point for a political response: poverty reduction and environmental protection must be forged into a coherent policy, involving civil society actors, from the local to the global level. Only an integrated approach can fulfil the guiding vision of sustainable development which emerged in Rio de Janeiro in 1992.

Breathing life into the partnership between industrialized and developing countries

Now more than ever, there is a need to forge alliances between the industrialized and developing countries so that they can jointly combat environmental problems and poverty. Both sides must take seriously the 'global partnership' agreed in Rio de Janeiro and honour their commitments to guarantee peaceful international development.

Since they are responsible for a substantial proportion of global environmental changes and in view of their economic and technological capacities, the industrialized countries have an obligation to change their consumption and production patterns at home while supporting viable modernization processes in developing countries. The present gap between the wealthy countries' rhetoric and their actual policies is undermining the developing countries' trust and confidence. The industrialized countries should honour the pledges that they have made at the world conferences: to open up their markets to products from the developing countries, to abolish the agricultural subsidies which distort competition, to cancel the poorest countries' debt, to provide more generous development assistance, and to improve access to technology and know-how.

In return, the governments of the developing countries must establish domestic political conditions which are conducive to good governance. This includes respect for basic human rights, government accountability, the separation of powers, and legal certainty for citizens and enterprises. People from all groups of society should have opportunities for social participation, for which more intensive funding of education and access to health care is a prerequisite. To ensure that economic development does not take place at the expense of the environment, the developing countries should embark on an environmentally sound development pathway as well.

Giving poverty and environmental problems the same high priority as security issues

The UN is a cumbersome organization which must improve its capacity to steer policy and become the institutional backbone of a global environmental and development partnership. This does not mean weakening the international financial institutions and the World Trade Organization (WTO), but integrating them more fully into a coherent global governance architecture under the UN's political leadership. This is the only way to overcome the much-lamented lack of coherence in the international institutional system and improve the enforceability of sustainability goals. As a long-term vision, WBGU therefore recommends the establishment of a new lead agency in the UN system: a Council on Global Development and Environment. It would provide the strategic and policy framework, coordinate the activities of the multilateral organizations working on development and environment – including the International Monetary Fund and the World Bank – and focus their activities towards the guiding vision of sustainable development. The UN Economic and Social Council (ECOSOC) would be subsumed within this new body. Until this reform project – for which an amendment to the UN Charter is necessary – can be achieved, coordination within the existing structures must be improved. As a further important reform measure, UNEP should be upgraded into a UN specialized agency. In WBGU's view, this would do much to enhance the importance attached to environmental issues within the UN system and improve coordination in this field.

Poverty reduction and environmental protection are financeable

WBGU estimates the transfer of financial resources from the industrialized to the developing countries that is required to implement internationally agreed poverty and environmental goals to run in the low hundreds of thousand millions of US dollars per year. This is broadly equivalent to the OECD countries' annual spending on agricultural subsidies, which total around US$350,000 million. Biodiversity conservation and compliance with the 'global warming guard rail' established by WBGU require additional resources. Provided that global biodiversity and climate protection policies are embedded in a coherent sustainable development and especially energy strategy, this is also likely to be achievable with less than US$400,000 million, on average, in international financial transfers annually. In WBGU's view, the internationally agreed targets on poverty and environment are financeable. A prerequisite is the restructuring of world economic conditions, especially by dismantling environmentally harmful subsidies and trade barriers which obstruct the poor countries' access to the industrialized countries' markets. Official development assistance must also be increased, especially for the least developed countries.

Poverty reduction and environmental protection are worthwhile for the industrialized countries too

Besides their ethical responsibility, poverty reduction and environmental protection accord with the industrialized countries' pragmatic interests as well. In specific terms, four positive dividends can be anticipated for industrialized countries:
- *Environmental dividend:* By protecting global public goods, environmental degradation and its costs are reduced in the industrialized countries too.
- *Development dividend:* Reducing poverty and environmental degradation worldwide creates markets and improves the climate for foreign direct investment in developing countries. The greater the success in implementing sustainability goals in these countries, the lesser the need for North-South transfers.
- *Trade dividend:* The removal of subsidies in the industrialized countries will boost world trade. The industrialized countries will also benefit in the medium to long term, not least because they will be able to import products more cheaply, and demand for their own products will increase as a result of rising per capita incomes worldwide.
- *Security dividend:* By maintaining natural life-support systems and successfully reducing poverty, the numbers of refugees fleeing from environmental degradation and poverty will decrease. This could lessen the industrialized countries' concerns about unwanted immigration and reduce costs, e.g. for deterring measures. Furthermore, improved living conditions, stronger entitlements and enhanced participation rights in the developing countries will narrow the enabling environment for terrorism.

This report affirms that linkage between global poverty reduction and environmental policy is essential in order to facilitate sustainable development. It also identifies appropriate policy options. This integrated approach proposed by WBGU is financeable and offers long-term benefits for the developing and the industrialized countries alike.

References   **8**

ADB (African Development Bank), Asian Development Bank and World Bank (2003) *Poverty and Climate Change. Reducing the Vulnerability of the Poor through Adaptation.* World Bank, Washington, DC.

Adger, W N and Kelly, P M (1999) 'Social vulnerability to climate change and the architecture of entitlements'. *Mitigation and Adaptation Strategies for Global Change* **4**: pp253–66.

AGI (Alan Guttmacher Institute) and UNFPA (United Nations Population Fund) (2004) *Adding it Up: The Benefits of Investing in Sexual and Reproductive Health Care.* AGI and UNFPA, New York, NY.

Alder, J and Sumaila, U R (2004) 'Western Africa: A fish basket of Europe past and present'. *Journal of Environment and Development* **13**: pp156–78.

Alliance 2015 (2004) *The EU's Contribution to the Millennium Development Goals.* Alliance 2015, Den Haag.

Alongi, D M (2002) 'Present state and future of the world's mangrove forests'. *Environmental Conservation* **2**: pp331–49.

Altvater, E and Brunnengräber, A (2002) 'NGOs im Spannungsfeld von Lobbyarbeit und öffentlichem Protest'. *Aus Politik und Zeitgeschichte* **B6–7**: pp6–14.

Amar, E C, Cheong, R M T and Cheong, M V T (1996) 'Small-scale fisheries of coral reefs and the need for community-based resource management in Malalison Island, Philippines'. *Fisheries Research* **25**: pp265–77.

Ananda, J and Herath, G (2003) 'Soil erosion in developing countries: a socio-economic appraisal'. *Journal of Environmental Management* **68**(4): pp343–53.

Anderson, K and Blackhurst, R (eds) (1992) *The Greening of World Trade Issues.* Harvester Wheatsheaf, New York and London.

Anderson, K, Dimaranan, B, Francois, J, Hertel, T, Hoekman, B and Martin, W (2001) *The Cost of Rich (and Poor) Country Protection to Developing Countries.* CIED Discussion Paper Nr. 0136. Adelaide University, Adelaide.

Angelsen, A and Wunder, S (2003) *Exploring the Forest-Poverty Link: Key Concepts, Issues and Research Implications.* Center for International Forestry Research, Jakarta.

Aninat, E (2000) 'Die Integration aller Länder in die immer globaler werdende Wirtschaft. Rede vor dem Wirtschafts- und Sozialrat der Vereinten Nationen in New York am 5. Juli 2000'. International Monetary Fund (IMF) website, http://www.imf.org/external/np/speeches/2000/070500g.htm (viewed 14. April 2004).

APEC (Asia Pacific Economic Co-operation) (2000) *Study Into the Nature and Extent of Subsidies in the Fisheries Sector of APEC Members Economies.* Report CTI 07/99T. APEC Secretariat, Singapore.

Arcand J-L (2001) 'Undernutrition and Economic Growth: The Efficiency Cost of Hunger'. Food and Agriculture Organization (FAO) website, http://www.fao.org/docrep/003/x9280e/x9280e03.htm (viewed 17. August 2003).

Asche, R and Schulze, E-D (1996) *Die Ragginer. 200 Jahre Volksmedizin in Südtirol.* Dr. Friedrich Pfeil, Munich.

Atkinson, A B (1999) *The Economic Consequence of Rolling Back the Welfare State.* MIT Press, Cambridge.

Aunan, K, Berntsen, T K and Seip, H M (2000) 'Surface ozone in China and its possible impact on agricultural crop yields'. *Ambio* **29**(6): pp294–301.

Austin, D, Faeth, P, da Motta, R S, Ferraz, C, Young, C E F, Ji, Z, Jungfeng, L, Pathak, M, Srivastava, L and Sharma, S (1999) *How Much Sustainable Development can we Expect from the Clean Development Mechanism?* Climate Notes. World Resources Institute (WRI), Washington, DC.

Averous, L (2002) *Financing Water Infrastructure: World Water Panel.* Lehman Brothers.

Baaden, A (2002) 'Bildung für Alle bis 2015? Die UNESCO und der Aktionsplan von Dakar'. *Entwicklung und Zusammenarbeit EZ* (**8/9**): pp246–8.

Balmford, A (2003) *Overview – The Global Costs and Benefits of Conserving Wild Nature. Presentation at the World Parks Congress, September 11, 2003.* Cambridge University, Cambridge, UK.

Balmford, A, Bruner, A, Cooper, P, Costanza, R, Farber, S, Green, R E, Jenkins, M, Jefferiss, P, Jessamy, V, Madden, J, Munro, K, Myers, N, Naeem, S, Paavola, J, Rayment, M, Rosendo, S, Roughgarden, J, Trumper, K and Turner, R K (2002) 'Economic reasons for conserving wild nature'. *Science* **297**: pp950–3.

Balmford, A, Gaston, K J, Blyth, S, James, A and Kapos, V (2003) 'Global variation in terrestrial conservation costs, conservation benefits, and unmet conservation needs'. *PNAS* **100**(3): pp1046–50.

Bannister, G J and Thugge, K (2001) *International Trade and Poverty Alleviation. Working Paper 91/54.* International Monetary Fund (IMF), Washington, DC.

Barber, C V, Johnston, S and Tobin, B (2003) 'User Measures. Options for Developing Measures in User Countries to Implement the Access and Benefit–Sharing Provisions of the Convention on Biological Diversity. 2nd Edition'. United Nations University – Institute of Advanced Studies website, http://www.ias.unu.edu/binaries/UNUIAS_User-Measures_2ndEd.pdf (viewed 25. October 2004).

Barbier, E B (1997) 'The economic determinants of land degradation in developing countries'. *Philosophical Transactions of the Royal Society of London Series B Biological Sciences* **352**(1356): pp891–9.

Barrett, C and Arcese, P (1998) 'Wildlife harvest in integrated conservation and development projects: linking harvest to household demand, agricultural production, and environmental shocks in the Serengeti'. *Land Economics* **74**: pp449–65.

Barrett-Lennard, E G (2002) 'Restoration of saline land through revegetation'. *Agricultural Water Management* **53**(1-3): pp213–26.

Bartholomäi, R (1997) *Sustainable Development und Völkerrecht. Nachhaltige Entwicklung und intergenerative Gerechtigkeit in der Staatenpraxis.* Nomos, Baden-Baden.

Bathgate, A and Pannell, D J (2002) 'Economics of deep-rooted perennials in western Australia'. *Agricultural Water Management* **53**(1-3): pp117–32.

Battikha, A-M (2003) *Structural Adjustment and the Environment: Impacts of the World Bank and IMF Conditional Loans on Developing Countries.* Faculty of the Virginia Polytechnic Institute and State University, Blacksburg, Virginia.

Bauer, S (2001) *Zur Zusammenarbeit internationaler Regierungsorganisationen in der internationalen Umweltpolitik.* University Hamburg, Hamburg. Mimeo.

Bauer, S and Biermann, F (2004) 'The debate on a World Environment Organization: an introduction'. In Biermann, F and Bauer, S (eds) *A World Environment Organization: Solution or Threat for Effective International Environmental Governance?* Ashgate, Aldershot, UK (in print).

Beckerman, W (1992) 'Economic growth and the environment - whose growth? Whose environment?' *World Development* **20**(4): pp481–96.

Beese, F O (2004) 'Ernährungssicherung als Produktions- bzw. Verteilungsproblem'. Expertise for the WBGU Report 'World in Transition: Fighting Poverty through Environmental Policy'. WBGU website, http://www.wbgu.de/wbgu_jg2004_ex01.pdf.

Belasquez, J and Malabed, J (2002) *Inter-Linkages in Financing Sustainable Development.* United Nations University (UNU), Tokyo.

Belle, A, Shyamsundar, P and Hamilton, K (2002) *Country Assistance Strategies and the Environment – Taking Stock.* World Bank Environment Strategy Notes No. 2, February. World Bank, Washington, DC.

Bénabou, R (1996) *Unequal Societies.* Working Paper No. 5583. National Bureau of Economic Research (NBER), Cambridge, MA.

Bichsel, A and Horta, K (1998) *Leapfrog into Mainstreaming and Jump-Start the Learning Process: Critical Steps for the Future of GEF Paper prepared for the GEF Assembly and Council Meeting, New Delhi March 29–April 3, 1998.* Swiss Coalition of Development Organizations and Environmental Defense Fund, Bern and Washington, DC.

Biermann, F (1997) 'Financing environmental policies in the South: experiences from the multilateral ozone fund'. *International Environmental Affairs* **9**(3): pp179–219.

Biermann, F (1998) *Weltumweltpolitik zwischen Nord und Süd: Die neue Verhandlungsmacht der Entwicklungsländer.* Nomos, Baden-Baden.

Biermann, F (2000) 'The case for a World Environment Organization'. *Environment* **20**(9): pp22–31.

Biermann, F (2002) 'Strengthening green global governance in a disparate world society: would a World Environment Organization benefit the South?' *International Environmental Agreements: Politics, Law and Economics* **2**: pp297–315.

Biermann, F and Simonis, U E (2000) 'Institutionelle Reform der Weltumweltpolitik? Zur politischen Debatte um die Gründung einer „Weltumweltorganisation". Zeitschrift für Internationale Beziehungen. Forumsbeitrag 1'. University Bremen website, http://www-user.uni-bremen.de/~iniis/zib/biersimo.htm#f13 (viewed 3. November 2004).

Biermann, F and Bauer, S (2004a) 'UNEP and UNDP'. Expertise for the WBGU Report „World in Transition: Fighting Poverty through Environmental Policy". WBGU website, http://www.wbgu.de/wbgu_jg2004_ex02.pd.f

Biermann, F and Bauer, S (2004b) 'Assessing the Effectiveness of Intergovernmental Organizations in International Environmental Politics'. *Global Environmental Change* (forthcoming).

Birdsall, N, Kelley, A C and Sinding, S W (eds) (2003) *Population Matters: Demographic Change, Economic Growth, and Poverty in the Developing World.* Oxford University Press, New York.

Birdsall, N, Ibrahim, A J and Gupta, R G (2004) *Interim Report of Task Force 3 on Primary Education. Millennium Project. Commissioned by the UN Secretary General and supported by the UN Development Group.* New York, UN.

Bishop, J and Allen, J (1989) *The On-site Costs of Soil Erosion in Mali.* World Bank Environment Working Paper No. 21. World Bank, Washington, DC.

Blaikie, P, Cannon, T, Davis, I and Wisner, B (1994) *At Risk: Natural Hazards, People's Vulnerability and Disasters.* Routledge, New York.

Bloom, D and Canning, D (2003) 'Cumulative causality, economic growth, and the demographic transition'. In Birdsall, N, Kelley, A C and Sinding, S W (eds) *Population Matters: Demographic Change, Economic Growth, and Poverty in the Developing World.* Oxford University Press, New York, pp165–81.

BMELF (Bundesminsterium für Ernährung, Landwirtschaft und Forsten) (1995) *Die FAO und die Mitwirkung der Bundesrepublik Deutschland.* Schriftenreihe des Bundesministeriums für Ernährung, Landwirtschaft und Forsten (446). BMELF, Münster.

BMU (Bundesministerium für Umwelt, Naturschutz und Reaktorsicherheit) (1997) *Umweltpolitik. Agenda 21. Konferenz der Vereinten Nationen für Umwelt und Entwicklung im Juni 1992 in Rio de Janeiro. Dokumente.* BMU, Bonn.

BMZ (Bundesministerium für wirtschaftliche Zusammenarbeit und Entwicklung) (no year) *Umwelt, Armut und Nachhaltige Entwicklung, Themenblätter zu Umwelt und nachhaltiger Ressourcennutzung in der Entwicklungszusammenarbeit.* BMZ, Bonn.

BMZ (Bundesministerium für wirtschaftliche Zusammenarbeit und Entwicklung) (1999a) *Förderung der Grundbildung in Entwicklungsländern – Sektorkonzept 1999.* BMZ-Konzepte Nr. 106. BMZ, Bonn.

BMZ (Bundesministerium für wirtschaftliche Zusammenarbeit und Entwicklung) (1999b) *Förderung sozialer Sicherungssysteme in Entwicklungsländern.* BMZ Spezial Nr. 98. BMZ, Bonn.

BMZ (Bundesministerium für wirtschaftliche Zusammenarbeit und Entwicklung) (2001a) *Aktionsprogramm 2015. Armutsbekämpfung – eine globale Aufgabe. Der Beitrag der Bundesregierung zur weltweiten Halbierung extremer Armut.* BMZ-Materialien Nr. 106. BMZ, Bonn.

BMZ (Bundesministerium für wirtschaftliche Zusammenarbeit und Entwicklung) (2001b) *Elfter Bericht zur Entwicklungspolitik der Bundesregierung.* BMZ, Bonn.

BMZ (Bundesministerium für wirtschaftliche Zusammenarbeit und Entwicklung) (2002a) *Report by the Federal Republic of Germany on Measures Taken to Assist the Implementation of the United Nations Convention to Combat Desertification (UNCCD) in Affected Country Parties.* BMZ, Bonn.

BMZ (Bundesministerium für wirtschaftliche Zusammenarbeit und Entwicklung) (2002b) *Auf dem Weg zur Halbierung der Armut, Zwischenbericht über den Stand der Umsetzung des Aktionsprogramms 2015.* BMZ, Bonn.

BMZ (Bundesministerium für wirtschaftliche Zusammenarbeit und Entwicklung) (2002c) *Sektorkonzept Wald und nachhaltige Entwicklung.* BMZ, Bonn.

BMZ (Bundesministerium für wirtschaftliche Zusammenarbeit und Entwicklung) (2003a) *Bessere Lebensbedingungen durch globales Handeln: die Ziele des BMZ bei der VN Konvention zur Bekämpfung der Desertifikation (UNCCD).* BMZ Spezial Nr. 80. BMZ, Bonn.

BMZ (Bundesministerium für wirtschaftliche Zusammenarbeit und Entwicklung) (2003b) *Informationsvermerk zu den vertraulichen Erläuterungen 2004 für die bilaterale Finanzielle und Technische Zusammenarbeit.* Ausschussdrucksache Nr. 15 (18) 90. BMZ, Bonn.

BMZ (Bundesministerium für wirtschaftliche Zusammenarbeit und Entwicklung) (2003c) *Soll-Ist-Vergleich 2002. Bilaterale Finanzielle und Technische Zusammenarbeit mit Entwicklungsländern.* Stand August 2003. BMZ, Bonn.

BMZ (Bundesministerium für wirtschaftliche Zusammenarbeit und Entwicklung) (2004a) *Biodiversity in German Development Cooperation.* GTZ, Eschborn.

BMZ (Bundesministerium für wirtschaftliche Zusammenarbeit und Entwicklung) (2004b) *Zweiter Zwischenbericht zur Umsetzung des Aktionsprogramms 2015 der Bundesregierung.* BMZ, Bonn.

Bode, T (2003) 'Die internationale Dimension in der deutschen Nachhaltigkeitspolitik, Challenger Report für den Rat für nachhaltige Entwicklung, 1.10.2003'. RNE website, http://www.nachhaltigkeitsrat.de/service/download/studien/Challenger_Report_Bode_01-10-03.pdf; (viewed 27. October 2003).

Bohle, H-G (1998) '20 Jahre „Grüne Revolution" in Indien. Eine Zwischenbilanz mit Dorfbeispielen aus Südindien'. *Geographische Rundschau* (**41**): pp1–9.

Bohle, H-G (2001) 'Vulnerability Article 1: Vulnerability and Criticality'. IHDP Update 2'. IHDP website, http://www.ihdp.uni-bonn.de/html/publications/update/IHDPUpdate01_02.html (viewed 25. October 2004).

Bohle, H-G, Downing, T E, Field, J O and Ibrahim, F N (1993) *Coping with Vulnerability and Criticality.* Verlag für Entwicklungspolitik, Saarbrücken.

Böjo, J and Reddy, R C (2003) *Poverty Reduction Strategies and the Millennium Development Goal on Environmental Sustainability. Opportunities for Assignment.* World Bank, Washington, DC.

Booth, D (Hrsg.) (2003) *Fighting Poverty in Africa. Are PRSPs Making a Difference?* Overseas Development Institute, London.

Bosselmann, F P, Peterson, C A and McCarthy, C (1999) *Managing Tourism Growth: Issues and Applications.* Island Press, Washington, DC.

Brachinger, H W and Schubert, R (2003) 'Messung von Armut. Was ist eigentlich Armut? Kann man Armut überhaupt messen?' *Universitas Friburgensis* (22.09.): pp11–3.

Branch, G M, May, J, Roberts, B, Russell, E and Clark, B M (2002) 'Case studies on the socio-economic characteristics and lifestyles of subsistence and informal fishers in South Africa'. *South African Journal of Marine Science* **24**: pp439–62.

Brand, U and Görg, C (2002) ',„Nachhaltige Globalisierung"? Sustainable Development als Kitt des neoliberalen Scherbenhaufens'. In Görg, C and Brand, U (eds) *„Rio+10" und die Sackgassen nachhaltiger Entwicklung.* Westfälisches Dampfboot, Münster.

Braun, R (2001) 'Konzerne als Beschützer der Menschenrechte?' In Brühl, T, Debiel, T and Hamm, B (eds) *Die Privatisierung der Weltpolitik.* Reihe EINE Welt - Texte der Stiftung Entwicklung und Frieden (SEF). SEF, Bonn: pp257–80.

Brenkert, E, Malone, A and Moss, R (2001) *Water, Development, and Vulnerability.* University of Maryland. Joint Global Change Research Institute, Maryland, MD.

Bridges, E M and Oldeman, L R (1999) Global assessment of human-induced soil degradation. *Arid Soil Research and Rehabilitation* **13**(4): pp319–25.

Brooks, N and Adger, W N (2003) *Country Level Risk Measures of Climate-related Natural Disasters and Implications for Adaptation to Climate Change.* Tyndall Centre Working Paper 26. Tyndall Centre for Climate Change Research, Norwich.

Bruce, N, Perez-Padilla, R and Albalak, R (2002) *The Health Effects of Indoor Air Pollution Exposure in Developing Countries.* World Health Organization (WHO), Geneva.

Brühl, T (2003) *Nichtregierungsorganisationen als Akteure internationaler Umweltverhandlungen.* Studien der Hessischen Stiftung Friedens- und Konfliktforschung. Campus, Frankfurt/M.

Brühl, T (2004) 'Funktionsweise und Effektivität der GEF'. Expertise for the WBGU Report „World in Transition: Fighting Poverty through Environmental Policy". WBGU website, http://www.wbgu.de/wbgu_jg2004_ex03.pdf

Brunnengräber, A, Klein, A and Walk, H (eds) (2001) *NGOs als Legitimationsressource. Zivilgesellschaftliche Partizipationsformen im Globalisierungsprozess.* Leske & Budrich, Opladen.

Bruns, B, Mingat, A and Rakotomalala, R (2003) *Achieving Universal Primary Education by 2015. A Chance for Every Child.* World Bank, Washington, DC.

Bundesregierung (2002) *Perspektiven für Deutschland. Unsere Strategie für eine nachhaltige Entwicklung.* Bundesregierung, Berlin.

Bundesregierung (2004) *Perspektiven für Deutschland. Unsere Strategie für eine nachhaltige Entwicklung. Fortschrittsbericht 2004.* Bundesregierung, Berlin.

Buntzel, R (1995) 'Hüter der Welternährung – Gedenken zum 50. Geburtstag der FAO.' *epd-Entwicklungspolitik* **18/19**: pp30–9.

Busch, P-O (2004) The Secretariat to the United Nations Framework Convention on Climate Change. *Global Governance Working Paper.* The Global Governance Project, Amsterdam, Berlin, Potsdam and Oldenburg (forthcoming).

Cai, X and Rosegrant, M (2003) 'World water productivity: current situation and future options.' In Kijne, J W, Barker, R and Molden, D (eds) *Water Productivity in Agriculture: Limits and Opportunities for Improvement.* Cabi Publishing, Wallingford: pp163–78.

Campbell, A (1990) 'The greening of Australia'. *Our Planet* **2**(1): pp7–8.

Campbell-Lendrum, D H, Prüss-Üstün, A and Corvalan, C (2003) 'How much disease could climate change cause?' In McMichael, A J, Campbell-Lendrum, D H, Corvalan, C, Ebi, K, Githenko, A, Scheraga, J and Woodward, A (eds) *Climate Change and Health. Risks and Responses.* World Health Organization (WHO), Geneva.

CBD (Convention on Biological Diversity) (2000) *Ecosystem Approach. Decision V/6.* UN Document UNEP/CBD/COP/5/23. CBD Secretariat, Montreal.

CBD (Convention on Biological Diversity) (2002a) *Strategic Plan for the Convention on Biological Diversity. Decision VI/26.* UN Document UNEP/CBD/COP/6/20. CBD Secretariat, Montreal.

CBD (Convention on Biological Diversity) (2002b) *Access and Benefit-sharing as Related to Genetic Resources. Decision VI/24.* UN Document UNEP/CBD/COP/6/20. CBD Secretariat, Montreal.

CBD (Convention on Biological Diversity) (2003) *Report of the Global Environment Facility.* UN Document UNEP/CBD/COP/7/9. CBD Secretariat, Montreal.

CBD (Convention on Biological Diversity) (2004a) *Protected Areas (Articles 8 (a) to (e)). Decision VII/28.* UN Document UNEP/CBD/COP/7/21. CBD Secretariat, Montreal.

CBD (Convention on Biological Diversity) (2004b) *Biological Diversity and Tourism. Annex: Guidelines on Biodiversity and Tourism Development. Decision VII/14.* UN Document UNEP/CBD/COP/7/21. CBD Secretariat, Montreal.

Chambers, R (1989) 'Vulnerability, coping and policy'. *IDS Bulletin* **20**: pp1–7.

Chambers, R (1995) *Poverty and Livelihoods: Whose Reality Counts?* IDS Discussion Paper No. 247. Institute of Development Studies (IDS), Brighton.

Chambers, R and Conway, G (1992) *Sustainable Rural Livelihoods: Practical Concepts for the 21st Century.* IDS-Discussion Papers 296. Institute of Development Studies (IDS), Brighton.

Chasek, P S and Corell, E (2002) 'Addressing desertification at the international level. The institutional system.' In Reynolds, J F and Smith, D M S (eds) *Global Desertification: Do Humans Cause Deserts?* Dahlem University Press, Berlin: pp275–97.

CID (Center for International Development) (2003) 'WTO Public Symposium 2003: Sustainability Impact Assessment and Trade Agreements'. CID website, http://www.cid.harvard.edu/cidtrade/geneva/sia.html (viewed 25. October 2004).

Cling, J-P (2003) 'A participatory process towards establishing new relationships between stakeholders.' In Cling, J-P, Razafindrakoto, M and Roubaud, F (eds) *New International Poverty Reduction Strategies.* Routledge, London: pp151–79.

Cohen, J E (2003) 'Human population: the next half century'. *Science* **302**: pp1172–5.

Coleman, J (1990) *Foundations of Social Theory.* Harvard University Press, Cambridge, MA.

Coley, P D, Heller, M V, Aizpria, R, Araúz, B, Flores, N, Correa, M, Gupta, M, Solis, P N, Ortega-Barría, E, Romero, L I, Gómez, B, Ramos, M, Cubilla-Rios, L, Capson, T L and Kursar, T A (2003) 'Using ecological criteria to design plant collection strategies for drug discovery'. *Frontiers in Ecology and Environment* **1**(8): pp421–8.

Collier, P (1998) *Social Capital and Poverty.* Social Capital Initiative Working Paper No. 4. World Bank, Washington, DC.

Commission on Global Governance (1995) *Our Global Neighborhood.* Oxford University Press, Oxford.

Commission on Macroeconomics and Health (2001) *Macroeconomics and Health: Investing in Health for Economic Development.* World Health Organisation (WHO), Geneva.

Commission on the Social Dimension of Globalization (2004) *A Fair Globalisation. Creating Opportunities for All.* The World Commission on the Social Dimension of Globalization, Geneva.

CONAGESE (Conseil National pour la Gestion de l'Environnement) (2002) *Deuxieme Rapport National sur la Mise en Oeuvre de la Convention des Nations Unies sur la Lutte Contre la Desertification au Burkina Faso.* Conagese, Ouagadougou.

Conzelmann, T (2003) 'Auf der Suche nach einem Phänomen: Was bedeutet Good Governance in der europäischen Entwicklungspolitik'. *Nord-Süd aktuell* **XVII**(3): pp468–77.

CORDIO (1999) *Coral Reef Degradation in the Indian Ocean. Status Reports and Project Presentations.* SAREC Marine Science Program, Department of Zoology, Stockholm University, Stockholm.

Corell, R, Cramer, W and Schellnhuber, H J (2001) 'Methods and Models of Vulnerability Research. Analysis and Assessment. Potsdam Sustainability Symposium. 8th November 2001'. PIK website, http://www.pik-potsdam.de/~dagmar/corelletal.pdf (viewed 25. October 2004).

Corvalan, C F, Kjellström, T and Smith, K R (1999) 'Health, environment and sustainable development. Identifying links and indicators to promote action'. *Epidemiology* **10**(5): pp656–60.

Cosgrove, W and Rijsberman, F-R (2000) *World Water Vision: Making Water Everybody's Business.* World Water Council (WWC) and Earthscan, London.

Costa Rica (2001) 'Second National Report to the Convention on Biological Diversity'. Government of Costa Rica website, http://www.biodiv.org/doc/world/cr/cr-nr-02-es.pdf (viewed 25. Oktber 2004).

Costanza, R, d'Arge, R, Degroot, R Farber, S, Grasso, M, Hannon, B, Limburg, K, Naeem, S, Oneill, R V, Paruelo, J, Raskin, R G, Sutton, P and Vandenbelt, M (1997) 'The value of the world's ecosystem services and natural capital'. *Nature* **387**(6630): pp253–60.

Daba, S (2003) 'An investigation of the physical and socio-economic determinants of soil erosion in the Hararghe Highlands, eastern Ethiopia'. *Land Degradation & Development* **14**(1): pp69–81.

Dalton, R (2004a) 'Bioprospectors hunt for fair share of profits'. *Nature* **427**: 576.

Dalton, R (2004b) 'Bioprospects less than golden'. *Nature* **42**: pp598–600.

Dasgupta, M (1987) 'Selective discrimination against female children in rural Punjab, India'. *Population and Development Review* **13**(1): pp77–100.

Dasgupta, S, Laplante, B, Wang, H and Wheeler, D (2002) 'Confronting the Environmental Kuznets Curve'. *Journal of Economic Perspectives* **16**: pp147–68.

Data Snapshots on Microfinance (2004) 'The Virtual Library on Microcredit'. The Global Development Research Center website, http://www.gdrc.org/icm/data/d-snapshot.html (viewed 11. October 2004).

Deacon, R T and Murphy, P (1997) 'The structure of an environmental transaction: the debt for nature swap'. *Land Economics* **73**(1): pp1–24.

Dearden, P, Chettamart, S, Emphandu, D and Tanakanjana, N (1996) 'National parks and hill tribes in Northern Thailand: A case study of Doi Inthanon'. *Society & Natural Resources* **9**(2): pp125–41.

Debiel, T (2003) 'Staatsversagen, Gewaltstrukturen und blockierte Entwicklung: Haben Krisenländer noch eine Chance?' *Aus Politik und Zeitgeschichte* (B 13-14): pp15–23.

Dehaan, R L and Taylor, G R (2002) 'Field-derived spectra of salinized soils and vegetation as indicators of irrigation-induced soil salinization'. *Remote Sensing of Environment* **80**: pp406–17.

Deininger, K and Squire, L (1998) 'New ways of looking at old issues'. *Journal of Development Economics* **57**: 259–87.

Deininger, K and Okidi, J (2002) *Growth and Poverty Reduction in Uganda, 1992–2000: Panel Data Evidence.* Economic Policy Research Council, Kampala.

Deutscher Bundestag (2002) *Globalisierung der Weltwirtschaft.* Leske und Budrich, Opladen.

Devarajan, S, Miller, M J and Swanson, E V (2002) *Goals for Development. History, Prospects and Costs.* World Bank, Washington, DC.

Development Committee of the World Bank (2004a) *Financing Modalities Toward the Millennium Development Goals: Progress Note.* International Monetary Fund (IMF) and World Bank, Washington, DC.

Development Committee of the World Bank (2004b) *Global Monitoring Report 2004. Policies and Actions for Achieving the MDGs and Related Outcomes.* World Bank, Washington, DC.

DFG (Deutsche Forschungsgemeinschaft) (ed) (1993) *Naturkatastrophen und Katastrophenvorbeugung. Bericht zur IDNDR.* VCH Wiley, Weinheim.

DGB-Bildungswerk (ed) (2003) *Auslandsinvestitionen und Unternehmensverantwortung zwischen ökonomischer Liberalisierung und sozial-ökologischer Regulierung.* DGB-Bildungswerk, Düsseldorf.

Dichtl, E and Issing, O (eds) (1994) *Vahlens Großes Wirtschaftslexikon.* Vahlen, Munich.

Diekwisch, H (2002) 'Riskante Partnerschaften. Public-Private-Partnerships für Gesundheit gefährden die Unabhängigkeit der WHO'. *epd-Entwicklungspolitik* 4: pp36–8.

Diesendorf, M (2003) 'Sustainable development in China'. *China Connections* (January-March): pp18–9.

Dlugokencky, E J, Houweling, S, Bruhwiler, L, Masarie, K A, Lang, P M, Miller, J B and Tans, P P (2003) 'Atmospheric methane levels off: temporary pause or a new steady state?' *Geophysical Research Letters* **30**(19) 1992, doi: 10.1029/2003GL018126.

DNR (Deutscher Naturschutzring), Nabu (Naturschutzbund Deutschland) and BUND (2004) 'Stellungnahme zum Konsultationspapier der Bundesregierung für den Fortschrittsbericht 2004 zur nationalen Nachhaltigkeitsstrategie'. DNR and BUND website, http://www.nachhaltigkeits-check.de/cms/upload/pdf/DNR-NABU-BUND-Stellungnahme 040303.pdf (viewed 13. May 2004).

Dobson, A P, Bradshaw, A D and Baker, A J M (1997) 'Hopes for the future: restoration ecology and conservation biology'. *Science* **277**: pp515–22.

Dollar, D and Kraay, A (2001) *Growth Is Good for the Poor.* World Bank Policy Research Working Paper No. 2587. World Bank, Washington, DC.

Downing, T E (1993) 'Concepts of vulnerability to hunger and applications for monitoring famine in Africa.' In Bohle, H-G (ed) *Coping with Vulnerability and Criticality.* Freiburger Studien zur Geographischen Entwicklungsforschung, Saarbrücken and Fort Lauderdale: pp205–59.

Downing, T E (2002) 'Linking sustainable livelihoods and global climate change in vulnerable food systems'. *Die Erde* **133**: pp363–78.

Dregne, H E (2002) 'Land degradation in the drylands'. *Arid Land Research and Management* 16: pp99–132.

Dregne, H E and Chou, N-T (1992) *Global Desertification Dimensions and Costs.* Texas Technical University, Lubbock.

Drèze, J and Sen, A (1989) *Hunger and Public Action.* Clarendon Press, Oxford.

Eagles, P F J, McCool, S F and Haynes, C D A (2002) 'Sustainable Tourism in Protected Areas: Guidelines for Planning and Management'. IUCN website, http://www.iucn.org/themes/wcpa/pubs/pdfs/tourism_guidelines.pdf (viewed 25. October 2004).

Easterly, W and Kraay, A (1999) *Small States, Small Problems?* World Bank Working Paper Nr. 2139. World Bank, Washington, DC.

Eberlei, W (2002) 'Entwicklungspolitische Nicht-Regierungsorganisationen in Deutschland'. *Aus Politik und Zeitgeschichte. Das Parlament* (6+7): pp23–8.

Eberlei, W (2004) 'Umweltrelevante Aspekte in Poverty Reduction Strategies'. Expertise for the WBGU Report „World in Transition: Fighting Poverty through Environmental Policy". WBGU website, http://www.wbgu.de/wbgu_jg2004_ex04.pdf

Eberlei, W and Siebold, T (2002) *Armutsbekämpfung in Afrika: Neue Ansätze oder alte Konzepte?* INEF Report 64. INEF, Duisburg.

Eberlei, W and Henn, H (2003) *Parlamente in Subsahara Afrika: Akteure der Armutsbekämpfung?* Study on behalf of the GTZ. GTZ, Eschborn.

Eberlei, W and Führmann, B (2004) *Die Bekämpfung von Armut und Korruption.* Study on behalf of the GTZ. GTZ, Eschborn.

Edwards, M and Hulme, D (eds) (1996) *Beyond the Magic Bullet: NGO Performance and Accountability in the Post-Cold War World.* Kumarian Press, West Hartford, Conn.

EIR (Extractive Industries Review) (2003) *Striking a Better Balance.* EIR Final Report. Volume I. World Bank, Washington, DC.

Eisermann, D (2003) *Die Politik der nachhaltigen Entwicklung. Der Rio-Johannesburg-Prozess.* Informationszentrum Entwicklungspolitik, Bonn.

Ekbom, A and Bojö, J (1999) *Poverty and Environment: Evidence of Links and Integration into the Country Assistance Strategy Process.* World Bank, Washington, DC.

Elliott, L (2005) 'The United Nations' record on environmental governance: an assessment.' In Biermann, F and Bauer, S (eds) *A World Environment Organization: Solution or Threat for Effective International Environmental Governance.* Ashgate Publishing, Aldershot.

Ellis, J, Corfee-Morlot, J and Winkler, H (2004) *Taking Stock of Progress under the Clean Development Mechanism (CDM).* COM/ENV/EPOC/IEA/SLT(2004)4/FINAL International Energy Agency (IEA), Paris.

Ellis-Jones, J (1999) 'Poverty, land care, and sustainable livelihoods in hillside and mountain regions'. *Mountain Research and Development* **19**(3): pp179–90.

Engberg-Pedersen, P and Jorgensen, H C (1997) 'UNDP and global environmental problems: The need for capacity development at country level.' In Fridtjof Nansen Institute (ed) *Green Globe Yearbook of International Co-operation on Environment and Development.* Oxford University Press, Oxford: pp37–43.

Engelhard, K and Otto, K-H (2001) 'Weltweite Disparitäten als Entwicklungsproblem'. *Geographie und Schule* **23**(133): pp 3–11.

Enquete Commission „Globalisation of the World Economy" (ed) (2002) *Schlussbericht der Enquete-Kommission – Herausforderungen und Antworten.* Bundestags-Drucksache 14/9200. German Bundestag, Berlin.

Environment Department, The World Bank Division of Technology, Industry and Economics, United Nations Environment Programme Fiscal Affairs Department and International Monetary Fund (2002) *Financing for Sustainable*

Development – Revised Consultation Draft. World Bank, Washington, DC.

Environmental Defense, Friends of the Earth and IRN (International Rivers Network) (2003) *Gambling with People's Lives. What the World Bank's New „High-Risk/High-Reward" Strategy Means for the Poor and the Environment.* IRN, Friends of the Earth and World Bank, Berkeley and Washington, DC.

Epiney, A (2003) 'Sustainable use of freshwater resources'. *Zeitschrift für ausländisches öffentliches Recht und Völkerrecht* (ZaöRV): pp377–96.

Epiney, A and Scheyli, M (1998) *Strukturprinzipien des Umweltvölkerrechts.* Nomos, Baden-Baden.

Esty, D C and Ivanova, M (2001) *Making Environmental Efforts Work: The Case for a Global Environmental Organization.* Yale Center for Environmental Law and Policy, New Haven, Conn.

European Commission (2001) *Europäische Rahmenbedingungen für die soziale Verantwortung der Unternehmen. Grünbuch der Europäischen Kommission.* European Commission, Brussels.

European Commission (2003) *Jahresbericht 2003 über die Entwicklungspolitik der Europäischen Gemeinschaft und die Außenhilfe im Jahr 2002.* European Commission, Luxemburg.

Ezzati, M and Kammen, D M (2001) 'Indoor air pollution from biomass combustion as a risk factor for acute respiratory infections in Kenya: an exposure-response study'. *Lancet* 358: pp619–24.

Ezzati, M, Vander Hoorn, S, Rodgers, A, Lopez, A D, Mathers, C D, Murray C J L and Comparative Risk Assessment Collaborating Group (2003) 'Estimates of global and regional potential health gains from reducing multiple major risk factors'. *Lancet* 362(9380): pp271–80.

FAO (Food and Agriculture Organisation) (ed) (1996) *State of the World's Plant Genetic Resources.* FAO, Rome.

FAO (Food and Agriculture Organisation) (ed) (2001a) 'Global Forest Resources Assessment 2000. FAO Forestry Paper 140'. FAO website, http://www.fao.org/forestry/foris/webview/ (viewed 25. October 2004).

FAO (Food and Agriculture Organisation) (ed) (2001b) *The State of Food Insecurity in the World 2001. Food Insecurity: When People Live With Hunger and Fear Starvation.* FAO, Rome.

FAO (Food and Agriculture Organisation) (ed) (2002) 'World Food Summit – Five Years Later'. FAO website, www.fao.org/worldfoodsummit/ (viewed 25. October 2004).

FAO (Food and Agriculture Organisation) (ed) (2003a) *World Agriculture: Towards 2015/2030. A FAO Perspective.* Earthscan, London.

FAO (Food and Agriculture Organisation) (ed) (2003b) *The State of Food Insecurity in the World 2003. Monitoring Progress Towards the World Food Summit and Millennium Development Goals Year.* FAO, Rome.

FAO (Food and Agriculture Organisation) (ed) (2003c) *Anti-Hunger Programme. A Twin-Track Approach to Hunger Reduction: Priorities for National and International Action.* FAO, Rome.

FAO (Food and Agriculture Organisation) (ed) (2004) 'The State of Food and Agriculture 2003–2004. Agricultural Biotechnology: Meeting the Needs of the Poor?' FAO website, http://www.fao.org/docrep/006/Y5160E/y5160e15.htm#p2 (viewed 25. October 2004).

Feiring, B (2003) *Indigenous People and Poverty. The Case of Bolivia, Guatemala, Honduras and Nicaragua. Macro Study.* Minority Rights Group International, London.

Feitz, A J and Lundie, S (2002) 'Soil salinisation: A local life cycle assessment impact category'. *International Journal of Life Cycle Assessment* 7(4): pp244–9.

Feldbrügge, T and von Braun, J (2002) *Is the World Becoming a More Risky Place?* ZEF Discussion Paper No. 46. ZEF, Bonn.

Feldt, H and Martens, J (2003) 'Der Dialogprozess „Umwelt und Auslandsdirektinvestitionen" – eine Kurzbewertung.' In DBG-Bildungswerk (ed) *Auslandsinvestitionen und Unternehmensverantwortung zwischen ökonomischer Liberalisierung und sozial-ökologischer Regulierung.* DBG-Bildungswerk, Düsseldorf: pp33–7.

Fenger, J (1999) 'Urban air quality'. *Atmospheric Environment* 33: 4877–900.

Ferreira, F (1999) *Inequality and Economic Performance – A Brief Overview to Theories of Growth and Distribution.* World Bank, Washington, DC.

Filmer, D and Pritchett, L (1999) 'The effect of household wealth on educational attainment: Evidence from 35 countries'. *Population and Development Review* 25(1): pp85–120.

Fischer, G, Shah, M and van Velthuizen, H (2002) *Climate Change and Agricultural Vulnerability.* IIASA, Laxenburg.

Fisher, J (1998) *Nongovernments: NGOs and the Political Development in the Third World.* Kumarian Press, West Hartford, CT.

Fogel, R W (1990) *The Conquest of High Mortality and Hunger in Europe and America: Timing and Mechanisms.* National Bureau of Economic Research (NBER) Working Paper No. H0016. NBER, Cambridge, MA.

French, H F (1995) *Partnerships for the Planet: An Environmental Agenda for the United Nations.* Worldwatch Paper 107. Washington, DC: Worldwatch Institute.

Fues, T (1998) *Das Indikatorenprogramm der UN-Kommission für nachhaltige Entwicklung: Stellenwert für den internationalen Rio-Prozeß und Folgerungen für das Konzept von Global Governance.* Europäische Hochschulschriften: Reihe 31 Politikwissenschaft. Peter Lang, Frankfurt/M, Berlin, Bern.

Fues, T and Hamm, B I (eds) (2001) *Die Weltkonferenzen der 90er Jahre: Baustellen für Global Governance.* Dietz, Bonn.

Fues, T and Messner, D (2003) 'Die Beziehungen zwischen Nord und Süd im Schatten der Irak-Krise: Perspektiven kooperativer Weltpolitik nach der Johannesburg-Konferenz.' In Hauswedell, C, Weller, C, Ratsch, U, Mutz, R and Schoch, B (eds) *Friedensgutachten 2003.* LIT-Verlag, Münster: pp51–60.

Gallagher, K S (2003) *Development of Cleaner Vehicle Technology? Foreign Direct Investment and Technology Transfer from the United States to China.* Paper presented at United Society for Ecological Economics 2nd Biennial Meeting. Saratoga Springs, May 2003.

Garenne, M (1996) 'Mortality in sub-saharan Africa: trends and prospects.' In Lutz, W (ed) *The Future Population of the World. What Can We Assume Today?* Earthscan Publications, London: pp149–69.

Garenne, M, Sauerborn, R, Nougtara, A, Borchert, M and Benzler, J (1997) 'Direct and indirect estimates of maternal mortality in a rural area of Burkina Faso (Nouna)'. *Studies in Family Planning* 28(1): pp54–61.

Garrity, D P, Amoroso, V B, Koffa, S, Catacutan, D, Buenavista, G, Fay, P and Dar, W (2002) 'Landcare on the poverty-protection interface in an Asian watershed'. *Conservation Ecology* 6(1): p12.

GEF (Global Environment Facility) (1996) *Incremental Costs.* GEF/C.7/Inf.5 of 29. February 1996. GEF Secretariat, Washington, DC.

GEF (Global Environment Facility) (2000) *GEF Contributions to Agenda 21. The First Decade.* GEF Secretariat, Washington, DC.

GEF (Global Environment Facility) (2002a) *Focusing on the Global Environment. The First Decade of the GEF Second Overall Performance Study (OPS2).* GEF Secretariat, Washington, DC.

GEF (Global Environment Facility) (2002b) *Summary of Negotiations on the Third Replenishment of the GEF Trust Fund.* GEF Secretariat, Washington, DC.

GEF (Global Environment Facility) (2002c) *The Challenge of Sustainability.* GEF Secretariat, Washington, DC.

GEF (Global Environment Facility) (2003a) *GEF Annual Report 2003.* GEF Secretariat, Washington, DC.

GEF (Global Environment Facility) (2003b) *Operational Program on Sustainable Land Management (OP#15).* GEF Secretariat, Washington, DC.

GEF (Global Environment Facility) (2004a) *GEF Assistance to Address Adaptation. GEF/C.23/Inf.8/Rev.1.* GEF Secretariat, Washington, DC.

GEF (Global Environment Facility) (2004b) *Status Report on the Least Developed Countries Trust Fund for Climate Change. GEF/C.23/10/Rev.1.* GEF Secretariat, Washington, DC.

GEF (Global Environment Facility) (2004c) GEF website, http://www.gefweb.org (viewed 02. November 2004).

GEF (Global Environment Facility) and UNDP (United Nations Development Programme) (2000) *Capacity Development Initiative. Assessment of Capacity Development in the GEF Portfolio. GEF-UNDP Strategic Partnership.* GEF Secretariat, Washington, DC.

George, C and Kirkpatrick, C (2003) *Sustainability Impact Assessment of World Trade Negotiations: Current Practice and Lessons for Further Development.* Impact Assessment Research Centre (IDPM) Working Paper No. 2. IDPM, University of Manchester, Manchester.

Ghassemi, F, Jakeman, A J and Nix, H A (1991) 'Human induced salinisation and the use of quantitative methods'. *Environment International* 17: pp581–94.

Gillwald, K (1996) 'Umweltverträgliche Lebensstile – Chancen und Hindernisse.' In Altner, G, Mettler-von Meibom, B, Simonis, U E and von Weizsäcker, E U (eds) *Jahrbuch Ökologie 1997.* Beck, Munich: pp83–93.

GKKE (Gemeinsame Konferenz Kirche und Entwicklung) (2004) *Halbierung der extremen Armut. Der Beitrag des Aktionsprogramms 2015 der Bundesregierung zu den Millenniumszielen.* GKKE, Berlin.

Glaesel, H (2000) 'State and local resistance to the expansion of two environmentally harmful marine fishing techniques in Kenya'. *Society and Natural Resources* 13: pp321–38.

Glagow, M (1992) 'Die Nicht-Regierungsorganisationen in der internationalen Entwicklungszusammenarbeit.' In Nohlen, D and Nuscheler, F (eds) *Handbuch der Dritten Welt. Band 1.* Dietz, Bonn: pp314.

Gleick, P H (2000) *The World's Water 2000–2001. The Biennial Report on Freshwater Resources.* Island Press, Washington, DC.

Glewwe, P and van der Gaag, J (1988) *Confronting Poverty in Developing Countries. Definitions, Information, and Policies.* Living Standards Measurement Study Working Paper 48. World Bank, Washington, DC.

GoBF (Government of Burkina Faso) (2003) *Poverty Reduction Strategy Paper.* GoBF, Ouagadougou.

Göthel, D (2002) *Die Vereinten Nationen. Eine Innensicht.* Auswärtiges Amt, Berlin.

Goldman, L and Tran, N (2002) *Toxics and Poverty: The Impact of Toxic Substances on the Poor in Developing Countries.* World Bank, Washington, DC.

Gorham, R (2002) *Air Pollution from Ground Transportation. An Assessment of Causes, Strategies and Tactics, and Proposed Actions for the International Community.* United Nations (UN), New York.

GRAIN (2004) GRAIN website, http://www.grain.org (viewed 25. October 2004).

Gray, L and Kevane, M (2001) 'Evolving tenure rights and agricultural intensification in Southwestern Burkina Faso'. *World Development* 29(4): pp573–87.

Green, D and Priyadarshi, S (2001) *Proposal for a 'Development Box' in the WTO Agreement on Agriculture.* Catholic Agency for Overseas Development (CAFOD), London.

Grepperud, S (1997) 'Poverty, land degradation and climatic uncertainty'. *Oxford Economic Papers – New Series* 49(4): pp586–608.

Griffin, K, Azizur, R K and Ickowitz, A (2002) 'Poverty and the distribution of land'. *Journal of Agrarian Change* 2(3): pp279–330.

Grootaert, C (1998) *Social Capital - The Missing Link. Social Capital Initiative.* Working Paper No. 3. World Bank, Washington, DC.

Grootaert, C (2001) *Does Social Capital Help the Poor? A Synthesis of Findings From the Local Level Institutions Studies in Bolivia, Burkina Faso and Indonesia.* Local Level Institutions Working Paper No. 10. World Bank, Washington, DC.

Grootaert, C and van Bastelaer, T (2001) *Understanding and Measuring Social Capital: A Synthesis of Findings and Recommendations From the Social Capital Inititiave.* Social Capital Initiative Working Paper No. 24. World Bank, Washington, DC.

Grossman, G M and Krueger, A B (1991) *Environmental Impact of the North American Free Trade Agreement.* NBER Working Paper 3914. National Bureau of Economic Research (NBER), Cambridge, MA.

Group of Like-Minded Megadiverse Countries (2003) 'Cancun Declaration of Like-minded Megadiverse Countries'. Group of Like-Minded Megadiverse Countries website, http://www.megadiverse.org/armado_ingles/PDF/three/three1.pdf (viewed 25. October 2004).

Gsänger, H (2001) 'Sozialkapital als Baustein für Afrikas Entwicklung'. *Entwicklung und Zusammenarbeit* (9): pp261–4.

GTZ (Gesellschaft für Technische Zusammenarbeit) (ed) (1994) *Ursachen der Bodendegradation und Ansätze für eine Förderung der nachhaltigen Bodennutzung im Rahmen der Entwicklungszusammenarbeit.* GTZ, Eschborn.

Gueorguieva, A and Bolt, K (2003) *A Critical Review of the Literature on Structural Adjustment and the Environment.* Environmental Economic Series Paper No. 90. World Bank, Washington, DC.

Gurung, C P and Coursey, M D (1994) *Nepal: Pioneering Sustainable Tourism. The Annapurna Conservation Area Project.* University of Reading, Reading, UK.

Hachicha, M, Cheverry, C and Mhiri, A (2000) 'The impact of long-term irrigation on changes of ground water level and soil salinity in northern Tunisia'. *Arid Soil Research and Rehabilitation* 14(2): pp175–82.

Haddad, L, Pena, C, Nishida, C, Quisumbing, A and Slack, A (1996) *Food Security and Nutrition Implications of Intra-household Bias: a Review of the Literature.* FCND Discussion Paper No. 19. Institute of Political Science and International Relations (ISPRI), Washington, DC.

Haites, E (2004) *Estimating the Market Potential for the Clean Development Mechanism: Review of Models and Lessons Learned.* World Bank, International Energy Agency (IEA), International Emissions Trading Association (IETA), Washington, DC.

Hamm, B (ed) (2002) *Public-Private Partnership und der Global Compact der Vereinten Nationen.* Report Nr. 62. Institut für Entwicklung und Frieden (INEF), Duisburg.

Hammer, K (1998) *Agrarbiodiversität und pflanzengenetische Ressourcen.* Schriften zu genetischen Ressourcen. Band 10. Zentralstelle für Agrardokumentation und -information (ZADI), Bonn.

Hanks, J (2001) 'Conservation strategies for Africa's large mammals'. *Reproduction Fertility and Development* 13(7-8): pp459–68.

Hansen, S (1989) 'Debt-for-nature swaps – overview and discussion'. *Ecological Economics* 1: pp77–93.

Harpham, T, Burton, S and Blue, I (2001) 'Healthy city projects in developing countries: the first evaluation'. *Health Promotion International* 16(2): pp111–25.

Hauff, V (2002) 'Erfolge, Defizite, Perspektiven – ein Resümee von Johannesburg und Perspektiven für die Umsetzung der Nachhaltigkeitsstrategie in Deutschland. Speech at a Symposium of the Friedrich Ebert Foundation and the Gesellschaft für Nachhaltigkeit, neue Umweltökonomie und nachhaltigkeitsgerechtes Umweltrecht e.V on 24.10.02'. Rat für Nachhaltige Entwicklung (RNE) website, www.nachhaltigkeitsrat.de/service/download/pdf/Vortrag Hauff_24-10-02.pdf (viewed 25. October 2004).

Heidbrink, K and Paulus, S (2000) *Nachhaltigkeitsstrategien im Dickicht nationaler Planungsprozesse.* GTZ, Eschborn.

Hemmer, H J (2002) *Wirtschaftsprobleme der Entwicklungsländer.* 3rd edition. Vahlen, Munich.

Henne, G (1998) *Genetische Vielfalt als Ressource. Die Regelung ihrer Nutzung.* Nomos, Baden-Baden.

Henne, G, Liebig, K, Drews, A and Plän, T (2003) 'Access and Benefit-Sharing (ABS) An Instrument for Poverty Alleviation. Proposals for an International ABS Regime'. German Development Institute website, http://www.biodiv.org/doc/meetings/abs/abswg-02/information/abswg-02-gdi-abs-en.pdf (viewed 25. October 2004).

Henry, R (1996) 'Adapting United Nations agencies for Agenda 21: programme coordination and organizational reform'. *Environmental Politics* 5(1): pp1–24.

Hertel, T and Martin, W (2000) 'Liberalising agriculture and manufactures in a millennium round: implications for developing countries'. *World Economy* 23(4): pp455–69.

Heydenreich, C (2003) 'Der Arbeitskreis „OECD-Leitsätze für Multinationale Unternehmen" im Bundeswirtschaftsministerium.' In DBG-Bildungswerk (ed) *Auslandsinvestitionen und Unternehmensverantwortung zwischen ökonomischer Liberalisierung und sozial-ökologischer Regulierung.* DBG-Bildungswerk, Düsseldorf: pp40–2.

Hewitt, K (1997) *Regions of Risk. A Geographical Introduction to Disasters.* Addison Wesley Longman, Essex.

Hinrichsen, D (1997) *Winning the Food Race.* Population Reports. Series M, Number 17. John Hopkins School of Public Health, Population Information Program, Baltimore.

Ho, C M (2003) 'Disclosure of Origin and Prior Informed Consent for Applications of Intellectual Property Rights Based on Genetic Resources: A Technical Study of Implementation Issues. UN Document UNEP/CBD/WG-ABS/2/Inf/2'. CBD Secretariat website, http://www.biodiv.org/doc/meetings/abs/abswg-02/information/abswg-02-inf-02-en.pdf (viewed 25. October 2004).

Hodgson, A, Smith, T, Gagneux, S, Adjuik, M, Pluschke, G, Kumasenu Mensah, N, Binka, F and Genton, B (2001) 'Risk factors for meningococcal meningitis in Northern Ghana'. *Transaction of the Royal Society for Tropical Medicine* 95(5): pp477–80.

Hoekman, B, Ng, F and Olarreaga, M (2002) *Reducing Agriculture Tariffs Versus Domestic Support: What's More Important for Developing Countries?* CEPR Discussion Paper No. 3576. Centre for Economic Policy Research (CEPR), Washington, DC.

Hoozemans, F M J, Marchand, M and Pennekamp, H A (1993) *A Global Vulnerability Analysis: Vulnerability Assessment for Population, Coastal Wetlands and Rice Production on a Global Scale.* Delft Hydraulics.

Holtz, U (2003) *Poverty Reduction Strategy Papers and Country Strategy Papers and Their Relationship to the Combat Against Desertification. The Role of Parliaments.* Paper Prepared for the Fifth Parliamentary Round Table During the Sixth Session of the Conference of the Parties to the UNCCD, September 2003.

Horta, K (1998) 'Global Environment Facility'. *Foreign Policy in Focus* 39(3): pp1–4.

Huang, J K, Pray, C and Rozelle, S (2002) 'Enhancing the crops to feed the poor'. *Nature* 418(6898): pp678–84.

Hüfner, K (2000) 'Agenda für Entwicklung.' In Volger, H (ed) *Lexikon der Vereinten Nationen.* Oldenbourg Verlag, Munich, Vienna.

Hulme, D and Shepherd, A (2003) 'Conceptualizing chronic poverty'. *World Development* 31(3): pp403–23.

Hurni, H, Messerli, P and Pfister, F (2004) 'Forschungspartnerschaften mit dem Süden'. *Zeitschrift Entwicklungspolitik* 18/19: pp54–6.

Ianchovichina, E, Mattoo, A and Olarreaga, M (2001) *Unrestricted Market Access for Sub-Saharan Africa: How Much is it Worth and Who Pays?* World Bank Development Research Group, Washington, DC.

Ibarra, A A, Reid, C and Thorpe, A (2000) 'Neo-liberalism and its impact on overfishing and overcapitalisation in the marine fisheries of Chile, Mexico and Peru'. *Food Policy* 25: pp599–622.

ICSU (International Council for Science), TWAS (Third World Academy of Science) and ISTS (Initiative on Science and Technology for Sustainability) (eds) (2002) *Science and Technology for Sustainable Development.* Series for Sustainable Development 9. ICSU, Paris.

IEA (International Energy Agency) (2002) *World Energy Outlook 2002.* IEA, Paris.

IEA (International Energy Agency) (2003) *World Energy Investment Outlook 2003.* IEA, Paris.

IFAD (International Fund for Agricultural Development) (2001) *Rural Poverty Report 2001. The Challenge of Ending Rural Poverty.* Oxford University Press, Oxford.

IFF (International Finance Facility) (2004) *International Finance Facility Proposals.* IFF, London.

IFPRI (International Food Policy Research Institute) (2003) *How Much Does it Hurt? The Impact of Agricultural Trade Politics on Developing Countries.* IFPRI, Washington, DC.

IFRC (International Federation of Red Cross and Red Crescent Societies) (2002) *World Disasters Report 2002.* IFRC, Geneva.

IISD (International Institute for Sustainable Development) (2004) 'Summary of the Eighth Special Session of the United Nations Environment Programme's Governing Council/Global Ministerial Environment Forum: 29–21 March 2004'. *Earth Negotiations Bulletin* 16(16): p15.

ILO (International Labour Organization) (ed) (1998) *Overview of Global Developments and Office Activities Concerning Codes of Conduct, Social Labelling and Other Private*

Sector Initiatives Addressing Labour Issues. GB.273/WP/SDL/1. ILO, Geneva.

ILO (International Labour Organization) (ed) (2001) *Women, Gender and Work.* ILO, Geneva.

Imber, M F (1996) 'The environment and the United Nations'. In Vogler, J and Imber, M F (eds) *The Environment and International Relations.* Earthscan, London: pp138–54.

IMF (International Monetary Fund) (2001) 'Poverty Reduction Strategy Papers (PRSP) Honduras'. IMF website, http://www.imf.org/External/NP/prsp/2001/hnd/01/ (viewed 21. October 2004).

IMF (International Monetary Fund) (2003) 'The IMF at a Glance – A Factsheet, September 2003'. IMF website, http://www.imf.org/external/np/exr/facts/glance.htm (viewed 24. March 2004).

IMF (International Monetary Fund) and World Bank (2002) *Market Access for Developing Countries. Selected Issues.* World Bank, Washington, DC.

IMF (International Monetary Fund) and World Bank (2004) *Heavily Indebted Poor Countries (HIPC) Initiative – Statistical Update.* World Bank, Washington, DC.

IPCC (Intergovernmental Panel on Climate Change) (ed) (2001a) *Climate Change 2001: The Scientific Basis. Contribution of Working Group I to the Third Assessment Report of the IPCC.* Cambridge University Press, Cambridge, New York.

IPCC (Intergovernmental Panel on Climate Change) (ed) (2001b) *Climate Change 2001: Impacts, Adaptation, and Vulnerability. Contribution of Working Group II to the Third Assessment Report of the IPCC.* Cambridge University Press, Cambridge, New York.

IPCC (Intergovernmental Panel on Climate Change) (ed) (2001c) *Climate Change 2001: Mitigation: Contribution of Working Group III to the Third Assessment Report of the IPCC.* Cambridge University Press, Cambridge, New York.

IRN (International Rivers Network) (2004) *The World Bank's Safeguard Policies Under Pressure. A Critique of the World Bank's New Middle Income Country Strategy.* IRN, Berkeley.

Isham, J and Kähkönen, S (1999) *What Determines the Effectiveness of Community-Based Water Projects? Evidence from Central Java, Indonesia on Demand Responsiveness.* Social Capital Initiative Working Paper No. 14. World Bank, Washington, DC.

Islam, M S (2003) 'Perspectives of the coastal and marine fisheries of the Bay of Bengal, Bangladesh'. *Ocean and Coastal Management* **46**: pp763–96.

IUCN (The World Conservation Union) (2004) *Options and Process for the Development of an International Regime on Access and Benefit-Sharing.* IUCN Law Centre, Bonn.

IWF (Internationaler Währungsfonds) (2000) 'Der IWF und Umweltfragen'. IWF website, http://www.imf.org/external/np/exr/ib/2000/deu/041400g.htm (viewed 19. March 2004).

James, A N, Gaston, K J and Balmford, A (1999) 'Balancing the Earth's accounts'. *Nature* **401**: pp323–4.

James, A N, Gaston, K J and Balmford, A (2001) 'Can we afford to conserve biodiversity?' *BioScience* **51**(1): pp43–52.

Jänicke, M (1998) 'Dematerialisierung als Prognose und Programm – die Hypothese vom Ende der „era of materials". FFU-report 98-4'. University Berlin website, http://www.fu-berlin.de/ffu/download/FFURep98_4.pdf (viewed 21. April 2004).

Jenkins, M, Scherr, S J and Inbar, M (2004) 'Markets for biodiversity services. Potential roles and challenges'. *Environment* **46**: pp32–42.

Jerve, A M (2002) *What Visions for Broad-based Growth and Sustainable Development in Africa? Exploring the Poverty-Environment Linkage in Five PRSPs.* Paper presented at the National Conference on Sustainable Development „Poverty and the Environment". Oslo, 6.–7. March 2002. Chr. Michelsen Institute, Oslo.

Jodha, N (1991) *Rural Common Property Resources: A Growing Crisis.* International Institute for Environment and Development (IIED) Sustainable Agriculture Programme Series No 24. IIED, London.

Johnson, N, Revenga, C and Echeverria, J (2001) 'Managing Water for People and Nature'. *Science* **292**(5519): pp1071–2.

Kaiser, R, Henderson, A K, Daley, W R, Naughton, M, Khan, M H, Rahmam, M, Kiezak, S and Rubin, C H (2001) 'Blood lead levels of primary school children in Dhaka, Bangladesh'. *Environmental Health Perspectives* **109**(6): pp563–6.

Kanbur, R (2002) *Conceptual Changes in Poverty and Inequality: One Development Economist's Perspective.* Cornell University, Cornell

Kappel, R (1999) 'Die entwicklungspolitischen Fehlleistungen von Lomé'. *Journal für Entwicklungspolitik* **15**(3): pp247–56.

Kappel, R (2003) *Kirschen und Kerne - Mehr Wohlstand für die Entwicklungsländer durch die Liberalisierung des Weltmarktes?* Paper for the SEF Workshop „Entwicklung: Mythos oder realistisches Politikziel?" on 24/25th January in Bremen. Mimeo.

Kasperson, R E and Kasperson, J E X (2001a) *International Workshop on Vulnerability and Global Environmental Change, October 2001. A Workshop Summary.* Stockholm Environment Institute (SEI), Stockholm.

Kasperson, R E and Kasperson, J E X (2001b) *Climate Change, Vulnerability and Social Justice.* Stockholm: Stockholm Environment Institute (SEI), Stockholm.

Kasperson, R E, Kasperson, J E X and Turner, B L (1995) *Regions at Risk: Comparisons of Threatened Environments.* United Nations University Press, Tokyo.

Kates, R W, Clark, W C, Corell, R, Hall, J M, Jaeger, C C, Lowe, I, McCarthy, J J, Schellnhuber, H-J, Bolin, B, Dickson, N M, Faucheaux, S, Gallopin, G C, Gruebler, A, Huntley, B, Jäger, J, Jodha, N S, Kasperson, R E, Mabogunje, A, Matson, P, Mooney, H, Moore III, B, O'Riordan, T and Svedin, U (2000) *Sustainability Science.* Belfer Center, Washington, DC.

Kaul, I, Grunberg, I and Stern, M A (1999) *Globale öffentliche Güter. Internationale Zusammenarbeit im 21. Jahrhundert.* Oxford University Press, Oxford, New York.

Kaul, I, Conceição, P, le Goulven, K and Medoza, R U (2003) *Die Bereitstellung globaler öffentlicher Güter. Globalisierung gestalten.* Oxford University Press, Oxford, New York.

Kelley, A C and Schmidt, R M (2001) 'Economic and demographic change: a synthesis of models, findings, and perspectives.' In Birdsall, N, Kelley, A C and Sinding, S (eds) *Population Matters: Demographic Change, Economic Growth, and Poverty in the Developing World.* Oxford University Press, Oxford, New York: pp67–105.

Kerkow, U, Martens, J and Schmitt, T (2003) *Die Grenzen der Freiwilligkeit. Handlungsmöglichkeiten und Erfahrungen von NGOs und Gewerkschaften bei der Anwendung freiwilliger Selbstverpflichtungen der Weltwirtschaft.* WEED, Bonn, Berlin.

Khan, M H (2002) *When is Economic Growth Pro-Poor? Experiences in Malaysia and Pakistan.* IMF Working Paper 02/85. International Monetary Fund (IMF), Washington, DC.

Khor, M (no year) 'Land Degradation Causes $10 Billion Loss to South Asia Annually'. Third World Network (TWN) website, http://www.twnside.org.sg/title/land-ch.htm (viewed 25. October 2004).

Klasen, S (2003) *In Search of the Holy Grail: How to Achieve Pro-Poor Growth?* IAI Discussion Paper No. 96. University Göttingen, Göttingen.

Klingebiel, S (1993) 'Globale Umweltfazilität. NGOs und Regierungen der 3. Welt wollen Reform'. *epd-Entwicklungspolitik* **9/10** (May): pp22–4.

Klingebiel, S (2000) 'Entwicklungsprogramm der Vereinten Nationen.' In Volger, H (ed) *Lexikon der Vereinten Nationen.* Oldenbourg Verlag, Munich: pp544–50.

Knack, S (1999) *Social Capital, Growth and Poverty: A Survey of Cross-Country Evidence.* Social Capital Initiative Working Paper No. 7. World Bank, Washington, DC.

Kößler, R and Melber, H (1993) *Chancen internationaler Zivilgesellschaft.* Suhrkamp, Frankfurt/M.

Köpke, R (2000) 'Verhaltenskodizes transnationaler Unternehmen.' In Enquete Commision „Globalisation of the World Economy" (ed) *Schlussbericht der Enquete-Kommission – Herausforderungen und Antworten.* Bundestags-Drucksache 14/9200. Deutscher Bundestag, Berlin.

Kolk, A (1996) *The World Bank and its Role in International Environmental Politics.* University Amsterdam, Amsterdam.

Krause, G and Sauerborn, R (2000) 'Comprehensive community-effectiveness of health care. A study of malaria treatment in children and adults in rural Burkina Faso'. *Annals of Tropical Paediatrics* **20**(4): pp273–82.

Krishna, A and Uphoff, N (1999) *Mapping and Measuring Social Capital: A Conceptual and Empirical Study of Collective Action for Conserving and Developing Watersheds in Rajasthan, India.* Social Capital Initiative Working Paper No. 13. World Bank, Washington, DC.

Krishna, A and Schrader, E (2000) *Cross-Cultural Measures of Social Capital: A Tool and Results from India and Panama.* Social Capital Initiative Working Paper No. 21. World Bank, Washington, DC.

Krüger, O and Graßl, H (2002) 'The indirect aerosol effect over Europe'. *Geophysical Research Letters* **29**(19), 1925: doi:10.1029/2001GL014081.

Krüger, O and Graßl, H (2004) 'Albedo reduction by absorbing aerosols over China'. *Geophysical Research Letters* **31**(2), L02108: doi:10.1029/2003GL019111.

Kulessa, M E (1998a) 'The economic and social effects of structural adjustment policy – theory and practice'. *Economics* **58**: pp47–71.

Kulessa, M E (1998b) 'World Trade Organization.' In Altmann, J and Kulessa, M E (eds) *Internationale Wirtschaftsorganisationen.* Lucius & Lucius UTB, Stuttgart: pp283–95.

Kulessa, M E (1999) 'Zur wirtschaftspolitischen Funktion des Staates im Strukturanpassungskonzept von Weltbank und IWF.' In Huhnholz, J H and Zeiler, I (eds) *Staat und Entwicklung.* Tübingen.

Kulessa, M E and Schwaab, J A (1998) 'Liberalisierung grenzüberschreitender Investitionen und Umweltschutz'. *Zeitschrift für Umweltpolitik & Umweltrecht* **1**: pp33–59.

Kulessa, M E and Ringel, M (2003) 'Kompensationen als innovatives Instrument globaler Umweltschutzpolitik'. *Zeitschrift für Umweltpolitik & Umweltrecht* **3**: pp263–85.

Kulessa, M E and Oschinski, M (2004) *Handelsliberalisierung und Armut in Entwicklungsländern – Zusammenfassung empirischer Studien und handelspolitische Schlussfolgerungen.* WWZ Research Report. Wirtschaftswissenschaftliches Zentrum (WWZ), Basel.

Labrador, D (2003) 'Refining green gold'. *Scientific American* (December): pp38–9.

Lal, R (1995) 'Erosion-crop productivity relationships for soils of Africa'. *Soil Science Society of America Journal* **59**: pp661–7.

Lal, R (2000) 'Soil management in the developing countries'. *Soil Science* **165**(1): pp57–72.

Lal, R, Blum, W H, Valentine, C and Stewart, B A (1997) *Methods for the Assessment of Soil Degradation.* CRC Press, Boca Raton.

Lambin, E F, Turner, B L, Geist, H J, Agbola, S B, Angelsen, A, Bruce, J W, Coomes, O T, Dirzo, R, Fischer, G, Folke, C, George, P S, Homewood, K, Imbernon, J, Leemans, R, Li, X B, Moran, E F, Mortimore, M, Ramakrishnan, P S, Richards, J F, Skanes, H, Steffen, W, Stone, G D, Svedin, U, Veldkamp, T A, Vogel, C and Xu, J C (2001) 'The causes of land-use and land-cover change: moving beyond the myths'. *Global Environmental Change Human and Policy Dimensions* **11**(4): pp261–9.

Laurance, W F, Oliveira, A A, Laurance, S G, Conditi, R, Nascimento, H E M, Sanchez-Torini, A C, Lovejoy, T E, Andrade, A, D'Angelo, S A, Ribeiro, J E and Dick, C W (2004) 'Pervasive alteration of tree communities in undisturbed Amazonian forests'. *Nature* **428**(11.03.): pp171–5.

Leisinger, K M (1999) *Die sechste Milliarde: Weltbevölkerung und nachhaltige Entwicklung.* Beck, Munich.

Lenton, R and Wright, A (2004) 'UN Millenium Project. Interim Report of Task Force 7 on Water and Sanitation'. UN Millennium Project Task Force 7 website, http://www.unmillenniumproject.org/html/tforce_7.shtm (viewed 25. October 2004).

Le Pestre, P G (1995) 'Environmental learning at the World Bank'. In Bartlett, R V, Kurian, P A and Malik, M (eds) *International Organizations and Environmental Problems.* Greenwood Press, Westport, CT: pp83–102.

Lindbeck, A and Snower, D J (2001) 'Insiders versus outsiders'. *Journal of Economic Perspectives* **1**: pp165–88.

Litwin, C (1998) *Trade and Income Distribution in Developing Countries.* Working Paper Series in Economics Nr. 9. University Göteborg, Göteborg.

Lonergan, S, Gustavson, K and Carter, B (2000) 'The Index of Human Insecurity. AVISO 6 (January)'. Carlton University Ottawa website, http://www.gechs.org/aviso/avisoenglish/six_lg.shtml (viewed 25. October 2004).

Lowell, B L and Findley, A (2001) *Migration Of Highly Skilled Persons From Developing Countries: Impact And Policy Responses. Synthesis Report.* International Migration Papers 44. International Labour Office, International Migration Branch, Geneva.

Lucas, R, Wheeler, D and Hettige, H (1992) 'Economic Development, Environmental Regulations and the International Migration of Toxic Industrial Pollution: 1960–1988.' In Low, P (ed) *International Trade and the Environment.* Discussion Paper No. 159. World Bank, Washington, DC.

Lutz W (ed) (1996) *The Future Population of the World. What can we Assume Today.* Revised Edition. International Institute of Applied Systems Analysis (IIASA), Laxenburg.

Lutz, W, Sanderson, W and Scherbov, S (2001) 'The end of world population growth'. *Nature* **412**: pp543–5.

Lvovsky, K, Hughes, G, Maddison, D, Ostro, B and Pearce, D (2000) *Environmental Costs of Fossil Fuels. A Rapid Assessment Method with Application to Six Cities.* Pollution Management Series Paper 78. World Bank, Washington, DC.

MA (Millennium Ecosystem Assessment Board) (ed) (2003) *Ecosystems and Human Well-being: A Framework for Assessment.* Island Press, Washington, DC.

Mainhardt-Gibbs, H (2003) *The World Bank Extractive Industries Review: the Role of Structural Reform Programs towards Sustainable Development Outcomes*. World Bank, Washington, DC.

Mantel, S and van Engelen, V W P (1997) *The Impact of Land Degradation on Food Productivity. Case studies of Uruguay, Argentina and Kenya*. Report 97/01. International Soil and Reference Information Centre (ISRIC), Wageningen.

Marr, S (2000) 'The southern bluefin tuna cases: the precautionary approach and conservation and management of fish resources'. *EJIL* **11**(4): pp815–31.

Masood, E (2003) 'GM crops: A continent divided'. *Nature* **426**(6964): pp224–6.

McGuigan, C, Reynolds, R and Wiedmer, D (2002) *Poverty and Climate Change: Assessing Impacts in Developing Countries and the Initiatives of the International Community*. Overseas Development Institutes (ODI), London.

McKeown, T (1989) 'The road to health'. *World Health Forum* **10**(3-4): pp408–16.

McNeely, J A (2003) 'Biodiversity in arid regions: values and perceptions'. *Journal of Arid Environments* **54**: pp61–70.

Meltzer, A.H (2000) *Report of the International Financial Institutions Advisory Commission*. World Bank, Washington, DC.

Menezes, A M B, Victora, C G, Barros, F C, Albernay, E, Menesey F S, Jannke, H A, Alves, C and Rocha, C (1996) 'Mortalidade infantile em duas coortes de base populacional no Sul do Brasil: tendências e deferenciais'. *Cad. Saude Publica* **12**(Suppl. 1): pp33–41.

Messner, D (ed) (1998) *Die Zukunft des Staates und der Politik. Reihe Eine Welt - Texte der Stiftung Entwicklung und Frieden (SEF)*. SEF, Bonn.

Messner, D (2004) 'The network based global economy: a new governance triangle for regions.' In Schmitz, H (ed) *Local Enterprises in the Global Economy: Issues of Governance and Upgrading*. Edward Elgar, Cheltenham.

Metternicht, G I and Zinck, J A (2003) 'Remote sensing of soil salinity: potentials and constraints'. *Remote Sensing of Environment* **85**: pp1–20.

Michaelis, N V (2003) *Nachhaltige Entwicklung und programmgebundene Kreditvergabe der Weltbank – Eine theoretische und konzeptionelle Analyse*. Doctoral thesis, University Kaiserslautern. Volkswirtschaftliche Schriften der Universität Kaiserslautern. Volume 26. Transfer Verlag, Regensburg.

Michaelowa, A, Butzengeiger, S, Jung, M and Dutschke, M (2003) 'Beyond 2012 – Evolution of the Kyoto Protocol'. Expertise for the WBGU Special Report „World in Transition: Climate Protection Strategies for the 21st Century. Kyoto and beyond". WBGU website, http://www.wbgu.de/wbgu_sn2003_ex02.pdf

Milazzo, M (1998) *Subsidies in World Fisheries, A Reexamination*. Technical Paper 406. Fisheries Series. World Bank, Washington, DC.

Mittermeier, R A, Myers, N, Gil, P R and Goettsch-Mittermeier, C (1999) *Earth's Biologically Richest and Most Endangered Terrestrial Ecoregions*. Cemex, Sierra Madre.

Molina, M J and Molina, L T (2004) 'Megacities and atmospheric pollution'. *Journal of the Air & Waste Management Association* **54**: pp644–80.

Molnar, A, Scherr, S J and Khare, A (2004) *Who Conserves the World's Forests? Community-driven Strategies to Protect Forests and Respect Rights*. Forest Trends, Ecoagriculture Partners, Washington, DC.

Münchner Rück (2002a) *Grafik Naturkatastrophen 2002. Volkswirtschaftliche Schäden – Versicherte Schäden*. pdf-Datei des NatCatSERVICE der Münchner Rückversicherung. Münchner Rück, Munich.

Münchner Rück (2002b) *Poster Naturkatastrophen 2002: Entwicklung (im Vergleich mit Monatsmittel 1992–2001 und Vorjahr 2001)*. Münchner Rück, Munich.

Münchner Rück (2002c) *Topics – 50 bedeutende Naturkatastrophen 2002*. Münchner Rück, Munich.

Münchner Rück (2003) *Jahresrückblick Naturkatastrophen 2002*. Münchner Rück, Munich.

Murphy, S and Suppan, S (2003) *Introduction to the Development Box – Finding Space for Development Concerns in the WTO's Agriculture Negotiations*. International Institute for Sustainable Development, Winnipeg, Canada.

Murray, C C J L and Lopez, A D (eds) (1996) *The Global Burden of Disease*. Harvard University Press, Harvard, MA.

Myers, N and Kent, J (2001) *Perverse Subsidies: How Misused Tax Dollars Harm the Environment and the Economy*. Island Press, Covelo.

Myers, N, Mittermeier, R A, Mittermeier, C G, de Fonseca, G A B and Kent, J (2000) 'Biodiversity hotspots for conservation priorities'. *Nature* **403**(24.02.): pp853–8.

Nelson, M, Dudal, R, Gregersen, H, Jodha, N, Nyamai, D, Groenewold, J-P, Torres, F and Kassam, A (1997) *Report of the Study on CGIAR Research Priorities for Marginal Lands*. Food and Agriculture Organization of the United Nations (FAO), Consultative Group on International Agricultural Research, Technical Advisory Committee Secretariat, Rome.

Newman, D J, Cragg, G M and Snader, K M (2003) 'Natural products as sources of new drugs over the period 1981–2002'. *Journal of Natural Products* **66**: pp1022–37.

Nicholls, R J, Mimura, N and Topping, J (1995) 'Climate change in South and Southeast Asia: some implications for coastal areas'. *Journal of Global Environment Engineering* **1**: pp137–54.

Nicholls, R J and Hoozemans, F M J (2000) 'Global Vulnerability Analysis. Prepared for Encyclopedia of Coastal Science'. Survas Project website, http://www.survas.mdx.ac.uk/docs/encyclop.doc (viewed 25. October 2004).

Nohlen, D (ed) (2002) *Lexikon Dritte Welt*. Rowohlt, Hamburg.

NRO Interventions (2003) *Compilation of NRO Interventions*. GEF Council Meeting, May 2003. GEF Secretariat, Washington, DC.

Nuffield Council on Bioethics (2003) *The Use of Genetically Modified Crops in Developing Countries - A Follow-up Discussion Paper*. Nuffield Council on Bioethics, London.

Nuscheler, F (2004) *Internationale Migration. Flucht und Asyl*. 2nd edition. Verlag für Sozialwissenschaften, Wiesbaden.

OECD (Organization for Economic Co-operation and Development) (ed) (1994) *The Environmental Effects of Trade*. OECD, Paris.

OECD (Organization for Economic Co-operation and Development) (ed) (1996) *Shaping the 21st Century: The Role of Development Co-operation*. OECD, Paris.

OECD (Organization for Economic Co-operation and Development) (ed) (2001) *Environmental Outlook for the Chemicals Industry*. OECD, Paris.

OECD (Organization for Economic Co-operation and Development) (ed) (2002a) *The DAC Guidelines. Integrating the Rio Conventions Into Development Co-operation*. OECD, Paris.

OECD (Organization for Economic Co-operation and Development) (ed) (2002b) *Poverty Environment Gender Linkages.* OECD, Paris.

OECD (Organization for Economic Co-operation and Development) (2004) *Agricultural Policies in OECD Countries: At a Glance. Highlights. 2004 edition.* OECD, Paris.

OECD (Organization for Economic Co-operation and Development) and WHO – World Health Organization (2003) *DAC Guidelines and Reference Series: Poverty and Health.* OECD and WHO, Paris, Geneva.

OECD DAC (Organization for Economic Co-operation and Development) - Development Assistance Committee (2001) 'Peer Review of Germany. Main Findings and Recommendations'. *DAC Journal* **2**(4).

OECD/DAC (Organization for Economic Co-operation and Development) - Development Assistance Committee (2002) *European Community. Development Co-operation Review.* OECD, Paris.

OECD DAC (Organization for Economic Co-operation and Development) - Development Assistance Committee (eds) (2003) 'DAC List of Aid Recipients as at 1 January 2003'. OECD website, http//:www.oecd.org/dataoecd/35/9/2488552. pdf (viewed 25. October 2004).

OECD DAC (Organization for Economic Co-operation and Development - Development Assistance Committee) (eds) (2004) 'Aid Statistics. Moderater Anstieg der Entwicklungshilfe im Jahr 2003'. OECD website, http://www.oecd.org/document/41/0,2340,en_2649_34447_31538025_1_1_1_1,00. html (viewed 23. September 2004).

OED (Operations Evaluation Division of the World Bank) (2004) *Brazil Country Assistance Evaluation.* Report 27629. World Bank, Washington, DC.

OED (Operations Evaluations Division), OEG (Operations Evaluation Group) and OEU (Operations Evaluation Unit of the World Bank) (2003) *Extractive Industries and Sustainable Development: An Evaluation of World Bank Group Experience.* World Bank, Washington, DC.

Oldeman, L R (1998) *Soil Degradation: A Threat to Food Security.* ISRIC, Wageningen.

Oldeman, L R, Hakkeling, R. T. A and Sombrock, W G (1991) *World Map of the Status of Human Induced Soil Degradation. Global Assessment of Soil Degradation (GLASOD).* ISRIC, Wageningen.

Olson, M L (1998) *Die Logik des kollektiven Handelns.* Mohr, Tübingen.

Osemeobo, G J (2001) 'Wild plants in everyday use: conservation towards sustainable livelihoods in Nigeria'. International *Journal of Sustainable Development and World Ecology* **8**: pp369–79.

Ott, H E (2001) 'The Bonn Agreement to the Kyoto Protocol – paving the way for ratification'. *Politics, Law and Economics* **1**: pp469–76.

Page, S E, Siegert, F, Rieley, J O, Boehm, H D, Jaya, A and Limin, S (2002) 'The amount of carbon released from peat and forest fires in Indonesia during 1997'. *Nature* **420**: pp61–5.

Painting, K and Wesseler, G (2003) 'Digital villages – A dream revisited'. *Entwicklung und ländlicher Raum* **37**(5): pp16–9.

Palmer, T N and Räisänen, J (2002) 'Quantifying the risk of extreme seasonal precipitation events in a changing climate'. *Nature* **415**(31.01.): pp512–4.

Panagariya, A (2004) *Aid Through Trade: An Effective Option?* Economics Working Paper Archive. International Trade 0403006. Economics Department of the Washington University, Washington, DC.

Pantoja, E (2000) *Exploring the Concept of Social Capital and its Relevance for Community-based Development: The Case of Coal Mining Areas in Orissa, India.* Social Capital Initiative Working Paper No. 18. World Bank, Washington, DC.

Paolisso, M, Gammage, S and Casey, L (1999) 'Gender and household-level responses to soil degradation in Honduras'. *Human Organization* **58**(3): pp261–73.

Parry, M and Livermore, M (eds) (1999) 'A new assessment of the global effects of climate change'. *Global Environmental Change* **9**: pp1–107.

Paudel, G S and Thapa, G B (2001) 'Changing farmers' land management practices in the hills of Nepal'. *Environmental Management* **28**(6): pp789–803.

Paul, J A (2001) 'Der Weg zum Global Compact.' In Brühl, T, Debiel, T and Hamm, B (eds) *Die Privatisierung der Weltpolitik.* Reihe EINE Welt – Texte der Stiftung Entwicklung und Frieden (SEF). SEF, Bonn: pp104–29.

Pauly, D, Christensen, V, Guenette, S, Pitcher, T J, Sumaila, U R, Walters, C J, Watson, R and Zeller, D (2002) 'Towards sustainability in world fisheries'. *Nature* **418**(08.08.): pp689–95.

Pearce, D and Warford, J (1994) *World Without End: Economics, Environment, and Sustainable Development.* Oxford University Press, Oxford, New York.

Pelletier, D L, Frongillo jr, E A and Schroeder, D G (1995) 'The effects of malnutrition on child mortality in developing countries'. *Bulletin of the World Health Organization* **73**(4): pp443–8.

Peltzer, R (2004) 'Armutsbekämpfung durch Baumwollanbau'. *Nord-Süd aktuell* **1**: pp114–7.

Pethiyagoda, R (2004) 'Biodiversity law has had some unintended effects'. *Nature* **429**: p129.

Petschel-Held, G, Sietz, D, Walkenhorst, O, Walther, C, Brooks, N and Matthies, F (2004) 'Armut und Umwelt in Burkina Faso und NO-Brasilien: Entwicklung und Anwendung eines Matrixkonzepts zur Beschreibung differenzieller Vulnerabilitäten gegenüber dem globalen Wandel'. Expertise for the WBGU Report „World in Transition: Fighting Poverty through Environmental Policy". WBGU website, http://www.wbgu.de/wbgu_jg2004_ex05.pdf

Pettifor, A and Greenhill, R (2002) *Debt Relief and the Millennium Development Goals 2002/3.* United Nations Development Programme. Human Development Report Office Occasional Paper. Background Paper for HDR 2003. UNDP, New York.

Picard, C H (2003) 'Post-apartheid perceptions of the Greater St Lucia Wetland Park, South Africa'. *Environmental Conservation* **30**(2): pp182–91.

Pigato, M A (2001) *Information and Communication Technology, Poverty, and Development in Sub-Saharan Africa and South Asia.* Africa Region Working Paper Series No. 20. World Bank, Washington, DC.

Pilardeaux, B (1997) 'Desertifikationsbekämpfung im Aufwind? 1. Vertragsstaatenkonferenz der UNCCD'. *Nord-Süd Aktuell* **XI**(4): pp744–9.

Pilardeaux, B (2003a) 'Verhandlungspoker statt Dialog über Umsetzung – Ergebnisse der 6. Vertragsstaatenkonferenz der Desertifikationskonvention (UNCCD)'. *Nord-Süd Aktuell* **XVII**(3): pp541–3.

Pilardeaux, B (2003b) 'Welternährungskonferenz + 5: Was ist mit der Allianz gegen den Hunger?' In Altner, G, Leitschuh-Fecht, H, Michelsen, G, Simonis, U E and von Weizsäcker, E U (eds) *Jahrbuch Ökologie.* Beck, Munich: pp72–9.

Pimentel, D, Harvey, C, Resudodarmo, K, Sinclair, D, Kurz, M, McNair, S, Crist, L, Spitz, L, Fitton, R, Saffouri, R and

Blair, R (1995) 'Environmental and economic costs of soil erosion and conservation benefits'. *Science* **267**: pp1117–23.

Porter, G (2001) 'Fisheries Subsidies and Overfishing: Towards a Structured Discussion'. UNEP website, http://www.unep.ch/etu/etp/acts/capbld/rdtwo/FE_vol_1.pdf (viewed 25. October 2004).

Posey, D (ed) (1999) *Cultural and Spiritual Values of Biodiversity. A Complementary Contribution to the Global Biodiversity Assessment.* United Nations Environment Programme (UNEP), Nairobi.

Prasad, E, Rogoff, K, Wie, S-J and Kose, M A (2003) *Effects of Financial Globalization on Developing Countries: Some Empirical Evidence.* International Monetary Fund (IMF), Washington, DC.

Primo, N (2003) *Gender Issues in the Information Society.* UNESCO Publications for the World Summit on the Information Society. UNESCO, Paris.

Proksch, P (2004) 'Bedeutung von Naturstoffen für die Pharmazie'. Expertise for the WBGU Report „World in Transition: Fighting Poverty through Environmental Policy". WBGU website, http://www.wbgu.de/wbgu_jg2004_ex06.pdf

Pryer, J (1990) 'Hunger and women's survival in a Bangladesh slum.' In Bernstein, H (ed) *The Food Question. Profits versus People?* Earthscan, London: pp125–33.

Psacharopoulos, G and Patrinos, H A (1994) *Indigenous People and Poverty in Latin America: An Empirical Analysis.* World Bank, Washington DC.

Putnam, R D, Léonardi, R and Nenetti, R (1993) *Making Democracy Work: Civic Traditions in Modern Italy.* Princeton University Press, Princeton, NJ.

Qadir, M, Ghafoor, A and Murtaza, G (2000) 'Amelioration strategies for saline soils: a review'. *Land Degradation & Development* **11**(6): pp501–21.

Rao, J M (1998) *Openness, Poverty and Inequality.* Paper Prepared for the Human Development Office, UNDP. UNDP, New York.

Rao, P K (2000) *Sustainable Development – Economics and Policy.* Oxford University Press, Oxford, New York.

Ravallion, M (1990) 'Rural welfare effects of food price changes under induced wage responses – theory and evidence for Bangladesh'. *Oxford Economic Papers* **42**(4): pp574–85.

Ravallion, M (2001) *Growth, Inequality and Poverty: Looking Beyond Averages.* Working Paper No. 2558. World Bank, Washington, DC.

Ravallion, M (2003) *The Debate on Globalization, Poverty and Inequality: Why Measurement Matters.* Policy Research Working Paper 3038. World Bank, Washington, DC.

Ravallion, M and Datt, G (2002) 'Why has economic growth been more pro-poor in some States of India than others?' *Journal of Development Economics* **68**(02): pp381–400.

Rawat, D S, Farooquee, N A and Joshi, R (1996) 'Towards sustainable land-use in the hills of Central Himalaya, India'. *International Journal of Sustainable Development and World Ecology* **3**(2): pp57–65.

Reddy, S G and Pogge, T W (2002) *How Not to Count the Poor?* Version 4.4. Columbia University, Columbia.

Reed, D H (1992) *Structural Adjustment and the Environment.* Macroeconomics for Sustainable Development Programme Office (MPO), WWF, London.

Reid, W V, Laird, S A, Gámez, R, Sittenfeld, A, Janzen, D H, Gollin, M A and Juma, C (1993) 'A new lease of life.' In Reid, W V, Laird, S A, Meyer, C A and Gámez, R (eds) *Biodiversity Prospecting.* World Resources Institute (WRI), Washington, DC: pp1–52.

Renaud, F, Bechstedt, H D and Nakorn, U N (1998) 'Farming systems and soil-conservation practices in a study area of Northern Thailand'. *Mountain Research and Development* **18**(4): pp345–56.

Resor, J P (1997) 'Debt-for-Nature-Swaps: A Decade of Experience and New Directions for the Future'. FAO website, http://www.fao.org/docrep/w3247e/w3247e06.htm (viewed 25. October 2004)

Reusswig, F, Gerlinger, K and Edenhofer, O (2002) 'Lebensstile und globaler Energieverbrauch. Analyse und Strategieansätze zu einer nachhaltigen Energiestruktur'. Expertise for the WBGU Report „World in Transition: Towards Sustainable Energy Systems". WBGU website, http://www.wbgu.de/wbgu_jg2003_ex08.pdf

Richards, K W (1993) 'Non-apis bees as crop pollinators'. *Revue Suisse de Zoologie* **100**: pp807–22.

RNE (Rat für Nachhaltige Entwicklung) (2003) *Gebrauchtgüterexporte und Baupraxis von Gebäuden. Empfehlungen des Rates für Nachhaltige Entwicklung an die Bundesregierung.* Texte Nr. 5. RNE, Berlin.

RNE (Rat für Nachhaltige Entwicklung) (2004) 'Schwerpunkte der nationalen Nachhaltigkeitsstrategie 2004. Stellungnahme des Rates für nachhaltige Entwicklung zum Konsultationspapier des Bundeskanzleramtes'. RNE website, http://www.nachhaltigkeitsrat.de/service/download/stellungnahmen/RNE_Stellungnahme_Konsultationspapier_01-03-04.pdf (viewed 13. May 2004).

Robb, C (1999) *Can the Poor Influence Poverty? Participatory Poverty Assessments in the Developing World.* World Bank, Washington DC.

Rodrik, D (2001) *The Global Governance of Trade – As If Development Really Mattered. Background Paper to the UNDP Project on Trade and Sustainable Human Development.* United Nations Development Programme (UNDP), New York.

Rozanov, B G (1990) 'Global assessment of desertification: status and methodologies.' In UNEP (United Nations Environment Programme) (ed) *Desertification Revisited: Proceedings of an Ad hoc Consultative Meeting on the Assessment of Desertification.* UNEP, Nairobi: pp45–122.

Sachs, W (1993) *Wie im Westen so auf Erden. Ein polemisches Handbuch zur Entwicklungspolitik.* Rowohlt, Hamburg.

Sachs, J (2000) 'Globalization and patterns of economic development'. *Weltwirtschaftliches Archiv* **136**(4): pp579–600.

Sachs, J (2004) 'Sustainable development (Editorial)'. *Science* **304**(30.04.): p649.

Sachs, J and Malaney, P (2002) 'The economic and social burden of Malaria'. *Nature* **415**: pp680–5.

Sands, P (2003) *Principles of International Environmental Law.* Cambridge University Press, Cambridge.

Santarius, T, Dalkmann, H, Steigenberger, M, and Vogelpohl, K (2003) *Grüne Grenzen für den Welthandel – Eine ökologische Reform der WTO als Herausforderung an eine Sustainable Global Governance.* Wuppertal Institut zur Globalisierung, Wuppertal.

Sauerborn, R, Nougtara, A and Latimer, E (1994) 'The elasticity of demand for health care in Burkina Faso: differences across age and income groups'. *Health Policy and Planning* **9**(2): pp185–92.

Sauerborn, R, Martens, P and Matthies, F (2004) *Global Environmental Change and Infectious Diseases: Impacts and Adaptation Strategies.* Springer, Berlin, Heidelberg, New York: (forthcoming).

Schaper, M (2004a) 'Internationale Harmonisierung von Umweltstandards im OECD-Rahmen. Aktuelle SWP-Dokumentation Reihe D, Nr. 41'. Stiftung Wissenschaft und Politik (SWP) website, http://marcus.schaper.com/publications/reihe_d_ecas.pdf (viewed 25. October 2004).

Schaper, M (2004b) 'Exportkreditagenturen und erneuerbare Energien: Chancen und Herausforderungen. Background Paper for the DIW and Germanwatch Workshop „Exportfinanzierung erneuerbarer Energien: Welchen Beitrag können die projektbeteiligten Exporteure, Betreiber, Banken und Exportkreditversicherer leisten?" on April 28, 2004'. Deutsches Institut für Wirtschaftsforschung (DIW) website, http://marcus.schaper.com/publications/040701ecas_und_ee.pdf (viewed 25. October 2004).

Scheffer, F and Schachtschabel, P (1998) *Lehrbuch der Bodenkunde*. Ferdinand Enke Verlag, Stuttgart.

Scherr, S (2003) *Halving Global Hunger*. Background Paper of the Task Force 2 on Hunger. UN Millenium Project. United Nations (UN), New York.

Schmidt, S (2002) 'Aktuelle Aspekte der EU Entwicklungspolitik'. *Aus Politik und Zeitgeschichte* **B19/20**: pp29–38.

Schneider, A-K (2002) 'Strukturanpassung contra nachhaltige Entwicklung'. weed website, http://www.weed-online.org/themen/iwf/17704.html (viewed 19. March 2004).

Schubert, R, Saladin, S and Spitze, K (2000) 'Wirtschaftliche Entwicklung und Umweltschutz. Zur Relevanz der Umwelt-Kuznetskurve.' In Scholing, E (ed) *Währung und wirtschaftliche Entwicklung, Festschrift für Vincenz Timmermann zum 65. Geburtstag*. Duncker & Humblot, Berlin: pp275–99.

Schwaab, J A and Busch, A (1999) *Direktinvestitionen und Umweltschutz: die empirische Evidenz*. Beiträge zur Wirtschaftsforschung Nr. 58. Institut für Wirtschaftsforschung (IFO), Mainz.

Schwertmann, U, Vogl, W and Kainz, M (1987) *Bodenerosion durch Wasser: Vorhersage des Abtrags und Bewertung von Gegenmaßnahmen*. Ulmer, Stuttgart.

Seely, M K, Zeidler, J, Henschel, J R and Barnard, P (2003) 'Creative problem solving in support of biodiversity conservation'. *Journal of Arid Environments* **54**(1): pp155–64.

SEF (Stiftung Entwicklung und Frieden) (1993) *Nach dem Erdgipfel: Global verantwortliches Handeln für das 21. Jahrhundert*. Kommentare und Dokumente. SEF, Bonn.

Seibel, S, Müller-Falcke, D and Bertolini, R (1999) *Informations- und Kommunikationstechnologien in Entwicklungsländern. Trends und Potentiale*. ZEF Discussion Papers on Development Policy 4. Zentrum für Entwicklungsforschung (ZEF), Bonn.

Seibold, B (2004) 'Verfügbar, verständlich und relevant – was Nutzer in Entwicklungsländern von Onlineinhalten erwarten.' In Beck, K, Schweiger, W and Wirth, W (eds) *Gute Seiten – schlechte Seiten. Qualität in der Onlinekommunikation*. Verlag Reinhard Fischer, Munich: pp168–89.

Sen, A (1981) *Poverty and Famines. An Essay on Entitlements and Deprivation*. Oxford University Press, Oxford.

Sen, A (1999) *Development as Freedom*. Oxford University Press, Oxford.

Shafik, N and Bandyopadhyay, S (1992) *Economic Growth and Environmental Quality – Time Series and Cross Country Evidence*. Discussion Paper Nr. 904. World Bank, Washington, DC.

Shams, R (1991) 'Hemmnisse der wirtschaftspolitischen Reformpolitik in Entwicklungsländern.' In Sautter, H (ed) *Wirtschaftspolitische Reformpolitik in Entwicklungsländern*. Schriften des Vereins für Socialpolitik. **209**. Duncker & Humblot, Berlin: pp135.

Shiferaw, B and Holden, S T (1998) 'Resource degradation and adoption of land conservation technologies in the Ethiopian Highlands: a case study in Andit Tid, North Shewa'. *Agricultural Economics* **18**(3): pp233–47.

Shiferaw, B and Holden, S T (1999) 'Soil erosion and smallholders' conservation decisions in the highlands of Ethiopia'. *World Development* **27**(4): pp739–52.

Shiferaw, B and Holden, S T (2001) 'Farm-level benefits to investments for mitigating land degradation: empirical evidence from Ethiopia'. *Environment and Development Economics* **6**: pp335–58.

Shively, G E (2001) 'Poverty, consumption risk, and soil conservation'. *Journal of Development Economics* **65**(2): pp267–90.

Shyamsundar, P and Hamilton, K (2000) *An Environmental Review of 1999 Country Assistance Strategies – Best Practices and Lessons Learned*. Environmental Economics Series Paper No. 74. Washington, DC, World Bank.

Shyamsundar, P, Hamilton, K, Segnestam, L, Sarraf, M and Fankhauser, S (2001) *An Environmental Review of 1999 Country Assistance Strategies – Best Practices and Lessons Learned*. The World Bank Environmental Department. Environmental Economics Series Paper No. 81, July 2001. World Bank, Washington, DC.

Singh, R B (2003) *Water as Driving Force for Poverty Alleviation and Environment Security in India*. Paper presented at the 2003 Open Meeting Human Dimension of Global Environmental Change. Montreal, Canada, 16.–18. October 2003.

SIPRI (Stockholm International Peace Research Institute) (2004) 'SIPRI Yearbook 2004. Armament, Disarmament and International Security'. SIPRI website, http://editors.sipri.se/pubs/yb04/pr04.html (viewed 25. October 2004).

Smith, K R, Samet, M J, Romieu, I and Bruce, N (2000) 'Indoor air pollution in developing countries and lower respiratory infections in children'. *Thorax* **55**: pp518–32.

Smith, K R and Mehta, S (2003) 'The burden of disease from indoor air pollution in developing countries: comparison of estimates'. International *Journal of Hygiene and Environmental Health* **206**(4-5): pp279–89.

Soete, B (2003) *Internationale Verhandlungen über Property Rights Regime und Verteilungskonflikte. Das Beispiel des globalen Umweltproblems Schwund biologischer Vielfalt*. Peter Lang, Frankfurt/M, Berlin, Bern.

Solh, M, Amri, A, Ngaido, T and Valkoun, J (2003) 'Policy and education reform needs for conservation of dryland biodiversity'. *Journal of Arid Environments* **54**(1): pp5–13.

Solomon, G M and Weiss, P M (2002) 'Chemical contaminants in breast milk: time trends and regional variability'. *Environmental Health Perspectives* **110**: A339–A347.

SRU (Rat von Sachverständigen für Umweltfragen) (2004) *Umweltgutachten 2004. Umweltpolitische Handlungsfähigkeit sichern*. Nomos, Baden-Baden.

Stephan, P (2001) 'Die Kommission für nachhaltige Entwicklung (CSD) Talkshop der Vereinten Nationen oder wirksame Institution zur Umsetzung der Agenda 21?' In Fues. T and Hamm, B (eds) *Die Weltkonferenzen der 90er Jahre*. Stiftung Entwicklung und Frieden (SEF), Bonn: pp126–57.

Stern, D I (2004) 'The rise and fall of the Environmental Kuznets Curve'. *World Development* **32**(8): pp1419–39.

Stockmann, R (1996) *Die Wirksamkeit der Entwicklungshilfe*. Westdeutscher Verlag, Opladen.

Stokke, O and Forster, J (eds) (1999) *Policy Coherence in Development Cooperation*. Portland, London.

Stokke, O S and Thommessen, O B (2003) *Yearbook of International Co-operation on Environment and Development*. The Fridtjof Nansen Institute, Stockholm.

Stolberg, F, Borysova, O, Mitrofanov, I, Barannik, V and Eghtesadi, P (2003) Caspian Sea. GIWA regional assessment 23. Global International Waters Assessment (GIWA) website, http://www.giwa.net/areas/reports/r23/giwa_regional_assessment_23.pdf (viewed 25. October 2004).

Stoll, P-T (2000) *Gestaltung der Bioprospektion unter dem Übereinkommen für biologische Vielfalt durch international unverbindliche Verhaltensstandards: Hintergründe, Möglichkeiten und Inhalte.* Berichte des Umweltbundesamts 4/00. Erich-Schmidt-Verlag, Berlin.

Stoll, P-T (2004) 'Armutsbekämpfung und Zugang zu genetischen Ressourcen'. Expertise for the WBGU Report „World in Transition: Fighting Poverty through Environmental Policy". WBGU website, http://www.wbgu.de/wbgu_jg2004_ex07.pdf

Stræde, S, Nebel, G and Rijal, A (2002) 'Structure and floristic composition of community forests and their compatibility with villagers' traditional needs for forest products'. *Biodiversity and Conservation* 11: pp487–508.

Strohscheidt, E and Hamm, B (2003) 'Normen für die menschenrechtliche Verantwortung der Privatwirtschaft'. *FOODFirst, FIAN-Magazin für die wirtschaftlichen, sozialen und kulturellen Menschenrechte* 2: p7.

Sullivan, C (2002) 'Calculating a Water Poverty Index'. *World Development* 30(7): pp1195–1210.

Sun, X, Katsigiris, E and White, A (2004) *Meeting China's Demand for Forest Products: An Overview of Import Trends, Ports of Entry, and Supplying Countries, With Emphasis on the Asia – Pacific Region.* Forest Trends, Chinese Center for Agricultural Policy und Center for International Forestry Research, Washington, DC.

Suri, V and Chapman, D (1998) 'Economic Growth, Trade and Energy: Implications for the Environmental Kuznets Curve'. *Ecological Economics* 25: pp195–208.

Swinton, S M and Quiroz, R (2003) 'Is poverty to blame for soil, pasture and forest degradation in Peru's Altiplano?' *World Development* 31(11): pp1903–19.

Tabuti, J R S, Lye, K A and Dhillion, S S (2003) 'Traditional herbal drugs of Bulamogi, Uganda: plants, use and administration'. *Journal of Ethnopharmacology* 88: pp19–44.

Technical Group on Innovative Financing Mechanisms (2004) *Action Against Hunger and Poverty.* Technical Group, New York.

ten Kate, K and Laird, S A (1999) *The Commercial Use of Biodiversity. Access to Genetic Resources and Benefit-Sharing.* Earthscan, London.

The Bellagio Child Survival Study Group (2003) 'The worlds forgotten children'. *Lancet* 361(9351): p1.

The Global Crop Diversity Trust (2004) 'Start With a Seed'. The Global Crop Diversity Trust website, http://www.startwithaseed.org/items/homepage.php (viewed 26. October 2004).

The Independent Working Group on the Future of the United Nations (1995) 'The United Nations in its Second Half-Century'. Ford Foundation website, http://www.ciaonet.org/wps/yuu01/ (viewed 25. October 2004).

The Microcredit Summit Secretariat (ed) (2002) *Microcredit Summit Report 2002.* Microcredit Summit Secretariat, Washington, DC.

Thomas, C (2004) 'A changed climate in Africa?' *Nature* 427: pp690–1.

Timoshenko, A and Berman, M (1996) 'The United Nations Environment Programme and the United Nations Development Programme.' In Werksman, J (ed) *Greening International Institutions.* Earthscan, London: pp38–54.

Tol, R S J and Verhejen, R (2004) 'State responsibility and compensation for climate change damages - a legal and economic assessment'. *Energy Policy* (32): pp1109–30.

Tomich, T P, van Noordwijk, M, Vosti, S A and Witcover, J (1998) 'Agricultural development with rainforest conservation: methods for seeking best bet alternatives to slash-and-burn, with applications to Brazil and Indonesia'. *Agricultural Economics* 19(1-2): pp159–74.

Troni, J, Moura Costa, P, Haque, N, Rodriguez, H, Sharma, A, Hession, M, Agbey, S, Gunaratne, L and Sokona, Y (2002) 'Managing Emissions Neutral Development (MEND) Final Technical Report'. Ecosecurities website, http://www.ecosecurities.com/mend/index.html (viewed 25. October 2004).

Turner II, B L, Kasperson, R, Matson, P A, McCarthy, J J, Corel, R W, Christensen, L, Eckley, N Kasperson, J X, Luers, A, Mertello, M L, Polsky, C, Pulsipher, A and Schiller, A (2003) 'A framework for vulnerability analysis in sustainability science'. *Proceedings of the National Academy of Science* 100(14): pp8074–9.

UN (United Nations) (1997) *Renewing the United Nations: A Programme for Reform.* Secretary General's Report (A/51/950). New York, UN.

UN (United Nations) (2000) *Die Millenniums-Erklärung der Vereinten Nationen.* New York, UN.

UN (United Nations) (2001a) 'United Nations Guide for Indigenous Peoples. Indigenous Peoples and the United Nations System: An overview. Leaflet no. 1'. UN Office of the High Commissioner for Human Rights website, http://www.unhchr.ch/html/racism/00-indigenousguide.html (viewed 25. October 2004).

UN (United Nations) (ed) (2001b) *Zedillo-Report of the High-Level Panel on Financing for Development.* New York, UN.

UN (United Nations) (2001c) *Road Map Towards the Implementation of the United Nations Millennium Declaration.* New York: UN

UN (United Nations) (2002a) *Bericht des Weltgipfels für nachhaltige Entwicklung, Johannesburg, 26. August - 4. September 2002 (translation in abstracts).* A/CONF.199/20. New York, UN.

UN (United Nations) (2002b) *Strengthening the United Nations: An Agenda for Further Change.* Report of the Secretary-General. A/57/387. New York: UN

UN (United Nations) (2003) *Follow-up to the Outcome of the Millennium Summit. Implementation of the United Nations Millennium Declaration.* Report of the Secretary-General (A/58/323). United Nations General Assembly. 2 September 2003. Fifty-eighth Session. New York, UN.

UN (United Nations) (2004a) 'Millennium Development Goals. Progress Report 2004'. UN website, www.un.org/millenniumgoals/mdg2004chart.pdf (viewed 21. September 2004).

UN (United Nations) (2004b) *Implementation of the United Nations Millennium Development Declaration.* Report of the Secretary-General to the Fifty-ninth Session of the General Assembly. Statistical Annex. Document NO-446540 (E). New York, UN.

UN (United Nations) (2004c) *Innovative Sources of Financing for Development.* New York, UN.

UN (United Nations) (2004d) *We the Peoples: Civil Society, the United Nations and Global Governance.* Report of the Cardoso-Panel of Eminent Persons on United Nations-Civil Society Relations. New York, UN.

UN (United Nations) (2004e) 'Partnerships for Sustainable Development'. Secretariat of the CSD UN website, http://

www.un.org/esa/sustdev/partnerships/partnerships.htm (viewed 03. November 2004).

UNAIDS (United Nations Programme on HIV/AIDS) (2004) *Financing the Expanded Response to Aids.* UNAIDS, Geneva.

UNCCD (United Nations Convention to Combat Desertification) - Committee for the Review of the Implementation of the Convention (2003) *Review of the Implementation of the Convention and of its Institutional Arrangements (ICCD/CRIC/(2)/3).* UNCCD, New York.

UNCCD (United Nations Convention to Combat Desertification) (2004) UNCCD website, http://www.unccd.int (viewed 2. November 2004).

UNCTAD (United Nations Conference on Trade and Development) (2002) *Least Developed Countries Report 2002.* UNCTAD, Geneva.

UNCTAD (United Nations Conference on Trade and Development) (2003) *E-Commerce and Development Report 2003.* UNCTAD, Geneva.

UNCTAD (United Nations Conference on Trade and Development) (2004a) *Least Developed Countries Report 2004. Linking International Trade with Poverty Reduction.* UNCTAD, Geneva.

UNCTAD (United Nations Conference on Trade and Development) (2004b) *World Investment Report 2003. FDI Policies for Development: National and International Perspectives.* UNCTAD, Geneva.

UN DESA (United Nations Department of Economic and Social Affairs) (2004) 'Multi-Year Programme of Work for CSD: 2004/2005 to 2016/2017'. UN DESA website, http://www.un.org/esa/sustdev/csd/csd11/CSD_multiyear_prog_work.htm (viewed 07. September 2004).

UNDP (United Nations Development Programme) (1997) *Human Development Report 1997. Human Development to Eradicate Poverty.* Oxford University Press, Oxford, New York.

UNDP (United Nations Development Programme) (2001a) *Human Development Report 2001. Making New Technologies Work for Human Development.* Oxford University Press, Oxford, New York.

UNDP (United Nations Development Programme) (2001b) 'UNDP Review of the Poverty Reduction Strategy Papers (PSRP)'. UNDP website, http://www.worldbank.org/poverty/strategies/review/undp1.pdf (viewed 28. April 2004).

UNDP (United Nations Development Programme) (2001c) *Evaluation of UNDP's Non-Core Resources. Note by the Administrator.* UN Doc. DP/2001/CRP.12. UNDP, New York.

UNDP (United Nations Development Programme) (2002) *External Partnership Review.* UNDP, New York.

UNDP (United Nations Development Programme) (2003a) *Executive Board of the United Nations Development Programme and of the United Nations Population Fund. UNDP Budget Estimates for the Biennium 2004–2005.* Report of the Administrator. UN Doc. DP/2003/28 of 11 June 2003. UNDP, New York.

UNDP (United Nations Development Programme) (2003b) *Making Global Trade Work for People.* UNDP, New York.

UNDP (United Nations Development Programme) (2003c) *Human Development Report 2003. Millennium Develpment Goals: A Compact Among Nations to End Human Poverty.* UNDP, New York.

UNDP (United Nations Development Programme) (2004a) *Reducing Disaster Risk: A Challenge for Development.* UNDP, New York.

UNDP (United Nations Development Programme) (2004b) *Human Development Report 2004. Cultural Liberty in Today's Diverse World.* UNDP, New York.

UNDP (United Nations Development Programme) (2004c) *2015: Mobilizing Global Partnerships. Annual Report 2004.* UNDP, New York.

UNDP (United Nations Development Programme) (2004d) *Evaluation of the Second Global Cooperation Framework of UNDP.* UNDP, New York.

UNDP (United Nations Development Programme) (2004e) *Annual Report 2003 of the Administrator.* UNDP, New York.

UNDP (United Nations Development Programme), UN DESA (United Nations Department of Economic and Social Affairs) and WEC (World Energy Council) (2000) *World Energy Assessment.* Oxford University Press, Oxford, New York.

UNEP (United Nations Environment Programme) (1999) *Environmental Impacts of Trade Liberalization and Policies for Sustainable Management of Natural Resources.* UNEP Country Projects, Round I. UNEP, Nairobi.

UNEP (United Nations Environment Programme) (2001) *Vulnerability Indices. Climate Change Impacts and Adaptation.* UNEP, Nairobi.

UNEP (United Nations Environment Programme) (2002a) *Issue Paper Concerning the Question of Universal Membership of the Governing Council/Global Ministerial Environment Forum of the United Nations Environment Programme.* Note by the Executive Director. UNEP/GC.22/INF/36 of 19 December 2002. Nairobi: UNEP

UNEP (United Nations Environment Programme) (2002b) *Global Environmental Outlook 3. Past, Present and Future Perspectives.* London, Earthscan.

UNEP (United Nations Environment Programme) (2002c) *Integrated Assessment of Trade Liberalization and Trade-Related Policies.* UNEP Country Projects. Round II A Synthesis Report. UNEP, Nairobi.

UNEP (United Nations Environment Programme) (2003) *Trade Liberalization in the Agriculture Sector and the Environment.* UNEP Country Projects. Round III. Nairobi: UNEP

UNEP (United Nations Development Programme) (2004a) *UNEP in 2003. Annual Report of the Executive Director.* UNEP, Nairobi.

UNEP (United Nations Development Programme) (2004b) *Women and the Environment.* UNEP, Nairobi.

UNEP (United Nations Environment Programme) (2004c) 'Partnership Agreements'. UNEP website, http://www.unep.org/rmu/en/Partnerships.htm (viewed 03. November 2004).

UNEP Chemicals (United Nations Environment Programme) Chemicals (2003) *Regionally Based Assessment of Persistent Toxic Substances.* UNEP Chemicals, Geneva.

UNEP GC (United Nations Environment Programme) Governing Council (2002) *Draft Report of the President of the United Nations Environment Programme Governing Council for Consideration by the Open-Ended Intergovernmental Group of Ministers or Their Representatives on International Environmental Governance.* UN Doc. UNEP/IGM/5/2 of 16 February 2002. UNEP, Nairobi.

UNEP (United Nations Environment Programme) and C4 (2002) *The Asian Brown Cloud: Climate and Other Environmental Impacts.* UNEP, Nairobi.

UNESCO (United Nations Educational, Scientific and Cultural Organisation) (1997) *UNESCO Statistical Yearbook.* UNESCO, Paris.

UNESCO (United Nations Educational, Scientific and Cultural Organisation) (1999) 'World Conference on Science for the 21st Century: A New Commitment'. UNESCO website, http://www.unesco.org/bpi/science/ (viewed 25. October 2004).

UNESCO (United Nations Educational, Scientific and Cultural Organisation) (2002) 'World Declaration on Education For All. The World Conference on Education for All (Jomtien, Thailand, 5-9 March 1990)'. UNESCO website, http://www.unesco.org/education/efa/ed_for_all/background/jomtien_declaration.shtml (viewed 25. October 2004).

UNESCO (United Nations Educational, Scientific and Cultural Organisation) (2003a) *The UN World Water Development Report. Water for People, Water for Life. World Water Assessment Programme.* UNESCO, New York.

UNESCO (United Nations Educational, Scientific and Cultural Organisation) (2003b) 'Education for All. Global Monitoring Report 2003/04'. UNESCO website, http://www.unesco.org/education/efa_report/chapter2.pdf (viewed 25. October 2004).

UNESCO (United Nations Educational, Scientific and Cultural Organisation) (2004) *EFA Global Monitoring Report 2003/2004.* UNESCO, New York.

UNFCCC (United Nations Framework Convention on Climate Change) (2002a) *Annotation Guidelines for the Preparation of National Adaptation Programmes of Action.* Least Development Countries Expert Group. UNFCCC Secretariat, Bonn.

UNFCCC (United Nations Framework Convention on Climate Change) (2002b) *SBSTA Methodological Issues, Scientific and Methodological Assessment of Contributions to Climate Change.* UNFCCC Secretariat, Bonn.

UNFCCC (United Nations Framework Convention on Climate Change) (2003) *Review of Implementation of Commitments and of Other Provisions of the Convention.* Draft Decision -/CP.9. Further Guidance to an Entity Entrusted with the Operation of the Financial Mechanism of the Convention, for the Operation of the Special Climate Change Fund. FCCC/CP/2003/L.8. UNFCCC Secretariat, Bonn.

UNFPA (United Nations Population Fund) (2001) *The State of the World Population 2001. Footprints and Milestones: Population and Environmental Change.* UNFPA, New York.

UNFPA (United Nations Population Fund) (2002) *The State of the World Population 2002. People, Poverty and Possibilities.* UNFPA, New York.

UNFPA (United Nations Population Fund) (2003) *Achieving the Millennium Development Goals. Population and Reproductive Health as Critical Determinants.* UNFPA, New York.

UNGA (United Nations General Assembly) (2003) *Report on the World Social Situation 2003.* A/58/153. Fifty-eighth Session. UNGA, New York.

UNICEF (United Nations Children's Fund) (2000) *The State of the World's Children 2000. Statistical Tables.* UNICEF, New York.

UNICEF (United Nations Children's Fund) (2004) *The State of the World's Children 2004. Girls, Education and Development.* UNICEF, New York.

UN Millennium Project (2004a) *Interim Report of Task Force 7 on Water and Sanitation.* New York, UN.

UN Millennium Project (2004b) *Interim Report of Task Force 1 on Poverty and Economic Development.* New York, UN.

UN Millennium Project (2004c) *A Global Plan to Achieve the Millennium Development Goals.* Draft Report for Public Consultation: 23 September 2004. New York, UN.

UN Millennium Project (2004d) *Interim Report of Task Force 2 on Hunger.* New York, UN.

UN OHRLLS (United Nations Office of the High Representative for the Least Developed Countries, Landlocked Developing Countries and the Small Island Developing States) (2004) 'The Criteria for Determining the LDCs'. UN OHRLLS website, http://www.un.org/special-rep/ohrlls/ldc/ldc%20criteria.htm (viewed 19. April 2004).

UN Population Division (2003a) 'World Population Prospects: The 2002 Revision Population Database'. Department of Economic and Social Affairs of the United Nations Secretariat website, http://esa.un.org/unpp/ (viewed 19. April 2004)

UN Population Division (2003b) *World Population Prospects: The 2002 Revision. Highlights.* Department of Economic and Social Affairs of the United Nations Secretariat, New York.

UN Population Division (2003c) 'New Survey Findings: The Reproductive Revolution Continues. Series M, Number 17'. Information and Knowledge for Optimal Health (INFO) website, http://www.infoforhealth.org/pr/m17/#contents. (viewed 25. October 2004).

UN SCN (United Nations Systems Standing Committee on Nutrition) (2004) 'The Fifth Report on the World Nutrition Situation: Nutrition for Improved Development Outcomes'. UN SCN website, http://www.unsystem.org/scn/Publications/AnnualMeeting/SCN31/SCN5Report.pdf (viewed 25. October 2004).

UN Statistics Division – United Nations Statistics Division (2003) *Progress Towards the Millennium Development Goals 1990–2003. Goal 7 – Ensure Environmental Sustainability.* UN Statistics Division, New York.

UNU (United Nations University) (2002) *International Environmental Governance.* UNU, Tokyo.

Unser, G (1997) *Die UNO. Aufgaben, Strukturen, Politik.* dtv, Munich.

Uphoff, N (2000) 'Understanding Social Capital: Learning from the Analysis and Experience of Participation.' In Dasgupta, P and Serageldin, I (eds) *Social Capital: A Multifaceted Perspective.* World Bank, Washington, DC: pp215–49.

Urgewald, weed, BUND, Germanwatch and FIAN (2003) 'Ernst machen mit der ökologisch-sozialen Reform der deutschen Außenwirtschaftsförderung. Stellungnahme'. weed website, http://www.weed-online.org/themen/hermes/18084.html (viewed 25. October 2004).

U.S. Census Bureau Population Division and International Programs Center (2004) 'International Data Base (IDB)'. U.S. Census Bureau website, http://www.census.gov/ipc/www/world.html (viewed 25. October 2004).

van Bastalaer, T (1999) *Does Social Capital Facilitate the Poor's Access to Credit? A Review of the Microeconomic Literature.* Social Capital Initiative Working Paper No. 8. World Bank, Washington, DC.

Vandemoortle, J and Roy, R (2004) *Making Sense of MDG Costing.* United Nations Development Programme (UNDP), New York.

Vaughan, J P, Mogedal, S, Druse, S, Lee, K, Walt, G and de Wilde, K (1996) 'Financing the World Health Organization: global importance of extrabudgetary funds'. *Health Policy* **35**(3): pp229–45.

Vavilov, N I (1926) 'Geographical regularities in the distribution of the genes of cultivated plants'. *Bulletin of Applied Botany* **17**(3): pp411–28.

Venetoulis, J, Chazan, D and Gaudet, C (2004) *Ecological Footprints of Nations. Redefining Progress.* Centro de Estudios para la Sustentabilidad, Xalapa, VeR, Mexico.

VENRO (Verband Entwicklungspolitik deutscher Nichtregierungsorganisationen) (2002) *Globale Armut – Europas Verantwortung.* VENRO, Bonn.

Vogel, J H (1994) *Genes for Sale. Privatization as a Conservation Policy.* Oxford University Press, Oxford, New York.

Vogel, M P (1999) *Environmental Kuznets Curves – A Study on the Economic Theory and Political Economy of Environmental Quality Improvements in the Course of Economic Growth.* Lecture Notes in Economics and Mathematical Systems 469. Springer, Berlin, Heidelberg, New York.

Volkert, J (1998) 'Nachhaltigkeit als Frage der politischen Durchsetzbarkeit. Eine Analyse der Interessenlagen mit Hilfe der Neuen Politischen Ökonomie Heft 2/98: Nachhaltige Entwicklung: Politisch-institutionelle Voraussetzungen schaffen'. Landeszentrale für Politische Bildung Baden-Württemberg website, http://www.lpb.bwue.de/aktuell/bis/2_98/bis982d.htm (viewed 25. October 2004).

von Bieberstein Koch-Weser, M (2002) 'Nachhaltigkeit und Wasserkraftpotenzial 2020–2050'. Expertise for the WBGU Report „World in Transition: Towards Sustainable Energy Systems". WBGU website, http://www.wbgu.de/wbgu_jg2003_ex01.pdf

von Braun, J, Wobst, P and Grote, U (2002) *'Development Box' and Special and Differential Treatment for Food Security of Developing Countries: Potentials, Limitations and Implementation Issues.* Working Paper No. 47. Zentrum für Entwicklungsforschung (ZEF), Bonn.

von Schirnding, Y, Bruce, N, Smith, K, Ballard-Tremeer, G, Ezzati, M and Lvovsky, K (2002) *Addressing the Impact of Household Energy and Indoor Air Pollution on the Health of the Poor.* Paper prepared for the Commission on Macroeconomics and Health. World Health Organisation (WHO), Geneva.

Vorhies, F (1999) *An Essay on Biodiversity and Globalisation.* The World Conservation Union (IUCN), Gland.

Walk, H and Brunnengräber, A (2000) *Die Globalisierungswächter. NGOs und ihre transnationalen Netze im Konfliktfeld Klima.* Westfälisches Dampfboot, Münster.

Walker, B L E (2001) 'Sisterhood and seine-nets: engendering development and conservation in Ghana's marine fishery'. *Professional Geographer* **53**: pp160–77.

Wapner, P (2003) 'World Summit on Sustainable Development: toward a post-Jo'burg environmentalism'. *Global Environmental Politics* **3**(1): pp1–10.

Wardle, D A, Bardgett, R D, Klironomus, J N, Setälä, H, van der Putten, W H and Wall, D H (2004) 'Ecological linkages between aboveground and belowground biota'. *Science* **304**: pp1629–33.

Warwick, H and Doig, A (2004) *Smoke – The Killer in the Kitchen.* ITDG Publishing, Bourton Hall, UK.

Watkins, K (2000) *The Oxfam Education Report.* Oxfam International, London.

Watts, M and Bohle, H-G (1993) 'The space of vulnerability: the causal structure of hunger and famine'. *Progress in Human Geography* **17**(1): pp43–67.

WBGU – German Advisory Council on Global Change (1994) *Basic Structure of Global People-Environment Interactions. 1993 Report.* Economica, Bonn.

WBGU – German Advisory Council on Global Change (1995a) *World in Transition: The Threat to Soils. 1994 Report.* Economica, Bonn.

WBGU – German Advisory Council on Global Change (1995b) *Scenario for the Derivation of Global CO_2 Reduction Targets and Implementation Strategies. Statement on the Occasion of the First Conference of the Parties to the Framework Convention on Climate Change in Berlin. 1995 Special Report.* WBGU, Bremerhaven.

WBGU – German Advisory Council on Global Change (1997a) *World in Transition: The Research Challenge. 1996 Report.* Springer, Berlin, Heidelberg, New York.

WBGU – German Advisory Council on Global Change (1997b) *Targets for Climate Protection 1997. A Study for the Third Conference of the Parties to the Framework Convention on Climate Change in Kyoto. Special Report 1997.* WBGU, Bremerhaven.

WBGU – German Advisory Council on Global Change (1998a) *World in Transition: Ways Towards Sustainable Management of Freshwater Resources. Report 1997.* Springer, Berlin, Heidelberg, New York.

WBGU – German Advisory Council on Global Change (1998b) *The Accounting of Biological Sinks and Sources Under the Kyoto Protocol - A Step Forwards or Back-wards for Global Environmental Protection? Special Report 1998.* WBGU, Bremerhaven.

WBGU – German Advisory Council on Global Change (2000) *World in Transition: Strategies for Managing Global Environmental Risks. 1998 Report.* Springer, Berlin, Heidelberg, New York.

WBGU – German Advisory Council on Global Change (2001a) *World in Transition: Conservation and Sustainable Use of the Biosphere. 1999 Report.* London, Earthscan.

WBGU – German Advisory Council on Global Change (2001b) *World in Transition: New Structures for Global Environmental Policy. 2000 Report.* London, Earthscan.

WBGU – German Advisory Council on Global Change (2001c) *The Johannesburg Opportunity: Key Elements of a Negotiation Strategy. WBGU Policy Paper 1.* WBGU, Berlin.

WBGU – German Advisory Council on Global Change (2002) *Charging the Use of Global Commons. Special Report 2002.* WBGU, Berlin.

WBGU – German Advisory Council on Global Change (2003) *Climate Protection Strategies for the 21st Century: Kyoto and beyond. Special Report 2003.* WBGU, Berlin.

WBGU – German Advisory Council on Global Change (2004) *World in Transition: Towards Sustainable Energy Systems. 2003 Report.* Earthscan, London.

WCD – World Commission on Dams (ed) (2000) *Dams and Development. A New Framework for Decision-Making.* WCD, London.

WCED – World Commission on Environment and Development (ed) (1987): *Our Common Future: 'The Brundtland Report'.* Oxford University Press, Oxford, New York.

Weber, E (2002) 'Die Klasse der Verwundbaren'. *iz3w* **244** (April): pp19–21.

Wells, M P (1994) 'The Global Environment Facility and prospects for biodiversity conservation'. *International Environmental Affairs* **6**(1): pp69–97.

Wells, M P (1996) 'The social role of protected areas in the new South Africa'. *Environmental Conservation* **23**(4): pp322–31.

WHO – World Health Organization (2000) *Guidelines for Air Quality.* WHO, Geneva.

WHO – World Health Organization (2001) *Macroeconomics and Health: Investing in Health for Economic Development.* Report of the Commission on Macroeconomics and Health. WHO, Geneva.

WHO – World Health Organization (ed) (2002) *The World Health Report 2002. Reducing Risks and Promoting Healthy Life.* WHO, Geneva.

WHO – World Health Organization (2003) *Proposed Programme Budget 2004–2005.* WHO, Geneva.

WHO – World Health Organization (2004a) *PRSPs: Their Significance for Health: Second Synthesis Report.* WHO, Geneva.

WHO – World Health Organization (2004b) *Financial Report and Audited Financial Statements for the Period 1 January 2002–31 December 2003 (Certified 30 March 2004). Annex: Extrabudgetary Resources for Programme Activities.* Fifty-seventh World Health Assembly. Provisional Agenda Item 15.1. A57/20 Add.1. WHO, Geneva.

WHO – World Health Organization (2004c) 'Financial Report and Audited Financial Statements for the Period 1 January 2002–31 December 2003 (Certified 30 March 2004) and Report of the External Auditor to the World Health Assembly (1 April 2004). Fifty-seventh World Health Assembly. Provisional Agenda Item 15.1. A57/20'. WHO website, http://www.who.int/gb/ebwha/pdf_files/WHA57/A57_20-en.pdf (viewed 25. October 2004).

WHO – World Health Organization and UNICEF – United Nations Children's Fund (2004) *Meeting the MDG Drinking Water and Sanitation Target. A Mid-Term Assessment of Progress.* WHO and UNICEF Joint Monitoring Programme for Water Supply and Sanitation, Geneva, New York.

WI – Wuppertal Institut (ed) (2004) *Wege von der nachholenden zur nachhaltigen Entwicklung.* WI, Wuppertal.

Wijetilleke, L and Suhashini, K A R (1995) *Air Quality Management. Considerations for Developing Countries.* World Bank Technical Paper 278 Energy Series. World Bank, Washington, DC.

Willets, P (ed) (1996) *The Conscience of the World. The Influence of Non-Governmental Organizations in the UN System.* Brookings Institution, Washington, DC.

Winchester, P (1992) *Power, Choice and Vulnerability. A Case Study in Disaster Management in South India 1977–88.* James and James, London.

Winpenny, J (2003) *Financing Water for All: Report of the World Panel on Financing Water Infrastructure.* World Water Council (WWC), Marseille.

WIPO – World Intellectual Property Rights Organization (2003) *Draft Technical Study on Disclosure Requirements Related to Genetic Resources and Traditional Knowledge.* UN Document UNEP/CBD/WG-ABS/2/INF/4. WIPO, Geneva.

Wissenschaftliche Arbeitsgruppe – Wissenschaftliche Arbeitsgruppe für weltkirchliche Aufgaben der Deutschen Bischofskonferenz (2000) *Das soziale Kapital. Ein Baustein im Kampf gegen Armut von Gesellschaften.* Deutsche Kommission Justitia et Pax, Bonn.

Wolf, S (1996) *Begrenzter Erfolg der Lomé-Abkommen.* Peter Lang, Frankfurt/M.

Wollny, C B A (2003) 'The need to conserve farm animal genetic resources in Africa: should policy makers be concerned?' Ecological Economics **45**(3): pp341–51.

Woolcock, M and Narayan, D (2000) 'Social capital: implications for development theory, research and policy'. *The World Bank Research Observer* **15**(2): pp225–49.

World Bank (1992) *World Development Report 1992. Development and the Environment.* World Bank, Washington DC.

World Bank (1993) *World Development Report 1993. Investing in Health.* World Bank, Washington, DC.

World Bank (1997) *World Development Report 1997. The Role of the State in a Changing World.* World Bank, Washington, DC.

World Bank (2000) *World Development Report 2000/2001. Attacking Poverty.* World Bank, Washington, DC.

World Bank (2001a) *Making Sustainable Commitments - An Environment Strategy for the World Bank.* World Bank, Washington, DC.

World Bank (2001b) *Poverty Trends and Voices of the Poor.* 4th edition. World Bank, Washington, DC.

World Bank (2001c) *The PRSP Source Book: Chapter 11.* World Bank, Washington, DC.

World Bank (2002a) *Development, Trade, and the WTO A Handbook.* World Bank, Washington, DC.

World Bank (2002b) *Costing the 7th Millennium Development Goal. Ensure Environmental Sustainability. Draft.* Environment Department and Development Economics Research Group. World Bank, Washington, DC.

World Bank (2003a) *Lifelong Learning in the Global Knowledge Economy: Challenges for Developing Countries.* World Bank, Washington, DC.

World Bank (2003b) *Putting Our Commitments to Work – Environment Strategy Implementation Progress Report.* World Bank, Washington, DC.

World Bank (2003c) *World Development Indicators 2003.* World Bank, Washington, DC.

World Bank (2003d) *World Development Report 2003. Sustainable Development in a Dynamic World. Transforming Institutions, Growth, and Quality of Life.* World Bank, Washington, DC.

World Bank (2003e) *Global Economic Prospects 2004. Realizing the Development Promise of the Doha Agenda.* World Bank, Washington, DC.

World Bank (2003f) *Global Development Finance 2003.* World Bank, Washington, DC.

World Bank (2004a) 'Country Classification'. World Bank website, http://www.worldbank.org/data/countryclass/countryclass.html (viewed 31. August 2004).

World Bank (2004b) *Water Resources Sector Strategy. Strategic Directions for World Bank Engagement.* World Bank, Washington, DC.

World Bank (2004c) *World Development Report 2004. Making Services Work for People.* World Bank, Washington, DC.

World Bank (2004d) *From Adjustment Lending to Development Policy Lending: Update of World Bank Policy.* World Bank, Washington, DC.

World Bank (2004e) 'Milllennium Development Goals. Maps: Population Below $1 a Day'. World Bank website, http://www.developmentgoals.org/tmaps.htm (viewed 21. September 2004).

World Bank (2004f) *Global Development Finance Report. Harnessing Cyclical Gains for Development.* World Bank, Washington, DC.

World Bank (2004g) *The World Bank Annual Report 2004, Volume 1. Year in Review.* World Bank, Washington, DC.

Worldwatch Institute (2004) *Zur Lage der Welt. Die Welt des Konsums 2004.* Fischer, Frankfurt/M.

WPC (World Parks Congress) (2003a) *Message of the Vth IUCN World Parks Congress to the Convention on Biological Diversity.* IUCN, Gland.

WPC (World Parks Congress) (2003b) 'Recommendations of the Vth IUCN World Parks Congress'. IUCN website, http://www.iucn.org/wpc2003/pdfs/outputs/wpc/recommendations.pdf (viewed 25. October 2004).

WPC (World Parks Congress) (2003c) 'The Durban Accord. Output of the World Parks Congress „Benefits beyond boundaries", Durban 2003'. IUCN website, http://www.iucn.org/wpc2003/pdfs/outputs/wpc/durbanaccord.pdf (viewed 25. October 2004)

WRI (World Resources Institute) (1996) *World Resources 1996–1997.* Oxford University Press, Oxford, New York.

WRI (World Resources Institute) (2003) *World Resources 2002–2004.* Oxford University Press, Oxford, New York.

278   **8 References**

WSSD (World Summit on Sustainable Development) (2002) *Plan of Implementation.* WSSD, Johannesburg.

WTO (World Trade Organization) (2002) *International Trade Statistics.* WTO, Geneva.

Würthwein, R, Gbangoub, A, Sauerborn, R and Schmidt, C M (2001) 'Measuring the local burden of disease. A study of years of life lost in sub-Saharan Africa'. *International Journal of Epidemiology* **30**: pp501–8.

WWC (World Water Council) (2000) *A Water Secure World. Vision for Water, Life, and the Environment.* World Water Vision. WWC, Marseille.

WWF (2002) *Changing the Balance of Trade.* WWF Briefing on Sustainability Assessment of EU Trade Policy. WWF UK, London.

WWF (2004) 'The Gold Standard - Quality Assurance for CDM and JI Projects'. WWF International website, http://www.edmgoldstandard.org (viewed 25. October 2004).

Xu, P and Shao, Y P (2002) 'A salt-transport model within a land-surface scheme for studies of salinisation in irrigated areas'. *Environmental Modelling & Software* **17**(1): pp39–49.

Yandle, B, Bhattarai, M and Vijayaraghavan, B (2004) *Environmental Kuznet Curves: A Review of Findings, Methods and Policy Implications.* PERC Research Study 02-1 Update, April 2004. The Property and Environment Research Center (PERC), Montana.

Young, Z (2002) *A New Green Order? The World Bank and the Politics of the Global Environment Facility.* Pluto Press, London.

Young, Z and Makoni, G (2001) *Green Aid in India and Zimbabwe – Conserving Whose Communities?* University of Hull. Mimeo.

Zack-Williams, A B (2000) 'Social consequences of structural adjustment.' In Mohan, G, Zack-Williams, T, Milward, B, Brown, E and Bush, R (eds) *Structural Adjustment – Theory, Practice and Impacts.* Routledge, London, New York: pp59–74.

Zhao, J Z, Wu, G, Zhao, Y M, Shao, G F, Kong, H M and Lu, Q (2002) 'Strategies to combat desertification for the twenty-first century in China'. *International Journal of Sustainable Development and World Ecology* **9**(3): pp292–7.

Agenda 21

A development and environmental programme of action containing policy recommendations for the 21st century, adopted at the ↑United Nations Conference on Environment and Development in Rio de Janeiro in 1992. It calls for a new global partnership for environment and development between the industrialized nations and the poor countries. Agenda 21 contains key development and environmental objectives such as poverty reduction, the sustainable management of natural resources, i.e. water, soil and forests, and mitigating global warming. It recognizes the importance of strengthening the role of major groups in political decision-making, and defines ↑sustainable development as the overarching political goal.

biophysical vulnerability

Describes the degree to which a system is susceptible to environmental changes or incapable of adapting to their effects. Biophysical vulnerability is a function of the type, extent and pace of the environmental changes to which a system is exposed, together with its sensitivity and adaptability.

capacity building

This refers to the development of a society's human, scientific, technological, organizational, institutional and financial capabilities. A fundamental goal of capacity building is to enhance a country's ability to achieve ↑sustainable development.

coping capacities

The capacity of countries and social groups to handle adversity and crisis. Coping capacities are highly dependent on the level of development achieved by the country concerned.

Clean Development Mechanism (CDM)

One of the flexible mechanisms introduced by the Kyoto Protocol. It allows investors in developed countries to achieve part of their reduction obligations through projects that reduce greenhouse gas emissions in developing and newly industrializing countries.

development policy lending

see ↑Structural Adjustment Programmes

developing countries

These are countries whose standard of living is far lower than in Europe (excluding Eastern Europe), North America and Oceania (Australia, New Zealand and Japan). The World Bank classifies national economies on the basis of per capita income according to the following thresholds: low income group = below US$765; lower middle income group = US$766–3,035; upper middle income group = US$3,036–9,385; high income group = US$9,386 or above. According to the UNDP and OECD, 137 countries from the first three categories are considered to be developing countries.

development cooperation (DC)

This comprises all the inputs provided through technical, financial and human resources cooperation. DC is carried out by private and public agencies in industrialized and developing countries. DC may take the form of material assistance (grants or concessionary loans) or non-material support (e.g. expertise/training).

Earth Summit Rio de Janeiro

↑United Nations Conference on Environment and Development in Rio de Janeiro

G7/G8 (Group of Seven/Group of Eight)

The group of major industrialized countries comprises Canada, France, Germany, Italy, Japan, the UK and the United States. Their heads of state and government meet annually at the G7 Summit to discuss economic issues. The G7 became the G8 in 1998, when Russia joined the discussions on political matters of global relevance. However, some G7 sessions on economic and financial policy are still held without Russia.

gender mainstreaming

Mainstreaming a gender perspective is the process of assessing the implications of any planned action for women and men, in terms of their different life situations and interests, combined with regular monitoring of progress, in order to promote gender equality.

global change

This refers to the linkages between global environmental changes, economic globalization, cultural transformation and a widening North-South divide.

global governance

This denotes the deepening of international cooperation and the creation and reinforcement of multilateral regimes in order to master the challenges arising from ↑globalization and threats such as global environmental changes or international terrorism. Global governance involves cooperation between states and non-government actors from the local to the global level.

global public goods, global commons

These are environmental goods such as the high seas and the world's atmosphere, which are universally accessible and for which no ownership or sovereignty rights exist. The term can be expanded to encompass financial stability, peace or health.

global structural policy

Global structural policy is intended to establish the framework conditions at international level that are necessary to improve the poorer countries' development prospects. It is based on the industrialized countries' recognition that they bear a share of the responsibility for, and may also be affected by, problems relating to development and the environment in other regions of the world. A key aim of global structural policy is therefore not only to implement relevant projects and programmes but also to reform national and international structures.

good governance

Good governance aims to promote and safeguard the rule of law and an independent judiciary, efficient public administration, government accountability and citizens' participation in the decision-making process. Nowadays, good governance in the partner countries is often a condition of development cooperation (conditionality).

Gross Domestic Product (GDP)

Currently the most frequently used indicator of the total output of an economy over a specific period of time. GDP is the sum of the market values, or prices, of all final goods and services produced within a country, minus the value of intermediate inputs.

Gross National Income (GNI)

An important indicator of the total output of an economy over a specific period of time. GNI is distinct from ↑Gross Domestic Product in that it comprises the total value of goods and services produced within a country together with net income (including interest and dividends) received from those institutions and individuals in other countries whose headquarters or place of residence are located in the economy in question. GNI is also known as Gross National Product (GNP).

guard rails

A concept introduced by WBGU. Guard rails are quantitatively defined limits to damage compatible with sustainable development. They demarcate the sustainable domain of development for the people-environment system. If guard rails are crossed, this has non-tolerable or even catastrophic effects. The pathways for sustainable development run within the domain defined by these guard rails.

HIPC Initiative (HIPC – heavily indebted poor countries)

An initiative launched by the International Monetary Fund and the World Bank in 1996 to reduce the external debt of the heavily indebted poor countries to a manageable level. The Enhanced HIPC Initiative (HIPC II) was adopted in 1999. The prerequisite for debt relief is the submission of a ↑Poverty Reduction Strategy Paper (PRSP). Countries benefiting under the HIPC Initiative are obliged to use the resources freed up by debt cancellation for the purpose of economic and social reform.

International Conference on Financing for Development (FfD), Monterrey

This UN conference was held in 2002 to discuss the financing of the ↑Millennium Development Goals (MDGs). It concluded with a reaffirmation of the existing commitment to spend 0.7 per cent of ↑Gross National Income on ↑Official Development Assistance (Monterrey Consensus) and a pledge to explore innovative sources of finance.

Johannesburg Summit

↑World Summit on Sustainable Development (WSSD)

Johannesburg Goals

These quantitative timebound goals were adopted by the international community at the ↑WSSD in

2002 to supplement the Millennium Declaration, with the aim of combating extreme poverty and protecting the environment.

Johannesburg Plan of Implementation

A set of agreements adopted at the ↑World Summit on Sustainable Development (WSSD) in Johannesburg in 2002. The Plan of Implementation (often known as 'JPoI') contains commitments on water, energy, climate, loss of biodiversity and natural resources, subsidies that have adverse environmental effects, and sound management of chemicals, together with timebound targets.

least developed countries (LDCs)

A subset of developing countries whose defining characteristics, besides low ↑Gross Domestic Product, are a poor standard of living, major economic vulnerability and a population below 75 million.

mainstreaming

This denotes the horizontal integration of a given theme into relevant policy fields, such as the integration of environmental measures into financial and economic policy.

Millennium Summit

Summit meeting of 147 heads of state and government, held in New York in September 2000. Against the background of United Nations reform, key issues were how to lift thousand millions of people out of abject poverty, make the United Nations more effective in maintaining peace and security, and identify better solutions to global environmental problems. The Summit concluded with the adoption of the ↑Millennium Declaration and the ↑Millennium Development Goals (MDGs).

Millennium Development Goals (MDGs)

The MDGs are set out in the United Nations ↑Millennium Declaration and draw together the main outcomes of the World Conferences held in the previous decade. The MDGs comprise a set of eight international development goals, together with a framework of 18 targets and 48 indicators to specify and operationalize the goals and measure progress. For most of the goals and targets, quantitative criteria and a timeframe were also adopted, generally to 2015 (the baseline year is 1990).

Millennium Declaration

Final declaration adopted at the ↑Millennium Summit. In it, 191 countries pledge to spare no effort to free people from the scourge of poverty and war, protect the environment more effectively, and strengthen the United Nations. The international community attaches great importance to the development objectives contained in the Declaration, known as the ↑Millennium Development Goals.

multilateralism

This denotes institutionalized cooperation between countries via international organizations (e.g. the UN) and regimes (such as the Climate Change Convention). Multilateralism is based on the recognition that effective management of global risks and the preservation of global public goods require cooperation among states, as well as binding regimes governing global action, and institutions with responsibility for setting and monitoring standards (↑global governance).

newly industrializing countries

This term is applied to developing countries undergoing a successful process of catch-up industrial development and which are thus poised to become industrialized countries. Their social development indicators, such as literacy, infant mortality, life expectancy or civil society development, may lag far behind economic indicators.

Official Development Assistance (ODA)

Official Development Assistance is defined as the resources provided, for the purposes of development, by the members of the OECD's Development Assistance Committee to developing countries on a bilateral basis or through multilateral institutions. In 2003, ODA reached US$68,500 million, or 0.25 per cent of the overall ↑Gross National Income of donor countries; however, these countries have pledged to achieve the target of contributing 0.7 per cent of Gross National Product to ODA over the long term.

poverty (absolute poverty)

Absolute poverty means a state in which a person's physical existence is in jeopardy. WBGU applies a broad concept of poverty, which it defines as a lack of access rights and entitlements. In addition to low per capita income (according to the World Bank's definition, less than US$1 a day) or unequal income distribution, poverty also means inadequate food, poor health and healthcare, a lack of access to education, and an absence of social capital and opportunities for participation.

Program of Action 2015

The German Government's contribution towards halving extreme poverty worldwide by 2015. The Program describes how the German Federal Government is working pro-actively towards attaining the goals defined in the ↑Millennium Declaration, the ↑Monterrey Consensus and the ↑Johannesburg Plan of Implementation. The AP 2015 was adopted by the Federal Cabinet in 2001.

Public Private Partnerships (PPPs)
Partnership initiatives between government, the private sector and/or civil society actors with the aim of providing public services previously deemed to be the responsibility of the state (e.g. infrastructure). The aim is to achieve sustained, mutually beneficial cooperation which serves the common good.

Poverty Reduction Strategy Papers (PRSPs)
PRSPs are produced by the developing countries in a participatory process involving civil society. Since 1999, the submission of a PRSP has been a condition for the granting of debt relief or concessionary loans by the World Bank, the IMF and the ↑G7.

Rio follow-up process
Political process to implement and monitor progress on the decisions adopted at the ↑United Nations Conference on Environment and Development in 1992 (↑Agenda 21, ↑Rio Conventions, follow-up agreements). The ↑World Summit on Sustainable Development (WSSD) reviewed the progress achieved during the ten years since Rio ('Rio+10').

Rio Conventions
A collective term for the United Nations Framework Convention on Climate Chance, including the Kyoto Protocol on the reduction of greenhouse gas emissions, the Convention on Biological Diversity, including the Cartagena Protocol on Biosafety, and the Convention to Combat Desertification. These agreements were developed as a result of the Earth Summit in Rio de Janeiro in 1992 (↑United Nations Conference on Environment and Development).

Rio Principles
These 27 principles are contained in the 1992 Rio Declaration. The most important are the precautionary approach and the principle of common but differentiated responsibilities.

social capital
This denotes social patterns of behaviour and formal/informal networks that stabilize social interactions over the long term. Despite continued differences over the definition of social capital, there is a general consensus that social capital strengthens social identity, promotes social participation and non-violent conflict management, and increases economic productivity.

social vulnerability
The risk faced by a social group that it may no longer be able to sustain its already minimal livelihood and may thus experience an existential crisis. A distinction is made between external factors, including both abrupt and gradual changes, and internal factors, such as a lack of protection or coping capacities.

Structural Adjustment Programmes (SAPs)
SAPs consist of a range of stabilizing and structural policy measures which the developing countries were required to undertake from the early 1980s onwards in order to secure loans from the World Bank or the International Monetary Fund. Due to the negative experiences and widespread criticism of these programmes, the World Bank modified its criteria on several occasions and finally recast the SAPs as 'developing policy lending' in 2004.

sustainable development
The Brundtland Commission in 1987 defined sustainable development as 'development that meets the needs of the present without compromising the ability of future generations to meet their own needs.' Today, many different definitions of sustainability exist; all recognize that sustainable development must be holistic and encompass the economic, social and environmental dimension.

trickle down effect
This refers to the widespread assumption among development economists that the benefits of economic growth in developing countries will automatically 'trickle down' to the poorest groups.

United Nations Conference on Environment and Development (UNCED, Earth Summit)
UNCED in Rio de Janeiro (1992) is seen as a milestone in terms of integrating environment and development policy measures. At the Conference, the international community established the concept of ↑sustainable development as a globally recognized guiding vision. The protection of natural life-support systems was accepted as an integral element of a development process that meets the needs of both present and future generations. The Conference concluded with the adoption of the ↑Rio Principles, ↑Agenda 21, the ↑Rio Conventions and the Statement of Forest Principles (see also ↑Rio follow-up process).

user charges
This fiscal instrument entails raising a charge for the use of global common goods, such as international airspace or the oceans. Through the payment

that has to be made, the scarcity of a resource and the costs of its provision are signalled to the user. It has both behaviour-modifying effect and a financing function, as the revenue from the charge must be deployed to mitigate the damage associated with the use of the resource.

vulnerability
This denotes the susceptibility of a social group or (environmental) system to crises and pressures. A distinction can be made between ↑social and ↑biophysical vulnerability.

World Summit on Sustainable Development (WSSD)
This conference was held in Johannesburg, South Africa, in 2002 and reviewed the progress made in the ↑Rio follow-up process. In the ↑Johannesburg Plan of Implementation, the international community agreed new objectives (↑Johannesburg Goals) and implementation measures to reduce poverty and protect the environment. In the Johannesburg Declaration on Sustainable Development, the heads of state and government reaffirmed the global importance of sustainable development and poverty eradication, climate and resource protection, changes to production and consumption patterns, and the need for socially and environmentally responsible management of the globalization process.

Index